1994

CORRECTIVE READING

CORRECTIVE READING
Sixth Edition

Zelda R. Maggart
University of New Mexico

Miles V. Zintz
University of New Mexico

WCB Wm. C. Brown Publishers

Book Team

Editor *Chris Rogers*
Developmental Editor *Cindy Kuhrasch*
Production Coordinator *Peggy Selle*

 Wm. C. Brown Publishers

President *G. Franklin Lewis*
Vice President, Publisher *George Wm. Bergquist*
Vice President, Publisher *Thomas E. Doran*
Vice President, Operations and Production *Beverly Kolz*
National Sales Manager *Virginia S. Moffat*
Advertising Manager *Ann M. Knepper*
Marketing Manager *Kathy Law Laube*
Production Editorial Manager *Colleen A. Yonda*
Production Editorial Manager *Julie A. Kennedy*
Publishing Services Manager *Karen J. Slaght*
Manager of Visuals and Design *Faye M. Schilling*

Cover design by Kay Dolby Fulton

Cover photo by Paul Lundquist

*To Harley B. Maggart
and Mary Hatley Zintz*

Contents

Preface

Reading is a major source of learning in today's society. Yet thousands of children are denied the opportunities to learn from print because they fail to master the process of reading. Instead they develop negative attitudes toward themselves and their own capabilities as well as toward books, teachers, reading, and schools. For teachers to learn as much about the teaching of reading as possible is of critical importance. It is equally important that they learn how to help those students who have yet to experience success with the task. No group of children is immune to reading difficulties, but children who are poor, hungry, neglected, or abused; children who speak little or no English; and children of the unemployed, migrant workers, isolated, rural communities, and shattered families are far more vulnerable to reading failure than others. Teachers need to learn and enthusiastically adopt the role of child advocate to make sure that *all* children have appropriate opportunities to become literate. Teachers will need to empower children so that they can make decisions about their own learning, become partners in the teaching and learning processes, and participate in the evaluation of learning. It is toward helping teachers respond to both the cognitive and affective needs of their students, whomever they may be, that *Corrective Reading* is oriented.

Philosophical Orientation

Corrective Reading is organized to promote the diagnostic teaching of reading. Teachers are encouraged to view boys and girls realistically and to accept all of their differences in outlook, achievement, interest, and ability. The text is oriented to the instructional model of preassessment, teaching, and postassessment for students at any achievement level.

The writers assume an awareness that reading is only one of the skills of communication and that oral language must be extended and enriched to make reading meaningful. The language-experience approach—"writing" books from the students' own verbalized stories—is a very logical way to move from the spoken to the written word. The first experiences with books may best come through wordless picture books; predictable books; and high-interest, low-vocabulary titles.

For many underachievers, writing is very difficult. To encourage them to write, teachers must look first at the story content and accept their work without criticism of misspellings, poor organization, and "bad" grammar. Teachers should also provide models for the children by being active writers and readers themselves. This text emphasizes such an approach.

Textbook Organization

The sixth edition of *Corrective Reading* has been prepared to address many of the problems that teachers face in providing reading instruction for the poor readers in their classrooms. In chapters 1 and 2 teachers will find a general overview of reading as one of the communication skills necessary for all children. Discussions of the nature of the reading process, methods of teaching reading, the humanistic side of learning, and mainstreaming to accommodate exceptional children in the classroom are included in these chapters. Regular classroom teachers can provide learning environments to accommodate in constructive ways all of the individual differences in the class—intellectual, linguistic, social, emotional, physical, and psychological.

Suggestions for working diagnostically with several of the better-known word lists and on the development of an understanding of print as a medium are provided in chapter 3. The need of teachers to be able to diagnose their students' strengths and areas for growth in reading is addressed in chapters 4, 5, and 6. The topic of chapter 4 is the informal reading inventory, its construction, administration, scoring, and interpretation. Updated information about standardized tests, including a discussion of the terminology used in reporting student performance in a statistical frame of reference, is provided in chapter 5. Teachers will find discussions and examples of a wide variety of informal ways of diagnosing reading difficulties, including measuring intelligence; using interviews, inventories, and anecdotal records; obtaining oral language data; and working with sociograms and bibliotherapy in chapter 6.

Managing the classroom so that there is time for corrective reading instruction for those children who require it is addressed in chapters 7 and 8. An approach to learning organized around themes that are derived from learner interests is stressed. Detailed information about teaching word recognition and comprehension is given in chapters 9 and 10. Chapter 11 focuses on study skills and reading in the content fields. Children who have reading difficulties must also study mathematics, social studies, and science; consult reference books; make use of libraries; and obtain and organize information. Chapter 11 is intended as a source of help for teachers as they work to improve the learning experiences of reading-disabled children in these areas.

The frequently ignored topic of the attitudes that teachers hold toward children who have difficulty in learning to read is discussed in chapter 12. This important chapter should stand as a reminder that little will be gained cognitively in learning to read unless the affective domain is properly considered. Chapter 13 addresses the need for teachers and parents to work cooperatively. It is becoming increasingly clear that success in learning to read is influenced by the community and family in which the child lives. The greatest progress will occur when there is ongoing, two-way communication between teachers and parents about the successes and problems that children experience in learning to read.

Chapter 14 explores the needs of the linguistically and culturally different children. New information about the limited-English-proficiency child is included in this chapter. Chapter 15 includes information from the previous edition on helping children with the most serious reading problems, while a variety of new methods and techniques for teaching these youngsters has been added.

Each chapter of this text is introduced by an outline of the content, a list of important vocabulary items, and a set of questions focusing on major concepts. Each question is assigned a cognitive level. The terminology used is adapted from the work of Bloom and others who have provided labels for levels of the cognitive domain.

This text includes seven appendixes. Appendixes A and C are composed of lists of references and reading tests that teachers may find helpful. An extensive annotated bibliography of high-interest, low-vocabulary books for disabled readers is included in appendix B. Details about teaching the directed reading lesson are given in appendix D. A sample informal reading inventory (IRI) may be found in appendix E. We hope that this sample will suggest ways for teachers to develop their own IRIs, uniquely suited to their students' interests and needs. A sample home information blank is given in appendix F as a suggested means of gathering useful information about students who need corrective instruction. Finally, appendix G is a list of instructional materials designed to support the teaching of word identification and comprehension.

Use of the Book

Corrective Reading is appropriate for undergraduate students. Many classroom teachers have recognized the practical nature of the text. No teacher, unaided, can solve all the problems of reading failure, so one must always be aware of special resources when they are needed. Because the emphasis in this text is *corrective,* not clinical, it is not research oriented and does not ask teachers to administer tests that require technical skills that they do not possess.

Zelda R. Maggart
Miles V. Zintz

CORRECTIVE READING

1
An Overview of the Reading Process

Vocabulary

affective environment
empowerment
advocacy
involvement
vicarious experiences
prior knowledge
first-hand experiences
feedback
reading readiness
"hurried" reader
method
approach
whole language
basal reader
skills
strategies
word-processing program
affective learning

Questions

1. Why should we consider the needs of children before we consider how to teach reading? **(Inference)***

2. How do *you* define reading? How does your definition compare with the definition and description of reading in this chapter? **(Application; Evaluation)**

3. What signs would you look for that would indicate that a child is ready for formal reading instruction? **(Recall)**

4. Describe the three methods of teaching reading. Identify an approach for teaching reading derived from each of the methods. **(Recall)**

5. In what ways are each of the four jobs of teaching reading important? **(Inference)**

6. What criteria would *you* employ to describe a good school reading program? **(Evaluation)**

*A cognitive level is indicated for each question. Cognitive levels are discussed in chapter 10.

Introduction

Reading involves thinking, and the process of teaching reading necessarily has cognitive components. Most teachers come to the classroom expecting to help students to achieve the four basic cognitive prerequisites to reading, including (1) learning some words to read with, (2) developing a system of self-help strategies for reading, (3) deriving meaning from print, and (4) practicing reading both in and out of school.

But even before we think "reading" and begin the process of teaching it, we must prepare to respond to students' individual needs. The abilities and interests of children vary greatly, and teachers need to recognize these differences in order to help students to read more effectively. In other words, teachers need to think about the children to be taught. In corrective reading, one might ask:

> Who are the children who need special help with reading?
> Why have they not learned to read as their classmates have?
> How fluent are they in the use of oral language?
> How large are their speaking vocabularies?
> Are they unilingual English speakers, or did they use another language at home before coming to school?
> Have they now learned negative behaviors that affect their retention of reading skills and strategies?
> Do they feel like failures?
> Do they manifest anxiety when trying to read?
> Are they afraid to take risks?

We need to consider ways to study the students whom we wish to help, to explore their attitudes, feelings, fears, and anxieties. We can ask the students to think about how they value reading as an achievement. If they have attended school for three or four years and have failed to learn to read, they may need a restructuring of their personalities to give them back some confidence and to reduce their anxieties.

We should discover their interests, or if we find no special interests, we may need to encourage them to develop some.

> Do they admire their parents or their caregivers very much?
> Would they be more comfortable in sharing events in their own lives *orally* or in *writing?*
> Are some kinds of games, toys, television programs, or pets of special interest?
> What captures and holds their attention? Watching the students play classroom games may provide information about their ability to concentrate or their willingness to take risks.
> How well are students accepted by their peers? Perhaps a sociogram mapping friendships will reveal varying degrees of acceptance by peers.
> Do they enjoy comics and cartoons in newspapers and magazines?

Ultimately, success in school depends more on the *affective environment* than on the cognitive process employed. Teachers find that by concentrating on the affective domain in children's lives, they can build positive relationships and promote successful learning experiences for children. They can also fulfill their teaching roles of *empowering, advocating for,* and *involving* students in planning the nature of their curricula. Although these concepts may not be familiar to teachers of corrective reading, they are vital in designing the kinds of flexible programs that can lead to success.

Empowerment

Teachers have a responsibility to empower students to feel good about themselves.[1] In order to feel free to take risks in anticipating meaning in reading, students need to have confidence and strong egos. How willing are they to approach new vocabulary through reading? Their course of study will be most effective if the children help to plan it themselves. Do they have the confidence to help to set their own goals?

Advocacy

Teachers must be willing to make whatever adjustments are necessary in the school curriculum to provide successful learning experiences. Public Law 94–142 requires the development of individualized education programs (IEPs) to meet the special needs of handicapped children. This law prescribes that handicapped or learning disabled children (and their parents) must be represented in the IEP process by an unbiased advocate who will understand the students' unique needs and will defend their rights to equal educational opportunities. The teacher's role includes this responsibility. Daily schedules and assignments must be flexible enough to allow for task completion and learning success.

Involvement

Teachers should involve students in planning and making alternative choices in the nature of their assignments. For example, in order to help individual students who are not proficient in English, teachers need to measure where the students are starting from and then *negotiate* with the students about what changes in language status they hope to make and what course of study they will undertake. If the students have been communicating in some manner to meet their personal needs, then they already have a language. First, we must *legitimize* their language; we should not disapprove of it, especially if it is the language of the parents. Second, we should plan with the students individual courses of study. Finally, we should offer positive reinforcement for learning.

In the classroom, teachers need to make adjustments (1) in recognizing that the evaluation of current achievement may lead to the need for different experiences and materials in the curriculum and (2) in negotiating with children what they might learn, how best they might learn it, and how to measure their success in learning it.

What Is Reading?

As stated earlier, reading is a thinking process. It requires some response on the part of the reader. People can utilize the reading they do to make different generalizations, to draw new inferences, and to plan new strategies on the basis of it.

Reading can provide for an endless flow of *vicarious experiences.* Utilizing reading in the classroom is a means of providing experiences for children that they cannot have in person. What was it like to be an Egyptian pharaoh? What does moon soil feel like under your feet? What would a person see inside an atom? Reading can help children to "live" such experiences.

However, successful reading depends on the past experiences of the readers. Often called *prior knowledge,* these experiences are the raw material out of which new concepts, generalizations, and inferences are made. If the children have seen modern royal persons on television, have visited a museum and seen Egyptian artifacts, have participated in electing a class leader, or have listened to a parent who recently visited Egypt, the teacher can utilize the experiences the children have had to lead them to imagine what it might have been like to be an Egyptian pharaoh, and to enjoy reading about it. *First-hand experiences,* then, form the basis of the vicarious experiences gained from reading.

Gray identified four different steps in the reading act: *word perception, comprehension, reaction,* and *integration.* The first step is word recognition, including both the ability to pronounce the word and to attach meaning to it as a concept. The second step is the ability to make individual words construct useful ideas as they are read in context. The third step requires judgmental action—a feeling about what the author has said. The final step is the crucial one: the ability to assimilate this idea or concept in the new reading into the background of experience so that it becomes a part of the total experience of the individual. These steps are completely interdependent in the meaningful use of reading as a tool in the solution of problems.[2]

Harris and Sipay wrote that "reading is the meaningful interpretation of printed or written verbal symbols."[3] They indicated that reading is the result of the interaction among the perception of graphic symbols, the language of the text, the language of the reader, cognitive (thinking) skills, and the world knowledge of the reader.

Smith described reading as "a matter of making sense of written language rather than of decoding print to sound" and as marked by four basic characteristics, "that it is *purposeful, selective, anticipatory,* and based on *comprehension.*"[4]

Ernest Horn emphasized the active nature of the reading process:

> The author does not really convey ideas to the reader; he merely stimulates him to construct them out of his own experience. If the concept is already in the reader's mind, the task is relatively easy, but if, as is usually the case in school, it is new to the reader, its construction more nearly approaches problem solving than simple association.[5]

Adams also emphasized reading as an active and constructive process:

The reading material in primers is typically based on simple, stereotyped schemata so that semantic difficulties will be minimized. However, the content of more advanced texts will shift away from information that children can retrieve and toward information that they must construct. Thus, semantic processing demands will increase and, at the same time, children will be less able to check their interpretations against things they already know.[6]

The Nature of the Reading Process

Reading is the process by which readers bring to lines of print the necessary understanding out of their backgrounds of experience so that they can construct new concepts, reinforce old concepts, or adjust previous thinking to fit a new idea. When readers combine what the eye fleetingly tells the brain with what the brain is already telling the eye, they construct meaning. This becomes a kind of chain reaction, since with each new reading assignment, readers add to their long-term memory storage something that they can bring to their next reading assignment.

For mature readers, reading is a pleasurable activity in which they rapidly absorb ideas with which to agree or to disagree, and new thoughts to ponder. For each reader, this is an individual, unique system.

Reading for mature readers who have already habituated all the necessary skills is a far different process than is reading for beginners who must acquire mastery of the written form of the words already common in the speaking vocabulary. For the students learning the first necessary skills, however, reading must provide for the anticipation and acquisition of meaning in context with the very first lessons. Children of six bring to school a fully developed language and possess all the skills of thinking, reasoning, and problem solving in oral communication. Instead of supposing that the children "don't know any words," teachers must recognize that beginning readers know thousands of words but have not met most of them in written form. By translating the children's personal experiences, conversations, and explanations of events into written form, teachers can show children that their language can be preserved in written form, and eventually they understand that the written message is merely an extension of the oral language that they have been using for some time. Thus the language-experience approach is a very logical way to extend children's listening and speaking skills to include reading and writing.

When children read from this frame of reference, they have three kinds of *feedback* to help them to evaluate how accurately they are anticipating meaning. First, they must make the printed word correspond to an idea or concept that they already know in the language. If they say it incorrectly, they should reject it as nonsense and arrive at a new response that makes sense. Second, they will know whether their pronunciation of a printed word fits the grammar of a sentence as correctly spoken in the vernacular. If they need a noun but supply a verb or an adjective, they should reject it because the syntax is not sensible. Third, they should continually test the appropriateness of the meaning of the sentence the way they have read it, and they should reject any words that do not make sense in relation to the context of the passage. So their knowledge of words, of grammar, and of semantic correctness provides *both* feedback about the quality of reading *and* the anticipation, to a remarkable degree, of what they are going to read next. The process then necessitates, for the novice, mediated steps in knowing what the words are in the lines of print.

Pleasurable reading depends on one's having an automatic vocabulary to draw upon in any reading situation. Independence and versatility in recognizing and using words are paramount in facile reading. Readers need many sight words in order to recode print easily into thoughts—they need a vocabulary as rich and extensive as possible to extend meanings, promote further growth, and develop permanent reading interests. A wide vocabulary increases interest in reading. Words that are colorful, descriptive, discriminating, or expressive add enjoyment to reading. A good vocabulary decreases dependence on slow, anxiety-laden analyzing of words. An extensive, lucid vocabulary augments the speed of comprehension of the phrase, the sentence, or the paragraph.

The Dimensions of Reading

1. Reading is a *social* process. It is augmented by self-reliance, social acceptance, and cooperation in a group. Attitudes affect reading: loyalties, prejudices, and conflicts. Negative factors affect reading: broken homes, second-language problems, and conflicting cultural values between home and school.
2. Reading is a *psychological* process. How one feels about oneself, how one feels about others, and how others feel about one all affect the reading process. Emotional stability, balance between egocentrism and sociocentrism, determine one's comfort in the reading situation. Defense mechanisms—rationalization, repression, inhibition, introjection, projection, aggression, compensation, and nervous mannerisms—are responses to anxiety in all types of situations.
3. Reading is a *physiological* process. One must be able to focus on a line of print and move along the line, to make return sweeps, to note likenesses and differences, and to discriminate figure-ground relationships. One needs skills in auditory discrimination, verbal expression, syntactical maturity, eye-hand coordination, and motor skills in order to execute all the mechanical skills associated with reading.
4. Reading is a *perceptual* process. It utilizes perceptual clues: size, shape, combinations of letters and sounds, figure-ground relationships, relationships of the part to the whole, sequencing, and ordering.
5. Reading is a *linguistic* process. It requires mastery of phoneme-grapheme relationships, and understanding of intonation, stress, pauses, and tone sequence. Reading is dependent on context meanings—grasping the idea in whole thought units. Reading requires acceptance of social variations in language: nonstandard usage, figurative language, and slang.
6. Reading is an *intellectual* process. It is dependent on vocabulary, verbal reasoning, perceiving relationships, generalizing, memory, critical judgment, and accommodation to extreme individual differences.

Making Connections 1.1: What Is Happening to School Children?

Children's ability to learn to read or to progress in reading is affected by many factors outside the classroom. In many instances what happens away from school is more powerful as a determiner of achievement than what happens in school.

Find two articles from newspapers and magazines that describe events and experiences occurring in the lives of children. You are sure to find articles about poverty, child abuse and neglect, latch-key children, Little League sports, recitals, and clothing bank drives, for example. Bring your articles to class at an agreed-upon time. You will find that sharing the articles with class members will make everyone more aware of the real forces impinging on children's lives.

Figure 1.1 defines graphically the complex process of reading. From the definition already given of the four-step process—perception, comprehension, reaction, integration—Robinson has circumscribed the process with the reader's speed of comprehension or facility in assimilating ideas through written language.[7] The necessary entry skills for success in learning to read—the cognitive factors in recognizing words, sequencing, and grasping sentence meaning described by Gibson and by Singer,[8] the linguistic factors in decoding, associating, and encoding the significant meanings in the language used,[9] and the affective factors exhibited in the self-concept, one's perception of self, and attitudes toward reading[10] have all been incorporated in the diagram.

Readiness for Reading

Because so many students do have problems with reading assignments in school, it behooves us to think briefly about the *readiness* of boys and girls when they enter school. Most people have known at least one child of age three or four who seemed to learn to read without ever being taught. And most people have known a few boys and girls whose reading ability remained almost nil even after years of tutoring. But we tend to categorize everyone as either successful or unsuccessful as if there were just two clearly defined groups. This is not true at all. The following paragraphs emphasize the great range of individual differences in interests, motivation, and achievement in students. In formal school programs with curricula that are much too inflexible, the system, that is, the school as an institution, *creates* the problems that this book has been written to help alleviate.

Many children know how to read some words or phrases when they enter first grade. They can quickly identify "Coca-Cola," "Stop," "Cheerios," "Crest," and a number of other labels and signs that have meaning in their lives. Occasionally children read fluently before they enter first grade. Though teachers sometimes suspect that these

Figure 1.1. The four parts of the circle show reading as a four-step thinking process: perception, comprehension, reaction, and integration. The cognitive process also includes interpretive or creative reading in a word recognition-sequencing process. The linguistic process includes the syntactic, semantic, and meaning (deep structure) in decoding-encoding print into meaningful concepts. The affective processes are interactions of self-concept, attitudes, and anxieties. All of these affect a reader's facility in assimilating ideas through written language—that is, the speed of comprehension in reading.

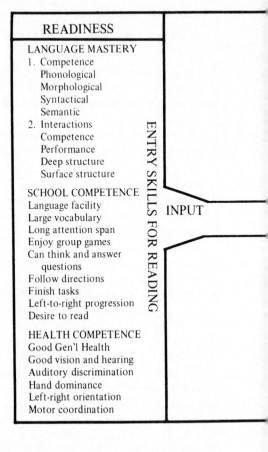

READINESS

LANGUAGE MASTERY
1. Competence
    Phonological
    Morphological
    Syntactical
    Semantic
2. Interactions
    Competence
    Performance
    Deep structure
    Surface structure

SCHOOL COMPETENCE
Language facility
Large vocabulary
Long attention span
Enjoy group games
Can think and answer
    questions
Follow directions
Finish tasks
Left-to-right progression
Desire to read

HEALTH COMPETENCE
Good Gen'l Health
Good vision and hearing
Auditory discrimination
Hand dominance
Left-right orientation
Motor coordination

ENTRY SKILLS FOR READING

INPUT

children begin to read early because their parents "push" them, some children do learn to read on their own by a variety of means. Some learn to read from the stories they have been read until they are memorized, others follow the commercials on television carefully, and others appear to make astute hypotheses about sound-symbol relationships by observing adults and asking questions. Terman, in 1925–26, found that about fifty of fifteen hundred gifted children in California were reading when they were five.[11] Print appears to be more readily available to small children now than it was sixty years ago. Labuda reported that half of the gifted children whom he studied had taught themselves to read, some even by age two.[12] To find a four- or five-year-old child among one's acquaintances who can do formal reading is not unusual.

Children who read early may be grouped into two distinct categories. The first category includes those children who are placed in groups to be *taught* reading as a series of lessons to be learned. The lessons are presented, and the children are expected to respond. In this frame of reference, many four-, five-, or six-year-olds are not motivated and may learn to avoid reading rather than to enjoy it. These children, literally, are being "pushed" into reading. Then there are those who learn to read entirely as a result of their own curiosity about words and who ask questions that are answered by sympathetic adults. The important point here is that these children learn to read on their

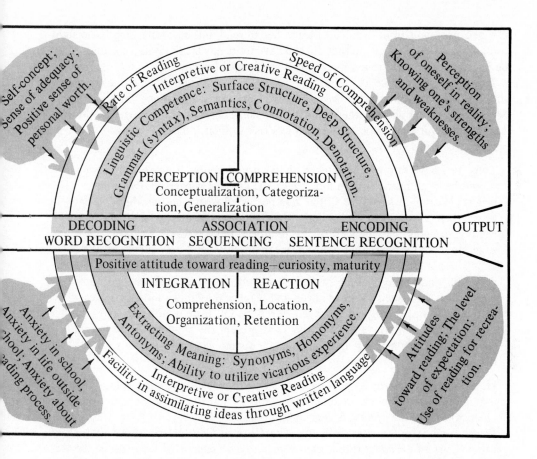

Self-concept; Sense of adequacy; Positive sense of personal worth.

Rate of Reading   Interpretive or Creative Reading   Speed of Comprehension

Linguistic Competence: Surface Structure, Deep Structure, Grammar (syntax), Semantics, Connotation, Denotation.

Perception of oneself in reality; Knowing one's strengths and weaknesses.

PERCEPTION │ COMPREHENSION
Conceptualization, Categoriza-
tion, Generalization

DECODING   ASSOCIATION   ENCODING   OUTPUT
WORD RECOGNITION   SEQUENCING   SENTENCE RECOGNITION

Positive attitude toward reading—curiosity, maturity

INTEGRATION │ REACTION
Comprehension, Location,
Organization, Retention

Anxiety in school, Anxiety in life outside school; Anxiety about reading process

Extracting Meaning: Synonyms, Homonyms, Antonyms; Ability to utilize vicarious experience.

Facility in assimilating ideas through written language

Interpretive or Creative Reading

Attitudes toward reading; The level of expectation; Use of reading for recrea-tion.

initiative; the adults only follow the children's lead in helping them to identify word symbols. This kind of learning to read informally is a happy situation. Debbie was a child who learned to read in this manner.

Debbie was a very bright little girl who talked fluently in sentences when she was one year old. She listened for long periods of time to *Mother Goose* when she was eighteen months old. She could study magazine pictures and "tell" four- and five-sentence stories about them when she was two. One day when she was three years old, she was sitting in the car downtown with her mother. Without warning, she spelled the name of the department store across the street, "B-A-R-N-E-Y-S," and asked, "What does that spell, Mother?" When Debbie was three and one-half years old, she began studying the comic strips in the newspaper and spelling out words for her mother to pronounce for her. When she had spelled out a series of words and waited each time for the pronunciation, she could, all by herself, keep in mind what the words were telling her and, at the end of the sentence, repeat the complete sentence. By the time Debbie was four, she was able to read sentences in a first reader without help. By the time she was five and one-half, she was able to read library books of her choice written at the third reader level. The crux of the matter here is that Debbie *did not* learn to read because some adult decided to teach her to read and began flashing basic sight words for her to recognize; neither did she have to memorize the isolated sounds of all the initial consonants through monotonous, prolonged lessons.

The urgency to expose all children at age six to formal reading must be countered with the differences among the six-year-olds who enroll in school. Such writers as Huey, Dewey, and Werner and Strother assure us that some children could learn well through other avenues for some time, with much less risk to their later well-being.

Huey wrote in 1908:

> Thus far I have said little about the child's use of *books,* because I think we should be in no hurry to have him use them. The age is over-bookish, and bright children, at least, are all too soon possessed with a notion which never leaves them that all knowledge lies within the covers of books. Reading, writing, drawing, may be learned and practiced in such ways as I have suggested and in others that will suggest themselves, and may supply all the child's needs for years, without the use of books. Languages, arithmetic, geography, nature may all be studied effectively, in the early stages, with no books other than such as the children and teacher may make for themselves. In the schools of the future books will surely be but little used before the child's eighth or ninth year. In the home at present the child should be taught to read them only as early and as fast as his spontaneous interest calls for them.[13]

Huey also cited Dewey as holding that early emphasis on reading is fatiguing for young children, requires too much drill on "form" that is monotonous, and makes a mechanical tool of the process of learning to read.[14]

Werner and Strother, citing Elkind's *The Hurried Child,*[15] considered the risk of creating *"hurried"* readers rather than "encouraged" ones. Hurried readers, the victims of a too-early emphasis on learning to read, often react negatively by being cautious and afraid to make mistakes. They tend to read for adult praise rather than for the pleasure to be gained from reading and come to find little satisfaction in reading or the school setting. Encouraged readers, by contrast, find pleasure in reading and receive support for whatever reading activities they attempt. The adults follow the child's lead, providing an atmosphere rich in print, respecting the child, and avoiding criticism and correction.[16]

Building Oral Language Competence

One of the most important tasks of the teacher both at the stage of beginning reading and all through the primary grades is to provide many activities for the children that will build their language competence. Some suggested activities are:

1. Using the Bill Martin *Sounds of Language,*[17] the Hap Palmer *Learning Basic Skills through Music,*[18] and any other tape-recorded materials that will give pleasure in assimilating the rhythm of the language.
2. Understanding words in different parts of speech; for example, "A feather is *light,*" "Turn on the *light,*" and "*Light* a fire, please."

3. Rhyming words: Listening and repeating *Mother Goose* and listening to such poems as "I Know an Old Lady Who Swallowed a Fly"[19] and "I Can't Said the Ant."[20]
4. Learning and repeating finger plays, tongue twisters, childhood songs, and jump rope jingles.
5. Telling riddles and jokes.
6. Composing (by dictating to the teacher) stories or language-experience charts such as:

> A Yellow Day
> The sun came up. It is *yellow*.
> We came to school. Our door is *yellow*.
> Julia is wearing a *yellow* sweater.
> We had *yellow* peaches for lunch.
> We read a book about a *yellow* school bus.
> We drew pictures of *yellow* bananas.

7. Finishing sentences or lines of poems in which the last word is left out.
8. Developing sensory awareness by experiencing different textures in a "feeling" box, tasting a variety of foods, or listening to the common sounds at home, which the teacher has captured on a cassette tape.
9. Organizing the daily events in the schedule.
10. Learning and repeating number rhymes and number concepts.
11. Hearing stories read and told; telling stories.
12. Discussing examples of idioms, slang, and figures of speech.
13. Dictating, illustrating, and binding books to be read and reread.
14. Reading, talking about, and binding into books labels from common household products—the package that contained a Milky Way candy bar, the front of a Jello box, a logo from the bag of a local supermarket.
15. Acting out stories. The role-playing may be preserved with video equipment so that the children can view their efforts and enjoy their interpretations of the story.

Judging Readiness for Reading

Facility with language is imperative because children are not going to learn how to read a language any better than they can understand it. The communication skills of listening, speaking, reading, and writing develop as a hierarchy of skills. Beginners must be able to understand and speak the language before they are ready to try to read it meaningfully.

So, first-grade teachers must plan some kind of room organization for the class of beginners. Soon they begin classifying roughly which children

1. Talk easily and use large vocabularies when they talk.
2. Have long attention spans and can get engrossed in a task for long periods.
3. Become engrossed in activities based entirely on language.
4. Become engrossed in active games or exercises of a manual nature.

5. Can think and answer the teacher's questions easily.
6. Follow directions and finish the jobs they start.
7. See and hear likenesses and differences.
8. Demonstrate increasing knowledge of how print functions.
9. Have motor control in writing their names and following lines.
10. Recognize left-to-right progression for following print.
11. Indicate basic training in how to handle books with care.
12. Exhibit a desire to read and indicate curiosity about print.

Measuring Readiness for Formal Reading

First-grade teachers may find it important and reassuring to support their observations and judgments of children's readiness for formal reading with testing. The 10 to 15 percent of six-year-olds who are apt *not* to retain basic sight words and may be required to repeat first grade must be identified and given the kind of developmental program that will increase motor skills; visual, auditory, and tactile discrimination; verbal fluency; and knowledge of concepts. It is disastrous to the self-concept of the children to push them into formal reading programs and then to "punish" them for not learning in the initial stages of reading instruction when they lack the minimum skills for achievement.

Several screening devices can help to alert first-grade teachers in their efforts to determine readiness for reading. A number of reading-readiness tests are available, along with manuals providing interpretation of the results. Typical of these tests are the *Metropolitan Readiness Test* by Joanne R. Nurss and Mary McGauvran (New York: Harcourt Brace Jovanovich, 1976) and the *Gates-MacGinitie Reading Readiness Test* by Arthur Gates and Walter MacGinitie (Boston: Houghton Mifflin, 1969).

Other assessments focus on the child's language development and its relationship to reading. Examples of these assessments are the *Preschool Language Assessment Instrument* (PLAI) by Marion Blank, Susan Rose, and Laura Berlin (Orlando, Fla.: Grune and Stratton, 1978) and the *Test of Language Development—Primary* (TOLD-P) by Phyllis Newcomer and Donald Hammill (Austin, Tex.: Pro-Ed, 1982).

Research suggests that a child's metalinguistic awareness, or his or her ability to reflect upon and think about language, is related to achievement in reading. Downing, Ayers, and Shaefer prepared the *Linguistic Awareness in Reading Readiness Test* (LARR)[21] to aid in the assessment of this ability to think about language.

Clay developed the *Concepts about Print Test,*[22] which has two forms, *Sand*[23] and *Stones.*[24] This instrument was designed to yield information about the child's understanding of print, book format, and the vocabulary used in reading instruction, such as the words "letter" and "word." Clay cited studies that suggest that children are slower than expected in developing these concepts. She stated that lack of knowledge in these areas contributes to many cases of reading failure.[25]

Sultman and Elkins tested 150 children at school entrance with a variety of measures and found that the *Sand* test correlated most highly with reading achievement when it was measured after a year in school.[26]

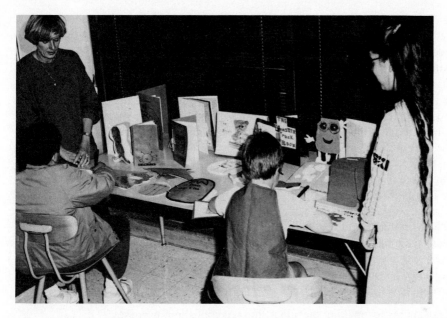

A class book fair is important to young authors. Two children write comments to authors of books on blank pages included in the backs of the books.

Methods of Teaching Reading

Numerous *approaches* to the teaching of reading exist.[27] They can be grouped under three *methods:* the analytic, the eclectic, and the synthetic. It is helpful to know about the beliefs behind each method and the better-known approaches derived from them. Most children are taught from the *basal reader,* which is usually an example of the eclectic method. Frequently, teachers using basal readers also include aspects of other approaches. As a result, many children have reading experiences that derive from all three methods of teaching reading.

The Analytic Method

The analytic method is well characterized by the language-experience approach to the teaching of reading. This approach is based on the belief that children read most easily those stories that use personally appropriate language to express familiar ideas. It is organized around children writing and reading their own stories. Children can talk about their own experiences, and their language can be written and later read.[28] The classroom in which the language-experience approach happens is a busy place filled with interesting, stimulating materials ranging from shell collections to scrapbooks of picture postcards and travel brochures to easels and paints. It is a setting in which children are encouraged to talk, to ask questions, to role-play, and to listen to and tell stories. The environment is rich with meaningful print. Experiences outside the classroom are frequent, but not necessarily elaborate, events. Children may have rich experiences by studying anthills and cloud patterns, as well as in taking trips to zoos and museums.

Whatever experiences the children have should evoke much language. Some of it can be recorded on charts or in class books or on the display of the microcomputer to be read and reread. Teachers can find library books related to the children's experiences to share. Art, music, and drama lessons can extend the experiences. During all of these activities, teachers can be alert to opportunities to extend the children's knowledge of the reading process by studying current abilities and needs. Future lessons can be designed to meet the needs that have been identified.

The language-experience approach starts with the meaningful language of the children. Smaller units of language are attended to as the teacher perceives the needs of individuals or small groups of children.

Whole language is often categorized as one application of analytic methodology. However, to think of whole language as a point of view or a set of beliefs about children, language, and learning is useful. Altwerger, Edelsky, and Flores wrote that whole language is based on the following ideas:[29]

1. Language is for making meanings, for accomplishing purposes.
2. Written language is language—thus what is true for language in general is true for written language.
3. The cuing systems of language (phonology in oral language, orthography in written language, morphology, syntax, semantics, pragmatics) are always simultaneously present and interacting in any instance of language in use.
4. Language use always occurs in a situation.
5. Situations are critical to meaning-making.

Any practices that are congruent with these premises may become whole language activities (for example, book writing, keeping journals, developing themes, or reading aloud to children). To the extent that whole language activities grow out of meaning and the language in which that meaning is expressed, they represent an analytical method. However, to think of whole language as a point of view rather than an approach is more accurate.

The Eclectic Method

Most reading instruction today is eclectic, utilizing the desirable facets of many different approaches. Emphasis is placed on the meaningful nature of reading at all times. Reading readiness continues when children begin a formal reading program. The children learn an *initial sight vocabulary* by a *word* method. This is achieved through chart reading, experience stories, labels in the room, chalkboard work, workbook lessons, and direct teaching on the part of the teacher of a specific list of words. Children read in selected series of basic readers to build systematically a larger and larger sight vocabulary. Simultaneously with building the sight vocabulary, they learn many *word-attack skills*. Early in their reading, they begin a systematic approach to word-attack skills by learning initial consonant sounds, a few consonant-blend sounds, and the structural elements *s, ed,* and *ing,* as well as some compound words. A free reading or supplementary reading program begins as soon as children have the vocabulary necessary to read other books at the level of difficulty that they have finished in the instructional program.

Learning the Sight Vocabulary

Because most children are able to master a controlled sight vocabulary by reading selected words in story context, writers of beginning reading books follow the pattern of using few words in the first book, introducing only one or two new words on a page and repeating all words several times through successive pages. They logically assume that children will be more strongly motivated to read stories with simple plots than to drill on structural and phonic elements in words for long periods of time.

Horace Mann recognized the advantages of the "whole word" approach and recommended it as a method of teaching in 1838. He stated:

> Presenting the children with the alphabet is giving them what they never saw, heard, or thought before. . . . But the printed names of known things (dog, cat, doll) are the signs of sounds which their ears have been accustomed to hear, and their organs of speech to utter. Therefore, a child can learn to name 26 familiar *words* sooner than the unknown, unheard of and unthought of letters of the alphabet.[30]

While children are learning the first fifty sight words, they are concomitantly strengthening their phonics training in *hearing* words that begin the same and rhyme.

In summary, the eclectic method attempts the following:

1. Emphasis on the *meaningful nature* of reading is always primary.
2. Reading readiness is continued with children while they are learning a sight vocabulary.
3. The children learn their initial sight vocabulary by a *word* method. This will be achieved through chart reading, experience stories, labels in the room, chalkboard work, workbook lessons, and direct teaching by the teacher of a specific list of words in their first reading books.
4. The children read a series of basic readers to build systematically a larger and larger sight vocabulary.
5. Simultaneously, children begin a systematic approach to word-attack skills.
6. Their reading, from the very beginning of preprimers, is supplemented by experience stories, chart reading, labels, and reading to follow directions.
7. A "free reading" or supplementary reading program begins as soon as the children have the vocabulary necessary to read other books at the level of difficulty that they have finished in their instructional program.
8. Thus, the reading program is:
   a. Developmental, to teach "learn-to-read" skills.
   b. Functional, requiring application of all these skills in order to "read to learn."
   c. Recreational, encouraging wide reading according to the individual's background of interests and abilities.

Teaching with Basals

Reading, as taught in most *basal reading* series, adheres to the following steps:

1. Children are taught to recognize words as whole units before they are asked to deal with letter components. The *word* is the smallest unit that the child needs to begin to read. As long as a student is learning a few elements so that she can read meaningful context, she can just as well memorize that "look" is the word *look* as she can learn that "l" is the letter *l.* McKee has illustrated how easily an adult can quickly learn a few "sight words" in a completely strange alphabet.

2. Children are being taught a complete course of study in phonic and structural analysis in the process of learning to read. The series of readers available today provide, in teachers' manuals and in pupils' workbooks, exercises for the teaching and learning of all the phonic and structural analysis skills needed to become an independent reader.

3. The all-important *result* is realizing that reading is a thinking process that necessitates comprehension and integration with one's experiential background. Overemphasis on phonics is apt to interfere with reading as a thought-getting process.

4. Books in series are developed from the preprimer level with a severely controlled vocabulary. It is often argued that the preprimer written with so few words (many have twenty or less) could not possibly be interesting. This may be true for an adult reader. Motivated children, however, show considerable interest and excitement in reading them. These books provide them with a great deal of repetitive practice. Most children need this practice.

The directed reading lesson plan is described and illustrated in appendix D.

The Synthetic Method

The synthetic method of teaching reading is exemplified well by the phonics approach to reading instruction. Those teachers who use a phonics approach believe that the child learns most readily when sounds and letters are introduced before reading stories begins. Usually a small set of letters and the sounds they frequently represent are introduced. Stories composed of the words that can be made from various combinations of these sounds are then read. For example, if the sounds /f/, /k/, /r/, /t/, and /s/ are introduced along with the short sound of *a,* and *the* is introduced as a sight word, the child can read such sentences as "The fat cat sat. The fat rat sat." The sentences and stories will become more varied as more letters, corresponding sounds, and rules are introduced.

The phonics approach focuses on the smallest units of language first: the sounds and the letters that represent them. Gradually, the child builds toward whole words and finally whole sentences and stories. The concept that print is meaningful and relevant is delayed until mastery of the many "pieces" of language is completed.

Various linguistic approaches that focus on the structure of language at different linguistic levels, such as syntactical and phonological levels, would generally be considered synthetic methods, also.

Making Connections 1.2: Methods of Teaching Reading

If you are a teacher in training, you should complete the first project in the following list. If you are a practicing teacher, complete the second activity.

1. Interview two teachers in some detail about the reading programs in their schools. It would be helpful if two or three of your peers worked with you to develop a set of questions that would gather a large body of specific information about each teacher's reading program.

    When you have conducted your interviews, analyze the responses in terms of the reading methods being used. Does the teacher use a single method, or does the teacher use elements of more than one method? How successful does the teacher feel the reading program is?
2. Examine the teacher's manual you follow or the prescribed reading program of your school for your grade level. Does the material base its approach on only one method, or does it draw from several methods? If it uses several strategies, list the elements in the program that are derived from each of the various methods.

Class members developing one of the activities may find it useful to share their findings with persons completing the other activity.

The School Reading Program

Each teacher is immediately responsible for the reading program of a single classroom. However, successful school reading programs are guided by consistent characteristics and goals from classroom to classroom. The faculty recognizes the cognitive and affective elements of reading instruction and works to address them.

Characteristics of a Good Reading Program

Some basic principles that guide the overall reading program in the school must be established. A complete reading program is based upon these generalizations:

1. Learning to read is a developmental process. This means that each individual arrives at the maximum state of readiness for learning at an individual time and that readiness must be achieved in all areas of growth: intellectual, academic, social, physical, and emotional. It means, further, that the reading program will emphasize differences in individuals while it must, of necessity, also utilize the homogeneity of interests, knowledge, and skills of groups within a class.
2. Classroom teachers will need to find methods of teaching that will span the differences in a single classroom. This will always include some type of grouping for reading instruction.

3. The language arts—reading, writing, speaking, and listening—are not developed as four compartmentalized subjects in a school day. They are interrelated aspects of a communication process that goes on all day, every day. Every teacher teaches the language arts. Every teacher is a reading teacher, an English teacher, a speech teacher, and a spelling teacher. These communication arts are the medium of instruction in all subjects.

4. The teacher has excellent manuals to use as guides for efficient methods of teaching reading and adequate information about the nature of children.

   a. First, a basic vocabulary must be developed. This is controlled, but leads step by step to higher levels of reading.

   b. Second, word-attack skills that help children to unlock new words are taught. These include picture or context clues, word form or configuration clues, phonic analysis, structural analysis, and the necessary dictionary skills to make that instrument useful and habitual with the student.

   c. The child reads *many* books at each level at all stages of reading. The school should provide many sets of readers within the school system and *many grade levels* of difficulty within every classroom.

   d. A variety of purposes for reading and varying methods of study to conform to these purposes are taught. As Francis Bacon has said:

   Read not to contradict and confute; nor to believe and take for granted; nor to find talk and discourse; but to weigh and consider. Some books are to be tasted, others to be swallowed, and some few to be chewed and digested; that is, some books are to be read only in parts; others to be read, but not curiously; and some few to be read wholly, and with diligence and attention. Some books also may be read by deputy, and extracts made of them by others; but that would be only in the less important arguments, and the meaner sort of books, else distilled books are like common distilled waters, flashy things. Reading maketh a full man; conference a ready man; and writing an exact man. And therefore, if a man write little, he had need have a great memory; if he confer little, he had need have a present wit; and if he read little, he had need have much cunning, to seem to know that he doth not. Histories make men wise; poets witty; the mathematics subtle; natural philosophy deep; moral grave; logic and rhetoric able to contend.[31]

   The teachers help the students to appreciate various types of reading matter and to evaluate their purpose in reading. Pupils adjust their speed in reading according to their purpose, select what is to be retained, and fix their sights on achieving a specific purpose so that they will retain what is significant.

5. All students must be accepted and respected at the level at which they can perform successfully, and they should be helped to grow from that point in the developmental skills in reading.

The Four Jobs in Teaching Reading

There are four major jobs to do in the teaching of beginning reading: (1) help students to develop a basic sight vocabulary; (2) teach word-attack skills (this has been called *phonics* or *self-help sounding* and is now popularly referred to as *decoding* or *breaking the code*); (3) teach that reading is always, and completely, a thinking process that requires understanding (far from being a word-calling process, reading is the interpretation of the ideas behind printed symbols); and (4) give every child a great deal of easy reading practice. Fluency is achieved through meaningful practice. Teachers should move children to the next higher level of reading difficulty *only* when they read comfortably and fluently at the lower level.

The Skills and Strategies of Reading

Teachers are confronted with conveying a wide variety of *skills* in word recognition and comprehension that are prescribed in the basal texts and curriculum guides. Students are expected to master these skills in order to be able to read with understanding and to be able to think about and to use the material that they have read.

Currently, in addition to emphasizing skill mastery, many programs focus on reading *strategies*. Teachers are encouraged to help children to employ prior knowledge, linguistic cues, and prediction and confirmation strategies to become thoughtful readers. Duffy and Roehler have suggested that teachers should turn the skills to be taught into additional reading strategies.

> Strategies are *plans* readers use flexibly and adaptively, depending on the situation. Skills, in contrast, are *procedures* readers overlearn through repetition so that speed and accuracy are assured every time the response is called for.
>
> Students who receive skills instruction learn to answer isolated exercises quickly and accurately. . . . Students who receive strategy instruction learn to reason adaptively with their knowledge about how reading works.[32]

Duffy and Roehler proposed that teachers can turn skills into strategies by describing, modeling, and providing practice in real situations where the strategy will work. By verbalizing the thinking processes needed to apply the strategies, teachers can gradually encourage the students to do likewise.[33]

The following is a list of important reading skills that may be taught as strategies to children. Students must learn all of the skills and strategies in word recognition and in comprehension so that they will be able to gain meaning readily. They are aided in word recognition by using the context of the reading wisely, by studying the picture clues provided, and by using structural and phonic analysis.

1. a. Phonic analysis is the application of a knowledge of consonant and vowel sound clues to the pronunciation of a word
   b. Phonic elements: single consonant letters, consonant blends, consonant digraphs, single vowel letters, vowel digraphs, diphthongs

2. a. Structural analysis is the means by which the parts of the word that form meaning units or pronunciation units are identified
    b. Structural elements: root words, compound words, prefixes, and suffixes
3. Vocabulary
4. Comprehending material is using content to predict meanings of words
    a. Understanding relevant and important details or facts
    b. Understanding the main idea or central thought
    c. Understanding the sequence of time, place, ideas, events, or steps
    d. Following directions
    e. Reading for implied meanings and drawing inferences
    f. Reading to understand characterization and setting
    g. Sensing relationships in time, place, cause, and effect
    h. Reading to anticipate outcomes
    i. Recognizing author's mood, tone, intent
    j. Understanding and making comparisons
    k. Drawing conclusions and making generalizations
    l. Skimming as a form of partial reading
5. Study skills
    a. Locating information
    b. Organizing information
    c. Interpreting visual aids to learning
    d. Presenting information
    e. Remembering
    f. Test taking
6. Oral reading skills

Developing Independence in Reading Power

The developmental process through which children must grow has been divided into five stages. The labels may be helpful in understanding the children's gradual progress toward the level at which they can read independently and effectively.

The first stage is getting ready to be introduced to formal reading, that is, *initial reading readiness*. The need for a broad experience background, good language facility, auditory and visual discrimination, physical coordination, ability to attend for longer and longer periods of time, ability to follow instructions, and a genuine desire to read—all have already been discussed as facets of the readiness program.

The second stage is *beginning reading*. Reading in this stage provides the pupils with a growing stock of sight words. In addition to readers, they read charts, labels, and much teacher-prepared material.

The third stage is the period of *rapid progress*. This includes the normal instructional program of the second- and third-grade levels. While comprehension is emphasized, an extensive course of study in word-recognition skills and strategies is taught to children reading at these levels. An abundance of reading materials is provided to give a great deal of easy, interesting practice.

The fourth stage is *wide reading,* generally designated as the fourth, fifth, and sixth grades. All the skills and strategies previously taught will be extended, and there will be much teaching of study skills. Children should do more and more independent reading both in and out of school.

The fifth stage is *refinement of reading skills and strategies.* The student in junior and senior high school needs practice in making value judgments, outlining, summarizing, and generalizing.

The ability to "shift gears in reading," that is, to adjust the speed of reading to the level of difficulty or type of writing so that understanding will result, is one indication of mature reading ability.

The Microcomputer

It is tempting to think of the microcomputer as a new method of teaching reading, but it is *not.* The microcomputer is a *tool* for learning and thinking that can be utilized to interface with any approach to reading instruction, provided that the appropriate software (the actual instructional program) is chosen. If the teacher is encouraging the writing of stories and books, several *word-processing programs,* such as KIDWRITER[34] and BANK STREET WRITER III,[35] are simple enough so that even young children can experience success with them. Other programs, such as PRINT SHOP[36] and NEWSROOM,[37] permit children to prepare class newspapers. Many programs are also available to support the skills of comprehension and word recognition that are congruent with the eclectic (basal) and synthetic methods.[38]

Much has been learned about how to prepare programs for children; more remains to be explored. Teachers should study the software that they contemplate using in their classrooms to be sure that the programs represent the best possible knowledge concerning the reading process, the needs of boys and girls, the development of language abilities, and instructional techniques. Teachers may find it helpful to read one or more of the periodicals that deal with microcomputers in the classroom; examples are *Electronic Learning*[39] and the *Computing Teacher.*[40]

Teachers need to arrange their classroom schedules so that *all* students have opportunities singly or in very small groups to work at a variety of tasks on the microcomputer (e.g., practice and tutorial exercises, simulations, interactive literature,[41] problem solving, word processing, and desktop publishing.)[42] Teachers must also arrange space to accommodate the microcomputer units, including keyboards, display screens, disk drives, and printers. Related materials such as bookmaking supplies, art materials, and a record-keeping system should be convenient and inviting. A display area should be nearby. Planning for the use of microcomputers in the classroom must also include arranging time to talk with children about what has been learned, since no matter how exotic the technology may seem, it *cannot* perform this vital function.

The Affective Side of Learning

The self-concept, attitudes toward learning, and anxieties that a child faces are *affective* processes that must interact positively with all the cognitive competence and language mastery the learner is trying to achieve. The affective features of the learning process are depicted in figure 1.1 as continuously affecting the language process.

Teaching in the elementary school requires that teachers respect children as people even though they are small. They have individual personalities to be nurtured, not thwarted. Valuing individual differences leads to the ultimate objective that children grow more different, not more alike, as they progress through the school.

Teaching is not at all synonymous with *telling*. Teaching is providing opportunities for learning; providing a rich environment for choices for children to explore; and providing guidance needed to solve problems. The physical environment for the children in school should be a safe, attractive place that invites the learners to use, to explore, and to feel good about the surroundings.

Because children are trying to "order" their worlds, they can make use of learning only as it meets their needs to further that ordering. They are unique (unlike anybody else); they have their own individual learning styles; and they bring to school a complete set of cultural values learned at home. With respect to what each child *will* learn, the relationship between the teacher and the child is more important than the intellectual content of the course of study.

Many teachers have never had any professional education to prepare them to interact with human feelings in the classroom. Neither have they had systematic feedback about responding to feelings expressed by others. Further, they may have an indefinite, undefined belief that feelings must be "left out" of the teaching process. With this point of view, teachers are sure to respond minimally to emotion and feeling in the classroom.

However, there is a positive and significant relationship between the teachers' levels of empathy, congruence, and positive regard for the students they teach and the levels of cognitive gain made by those students as measured by standardized tests. The classroom social-emotional setting directly affects what the pupils try to do and what they learn. Teachers who are skilled in listening to, accepting, and reflecting feelings as they hear students' cognitive responses use a great deal of praise and encouragement, let the students know that their feelings are accepted, and attempt to avoid criticism. These positive behaviors enable the students to perceive themselves in a wholesome manner and to respond more successfully. Looking for and reinforcing desirable behavior and ignoring all possible undesirable behavior is helpful. Teachers who accept and reflect feelings in a positive way and respond to expressed concerns and feelings help students to overcome frustration, hostility, indifference, and timidity.[43]

Nonverbal Communication

Teachers and students are communicating all through the school day with messages that are sent by means other than the use of words. Teachers "say" more to the students in their classrooms in nonverbal ways than they do in verbal ways. Generally speaking, the students in school are young, in need of adult support, and on the defensive when they do something wrong, make a mistake, or feel inadequate. Recognizing these conditions, then, it is easy to understand the importance of giving a smile or withholding a smile; using a pleasant voice or a stern unfriendly voice; or maintaining a friendly, close proximity to the student or a distant, standoffish nature. Even eye behavior can be a significant source of nonverbal communication: The middle-class Anglo culture requires that the interested person look directly into a person's eyes to communicate. Personal grooming, mode of dress, presence or absence of perfume, or even the contrast of stiff or relaxed posture—all of these things are communicating messages all day long. Many teachers need to recognize the great variety of ways in which approval or disapproval is expressed. Such behaviors as simply recognizing the child, giving attention to the child, being close to the child, gesturing, touching, or smiling may be the support the child needs. If the teacher says, "I'm sure you did the best you could," but has a cold, rejecting manner, the child will attribute more value to the nonverbal behavior observed than to the verbal expression.

Humanistic processes can help the student to build awareness and acceptance of self. This awareness and acceptance will lead to positive self-concept and increase each individual's level of trust. Quandt writes:

> Acceptance is a value of oneself that enables that person to see himself as important and worthwhile. It develops when there is no threat that others will express judgments about the person. Acceptance leads to risk taking, an atmosphere in which an individual is willing to uncover and confront his or her own emotions, attitudes, and values. Risk taking leads to openness, a condition under which individuals share their emotions, attitudes, and values with others without fear of nonacceptance.[44]

Summary

Reading is a process by which the graphic symbols are translated into meaningful sound symbols in the reader's experience. Meaning is the key: Learning to read necessitates mastery of all the linguistic cues that facilitate anticipation of meaning in a line of print.

Perhaps too much emphasis has been placed on the techniques of teaching reading and not enough on the peculiar nature of the children who do not learn what they are taught. The myriad of different abilities of children varies extremely so that teachers need to be continually evaluating the children as individuals in order to help them learn to read more effectively.

Learning to read is a developmental process and requires an extended period of time for most people to grow into mature readers. Reading is a part of the communication process and must be seen in the integrated hierarchy of listening with understanding, speaking, reading, and writing.

The four major cognitive tasks in learning to read are (1) acquiring a sight vocabulary of words, (2) learning word-attack skills and strategies for decoding strange words, (3) learning comprehension and study skills and strategies, and (4) practicing extensively and meaningfully. Analytic, eclectic, and synthetic methodologies can be applied to help students to master these jobs. *157082*

For Further Reading

Anderson, Richard C., et al. *Becoming a Nation of Readers: The Report of the Commission on Reading.* Washington, D.C.: National Academy of Education, National Institute of Education, and Center for the Study of Reading, 1985. An important summary of the state of reading instruction in the mid-1980s.

Goelman, Hillel, Antoinette Oberg, and Frank Smith, eds. *Awakening to Literacy.* Portsmouth, N.H.: Heinemann Educational Books, 1984. A collection of essays by major writers on the reading process and reading instruction.

Goodman, Kenneth. *What's Whole in Whole Language?* Portsmouth, N.H.: Heinemann Educational Books, 1986. An attempt to capture the essence of the meaning and application of whole language theory.

Jewell, Margaret G., and Miles Zintz. *Learning to Read Naturally.* Dubuque, Iowa: Kendall/Hunt Publishing Co., 1986. A theoretically sound handbook in the development of literacy abilities in young readers. Many lists of references, materials, and instructional ideas.

McKee, Paul. *A Primer for Parents.* Rev. ed. Boston: Houghton Mifflin Co., 1975. Parents can experience what it means to be a beginning reader as they struggle to read using a strange code.

Smith, Frank. *Reading without Nonsense.* 2d ed. New York: Teachers College Press, 1985. A cogent and readable statement of psycholinguistic theory as it applies to reading.

Taylor, Denny. *Family Literacy: Young Children Learning to Read and Write.* Exeter, N.H.: Heinemann, 1983. A study of the development of literacy in young children in six families. The context is the support for literacy within the homes.

Walker, Barbara J. *Diagnostic Teaching of Reading: Techniques for Instruction and Assessment.* Columbus, Ohio: Merrill Publishing Co., 1988. A current textbook in the field of reading that assumes a diagnostic approach to teaching.

Notes

1. Jim Cummins, "Empowering Minority Students: A Framework for Intervention," *Harvard Educational Review* 56 (February 1986): 18–36.
2. William S. Gray, *On Their Own in Reading* (Chicago: Scott, Foresman, 1948), 35–37.
3. Albert J. Harris and Edward R. Sipay, *How to Increase Reading Ability,* 8th ed. (New York: Longman, 1985), 12.
4. Frank Smith, *Understanding Reading,* 3d ed. (New York: Holt, Rinehart and Winston, 1982), 2–3.
5. Ernest Horn, *Methods of Instruction in the Social Studies* (New York: Charles Scribner's Sons, 1937), 154.
6. Marilyn Jager Adams, "Failures to Comprehend and Levels of Processing in Reading," in *Theoretical Issues in Reading Comprehension,* ed. Rand J. Spiro, Bertram C. Bruce, and William F. Brewer (Hillsdale, N.J.: Lawrence Erlbaum Associates, Pub., 1980), 28.
7. Helen M. Robinson, "Major Aspects of Reading," in *Reading: Seventy-five Years of Progress,* ed. H. Alan Robinson (Chicago: University of Chicago Press, 1966), 28.
8. Eleanor J. Gibson, "Learning to Read," and Harry Singer, "Conceptualization in Learning to Read," in *Theoretical Models and Processes of Reading,* 3rd ed., ed. Harry Singer and Robert B. Ruddell (Newark, Del.: International Reading Association, 1985), 222–55.

9. Robert B. Ruddell and Martha R. Haggard, "Oral and Written Language Acquisition and the Reading Process," in *Theoretical Models,* 63 and 80; and Miles V. Zintz and Zelda R. Maggart, *The Reading Process,* 5th ed. (Dubuque, Iowa: Wm. C. Brown Co. Publishers, 1988).

10. Grover C. Mathewson, "Toward a Comprehensive Model of Affect in the Reading Process," in *Theoretical Models,* 841–56.

11. Lewis M. Terman, *Genetic Studies of Genius* (Stanford, Calif.: Stanford University Press, 1925, 1926), 1: 271–72; 2: 247–55.

12. Michael Labuda, ed., *Creative Reading for Gifted Learners: A Design for Excellence,* 2d ed. (Newark, Del.: International Reading Association, 1985), 4.

13. Edmund Burke Huey, *The History and Pedagogy of Reading* (New York: Macmillan, 1918; Cambridge, Mass.: Massachusetts Institute of Technology, 1968), 145.

14. Ibid., 120.

15. David Elkind, *The Hurried Child: Growing Up Too Fast Too Soon* (Reading, Mass.: Addison Wesley, 1981).

16. Patrice Holden Werner and JoAnna Strother, "Early Readers: Important Emotional Considerations," *Reading Teacher* 40 (February 1987): 538–43.

17. Bill Martin, Jr., and Peggy Brogan, *The Sounds of Language* (New York: Holt, Rinehart and Winston, 1972–73).

18. Hap Palmer, *Learning Basic Skills through Music,* 2 vols. (Freeport, N.Y.: Educational Activities, Inc., 1980), record or cassette.

19. "I Know an Old Lady" in Tom Glazer, *Eye Winker, Tom Tinker, Chin Chopper, Fifty Musical Fingerplays* (New York: Doubleday, 1973).

20. Polly Cameron, *I Can't Said the Ant* (New York: Scholastic Book Services, 1961).

21. John Downing, D. Ayers, and B. Shaefer, *Linguistic Awareness in Reading Readiness Test* (Scarborough, Ontario: Nelson Canada Ltd., 1983).

22. Marie M. Clay, *The Early Detection of Reading Difficulties: A Diagnostic Survey with Recovery Procedures,* 3d ed. (Auckland, New Zealand: Heinemann Educational Books, 1985).

23. Marie M. Clay, *Sand* (Auckland, New Zealand: Heinemann Educational Books, 1972).

24. Marie M. Clay, *Stones* (Auckland, New Zealand: Heinemann Educational Books, 1979).

25. Marie M. Clay, *The Early Detection of Reading Difficulties,* 27; and Marie M. Clay, *Reading: The Patterning of Complex Behaviour,* 2d ed. (Auckland, New Zealand: Heinemann Educational Books, 1979).

26. William F. Sultman and John Elkins, "Readiness Assessment and Early Reading: A Multiple Regression Analysis," *Reading Education* 7, no. 1 (Autumn 1982): 25–31.

27. Robert C. Aukerman, *Approaches to Beginning Reading,* 2d ed. (New York: John Wiley and Sons, 1984).

28. Roach Van Allen, *Language Experiences in Communication* (Boston: Houghton Mifflin Co., 1978), 23–24.

29. Bess Altwerger, Carole Edelsky, and Barbara Flores, "Whole Language: What's New?" *Reading Teacher* 41 (November 1987): 145.

30. Lillian Gray, *Teaching Children to Read,* 3d ed. (New York: Ronald Press, 1963), 47, citing Horace Mann's *Report to the Board of Education in Massachusetts in 1838.*

31. Francis Bacon, *Essays, Civil and Moral, and the New Atlantis,* vol. 3 of *The Five Foot Shelf of Books, The Harvard Classics,* ed. Charles W. Eliot, (New York: P. F. Collier and Son, 1909), 128–29.

32. Gerald G. Duffy and Laura R. Roehler, "Teaching Reading Skills as Strategies," *Reading Teacher* 40 (January 1987): 415.

33. Ibid., 416–17.
34. *Kidwriter* (Cambridge, Mass.: Spinnaker Software Corp.).
35. *Bank Street Writer III* School Edition (New York: Scholastic Software).
36. *Print Shop* (San Rafael, Calif.: Broderbund Software).
37. *Newsroom* Scholastic Edition (New York: Scholastic Software).
38. See the various volumes of *The Digest of Software Reviews, Education, and Computers, Reading and Language Arts* (Modern Learning Publishers, Inc., 1308 E. 38th St., Oakland, Calif.).
39. *Electronic Learning* (Scholastic Inc., P.O. Box 2041, Mahopac, N.Y. 10541).
40. *The Computing Teacher* (University of Oregon, 1787 Agate St., Eugene, Ore. 97403–1923).
41. Dennis M. Adams, "Interactive Children's Literature: Moving from Print to Electronic Literacy," *Reading Horizons* 26 (July 1986): 246–51.
42. Robert McCarthy, "Stop the Presses! An Update on Desktop Publishing," *Electronic Learning* 7 (March 1988): 24–30.
43. Ron Brandt, "On Student Needs and Team Learning: A Conversation with William Glasser," *Educational Leadership* 45 (March 1988): 38–45.
44. Ivan J. Quandt, *Teaching Reading: A Human Process* (Chicago: Rand McNally, 1977), 31.

2
Getting Ready for Corrective Instruction

Vocabulary

diagnostic approach
chronological age
mental age
intelligence quotient (IQ)
test ceiling
background of experience
readiness
mental retardation
educational retardation
expected reader level
range of achievement
general reading immaturity
specific reading immaturity
limiting reading disability
complex reading disability
discouraged learners
Public Law 94–142
individualized education
    program (IEP)
mainstreaming
Regular Education
    Initiative
self-concept
corrective reading
remedial reading
learned helplessness
depression

Questions

1. What are the major factors that contribute to success or failure in learning how to read? (**Recall**)
2. What important issue does the section in this chapter on mental retardation versus educational retardation highlight? (**Inference**)
3. What are two ways to identify the expected reader level? (**Recall**)
4. Why will the differences in a group of children increase as they progress through school, especially with good teaching? (**Inference**)
5. What should *every* teacher know about P.L. 94–142? (**Recall**) How is that law related to corrective reading in the regular classroom? (**Inference**)
6. How does the Regular Education Initiative affect the teaching of reading in the regular classroom? (**Inference**)
7. What do the relationships between emotional difficulties and learning to read mean to you, as the teacher in the classroom? (**Application**)
8. What are some specific things that you can do to help children to grow in positive attitudes toward themselves? (**Application**)
9. Distinguish between corrective and remedial reading. (**Recall**)

Introduction

Among the students in any teacher's classroom will be several children who read more poorly than most of their peers. These children constitute a challenge to the teacher to meet their needs and to guide their reading growth for the year.

> Poor readers present a special challenge to the classroom teacher. It would be a far easier task to teach them if their only difficulties lay in decoding and comprehending the written word. But along with reading difficulties, poor readers may exhibit a number of behavioral, cognitive, and emotional problems. . . . Often they experience difficulty in such areas as initiating or completing tasks, working accurately, maintaining concentration, following oral and written directions, staying in their seats. . . . In addition, poor readers may have a maladaptive learning style. . . . And associated with their learning difficulty may be emotional issues; poor self-concept, low frustration tolerance, and defeatist attitudes may contribute to impaired concentration or decreased willingness to attempt or persevere at tasks.[1]

How will the teacher proceed? Background knowledge about the range of differences that is normal in the classroom, about factors that make for success or failure in teaching troubled readers, and about support systems will be helpful. A *diagnostic approach* that guides the teacher in building a broad picture of the students' strengths and weaknesses and designing an instructional program based on that knowledge will shape and support the teacher's work.

Background Knowledge

One of the first realities to be faced by the classroom teacher upon meeting the new class at the opening of the school term will be the range of differences among the individuals in the group. These differences will evidence themselves in physical appearance, in facial expression, in motivations to work with or against the teacher, in interests, aptitudes, and aspirations, and in varying abilities to achieve in all of those academic skills commonly accepted as criteria of school success. The teacher may think of these behaviors, learned since infancy, as affective, cognitive, or psychomotor. The emphasis is, nevertheless, upon the range of differences. And since reading success or failure is an integral part of all these behaviors, this book attempts (1) to help classroom teachers to organize what they already know cognitively about effective classroom management and (2) to present new ideas that are designed to enable each child to grow in the ability to read. Because reading is still the basic requirement for success in our schools as they are presently organized, classroom teachers have to assume a heavy responsibility for coping with the idiosyncratic behaviors of the students and meeting the needs of those students.

Figure 2.1. A paragraph by Anita

Anita Wants to Read and Write the Way Her Sisters Do

Anita is nineteen and has just graduated from high school. She has two sisters who are enrolled in college and are successful there. She has no particular desire to go to a liberal arts college, but she is deeply frustrated because she cannot read or write adequately for the pursuit of further education at any kind of school. She attended many schools in getting through the twelfth grade because her family moved from Michigan to Florida, and on to Okinawa, West Germany, and Alaska. Her mother had been a teacher in high school and thought Anita probably needed to be taught by a phonics method, but none of the schools had used that method, as far as she knew. All Anita remembers now about her first years in school is that she never did "get the hang of reading" the way everybody else apparently did.

Figure 2.1 contains a paragraph written by Anita during the summer after she finished high school. Anita's paragraph reveals that she does not begin sentences with capital letters; *C* words can begin with *S*; *m's* and *n's* are alike; "real" and "really" must sound like "rile" and "rilley"; and sometimes *W* is made correctly and sometimes it isn't. Perhaps the paragraph was intended to read:

> Living in Alaska is the best life I know. You are not hurried like in a big city. The summers are warm and sweaty, and the days are long. If you are a real outdoor person you would really like it. You can go fishing in any of the streams and come up with a trophy. Or you can go hunting and bag a moose. But Anchorage is a modern city with all its city problems.

One cannot help but feel that if Anita's teachers of some ten or twelve years before had been sophisticated about the learning disabilities of many children, Anita might have had the kind of listening, reading, and writing instruction that would have made schoolwork a much more successful adventure for her.

Factors Influencing Success

In chapter 1 we indicated four major jobs to be done in teaching beginning reading: teach a basic sight vocabulary, teach word-attack skills, develop comprehension in reading, and give lots of easy reading practice. These tasks are specific and clear-cut. Problems arise, however, when the teacher attempts to perform these four major jobs with a class of, perhaps, thirty students. The technical difficulties are not apt to arise in the development of these reading techniques but in the differences within the heterogeneous group of students. *All* students do not learn as the teacher teaches. The causes of individual differences have been categorized by Monroe and Backus as constitutional, intellectual, environmental, emotional, and educational.[2] Taylor, Harris, and Pearson in 1988 emphasized educational, environmental, psychoemotional, and neurological (constitutional) problems as the categories for explaining reading difficulties.[3] Pupils' learning at school is conditioned by these factors in their life experiences. An attempt has been made to show this diagrammatically in figure 2.2. Constitutional factors include chronological age; status of physical health, rest, and sleep; and the presence or absence of handicapping conditions in speech, hearing, and coordination. Intellectual factors are closely related to general learning ability and the development of reading skills. The range of intelligence in any class will be several years unless students are specifically grouped on this basis. Environmental factors include the parental understanding of the school and its program, the socioeconomic levels of school patrons, mobility, and foreign language background.

Emotional factors relate to the psychological needs of children: development of the self-concept, recognition of the need for new and varied experiences, reduction of tensions, and fear of failure. Educational factors are those factors in experience background: understanding of concepts, understanding of the language of the school, adequate materials, adequate subgroupings in the room, appropriate instruction, and motivation techniques that are rewarding.

Figure 2.3 emphasizes concisely the many factors upon which the pupil's learning depends. *Chronological age* (C.A.) is the most tangible factor now used to determine children's placement within the school. It is probably the least important of all the

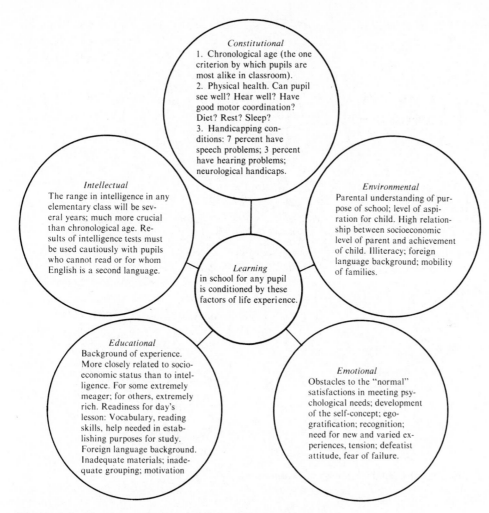

Figure 2.2. Factors explaining individual differences

factors with respect to how successful children will be in learning. For the chronological age spread in a classroom to be only one year is not unusual. In this respect, groups are extremely homogeneous.

The range in *mental ages* (M.A.) in any given classroom will be much greater, however. Six-year-olds in the first grade may have a mental age range from less than four years to more than nine years as measured by intelligence tests administered individually. To the teachers, this range in general learning ability is much more significant than is the chronological age status of the pupils. In fact, many teachers understand the theoretical ceiling on learning in children in terms of their intelligence but have difficulty putting this understanding into practice in everyday teaching. Figure 2.4 shows the range in mental ages of six-year-olds with *intelligence quotients* (IQs) from 50 to

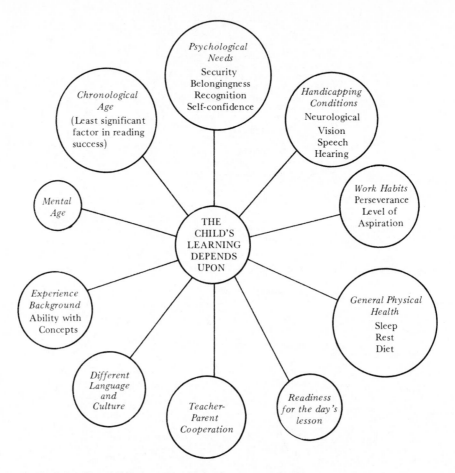

Figure 2.3. The child's learning depends on many factors.

150. It also shows that this range of six years has doubled by the time the pupils are twelve years old. If the IQ spread is as great as 50–150 in a large group of twelve-year-olds, the range of mental ages is from six to eighteen—a spread of twelve years.

In addition, the child with an IQ of 50 reaches a *ceiling* at adulthood of about seven years and six months mental age; the child with an IQ of 75 reaches a ceiling at adulthood of eleven years and three months. The normal adult mental age is fifteen years. As measured by tests currently in use, these are arbitrary differences that can never be reconciled. They will always exist. They arbitrarily fix limits on achievement.

Teachers must, however, always be realistic about the fallibility of test measurements. One must accept inflexible limitations cautiously and recognize that if cultural, social, or emotional difference exists, the "true" measure of potential has not been assessed.

Not all children will have had the same first-hand experiences before they come to school. By the time they are in first grade, many children have had a rich *background of experience*. They have been talked to, listened to, read to, taken many places in the

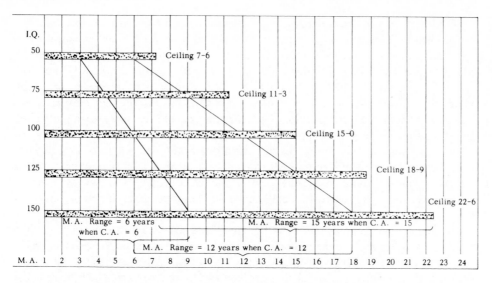

Figure 2.4. Ranges of mental development at ages six, twelve, and fifteen for different IQ levels as measured by intelligence tests administered individually.

company of supportive adults, and provided with a variety of challenging materials with which to interact. For others the background of experience has been extremely meager. Background of experience is not necessarily related to mental age, although the children with the higher mental ages will be much better able to assimilate the experiences to which they are exposed and to understand and make use of them.

Evaluating the children's work habits and their perseverance at a school task can be helpful. Pupils of lesser ability but who work hard will probably get much more done than bright pupils who do not develop good work habits or "drive" for achievement.

Readiness is an important part of the learning tasks of the pupil all the way through school. The idea that teachers teach readiness for several weeks in first grade and then reading the rest of the year is a *false* concept. Readiness should technically be thought of as the "getting ready" period for studying *any* lesson one has to do. Relating the new lesson to the previous experiences in the pupil's background is important all the way through school if learning is to be meaningful.

The health habits and possible handicapping conditions of a child have a direct bearing on his or her ability to make progress in school. When a child fails to progress, the classroom teacher should consult first with the school nurse. In the absence of a school nurse, the teacher should request from the parents a report of a general physical examination by the family physician or the child's pediatrician. If all these factors—impaired vision, hearing, or motor coordination; fatigue; malnourishment; and infections—can be ruled out, then the teacher must look to some other cause for the failure to progress. If these physical factors *do* help to explain the difficulty, they should be corrected *first*. In the event that they cannot be corrected, the best possible adjustment must be made to the handicap.

While defective vision is the first impairment usually considered, and one always to be checked by a vision specialist, there are other less-obvious physical handicaps limiting many children's progress. Obese children referred to family physicians have been found to have conditions of underactive thyroid or very low basal metabolism or both (see Case II: Betty, in this chapter), which may explain lethargic behavior or a complete lack of intrinsic motivation. Asthmatic conditions and allergies may handicap children's general well-being to the extent that they never "feel like" learning to read. Because of the extreme importance of learning auditory discrimination of sounds and developing acuity in this ability, hearing impairment must be evaluated as a possible contributing factor to failure to learn to read. A hearing disability may be of only a temporary nature, and a second-grade child who has a head cold for several weeks or an ear infection of some duration may have some temporary hearing impairment for many weeks and so "miss" much of the second-grade course of study in phonic analysis.

Finally, the psychological needs of the child have significant ramifications in child behavior, but they may be the most difficult for the teacher to change or accommodate. If the children have group recognition and approval, feel that they belong and are accepted in their groups, and are challenged by a variety of new experiences, their needs usually will be adequately met.

The home environment, however, is the primary agent in determining whether a child's psychological needs are met. Many parents have difficulty in responding to the overt behavior problems of their children. Serious psychological needs may develop in latchkey children,[4] in children living with substance abusers,[5] in malnourished children, and in abused children. These problems derive from the home and community

---

Making Connections 2.1: What Makes Successful Readers?

Reading teachers are encouraged to be aware of factors that frequently contribute to reading difficulties for certain children. Knowledge of these factors may help teachers and parents to arrange positive experiences for students learning to read.

It is equally useful to find out what factors contribute to success in learning to read. Such insights can lead to community and school planning for optimum learning experiences. Plan to interview at least two persons of high school age or older who see themselves as successful readers. Ask each to share with you what factors contributed to their success in learning to read and enjoying reading.

When each class member has completed his or her interviews, prepare a composite list of factors contributing to success in reading. Did some factors appear more than once? Were some factors prevalent among particular subgroups of the total group that was interviewed? Do the identified factors fall into a few large categories? Perhaps you can prepare a statement that suggests what factors seem to contribute to success in learning to read.

environment rather than from the schoolroom, but they may have serious consequences in education. Adults in the home establish the values that the child holds for education, including the purpose of learning, the importance of reading as an activity, and the intrinsic motivation to learn. These values are likely set by the time the child enters first grade.

Mental Retardation versus Educational Retardation

Problems also arise as a result of children being "labeled" as *mentally retarded* when they are not. Wide discrepancies sometimes exist between children's achievement levels and their tested intelligence. Occasionally pupils who manifest a "normal" IQ score when given an individual test fail completely to learn to read in the elementary school. When this problem is not adequately faced by those concerned—the parents, the teachers, the school principal, the school psychologist, and the school social worker— such children occasionally get all the way into, or even through, the senior high school. They are usually then given diplomas because they have good attendance records, are socially adjusted with their peers, and practice some of the social amenities. Frustrated teachers have not known what to do or where to turn for help in specific situations and so have passed the students through school. In spite of their inability to read, these students are not mentally retarded.

Jerry was referred for a reading analysis by his minister. The minister described him as a fifteen-year-old boy who *seemed* bright enough and who had excellent social behavior but who could not read. An individual intelligence test indicated perfectly normal intelligence (Wechsler IQ 100). A speech check indicated such serious speech articulation difficulties as to render his speech almost unintelligible to many listeners. A reading test established his status as a nonreader. This profile of abilities is diagrammed in figure 2.5. Obviously, Jerry had tremendous potential for reading and language growth.

The case history provided by the family explained much of *why* the situation existed. Attendance in several schools in three states during the primary grades concomitant with a serious asthmatic condition that was not arrested until he was ten years old were given as causes of failure to learn to read.

Eighteen months after tutoring was started, Jerry was attending high school classes, reading fairly well at sixth- or seventh-grade level, had developed an easily understood speech pattern, played on the high school football team all fall, and had earned passing grades at the first reporting period in the senior high school. "He attended the high school prom after their homecoming football game and appeared on the dance floor completely indistinguishable from any of his football teammates," according to his school superintendent. Yet this boy and the many who have similar school learning problems are often referred to as mentally retarded or as slow learners. In cases such as these, problems are correctable, and any description alluding to mental deficiency does not apply.

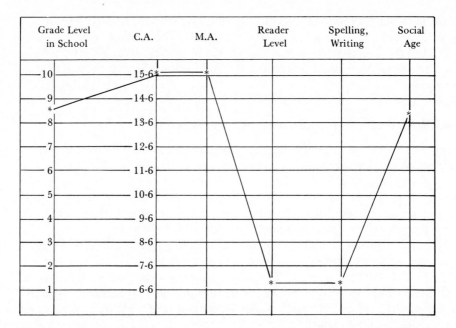

Grade Level in School	C.A.	M.A.	Reader Level	Spelling, Writing	Social Age
—10	15-6*	—————*			
—9	14-6				
*					
—8	13-6				*
—7	12-6				
—6	11-6				
—5	10-6				
—4	9-6				
—3	8-6				
—2	7-6				
—1	6-6		*	*	

Figure 2.5. Jerry's profile of abilities. Jerry's individual intelligence test results showed normal intelligence. His behavior in social situations was judged to be "normal" for one in the eighth grade. He could not, however, read or write.

While a wide range of achievement is normally expected in a class, many of the poor achievers need instruction in remedial reading. Pupils who need remedial reading in such a class are underachievers. Pupils whose capacity for learning is below the average of the class but who are achieving as well as their ability permits are not underachievers. The difference is estimated on the basis of an *expected reader level*.

Expected Reader Level

If teachers had accurate measures of the mental ages of their pupils (group intelligence tests have no value in assessing the abilities of poor readers), they could get a *rough estimate* of expected reader level by *subtracting five and one-half years* from the mental age, since six and one-half is the average age of beginning first graders. Formulae have been derived for more accurately estimating this expected reader level. Bond et al. found that using a formula of years in school times IQ (expressed as a decimal; for example, 100 equals 1.00) plus 1.0 gave a practical estimate of grade achievement expectancy.[6] Thus a child in the middle of fourth grade with an IQ of 120 has a reading expectancy of 3.5 times 1.20 plus 1.0, or 5.2. This child would be mentally capable of reading at the fifth reader level. If the child is reading only at the third-grade reader level, the child is underachieving, or *educationally retarded,* by two grade levels.

TABLE 2.1. Educational Retardation Is the Difference between Expected and Present Reading Levels

Name	C.A.	M.A.	IQ	Years in School	Expected Reading Grade (Bond-Tinker)	Present Reading Level	Educational Retardation (Bond-Tinker)
Betty	12–6	13–4	108	6	7.48	Second Grade	About 5 years
George	14–11	14–9	99	8	8.9	First Grade	About 8 years
Bill	9–8	9–11	102	3.5	4.5	First Grade	About 3½ years
Tom	9–0	13–6	150	4.0	7.0	Fourth Grade	About 3 years
Mary	7–6	6–6	87	1.5	2.3	Beginning Reader	None
Jim	12–8	10–0	79	6.0	5.7	Easy fifth	None
Sally	12–0	9–0	75	4.0	4.0	Hard third	None

The amount of educational retardation for seven students, based on Bond and Tinker's formula for estimating expected reader level, is illustrated in table 2.1.

Betty is underachieving by five years, educationally speaking; George, eight years; Bill, three and one-half years; and Tom, three years. The expected reading level column in the table shows the level at which each child would be achieving if he or she were performing at his or her so-called capacity level. Sally, Mary, and Jim, on the basis of mental age given in table 2.1, are achieving at approximately capacity level. They are not educationally retarded.

When children enter the fourth grade and again when they enter the junior high school they face a crucial test. At the fourth grade, students are expected to begin the study of content area texts, and in junior high school, students are expected to study more independently and are not afforded as much individual attention. A great deal of pressure is exerted to make sure that the school teaches them what it has in mind for them to learn, but it often does not vary the assignments to give them a chance to learn what they are ready to learn.

To clarify further the distinction between mental retardation and educational retardation, we will present three brief illustrative cases. The first is a mentally retarded boy for whom the school should provide an adjusted program. This boy is *not* a remedial case. The other two cases are students with "normal" ability who need remedial teaching of basic reading skills.

Case I: Ronald

Ronald was thirteen and in the sixth grade. The results of the Stanford-Binet Intelligence Scale, Form L, showed his IQ to be 68. He was referred for testing so that some evidence could be obtained to determine whether he was mentally retarded and the extent to which his reading retardation might be explained by low intelligence.

The intelligence test indicated that Ronald's mental age was about nine years and that the things expected of him in his schoolwork ought to be no more difficult than would be expected of a nine-year-old child.

Technically, a diagnosis of mental retardation is never made on the basis of the administration of the Stanford-Binet test alone. A complete case study of a child (see chapter 8) necessitates medical examinations, a psychological evaluation of many behaviors, a social case history, and a consideration of life values, motivations, and aspirations. From the point of view of the classroom teacher, however, this test of intelligence has revealed extremely valuable information about Ronald's present ability to function. It may perhaps be all the information immediately available to the teacher, and the teacher must plan something for Ronald *now*.

The teacher's major problem is to help Ronald make a contribution to the group and to help the group understand and appreciate him. His classmates need to learn to recognize his limitations and his contributions, and to be helpful. Ronald will be accepted by many as a friend; by many he will often be ignored.

Ronald can make a satisfactory adjustment as an adult if he is supervised and taught some personal, social, and occupational skills as he grows older (if he is retarded, as this test result indicated).

Ronald's teacher, who is one of the primary factors in his success, must maintain for Ronald standards that will result in success rather than failure. The teacher must remember always to start *where Ronald is* and to move slowly from one step in learning to another. Sixth-grade standards have no place in the teacher's approach with him.

Since Ronald can now read at third-grade level, he is not seriously retarded in reading, if the intelligence test score is reliable. During the class period when the other children work on strategies, the teacher should make sure that Ronald gets adequate instruction and practice using work-type reading of third-grade level. Because his teacher teaches social studies and science by the unit method and provides reading materials in the classroom covering a range of several years of reading difficulty, Ronald will be able to participate in the class as well as others who read poorly. In addition to providing practice in the three R's, his teacher will utilize whatever talents he may have in drawing or illustrating, mounting pictures, making bulletin boards, or making models to clarify concepts. Ronald may find some microcomputer programs useful and may enjoy recording his ideas in books that he designs.

Mentally retarded children may also be educationally retarded. Mentally retarded children who have a capacity to achieve higher than their achievement level will profit from corrective reading, although their rate of growth will be slower, corresponding to their rate of mental development.

If children are mentally retarded, they need to work at *their* reader levels, and the teacher should conscientiously remember to "go back to where they are" just as the teacher would for children who are not mentally retarded.

Case II: Betty

Betty was referred to the educational clinic in May, at the end of her sixth-grade school year. The sixth-grade teacher had decided to move Betty to special education in the elementary building for next year's assignment because she could not read, had no aptitude for schoolwork, seemed tired all day, and responded to no type of motivation. Her referral to the clinic was made through the school psychologist, who found that Betty's IQ score on the Stanford-Binet test was 114. The psychologist could not approve Betty's transfer to the room for the educable mentally retarded and made the referral for an analysis of reading ability.

The reading analysis showed that Betty's reading abilities were somewhat as follows:

Reader level as found in a series of readers	Second grade, first semester (2')
Grade placement on Gates-MacGinitie Reading Tests	3.2
Vocabulary	3.0
Comprehension	3.4
Spelling grade placement	Third grade
Word-attack skills	End of grade 2
Dolch Basic Sight Vocabulary of 220 service words	Score of 192—second-grade level
	(See table 3.2)

Betty's chief expressed interest was in horses. The clinic director made use of this interest by giving her many stories about horses and employing her talents in drawing and writing about them.

It was concluded that if Betty were to be helped, her remedial program should begin with all the developmental skills and strategies at the second-grade level.

Her mother and father accompanied her for the analysis and were much interested in the results. They were determined that she should not be transferred to the class for retarded children. The father expressed the greater interest in having Betty achieve success in reading. Betty's vision and hearing had been checked at the teacher's suggestion during the school year. Since Betty was overweight, this physical condition was discussed with her parents. They indicated that Betty was sixty pounds too heavy; they had tried to keep her from eating sweets until she felt that they nagged at her about eating anything; and they recognized that she often seemed tired.

Her mother insisted that Betty got sufficient sleep, as much as ten hours a night. She had taken Betty to the doctor, who found Betty to have a very low metabolism rate and had prescribed medication. Betty's mother expected Betty to accept the responsibility for taking the medicine, however, and had not supervised it. No one in the family seemed to recognize the seriousness of this and the interrelationship between Betty's lethargy, her excess weight, and her lack of motivation. The clinic director suggested that the parents have Betty again visit the doctor and that they follow through carefully on any advice for Betty's taking medication regularly.

The first step in remedial teaching was to assure Betty that she was bright, that she could learn to read, and that if she were willing to work at it, she would be able to catch up with her class and eventually be able to read and write as well as they could. Since Betty was now ready to transfer to junior high school and that challenge made a considerable impression, to convince her that her situation could be remedied was not difficult.

Betty attended the reading clinic during the eight-week summer school. In the fall, she attended the clinic two hours each day and went to junior high school at 11:00 A.M. This program continued until the following May when Betty's reader level had progressed to sixth-grade level. Her last tests in the clinic revealed the following scores:

Reading vocabulary	7.2
Paragraph meaning	6.4
Total	6.8

Conferences with her mother indicated that her parents had not given Betty much encouragement and praise for the rather remarkable growth that she had effected during seventh grade. They were counseled to give her encouragement, to spend time with her and to appreciate her as a person. The parents were encouraged to help her to understand her physical problem, since she was still much overweight. They were counseled that while she did not read at eighth-grade level, she would be able to read competently enough to complete eighth-grade work, and that in her free reading she would be able to find plenty of reading material at her reading level.

The clinic program for Betty had been primarily one of:

1. Starting where she was and building security and confidence.
2. Following the same steps that are necessary in good first teaching of reading.
3. Building attitudes toward reading that helped her to accept herself and her schoolwork, and encouraged personal reading outside of the schoolwork.

In Betty's case, the program included giving attention to health problems that would make her feel like working and encouraging the parents to be more interested in and to give greater acceptance to her school effort. Not the least task, by any means, was convincing Betty that she was a bright girl who would meet expectations.

Case III: George

George was 14–11 (C.A.) and in the seventh grade in a three-teacher rural school when he was identified on a reading screening test as a nonreader. On the Gates-MacGinitie Reading Tests given to all the children in grades three through eight, George attempted only a few answers and missed so many of those that one could only conclude that he was guessing. An individual reading inventory disclosed that his reader level was primer. His sight vocabulary was limited, and he had little knowledge of useful reading strategies or specific skills.

George was quiet; however, his conversation with the psychologist suggested that he was not mentally retarded. On the Stanford-Binet, George earned an IQ score of 99. His performance in problem solving, immediate recall, and memory for digits was good; his scores on vocabulary and items requiring much use of the language were more limiting.

George's school record showed that he had been promoted each year through the fourth grade. At that point, the fourth-grade teacher found that George could not read and put him back into the second grade. He had since been promoted regularly and was now in the seventh grade. His family history showed that his father had died when George was six and that at the age of twelve George had acquired a stepfather.

George's present teacher had never considered the possibility of teaching him *how* to read. She read a lot of his subject matter to him and hoped that he would be allowed to graduate from the eighth grade!

In a conference with the teacher, it was decided that George could be excused from regular seventh-grade spelling, language arts, and reading. In their place he could learn to spell the basic words that he would need in stories that he would write himself. At first, he would dictate stories to a retiree from the community who helped in the class twice weekly. Later, he would be encouraged to write his own stories, seeking help with words and the organization of sentences as needed. It was planned that he would have many chances to read his stories to the teacher, to the helper, to younger boys and girls, and to the principal who was in charge of three schools and worked in George's school two days a week.

When several stories had been written, George was encouraged to bind them into a book just as other class members bound their writings. The teacher planned that the community helper would take time to read to George each day that he was in the classroom. The helper would also aid George in finding interesting books in the small library for the boy to read to him. The teacher suggested several books that had excellent story structures so that George could experience how good narratives are formed.

By the end of the year George had heard a dozen trade books read to him. He had written eight books and had read nineteen library books. At first the books had been comparable to a primer level of difficulty. By the end of the year George was able to read a library book on his favorite subject, horses, that was approximately of fourth-grade difficulty; he was able to use prediction and confirmation strategies, due in part to his prior knowledge of horses. While his reading still lacked fluency, George was pleased with his progress and anxious to continue reading during the summer months and in eighth grade.

The point to recognize is that George read many interesting books at increasingly harder levels. By using library materials and books that George had written, the teacher provided lots of easy practice with materials that did not look like primers. George experienced writing, spelling, and word-identification skills and strategies at the level at which he was able to work at any given time.

TABLE 2.2. Range of Reading Ability in a Fifth Grade: The Nelson Reading Test for Grades 3 to 9* Revised Edition, Form A

| | | | | | Grade Norm: 5.9 |
| | | | | | Class Median: 6.5 |
Student	Raw Score	Grade Equivalent	Student	Raw Score	Grade Equivalent
F — 1	133	10.5	M — 7	81	6.5
M — 1	125	10.5	M — 8	80	6.4
F — 2	122	10.4	F — 10	80	6.4
F — 3	111	9.4	M — 9	77	6.2
M — 2	107	9.1	M — 10	73	6.0
F — 4	106	9.0	F — 11	67	5.7
F — 5	105	9.0	M — 11	67	5.7
M — 3	100	8.6	F — 12	67	5.7
M — 4	98	8.3	M — 12	65	5.6
F — 6	95	7.9	F — 13	55	5.0
M — 5	95	7.9	F — 14	55	5.0
M — 6	92	7.5	F — 15	49	4.6
F — 7	91	6.7	F — 16	47	4.4
F — 8	81	6.5	F — 17	40	3.9

*M. J. Nelson, *The Nelson Reading Test* (Boston: Houghton Mifflin Co., 1962).

Range of Achievement within the Class

In view of recognized principles of human growth and development, one must accept that boys and girls grow at different rates, and that they arrive at different destinations in varying lengths of time. All children *will not* learn the *same* lessons in the *same* amount of time with the *same* amount of practice. A most important concept for teachers follows: *The range of differences in a given class will increase through the year and from year to year as the class progresses through school.* If the range of reading ability in second grade is four years on standardized reading tests, it is to be expected that with good teaching this range will, by the eighth grade, be about ten years. Teachers who feel a strong compulsion to work especially hard with the slowest group in the class, hoping to get them to achieve at grade level, not only are attempting the impossible but also may be neglecting the other groups who have greater capacity.

The reading level of the class may be defined as that level at which the "middle child" reads. Measured by a standardized test, it is the level above which and below which half of the class reads. The scores on the Nelson Reading Test, Form A, administered to a fifth grade at the end of the school year, presented in table 2.2, show the class median to be 6.5 (fifth month of sixth grade) while the grade norm is 5.9 (the last month of the fifth-grade year). The class, as a group, is performing above grade level. The scores on the California Reading Test, Form W, administered to a sixth grade at the beginning of the school year, presented in table 2.3, show the class median to be 5.0 (beginning fifth grade) while the grade norm is 6.0 (beginning sixth grade).

TABLE 2.3. Range of Reading Ability in a Sixth Grade: The California Reading Test, Intermediate, Form W*

Grade Norm: 6.0
Class Median: 5.0

Student	Grade Equivalent			Student	Grade Equivalent		
	Vocab.	Comp.	Total		Vocab.	Comp.	Total
No. 1	8.4	7.0	7.7	No. 17	5.3	4.7	5.0
No. 2	6.8	7.7	7.3	No. 18	4.2	5.5	4.9
No. 3	7.1	7.2	7.2	No. 19	4.2	5.5	4.9
No. 4	7.5	6.6	7.1	No. 20	4.9	4.6	4.8
No. 5	7.3	5.7	6.5	No. 21	5.0	4.4	4.7
No. 6	5.8	7.1	6.5	No. 22	4.3	4.8	4.6
No. 7	5.9	6.9	6.4	No. 23	4.5	4.6	4.6
No. 8	5.4	7.1	6.3	No. 24	4.3	4.9	4.6
No. 9	5.9	6.0	6.0	No. 25	3.8	4.9	4.4
No. 10	6.7	5.2	6.0	No. 26	4.5	3.8	4.2
No. 11	5.0	6.7	5.9	No. 27	4.5	3.8	4.2
No. 12	5.9	5.6	5.8	No. 28	4.1	4.0	4.1
No. 13	6.2	4.9	5.6	No. 29	3.8	4.0	3.9
No. 14	4.7	6.5	5.6	No. 30	3.0	4.7	3.9
No. 15	4.9	5.2	5.1	No. 31	4.1	2.8	3.5
No. 16	4.7	5.3	5.0	No. 32	3.3	2.8	3.1

*California Test Bureau, Del Monte Research Park, Monterey, Calif., a Division of McGraw-Hill Publishing Company.

The class, as a group, is performing one year below grade level expectancy. The reader will note that the range of differences in the fifth-grade performance on the Nelson Reading Test is 6.6 (six years, six months) while the range of the sixth grade on the California Reading Test is only 4.6 (four years, six months). The greater range is the more desirable because it indicates that the more able students are appropriately challenged to achieve at higher levels.

Teachers must not permit children with special learning problems to go beyond the primary school without bringing to light the nature of their problems in reading and finding out which specialized techniques need to be used. Such a procedure will preclude students from "going through" the grades with their age-mates without learning reading skills and strategies.

Probably the best way to help children with reading is to combine the teaching of "how to read" with counseling for whatever social or emotional problems exist concurrently with the reading failure. This attacks the so-called blocks to learning that may lie behind the inability to learn, and as children's minds become "free" to learn, they are successfully retaught "how to read." The problems of cause and effect go together and are often inseparable. Sometimes it is not possible, and perhaps not necessary, to say that the poor reading resulted in delinquent or disturbed behavior or that the delinquent or disturbed behavior caused the poor reading. The classroom teacher can assess where children are in the reading process and try to alleviate both the bad behavior and poor reading by giving those children success experiences, building up their feelings of importance, and adding to their security in the classroom and to their feelings of belonging and contributing something worthwhile to the group.

The aim of the diagnosis is not so much to be able to say that one particular factor (for example, poor teaching, poor vision, poor home environment, or lack of motivation to learn) is the cause of failure, but to learn as much as possible about all the causal factors and correct as many contributing conditions as possible.

Psychological, physical, and sociological factors that explain individual differences in learning need to be explored. The fact is that disabled readers are with us in almost every classroom, and their presence must be acknowledged by every competent classroom teacher. The regular teacher is the key person who must accept the responsibility for identifying the child who is not making satisfactory progress.

Characteristics of Poor Readers

In general, poor readers are those students who are not able to function as well in reading ability as their general learning ability would indicate that they should. If they are of "normal" intelligence, they should, all other things being equal, progress "normally" in developmental reading. Students may have problems even though most of their reading skills and strategies are adequate if they are deficient in a few specific areas. Many children are hindered all the way through school because they did not learn how to "attack" polysyllabic words. They may have adequate sight vocabulary but may not know what a syllable is or how to divide words into parts. Other students may not have learned to use their prior knowledge in making predictions and confirming them concerning the print on the page. Still others may pronounce words remarkably well but have very poor comprehension; they may be so focused on sounding or even on accuracy in naming words that they do not attend to the total meaning of sentences and paragraphs, or they do not bring their prior knowledge to bear in applying what was read, making inferences, drawing conclusions, and arriving at judgments.

Poor readers include the boys and girls who have either emotional problems that overlay their ability to attend and prevent their learning what the teacher teaches, or organic problems such as *neurological disorders, minimum brain dysfunction,* or a number of other conditions.

Bond et al. classified poor readers according to:

1. *General reading immaturity.* Simple retardation suggests general immaturity in reading. Fourth graders who have average general learning ability but whose profiles of skills consistently indicate an ability to use only second-grade material are an example. They need to be motivated to learn all the developmental skills that they have missed.
2. *Specific reading immaturity.* This category is used to describe the student whose general profile shows one or two serious deficiencies but who otherwise performs normally. Such deficiencies might be (1) the inability to sense and use syllabication, (2) the inability to read and follow directions, or (3) the inability to organize and remember material read.

3. *Limiting reading disability.* The term *limiting reading disability* is used to describe the student who shows "gaps" in skill learning or who is seriously deficient in school learning. An example is the student whose word recognition and general vocabulary are adequate for grade level but whose ability to understand and remember ideas in content reading is inadequate. Such a student who has average learning ability can be taught the missing skills. Such a student who lacks basic skills in comprehension will need to be taught all the skills basic to analysis, synthesis, and evaluation of paragraph units.
4. *Complex reading disability.* Complex reading disabilities are limiting disabilities further complicated by negative attitudes, poor self-concepts, or sensory or other handicaps. Limiting disability cases should be identified, diagnosed, and rehabilitated *before* they become complex.[7]

Dechant described poor readers as slow learners or reluctant, disadvantaged, or retarded readers.[8] The slow learners are limited by general learning ability; the reluctant readers lack the desire to read; the disadvantaged readers may fail to see the relevance of the school to their personal lives, and they may need to learn "how to learn"; the retarded readers include all those who are performing in reading considerably below their potential level of performance.

Sagor discussed *discouraged learners:*

These are the students who could succeed at school, but who don't think they have a reason to try. They don't believe school offers them anything to make their lives better . . . they get constant feedback on their academic incompetence . . . they don't feel they have any control over their lives at school.[9]

Gentile and McMillan noted that poor readers perceive reading as a threat and exhibit fight-or-flight stress reactions when they read.

Poor readers also display self-deprecation, lack of clear goals or values, vulnerability to disparagement by others, immature relationships with parents and teachers, lack of insight into personal problems, or pervasive depression.[10]

These children represent a serious challenge for the classroom teacher along with all of the other problems associated with teaching reading (e.g., too many students; three, four, or more reading groups; inadequate materials; pressure to complete basal texts, skills lists, or curriculum guides; and responsibility for all other curriculum areas). Yet, if classroom teachers do not meet the reading needs of most children, there is little hope that these needs will be met at all.

Under some pressure about her responsibility to children who have reading problems, one fifth-grade teacher said:

I think of a teacher as being all day in the classroom with thirty-five or even forty children. Perhaps one-fourth need individual conferences, extra time, parent conferences, and some need remedial tutoring. Not always can I refer a child to the school's centralized guidance services and have any results of diagnosis from the psychologist in time to help me during the school term.

The comments of this teacher are directly related to the philosophy of this book. The existence of the problem is not new; a great deal of awareness of it may be new. The solution, to a considerable degree, is dependent upon classroom teachers.

Mainstreaming and the Education of All Handicapped Children Act of 1975

Public Law 94–142, the Education of All Handicapped Children Act of 1975, reflects a present-day concern that all handicapped learners have optimum educational opportunity. This requires that all people be educated in the least restrictive environment in which they can function.

The classification of children by "labels" has produced problems. Assigning labels has created stereotyped behavioral expectations for many who can modify their behavior. Decisions for placing children in any situation should be made cooperatively with the parents and after learning as much as possible about all aspects of the individuals' lives. Certainty that language facility, cultural heritage, and experience background will not discriminate against the children is needed in testing and evaluation. The school can no longer use such arguments as: "The children cannot learn"; "Their handicaps are too severe"; or "A program for these children does not exist." The 1975 law requires constructive, individual programs. *Individualized educational programs* (IEPs) must be provided for all children based on a thorough evaluation of the children's strengths and weaknesses.

The major requirements of P.L. 94–142 include:

1. Extensive child identification procedures.
2. Assurance of full service with a projected timetable.
3. Guarantee of *due process* procedures.
4. Regular parent or guardian consultation.
5. Comprehensive personnel development (in-service training).
6. Full service in the least restrictive environment.
7. Nondiscriminatory testing and evaluation.
8. Guarantee to protect the confidentiality of data.
9. Maintenance of an IEP for all handicapped children.
10. Guarantee of appropriate, public education at no cost.
11. Assurance of a responsible adult to act in lieu of parents when parents are unknown or unavailable.

Federal law required that all eleven of these provisions be in effect as of 1 September 1978. The implications of this law are profound. All children must be provided with an opportunity to learn since it is now accepted that all children can learn something. The law also provides that parents who do not feel that the program of the school is adequate can receive independent evaluations of their children or report to regional federal offices their dissatisfaction.

This major change in education specifies that education will take place in the least restrictive environment. School administrators, generally, accept some form of mainstreaming as the least restrictive. *Mainstreaming* provides that all children who can profit from doing so must be accommodated in a regular classroom for some part of each school day. Thus mainstreaming serves major purposes in the social, psychological, and environmental aspects of the development of the handicapped children.

Public Law 94–142, Section 612, 5B, provides:

> To the maximum extent appropriate, handicapped children, . . . are educated with children who are not handicapped, and special classes, separate schooling, or other removal of handicapped children from the regular education environment occurs only when the nature or severity of the handicap is such that education in regular classes with the use of supplementary aids and services cannot be achieved satisfactorily.[11]

The emphasis throughout the law is that all decisions must be made on an individual basis. All students must be given the education that is appropriate to their individual needs. This law, in its broadest application, relates also to those children who may be taught in remedial reading centers in local schools or sent to special reading clinics in city schools. The children may be helped more in their total development if their remedial programs can be worked out within the classroom. Such programs could include specific help to the teacher from the reading specialist or supervisor, provisions for an itinerant teacher to work in the classroom during the school day, provision for peer tutoring or cross-age grouping, and specific lessons designed to teach students the developmental skills that they need to learn. With respect to the child who may have been labeled as dyslexic, Simpson said:

> It is not the specific difficulty with words that makes the dyslexic's problem so serious. It is the massive, relentless pressure brought to bear on him through the anxiety of parents and the demands of the school.[12]

Classroom Teachers and Individualized Education Programs

Classroom teachers should be aware that special programs for individual special education students have been used for some years now, and individual teachers are, in some measure, accountable for the part of an individualized education program that should transpire in the regular classroom. The National Association for Children with Learning Disabilities has pointed out that misunderstandings may be avoided when school systems:

1. Follow carefully the guidelines disseminated at the federal level. Parents must be notified about any meeting concerning their child, and parent participation is extremely important. Evaluations must be complete and up to date. Such meetings must not become lax and disorganized.
2. Make sure that the personnel who work directly with the student are at the meetings with the parents. Classroom teachers, rather than supervisors who consult occasionally with teachers, should discuss the children's behavior with the parents.

Making Connections 2.2: Utilizing Support Personnel

The roots of difficulties in learning to read have already been identified in this text as being extremely complex. Frequently, the classroom teacher is not able to deal effectively with the problems, since they reside in the conditions of the family or the community.

Support personnel within the school system can often be effective in helping the teacher to resolve some problems so that the child can get on with the business of learning. The principal, the nurse, the speech therapist, the psychologist, the counselor, the special education teacher, the librarian, the physical education teacher, and the home-school liaison person are examples of professional people who can help.

Make arrangements to interview at least two support persons in a school concerning *specific* ways in which they can help the classroom teacher with children who are having unsuccessful experiences in learning to read. You will want to find out how teachers can make arrangements to work with the support personnel and how communication is maintained.

Bring notes from your interviews to share with your class when all members have completed the assignment. In addition to comparing services of persons in different jobs, also note what different people holding the same job see as possible ways that they can help.

---

3. Set up evaluation conferences to respond to the concerns of the parents, the teachers, the therapists, and any others who may work with the child. Evaluations must be kept "open" and broad. The school needs to understand the student's *abilities, disabilities,* and *possibilities.* Good evaluations are multidisciplinary. Also, if parents bring independent evaluations, schools are required by federal guidelines to study them carefully.

4. State IEPs clearly, so that parents can understand the specific objectives that the student will work on during the time period.

5. Include in IEPs all the needed related services such as physical therapy, occupational therapy, and speech therapy.

6. Do not "mainstream" students into regular classrooms with vague objectives that do not meet the social-adjustment needs of a student. What is available may not be what the individual student needs! The school is required by law first to accurately diagnose the student's need and then to provide the service that meets that need.

7. Make sure that the IEP for any student is properly communicated to each regular classroom teacher who will teach him or her. There have been instances in which classroom teachers have never seen the IEP for students who have spent parts of their school days in their rooms for long periods of time.

8. The student's program is worked out and mutually discussed by the parents and everyone who will work with the student. It is most unfortunate if school officials convey to the parents that the school system is doing the parents a great favor by accommodating their child.

Classroom teachers are wise to cultivate the best skills possible in their public relations with patrons of the community.

The Regular Education Initiative

The Regular Education Initiative is a new movement designed to respond to the requirement of the least restrictive environment. The general feeling is that many mildly handicapped children, usually children labeled as learning disabled, can receive *all* of their education in regular education classrooms and that all pullout programs for these students are unnecessary.[13] Shepard wrote that 90 percent of the children presently being served as learning disabled have very mild handicaps and could be educated in regular education classrooms.[14] Others have made note of overreferrals. Kauffman, Gerber, and Semmel have reported that teachers generally believe that students should be identified for special services only when necessary and should spend as much time as possible with their nonhandicapped peers, leaving special educators to focus their efforts and services on those needing specialized services.[15]

Not all specialists in the education of the mildly handicapped feel sure that the Regular Education Initiative is wise. They are concerned that low achievers will remain low achievers even when the label of "learning disabled" is removed and that placement in a regular education classroom will do little to bolster self-concept. They are also concerned that overworked teachers will be forced to "maximize mean performance of the group . . . improving the performance of the most able learners, or minimize the variance in performance of the group" by concentrating on the least able students.[16]

The Regular Education Initiative means that the regular classroom teacher will have a few more children in each class who will need special attention and careful planning for their instruction if they are to learn satisfactorily. The teacher will need to be well informed of the results of diagnostic tests given to individuals and of other data that will provide information for program planning. The regular classroom teacher will also need to carry out evaluations in the course of the school day and find times to observe children as they go about their work to assess the value of instructional procedures, materials, and management strategies.

Appraising Problems: The Affective Component in Reading

Now that some background knowledge about the students and the expectations for their success in school have been presented, we will look at three important affective aspects of a school program to meet the needs of those who have difficulties in reading and writing. These affective aspects are (1) the self-concept: success and failure; (2) corrective versus regular reading programs; and (3) emotional problems and reading.

The Self-Concept

Children who have strong *self-concepts* appear consistently to make better progress in reading. The teacher is a powerful force in building, repairing, and maintaining strong self-concepts in students.

No one questions the destructive power of unbridled criticism or sarcasm on the fragile feelings that children have about themselves. However, perhaps surprisingly, praise of students and their work can also have negative effects on self-perceptions, which include both self-concept and self-esteem. Praise of children's work or behavior may cause them to be dependent on teacher judgments instead of on their own perceptions of worth. Teachers can support the growth of self-worth by using the language of encouragement. An example of a praise statement might be, "You read that page well today." A restatement of that idea as encouragement might be, "It is obvious how hard you worked to read that page today." The use of the language of encouragement "recognizes the growth and contributions that students make and promotes within them self-reliance, self-direction, and cooperation."[17]

Ford and Ohlhausen[18] made several suggestions which ultimately address self-concept that may be useful when working with poor readers:

1. Find out what motivates each individual.
2. Set reasonable goals that may be achieved by a variety of means for each student.
3. Set encouraging measures of progress. For example, measure progress in time spent on reading rather than in how many books or pages are read. The amount read by poor readers may be too little to be meaningful to them.
4. Encourage children to compete with themselves, not with others.
5. Keep progress records private; public displays of progress may be embarrassing to poor readers.
6. Utilize instructional strategies that encourage group cooperation, not competition.

Additional suggestions for supporting the self-concept would also include minimizing ability grouping, keeping up a fast pace in the classroom (which discourages passivity and complacency), attending to learning styles, helping children to understand cause and effect (which relate to progress in reading), and becoming a child advocate.[19]

Schools are organized to accommodate groups. Many times they are not as well organized to meet the needs of the individual. The traditional organization places all the values and rewards on conformity and achievement. In this pattern:

1. Children are lumped together in large groups.
2. Children are given identical assignments with the expectation that everyone will complete them and hand them in.
3. Teachers are apt to express, overtly or covertly, some displeasure at poor, incomplete work.
4. Teachers are apt to unconsciously think "he can't," "he's dull," "he won't get far," "he should have had help before," or "he's inadequate."

Teachers need to be admonished *not to rationalize* the problems of the under-achiever: (1) that the classes are too large to give such a student help, (2) that there is too little time in the school day (the student will be here six hours and needs to fill all that time with constructive work), (3) that there are not any materials to work with (the student cannot help this, either), or (4) that underachievers have developed negative behaviors and do not want to try.

Many people begin their efforts with much zeal and are sincere in their desire to be helpful to children, but when children do not respond to the methods of teaching, teachers allow their zest to cool and begin saying, "Yes, but."

Don'ts That May Encourage the Teacher

The following *don'ts* may be helpful:

1. Don't have any preconceived notions of quick success. You may have it and that will be fine, but you should not anticipate it.
2. Don't feel guilty because you have a pupil in your room who cannot read. All teachers have had seriously underachieving pupils, and many are alert to the existing needs.
3. Don't feel expected to "get them up to grade level."
4. Don't blame former teachers for lack of success.
5. Don't lose patience and say sarcastic things to the child.
6. Don't feel that everybody expects you to know how to teach every child how to read. If they do, they shouldn't.
7. Don't decide that the student is stupid just because you do not make progress. There are probably lots of specialized techniques that you have not tried. Rather, if you feel that you have failed up to now, try to think of the child as your challenge and begin looking for new ideas to try . . . or of other people who may be able to help.

A negative self-concept, which may be the consequence of poor achievement in school, may be irreversible in our present-day schools by the time the student reaches the sixth grade. Dealing with aggression from students in ways to make follow-up positive instead of negative is very difficult for many teachers. Confluent education emphasizes that there are two components in learning: the affective and the cognitive. Rogers wrote: "The facilitation of significant learning rests upon certain attitudinal factors that exist in the personal relationships between the facilitator and the learner."[20] All the variables—interest, anxiety, appreciation, values, motivation, self-concept, and self-acceptance—are part of the affective domain of the student.

Rucker mentioned such words as *lonely, hunger, want of love, poor self-concept, confusion* in describing the affective qualities found in some poor readers. These are some of her direct quotes from different Johnnies:

"You've got to let me cover the other words in the row or I can't read."
"Readin ain't real. Real is outside that window."
"Every time you have that readin class, I have to go to the john."
"Them kids won't sit beside me cause they say I stink. I smell all right to me."
"Mom says I'll end up in the pen like my dad."
"You don't say 'good' when I read, teacher."[21]

Sparks describes the student who gets sent to the office: downcast, general air of detachment, defensive, seems to neither know nor care what is going to happen next. Sparks suggests this student is too often an unwanted child, may be the victim of multiple divorce and remarriage, may be ethnically different, may be the child of overzealous, struggling middle-class parents, or there may be many other causes for the behaviors he or she has learned.[22]

Attitudes toward Success

Sociologists have defined for teachers the narrow scope of life experience that the curriculum of the school encompasses. A rather narrow, inflexible set of values aptly describes the behavioral pattern of teachers in their overt judgmental reactions to students. This set of values places strong rewards on succeeding, working hard, doing good, being right, saving, planning for a bigger and better future, climbing the ladder of success, and shaping one's future destiny.

Many teachers have internalized these values and have perpetuated the narrow channeling of acceptable behavior. In their implementation of the curriculum, they cause a great deal of frustration because of unreconciled conflict in purposes between the teacher and the student. Students who are of lower-class socioeconomic status do not have the same values as their teachers. Those American Indians not acculturated to a middle-class life-style and the many Spanish-speaking children throughout the country who come from homes where language, culture, and experience have not prepared them for the ideology that the teacher takes for granted will find difficulty. The Protestant ethic, to which teachers universally subscribe, refers to the complex of ideas that includes the notion of personal responsibility, personal obligation, the desirability of hard work, thrift, and accumulation of wealth.

Rist noted these values in the assignment and instruction of children in a kindergarten classroom. He found that:

> Those attributes most desired by educated members of the middle class
> became the basis for [the teacher's] evaluation of the children. . . . Highly
> prized middle-class status for the child in the classroom was attained by
> demonstrating ease of interaction among adults; high degree of verbalization
> in Standard American English; the ability to become a leader; a neat and
> clean appearance; coming from a family that is educated, employed, living
> together, and interested in the child; and the ability to participate well as a
> member of a group.[23]

Corrective versus Regular Reading Programs

Corrective reading is for people whose functioning levels in reading are below their capacity levels for reading. In other words, in terms of individuals' abilities as they are assessed, they should be able to read better than they are now reading. Instruction that will narrow the gap between their present functioning and their potential for performing is corrective or *remedial reading* instruction. If this work is done in the classroom by the regular teacher, it is usually designated as *corrective reading* in contrast to the remedial instruction that takes place under "special" arrangements outside the usual class procedure.

Corrective reading instruction is exactly the same process as good teaching of developmental reading, except that it is planned in a very different setting and is directed toward some additional and difficult goals. In the *first* place, the student has experienced failure which, in our culture, is often a traumatic experience. Depending on the nature and extent of this failure, reading instruction will now need varying degrees of adjustment. In the *second* place, remedial instruction is usually done in very small groups or with individual students. Of course, if original instruction could have been individual or nearly so for many of these cases, the instruction might have been effective the first time. The fact that remedial work is highly individualized makes it much different from regular teaching. In the *third* place, it is expected that the children will learn to read, beginning at some level of difficulty below their grade placements. If their regular day-by-day work had been so adjusted, they might have made desired progress without "special" help. When the work is *labeled* corrective or remedial, it is apparently easier to *accept* the below-grade performance and thus reduce the tensions that the children may feel otherwise. In the more permissive atmosphere, the students are allowed to reestablish some confidence, rebuild their egos, learn at their rates, compete only with their own past records, and accept their performances as adequate for them. After these criteria are met, most disabled readers can learn to read. In the *fourth* place, the search for causes of lack of success is continued. Reference will be made frequently to continuing diagnosis. Reading teachers search for causes of nonachieving while they teach the reading skills that the students lack.

One does need to *know more* to deal successfully with the student who has failed. There are additional problems in motivation, in reward, in conferring with a troubled parent, and in adequately planning a learning program for the entire day with the underachiever. But these are not strange and mysterious tasks. These must be incorporated in the "standard" operating procedure of the conscientious teacher.

Corrective reading should be aimed at any individual who is missing any skills or strategies that have already been taught. Primary-grade children are usually not referred to clinics for special tutoring because two years of retardation is sometimes used as a guide for teachers making referrals. But many who are two years behind can be helped adequately in classroom programs, and many who are less than two years behind should have help early so that they will not continue to get farther behind. The only valid criterion for the teacher is to help any children who are not achieving their potentials.

The person who teaches corrective reading needs to know more than just the basic reading skills to be taught. Nevertheless, the best teaching practices are the best remedial practices. The prerequisites to success are patience, understanding, optimism, and ingenuity. It is the classroom teacher's task to determine where the children lost their way, to get them back to their point of departure, and to help them move forward.

Emotional Problems in Reading

Emotional disturbance is evidenced in the behavior of students by mannerisms such as nail biting, stuttering, having extremely short attention span, behaving defiantly, and daydreaming. Other manifestations may be the haggard, tired-out expression; inhibited, withdrawn behavior; hyperactivity and the inability to sit still; or aggression. In deciding what to do about these behaviors, the teacher must be cognizant of the fact that the emotional disturbances may be the cause of poor reading habits, the result of poor reading, or the two behaviors may not have a direct cause-effect relationship. The teacher must attempt, however, to improve reading ability and to adjust the behavior as much as possible.

First of all, the teacher can obtain information about the pupils through careful observation of their total behavior throughout the school day—their play activities, the way they come to and leave the school ground, their comments in casual conversation, their responses as the teacher subtly pursues their interests, their attitudes, and their aspirations. If the teacher can, through the remedial reading effort, meet the pupils' needs sufficiently to rebuild the students' egos and help them to attain greater emotional stability, they may need no further psychological help. In most cases, however, special help for these pupils is desirable.

The second step is to request the school psychologist to obtain further data concerning each pupil's total behavior pattern by using projective tests of a structured or an unstructured nature. The interpretation of the results of such tests requires the skills of a specialist.

A third step in preparing to help most remedial cases is contact with the parents of the pupil. This will best be done by the school social worker, who is in a position to help the parents to analyze their problems in relation to their child, and to plan some kind of rehabilitation if a parent-child relationship is the major cause of the difficulty. In the absence of the school social worker, it is imperative that the teacher visit the parents, report observations of the child, and ask the parents for their evaluation. The child's reading difficulty may not be the basic problem in failure to learn at school. Techniques for recognizing family problems, helping parents to analyze their difficulties, and helping them to solve their problems, to work out constructive solutions and put them into practice—these skills are not within the scope of classroom teachers, but are the basic techniques used in social casework. The reconstruction of the family pattern of living is often basic to a satisfactory solution of the child's school learning problems.

Gearheart[24] has reminded teachers that if a student's *primary* disability is found to be emotional disturbance (a behavior disorder), then the child may not be labeled *learning disabled* in most states. The emotional problem takes precedence over the learning or reading problems, and until it is remedied, it will be considered a factor in causing and continuing the learning problem.

Ephron aptly described the frustration that many teachers feel when adolescents whom they try to teach fail to learn. She entreated teachers never to use words for labels that do not explain.

> Johnny is not responding to our tutoring him. I have a feeling he is resisting.
> His parents always put too much pressure on him, and now he is resisting
> them. He wants to defeat them. He is being contrary, defiant, uncooperative.
> But he's so foolish to cut off his nose to spite his face. Doesn't he realize it's
> his own life that's at stake? Defeating his parents won't help him any, nor do
> him any good.

The adolescent boy is being "negative." Why does he cling so stubbornly to his "negativism"? If our understanding of the boy stops here, we are indeed defeated, and so is the boy.

The words "resistance," "negativism," "defiance," "stubbornness," "spite"—all these words (like "lazy") are pawns being pushed back and forth across the chessboard. They are busy words, much in use, which explore no depth and explain nothing.[25]

Ephron further pointed out, following one of her interviews with a student named Donald, that teachers need to be aware of the inflexible situations within which many schools operate, and that life experiences are not always "either-or" situations. "Either-or-ness" forces people into anxiety states caused by the pressure to demonstrate immediate success.

[Donald's] statement, "You either know or you don't," is an interesting reflection of education's emphasis on absolute accuracy. Education impresses upon children the *need to be right,* and they grow up under the tyranny of immediacy and unrelenting accuracy. There is desperation in rushing to be right, with the accompanying fear of being hurled down the abyss of rejection if one is *wrong* instead of *right.* Therefore, Donald feels that one either knows or does not know, almost by magic, and without the trust in his own good mind to stay with a problem and reason it out.[26]

A Case Study: Fred

Fred (an emotionally disturbed boy to whom psychotherapy and remedial reading instruction were given concurrently) was ten years old and was tested in March of his fourth-grade year.

Fred attended an elementary school where he had a succession of excellent classroom teachers. When he was in the fourth grade, he was referred to the psychoeducational clinic for tutoring in remedial reading.

A reading analysis was made, and tutoring began at the preprimer level. While Fred had an individual intelligence test score of 122 and appeared to be interested and cooperative with his clinician, he was no more ready to move into more difficult material at the end of twelve weeks of tutoring than he had been at the beginning.

An analysis of his relationship with his mother suggested to the remedial reading supervisor that Fred was overdependent and was having some difficulty growing up. Fred had two older sisters who were already married and had children of their own. His interests and abilities in play were with younger children, and he often engaged in solitary play much more characteristic of younger boys.

The remedial reading supervisor suggested to the mother that, since the remedial reading clinic did not seem to be helping, she and Fred should visit the child guidance clinic in the community. It was explained that the clinic would expect her to appear for interviews and some counseling. Fred's mother accepted this willingly, and the two entered therapy sessions in June after school closed in May. The following fall, Fred came to the reading clinic four days a week and attended the guidance clinic the fifth day for the hour. He began making progress in his remedial reading instruction, and at the end of his fifth grade in the elementary school, he was able to read successfully for instructional purposes at the third-grade level.

The "apron strings" should be severed gradually, but they must be severed. A child who has not learned to be responsible for his or her own actions may not feel the importance of learning to read. The responsibility for effecting such changes in children's behavior may require special services outside the classroom, as indicated in Fred's case.

It is true that with determination and persistence the reading clinician might have measured some success in Fred's reading, but the primary problem was apparently psychological, and Fred needed the clinical psychologist to help him find himself, to strengthen his ego, to make a person of him "in his own right," and to free him of his dependence on his mother.

Most parents want to cooperate with school personnel when they recommend examinations of hearing, vision, or psychological factors. They also want a clear explanation of the problem and some interpretation of the results of testing. Parents of children with reading problems indicate almost unanimously that the schools should provide guidance services in the lower grades of the elementary school to prevent as many problems as possible.[27]

The Relationship between Reading Disability and Emotional Disturbance

There are three possible ways in which remedial reading and emotional disturbances may be related:

1. Some children are emotionally disturbed before they try to learn to read, and as a result, fail.
2. Some children fail in reading and become emotionally disturbed as a result of the reading failure.
3. Some children experience emotional problems and reading failure as a concomitant experience.

Harris and Sipay[28] have stated that most children with reading disabilities show signs of emotional maladjustment ranging from mild to severe. Researchers throughout this century have agreed with them.

Arthur Gates,[29] summarizing his studies of emotional and personality problems in relation to reading disability, reported that emotional instability was present in about 75 percent of the disabled readers studied but *caused* the reading disability in only about 25 percent of the cases.

Grace Fernald[30] reported that only four of seventy-eight severely disabled readers in her clinic showed no signs of emotional disturbance when entering school. Extreme emotional reactions did not occur, however, until after the children had experienced repeated difficulties and lack of success. Such experiences produce a deep-seated sense of inferiority in many children and kill their incentive to try to learn. Sometimes an aggressive, irritable personality develops, and the child tries to compensate for the inability to learn by compelling extra attention from parents and teachers.

Robinson[31] found in her study of twenty-two cases of reading disability that emotional problems existed in 41 percent of the cases but were considered the cause of the reading failure in only 32 percent. Robinson noted that the criteria used for defining emotional disability were stringent, perhaps accounting for the lower percentages than those found in other studies.

The Educational Clinic of Boston University reported that 39 percent of the children with reading disabilities who were analyzed "showed an emotional disturbance of some kind."[32] In these cases, discouragement, nervousness, and family trouble were the three causes mentioned most frequently.

Bond and others stated that in the great majority of cases teaching the child adequate reading skills reduces the anxiety and alleviates the emotional problem.[33]

However, some children exhibit *learned helplessness,* a condition characterized by an unwillingness to learn what one is capable of learning, a reluctance to invest effort in assigned tasks, and a negative outlook on one's capabilities and chances of success. Children probably arrive at this point because they perceive that they have no control over their environment and the outcomes of their efforts.[34] They feel that the *locus of control* is *external* to them and that they are powerless over decisions in their lives and the results of those decisions. Helping such children is difficult because they usually refuse to try even tasks that they could complete because they are sure that they will fail. Teachers and parents may help such youngsters by strongly encouraging them to try tasks at which they can be successful and then supporting them to persist until they are successful.

Until recently most persons assumed that *depression* was an adult disorder. However, children of all ages may become victims of depression. Vincenzi reported a study of sixth-grade children which linked the level of depression significantly to reading achievement and reading level.[35] Other studies have supported his findings.[36]

The writers of this text have found that most of the pupils who are referred to clinics for reading analyses exhibit anxiety and nervous mannerisms. However, when reading clinicians demonstrate that these children are "being accepted as they are," their tensions are reduced quickly. Further, as children observe others working at instructional levels far below assigned grade levels, they are willing to "begin at any level" if it means that they can successfully learn to read.

According to Sires:

Many children in analyzing their own problems say, "I got lost in the first grade." How much would be gained if each child spent enough time on the primer level, for example, to become a fluent and thoughtful reader before moving on to first-reader materials! This plan does not involve a non-promotion policy but simply that the teachers become less conscious of grade lines and accept children as they are. If we did this in the primary grades, our middle grade "remedial reading problems" would decrease.[37]

Louttit tells us:

The remedial teacher has the task of helping the child with his disability. He cannot hope to affect parental rejection or inconsistency. He cannot undertake psychotherapy with the child. But he can accept the child as he is, give him support and security, appreciate and encourage him in his positive characteristics, and in this way afford a more wholesome atmosphere in which the child can attack his specific problem.[38]

Even when an emotional problem has been identified and is apparently causing the reading difficulty, one must remember that other children with similar emotional problems learn to read without difficulty. Often, there is a concomitant factor such as an unidentified vision problem, directional confusion, a temporary hearing loss due to head colds, or poor teaching.[39]

The types of problems that children have are sometimes difficult to define, and teachers many times must work with very little information. When children are assigned to classes, teachers should hope that they will respond and progress normally. When emotional distress is evident, teachers must proceed as if these children will be able to learn through group teaching and give as much individual help as possible.

When emotional factors are the primary cause of reading disability, classroom teachers should attempt the following:

1. Become the child's friend (first and most important).
2. Study the child's past history and gain understanding of his or her emotional makeup.
3. Help the child to talk freely about likes and dislikes, fears and hopes, hobbies and interests, friends, and family. With this information, try to discover causes for emotional states and take steps to help each child to adjust. Be a sympathetic listener.
4. Try to determine whether the child failed to read because of emotional instability or whether emotional instability caused the failure to learn. Are reports available from a mental health center or a child guidance clinic?
5. If the child is not seriously disturbed, give reassurance of the ability to read, and motivate and encourage with a good corrective reading program.
6. If there is evidence of a severe emotional disturbance, refer the child for a psychological evaluation before undertaking remedial work.
7. Maintain a classroom atmosphere that has maximum permissiveness.

Summary

In this chapter, the problems of the students who do not make adequate progress in reading were discussed. Studies suggest that these children are, on the average, from the dull normal and normal ranges of intelligence.

Factors influencing learning are constitutional (physical), intellectual, environmental, educational, and emotional. How much pupils learn depends upon their mental ages, experience backgrounds, linguistic differences, general health, work habits, physical handicaps, and psychological needs; and the degree to which the conditions surrounding these factors can be improved to accommodate the learners.

Case studies were cited to distinguish educational retardation, mental retardation, and mental *and* educational retardation. The problem of educational retardation was further illustrated by the contrast between expected reader levels and present reading levels of students selected by classroom teachers for work in corrective reading.

Causes of reading failure are rooted in the fact that individuals are different from one another, that they learn at different rates, and that motivation and drive have much to do with their enthusiasm for learning. Causes of reading failure are sometimes persistent and long-standing. Failure may be rooted in the cultural difference between the middle-class life-style of the school and the home background, the mobility of much of our present-day population, the almost universal acceptance of automatic (social) promotion *without* adequate study of why the child failed, and the greater holding power of the school, so that more children with all levels of ability remain in classrooms longer.

When a case of reading disability is carefully studied, multiple causes are usually found. To sort out the relative importance of the effects of the various causes is almost impossible. Since this is the case, the teacher must be always alert to new information about the reading problem and its implications. In short, each teacher must be a diagnostic teacher of reading, especially when working with children with reading disabilities.

For Further Reading

Campbell, N. Jo, Judith E. Dobson, and Jane M. Bost. "Educator Perceptions of Behavior Problems of Mainstreamed Students." *Exceptional Children* 51 (January 1985): 298–303. Results of the study suggest a need for regular education teachers to understand behavior management of handicapped students.

Carbo, Marie. "Deprogramming Reading Failure: Giving Unequal Learners an Equal Chance." *Phi Delta Kappan* 68 (November 1987): 197–201. Citing the fact that 18.8 percent of "disadvantaged" children never become proficient readers, the author states that no one right way to teach reading exists.

Cunningham, Patricia M. "When All Else Fails . . ." *Reading Teacher* 41 (April 1988): 800–805. In an issue totally devoted to reading disability, the author makes specific recommendations for older readers who need to start over.

Ekwall, Eldon E., and James L. Shanker. "Diagnosis and Remediation of Psychological and Sociological Problems." In *Diagnosis and Remediation of the Disabled Reader.* 2d ed., 238–78. Boston: Allyn and Bacon, 1983. Gives a comprehensive look at issues appropriate to the topic, including IQ and reading.

Haynes, Norris M., et al. "An Analysis of the Relationship between Children's Self-Concept and Their Teachers' Assessments of Their Behavior: Implications for Prediction and Intervention." *Journal of School Psychology* 25 (Winter 1987): 393–97. With teacher assessments of 142 elementary students accounting for 72 percent of the variance in school-related self-concept, teacher assessments appear to have much to do with how children view themselves.

Heath, Shirley Brice. *Ways with Words: Language, Life and Work in Communities and Classrooms.* Cambridge, Mass.: Cambridge University Press, 1983. An important study of the matches and mismatches between the purposes and uses of language in communities and classrooms.

Pellicano, Roy R. "At Risk: A View of 'Social Advantage.' " *Educational Leadership* 44 (March 1987): 47–49. To keep schools from simply reproducing society, educators must recognize and respond to the social diversity and fragility of their students.

Stipek, Deborah J. *Motivation to Learn: From Theory to Practice.* Englewood Cliffs, N.J.: Prentice-Hall, 1988. A comprehensive discussion of motivation that is well researched and rich with practical suggestions and lists.

Notes

1. Judith S. Beck, "A Problem Solving Framework for Managing Poor Readers in Classrooms," *Reading Teacher* 41 (April 1988): 774.
2. Marion Monroe and Bertie Backus, *Remedial Reading* (Boston: Houghton Mifflin Co., 1937), 17–33.
3. Barbara Taylor, Larry Harris, and P. David Pearson, *Reading Difficulties: Instruction and Assessment* (New York: Random House, 1988), 24–41.
4. Bryan E. Robinson, Bobbie H. Rowland, and Mick Coleman, "Taking Action for Latchkey Children and Their Families," *Family Relations* 35 (October 1986): 473–77.
5. National Institute on Alcohol Abuse and Alcoholism, "Helping Children from Alcoholic Families: Approaches and Caregivers," *Children Today* 15 (January–February 1986): 13–16.
6. Guy L. Bond et al., *Reading Difficulties: Their Diagnosis and Correction,* 5th ed. (Englewood Cliffs, N.J.: Prentice-Hall, 1984), 43.
7. Ibid., 45–47.
8. Emerald V. Dechant, *Improving the Teaching of Reading,* 2d ed. (Englewood Cliffs, N.J.: Prentice-Hall, 1970), 455.
9. Richard Sagor, "Discouraged Learners: Teetering on the Edge of Failure," *Learning* 17 (April 1988): 29.
10. Lance M. Gentile and Merna M. McMillan, "Stress and Reading Difficulties: Teaching Students Self Regulating Skills," *Reading Teacher* 41 (November 1987): 170.
11. Cited by Alan Abeson and Jeffrey Zettel in "The End of the Quiet Revolution: The Education of All Handicapped Children Act of 1975," *Exceptional Children* 44 (October 1977): 125.
12. Olive C. Simpson, "Fifty Years of Dyslexia: A Review of the Literature, 1925–1975, II Practice," *Research in Education,* no. 15 (May 1976).
13. Daniel P. Hallahan et al., "Questions about the Regular Education Initiative," *Journal of Learning Disabilities* 21 (January 1988): 3.
14. L. A. Shepard, "The New Push for Excellence: Widening the Schism between Regular and Special Education," *Exceptional Children* 53 (1987): 327–29.

15. James M. Kauffman, Michael M. Gerber, and Melvyn I. Semmel, "Arguable Assumptions Underlying the Regular Education Initiative," *Journal of Learning Disabilities* 21 (January 1988): 6.

16. Ibid., 10.

17. Lowell Madden, "Do Teachers Communicate with Their Students as if They Were Dogs?" *Language Arts* 65 (February 1988): 145.

18. Michael P. Ford and Marilyn M. Ohlhausen, "Classroom Reading Incentive Programs: Removing the Obstacles and Hurdles for Disabled Readers," *Reading Teacher* 41 (April 1988): 796–98.

19. Sagor, "Discouraged Learners," 32–33.

20. Carl A. Rogers, *Freedom to Learn* (Columbus, Ohio: Merrill Publishing Co., 1969), 106.

21. Helen Rucker, "Why Can't You Read, Johnny?" *Instructor* 83 (March 1974): 14.

22. Richard Sparks, "The Walking Wounded in Our Schools," *Instructor* 83 (June/July 1974): 12.

23. Ray C. Rist, "Student Social Class and Teacher Expectations: The Self-Fulfilling Prophecy in Ghetto Education," in *Challenging the Myths: The Schools, the Blacks, and the Poor,* Reprint Series No. 5 (Cambridge, Mass.: Harvard Educational Review, 1979), 81.

24. Bill R. Gearheart, *Learning Disabilities: Educational Strategies,* 4th ed. (St. Louis: Times Mirror/Mosby, 1985), 3–4.

25. Beulah Kanter Ephron, *Emotional Difficulties in Reading* (New York: Julian Press, 1953), 13.

26. Ibid., 98.

27. E. A. Tufvander and Miles V. Zintz, "Follow-up Study of Pupils with Reading Difficulties," *Elementary School Journal* 58 (December 1957): 156.

28. Albert J. Harris and Edward R. Sipay, *How to Increase Reading Ability,* 8th ed. (New York: Longman, 1985), 309.

29. Arthur I. Gates, "The Role of Personality Maladjustment in Reading Disability," *Journal of Genetic Psychology* 59 (1941): 77–83.

30. Grace Fernald, *Remedial Techniques in Basic School Subjects* (New York: McGraw-Hill, Inc., 1971), 8.

31. Helen Robinson, *Why Pupils Fail in Reading* (Chicago: University of Chicago Press, 1946), 225.

32. Helena H. Zolkos, "What Research Says about Emotional Factors in Retardation in Reading," *Elementary School Journal* 52 (May 1951): 514.

33. Guy L. Bond et al., *Reading Difficulties: Their Diagnosis and Correction,* 5th ed. (Englewood Cliffs, N.J.: Prentice-Hall, 1984), 252.

34. John G. Greer and Chris E. Wethered, "Learned Helplessness: A Piece of the Burnout Puzzle," *Exceptional Children* 50 (April 1984): 524–30.

35. Harry Vincenzi, "Depression and Reading Ability in Sixth-Grade Children," *Journal of School Psychology* 25 (Summer 1987): 155–60.

36. Roger Brumback and Dennis Staton, "Learning Disability and Childhood Depression," *American Journal of Orthopsychiatry* 53 (April 1983): 269–81; and W. Reynolds, G. Anderson, and N. Bartell, "Measuring Depression in Children: A Multimethod Assessment Investigation," *Journal of Abnormal Child Psychology* 13 (1985): 513–26.

37. Louise Sires. *Newsletter* (New York: Macmillan Co., 1950).

38. C. M. Louttit, "Emotional Factors and Reading Disabilities," *Elementary School Journal* 56 (October 1955): 72.

39. James A. McLoughlin and Rena B. Lewis, *Assessing Special Students,* 2d ed. (Columbus, Ohio: Merrill Publishing Co., 1986), 214–40. Provides ideas of behaviors to identify and formal and informal assessment tools.

3
Evaluating Word-Recognition Abilities

Vocabulary

"trying the book on for
   size"
running words
service words
basic sight vocabulary
miscue
reader level
phonics
phonic elements
reversals
confusions
compound word
Concepts about Print
environmental print

Questions

1. How would you explain to the parent of a child in your class the purpose for administering a word-recognition test? (**Application**)
2. What is important about the fact that different word lists identify the same words as being the most frequent in the language? (**Inference**)
3. Why should a teacher know the content of phonics very well? (**Recall**)
4. What are the different forms that you can expect reversals to take? What can you do about them? (**Recall**)
5. How are reversals distinguished from confusions? (**Recall**)
6. Why should the reading teacher be concerned about the child's spelling ability? (**Inference**)
7. What concepts should the reader have about the nature of print? (**Recall**)

Making a Quick Class Survey

The classroom teacher inventories the oral reading abilities of the students at the beginning of the school year. This can be done, superficially but quickly, by asking individuals to read parts of a story that has been selected and reviewed for them. Preferably the teacher will be able to assemble the students in subgroups of six or eight. The teacher asks the students to read aloud in turn. The pupils who read fluently and keep the attention of the audience may read longer passages. The pupils who show immediate signs of difficulty may read only one sentence. The students who experience considerable difficulty are the ones about whom the teacher needs more information quickly.

With some practice, the teacher learns to *"try the book on for size"* very quickly by asking students to read a passage that they have not previously seen to find out if they make more than one miscue in twenty consecutive words. If not, then the book meets the criterion for the instructional level of reading, which will be defined later in the text. Reading orally as described here is sight reading, without previous practice, because this constitutes a "test" situation for the teacher to learn about the students' word-recognition abilities.

Another "rule of thumb" that many teachers give students is this: "Select a page in a book you'd like to read. Begin reading and turn down a finger when you come to a word that you do not know. If you turn down all the fingers on one hand before you finish reading the page, this is a strong indication that this book is too difficult for you to read. Put it back and select an easier one."

Much of the reading for the quick class survey will be done from the basal readers on classroom teachers' bookshelves. Because this is true, attention is now directed to those basal readers with severely controlled vocabularies and the need for teachers to be aware of some of the abbreviated word lists.

In the basal reading series published during the past four decades, the general practice has been to introduce up to thirty words in the first book, and an additional fifteen or twenty in each of two succeeding books (designated as the preprimers). The preprimers teach from sixty to one hundred words before the child is introduced to the first hardbound reader in the individual reading series.

Before 1935, many teachers introduced children to reading through the writing of dictated stories of common interest to the group. During the years of the basal reader, many competent first-grade teachers have consistently introduced reading to children through what is now commonly called the language-experience approach. This approach applied to reading has many advantages because it makes use of the child's language, it uses the experiences of the child for its story content, and the child will use the same vocabulary when writing his or her own books of stories.

One can readily see strong psychological advantages to this method for all children. In corrective reading particularly, following unsatisfactory encounters with print, students need to learn that reading is one facet of communication. They can begin by reading what they want to read about, and they can compose their own stories.

One of the problems with using preprimers and the basal approach is determining which words should be taught first. What are the most important words to be used, overlearned, and made a part of the instant recognition vocabulary?

Abbreviated Word Lists

Several reading researchers have demonstrated that a relatively small nucleus of words exists that boys and girls must learn as quickly as possible in order to progress in beginning reading from the task of mediating what words are, to reading ideas rapidly. The study of Durr showed that only 188 different words constituted 68.41 percent of all the *running* words in eighty trade books selected by elementary school students for their free reading.[1]

Ten words that appeared most frequently in Durr's study—*the, to, and, he, a, I, you, it, of, in*—occurred a total of 25,010 times in a total word count of 105,280 in the eighty trade books. These ten little words represented 23.76 percent of all the *running* words in the study. When fifteen more words are added—*was, said, his, that, she, for, on, they, but, had, at, him, with, up, all*—the twenty-five most frequently used words constituted 35 percent of the *running* words tabulated. This finding suggests that teachers need to teach these most common words early in the reading program and that teachers must provide sufficient relevant practice to ensure permanent learning of these words.

Eeds[2] identified 400 children's literature books judged to be suitable for teaching reading to primary children. A computer analysis of the words in the books resulted in a list of 227 words that accounted for an average of 73 percent of all running words in the texts. The ten least-common words appeared at least twenty times on the list.

McNally and Murray found that the twelve most frequently used words were *a, and, he, I, in, is, it, of, that, the, to,* and *was.* They stated that these words accounted for about 25 percent of the running words in their print sample.[3] All of their words except *is* appeared in Durr's high-frequency list of twenty-five words; nine of McNally and Murray's twelve words were in Durr's first ten. The essence of the word count data is that a very few words account for a high percentage of the running words in print. To achieve fluent reading, it is essential that these words be known well. The best way for most children to learn these words is to engage in lots of meaningful reading and writing, since these high-utility words are bound to appear again and again.

Some of the useful abbreviated word lists teachers may wish to use include:

1. Edward W. Dolch, *The Basic Sight Word Test: Parts I and II* (Champaign, Ill.: Garrard Publishing Co., 1955).
2. Eldon E. Ekwall, "300 Sight Words, Graded in Levels from Pre-Primer to Third Grade," *Diagnosis and Remediation of the Disabled Reader* (Boston: Allyn and Bacon, 1976), 69–71. This list contains all of the Dolch 220 sight words and the first 200 of the Fry list.
3. Peter Edwards, "The 100 Most Frequent Words," and "The Edwards List of 800 Easy Words," *Reading Problems: Identification and Treatment* (London: Heinemann Educational Books, 1978), 77–80.
4. Edward B. Fry, "The Instant Words" (a 600-word basic vocabulary, graded according to frequency and approximate grade level of difficulty), in *Elementary Reading Instruction* (New York: McGraw-Hill Book Co., 1977), 73–74.

5. Albert J. Harris and Milton D. Jacobson, *Basic Reading Vocabularies* (New York: Macmillan Co., 1982). Words common to four or more series of basals are given in order of frequency, in alphabetical order, and in order of teaching.

6. Robert L. Hillerich, "Word Lists—Getting It All Together," *Reading Teacher* 27 (January 1974): 353–60.

7. J. McNally and W. Murray, *Key Words to Literacy* (London: Schoolmaster Publishing Co., Ltd., 1968), 1.

8. Wayne Otto and Robert Chester, "Sight Words for Beginning Readers," *Journal of Educational Research* 65 (July/August 1972): 435–43.

9. Lillie Pope, "Sight Words for the Seventies," *Academic Therapy* 10 (Spring 1975): 285–89.

10. Clarence R. Stone, "One Hundred Important Words for Prebook, Preprimer, and Early Primer Reading," *Progress in Primary Reading* (New York: McGraw-Hill, Inc., 1950).

Word-Recognition Tests

The tests discussed in this section are the San Diego Quick Assessment, The Slosson Oral Reading Test, The Wide Range Achievement Test, and the Dolch Basic Sight Word Test. The San Diego Quick Assessment includes instructions for administering and interpreting the results. The Slosson Oral Reading Test's discussion involves the test's interpretation, while the consideration of the Wide Range Achievement Test deals with both administration and interpretation. The discussion of the Dolch Basic Sight Word Test includes a methodology for analyzing students' errors and estimating a grade equivalent based on number of words recognized at sight.

The San Diego Quick Assessment

The San Diego Quick Assessment is a word-recognition test that provides ten words at each grade level, beginning with preprimer level and continuing through grade eleven.[4] The instructions suggest giving the student the ten words for one level typed on an index card. For primary grades it will be well to use a primary-type typewriter. By starting two grades below the students' grade levels, most students will be able to begin successfully. This test is easy to administer and requires very little time. Teachers report a high degree of agreement between the performance on this test and the Informal Reading Inventory (IRI). Teachers should use this test before administering an IRI to determine the appropriate grade level for the student to begin in the series of passages of the IRI. The San Diego Quick Assessment, the suggestions for the teacher, and the directions for administering it are presented in figure 3.1.

Suggestions to the Teacher

1. Have the students read lists until they miss three words in one list.

2. The list in which students miss no more than one of the ten words is the level at which they can read independently. Two errors indicate their instructional level. Three or more words identify the level at which reading material will be too difficult.

3. Be sure to analyze the errors.

4. Observe behaviors that accompany the reading.

Administration

1. Type out each list of ten words on index cards, one list to a card. If available, type the first three or four lists with primary type.

2. Begin with a card that is at least two years below the students' grade level assignments.

3. Do not put the reading level on the cards where the students can read it. Do your coding on the back of the card.

4. Ask the students to read the words aloud to you. If they misread any on the list, drop to easier lists until they make no errors. This indicates the base level.

5. Write down all incorrect responses or write them on the copy of the test.

6. Encourage the students to read words they do not know so that you can identify the techniques they use for word identification.

7. Keep reading lists until they miss three words on any one list or all lists are exhausted.

PP	*Primer*	*1*	*2*
see	you	road	our
play	come	live	please
me	not	thank	myself
at	with	when	town
run	jump	bigger	early
go	help	how	send
and	is	always	wide
look	work	night	believe
can	are	spring	quietly
here	this	today	carefully

Figure 3.1. San Diego Quick Assessment (From Margaret La Pray and Ramon Ross, "The Graded Word List: Quick Gauge of Reading Ability," *Journal of Reading* 12 [January 1969]: 305–7).

3	4	5	6
city	decided	scanty	bridge
middle	served	certainly	commercial
moment	amazed	develop	abolish
frightened	silent	considered	trucker
exclaimed	wrecked	discussed	apparatus
several	improved	behaved	elementary
lonely	certainly	splendid	comment
drew	entered	acquainted	necessity
since	realized	escaped	gallery
straight	interrupted	grim	relativity

7	8	9	10
amber	capacious	conscientious	zany
dominion	limitation	isolation	jerkin
sundry	pretext	molecule	nausea
capillary	intrigue	ritual	gratuitous
impetuous	delusion	momentous	linear
blight	immaculate	vulnerable	inept
wrest	ascent	kinship	legality
enumerate	acrid	conservatism	aspen
daunted	binocular	jaunty	amnesty
condescend	embankment	inventive	barometer

11	
galore	exonerate
rotunda	superannuate
capitalism	luxuriate
prevaricate	piebald
risible	crunch

Figure 3.1. —*Continued.*

The Slosson Oral Reading Test

The Slosson Oral Reading Test (SORT) measures the ability to pronounce words at different levels of difficulty.[5] The words, in lists of twenty, by level of difficulty, range from preprimer level to high school level. The entire test contains two hundred words. The students should pronounce first the list of twenty words that the teacher estimates that the students will be able to get right. Then they pronounce words that are progressively more difficult until they indicate that they know no more of the words. Their raw scores are the number of words pronounced correctly, and if they did not begin with the easiest words, they get credit for having pronounced all of those also. Their raw scores convert to grade placement scores. Teachers generally have reported that the Slosson test assigns a grade placement value about one year above the instructional level determined by the IRI. Knowing that it may not be completely accurate, the teachers can adjust the reading levels determined for the children. We want to emphasize that this is only a word-recognition test. It is not a reading test, as the title indicates, because it does not test comprehension.

The Wide Range Achievement Test

The Wide Range Achievement Test (WRAT) is a standardized test that measures ability in reading (word recognition), spelling, and arithmetic computation.[6] Its administration is divided into two levels: Level I for children between the ages of five and twelve and Level II for persons twelve years through adulthood. The reading subtest has some utility for Level II because the people taking the test are asked to pronounce a relatively long list of words (seventy-five) that become progressively more difficult. Some of the word lists are too easy to test the adult level. The test can be administered in about ten minutes and gives a rough estimate of word-recognition ability. The raw score earned can be converted to a grade placement score. While it is labeled as a reading test, it is only a test of word-recognition ability. It does not test comprehension.

For students in corrective reading, the spelling subtest of the WRAT may also be useful. The examiner dictates from a list of forty-five words ranging from very easy to quite difficult, and the raw score can be converted to a grade placement value. As a screening test, it will alert the teachers to the kind of writing to expect from the students when corrective reading classes begin.

The Dolch Basic Sight Word Test

Dolch wanted a list of words that would be useful for the classroom teacher, especially in the primary grades. In the mid–1930s he selected three word lists, arranged them in dictionary order in juxtaposition, and chose the words common to these three lists as the most needed *service words*.[7] The first list was published by the Child Study Committee of the International Kindergarten Union.[8] It was a study of the vocabulary of children before they entered first grade, based on detailed observations in kindergarten. It contained 2,596 words. Only those with a frequency of 100 or more were selected, making a list of 510 words often spoken in kindergarten.

The second list that Dolch used was the first 500 words of the Gates List, which has been used as a basis of many studies in reading vocabulary. It is recognized as containing words of first importance in children's reading.[9]

The third list was that compiled by Wheeler and Howell, consisting of 453 words found in ten primers and ten first readers published between 1922 and 1929.[10] This list represents the actual reading vocabulary used in grade one, and therefore the vocabulary upon which all later reading was built in those series of readers.

When the words common to all three lists were identified, they totaled 193 words. Dolch then arbitrarily selected 27 words common to two of the lists that he felt "rounded out" the list. The 27 words that appeared on only two of the three lists were included since they "seemed to belong"—*which* with *who* and *that; done* and *does* with *did* and *do; start* with *stop;* and *write* with *read.* The number words (*six, seven*) under ten not included were added, since some of them were in the list.

1. by	at	a	it	sit	me	to	the
2. in	I	be	big	not	of	we	so
3. did	good	do	go	red	too	seven	walk
4. all	are	any	an	six	start	show	stop
5. had	have	him	drink	put	round	right	pull
6. its	is	into	if	no	on	or	old
7. ask	may	as	am	yellow	you	your	yes
8. many	cut	keep	know	please	pick	play	pretty
9. does	goes	going	and	take	ten	they	today
10. has	he	his	far	my	much	must	together
11. but	jump	just	buy	own	under	off	over
12. black	kind	blue	find	out	new	now	our
13. fast	first	ate	eat	open	one	only	once
14. help	hot	both	hold	try	myself	never	two
15. brown	grow	bring	green	us	up	upon	use
16. four	every	found	eight	with	white	was	wash
17. from	make	for	made	shall	she	sleep	small
18. around	funny	always	because	who	write	would	why
19. long	let	little	look	some	very	sing	soon
20. away	again	after	about	wish	well	work	will
21. cold	can	could	clean	ran	read	run	ride
22. full	fall	five	fly	then	tell	their	them
23. before	best	better	been	see	saw	say	said
24. live	like	laugh	light	that	there	these	three
25. her	here	how	hurt	when	which	where	what
26. down	done	draw	don't	thank	those	this	think
27. give	get	gave	got	want	went	were	warm
28. came	carry	call	come				

Figure 3.2. Dolch Basic Sight Word List (From E. W. Dolch, *Dolch Basic Sight Word Test.* Copyright 1942 by Garrard Publishing Company, Champaign, Ill.)

The Dolch Basic Sight Words are, as the name implies, a short list of words that children should recognize "at sight"; they should not expect to "sound out" or otherwise hesitate on these crucial service words. The 220 words of the Dolch Word List are *service* words, and "service" in this frame of reference means that these are the most common words used in all reading and writing—making up over half of all the running words that children read in their elementary textbooks. No nouns are included in the service words, since nouns change with the subject matter and, for young children, are often identifiable from the illustrations on the pages of the reading material.

TABLE 3.1. Percentage of the Basic Sight Vocabulary in Running Words in School Textbooks

Textbook	Number of Series	Grade					
		1	2	3	4	5	6
Reading	4	70	66	65	61	59	59
Arithmetic	2			62	63	57	57
Geography	2				60	59	54
History	2				57	53	52

From E. W. Dolch, *Teaching Primary Reading* (Champaign, Ill.: Garrard Press, 1941), 208. By permission.

The Dolch Basic Sight Word List becomes an extremely valuable list of words in classroom work—if used appropriately. Suggestions for its use as a teaching aid are given later in this chapter.

The greatest value of the list of 220 words is to emphasize the importance of a few service words *in all reading.* The complete Basic Sight Word List is presented in figure 3.2.

Based on a 1,000-word sampling of each book, Dolch determined what percentage of all the running words in textbooks used in the elementary school were sight words. Sampling of four first readers showed that 70 percent of the running words were on the service list; for the four second readers, 66 percent were service words; of four sixth-grade readers, 59 percent were service words. This emphasizes the extreme importance, for every child, of having complete mastery of these words. These percentages, and those for word counts in arithmetic, geography, and history textbooks, are given in table 3.1.

Finding the Children's Instructional Levels Using the Test

Two methods of testing knowledge of *basic sight vocabulary* are presented here. The Basic Sight Word Test can be administered either as a recognition test or as a recall test. The differences seem significant. A recognition test is one in which the teacher reads one word in each row of four words and asks the children to find and circle it. This is the method suggested for classroom teachers to use when packages of the Basic Sight Word Tests are used with groups. However, a recall test is one that requires the child, without any stimulus, to say each word. The teacher has a better measure of how many sight words that each child knows if the teacher asks the children to pronounce every word in each row, progressing down the page. This is a recall test.

A Scale for Determining Reader Level

The 220 words in the Dolch Basic Sight Word List constitute more than 60 percent of all the running words in primary-grade reading materials and about 50 percent of all the running words in intermediate-grade reading materials. This emphasizes their importance as *service words* in all children's reading. If children recognize these at sight, they will be less handicapped if they must hesitate to figure out other words in general elementary reading. These should not be analyzed phonically, but learned as "automatic" sight words. All children reading at third-grade level need to know all 220 of these words as sight words. *A Scale for Determining a Child's Reader Level* has been prepared for testing the children's knowledge of these words and then estimating their reader levels on the basis of the number of these words that they can recognize.[11]

In establishing the scale, each child was asked to pronounce the words as a recall test. The words were presented from flash cards,[12] one at a time, or in groups arranged on the children's desks; or the teacher used the Dolch Basic Sight Word Test, Parts I and II.[13] The children, supplied with a three-by-five-inch index card or similar marker, were asked to pronounce all four words in each line across the page. Sliding the marker down one line at a time, they proceeded in this fashion down the page.

The test can usually be completed in one sitting. If the children make many miscues, there may be no value in continuing. If the children know very few of the words at the top of Test I, they need not continue. Younger children, or less successful ones who work slowly, may complete successive parts of the 220-word test over more than one work period, or identify the words on flash cards presented a few at a time.

The following criteria serve as a basis for computing scores on the test.[14]

1. The child should respond within a few seconds (ten or less); if not, encourage the child to go on to the next word.
2. The teacher may indicate children's responses in the following ways:
    a. If the word is called properly, draw a line through it.
    b. If the word is miscalled and then corrected before going on, write above the word what the child said and then indicate with a *C* in front of the word that it was corrected.
    c. If the word is miscalled but not corrected, write the children's pronunciation above the word.
    d. If the child is willing to skip a word or move on without identifying it in any way, do not mark it.
    e. If the child makes several guesses and seems to get the word right only by guessing, write the mispronunciation but do not draw a line through the word.
    f. The child's score on the total test is the number of words lined through.
    g. If the child makes pertinent comments about words, jot them down on the margin of the page; for example:
        (1) Spelling out each word: "c-a-n, that's can."
        (2) "Oh, I know it but I just can't say it."
        (3) "I had that word in spelling just this week."
        (4) "It's 'on' or 'no' but I don't know which."
        (5) "Am I doing all right? Is this good?"

TABLE 3.2. Approximate Reader Levels Based on the Dolch Basic Sight Word Recall Test

Dolch Words Known	*Equivalent Reader Levels*
0–75	Preprimer
76–120	Primer
121–170	First Reader
171–210	Second Reader or Above
Above 210	Third Reader or Above

3. The scale for determining *reader level* on the basis of this score devised by McBroom, Sparrow, and Eckstein is shown in table 3.2.[15]

Standards used in giving the Dolch Basic Sight Word Test individually were developed by Sparrow and Eckstein and include the following:[16]

1. The criteria upon which children are given credit for knowing a word are:
   a. If they can pronounce it at sight;
   b. If they can sound it out and then pronounce it on first trial;
   c. If they correct themselves immediately after miscalling it and then pronounce it correctly.
2. In no case are children given credit for knowing a word if any of the following occur:
   a. If they miscall it and then (after correctly pronouncing one or several others in the list) come back to that word and pronounce it correctly.
   b. If they take more than one trial of sounding to get it.
   c. If they miscall it and give more than one original mistaken word before finally getting the right one. Example: If for the word *could* children say *called, cold,* and then *could,* they are given no credit.
   d. If they omit the word and then later come back and give it correctly.
   e. If they hesitate longer than fifteen seconds before giving the word.[17]

The scale is useful in selecting an appropriate beginning level for the informal reading inventory, but the San Diego Quick Assessment is quite accurate, requires much less time, and allows the teacher to assess students' reading at even high school levels.

Administering the Basic Sight Word Test and Analyzing the Miscues Made

Part I of the Dolch Basic Sight Word Test was administered to a sixth-grade boy enrolled in a reading clinic. The scoring of the test is reproduced in figure 3.3. Because he made many miscues and omissions, he was not given the second half of the test. It was possible to estimate subjectively a score on the total test to compare with the scale of known Dolch words in figure 3.3 by multiplying his score on Part I by two.

b̸y	a̸t	a̸	i̸t	*down* brown	*good* grow	*drink* bring	gre̸en
i̸n	I̸	b̸e	bi̸g	fou̸r	*it* every	found	ei̸ght
di̸d	goo̸d	*don't* do	g̸o	*if* from	ma̸ke	fo̸r	made
al̸l	ar̸e	any	*and* an	aro̸und	fun̸ny	*away* always	be̸cause
he have	*very* had	hi̸m	*did* drink	long	let	lit̸tle	loo̸k
set its	is̸	int̸o	if̸	aw̸ay	*into* again	aft̸er	about
as ask	*my* may	as	am	co̸ld	*an* can	could	clean
many	*cat* cut	*be* keep	kno̸w	full	fall	fiv̸e	fl̸y
don't does	*go* goes	goi̸ng	an̸d	be̸fore	best	*butter* better	been
has	his	H̸e	far	liv̸e	li̸ke	lau̸gh	light
bu̸t	jum̸p	just	buy	*he* her	*has* here	how	hurt
back black	kind	bl̸ue	find	do̸wn	*down* done	draw	*didn't* don't
fast	first	*eat* ate	*ate* eat	give	get	*good* gave	got
he̸lp	hot	both	ho̸ld	*Come* came	*Call* carry	*all* call	*came* come

Score 47

Errors and Omissions 65

Figure 3.3. The Dolch Basic Sight Word Test: Part I (From E. W. Dolch, *Dolch Basic Sight Word Test*. Copyright 1942 by Garrard Publishing Company, Champaign, Ill.)

Since the words are to be recognized *at sight*, children are *not* taught to use word-analysis techniques in identifying them unless a severe perceptual or neurological condition exists.

To make a detailed analysis of the miscues made on this recall test is possible. The miscues can be grouped as *wrong beginnings, wrong middles, wrong endings, reversals, wrong several parts, miscellaneous,* and *omissions* (words failed to pronounce). A sheet of paper divided into spaces for recording miscues with these suggested headings is shown in figure 3.4. Figure 3.4 shows an analysis of George's miscues recorded in figure 3.3. Other headings may be indicated, but these will contain most of the miscues.

Wrong Beginnings	Wrong Middles	Wrong Endings	Reversals	Wrong Several Parts	Omissions		Miscellaneous
black-back	may-my	do-don't	its-sit	drink-did	any	full	had-very
					long	fall	
can-an	cut-cat	an-and	eat-ate	have-he	as	best	keep-be*
					am	been	
down-brown	always-away	ask-as	ate-eat	grow-good	many	how	
call-all	better-butter	does-don't	from-if	bring-drink	his	light	
					has	hurt	
	don't-didn't	goes-go	again-into	every-it	far	draw	
					just	got	
	came-come	done-down		gave-good	buy	get	
	come-came	carry-call			kind	give	
					find		
		her-he			fast		
					first		
		here-has			hot		
					both		
					found		
					let		
					about		
					could		
					clean		

Figure 3.4. Analysis of miscues made on Dolch Basic Sight Word Test: Part I (See figure 3.3 for errors.) *May be a reversal of *p* and *b*.

If George performs equally well on Part II, his total score will be 94. He will need to read from primer (or easy first grade) reader level. The analysis shows that he makes all types of miscues. Probably the teacher will concentrate first on correcting wrong beginnings. This individual makes only a few miscues on beginning sounds. Omissions—failing to attempt the word—account for his greatest number of miscues.

One objective in teaching reading is to build up the stock of basic sight words quickly. However, there are some cautions and suggestions to be pointed out in teaching the Dolch Sight Word List to a child.

1. Since uninteresting, unmotivated, meaningless drill on word pronunciation of the list is apt to intensify dislike for reading, offer the needed practice through personalized, relevant reading and writing activities. The Dolch words will likely constitute at least half of the words that children read and write.
2. Since words in a list are devoid of contextual clues to meaning and pronunciation, be sure that practice activities and games provide contexts to aid the reader. This is the normal way that word identification is accomplished, and the children should learn to employ a variety of clues to identification.
3. When new words are added too fast, the usual result is confusion and frustration. Let children have many chances to read and reread stories containing new words. Reading experiences may be planned with basals, trade

books, or stories that the children have written. Children can also get meaningful word-recognition experience with signs, labels, announcements, and directions posted in the classroom and changed frequently.

4. Children are likely to have trouble spelling words that they do not read. They should have a variety of meaningful opportunities to use the words that they meet in their reading. Developing personal dictionaries or card files may be helpful.

Is the Dolch Basic Sight Word List Still Satisfactory?

Because the Dolch Word List is based on word counts made in the 1920s, several writers have questioned whether the list is still sufficiently relevant to the reading of six-year-olds today. Haven't television, home computers, space travel, and the continuous influx of new technologies outmoded most of the life of the twenties?

Hillerich has summarized the results of fourteen different studies and arrived at some very significant conclusions: (1) The recency of a list is no assurance of its importance; (2) the language base of the word count may be more important than the date it was compiled; (3) even though language is continually changing, the *structure* words tend to remain constant; and (4) while the Rinsland list contains some rural and childlike words little used today, the Dolch list does not seem particularly outmoded.[18] The Hillerich list of 240 words that were drawn from the composite certainly contains no words that young children will not soon need to recognize.[19] However, he included 40 nouns that Dolch deliberately omitted. Dolch believed that nouns would be dependent upon context and many times included in illustrations. Disregarding the nouns, however, Hillerich included 42 words not selected by Dolch, while Dolch included 62 words not selected by Hillerich. Be that as it may, they are all common sight words, common enough that children must readily master all the words on both lists.

Do word lists as basic as that containing the Dolch words become outdated in the course of a few decades? It is true that language is constantly changing because of the infusion of new concepts and changing societal behaviors. However, the converse, that language changes very slowly, is just as true. Further, the most basic words, such as those in the Stone list of 100 most common words[20] (including *and, at, big, for, go, on, said, she, the, to,* and *up*) have been basic for a long time, and we may expect them to remain so for some time to come.

Shakespeare's famous lines about the seven ages of man that appear in *As You Like It* (Act II, Scene VII) were written more than 350 years ago, yet approximately 50 percent of the total running words appear as service words on the Dolch list:

Jaques:

All the world's a stage,
And all the men and women merely players:
They have their exits and their entrances;
And one man in his time plays many parts,
His acts being seven ages. At first the infant,
Mewling and puking in the nurse's arms.

And <u>then</u> <u>the</u> whining school-boy, <u>with</u> <u>his</u> satchel
<u>And</u> shining morning face, creeping <u>like</u> snail
Unwilling <u>to</u> school. <u>And</u> <u>then</u> <u>the</u> lover,
Sighing <u>like</u> furnace, <u>with</u> <u>a</u> woeful ballad
<u>Made</u> <u>to</u> <u>his</u> mistress' eyebrow. <u>Then</u> <u>a</u> soldier
<u>Full</u> <u>of</u> strange oaths <u>and</u> bearded <u>like</u> <u>the</u> pard,
Jealous <u>in</u> honor, sudden <u>and</u> quick <u>in</u> quarrel,
Seeking <u>the</u> bubble reputation
Even <u>in</u> <u>the</u> cannon's mouth. <u>And</u> <u>then</u> <u>the</u> justice,
<u>In</u> fair <u>round</u> belly <u>with</u> <u>good</u> capon lined,
<u>With</u> eyes severe <u>and</u> beard <u>of</u> formal <u>cut,</u>
<u>Full</u> <u>of</u> wise saws <u>and</u> modern instances;
<u>And</u> <u>so</u> <u>he</u> <u>plays</u> <u>his</u> part.[21]

In the first 141 words of this passage, 73 are sight words on the Dolch list. The three forms of "play" are also used and, if also counted, make 76 of 141 words, or 54 percent of the total.

Palmer conducted a study of the Dolch words' continuing relevance. The words in levels 4 through 8 of four major basal series of the late 1970s and early 1980s were analyzed. It was found that, with one exception, the Dolch words made up at least 60 percent of the vocabulary in the passages studied. The relevance of the Dolch list is clear. "If six out of ten words in these materials are Dolch words, young readers must be able to read them well if they are to have a chance of being successful readers."[22]

The important principle to guide the teacher is that any of these abbreviated lists can serve as a guide to common words. Students should use *their* words in the beginning reading situation, and after they have learned perhaps 100 words through their language-experience stories, they are ready to broaden their base of word recognition by reading meaningful ideas in context, using phonic and structural skills, and remembering sight words.

Strengths and Weaknesses of Word-Recognition Tests

Any reading test has both strengths and weaknesses. Word-recognition tests are no exception. These tests generally require students to name lists of words, and they offer a quick estimate of the reading ability of individual students. The San Diego Quick Assessment may require five minutes; at the other extreme, the Dolch list may take twenty minutes to administer. The Ekwall Quick Check for Basic Sight Word Knowledge is another very brief word-recognition test.[23] Word-recognition tests are easy to administer and are relatively easy for children to complete because the testing stops when the words become too difficult. Interpretation of the results is straightforward with immediately useful applications. If the test is repeated at intervals throughout the school year, pupil progress may be quickly identified and quantified. Finally, a word-recognition test may be used to suggest a likely entry point on the informal reading inventory.

Reading is more than word recognition; the ability to recognize words is only one step in the process. Word-recognition tests should never be confused with reading tests, which provide a much broader assessment of reading abilities, including comprehension. Final decisions about assigning children to groups, placing children in textbooks, or referring children for special services should never be made on the basis of word-recognition test scores alone. Some children become adept at naming words yet have little understanding of their meanings. Others name words efficiently but have extremely poor comprehension strategies. Still other students may have difficulty naming words in lists but have strong predicting and confirming strategies when words are in context. These youngsters may have excellent comprehension, even though naming words in isolation is difficult for them.

The San Diego Quick Assessment and the Slosson Oral Reading Test each have short lists of words for the reader to pronounce at each level of difficulty. While this is an advantage in terms of the time needed for administration, it may also be a weakness. Such small numbers of words selected from all the possible words at each reading level suggest that some children could know many words at a level, but not the particular ones on the list. Or, some readers could know the words on the list but not many other words at the level represented by the list. The problem could be greater at the higher levels where the number of words from which the selection is made is much more extensive.

Word-recognition tests have multiple uses in the classroom. The teacher should be aware of both their strengths and their weaknesses. They *can* be used wisely for appropriate purposes.

Making Connections 3.1: How Many Sight Words Do You Find?

Select a piece of printed material about two hundred words in length. It might be from the newspaper, from this textbook, from a basal reader, or from a story written by a child.

Complete an analysis of the passage in terms of the number of Dolch words included in the running words. Simply slash out each word that is on the Dolch list. After you have marked through all the words that appear on the list, figure the percentage of Dolch words in the running words in the passage by dividing the number of words with the slash marks by the total number of words in the passage. You will obtain a decimal for your answer; the decimal may then be changed to a percentage.

This activity will be particularly useful if several people evaluate different kinds of materials judged to be at a variety of levels of difficulty. The shared findings will undoubtedly suggest the value of readers knowing well a small, but high-utility, collection of sight words.

Other Methods of Testing for Reader Level

Other methods for finding the reader level are summarized here.

1. The teacher can estimate children's abilities to read new books by:
   a. Selecting passages near the beginning of the books and asking the child to read aloud. If more than five errors in one hundred words are made, an easier book to improve context reading is indicated.
   b. Pronouncing words here and there on selected pages and asking the pupil to point to them.
2. A selection of twenty-five or fifty words can be compiled by choosing every fourth or fifth word from the vocabulary list of a given book. If no such list is given, the teacher may pick words at random. Ask the child to pronounce each word and give the meaning. This may be done by using the word in a sentence. If the child can pronounce and know the meaning of twenty of the twenty-five words in the test, or forty of the fifty-word test, the child probably can read adequately from that book. This is the procedure:
   a. Turn to the total list of words in the back of the book.
   b. Select twenty-five or fifty words by some method, such as choosing every fourth or fifth word.
   c. Make two copies of these words, one for yourself and one for the child. Use manuscript writing if the child cannot read cursive writing.
   d. Ask the child to pronounce the word as you point to it.
   e. Record on one sheet the errors made.
   f. Next, ask the child for the meaning of each word. The word may be used in a sentence.
   g. The child should be able to pronounce twenty of twenty-five or forty of fifty words without much hesitancy, and know the meanings.

Inventorying Phonic and Structural Skills

Teachers cannot assume that all students know the names or the sounds of all the letters of the alphabet, and some students may not know how to write them. It is a simple task to:

1. Show the students a card with the letters in mixed-up order:

c	i	d	f	m	g	k	x
a	l	b	h	p	r	y	e
j	n	s	o	v	t	w	u

   Then point to some of the letters, and ask the students to name them. If the teachers circle only those that the students do not know, the teachers have a written record to show which ones the students have been able to identify.
2. Ask the students to write all of the letters of the alphabet in their alphabetical order. It will be apparent which ones they omit, which ones they confuse, and which ones they reverse.

3. Provide the students with a piece of paper. Direct them to write the letters that you name, and then ask them to say some of the names of the letters.
4. Be sensitive to the fact that the children may never have been taught how to make the letters properly. Or, they may make the letters with "upside-down movements" that will make rapid writing during the school day very difficult. Patiently teach the students how to form the letters that they cannot make properly.
5. It is easy to sample knowledge of the sounds of the most-used consonants by asking each child to identify the first letter in a word. Give a short list of words orally: *bear, cow, dog, fox, kitten, top, milk, lion, pony, rooster.*

Pictures like those found in figure 3.5 can be used to elicit beginning or ending sounds.

Clay's *The Early Detection of Reading Difficulties*[24] has several diagnostic surveys that will provide valuable information about the child's knowledge of letter names and the sounds that letters represent. These include "Text Reading," "Writing Vocabulary," "Dictation Test," "Word Tests," and "Letter Identification."

All of the *phonic elements* are presented in table 3.3. Most students will learn the consonants and consonant combinations with a minimum of oral practice. For some students, practice lessons in hearing minimal pairs may be helpful. Minimal pairs of words are those that sound exactly alike except for one phonemic difference. For example, in *big* and *pig* the words are the same except for the phonemes *b* and *p*.

Also, the chart of phonic elements makes clear that there are not a great many sounds to be distinguished and remembered. More importantly, the sounds need to be presented or taught in the order that they are being used as sounds in words that distinguish meaning. Thus, *one* sequence for teaching a series of sounds is not necessary since teachers who use a great deal of language-experience work should teach those sounds needed to discriminate the sounds in the words that the boys and girls use in their stories. Also, if children can hear sounds clearly and can decode words, they have no need for further lessons in phonics as far as reading is concerned. If difficulties arise in spelling, that problem needs to be seen as a spelling problem.

Teachers' Knowledge of Phonics

Teachers need to have a strong knowledge of phonics themselves before they attempt to test that knowledge in children or before they teach students the use of phonics as a word-identification tool. A knowledge of phonics will help teachers to avoid spending a lot of time testing students' phonic knowledge, since they will be more able to observe students' reading behaviors and detect specific needs for information or practice that are phonic in nature.

Teachers often feel that they know no phonics and state that "it wasn't taught when I was in school." Others may not realize the range of information about letters and sounds that collectively is called phonics. Making Connections 3.2 is a phonics test for teachers. It may be useful to take the test to demonstrate how much you do know already, to discover the range of information that is designated as phonics, or to learn some of the phonics rules if you have not worked with them before. (The reader is referred to chapter 1 for a discussion of the synthetic method of teaching reading.)

Hearing Beginning Sounds. Tell me the name of each picture. What is the letter each picture begins with?

Hearing Final Sounds. Tell me the name of each picture. What is the letter that makes the sound you hear at the end of each word?

Figure 3.5. Pictures can be used to elicit beginning or ending sounds.

TABLE 3.3. The Phonic Elements

Consonants		*Vowels*			
Single Consonants	Consonant Combinations	Single Vowels	Vowel Combinations	Vowel-Consonant Combinations	The Schwa
Single consonants (one phoneme):	Consonant blends:	Single vowels (May be long or short):	Vowel digraphs:	Vowels A followed by "l" or "w":	(ə)
b d f h	bl br sc tw	a e i	ai in *sail*	"aw" in *bawl*	*pencil*
i k l m	cl cr sk scr	o u	ay *day*	"al" in *wall*	*about*
n w y z	fl dr sm spr	y (sometimes)	ea *beat*		*beckon*
	gl fr sn str		ea *head*	Vowels followed by "r":	*latent*
Single consonants with two or more common sounds:	pl gr sp shr		ea *tea*	a in *arm*	
	sl pr st spl		ee *sleep*	e *fern*	
"c" as "k"	dw tr sw sch		ei *receive*	i *dirt*	
"c" as "s"	wr thr		ie *believe*	o *word*	
"g" as "g"			ey *key*	u *hurt*	
"g" as "j"	Consonant digraphs:		ey *they*	y *martyr*	
"s" in hiss	One sound:		oa *boat*		
rose	gh, ph, sh, ck, ng, nk		oe *toe*	q and u	
sugar	Two or more sounds:		ow *show*	qu in *quick*	
"x" in six	th: *this, thin*			squ *squirrel*	
xylophone	wh: *what, who*		Vowel blends (diphthongs):		
exact	ch: *chin,*		oi in *soil*		
	chalet		oy *boy*		
	choir		ue *true*		
			ew in *new*		
			ow *now*		
			ou *though*		
			oa *goal*		

Making Connections 3.2: A Phonics Test for Teachers

Why a phonics test for teachers? We know that phonics is just one tool to aid in word identification, so why give it so much time? The answer may be helpful. If the teacher has extensive knowledge of the subject, he or she can recognize when the student needs information in the area of phonics and can give it accurately and economically. When the teacher does not have a thorough knowledge of the subject, he or she will usually find it necessary to follow one of two approaches:

1. Skip the subject altogether (which is not helpful).
2. Teach everything in the teacher's manual (which is also not helpful).

Knowledge of the subject will allow the teacher to make professional decisions about what, how much, and when phonics will be taught.

Now try your hand at these questions:

1. Underline seven words in this sentence starting with a single consonant sound.
2. Circle the words below that contain consonant blends:
   Irish   trigger   flag   clip   bland   picture   blot
3. Two three-letter blends are _____ and _____ .
4. What is a consonant digraph? _____
   _____
5. The word *diphthong* contains three consonant digraphs. They are _____ ,
   _____ , and _____ .
6. Six words that might help a child decide how to pronounce words with
   "hard" *g* are _____ , _____ , _____ , _____ , _____ , _____ .
7. A "soft" *g* is in the word: got   ghost   frog   wage
8. After each of these nonsense words, write *H* if the *c* is "hard" or *S* if the *c* is "soft."
   calum ____ , cebut ____ , cinky ____ , cottle ____ , cuve ____ , cybers ____ .
9. "Th" is *unvoiced* in: them   thimble   thistle   thin   they
10. Following are four nonsense words containing various sounds that *y* often represents. Match them with words that contain the same sounds usually represented by *y*.
    deyorg   syntax   tyth   twenty   gry   yellow   perry   my
11. The letter *x* stands for three sounds. Write a word to represent each of these three sounds: _____ , _____ , _____ .
12. The letter *q* stands for two sounds. Words that contain examples of each of these are _____ and _____ .
13. On words ending in *s,* you may hear either an *s* or a *z* sound. Write *s* or *z* after each word, indicating which sound you hear at the end:
    hands _____ , baths _____ , bathes _____ , hats _____ .
14. There is a silent consonant in each of these words. Circle each silent consonant: comb   wren   talk   knew   listen   often

15. Write an *L* or an *S* after each of these words, depending on whether the word contains a long or a short vowel sound. Write *X* if the word contains neither.
    pipe _____ , ways _____ , sounds _____ , salve _____ , which _____ , use _____ , fold _____ , have _____ , leek _____ , word _____ , tint _____ .

16. In the nonsense word *dode,* the letter *o* would probably represent the sound that the *o* represents in: on   out   comb   hotter   brown

17. In the nonsense word *oap,* the letter *o* would probably represent the sound that the *o* represents in: rot   round   fox   Rome

18. A vowel digraph is in the word: slam   goat   bugle   couch   funnel

19. A diphthong is _____ .
    Circle all the diphthongs in these words: couch   boy   through
    oil   now   known

20. The *schwa* sound is represented in the dictionary by a _____ .

21. Circle the vowel in each word below that represents the *schwa* sound:
    balloon   eaten   ago   golden   beautify   silent   button
    circus   consistent   modify   second

22. Circle all of the following nonsense words that are correctly divided into syllables: ham/ner   de/fort/ly   deg/or   mec/hor

23. The word *polysyllabic* contains _____ syllables.

24. Write *O* or *C* after each word to show whether the syllable is open or closed: like _____ , no _____ , tend _____ , thee _____ , ban _____ , it _____ .

25. A grapheme is _____ .

26. A phoneme is _____ .

You will find the answers on page 97.

Phonics Tests for Students

If teachers want to assess phonic knowledge beyond the informal devices that they create in their own classrooms, they may choose from a number of commercial phonics tests:

1. The Sipay Word Analysis Tests (SWAT), a series of sixteen individually administered subtests, provide the teacher a great deal of information. (Edward R. Sipay, Cambridge, Mass.: Educators Publishing Service, Inc., 1974.)
2. The "El Paso Phonics Survey" in the *Ekwall Reading Inventory* by Eldon E. Ekwall (Boston: Allyn and Bacon, 1986). A detailed analysis most valuable when used with the other parts of the broader reading evaluation.
3. "Baumann Informal Phonics Test" in James F. Baumann, *Reading Assessment: An Instructional Decision-Making Perspective* (Columbus, Ohio: Merrill Publishing Co., 1988), 307–12. This test has three parts: "Consonant Letter/

Sound Correspondences," "Vowel Letter/Sound Correspondences," and "Vowel Generalizations and Reversals." Each part may be used independently.

4. The Word Attack Test of the Woodcock Reading Mastery Tests. (Circle Pines, Minn.: American Guidance Service, 1973.) This test requires the reader to demonstrate knowledge of phonic elements by reading nonsense words that demonstrate important rules governing English words.

5. Wilma H. Miller, in the *Reading Diagnosis Kit,* 2d ed. (West Nyack, N.Y.: Center for Applied Research in Education, 1978), presents some useful phonics tests on pages 230 through 233. They are meant for readers who are at or beyond the upper-primary reading level.

6. Margaret LaPray, in *On the Spot Reading Diagnosis File* (West Nyack, N.Y.: Center for Applied Research in Education, 1978), includes a test of applied phonics on pages 75 through 79. Phonics knowledge ranging from initial consonants to syllabication rules is assessed.

7. Phonics assessments that accompany commercial informal reading inventories. Examples are the *Bader Reading and Language Inventory* by Lois A. Bader (New York: Macmillan Co., 1983) and *Individual Evaluation Procedures in Reading* by T. A. Rakes, J. S. Choate, and G. L. Waller (Englewood Cliffs, N.J.: Prentice-Hall, 1983).

Reversals and Confusions

In making an informal reading analysis, one should be observant of any errors the students make that may relate to directional orientation on the page. Do they say "was" for *saw,* "day" for *bay,* or "form" for *from?* Kennedy concluded that while a high percentage of *reversal* tendencies exists in kindergarten, they tend to practically disappear by the third grade.[25] On one form of her test, internal interchanging of letters, for example, *from* to *form,* decreased from 38.5 percent in low kindergarten to 11.5 percent in high grade two. Also, such reversals as *b* for *d* or *p* and *n* for *u* decreased from 22.1 percent in low kindergarten to 3.07 percent in high second grade when both groups were tested in multiple-choice selection in isolation.

Awareness of the reversal problem and having a few constructive techniques to help the children to habituate left-to-right progression in word identification will help the teachers provide the correct practice for the children.

Types of Reversals and Confusions

Reversals and *confusions* may be:

1. Reversing whole words:
   "was" for *saw;* "on" for *no;* "pot" for *top;* "rats" for *star*
2. Rearranging letters within words:
   "paly" for *play;* "how" for *who;* "spot" for *stop*
3. Confusing word configuration:
   "and" for *said;* "when" for *then;* "there" for *three;* "for" for *from*

4. Rearranging whole phrases:
   "once there was" for *there once was;*
   the boy saw the dog read as "the dog was a big"
5. Interchanging letters:
   "b" for *d* or *p;* "m" for *w;* making the slant line in *N* or *z* backwards

Monroe gave the following examples of rearranging whole phrases.[26]

A boy saw a dog on the street read as "A doy was a god no the treest"
The boy saw the dog read as "The boy was good"
He felt sad read as "He left home"
The boys had no caps read as "The boys had on caps"

One fifteen-year-old girl wrote these sentences early in her remedial program in a clinic situation:

For:	*She wrote:*
I can work and play.	I cna wrck adn paly.
Who did it?	How idd ti?
The old crow sat on its perch.	The eld corw saw no sit perch.

Overcoming Reversals

Specific teaching suggestions for children who lack directional sense include the following:

1. Underline the first letter in each of the words confused. This directs the children to the beginning of the word.
2. In making lists of words for children to read, begin at a "starting line" or margin that is identifiable as the beginning point. For example, if you put words on the chalkboard, make the list at the extreme left side of the board. Help the children to see the starting place.
3. Over and over, uncover words from left to right.
4. Make the first letter with a different color.
5. Use medium-grained sandpaper and cut out letters in either cursive or manuscript. The letters should be two-to-three-inches high. The children should trace over them with the middle and index fingers of the hand with which they normally write. This is one more way to emphasize the kinesthetic-tactile dimension in the VAKT (visual-auditory-kinesthetic-tactile) method of overcoming reversals or confusions.
6. For individual letters, figure out any mnemonic device that works and let the children use it as a crutch until their habit pattern accommodates the correct response. For example, one teacher found that a child could remember to distinguish *b* from *d* by thinking that *c* had to come before *d* in the alphabet, and in writing he could not make a *d* unless he made a *c* first. As long as his *c* was correct, he could use this device. The converse, that he could not make *c* before *b* was a part of the device.

7. Have the students write the words being learned, using a meaningful context. If the children are old enough to do cursive writing instead of manuscript, have them use cursive writing because all letters are joined and reversing is less plausible. Some children find writing words on the typewriter useful.

The teacher must watch for reversals in the spelling papers of pupils at any grade level, but especially at the primary level. The spelling paper in figure 3.6 that was written by a second-grade boy was returned by his classroom teacher with the following notation across the top: "Too many mistakes." Actually, both letter reversals and confusion of order of letters appear several times in this paper. If this happened to be the first paper the teacher saw that had been written by this child, the teacher should watch carefully to see whether the reversals persist. If they do tracing, copying, comparing two words often confused, and filling blanks especially prepared to distinguish between two often-confused words in context are all possible methods that the teacher can use to help the pupil establish the proper habits of left-to-right orientation on the page. If the *habit* of reversing or of being utterly confused has persisted through several years, it will be necessary first to erase the old habits and then to form new ones.

In the primary grades many children will reverse letters, words, and numerals. The teacher will want to watch carefully the reversal tendencies of each child who experiences these difficulties. The teacher should expect the pattern of errors and the frequency of reversals to decline gradually and finally to disappear. It is the pattern of lessening of the problem over the primary years that the teacher should note. If reversal problems continue into the middle grades, the classroom teacher may need to seek help from specially trained school personnel.

A fifth-grade boy was once asked to write on the chalkboard the word *shade*. He thought a minute and then wrote: *shade* . When the examiner asked him whether the letter was a *b* or a *d* in the word, the boy said that when he wrote it that way, the teacher counted it right if it was a *b* and right if it was a *d!* Another boy in the sixth grade was asked to pronounce *dab* and *bad* when they were written on the chalkboard. He said, "One of them is *bad,* but I don't know which one."

Specific exercises need to be provided to help those having difficulty with letters or words that cause confusion; for example:

was-saw confusion	*how-who* confusion
He *was* here.	*Who* came in?
I *saw* the boy.	I see *how* to do it.
It *was* my pet.	He saw *who* I was.
The dog *saw* the rabbit.	*How* did he do that?

Predicting and confirming strategies should be used by children experiencing difficulty with pairs of similar words. Children need to ask themselves, "Which one of these words makes sense here?" Then they should try the words, thinking about which one fits the meaning of the sentence. Occasionally, either word will fit the syntactic and semantic requirements of the sentence, but in most instances that will not be the case.

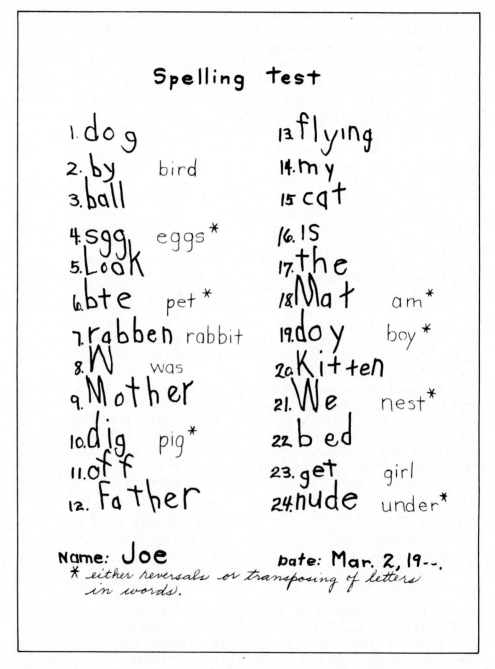

Figure 3.6. Spelling test discloses letter reversals and confusion of letter sequence.

Sentences in which the pupil selects the appropriate one of a pair of confused words have been found helpful. It may be best to work on only *one* word first, then the second word of the pair before using sentences such as the following:

Choose *on* or *no:*

1. My birthday is _____ the first of May.
2. Mrs. Hill said, "_____ , thank you."
3. The street was empty. There were _____ people there.
4. He is sitting _____ a bench in the park.

Choose *where* or *there:*

1. How long will it take to get _____ ?
2. _____ is a glass on the table.
3. _____ are you going?
4. I don't know _____ the boys went.

Other Word-Recognition Abilities

1. *Knowledge of compound words.* The teacher wishes to know whether the children see quickly how to divide compound words into two parts. A list of compound words from three representative second readers appears in table 3.4. Until the children do pronounce these words easily, they will not profit from instruction in syllabication of words.
2. *Ability to pronounce pairs of often-confused words.* If the children have completed the other word-attack tests somewhat successfully, ask them to pronounce the forty words in either of the two lists of paired words often confused, found in tables 3.5 and 3.6. The teacher can use such exercises as "bolt-blot" flash card drill or completion sentences to help children who make such errors. If the more difficult words (table 3.6) present many problems in pronunciation, ask the pupils to pronounce the more elementary list (table 3.5).

Spelling Ability

When considering the ability of given students to spell words correctly, teachers need to remember that:

1. Children should not be trying to learn to spell words that they cannot pronounce.
2. Children should not be trying to learn to spell words if they do not understand their meanings.
3. Children do not need to learn to spell words that will not be used in writing. *It is a waste of time for both the children and the teacher for the pupils to study spelling words at the fifth-grade level if they are reading at the second-grade level.*

TABLE 3.4. Compound Words Found in Representative Second-Grade Readers

somebody	something	tonight
daytime	peanut	workbag
another	grandmother	farmhouses
birthday	lonesome	anyone
himself	everywhere	haystack
firemen	schoolhouse	boxcar
railroad	package	waterfall
runway	lemonade	maybe
downtown	popcorn	blueberries
spaceship	policewoman	watchdog
postman	sandwiches	tablecloth
whoever	campfire	bedroom
popover	sometimes	housekeeper
schoolbook	overalls	without
snowbank	everything	indeed
schoolroom	afternoon	fireplace
gatepost	jackknife	anything
buttermilk	scarecrow	whatever
blackboard	Thanksgiving	somewhere
airplane	bedtime	grandchildren

TABLE 3.5. Words Often Confused in Primary Reading

stop	pots	tops
who	how	now
and	said	new
star	rats	tars
was	saw	on
no	not	ton
or	our	off
for	of	from
tap	pat	apt
tub	but	put
team	meat	yes
eyes	say	net
dab	bad	add
pal	lap	alp
god	dog	nap

TABLE 3.6. Paired Words Often Confused—Second List

left	very	even
tired	freight	tried
pitcher	angle	fright
spilt	verse	felt
scared	quit	ever
broad	spotted	nowhere
trial	trail	blot
serve	through	fight
angel	board	picture
form	quiet	from
quite	weather	stopped
though	every	sacred
whether	thought	
bolt	split	

The correlation between reading and spelling abilities is a highly positive one. This fact would suggest that children who have reading difficulties might profit from work on spelling, especially work that emphasizes auditory discrimination and special attention to the order of letters in words. Writing practice directed toward habituating the spelling of most common service words is recommended. This writing practice must be motivated and purposeful. In other words, it should take the form of book, story, or script writing, among many possibilities. Teach children initially to get their ideas recorded. Then, they can focus on writing mechanics, including spelling.

When an informal reading inventory is being completed, the teacher should measure the student's ability to spell words correctly. This is true because students within the classroom must complete some types of work that require writing. Many boys and girls are very reluctant to write because they know they do not have adequate spelling skill. One of the best ways to improve spelling ability is for the students to write about topics of interest to them and to have the opportunity to talk about the types of errors that they can correct.

There are several ways that the teacher can sample the students' abilities to spell:

1. The 220 Dolch Basic Sight Words or the first 300 of the Fry Instant Words are good lists to use for spelling. They contain the words used most often.
2. A list of spelling words from a graded speller can serve adequately. The students need to begin with a list from which they can write about 60 percent of the words correctly after pronouncing them with the teacher but before study. For example, fifth-grade students might be able to write correctly before study twelve of the twenty words in a third-grade list. If so, this is 60 percent correct, and they could begin working with words for writing at this level.

3. The Written Expression Subtest of the Gates Reading Diagnostic Test. Arthur I. Gates and Anne McKillop, *Gates-McKillop-Horowitz Reading Diagnostic Tests* (New York: Teachers College Press, 1981).
4. Spelling Test for Grades Two and Three; Spelling Test for Grade Four and Above, *Durrell Analysis of Reading Difficulty.* Donald D. Durrell, *Durrell Analysis of Reading Difficulty, Manual of Directions* (New York: *Harcourt Brace Jovanovich,* 1980).

Huelsman developed a word-discrimination test to study the ability of the reader to select the correct spelling of a word when it appears with four foils in a line of print.[27] A few students may need "extra" help with the order of letters in words and with the quick perception of the configuration of common words.

Sample items from the Huelsman test include:

1. eht tle the thc lhe
2. hittle ilttle fittle lihhle little
3. yonp pouy pony ponv pnoy

Concepts about Print

Clay[28] has made teachers aware of the need to consider more than word recognition in helping children to gain an understanding of the nature of print. She found that readers frequently experienced reading problems, not because they were having trouble memorizing sight words, but because they did not have adequate concepts about letters, words, sounds, directionality of print, the role of pictures in books, and the organization of books. Without these and other related concepts, children experience confusion when teachers give directions or talk to them about the reading process. Clay has developed two tests, *Sand*[29] and *Stones,*[30] which appear to be simple story books but can yield important information about the child's understanding of the vocabulary used in reading instruction and in discussion of the reading process. Clay intended that one of these tests would be used in conjunction with a large collection of tests aimed at giving a comprehensive picture of the child's reading status.

Several researchers have reported that young children usually become aware of *print* in the *environment* (such words as "Coke," "Stop," and "Safeway") and that these observations contribute to the growing concepts about words and reading. It may be useful to develop a collection of common environmental signs—both words and phrases—to show to children for identification. The teacher can observe the children's responses and infer the attention that is being paid to environmental print, the growing understanding of the meaningfulness of print, and the children's curiosity about these print examples.[31] It is encouraging to children to see in school the print that they have seen away from school and to have a sense that they actually "can read"; this knowledge may be very useful as the child confronts the more common print forms of the classroom.

Summary

This chapter presented suggestions for evaluating word-recognition abilities, dealing with problems of reversals and confusions, and helping children to understand important concepts about print and reading. The results of word-recognition tests help teachers to select materials at the students' instructional levels of reading and to begin teaching at that level *while* searching for further information about the students and the causes of their reading disability.

Answer Key to a Phonics Test for Teachers

 1. seven, words, sentence, with, single, consonant, sound
 2. trigger, flag, clip, bland, blot
 3. for example, *spl, spr, str, (thr* is a digraph plus *r)*
 4. (something like this): two letters that represent a sound different from the individual sounds represented by each letter
 5. *ph, th, ng*
 6. get, got, gum, gave, game, goose, geese, gush are examples
 7. wage
 8. calum H, cebut S, cinky S, cottle H, cuve H, cybers S
 9. thimble, thistle, thin
10. deyorg—yellow; tyth—syntax; gry—my; perry—twenty.
11. *z*—xylophone; *ks*—box; *gs*—exaggerate
12. *kw*—queen; *k*—antique are examples
13. hands—z; baths—s; bathes—z; hats—s
14. com*b* *w*ren ta*l*k *k*new lis*t*en of*t*en
15. pipe—L; ways—L; sounds—X; salve—S; which—S; use—L; fold—L; have—S; leek—L; word—X; tint—S
16. comb
17. Rome
18. goat
19. Two vowels that both affect pronunciation—there is a change in mouth position in the production of the new sound. *c*ouch, b*oy,* through (*ou* is not a diphthong here), *oi*l, n*ow,* known (*ow* is not a diphthong here)
20. ə
21. b*a*lloon, eat*e*n, *a*go, gold*e*n, beaut*i*fy, sil*e*nt, butt*o*n, circ*u*s, c*o*nsistent, mod*i*fy, sec*o*nd
22. ham/ner, de/fort/ly
23. five
24. like—C; no—O; tend—C; thee—O; ban—C; it—C
25. A written form
26. A smallest unit of sound

For Further Reading

Anderson, Richard C., et al. "Do Errors on Classroom Reading Tasks Slow Growth in Reading?" *Elementary School Journal* 88 (January 1988): 267–80. Because reading errors result in a degree of tension, their corollary may be attention and a greater effort to obtain meaning. Reading errors may have positive results.

Clay, Marie M. "The Visual Perception of Print." In *Reading: The Patterning of Complex Behaviour*. 2d ed., 216–43. Auckland, New Zealand: Heinemann Educational Books, 1979. Focuses on the young reader's attention to letters and on how letters are discriminated and remembered.

Ekwall, Eldon E. *Locating and Correcting Reading Difficulties*. 4th ed. Columbus, Ohio: Merrill Publishing Co., 1985. Contains suggestions for remediating specific difficulties.

Fry, Edward B. "Picture Nouns for Reading and Vocabulary Improvement." *Reading Teacher* 41 (November 1987): 185–91. One hundred picture nouns are identified by categories. The author suggests that they be used in semantic maps.

Fry, Edward B. *The Reading Teacher's Book of Lists*. Englewood Cliffs, N.J.: Prentice-Hall, 1984. A good reference for any teacher of reading.

Fry, Edward, and Elizabeth Sakiey. "Common Words Not Taught in Basal Reading Series." *The Reading Teacher* 39 (January 1986): 395–98. The authors state that basals teach only 50 percent to 59 percent of the three thousand most common words. Basals may not be as comprehensive as was thought.

Harris, Albert J., and E. R. Sipay. "Assessing Reading Performance." In *How to Increase Reading Ability*. 8th ed., 160–228. New York: Longman, 1985. Includes an in-depth summary of information on word recognition on pp. 211–20.

Leslie, Lauren, and Brenda Thimke. "The Use of Orthographic Knowledge in Beginning Reading." *Journal of Reading Behavior* 18, no. 3 (1986): 229–41. The results of this study suggest that as children grow in orthographic knowledge, they also grow in the recognition of words and reading rate.

Samuels, S. Jay. "Decoding and Automaticity: Helping Poor Readers Become Automatic at Word Recognition." *Reading Teacher* 41 (April 1988): 756–60. The author suggests that direct teaching of decoding skills and practice with materials at a comfortable level of difficulty will result in automaticity in decoding.

Samuels, S. Jay. "Word Recognition." In *Theoretical Models and Processes of Reading*. 3d ed., edited by Harry Singer and Robert B. Ruddell, 256–75. Newark, Del.: International Reading Association, 1985. Provides a detailed review of the literature on word recognition in both alphabetic and nonalphabetic languages.

Simons, Herbert D., and Donald J. Leu, Jr. "The Use of Contextual and Graphic Information in Word Recognition by Second-, Fourth-, and Sixth-Grade Readers." *Journal of Reading Behavior* 19, no. 1 (1987): 33–47. The results of this study indicate that the use of graphic information in word recognition increases with development, while the use of contextual information tends to decrease.

Taylor, Barbara, Larry A. Harris, and P. David Pearson. "Word Recognition Assessment." In *Reading Difficulties: Instruction and Assessment,* 173–99. New York: Random House, 1988. Chapter 7 provides a variety of means for testing and teaching word recognition.

Notes

1. William Durr, "Computer Study of High Frequency Words in Popular Trade Juveniles," *Reading Teacher* 27 (October 1973): 37–42.
2. Maryann Eeds, "Bookwords: Using a Beginning Word List of High Frequency Words from Children's Literature K–3," *Reading Teacher* 38 (January 1985): 418–23.
3. J. McNally and W. Murray, *Key Words to Literacy* (London: Schoolmaster Publishing Co., Ltd., 1968), 1.
4. Margaret LaPray and Ramon Ross, "The Graded Word List: Quick Gauge of Reading Ability," *Journal of Reading* 12 (January 1969): 305–7.
5. Richard L. Slosson, *The Slosson Oral Reading Test* (140 Pine St., East Aurora, N.Y.: Slosson Educational Publications, Inc., 1963).
6. J. F. Jastak and S. R. Jastak, *The Wide Range Achievement Test* (1526 Gilpin Ave., Wilmington, Del.: Guidance Associates of Delaware, Inc., 1965).
7. E. W. Dolch, *Teaching Primary Reading* (Champaign, Ill.: Garrard Press, 1941), 196–215.
8. Child Study Committee of the International Kindergarten Union, *A Study of the Vocabulary of Children before Entering First Grade* (Washington, D.C.: The International Kindergarten Union, 1928).
9. Arthur I. Gates, *A Reading Vocabulary for the Primary Grades* (New York: Teachers College, Columbia University, 1926).
10. H. E. Wheeler and Emma A. Howell, "A First Grade Vocabulary Study," *Elementary School Journal* 31 (September 1930): 52–60.
11. Maude McBroom, Julia Sparrow, and Catherine Eckstein, *A Scale for Determining a Child's Reader Level* (Iowa City: Bureau of Publications, Extension Division, State University of Iowa, 1944).
12. *The Popper Words,* Dolch Basic Sight Word Cards (Champaign, Ill.: Garrard Press, 1942).
13. *The Dolch Basic Sight Word Test* (Champaign, Ill.: Garrard Press, 1942).
14. McBroom, Sparrow, and Eckstein, *A Scale,* 9–10.
15. Ibid., 11.
16. These standards, as well as the limits for the scale, were summarized from the two following studies: Catherine Eckstein, "Use of the Dolch Basic Sight Word List as a Measure to Determine Reader Level" (Master's thesis, State University of Iowa, 1944); and Julia Sparrow, "Accomplishment on the Dolch Basic Sight Word List as a Measure of Reader Level" (Master's thesis, State University of Iowa, 1944).
17. Ibid., 10.
18. Robert L. Hillerich, "Word Lists—Getting It All Together," *Reading Teacher* 27 (January 1974): 353–60.
19. Ibid., 357.
20. Clarence R. Stone, *Progress in Primary Reading* (New York: McGraw-Hill, Inc., 1950).
21. William Shakespeare, *The Plays and Sonnets of William Shakespeare,* vol. 1, edited by William George Clarke and William Aldis Wright. *Great Books of the Western World,* vol. 26 (Chicago: Encyclopedia Britannica, 1952), 608.

22. Barbara C. Palmer, "Is the Dolch List of 220 Basic Sight Words Still Relevant?" *Reading Improvement* 23 (Fall 1986): 227–30.

23. Eldon E. Ekwall and James Shanker, *Diagnosis and Remediation of the Disabled Reader* (Boston: Allyn and Bacon, 1983), 94–95.

24. Marie M. Clay, *The Early Detection of Reading Difficulties,* 3d ed. (Portsmouth, N.H.: Heinemann Educational Books, 1985), 42.

25. Eloise Kennedy, "Reversals, Reversals, Reversals!" *Journal of Experimental Education* 23 (December 1954): 161–70.

26. Marion Monroe, *Children Who Cannot Read* (Chicago: University of Chicago Press, 1932), 127–28.

27. Charles B. Huelsman, *The Huelsman Word Discrimination Test,* Forms A and B (Oxford, Ohio: Miami University, 1958).

28. Marie M. Clay, *Early Detection of Reading Difficulties,* 3d ed.

29. Marie M. Clay, *Sand* (Auckland, New Zealand: Heinemann Educational Books, 1972).

30. Marie M. Clay, *Stones* (Auckland, New Zealand: Heinemann Educational Books, 1979).

31. Kenneth Goodman and Yetta Goodman, "Learning to Read is Natural," in *Theory and Practice in Early Reading,* vol. 1, ed. Lauren Resnick and Phyllis Weaver (Hillsdale, N.J.: Lawrence Erlbaum Associates, 1979); Elfrieda Hiebert, "Developmental Patterns and Interrelationships of Preschool Children's Print Awareness," *Reading Research Quarterly* 16, no. 2 (1981): 236–60; and Margaret G. Jewell and Miles V. Zintz, *Learning to Read Naturally* (Dubuque, Iowa: Kendall/Hunt Publishing Co., 1986), 165–66.

4
The Informal Reading Inventory

Chapter Outline

Vocabulary

informal reading inventory
   (IRI)
independent level
instructional level
frustration level
capacity level
narrative
expository text
passage-dependent
questions
passage-independent
questions
miscue
substitution
mispronunciation
omissions
insertions
hesitations
repetitions
comprehension
reinspection
sight reading
commercial informal
   reading inventory

Questions

1. What do you see as the advantages and importance of the informal reading inventory? **(Inference)**
2. Define the criteria for each of the four reading levels—independent, instructional, frustration, and capacity. **(Recall)**
3. In the word-recognition portion of the IRI, what are the reading behaviors that are counted as kinds of miscues? **(Recall)**
4. What behaviors should be noted but are not counted as miscues? **(Recall)**
5. How would you go about making an informal reading inventory for your classroom? **(Application)**
6. Detail the steps in administering and scoring the informal reading inventory. **(Recall)**

Introduction

One of the most serious problems in elementary school classrooms today is the very large percentage of children who are kept reading at their *frustration* level. If a book is too difficult, if too many new concepts appear and are not repeated several times, and if the decoding process of unlocking new words combined with predicting and confirming strategies have not been learned, boys and girls spend much time in school trying to gain information that is beyond their grasp. At the same time, when teachers look at standardized test results and arbitrarily assign all the children in their rooms to three reading groups, they may be asking some children to stay frustrated all day long. Learning does not progress when children work at the frustration level.

While standardized reading achievement tests have a very important place in assessing the total school reading program, and they provide teachers with a distribution of their students from best to poorest performer, they do not provide the teachers an adequate measure of what books are the appropriate ones for children to read at their *instructional* levels. The standardized test is a power test and may more nearly measure children's frustration levels of reading when they read for a short period of time.[1]

Standardized test scores may yield grade placement equivalents one or more years higher than children can actually read with understanding. Wheeler and Smith found that the grade placement scores on standardized reading tests in the primary grades often have little relationship to the children's actual instructional reading levels.

The teachers cannot meet all children at their levels of functioning and provide instruction from which they can profit unless the teachers can somehow determine with a fair degree of accuracy what those functioning levels are. An *informal reading inventory (IRI)* will provide the classroom teachers with this fundamental information.

The advantages of the IRI for finding where to begin to instruct the children are:[2]

1. The teachers use the materials they have at hand; there is little cost.
2. With direct and rapid administration, the teachers get some needed answers quickly.
3. In terms of textbook reading the children are capable of doing, the IRI is more valid than other tests.
4. IRIs can be either group or individual for appropriate purposes.
5. The students can be made aware of how well they read.
6. The students can be made aware of progress as they achieve it.
7. As achievement is appraised, specific needs are revealed.
8. Interesting materials can be selected to use in the inventory.
9. Readability of materials can be checked in series of texts.
10. The test situation can be a valuable instructional situation.

What Is the Informal Reading Inventory?

The IRI is an individual test in which the child reads both orally and silently from increasingly difficult material until the material becomes frustrating in terms of either accuracy of pronunciation or understanding of ideas in the content. The informal reading test is diagnostic in that it reveals many specific areas of difficulty in reading for the observant teachers. Clearly, the values derived from administering the IRI depend entirely upon the competence of the teacher, who must make judgments as the child reads. An informal reading inventory should provide a selection of reading at each level from preprimer through the sixth grade for both oral and silent reading. Comprehension questions must be provided to obtain a measure of the child's understanding of what is read.

The child should read from the book while the teacher has a reproduced copy for marking miscues, making notes, and evaluating. The child continues to read increasingly difficult material until he or she makes too many miscues for the instructional level, either in comprehension or pronunciation. Then the teacher begins reading one passage orally at each reading level and asking the prepared questions to measure the child's capacity for understanding ideas heard when listening to someone else read the material. This is referred to as the *capacity level, listening level,* or *hearing comprehension level.*

The Four Reading Levels to Be Defined

The IRI will enable the teacher to establish an *independent* level of reading for the student; the *instructional* level of reading; the *frustration* level; and the *capacity* level. These are defined below.

The *independent* level of reading is the *highest* level at which the child can read fluently and with personal satisfaction without help. In independent reading, the child encounters practically no mechanical difficulties with the words and no problems with understanding the concepts in the context. The level is generally defined as that level where the child makes no more than one miscue in one hundred words in the mechanics of reading and where there are no difficulties in comprehension. Much of the material that the child selects for free reading from the library should be at this level, as well as some of the collateral reading for unit work in social studies and science.

The *instructional* level of reading is the teaching level. This is defined as the *highest* level at which the child makes no more than five uncorrected miscues in reading one hundred running words with at least 75 percent comprehension of the ideas in the text. Such materials are difficult enough to be challenging but sufficiently easy that the student can do independent seat work with only the usual readiness help from the teacher when assignments are made. The most important tasks of the elementary teacher are to establish for all children their instructional levels of functioning in reading and to provide them with work at those levels. Instructional reading material should be read silently before being read orally. Then no difficulties with phrasing, punctuation, finger pointing, or tension will arise. Many children are not given the opportunity to read at this level at school. The instructional level is reached when the child uses a conversational tone, without noticeable tension, with satisfactory rhythm, and with suitable phrasing, making proper use of word-recognition clues and strategies.

The *frustration* level is the *lowest* level at which obvious difficulties cause confusion, frustration, and tension in the reading situation. Betts listed inability to anticipate meanings, head movements, finger pointing, tension, slow word-by-word reading, vocalization, and too many substitutions, omissions, repetitions, and insertions as evidences of frustration.[3]

There is not always a clear line of separation between what is instructional level and what is frustration. The teacher's purpose is to keep the child on the growing edge of learning without pushing along too fast. The teacher will do well to choose the lower of two possible reader levels when there is a question about which is appropriate for given individuals. To let students have more practice at easier levels and strengthen their abilities and skills is preferable to moving them into material that is too difficult and stopping their progress.

The *capacity* level for reading is the *highest* level at which the child can understand the ideas and concepts in informational material that is read aloud. The teacher begins reading to the student at the level of difficulty at which oral or silent reading stopped because of frustration. The same questions prepared to test the child's oral or silent reading comprehension are now also appropriate to ask after the teacher reads the material. The standard expected for instructional level, 75 percent comprehension, is an adequate measure of establishing capacity for understanding reading.

The capacity level measures the level at which the readers would function if they were able to use all their innate abilities for reading. So, if their instructional level is third grade but their capacity level (listening or understanding level) is fifth grade, they should be able to profit from remedial instruction and raise their reading levels by two years.

Importance of the Informal Reading Inventory

Practice by any classroom teacher will provide a great deal of confidence in use of the IRI and will demonstrate its absolute necessity. It is the most accurate test measure that can be provided to evaluate the child's ability to use textbooks for instructional purposes. The reading inventory should be the very core of the teacher's whole reading-work program for the year. The teacher can learn to prepare a reading inventory and to use it to study the abilities and disabilities of the boys and girls in the classroom with respect to developmental reading.

Since the child is reading only brief passages and the test situation represents only one small sample of the child's total behavior, some facets of reading may not be adequately assessed. It is also possible that on another day or at another time, the same individual might perform somewhat differently.

The individual texts in the reading series may not be accurately graded so that a readability formula may need to be applied to determine the level of difficulty. Fry's Readability Graph (see figure 7.7) may be used for this purpose.

The classroom teachers are the ones who, in the final analysis, *must make all the decisions* about the child's reading ability in day-to-day work. The teachers must *unavoidably* select their reading materials in language arts, social studies, arithmetic, science, and literature.

An excellent way for a teacher to get initial skill in administering an informal reading inventory is to record the children's oral reading on the tape recorder so that it can be played back a number of times. Most clinicians are apt to hear a few miscues the second time that they missed completely the first time. Without a specific plan of what to listen for and some practice, the listener may not be able to make an objective summary of the results of the oral reading.

Construction of the Informal Reading Inventory

The first step in preparing the inventory is the selection of a series of books, probably a series of readers. Preferably, a series of readers not already familiar to the children being tested should be used. While there are many words *not common* to two series of readers, the controlled vocabularies, the picture clues, and the context clues all help the children to anticipate meanings, and most of the words are already in the children's speaking vocabularies.

Selections from preprimers, primers, and first and second readers need to contain 60 to 125 words and to be sufficiently informational in nature that questions can be asked to measure understanding of the ideas about what is read. For grades three to six, passages need to be somewhat longer, perhaps 100 to 200 words in length.

One selection must be identified to be read orally and one to be read silently. The selection from each book should be taken at the end of about the first one-third of the book. This follows the first few stories containing mostly review words from previous books in the series.

Most basal reader selections are *narrative* in nature; Flood and Lapp[4] found that 72 percent of the pages in the basals examined contained narratives or poems. Narratives, or stories, have a form that often includes a setting, a beginning action, a reaction to the beginning, a goal of the main character, an attempt to reach the goal, an outcome, and an ending.[5] More than one action and reaction may be included in the story. Readers seem to use knowledge of story structure, which has been developed over years of hearing and reading stories, to help them to understand and remember narratives.

Expository texts, which are not common in basal readers, do not have the single, basic structure that narratives do. Instead, several organizational patterns may be used, such as cause-effect, description, enumeration, and comparison, to present content material. Children have had far fewer opportunities to experience expository writing and may find it more difficult to read and understand than narratives.

When informal reading inventory passages are being chosen, it is wise to select only narrative passages or only expository texts. If the two types of writing are mixed in the informal reading inventory, the teacher may find it difficult to determine whether comprehension problems are the result of the text structure or difficulties with vocabulary or concepts. Gillis and Olson have commented:

> When a student's comprehension scores are erratic from level to level, examine the passages to see if the variability could be due to shifts between types of text or between well and poorly-organized passages.[6]

When the children read, they must be given an introduction to the story and a motivation question to set a purpose for reading. These should be prepared and printed on the scoring sheets so that the teacher makes consistent introductory statements. It is wise to select the silent reading passage immediately following the oral reading selection so that the children can continue reading without teacher explanation, thus saving time.

The comprehension questions should be carefully thought out so that they measure understanding as completely as possible. Levels of questioning are pertinent: factual or memory items; inferential items requiring reading between the lines; vocabulary items to test concepts; and items to test ability to interpret and evaluate. Authors need to provide meaningful concepts for new or difficult vocabulary items: "A transformer, a device to change alternating current to higher or lower voltages, allows electricity from a power line to be used in homes." The careful reader can now answer the question, "What is a transformer?"

When choosing selections for the informal reading inventory, teachers should consider the nature of the context material. Can good comprehension questions be derived from the story? Vocabulary, sentence structure, human interest, and the number and complexity of the ideas dealt with influence the comprehension level of the material. Teachers should ask questions requiring recall, rather than those requiring only an answer of yes or no. For example, ask "What color was the hound?" not "Was the hound in the story red?"

To develop comprehension questions that cannot be answered without having read the passage is important. These are called *passage-dependent questions. Passage-independent questions* are those that can be answered without having read the material; they do nothing to measure a reader's comprehension of the passage. After developing a set of questions for a selection, the teacher may ask a child who has not read the material to answer them. If the questions can be answered, they are passage independent; new questions need to be written.[7]

Making Connections 4.1: Creating an IRI Passage

One skill that each reading teacher needs is the ability to create an informal reading inventory. For this Making Connections, the task will be to prepare one oral and one silent reading passage. The following steps will be helpful.

1. Select a basal reader designated for a particular reading level. (In a later chapter, you will be given information about how to estimate reading levels independent of the publishers' stated levels.)
2. Identify a passage long enough to be divided into oral and silent parts. Each part should be of suitable length for the estimated reading level.
3. Develop questions to accompany your two reading passages. Follow the guidelines given in the chapter for comprehension questions.
4. Type the two passages, the accompanying questions, the number of words in each passage, and the motivating statements. Using the IRI in appendix E as a guide, prepare the chart for showing percentages for correct word recognition and comprehension.
5. Type the pupil's copies of the two passages; remember, the pupil's copy has nothing on the pages except the stories.

Bring your work to class to share with others. Each student should receive feedback from peers so that the best possible IRI can be produced.

Administering the Informal Reading Inventory

Before the teacher can decide what selection to give the child to read, some idea of the child's functioning level is needed. Several ways to obtain information for making this decision follow:

1. One way to decide at what grade level to begin the IRI with given students is to have them complete the San Diego Quick Assessment. If nine out of ten words are correct at grade three but several are missed at grade four, the reader begins the IRI at grade three.
2. In September, the teachers can check the cumulative records from the previous year and see which books the children were reading when the last school year ended. Such a listing may be in error, but if the selection is too difficult, the teachers will move to easier material.
3. The teacher may be able to assemble subgroups of children in a reading circle very early in the year and ask them to "read around the circle" (sampling a story for which the teacher has developed readiness). For those who have difficulty, only one sentence is sufficient. For those who read well, a much longer passage is fine.[8]

4. If the teacher estimates that a particular book is appropriate, a sampling of words can be made from the list in the back of the book to make a word-recognition test of twenty words. The sample will be obtained by dividing the total number of words in the list by twenty and selecting words from the list at intervals of that quotient. For example, if there are two hundred words in the list, two hundred divided by twenty is ten, so the teachers will select every tenth word. If the child knows at least 80 percent of these words at sight, this book may be at his or her instructional level of reading.

The following list of twenty words was selected from the word list, including both "introduced" and "glossary" words, in the back of the teacher's manual for the basal *Hidden Wonders*,[9] level 7, a 3¹ reader (first semester, third reader), by selecting the first word on the list and every twentieth word thereafter from a total list of 391 words.

hippopotamus	biscuit	climate	design
trophy	theatre	mahogany	avocado
carriage	rearrange	conveyor	Chicago
Oklahoma	thoughtfully	ultimate	license
plume	chore	frame	average

If a child can read sixteen or more of these words at sight, this would be an appropriate book to sample for the instructional level of reading.

The easiest way to establish rapport with the child is to explain exactly what it is that you are doing and why determining the instructional level of reading is so important. If the child is interested, discuss the changing sizes of print in more difficult books, the amount of reading on a page, and the decrease in the use of pictures. The child must not be made to feel that the test is a "threat" to acceptance, and if the child continually asks for reassurance ("Am I doin' good?"), the teacher needs to be completely reassuring.

If the child makes more than five uncorrected *miscues* in 100 running words in reading the first selection attempted, the teacher may select an easier one and continue the reading until a satisfactory instructional level is found. Occasionally a child will make more miscues on the first passage than on the next, more difficult one, so the teacher has to be alert for any psychological factors that may cause this to happen and be sure to find the highest level at which the student meets the criterion for instructional level.

While the pupil is reading, the teacher will record all word substitutions, hesitations, words not pronounced, repetitions, omissions, and insertions. It will be most helpful to record the pupil's reading on the tape recorder so that the teacher can replay it when the child is gone and give more attention to the reading. Try to arrange the work of the rest of the class in independent activities, so that you can spend fifteen or twenty minutes with the child in one corner of the room where the child can complete the inventory. The relatively uninterrupted environment is necessary. A properly conducted informal reading inventory is the best instrument that classroom teachers have to determine most adequately what the child can and cannot do in formal reading.

Type of Miscue	Rule for Marking	Example
1. Substitutions.	Write in the substituted word.	*black* The boy is back of . . .
2. Mispronunciations.	Write in the word phonetically or draw a line through the word.	~~symbolic~~ or / sim bŏl ĭk
3. Hesitations. A pause of two seconds or more.	Make one check above the word on which the hesitation occurs. (Two seconds or more.)	✓ It is a fascinating
4. Word pronounced by teacher. Word on which child hesitates more than five seconds.	Make two checks above the word pronounced. (Five seconds or more.)	✓✓ It is a fascinating story.
5. Repetitions.	Draw a wavy line beneath word or words repeated.	He thought he saw a whale.
6. Omissions.	Encircle the word or punctuation omitted.	It is the largest ⟨living⟩ animal. It is a whale
7. Insertions.	Use caret and write in inserted words or punctuation.	*is a* This ᵥbig fellow from the jungles of Africa,

Figure 4.1. Recording miscues in oral reading. John V. Gilmore and Eunice C. Gilmore, *Gilmore Oral Reading Test, Manual of Directions* (Harcourt, Brace, & World, Inc. 1968), general directions modified by the writers. With permission.

Method of Marking and Analyzing Miscues

The miscues to be noted include *substitutions, mispronunciations, omissions, insertions, hesitations, words pronounced by the examiner,* and *repetitions.* To have a definite, well-learned system of marking that will be meaningful is important. By such a method, a child may read a passage of 300 words, for example, in which twenty miscues are made in the mechanics of reading. If three months later the same passage is read with only five miscues in mechanics, the teacher has a favorable measure of the student's growth. However, the use of the system of recording miscues must be consistent if the pre- and post-test record is to have value.

The system used here is borrowed from the manual of directions of the Gilmore Oral Reading Test.[10] The use of that test will be discussed later, in chapter 5. The teachers should become habituated to one marking system and use it in all the individual testing that they do. Marking of miscues is explained in figure 4.1.

With only a minimum amount of practice, groups of experienced teachers find that they mark children's oral reading with a very high percentage of agreement. So, even though the administration of the IRI has subjective qualities, and many judgments must be made informally by the teacher very quickly, with some practice the results become quite objective for the competent teacher.

The following types of oral reading miscues constitute most of the children's difficulties (see figure 4.1):

1. *Hesitations.* Mark after two seconds of hesitation with a (✓). Proper nouns are given to the child as needed and are not scored as miscues unless the proper noun is a word that most children would know. Examples: *Big, Brown.*

2. *Word pronounced for the child.* If the pupil hesitates for approximately five seconds on a word, pronounce it and make a second check mark (✓✓) above it.

3. *Mispronunciations.* This results in a nonsense word that may be produced by (1) false accentuation, (2) wrong pronunciation of vowels or consonants, or (3) the omission, addition, or insertion of one or more letters, without creating a real or new word. Example: *cret ik* for *critic.* Write the child's pronunciation above phonetically. Notice word-attack methods and enunciation. If miscues come too rapidly for recording, draw a line through mispronounced words. Do not count foreign accent or regional speech mannerisms.

4. *Omissions.* Encircle the omitted word, syllable, letter sound, or endings. Count as one miscue the omission of more than one word of consecutive print.

5. *Substitutions.* This occurs when one sensible or real word is put in the place of the word in print. Write the substituted word directly above the word presented in print. Note whether it makes sense or whether it is irrelevant to the context.

6. *Insertions.* These are words that do not appear in the printed material. Place a caret (∧), and write the added word or words. Count as one miscue the insertion of two or more words consecutively.

7. *Repetitions.* A word, part of a word, or groups of words that are repeated should be marked; this may indicate that the child is having trouble understanding what he or she reads. Draw a wavy line under the repeated words.

One uncorrected miscue in twenty consecutive words is often interpreted as one mispronounced word or one unknown word. In this text, hesitations, repetitions, insertions, and omissions are also considered; however, many repetitions are made only to correct a substitution miscue. The subjective judgment therefore must be made in each case whether two or three recorded miscues represent only one miscue in reading in terms of accuracy in mechanics.

For example:

. . . one . . . [after] another . . . one after another . . .

The reader fails to pronounce "after." After reading falteringly through "one . . . [after] . . . another" with help, the child repeats it to regain the thought, perhaps, before continuing. This is recorded in the tabulation of miscues as one word *failed to pronounce,* and not as a repetition. However, if the reader reads:

. . . one . . . after another . . . one after another . . .

this repetition is a miscue counted in the tabulation, because the mere fact that the phrase is repeated indicates that the reader is having difficulty for some unknown reason. Often, by reducing the level of difficulty of material, pupils who do much repeating will no longer need to do so.

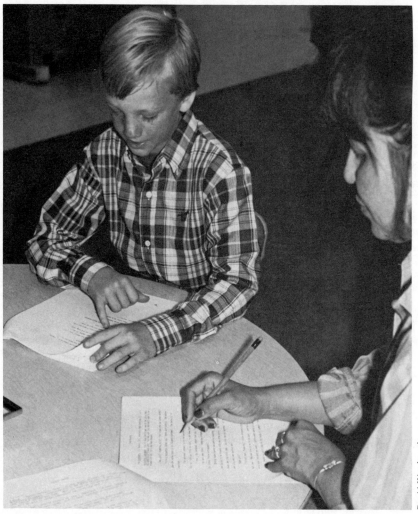

David Woodward

Completing an informal reading inventory provides the teacher with critical information needed for planning a successful reading program for a child.

The teacher needs a series of readers from which pupils can read. In order to establish a satisfactorily easy level for some, a complete series beginning with the pre-primer or primer and continuing through the sixth-grade level will be needed.

The child begins reading selections and continues to read until the frustration level is reached. Then the teacher reads one selection at each level beyond that to the child and checks the comprehension score. This will provide a measure of the *understanding* of context material read aloud, or the capacity level of reading.

Figure 4.2 is an illustration of the marking of oral reading done by Mary, a seventh-grade student. The method of marking miscues is that found in figure 4.1. The reader is reminded that proper nouns are not counted and that if a word is pronounced more

---

A Hunting Guide

When Robert Gonzales was 18, he signed up as an apprentice mountain porter and hunting guide. As an apprentice, he helped the other guides when extra men were needed on the climbing rope or on a pack trip.

After a year as a porter, Robert was ready for the test to become a guide. This tricky test lasted three days. It was given by the "guide chief" appointed by (the) Park Service. Many of the test questions stressed the safety rules a guide must follow. *starting* Part of the test was taken right on the mountains. Robert had to show that he could do all the work *for* of a guide—from getting a man out of trouble to giving first aid.

At the end of three days, Robert was taken on a climb by the guide chief. Robert led (on) *taking* the rope, while the chief watched every move he made. The climb called for every sort (of) *waited for* *short* climbing technique: step-cutting in snow and ice, "balance climbing" on smooth slabs, and *bal* *slabs* many knots of the rope.

Level of difficulty of this passage: fifth grade on Fry Readability graph. Mary is in the seventh grade.

Total words in passage: <u>169</u>. Maximum permissible miscues for the instructional level of reading: 8 or 9.

Questions to check comprehension:	*Scoring the oral reading:*	
+ 1. How old was Robert when he signed up as a guide? (18)	Substitutions	<u>6</u>
	Mispronunciations	<u>1</u>
− 2. How long did he work as a guide? (one year)	Hesitations-	____
	Words pronounced	
− 3. What was a guide supposed to do? (Make dangerous climbs safely.)	by examiner	<u>3</u>**
	Repetitions	____
+ 4. What did Robert have to do to pass his test? (Know safety rules and go on a climb)	Omissions	<u>3/4</u>
	Insertions	<u>1</u>
	TOTAL ERRORS	14/15
+ 5. Would you trust Robert if he passed the test? Why? (Yes, he'd have the skills)		

*Omitting "of" makes sense; doesn't need "of" with short.
**Do not count proper names (Gonzales) "apprentice" is counted only once.

Figure 4.2. An illustration of marking oral reading miscues than once for the student, it is counted as only one miscue. Questions for checking comprehension are given below the reading (70 or 75 percent is a minimum level of acceptable comprehension), and a list of oral reading miscues is given so that the total miscues with the mechanics of reading can be computed. The story is part of an unpublished informal reading inventory prepared in a class at the University of New Mexico under the direction of Dr. Robert White.

With respect to comprehension, Mary answered three questions correctly, as indicated by the three pluses, and missed two questions, as indicated by the two minuses. One cannot judge from only one sample such as this, but 60 percent suggests frustration level. Fourteen or fifteen uncorrected miscues in oral reading is nearer to one miscue in twelve running words than it is to one miscue in twenty words. Mary needs to read other passages, but this exercise suggests a frustration level of reading.

The examiner must record these reading behaviors:

1. *Corrections.* Write a *C* by the mistake when the child corrects the miscue.
2. *Phrasing.* Use a diagonal mark to indicate undue pauses or incorrect phrasing.
3. *Punctuation.* Put an *X* on punctuation marks that the child ignores or passes over.
4. *Rate.* As difficulty increases, the child may read "slowly" or "haltingly." Indicate this. One must record reading time in seconds for each selection in order to determine words per minute.

In scoring the oral reading inventory, it seems logical to:

1. Count only one miscue at any place in the reading. If the child repeats a phrase to correct a word substitution, the important miscue is that of sight word substitution.
2. If a phrase of two or three words is omitted, count it as only one miscue.
3. If a phrase of two or three words is inserted, count it as only one miscue.
4. If the child makes one substitution miscue and then in the same sentence makes a second miscue to get proper grammatical structure with verbs or pronouns, count this as only one miscue.
5. If the proper names are unusual or difficult, do not include them in the miscue count. If they are common names like *Brown, Green,* or *Smith,* they should be counted as miscues. If the proper names are miscalled several times in one passage, the teacher must decide whether to count this as only one miscue. For example, a child may have read regularly about Tom and Betty previously, then in the IRI consistently pronounces *Juan* as *Tom.* This should be counted as only one miscue.
6. In basic sight word substitutions, the miscue should be counted each time it occurs. If the reader says "then" for "when" three times, this is three miscues.

Method of Recording Oral and Silent Reading Comprehension

The teacher must record the child's responses to the *comprehension* questions as they are given so that an accurate measure will result. When the child's comprehension falls below 70–75 percent, there is no need to continue the reading even if the child has few mechanical difficulties.

The teacher needs to think about the conditions under which the child will be asked to respond to comprehension questions. The usual practice has been to expect the child to answer the questions without referring back to the passage that has just been read. That practice confuses memory for what has been read with comprehension of the material. In order to determine comprehension alone, it may be appropriate to allow the reader to look back if needed. Kender and Rubenstein found that children could not look back and find answers if they did not comprehend the material.[11] It would seem that comprehension scores will not be significantly inflated if children are allowed to keep the material they have just read and look back as needed.

Cardarelli also supported *reinspection:*

> In the conventional administration of the IRI, comprehension diagnosis is inordinately influenced by the reader's ability to recall information. Reinspection restores recall to its proper function . . . . reinspection may also indirectly promote the generation of better questions by teachers, demanding higher cognitive operations by students.[12]

Interpreting the IRI

The teacher will be able to summarize the results of the reading of the IRI in a chart, as in figure 4.3.

General Reading Habits

Nervous mannerisms such as fidgeting, hair twisting, nose picking, drawing a heavy sigh, or exhibiting undue restlessness indicate discomfort and frustration. These should be noted on the child's test. Also, teachers should notice such difficulties as losing the place in the story, holding the book close to the face, pointing with the fingers, or moving the head.

In silent reading, the child may vocalize everything, read very slowly, or need encouragement to keep on reading.

Observations about Reading Performance

In determining the child's instructional level of reading from a series of readers, the following points are made:

1. This is *"sight reading."* That is, the child is reading the material orally without first *studying* it silently. This is a test situation; in everyday work, children should have the opportunity to read silently any material they will be expected to read well orally. Here the teacher is trying to find out what the child *can* read.
2. The first concern in this basic step in establishing corrective instruction is to measure the ability to pronounce the words. However, understanding of the content read is basic and must be measured also.

ORAL					
Level of Book	Total Words	Total Miscues	Percent of Miscues	Percent Accuracy	Suitability of Level of Difficulty
_____	_____	_____	_____	_____	_____
_____	_____	_____	_____	_____	_____
_____	_____	_____	_____	_____	_____

SILENT					
Level of Book	Total Words	Time in Seconds	Rate per Minute	Percent of Comprehension	Suitability of Level of Difficulty
_____	_____	_____	_____	_____	_____
_____	_____	_____	_____	_____	_____
_____	_____	_____	_____	_____	_____

Figure 4.3. Chart for summary of IRI reading

3. All the miscues that the child corrects immediately without help are deducted in arriving at a figure to compute percentage of error or percentage of accuracy. If the child makes two miscues in the same place in reading, this will usually be counted as one miscue. For example, repeating a phrase where a word has been omitted so the reading can be corrected constitutes an *omission*.
4. The instructional level sought is the *highest level* at which the child reads orally with 95 percent accuracy in the mechanics and has at least 75 percent comprehension.

5. One of the common defects in oral reading is nonfluency or word-by-word reading. The word caller plods along slowly, tending to make a noticeable pause after each word. Word callers may not phrase adequately; they may not group words together; and they may disregard and misuse punctuation marks. Keeping the place with the finger is common. Getting the sense of what they read is hard for students who struggle to pronounce the words.

6. In evaluating the oral reading sample, the teachers should identify the "context reader." They may read rapidly enough, but quite inaccurately. They may skip over words or add words, but their most usual miscue is in substituting freely what they think the story will say. Below are three textbook sentences with children's context reading of them:

The story reads:	*The child says:*
"The little rabbit went down the road."	"The small bunny hopped down the lane." (The picture at the top of the page gave the idea clearly.)
"Come out of the back door."	"Come out on the back porch."
"Behind the band came a man on a big elephant."	"After the band wagon went, a man came by on an elephant."

Organizing and Reporting Test Information

After several tests have been given to a child and information from other sources has been gathered, the teacher must find a way to arrange all of the data for use in planning the reading program. An easy way to accomplish this task is to devise a sheet such as the one in figure 4.4. All of the test scores are recorded in one place, along with summaries of inventories and previous records. At the bottom of the sheet, space should be provided for a brief plan for meeting the needs of the student. It is most important that such a summary sheet be dated if it is to have usefulness at some later time.

Strengths and Potential Weaknesses of the IRI

Examining briefly the strengths and potential weaknesses of the informal reading inventory may be helpful. Many of the strengths were presented in the introduction to this chapter. They center around the low cost of the inventory, its validity, the information that can be supplied to the student, the variety of materials that may be used, and the instructional nature of the testing situation. And, most importantly, the teacher has information that will allow the student to be given reading materials of suitable difficulty.

The potential weaknesses center around the skills of the teacher giving the test, the quality of the passages selected to be read, and the comprehension questions. The accuracy of the administration of the test will determine its effectiveness as a diagnostic and placement tool. Passages to be read must be selected carefully, taking into account knowledge about narrative and expository text, appropriate length, sufficient content,

A Quick Screening Report about the disabled reader in your room.

Name _____ Grade _____ Age _____ School _____

Date Collected   *Comments:*

1. Last year's report in
   cumulative folder: _____

2. Informal Reading Inventory:

   Independent Level: _____

   Instructional Level: _____

3. San Diego Quick Assessment: Raw Score _____

   Grade Level _____

4. Spelling Test: (Source of word list) _____

5. Writing sample: (Specific types of problems) _____

   _____

6. Keystone Visual Survey Test: (Need for referral)   Yes _____ No _____

7. Interest Inventory: _____

8. Interview about reading: _____

   _____

9. Parent Interview: _____

   _____

10. Vocabulary measure; _____

11. Wepman Auditory Discrimination Test: (Need for referral)

    Yes _____ No _____   (This test is discussed in Chapter 6)

12. Status summary: What can you do in the immediate future to make constructive use of
    the student's time? Who is available in your school to help you get further information?

Figure 4.4. A Quick Screening Report

and attractiveness of the materials. Questions, if they are to be effective, must be passage dependent, varying from recall to evaluative, and of sufficient number. The major weaknesses of the informal reading inventory can be avoided if the test is well planned. Thus, the IRI can be a most important tool in carrying out an effective reading program.

Commercial Informal Reading Inventories

Within recent years, a number of informal reading inventories, as such, have been published in formats that make them appear to be formal. With an increase in the extent to which rigid steps are outlined for their administration and technical skills are required for the interpretation of their results, they have tended to lose their "informality." However, they are labeled as informal inventories when they are designed to help the teacher estimate rather quickly *instructional* levels of reading (both oral and silent), the *frustration* level where difficulties show up, and (if the teacher then reads to the student) the understanding or *capacity* level of the student.

Inventories currently in use include:

1. Lois A. Bader, *Reading and Language Inventory* (New York: Macmillan Co., 1983). Levels preprimer through grade twelve. Part of an extensive diagnostic battery of tests.
2. Paul C. Burns and Betty D. Roe, *Informal Reading Assessment,* 2d ed. (Chicago: Rand McNally College Publishing Co., 1985). Word lists and reading passages, preprimer through grade twelve.
3. Eldon E. Ekwall, *Ekwall Reading Inventory,* 2d ed. (Boston: Allyn and Bacon, 1986). Includes eleven graded passages and eleven graded word lists.
4. Edward B. Fry, *Reading Diagnosis: Informal Reading Inventories* (Providence, R.I.: Jamestown Publishers, 1981). Tests oral reading and silent reading comprehension through elementary grades.
5. Jerry L. Johns, *Basic Reading Inventory: Preprimer–Grade 8,* 3d ed. (Dubuque, Iowa: Kendall/Hunt Publishing Co., 1985). Graded word lists and passages, preprimer through grade eight.
6. Wilma Miller, *Reading Diagnosis Kit,* 2d ed. (New York: Center for Applied Research in Education, 1978). Levels primer through grade twelve.
7. Nicholas J. Silvaroli, *Classroom Reading Inventory,* 5th ed. (Dubuque, Iowa: William C. Brown Co. Publishers, 1986). Graded reading passages, preprimer through grade eight.
8. Mary Lynn Woods and Alden J. Moe, *Analytical Reading Inventory,* 3d ed. (Columbus, Ohio: Merrill Publishing Co., 1985). Graded passages, primer through grade nine.

Making Connections 4.2: Administering the IRI

Each teacher needs to be able to administer an IRI quickly and effectively. Only practice will aid the teacher in achieving this goal.

Plan to do one of these two activities:

1. Administer the IRI passages that you prepared in Making Connections 4.1 to three children who should be able to read them. Tape record each child's reading, and score the word recognition and comprehension tasks carefully. Compare the performances of the three readers. Plan to share your results with other class members.
2. Administer the informal reading inventory found in appendix E to one child. Tape record and then evaluate carefully the child's reading. Were you able to find any of the reading levels of your reader with this abbreviated IRI? Prepare a description of the many observed reading behaviors of the child you tested. Plan to share your findings with peers.

Summary

Classroom teachers have no alternative to administering informal reading inventories to students in their classes. There is no other way to help students to find the books that they can read adequately for study. All teachers may not construct or administer their informal reading inventories in exactly the same ways, but each teacher's consistent judgment may be more important. The classroom teacher is ultimately responsible for assigning appropriate materials for each child. Creating and administering teacher-made IRIs will provide insights into the reading process rarely found elsewhere. Commercial informal reading inventories are not as useful to competent teachers as their own abilities to take a book off the shelf and ask the students to "try it on for size." The published inventories do give teachers valuable pre- and post-test results and are easily available for use with many students. But teachers also need to be able to try the geography text, the science text, or any other to determine the level of difficulty for any one student.

As Powell has very aptly concluded:

> The strength of the IRI is not as a test instrument but as a strategy for studying the behavior of the learner in a reading situation and as a basis for instant diagnosis in the teaching environment.[13]

For Further Reading

Anderson, Betty, and Rosie Webb Joels. "Informal Reading Inventories." *Reading Improvement* 23 (Winter 1986): 299–302. The authors question the scoring of repetitions based on a study of 136 elementary students.

Betts, Emmett A. *Foundations of Reading Instruction.* New York: American Book Co., 1946. Betts developed the concept of the IRI and many of the rules of its administration, scoring, and interpretation.

Duffelmeyer, Frederick A., and Barbara B. Duffelmeyer. "Main Idea Questions on Informal Reading Inventories." *Reading Teacher* 41 (November 1987): 162–66. When developing IRI questions, distinguishing between main idea questions and questions about the topic of the passage is important.

Ekwall, Eldon E. "Using Informal Reading Inventories, the Cloze Procedure, and the Analysis of Reading Scores." In *Diagnosis and Remediation of the Disabled Reader,* 366–411. Boston: Allyn and Bacon, 1983. A basic textbook presentation on the IRI and other assessments.

Englert, Carol Sue, and Elfrieda H. Hiebert. "Children's Developing Awareness of Text Structures in Expository Materials." *Journal of Educational Psychology* 76 (February 1984): 65–74. The authors report research that indicates that understanding of expository text is related to grade level and reading ability.

Henk, William A. "Reading Assessments of the Future: Toward Precision Diagnosis." *Reading Teacher* 40 (May 1987): 860–70. The author identifies a number of changes to be made in IRIs to make them more precise for disabled readers.

Johnson, Marjorie Seddon, Roy A. Kress, and John J. Pikulski. *Informal Reading Inventories.* 2d ed. Newark, Del.: International Reading Association, 1987. An important and comprehensive publication concerning the IRI.

Krein, Evelyn L., and Jane A. Zaharias. "Analysis of Able and Disabled Sixth-Grade Readers' Knowledge of Story Structure: A Comparison." *Reading Horizons* 27 (Fall 1986): 45–53. The results of this study indicate that good readers have a better understanding of story structure than do disabled readers. Several suggestions for helping disabled readers to learn about story structure are given.

McKenna, Michael C. "Informal Reading Inventories: A Review of the Issues." *Reading Teacher* 36 (March 1983): 670–77. As the title suggests, this is a broad-ranging review of questions about IRIs.

Notes

1. Page Simpson Bristow, John J. Pikulski, and Peter L. Pelosi, "A Comparison of Five Estimates of Reading Instructional Level," *Reading Teacher* 37 (December 1983): 273–79; and Lester R. Wheeler and Edwin H. Smith, "A Modification of the Informal Reading Inventory," *Elementary English* 34 (April 1967): 224.

2. Emmett A. Betts, *Foundations of Reading Instruction* (New York: American Book Co., 1950), 478–79.

3. Ibid., 448.

4. James Flood and Diane Lapp, "Forms of Discourse in Basal Readers," *Elementary School Journal* 87 (January 1987): 299–306.

5. Dixie Lee Spiegel and Jill Fitzgerald, "Improving Reading Comprehension through Instruction about Story Parts," *Reading Teacher* 39 (March 1986): 477–78.

6. M. K. Gillis and Mary W. Olson, "Elementary IRIs: Do They Reflect What We Know about Text Type/Structure and Comprehension?" *Reading Research and Instruction* 27 (Fall 1987): 42.

7. Frederick A. Duffelmeyer, Jennifer Long, and Anne Kruse, "The Passage Independence of IRI Comprehension Question Categories: Evidence of Non-Uniformity," *Reading Improvement* 24 (Summer 1987): 101–6.

8. E. W. Dolch, "How to Diagnose Children's Reading Difficulties by Informal Classroom Techniques," *Reading Teacher* 6 (January 1953): 10–14.

9. Ira E. Aaron et al., *Teacher's Manual for "Hidden Wonders,"* Level 7 (Glenview, Ill.: Scott, Foresman and Co., 1985), T113–T115.

10. John V. Gilmore, *Manual of Directions, Gilmore Oral Reading Test* (New York: Harcourt, Brace, 1968).

11. Joseph Kender and Herbert Rubenstein, "Recall Versus Reinspection in IRI Comprehension Tests," *Reading Teacher* 30: (April 1977): 776–79.

12. Aldo F. Cardarelli, "The Influence of Reinspection on Students' IRI Results," *Reading Teacher* 41 (March 1988): 666.

13. William R. Powell, "The Validity of the Instructional Reading Level," in *Elementary Reading Instruction: Selected Materials,* 2d ed., ed. Althea Beery, Thomas C. Barrett, and William R. Powell (Boston: Allyn and Bacon, 1974), 89–96.

5
Standardized Tests and Records of Progress

Vocabulary

standardized tests
validity
reliability
norms
raw scores
grade equivalent scores
percentiles
stanines
norm-referenced tests
criterion-referenced tests
Buros Institute of Mental
  Measurements
oral reading test
silent reading tests
diagnostic reading tests
lines of importance
progress indicators
group test
Reading Miscue Inventory

Questions

1. Compare the terms *validity* and *reliability*. **(Recall)**

2. What problems do you see in using grade equivalent scores? Percentiles? Stanines? **(Application)** Which would you prefer to use? Why? **(Evaluation)**

3. Describe the critical differences between norm- and criterion-referenced tests. **(Critical)**

4. What are the major limitations of standardized tests? **(Recall)** What role could standardized tests play in the teacher's diagnostic plans? **(Inference)**

5. Describe any one of the tests discussed in some detail in this chapter. From the description given, what could be the test's strengths and weaknesses? **(Recall; Inference)**

6. What is meant by *miscue analysis?* How is the Reading Miscue Inventory different from other reading tests described in this chapter? How is it different from an IRI? **(Recall; Evaluation)**

Introduction

Early in the school year, teachers will complete several informal measures of reading abilities in an attempt to get the necessary information to assign work to individuals, to small groups, and to the whole class. Some informal reading inventories provide a great deal of information about students. Also evaluating the students' abilities to write paragraphs, to complete seat-work assignments, and to successfully complete spelling exercises will help the teacher to understand the range of abilities in the class.

Beyond these measures, a few students may need referrals to other specialists for hearing, vision, or personality tests.

Some few students need referral to the reading diagnostician for further testing in reading. In order to know when to make such referrals and to be able to dialog with consultants, teachers must have some understanding of the terminology used in interpreting *standardized tests* used with their students.

Terminology Used to Interpret Standardized Tests

To use and understand information about standardized tests, teachers should know the terms used in statistical measurement. Also, a clear distinction needs to be made between norm-referenced and criterion-referenced tests.

Validity

The *validity* of a test is a measure of the extent to which the test measures what it was designed to measure. For example, a test that is labeled an "intelligence" test will be valid to the extent that it is, in reality, a true measure of global intelligence. Since intelligence is a very complex set of factors, it is doubtful whether any one test can be a valid measure of all the facets of intelligence. Certainly, group intelligence tests, which require much reading, cannot be considered valid measures of intelligence, especially for poor readers who will miss many items because of reading difficulties.

As another example, teachers must be aware that a *reading* test that is actually composed of lists of words to be named can not be a *valid* test of reading. A reading test is a composite of many strategies, skills, and affective and psychomotor components. Naming words in isolation is only one small facet of the complex process.

Reliability

The *reliability* of a test is a measure of the extent to which it measures consistently over time whatever it is designed to measure. If people complete a test today and then complete the same test (or an equivalent form) six weeks from today and earn approximately the same score, the test is apparently reliably measuring their ability to perform on those test questions. With respect to the intelligence test just referred to, it would have little *validity* if it did not sample global intelligence; however, the test could consistently yield the same results and, therefore, have high reliability.

TABLE 5.1. Norms for Test Evaluation

Student	Raw Score	Grade Placement	Percentile	Stanine
John Doe	42	4.5	50	5
Bill Doe	72	8.2	97	9
Tom Doe	21	2.8	07	2

Intelligence tests that are heavily loaded with vocabulary items, testing the students' knowledge of word meanings, may be extremely reliable when administered to large groups of students. What this tells us is that some students always get high scores on vocabulary tests and others always get low scores. However, in the frame of reference that global intelligence is one's ability to cope with new situations and solve problems, a vocabulary test is not a valid test of general ability.

Norms

Norms provide information about the typical performance for students for whom a test has been constructed. To determine the "typical performance," the test is given to a large number of students representative of the population for whom the test is intended. The students' *raw scores,* usually the actual number of correct answers identified,[1] are then changed to norms, which are intended to facilitate evaluation of pupil progress through time and are expressed in such units as grade placements, percentiles, and stanines. These are illustrated in table 5.1. Norms on tests provide a basis for comparing a given individual's performance with the standard reference group.

Table 5.1 shows us that John Doe earned a grade placement score of 4.5, which ranked him at the fiftieth percentile and at the fifth stanine. If John Doe is in the fourth grade, this test would indicate that he is performing normally in the "middle" of the distribution for his class. Bill, with a grade placement of 8.2, performs much better than the average of his class if he is in the fourth grade, and Tom is achieving below grade level if he is also in grade four.

Grade Equivalent Scores

Grade equivalent scores are usually provided by test publishers so that teachers can translate raw scores into ratings easily understood as school achievement. If John's grade placement is 4.5 (the four represents the school grade, fourth, and the second number represents the month of the school year, fifth), he is performing at the norm for one who is now halfway through the fourth grade. The grade equivalents for the fourth grade are 4.1 to 4.9. A tenth of a point needs to be accounted for so that the first month of fifth grade can be represented by 5.1, so the scoring allows one month of growth for the summer vacation period. This accommodates to an easy plan for assigning ten "parts" to the year of growth.

John's score of 4.5 may be an "average" score at midyear in fourth grade, *but* this is telling us, statistically, that half of his group tested above this score and half tested below it. *Average,* equivalent to the fiftieth percentile, means that half of the students must be either above or below this level of achievement.

Grade equivalents encompass the grade range of the public school, from 1.0 to 12.9. One limitation of this range of scores that teachers will understand is that the *sizes* of units of learning representing what constitutes grade one, four, eight, or eleven are not necessarily equal units. It is difficult to say, for example, whether growth from 7.1 to 8.0 in reading is equivalent to the rapid growth a child may make in reading from 2.1 to 3.0.

Teachers need also to recognize that while achievement at 5.0 means beginning fifth grade *for fifth graders,* achievement of an 8.0 on a test for fifth graders means that they are achieving extremely well, but not that they are able to perform as beginning eighth graders. The only standard to which the fifth graders are being compared is the range of performance of all of the fifth graders.

Percentiles

A *percentile rank* is a point on a distribution that defines the relative position of one individual with respect to the total group. Expressed in terms of 100 percent, it has an absolute value that is independent of the number of cases with which it is being compared, and it is clearly understandable. For example, a percentile rank of 58 means that 42 percent of all those tested performed better and 58 percent performed less well. Percentile ranks afford a direct and ready means for interpreting an individual performance in comparison with the whole group. Students who rank at the seventy-fifth percentile have done very well; they have exceeded the performances of 75 percent of their peers. The students who rank at the tenth percentile have exceeded the performance of only 10 percent of their group or of only ten in one hundred of their peers.

Because percentiles are easy to compute, interpret, and understand, they are frequently used for local norms in a school district. Publishers almost always provide percentile norms with their test data. However, percentile norms are meaningful only in terms of a specific test administered to a particular group at a given time. And local percentile norms may be different from the national norms.

Percentiles are not based on a scale of equal units of difference. For example, the raw score difference between the ninetieth and the ninety-fifth percentiles may not be the same number of raw score points between the forty-fifth and the fiftieth percentiles. Raw scores tend to cluster around the mean of the distribution so that many scores will be the same or nearly the same at the middle, or fiftieth percentile.

Stanines

The *stanine* is a norming term expressed in the numbers from one to nine. The distribution of raw scores is divided into nine parts. The fifth stanine accounts for all the students whose raw scores cluster at the middle of the distribution. A stanine of nine is the highest level and a stanine of one is the lowest level. The same caution that was earlier stated for percentiles applies to stanines; stanines are not of equal value in the

TABLE 5.2. Distribution of Stanine Levels

Percent of cases:	4%	7%	12%	17%	20%	17%	12%	7%	4%
Stanines:	1	2	3	4	5	6	7	8	9

range of raw scores. Stanines tell us that the fifth stanine is the performance of the large group in the middle (20 percent of the total population); the fourth and sixth stanines are those below and above average (each stanine accommodates 17 percent of the total population); stanines three and seven include those students farther above and farther below average. The lowest achievers are in stanines one and two, and the highest achievers are in stanines eight and nine. The distribution of the percentages of the test population is shown in table 5.2.

If teachers keep in mind that 54 percent of a distribution falls in stanines four, five, and six, they will know that stanines one, two, and three account for the bottom 23 percent of the distribution and stanines seven, eight, and nine account for the 23 percent at the top of the distribution.

In summary, norms are a more consistent way of talking about and making evaluations of achievement from one test to another. Norms, as grade equivalents, express average performance of students at various grade levels. Norms, as percentiles, describe students' places in a distribution in terms of the percent of students who scored lower and higher. Stanines indicate how far above or below the average given students are in the norming group.

Interpretations of test results, however, require more information than just knowledge of norms. One must know what the test is measuring, the language and cultural background of the students being tested, and the kind of motivation for school success learned at home.

Norm-Referenced Tests and Criterion-Referenced Tests

The norms discussed earlier have traditionally been applied to tests standardized on one large population and then administered to any selected group. These tests are *norm-referenced* and provide comparisons of a specific group with the population on which the test was normed. Statewide reading tests, for example, are norm-referenced. When all students, regardless of their special status, take the tests, state departments of education and school systems have data for evaluating progress, identifying groups of students who need additional help, and making curricular decisions.

Criterion-referenced tests are those developed in response to criteria specified in the objectives that teachers develop. They set out to teach a specific body of subject matter, or a set of principles, agreed upon before the teaching starts. Then they design a test that measures whether students learned what they were taught. Criterion-referenced tests are tailored to more individual purposes.

Making Connections 5.1: Exploring Test References

It is important for teachers to have access to organized and objective reports about current standardized tests. *Tests in Print III* from the Buros Institute of Mental Measurements is undoubtedly the best reference available.* From time to time, newer editions are prepared.

Most of the standardized tests mentioned in this chapter are listed and described in this reference. You will also find extensive bibliographies of articles and reports in which each particular test has been reviewed or employed in research.

Look up at least three of the tests described in this chapter. Obtain as much information as possible about the forms of the test, grades for which various forms are intended, author(s), publisher, publication dates, previous editions, and so on. Also, locate and read at least one of the references cited for each test.

Bring all this information to class for sharing. Your group may decide to "pool" the information collected into a useful handbook for class members.

* James V. Mitchell Jr., ed. *Tests in Print III* (Lincoln, Nebr: University of Nebraska, Lincoln, 1983).

Limitations of Standardized Tests

Silent reading tests are useful for surveying the general abilities of students. Such tests measure vocabulary ability and the ability to associate ideas in print. The clinician can identify some strengths or weaknesses of given students by comparing their performances with the performances of a large number of their peers on whom the test was normed.

Silent reading group tests are *not* diagnostic and have limitations with respect to testing any specific comprehension or study skills. If students have any knowledge of a subject, they may be able to answer literal-level questions for a paragraph as well *without* reading it as after reading it. The purpose of the silent reading test will be to measure the level at which given students perform when they are compared with a large number of their peers.

Since most silent reading tests measure vocabulary, literal comprehension, and possibly relationships such as cause and effect, clearly they are severely limited in helping teachers to find strengths and weaknesses in students' abilities to use discrete comprehension or study strategies. Therefore, the teacher, after examining the grade placement scores received by students, should plan repeated opportunities for them to learn many of the strategies and skills included in chapters 10 and 11 on comprehension and study skills.

Selected Reading Tests

A discussion of several well-known reading tests follows. The tests are grouped under the headings of oral and silent reading tests, diagnostic reading tests, criterion-referenced tests, reading tests accompanying basal readers, and the Reading Miscue Inventory. Additional information about a selected group of tests is included in appendix C. If more information and evaluations of specific tests are needed, the teacher should consult *Tests in Print III* from the Buros Institute of Mental Measurements[2] (see Making Connections 5.1) or *Tests: A Comprehensive Reference for Assessments in Psychology, Education and Business* from Test Corporation of America.[3]

Oral Reading Tests

The *oral reading test* is a well-known form of standardized reading tests. It resembles the informal reading inventory because it includes paragraphs for the child to read orally; a marking code for the teacher to use to record word-recognition problems; comprehension questions to be asked for each oral passage; and a table for converting errors, time required for reading, and accuracy of comprehension into a reading score. This type of reading test requires that the teacher or diagnostician have approximately half an hour of uninterrupted time in which to administer the test.

Gilmore Oral Reading Test

The Gilmore Oral Reading Test[4] analyzes *oral* reading abilities at grade levels one through eight. The test provides grade placement scores for accuracy of oral reading, comprehension of material read, and rate of oral reading. *A* and *B* and *C* and *D* forms provide equivalent tests for use at the beginning and ending of a learning period. About twelve to fifteen minutes are required for administration of the test to an individual; however, some cases may take up to twenty minutes.

The manual provides for a system of recording errors as the pupil reads. The errors to be recorded include substitutions, mispronunciations, words pronounced by the teacher, hesitations, repetitions, insertions, omissions, and disregard of punctuation. The recording of errors in informal reading made use of this system (see chapter 4); thus, the teacher should already have learned the method for administering this test. In scoring the test, the result will be in *grade placement scores,* rather than in the percentage of accuracy in mechanics and comprehension.

On the Gilmore Test, the individual establishes a beginning level with the paragraph in which no more than two errors in reading mechanics are made. The reading continues until ten or more errors are made in a paragraph. Degree of accuracy determines the level at which the pupil stops reading. However, the comprehension score is computed by reducing the paragraph comprehension scores successively by one point for each level more difficult than the first paragraph in which ten errors were made. This

NAME *Paula*

TEST SUMMARY   Form C

PARA-GRAPH	ACCURACY		COMPREHENSION	RATE	
	ERRORS	10 MINUS NO. ERRORS	NO. RIGHT (OR CREDITED)	WORDS IN ¶	TIME IN SEC.
1	*O*	*10*	*5*	24	*18*
2	*3*	*7*	*5*	45	*32*
3	*8*	*2*	*5*	50	*62*
4	*11*	*0*	*4*	73	*80*
5			*3*	103	
6			*2*	117	
7			*1*	127	
8			*0*	161	
9				181	
10				253	

Basal — (row 1)
Ceiling — (row 3)

	ACC. SCORE (TOT. "10 MINUS NO. ER-RORS" COLUMN)		COMP. SCORE (TOT. NO. RIGHT OR CREDITED)	(1) NO. WORDS READ*	*95*
		19	*25*	(2) TIME IN SEC.*	*94*
STANINE	*3*		*7*	(1) ÷ (2)	X 60
GRADE EQUIV.	*2.8*		*5.1*	RATE SCORE (WPM)	*60*
RATING	*Below Ave.*		*Above Ave.*	*Slow*	

*Do **not** count "ceiling" paragraph or paragraphs below "basal."

COMMENTS: *Paula is finishing third grade, has a W.I.S.C. Iq. of 120, and would be an excellent student if she could master quick word-recognition skills.*

Figure 5.1. Gilmore Oral Reading Test Summary for Paula (Reproduced from John C. Gilmore and Eunice C. Gilmore, *Gilmore Oral Reading Test*, copyright 1968 by Psychological Corporation. Reproduced by special permission.)

TABLE 5.3. Improvement in Gilmore Test Performance for Martha (High Average IQ)

Date	Form	Accuracy	Grade Equivalents Comprehension	Speed Rating
February 26, 1975	B	4.4	9.8 +	Very slow
July 28, 1975	A	5.9	9.8 +	Slow
July 16, 1976	B	8.6	9.8 +	Slow
Improvement		4.2		

"compensation" in computing the comprehension score helps in some cases to approximate more closely the expected level of comprehension for the disabled reader. The total raw score is converted to a grade equivalent score and rating by use of tables in the manual of directions. See the test summary for Paula in figure 5.1.

Improving oral reading with remedial reading cases should decrease errors in silent reading, improve auditory abilities in discriminating similar sounds, and build the individual's confidence.

Martha was fourteen and in the ninth grade when she was given the Gilmore Oral Reading Test. She made many substitutions of easy words, many repetitions of words and phrases, and hesitated too long on many polysyllabic words. Her accuracy score was 4.4. Her ability to answer the comprehension questions was good, even when she made more than the maximum of ten errors. Martha attended a reading clinic during an eight-week summer school session where she did a great deal of easy oral reading, completed speed of comprehension exercises, and worked on roots, prefixes, and suffixes. At the end of the tutoring program, she was again given the Gilmore Test and earned an accuracy score of 5.9. She was given the Gilmore Test, Form B, one year later as a follow-up. This time her accuracy score was 8.6. The small amount of individual tutoring had apparently helped a great deal. These three administrations of the test are summarized in table 5.3.

Gray Oral Reading Test

The Gray Oral Reading Test[5] is another useful instrument that any classroom teacher can use. The score is based on errors made in the mechanics of reading and the time required for reading. The comprehension score is not used directly in determining a reading level. However, the test does provide the teacher with a check on comprehension of ideas within the content read. The cover page of the Gray Oral Reading Test is presented in figure 5.2, giving the summary and the types of reading errors made by a fourth-grade child who functions at first-grade reading level.

EXAMINER'S RECORD BOOKLET

for the

GRAY ORAL READING TEST

FORM A

Name *Audrey Jackson*   Grade   4   Age *10 – 3*
School *Washington Elementary*   Teacher *Smith*   Sex *F*
City_____   State_____
Examiner *Mrs. Maggart*   Date *July 24, ——*

SUMMARY

Passage Number	No. of Errors	Time (in Seconds)	Passage Scores	Comprehension
1.	3	13	6	3½
2.	4	23	3	3
3.	6	52	0	4
4.	8	55	0	3
5.				
6.				
7.				
8.				
9.				
10.				
11.				
12.				
13.				
Total Passage Scores		9		
Grade Equivalent		1.6		

TYPES OF ERRORS

1.	Aid	1
2.	Gross Mispronunciation	
3.	Partial Mispronunciation	
4.	Omission	
5.	Insertion	2
6.	Substitution	12
7.	Repetition	4
8.	Inversion	2
		21

OBSERVATIONS
(Check statement and circle each part)

_____ Word-by-word reading
✔ Poor phrasing
_____ Lack of expression
_____ Monotonous tone
_____ Pitch too high or low; voice too loud, too soft, or strained
✔ Poor enunciation
✔ Disregard of punctuation
✔ Overuse of phonics
✔ Little or no method of word analysis
partial Unawareness of errors
_____ Head movement
_____ Finger pointing
_____ Loss of place

COMMENTS: *Little awareness of the end of a sentence. Nearly all errors begin the same as the correct word.*

THE **BOBBS-MERRILL** COMPANY, INC.
A SUBSIDIARY OF HOWARD W. SAMS & CO., INC.
Publishers • INDIANAPOLIS • NEW YORK

Copyright © 1963, The Bobbs-Merrill Co., Inc. Indianapolis 6, Indiana

Figure 5.2. Audrey takes the Gray Oral Reading Test. (Reproduced from Examiner's Record Booklet, *Gray Oral Reading Test,* Form A. Copyright 1967 by Psychological Corporation. Reproduced by permission.)

Silent Reading Tests

Silent reading tests are designed to be used with more than one child at a time. In fact, large numbers of children frequently take these tests simultaneously in school settings. These tests are designed to provide school personnel with scores expressed in stanines, percentiles, and grade scores. They provide little useful diagnostic information. Computer printouts of pupils' responses on individual test items may suggest a greater degree of diagnostic usefulness than is justified. The teacher must also be careful not to make inferences about the child's oral reading skills based on information obtained from silent reading tests. Research has yet to confirm that oral and silent reading are similar enough to enable the teacher to evaluate only either the oral or the silent reading.

Group Standardized Silent Reading Tests

1. *Gates-MacGinitie Reading Tests,* 2d ed. (Riverside Publishing Co., 1978). This series of tests measures vocabulary, comprehension, speed, and accuracy. The levels are Primary A (grade one); Primary B (grade two); Primary C (grade three); Survey D (grades four–six); Survey E (grades seven–nine); and Survey F (grades ten–twelve).
2. *Nelson Reading Skills Test,* revised by Gerald Hanna, Leo M. Schell, and Robert L. Schreiner, (Riverside Publishing Co., 1977). Comes in three levels: A (3.0–4.5), B (4.6–6.9), and C (7.0–9.9). Tests vocabulary and comprehension. Optional tests are word parts and rate tests. Grades three to nine. The time required is thirty minutes for vocabulary and comprehension.
3. *Stanford Achievement Test: Reading* (New York: Psychological Corp., 1982). Primary levels I, II, III; intermediate levels I, II; and advanced level. Most levels measure word-study skills, word reading, comprehension, vocabulary, and listening.
4. *California Achievement Tests: Reading* (Monterey, Calif.: California Test Bureau/McGraw-Hill, 1978). Tests vocabulary and comprehension. Level 1, grades one and two; Level 2, grades two–four; Level 3, grades four–six; Level 4, grades six–nine; and Level 5, grades nine–twelve. Forms C and D (1977).

Diagnostic Reading Tests

There are many *diagnostic reading tests* among which teachers and school diagnosticians may choose. A diagnostic reading test is usually designed for a particular group of children's reading levels and skills. The reading teacher should become familiar with several of these tests so that one can be selected that best fits the child who will take it. Diagnostic tests tend to be exhaustive in their coverage of reading skills and to require over an hour of working time with a child. In many cases, the responses on a few subtests will provide sufficient information to guide decisions about the child's reading problems.

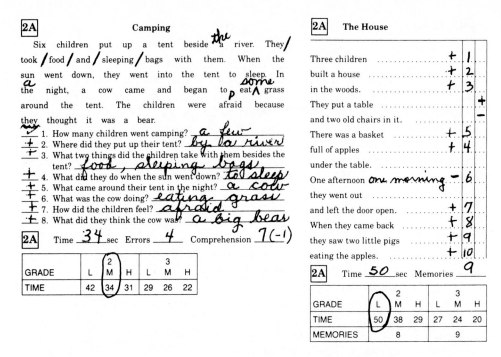

2A   Camping

Six children put up a tent beside *the* river. They took food and sleeping bags with them. When the sun went down, they went into the tent to sleep. In the night, a cow came and began to eat *some* grass around the tent. The children were afraid because they thought it was a bear.

1. How many children went camping? *a few*
2. Where did they put up their tent? *by the river*
3. What two things did the children take with them besides the tent? *food, sleeping bags*
4. What did they do when the sun went down? *to sleep*
5. What came around their tent in the night? *a cow*
6. What was the cow doing? *eating grass*
7. How did the children feel? *afraid*
8. What did they think the cow was? *a big bear*

2A   Time *34* sec Errors *4* Comprehension *7 (-1)*

GRADE		2			3	
	L	M	H	L	M	H
TIME	42	34	31	29	26	22

2A   The House

Three children	+	1
built a house	+	2
in the woods.	+	3
They put a table		+
and two old chairs in it.		−
There was a basket	+	5
full of apples	+	4
under the table.		
One afternoon *one morning*	−	6
they went out		
and left the door open.	+	7
When they came back	+	8
they saw two little pigs	+	9
eating the apples.	+	10

2A   Time *50* sec Memories *9*

GRADE		2			3	
	L	M	H	L	M	H
TIME	50	38	29	27	24	20
MEMORIES		8			9	

Figure 5.3. Marking errors and scoring oral and silent reading in the *Durrell Analysis of Reading Difficulty*, 3d ed. (Reproduced by permission from *Durrell Analysis of Reading Difficulty:* Third Edition. Copyright © 1980, by Harcourt Brace Jovanovich, Inc. All rights reserved.)

Durrell Analysis of Reading Difficulty

This test is an individually administered test that yields a profile of grade equivalent scores ranging from low-first to high-sixth grade.[6] The abilities tested are oral reading, silent reading, listening (a kind of capacity test), flash-word recognition, word analysis, spelling, and handwriting. The test can be administered in about thirty minutes. It provides one subtest in word association for the nonreader. While requiring extended training in reading and its diagnosis to handle the subjective nature of the scoring system, this test is one of the best of the individual diagnostic reading tests.

Speed of reading is the determining factor in finding the pupil's reading grade level in the Durrell Analysis. Scoring is detailed for the teachers in the manual of directions. Figure 5.3 shows errors marked and scored for the third paragraph for both the oral and silent reading subtests.

Figure 5.4 shows the recording of errors and scoring of one pupil's performance on the word-recognition and word-analysis subtests. Teachers using the test will do well to learn to use such devices for quick scoring as *NR* for "no response," *C* for "correct" when they get something right after failing to respond or after responding incorrectly, and *dk* for "don't know" when they say they don't know. Further, teachers can record on the margins of test pages useful information about types of responses that children make or fail to make.

Word Recognition/Word Analysis

LIST A—GRADE 1 READING LEVEL

Flash		Analysis
+	1. you	
+	2. look	
+	3. little	
+	4. me	
+	5. day	
+	6. tree	
+	7. all	
+	8. come	
+	9. away	
ate	10. are	+
+	11. run	
+	12. father	
+	13. children	
make	14. morning	−
+	15. sleep	
+	16. fish	
+	17. around	
+	18. name	
+	19. chair	
+	20. live	
+	21. rain	
+	22. seen	
+	23. breakfast	
mother	24. other	+
+	25. hole	

LIST 1—ABOVE GRADE 1 READING LEVEL

Flash		Analysis
+	1. red	
+	2. tree	
+	3. glad	
house	4. horse	+
+	5. large	
+	6. rain	
+	7. dress	
+	8. dime	
+	9. music	
+	10. lunch	
+	11. leaf	
+	12. words	
+	13. march	
+	14. year	
please	15. pleased	+
+	16. scare	
+	17. hike	
+	18. fear	
+	19. whistle	
+	20. flash	
+	21. glow	
+	22. delight	
+	23. sprinkle	
+	24. huge	
enermet	25. enormous	−

WORD RECOGNITION/WORD ANALYSIS

	Score		Grade	
	Flash	Analysis	Flash	Analysis
List A	*22*	*24*	*H-1*	*H-1*
List 1	*22*	*24*		
List 2	*10*	*14*		
List 3	*4*	*5*		
Total	*36*	*43*	*L-4*	*M-4*

	List A			Lists 1, 2, 3														
		1			2			3			4			5			6	
GRADE	L	M	H	L	M	H	L	M	H	L	M	H	L	M	H	L	M	H
FLASH	5	14	(19)	20	22	25	27	31	33	(36)	38	40	43	46	48	49	50	52
ANALYSIS	7	17	(23)	21	27	29	30	36	38	40	(43)	46	47	50	52	53	55	60

Figure 5.4. Marking errors and scoring word recognition and word analysis in the *Durrell Analysis of Reading Difficulty,* 3d ed., Grade one reading level. (Reproduced by permission from *Durrell Analysis of Reading Difficulty:* Third Edition. Copyright © 1980, by Harcourt Brace Jovanovich, Inc. All rights reserved.)

Examples of notes made by a teacher when testing word recognition are:

Harold was unable to pronounce *away* but knew *way* when I covered the *a*.
Even after pronouncing *way,* he was unable to add the vowel and pronounce *away.*
Harold may be "reversing" in *near* for *rain* and in *feel* for *leaf.*

Bobby's profile on the Durrell Analysis is presented in figure 5.5. Bobby was a very bright boy (WISC IQ 125) who needed tutorial help to make reading make sense for him.

Silent Reading Diagnostic Test

The Silent Reading Diagnostic Test[7] can be administered to all the pupils in a reading group at the same time. Separate subtests can be given during different work periods so that the teacher can fit the test to the time available. This test is effective with children whose reading abilities range from grade two to grade six. It provides an adequate check on needed word-perception skills in silent reading. The profile contains eight subtests: (1) words in isolation, (2) words in context, (3) visual-structural analysis, (4) syllabication, (5) word synthesis, (6) beginning sounds, (7) ending sounds, and (8) vowel and consonant sounds.

A profile on the test cover shows graphically the results of all the subtests. Raw scores convert to grade placement scores. The teacher's manual explains clearly the methods to be followed. It is necessary to draw *lines of importance* on the profile to determine those subtests on which the pupil's performance indicates need for remedial teaching. Bond et al. suggested limitations for lines of importance—one-half year on either side of the student's reading level.[8] One year constitutes the expected range of ability.

Those subtests on which scores fall below the left line of importance indicate need for reteaching of specific word-perception skills. Appropriate use of this test by classroom teachers, and corrective teaching as a result, could help to eliminate many of the difficulties of retarded readers in the schools.

In summary, then, this test measures vocabulary, word recognition, visual and auditory abilities in word forms, and word synthesis. It differs from the other tests in that it is a *group test* and measures abilities involved in silent reading. The Silent Reading Diagnostic Test helps the teacher to become familiar with the specific skills that should be checked when identifying the weaknesses of disabled readers. The test has value in that it enables the teacher to be more alert to gaps in the pupils' development of reading skills.

Stanford Diagnostic Reading Test

The Stanford Diagnostic Reading Test[9] is available in four levels: Red (grades 1.5–3.5 or above with low achievers), Green (grades 3.5–5.5 and above with low achievers), Brown (grades 5.5–8.5 and above with low achievers), and Blue (grades 7.5–13.0). Two forms of the test are available. It assesses phonic skills on all four levels; other

Durrell Analysis of Reading Difficulty
THIRD EDITION

INDIVIDUAL RECORD BOOKLET

Donald D. Durrell and Jane H. Catterson
Professor Emeritus, Boston University   Professor of Education, University of British Columbia

NAME _Bobby G._   DATE _9/17/8_
                               Mo/Day/Yr

SCHOOL _Hill Top Elem._   EXAMINER _Carol James_

                        REPORT TO _____

PHONE _____   ADDRESS _____

AGE _11_ GRADE _5_

DATE OF BIRTH _4/2/7_   PHONE _____
                 Mo/Day/Yr

Profile Chart

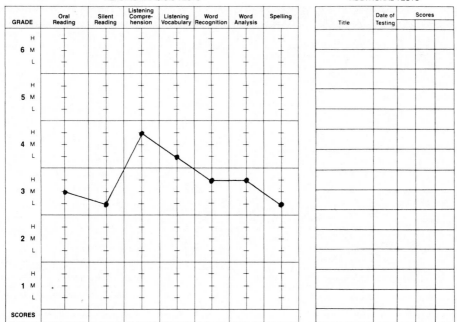

READING ANALYSIS TESTS   ADDITIONAL TESTS

Figure 5.5. Cover page of the *Durrell Analysis of Reading Difficulty* used for Bobby's reading. (Reproduced by permission from *Durrell Analysis of Reading Difficulty:* Third Edition. Copyright © 1980, by Harcourt Brace Jovanovich, Inc. All rights reserved.)

Name: **Malley** Last   **Betty** First   **T.** MI

School: **Pine View**

Teacher: **Raymond**

Examiner: **Willis**   Code: _____   Sex: **F**

Grade: **5**

Date of Testing: **198-** Yr / **9** Mo / **16** Day

Date of Birth: **197-** Yr / **9** Mo / **12** Day

Age at Testing: **11** Yr / **—** Mo / **—** Day

SUMMARY SCORES

	Grade Scores					Age Scores					Grade-Referenced Placement	Writing Sample Used:
	Total Raw Score	PR	S	GE	SS	Total Raw Score	PR	S	AE	SS		Grade _____
												Below Average / Average / Above Average (circle one)
MATHEMATICS												
READING	**50**	**42**	**5**	**4.8**	**97**	**50**	**32**	**4**	**10.3**	**93**		
SPELLING												**BASIS**

MATHEMATICS TALLY

Cluster Grade	No. Right	Base Score
Readiness		0
1		6
2		14
3		22
4		30
5		38
6		46
7		54
8		62
Total No. Right	+	
TOTAL RAW SCORE		

DIRECTIONS FOR TALLYING AND SCORING

Read these instructions before completing the above Tally charts and the box for Summary Scores. More detailed instructions can be found in the Manual.

1. Follow carefully the scoring directions for each test as described in the Manual, and indicate on each item in the Record Form whether it is correct or incorrect.

2. For each test, determine the *lowest* grade-referenced cluster administered. Circle this Cluster Grade on the Tally charts.

3. Circle the Base Score in the same row as the circled Cluster Grade. Record this Base Score at the bottom of the "Base Score" column to the right of the "+".

READING TALLY

Cluster Grade	No. Right	Base Score
READINESS		
Letter Ident.		0
Visual Disc.		
BEGINNING READING		
Word Rdg.		8
Sentence Rdg.		
PASSAGES		
P-1		16
P-2		
P-3		
(1-1)	**3**	(22)
1-2	**2**	
2	**5**	28
3	**5**	34
4	**4**	40
5	**5**	46
6	**3**	52
7		58
8		64
Total No. Right	**27** + **22**	
TOTAL RAW SCORE	**50**	

Directions Continued

4. For each grade-referenced cluster administered, count the number of items the student answered correctly, obtaining this information from the appropriate Record Form page. Then, opposite the appropriate cluster in the Tally chart, enter each count in the "No. Right" column.

5. Add the entries in the "No. Right" column and enter the sum at the bottom of the column in the "Total No. Right" row (to the left of the "+"). Add this number to the Base Score and write the sum in the "Total Raw Score" line. Copy this Total Raw Score into the appropriate "Total Raw Score" column of the "Summary Scores" above.

6. See the Manual for converting Total Raw Scores into Grade or Age Scores.

SPELLING TALLY

Cluster Grade	No. Right	Base Score
1		0
2		6
3		12
4		18
5		24
6		30
7		36
8		42
Total No. Right	+	
TOTAL RAW SCORE		

12

Figure 5.6. Cover page from the *Basic Achievement Skills Individual Screener.* (Reproduced by permission from *Basic Achievement Skills Individual Screener.* Copyright © 1983 by Harcourt Brace Jovanovich, Inc. All rights reserved.)

skills measured are auditory vocabulary at the Red and Green levels, word recognition and comprehension at all levels, reading rate at the Brown and Blue levels, and knowledge of affixes, skimming, and scanning at the Blue level.

The Stanford Diagnostic Reading Test identifies test items that assess particular skills. The groups of items are called *progress indicators.* Student summary scores on these special groups of items may be compared to cutoff scores. Use of this information should enable the teacher to diagnose strengths and weaknesses when these data are combined with other evidences of reading abilities.

Basic Achievement Skills Individual Screener

The Basic Achievement Skills Individual Screener (BASIS)[10] is a useful test for examining not only reading abilities but also mathematics and spelling skills. The test is designed for levels from primer through grade eight. All of the reading paragraphs require students to fill in cloze exercises. The cover sheet for the BASIS is shown in figure 5.6.

Making Connections 5.2: Administering a Standardized Reading Test

Work with your instructor to select a standardized reading test for you to administer. Plan to work on this project with a peer. Once the test has been identified, study the manual well so that you know as much about the test and its administration as possible.

The next step is to identify a child whose age and reading ability appear suitable for the test in question. Then make plans for appropriate space and time for administering the test. If permission to test is required, be sure you obtain the necessary approval. As you administer the test, take turns with your partner in administering the various subtests or parts. During the time that each of you is the observer, take detailed notes of the language and nonlanguage behaviors observed. It will also be helpful to tape record the entire session.

After the testing session is completed, work on three analyses:

1. Analyze the child's performance on the test, and prepare appropriate recommendations about the instruction of this reader.
2. Analyze the test-administration techniques of you and your partner. One of the best ways to grow professionally is to observe and be observed and then to engage in analysis sessions.
3. Analyze the particular test in terms of the information that you were able to obtain, its appropriateness for the child you tested, the ease with which the test may be given, and the way(s) in which raw scores are converted to some kind of standard scores.

Prepare a joint report to your instructor, providing information about the three analyses completed after the test was administered.

Criterion-Referenced Tests

Criterion-referenced tests are part of an instructional testing system. Instructional objectives written in behavioral terms are prepared for individual children. Sometimes the objectives are prepared by the publishers of systems approaches to reading; in other situations, the child's teacher may prepare the objectives. Then materials are identified that will help the child to meet each objective. After the child has done the required reading, skills work, and other related activities required to meet a particular objective or small group of objectives, the child takes the criterion-referenced test for those objectives. If the child answers the questions to the level of accuracy stated in the behavioral objectives, then work is begun on a new set of objectives. If the child fails to meet the stated criterion, then more work must be done on those particular objectives, and the test must be taken again.

1. *Prescriptive Reading Inventory (PRI)* (Monterey, Calif.: California Test Bureau/McGraw-Hill, 1977). Criterion-referenced tests that assess many different reading skills taught in the elementary school are: Red book, grades 1.5–2.5; Green book, grades 2.0–3.5; Blue book, grades 3.0–4.5; and Orange book, grades 4–6. The inventory includes ninety objectives. There are also thirty objectives for kindergarten.
2. *Wisconsin Design Tests of Reading Skill Development* (Madison, Wis.: Learning Multiple Systems, 1977). See chapter 7 for an expanded description.
3. *Comprehensive Tests of Basic Skills: Reading* (Monterey, Calif.: California Test Bureau/McGraw-Hill, 1981). This test is designed for grades K–12. It has two forms. Word-attack skills, vocabulary, and comprehension are tested. The CTBS may be considered as a criterion-referenced test, since computer scoring and analysis provide teachers with item analyses from which instructional objectives and plans may be made.
4. *Sipay Word Analysis Tests* (Cambridge, Mass.: Educators Publishing Service, 1974). Tests from grade one through grade six; may be used with disabled readers through the adult level. Sixteen tests cover many aspects of phonics and contractions.

Normed Tests Accompanying Basals and Children's Newspapers

Basal readers provide tests to be administered to students either after they finish sections of the book and workbook or after they complete the entire book. These tests measure the degree to which students have mastered the skills taught in that reading series. Teachers who have access to such tests will do well to use them regularly for their diagnostic value.

Also, the current-events newspapers published weekly often provide tests of comprehension skills in reading with normed scores for the grade for which the test is intended. These tests also help teachers to identify strengths and weaknesses of students.

Reading Miscue Inventory

The Reading Miscue Inventory is a measure of the accuracy with which students read a passage orally.[11] The examiners will study the "mismatch" between the exact wording of the passage and the language used by readers in reproducing the text. *Miscue* is the term used to describe the oral response that differs from the word in the text. The inventory allows teachers to make a clear distinction between reading miscues that preserve meaning and may be overlooked and reading miscues that represent the traditional "inability to read well" to which so much attention is given in the informal reading inventory.

According to Goodman and Watson:

> The Reading Miscue Inventory provides a view of a student's reading performance that is very different from the ones provided by the traditional standardized reading tests or by informal reading inventories. During the oral reading, the student receives no external help; he must rely on his own strategies. His miscues are evaluated to see if he makes appropriate use of syntactic and semantic information. The results of the inventory register the reader's strengths and give information about ineffective and inefficient uses of strategies. It also provides the teacher with information about causes and quality of miscues.[12]

The Reading Miscue Inventory provides for the examiners to analyze grammatical function, semantic acceptability, intonation patterns, and dialect differences. The rationale and interpretation of the inventory are valid when the students are reading narrative passages to which they should be able to relate. However, in subject matter where terminology may be unfamiliar, the students will have to rely on phonic or structure clues for word recognition. Karlin's summary seems appropriate:

> The Reading Miscue Inventory provides a qualitative and quantitative analysis of reading proficiency based on psycholinguistic theory. It is a tool for matching materials to readers, for analyzing the reading strategies students use, and for planning lessons. Its use by classroom teachers will be limited by the extent to which they can become familiar with its rather complicated procedures. Until those procedures are simplified, the inventory will probably be used mainly by reading specialists.[13]

Hood has raised the question of whether or not the analysis of the Reading Miscue Inventory is a practical exercise for the busy classroom teacher. What do the classroom teachers need to know in order to find the proper book for each child in the class? It is clear that miscue research has much value for the clinician and the researcher. It has value for the classroom teacher, too, if enough practice in analysis of miscues is done so that in the classroom the teacher will use this knowledge in making many of the on-the-spot decisions that need to be made every day.[14]

Classroom teachers *do* need to decide whether reading miscues are of an "acceptable" or "excusable" variety or whether they are "wrong" in the sense that meaning will be lost if they are not corrected. If the students read "frightened" for "afraid" or "put the tent up" for "put up the tent," these are obviously acceptable miscues since no meaning is lost.[15] However, if the readers read "The message was brought by the teacher to the children" instead of "The message was brought to the teacher by the children," the meaning is lost and the miscue needs to be corrected for meaning. Some experience with the Reading Miscue Inventory will develop teacher sensitivity to the types of miscues that students make in oral reading. This achievement will be useful to the teachers every day. However, Hood concluded that the classroom teachers can continue to select reading material for the students by means of total miscue scores.[16]

Children's performances on the Reading Miscue Inventory can now be scored and analyzed using the computer. Such a program makes it more possible for the teacher to consider the type of data that can be obtained from the inventory in planning children's reading experiences. Several abbreviations of the full Reading Miscue Inventory have also been developed.

Summary

This chapter has presented information about testing: norms, grade placement scores, percentiles, stanines, and differences between norm-referenced and criterion-referenced tests. Silent reading standardized tests have cumulative value in measuring gains in achievement, although their limitations in measuring different comprehension skills has been explained. There are also basal reader tests and such reading tests as supplied by *My Weekly Reader* that also have value for the teacher.

As the teachers continue to teach corrective reading to pupils in the class, formal tests are needed to help them to evaluate the pupils' progress and to show tangible evidence of success. While many tests and rating scales are available, the Gilmore Oral Reading Test, the Gray Oral Reading Test, the Silent Reading Diagnostic Test, the Durrell Analysis of Reading Difficulty, the Stanford Diagnostic Reading Test, and the Basic Achievement Skills Individual Screener (BASIS) have been described here. In addition, the basic reading tests for graded readers were discussed. Ability to perform well on these tests is a good indication that the students are ready to progress to the next higher level of reading. The Reading Miscue Inventory has also been described as a means of evaluating a child's reading.

For Further Reading

Anderson, Richard C., et al. "Testing and Reading." In *Becoming a Nation of Readers: The Report of the Commission on Reading,* 95–101. Washington, D.C.: National Academy of Education, National Institute of Education, and Center for the Study of Reading, 1985. A national statement on the relationships between testing and reading that should be read and *evaluated critically* by all educators.

Baumann, James F. "Interpreting Scores from Standardized Reading Tests." In *Reading Assessment: An Instructional Decision-Making Perspective,* 35–48. Columbus, Ohio: Merrill Publishing Co., 1988. This is a thorough presentation of statistical terms and information relating to standardized tests and their interpretation.

Baumann, James F., and Jennifer A. Stevenson. "Understanding Standardized Reading Achievement Test Scores." *Reading Teacher* 35 (March 1982): 648–54. A clear and succinct explanation of the meanings of important terms related to standardized tests. Several diagrams add to the written explanations.

Buros, Oscar K. *Reading Tests and Reviews* II. Highland Park, N.J.: Gryphon, 1975 and 1968. All available reading tests prepared to the date of publication are reviewed. This is an important reference.

Ekwall, Eldon E., and James L. Shanker. "Interpreting Test and Research Results in Reading." In *Diagnosis and Remediation of the Disabled Reader.* 2d ed., 579–95. Boston: Allyn and Bacon, 1983. A comprehensive textbook presentation of standardized testing and accompanying concepts and terminology.

Farr, Roger, and Robert F. Carey. *Reading: What Can Be Measured?* 2d ed. Newark, Del.: International Reading Association, 1986. A significant publication, one every reading teacher should have as a reference.

Wixson, Karen K., et al. "New Directions in Statewide Reading Assessment." *Reading Teacher* 40 (April 1987): 749–54. Presents the Michigan Educational Assessment Project as a model of what can be accomplished when policymakers, curriculum specialists, test developers, and reading educators all work together for the benefit of education.

Notes

1. Some tests are designed so that the pupil's raw score must be corrected for the *guessing factor.* Usually the number of wrong responses is subtracted from the total of correct responses.
2. James V. Mitchell, Jr., ed., *Tests in Print* (Lincoln, Nebr.: University of Nebraska at Lincoln, 1983).
3. Richard C. Sweetland and Daniel J. Keyser, eds., *Tests: A Comprehensive Reference for Assessment in Psychology, Education and Business,* 2d ed. (Kansas City, Mo.: Test Corporation of America, 1986).
4. John V. Gilmore and Eunice C. Gilmore, *Gilmore Oral Reading Test* (New York: Psychological Corp., 1968).
5. William S. Gray, *Gray Oral Reading Test* (New York: Psychological Corp., 1967).
6. Donald D. Durrell and Jane H. Catterson, *Durrell Analysis of Reading Difficulty,* 3d ed. (New York: Harcourt Brace Jovanovich, 1980).
7. Guy L. Bond, B. Balow, and C. J. Hoyt, *Silent Reading Diagnostic Test,* rev. ed. (Chicago: Rand McNally, 1970).
8. Guy L. Bond, et al., *Reading Difficulties: Their Diagnosis and Correction,* 5th ed. (Englewood Cliffs, N.J.: Prentice-Hall, 1984), 219.
9. *Stanford Diagnostic Reading Test* (New York: Psychological Corp., 1984).
10. *Basic Achievement Skills Individual Screener, BASIS* (New York: Psychological Corp., 1982).
11. Yetta Goodman and Carolyn Burke, *Reading Miscue Inventory: Procedure for Diagnosis and Evaluation* (New York: Macmillan Co., 1972).

12. Yetta Goodman and Dorothy J. Watson, "A Reading Program to Live with: Focus on Comprehension," *Language Arts* 54 (November/December 1977): 868–79.

13. Robert Karlin and Andrea Karlin, *Teaching Elementary Reading: Principles and Strategies,* 4th ed. (New York: Harcourt Brace Jovanovich, 1987), 98.

14. Joyce Hood, "Is Miscue Analysis Practical for Teachers?" *Reading Teacher* 32 (December 1978): 260–66; reprinted in *Readings on Reading Instruction,* 3d ed., ed. A. J. Harris and E. R. Sipay (New York: Longman, Inc., 1984), 170–76.

15. Ibid., 262.

16. Ibid., 266.

6
Additional Data Needed for Further Diagnosis

Vocabulary

diagnosis
case history
cumulative folders
group intelligence test
individual intelligence test
reading potential
vocabulary test
auditory discrimination
audiogram
audiologist
ophthalmologist
color blindness
hypothyroidism
allergies
interest inventory
Incomplete Sentences Blank
interview about the reading
    process
parent interview
sociogram
bibliotherapy
identification
catharsis
insight
storytelling as assessment
story grammar
character goals,
    motivations, and
    feelings
cohesive ties
fluency
writing sample
story frames
holistic scoring
cloze procedure
anecdotal records
video recording
areas of exceptionality

Questions

1. Outline the steps in gathering data and preparing a diagnosis of a reading difficulty. **(Recall)**
2. What relationships appear to exist between intelligence and reading? **(Recall)** What cautions should one observe in assessing the intelligence of a disabled reader? **(Recall)**
3. List the major points that you think a teacher should remember about vision and hearing. **(Application)**
4. Make a list of health problems that could be factors in reading success or failure. **(Recall)** What problems could you add to the list discussed in the text? **(Critical)**
5. Why should a teacher want to find out about the interests of the children in the classroom? **(Inference)**
6. How might personality data be useful in planning reading instruction? **(Inference)**
7. What kinds of information might one expect to acquire from the varied kinds of interviews and observation strategies? **(Inference)**
8. What is bibliotherapy, and how might it be used in the classroom? **(Recall; Application)**
9. How could assessments such as storytelling, a writing sample, and a cloze test provide important information to the teacher? **(Inference)** How could such information be used? **(Application)**

Introduction

In order to plan more efficiently with the pupils those study jobs that will help them most quickly to learn to read, the teacher must obtain further information in order to round out as complete a case history as possible. Specialists in the school system may be able to provide information relating to intelligence factors, physical factors, and social and emotional factors. However, because many of the learning problems of children cannot be resolved without the close cooperation of the parents, chapter 13 will be devoted to this tremendously important factor.

Steps in Diagnosis

The first characteristic of a sound reading program for a school system is a well-worked-out statement of purpose in developing language arts skills from kindergarten through the senior high school. It will not be possible to attain maximum efficiency in reading in this program unless adequate diagnostic facilities are provided for students with learning difficulties.

Resources for Special Services

Teachers need support and counsel about the nature of children's problems and the types of assessments, both formal and informal, that are available. This aid may come from a variety of sources, including school psychologists and social workers, school doctors and nurses, special education specialists and diagnosticians, Chapter I reading teachers, school counselors, and administrators with special training in identifying learning needs and selecting suitable assessment tools. Teachers may also find support for obtaining the information needed to plan programs for children from family doctors, from psychologists and psychiatrists in community health clinics, and from state and local social workers and community liaison personnel. Table 6.1 lists several areas of health, behavior, language development, general learning ability, and neurology in which special services are needed for children with reading difficulties in regular classrooms. Once these areas have been considered, the next step is to press for a formal diagnosis.

The school social worker, psychologist, and diagnostician are key personnel in providing teachers with needed information about the students in their classrooms. The school social worker will obtain the intake history with the parents and analyze those problems that deter learning in school. These problems may be interpersonal conflicts within the family, or they may be primarily economic. Social workers may need to make repeated home visits to resolve difficulties before instruction can be effective. The school psychologist or diagnostician is prepared to obtain intelligence test data, school achievement data, and limited information relative to personality problems that the pupils may face.

TABLE 6.1. Special Services Needed for Children with Reading Problems

Areas Where Possible Causes May Exist	Professional People Who Offer Help in this Area	Adjustments that May Be Necessary on the Part of the Classroom Teacher
1. General health	The family doctor needs to give a general medical examination.	Students may have special needs in response to physical health and general growth and development.
2. Behavior of the student in the classroom	The school counselor can discuss with the teacher current report card data: uses self-control; accepts guidance; is courteous; works and plays well with others; uses good judgment; is cooperative; contributes to activities of group; assumes responsibility. The counselor may administer the Vineland Adaptive Behavior Scales.[a]	Six-year-olds generally are active, curious, eager to explore the environment; they like to manipulate things, need time to work in groups but time to work alone also; they are not very responsible for finishing tasks and not very understanding of rigid time sequences.
3. Thinking processes	The school psychologist can test convergent and divergent thinking, putting things in categories, acquisition of meaning, classifying, creative/innovative thinking, cognitive levels as defined by Piaget.[b]	Activities can be provided for: putting things in categories (colors, names, days of the week, domestic animals); interpreting pictures, making inferences, creating stories; classifying; working in art, carpentry, block, or housekeeping centers.
4. Use of language	The language specialist can observe oral language use, auditory discrimination and awareness, ability to retell a story. Administer the Illinois Test of Psycholinguistic Abilities[c] or the Test of Language Development Primary (TOLD-P).[d]	Encourage verbal expression, adequate English syntax, auditory decoding, auditory association, listening, concept development through oral language, listening to and telling stories.
5. Psychological examinations	The school psychologist can administer the Wechsler Preschool and Primary Scale,[e] the Wechsler Intelligence Scale for Children,[f] the Wechsler Adult Intelligence Scale,[g] other tests or observations.	The open classroom concept accommodates the wide range of differences in many abilities. Teachers can plan for a wide range of achievement in a class; learning centers may be an option.
6. Neurological factors (Perceptual skills)	The psychologist, diagnostician, or the reading specialist may administer the Visual Motor Gestalt,[h] the Identifying Children with Specific Learning Disabilities,[i] or the Developmental Test of Visual-Motor Integration.[j]	Activities can be provided to teach motor coordination, directional sense, visual-motor coordination; language and concept development; space relationships; perceptual constancy.

a. S. Sparrow, D. Balla, and D. Cicchetti, *Vineland Adaptive Behavior Scales* (Circle Pines, Minn.: American Guidance Service, 1984). Formerly called the Vineland Social Maturity Scale. This scale requires an in-depth interview with a parent or parent substitute and measures social development based on observation and information about the client's habits and practices.

b. John L. Phillips, Jr., *The Origins of Intellect: Piaget's Theory,* 2d ed. (San Francisco: Will Freeman, and Co., 1975); and Ed Labinowicz, *The Piaget Primer* (Reading, Mass.: Addison Wesley, 1980).

c. S. A. Kirk, J. J. McCarthy, and W. D. Kirk, *The Illinois Test of Psycholinguistic Abilities,* ITPA, revised edition (Urbana: Univ. of Illinois Press, 1968). This test measures the child's language reception, word association, and ability to give information through language. The test is composed of ten subtests.

d. Phyllis L. Newcomer and Donald D. Hammill, *Test of Language Development-Primary,* rev. ed. (Austin, Tex.: Pro-Ed, 1982). This test measures English language proficiency for children, ages 4.0 to 8.11. There are seven subtests.

e. *Wechsler Preschool and Primary Scale of Intelligence,* WPPSI (New York: Psychological Corp., 1967). This is an individually administered general intelligence test with norms for young children ages 4.0–6.5.

f. *Wechsler Intelligence Scale for Children,* rev. ed., WISC-R (New York: Psychological Corp., 1974). This scale measures general intelligence for ages 6–16.

g. *Wechsler Adult Intelligence Scale,* WAIS (New York: Psychological Corp., 1955). This scale is for ages 15–adult. The Wechsler tests provide verbal, performance, and full-scale scores (intelligence quotients) and is to be used only by qualified psychologists.

h. Lauretta Bender, *The Bender Visual Motor Gestalt Test* (New York: Psychological Corp., 1938).

i. Beth Slingerland, *Identifying Children with Specific Learning Disabilities* (Cambridge, Mass.: Educators Publishers Service, 1974).

j. K. E. Beery, *Developmental Test of Visual-Motor Integration* (Cleveland, Ohio: Modern Curriculum Press, 1982). For ages 2–15.

Figure 6.1 diagrams the process for obtaining and channeling to principals and teachers necessary information that will enable them to plan constructively for goals through which the individual will more nearly achieve self-realization.

A Diagnostic Program

A program of *diagnosis* must include the following steps:

1. Provide a means for the initial referral of cases.
2. Gather together all pertinent data needed for building a case history.
3. Evaluate the effects of observed conditions upon the pupil's behavior.
4. Make suggestions for remedial measures to improve the pupil's adjustment.
5. Reevaluate the case at intervals to see if the progress has been satisfactory.

As diagrammed in figure 6.1, five types of information are needed about the pupils in preparing their case studies. These involve:

1. A *case history* interview that provides family background, general significance of reading success in the family, and reasons given by the parents for pupils' reading failure.
2. A medical examination that evaluates visual and hearing acuity and general physical development. Especially important are referrals by the family doctor to various specialists for further study of possible neurological problems, problems of basal metabolism, or convulsive disorders.

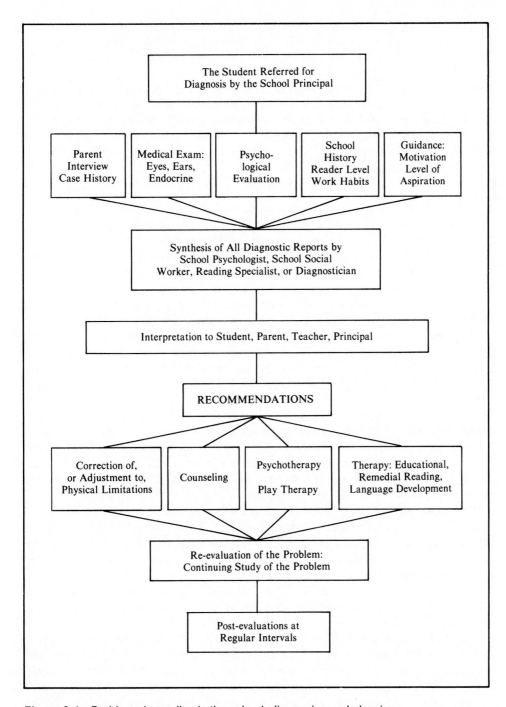

Figure 6.1. Problems in reading in the school: diagnosing and planning

3. A psychological evaluation that may include both tests of general intelligence and structured or unstructured tests of personality. Further testing by clinical psychologists—with such tests as the Rorschach or referral to a consulting psychiatrist—may be indicated.
4. A summary of the student's school history that reveals such evidence as grades repeated in school, attendance in kindergarten prior to encountering formal reading, persistence of learning problems through the years, membership in special education classes, and teachers' evaluations of work habits.
5. Guidance information revealing motivations, aptitudes, and levels of aspiration. This information helps to show how the students view themselves in their world, how they view others, and how they view the world around them.

This body of information must be synthesized by a guidance counselor, school psychologist, school social worker, diagnostician, or reading specialist; then it must, in turn, be interpreted to the pupil, the parents, and the pupil's teachers and principal.

A plan of action to correct or alleviate the situation must be worked out. Some pupils may have medical problems for which there may be correction or to which they must make an adjustment. For example, some pupils with visual limitations cannot have their vision improved, but the school program can be adapted to serve them. A change in seating within the classroom, use of sight-saving print, early use of the typewriter or microcomputer for completing assignments, counseling, and in more disturbed cases, psychotherapy may make regular class attendance possible.

In many instances the major problem lies in adapting the teaching to the individual, that is, remedial procedures. The teacher needs to understand what can and cannot change. The schoolwork must be geared to the pupil rather than the pupil to the schoolwork. The teacher should be an expediter of growth by starting where the pupil is and using knowledge of the growth and development of children.

Finally, after the pupil's problem has been studied and remedial programs effected, the case must be reevaluated on a continuing basis. Whatever the initial prognoses may have been, continuing evaluations are necessary for the purpose of adjusting the recommendations to ensure maximum learning opportunities for the pupils.

It may be well that the recommendations resulting from the case studies are all related to language development and *intensive* reading instruction. This challenges the teacher—supported by the school social worker and the school psychologist—to find adequate teaching techniques for diminishing the gap between the pupils' functional levels in reading and their grade placement.

If teachers refer only severely disabled readers for case study, however, almost certainly there will be concomitant problems that need to be met through medical or psychological therapies.

If the services of school social workers or school psychologists are nonexistent in a school system, this only means that greater responsibility rests with the principal and the teachers. The problems exist whether or not the specialists are there to help. Teachers and principals must follow as systematic a program as possible for gathering information for diagnosing problems. They can obtain information about the child's family from the parents and about the child's problems at school from previous teachers, standardized test results, and available medical reports. On the basis of the information secured, they must plan the best possible program for the pupil.

To illustrate, the classroom teachers, without benefit of the services of a school social worker or psychologist, are applying this procedure in its most common form when they encounter pupils who cannot read, and act upon the situation promptly. If they talk with the pupil's parents about the problem; if they make the best possible subjective judgments about behavior and performance at various tasks and decide that the pupil probably has "normal" intelligence; if they test present specific abilities in reading; if they interpret to the child and the parents the nature of the reading problem as they see it; and if they make time during the school day for the pupil to learn how to read by the same methods used in good first teaching of reading, then the teachers have applied these principles in the solution of the problem.

As a specific example, we illustrate how Victor and his fourth-grade teacher met the problem together without the help of others.

Miss Jones, fourth-grade teacher in a small midwestern town, placed Victor's name on the list to be tested by the visiting school psychologist because Victor was unable to read. Victor appeared with a well-scrubbed look, wearing faded jeans. He seemed to be a very normal, alert nine-year-old. The IQ score earned on the Stanford-Binet, Form L, was 97 (C.A. 9–10, M.A. 9–7). The psychologist wrote the following statement:

> This report is of necessity a superficial one. Its accuracy needs to be tested further by the teacher's observations. Victor gives evidence of being a child with very limited first-hand experiences. He has recently moved from an extremely isolated area in a neighboring state. He apparently got off to a bad start in beginning reading. His reader level in context is first grade. He recognized only 182 of the 220 sight words of the Dolch Basic Word Test. Since the school nurse found nothing wrong with his vision or hearing, he needs to begin with easy first-grade reading, including stories he has written, and learn all the developmental strategies and skills in both word recognition and comprehension and move as rapidly as possible to catch up to his present grade placement.

The fourth-grade teacher asked for and was given permission to discuss retention with the parents and, with their consent, retained the boy in her fourth-grade room the following year.

The next spring when the visiting school psychologist called at the school, he asked the fourth-grade teacher about Victor. She seemed surprised that there would be any question about Victor until the psychologist showed her the results of the previous year's testing. She reported that he was doing good work in her middle group in fourth grade. Then she told the psychologist that Victor had been very pleased to stay with her when she had convinced him that she could teach him, and that occasionally she had talked with his mother, who had been much relieved to see Victor's progress.

Other teachers had shared work sheets that were appropriate for a ten-year-old working at primary level. Victor's teacher had arranged for a retired man in the community to come three times weekly to read to Victor, to listen to Victor read, and to help him write stories.

Inventorying Abilities at the Beginning of the Year

While teachers need to make more detailed studies of pupils who present learning difficulties, cumulative folders in most schools do provide accumulated information about all pupils as they progress through the grades. During the first few weeks of the school year, the teachers collect, coordinate, and study all the information they have available on their pupils. This information will be found in:

1. *Cumulative folders.* All pupils should have cumulative folders in which are included each year's data concerning physical health, school achievement, standardized test results, and other pertinent information.
2. *Health records.* School nurses often have valuable information about vision, hearing, or special physical handicapping conditions.
3. *Anecdotal records of behavior.* Notes written by previous teachers may reveal persistent problems such as concern with reading, continual absences from school, and reports from social agencies or private clinics.

Using such information, the teachers can:

1. Compare mental test results with reading test results to see that reading capacity and achievement correspond.
2. Evaluate previous indications of a reading problem identified by previous teachers or by the parent, or of unusual attitudes of the pupil.

In addition to the reading tests discussed in chapters 4 and 5, the teacher should obtain data on intelligence, health status, interests and attitudes toward reading, social and psychological information, and language and special reading abilities. Additional information may be obtained by the use of anecdotal records and ongoing teacher observation.

Measuring Intelligence

Intelligence is probably the one most important factor in the determination of how well pupils can be expected to read. The correlations between IQ and reading ability appear to become higher as pupils move through the grades.[1] This is probably due to the increasing complexity of the reading tasks and the greater cognitive abilities necessary for adequate comprehension.

Group versus Individual Intelligence Tests

Group intelligence test scores for pupils with learning disabilities are frequently invalid. Decisions based on such scores are often faulty and harmful to the best interests of students. Because of the dangers of program planning based on group intelligence test scores, it is now mandated that the evaluations of students suspected of having learning disabilities must include an *individual intelligence test.*[2]

Since reading is required for the completion of most group intelligence tests, reading-handicapped students will surely obtain low IQ scores, suggesting an invalid reason for the reading problem. They may then not receive the remediation that they need because it is presumed that they cannot be expected to read better, based on the IQ scores. Ekwall and Shanker stated that such tests are not suitable for poor readers because they obviously do not measure their intellectual abilities accurately.[3]

Clymer concluded that certain group intelligence tests were of *no* value in testing general mental ability of fifth-grade pupils who test in the lowest 40 percent in reading ability.[4] This is to say that for practically all those pupils under consideration in corrective reading programs, because they would test in reading in the lower two-fifths of their classes, the group intelligence test results are of no value to the teachers. Pupils with reading disabilities should be given the advantage of individual intelligence tests when they are being tested to assess their learning potentials.

There are two such individual intelligence tests in common use by psychologists and psychometrists. They are the Stanford-Binet Intelligence Scale and the Wechsler Intelligence Scale.[5]

A few years ago, a fifteen-year-old boy in the seventh grade was given the California Test of Mental Maturity in a group. His IQ score was computed as 76. A few weeks later he was given the Stanford-Binet, Form L, and his IQ score was computed as 99. He proved to be a lad of perfectly normal intelligence who had a serious reading disability. His reader level, when tested, was primer level. To have classified this boy as mentally retarded on the basis of the group test would have been entirely unjustified.

Farr has written specifically and pertinently about the limitation of tests involving reading skill as measures of student *ability:*

> . . . a student's score on any reading skill test represents *one* sampling of behavior, on *one* operational definition of that skill, under *one* specific set of conditions, at *one* particular point in a student's development: . . . what is really needed for valid and reliable evaluation is the sampling of *many* sets of conditions, at *many* points in a student's development.[6]

School psychologists will have other individual tests in their repertoire and, at times, will need to administer one or more to an individual. Teachers need to study carefully the interpretations of the test results, written by the psychologist who administers the test, because individual intelligence tests also have their limitations. This is evidenced by the comments on the Wechsler Intelligence Scale—Revised (WISC-R) test profile for José, who has both a learning disability and second-language interference (see figure 6.2).

Reducing Bias in Aptitude Testing

In recent years parents and teachers, as well as diagnosticians and others who administer intelligence tests, have become aware that tests contain biases that may discriminate against bilingual and minority children. A few tests have been designed to address these concerns. The *System of Multicultural Pluralistic Assessment*[7] is an effort to develop a test of general learning aptitude for children from ages five to eleven "to aid

WISC-R RECORD FORM

Wechsler Intelligence Scale
for Children—Revised

NAME _José_ AGE _12-0_ SEX _M_

ADDRESS

PARENT'S NAME

SCHOOL _____ GRADE _5th_

PLACE OF TESTING _____ TESTED BY

REFERRED BY

WISC-R PROFILE

Clinicians who wish to draw a profile should first transfer the child's scaled scores to the row of boxes below. Then mark an X on the dot corresponding to the scaled score for each test, and draw a line connecting the X's.*

	Year	Month	Day
Date Tested	75	7	28
Date of Birth	63	8	8
Age	11	11	20

VERBAL TESTS — Information, Similarities, Arithmetic, Vocabulary, Comprehension, Digit Span

Scaled Score: 5, 6, 5, 4, 3, [ ]

PERFORMANCE TESTS — Picture Completion, Picture Arrangement, Block Design, Object Assembly, Coding, Mazes

Scaled Score: 7, 8, 5, 4, 4, [ ]

*See Chapter 4 in the manual for a discussion of the significance of differences between scores on the tests.

	Raw Score	Scaled Score
VERBAL TESTS		
Information	9	5
Similarities	9	6
Arithmetic	6	5
Vocabulary	4	4
Comprehension	16	3
(Digit Span)	( )	( )
Verbal Score		23
PERFORMANCE TESTS		
Picture Completion	9	7
Picture Arrangement	25	8
Block Design	6	5
Object Assembly	10	4
Coding	22	4
(Mazes)	( )	( )
Performance Score		28

	Scaled Score	IQ
Verbal Score	23	66
Performance Score	28	69
Full Scale Score	51	64

*Prorated from 4 tests, if necessary.

NOTES _This test suggests a need for a much more complete evaluation for José. This is not a valid measure of general ability. José has much difficulty with English syntax. He speaks Spanish all the time at home and has been chastised for not doing so. His vocabulary score shows a lack of common English concepts. His block-design and object assembly show perceptual problems of a severe nature. He perseverated in similarities, picture completion, and arithmetic. He wants help._

Figure 6.2 The WISC-R Test profile record for José (From the record form of the *Wechsler Intelligence Scale for Children—Revised.* Copyright 1971, 1974, by the Psychological Corporation, New York, N.Y. Used by permission.)

in the evaluation of students from diverse sociocultural backgrounds and white, Black and Hispanic ethnic groups." The children are evaluated from medical, social system, and pluralistic viewpoints. The WISC-R is included as part of the social system viewpoint. Adequacy of individuals within their social settings is assessed in the pluralistic component of the battery.

Estimating General Alertness and Ability for School Tasks When Individual Intelligence Test Results Are Not Available

The teachers have some means at their commands to judge general intelligence even when there are no standardized tests of any kind on record, as, for example:

1. The teachers should observe leadership qualities both on the playground and in the room, mechanical aptitude, ingenuity in problem solving, and maturity in interpersonal behavior.

2. After selecting a story from a graded book (such as fourth-, eighth-, or ninth-grade level), the teacher should prepare a list of questions to test comprehension of ideas, then read a selected passage from the story aloud, telling the student beforehand that he or she will be asked questions. If the student answers more than 75 percent of the questions correctly, it can be assumed that the student has the *capacity* for understanding reading material at that level. To establish any ceiling for the student's capacity, however, it is necessary to sample the *most difficult* level from which the student can grasp 75 percent of the ideas. Obtaining the capacity level on the informal reading inventory provides this information.

3. The teacher can administer a commercially prepared picture vocabulary test for which there are norms in terms of grades and ages. Two such tests are:

   a. The Durrell Listening-Reading Series of Tests. Donald D. Durrell and Mary T. Hayes, *Durrell Listening-Reading Series: Primary Level, Intermediate Level,* and *Advanced Level* (New York: Harcourt Brace, 1969). This is a group test designed specifically to measure *reading potential* through measuring listening comprehension—without requiring the students to read context. The test is done by classifying or categorizing vocabulary words, sentences, or ideas from paragraphs read to the students. Raw scores are converted into grade placement or percentile values. Pupils who are reading at the second-grade level but show listening ability at the fourth-grade level may be considered to be two years retarded in reading ability. These tests replace the 1937 edition of the Durrell-Sullivan Reading Capacity and Achievement Tests. If the children come from homes where a language other than English is spoken, the Listening Test will reveal their present functioning level or could measure their progress in understanding the English language.

   b. The *Peabody Picture Vocabulary Test* by L. M. Dunn and L. M. Dunn (Circle Pines, Minn.: American Guidance Service, 1981). The test consists of 175 plates arranged in order of ascending difficulty designed to test an age range of two and one-half to forty years. One stimulus word is illustrated on each plate. Receptive language is assessed; no language is required from the child. Standard scores, percentiles, stanines, and age equivalent scores are provided, based on a population of 4,200 persons.

4. The teacher can administer an oral *vocabulary test*. The oral vocabulary subtest of the *Gates-McKillop-Horowitz Reading Diagnostic Tests* (New York: Teachers College Press, 1981) is an example. The examiner reads to the students the stem of a question and four possible answers and asks the students to select the correct one:

   "A *head* is a part of a *coat   saw   man   box*."
   "*Gaudy* means *certainly   wealthy   beautiful   showy*."

   The raw score on the vocabulary test has a grade placement equivalent.

5. Bond and Brueckner suggested that teachers should observe the extensiveness of the pupils' vocabularies, their achievement in other subjects such as arithmetic, their abilities to apply school learning to solve problems, the knowledge they have been able to gain from radio and television, and the contributions to discussions they make from their first-hand experiences.[8] They also reminded teachers that the aggressive or talkative students, the popular, quiet ones, and the overaverage ones are likely to be overestimated; the unattractive, shy, or rejected students are likely to be underestimated.

These measures for the classroom teachers to use to estimate subjectively what can be expected of pupils are not intended to substitute for more accurate testing by a counselor or school psychologist. The classroom teachers must make use of as many ways as possible to assess the potential of the students they teach, but it should be clearly understood that these supplement, but do not substitute for, examinations by a counselor or school psychologist.

Health Status

All available evidence points toward positive relationships between success in school and good general health. It is reasonable to expect that children who are free from illnesses, who have abundant energy, who see and hear adequately, who get sufficient rest and nourishment, and who are free of handicapping conditions are far more likely to devote attention to learning in school than children who have problems in these areas.

Hearing

The teacher should be alert to any symptoms suggesting that students who have difficulty learning how to read may have vision or hearing problems. Nurses usually give vision tests, and either nurses or speech and hearing therapists give hearing tests. All pupils who fail to pass screening tests should be referred to the vision specialist or to the audiologist. Teachers should discuss in personal conferences with parents any problems in the area of health that may explain learning difficulty. Parents are usually anxious to take their child for a physical examination when the teacher has evidence that such is indicated. Public health nurses or social workers can often obtain services

A child taking Peabody Picture Vocabulary Test points to the picture he thinks matches the stimulus word, while his teacher marks his response on the record blank.

for children whose parents are not financially able to pay for them. The teacher should be alert to the techniques for helping the pupil with limited vision or impaired hearing to make the best use of his or her abilities.

All pupils with school learning problems should be referred routinely for hearing and vision tests. The Auditory Discrimination Test (figure 6.3) can serve as a basis for referral for further hearing evaluation. According to the manual for the Auditory Discrimination Test, Revised, scoring is arrived at as follows:

Directions: Do the pairs of words sound alike or different? If the children make a score of less than 10 (out of 30 items) in the *different* column or less than 7 (out of 10) in the *same* column, the test should be considered invalid . . . and other means of assessing hearing discrimination should be found. Only the *different* column counts in scoring:
Threshold accuracy for

age	5	6	7	8+
is	18	20	24	25

The median scores earned by large numbers of children were:

age 5	median	23.8
age 6	median	24.6
age 7	median	26.3
age 8+	median	27.3

Figure 6.3. Auditory Discrimination Test as used with Paul (From *Auditory Discrimination Test, Revised* by Joseph M. Wepman. Copyright 1973 by Language Research Associates, Inc., 175 E. Delaware Place, Chicago 60611. Used with permission.)

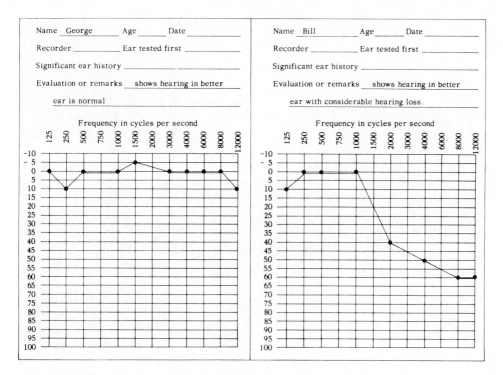

Figure 6.4. Sample audiograms (Form developed in the Speech and Hearing Center, University of New Mexico.)

The *Goldman-Friscoe-Woodcock Test of Auditory Discrimination*[9] is another assessment tool that may be used to gather data on *auditory discrimination* abilities. The child is required to select from four pictures the one that represents the stimulus word.

In figure 6.4 the *audiogram* on the right shows the results of a severe hearing loss in both ears, although the student insisted that his hearing was perfectly normal. The audiogram on the left shows normal hearing.

A list of specific behaviors that may signal that a child is experiencing some hearing difficulties follows:

1. Fails to talk in appropriate tones (speech too loud).
2. Ignores comments (either negative or positive).
3. Constantly asks teachers or classmates to repeat.
4. Has difficulty learning and retaining word sounds or spelling words.
5. Frequently picks or probes the ear.
6. Strains to hear: tilts the head, cups hand behind ear, leans toward speaker, maintains stiff or restrained posture while listening.
7. Enunciates poorly.
8. Scores low on auditory discrimination or auditory memory tests.

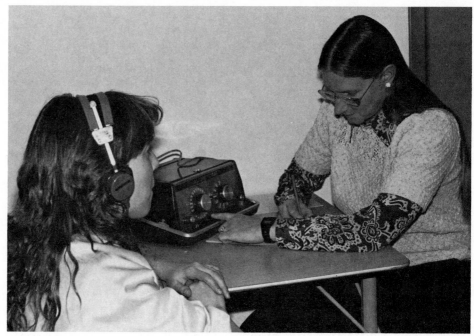

David Woodward

Since the teacher needs to know about any hearing problems that the child might have before reading instruction is begun, an examination with the audiometer is important.

9. Misses or misinterprets details in oral directions. Responds to written instructions better than to oral instructions.
10. Has physical evidence of ear problem (discharge, ringing sound).
11. Shows low attention span while oral activities are going on.
12. Has colds frequently; history of ear infections.
13. Tends to withdraw from peers and to play alone.
14. Tends to avoid listening-center activities.
15. Is easily distracted.
16. Complains of noise. Cannot concentrate in a noisy environment because of the confusion of many sounds.
17. Opens mouth while listening.
18. Watches the speaker closely as if lip-reading.

More and more school systems are using the services of skilled *educational* audiologists who are able to analyze the problems of school achievement in children with hearing difficulties. Occasionally a child is identified who has had serious hearing difficulty for a long time but has never had appropriate medical attention. An educational audiologist performs a most valuable service for such children. Anderson has described the learning problems of the child who has fluctuating hearing loss caused by the buildup of fluid behind the eardrum. Anderson asked the school system to provide these services:[10]

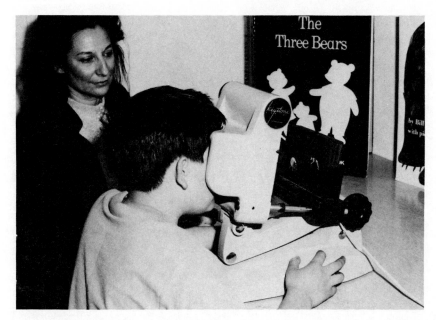

Near a display of big books, a student has his vision screened with the Keystone Telebinocular Visual Survey.

1. Improve the identification of children who are likely to do poorly in school due to hearing problems;
2. Improve methods used to screen for significant ear/hearing problems;
3. Consider the needs of the child from an educational point of view as well as from a medical one;
4. Help the students *early;*
5. Share management strategies with classroom teachers to help the child to cope in the classroom;
6. Boost the loudness of the teacher's voice so listening is easier;
7. Contact an educational audiologist for help.

Vision

It is generally accepted that information revealed by the Snellen Chart and the AMA Visual Survey Chart is very limited. Many types of visual difficulties are not revealed by these tests. The *Keystone Telebinocular Visual Survey*[11] and the *Orthorater*[12] are instruments used for screening and for referral to vision specialists for diagnosis of eye difficulties. The *Eames Eye Test*[13] is an inexpensive visual survey that possesses many of the qualities of more expensive tests. A *Keystone Visual Survey Test* for José, who apparently had a visual problem, appears in figure 6.5.

A competent ophthalmologist can determine whether or not visual defects contribute to the reading difficulty; an audiologist can assess hearing problems that may prevent learning by usual auditory methods.

Figure 6.5. *Keystone Visual Survey Test*—marked for José. (School Survey Cumulative Record Form No. 5A. Copyright 1961 Keystone View Division. Mast Development Co., Davenport, Iowa. Used by permission.)

The teacher should note symptoms of visual problems as they occur in the class-room. Typical behaviors indicating possible visual difficulties include:

1. Rubs eyes when reading.
2. Needs to hold the book very close to eyes to read.
3. Squints.
4. Has difficulty copying from the chalkboard. Makes lots of mistakes when copying.
5. Skips lines when reading. Unable to keep or find place.
6. Turns head at unusual angle to try to see better.
7. Has frequent headaches.
8. Holds hand over one eye to block it out.
9. Has watery, bloodshot eyes.
10. Is unable to continue reading very long.
11. Points to words while reading.
12. Has prescription glasses but never wears them.
13. Prefers to sit very close to TV screen.
14. Is inattentive when activity involves reading.
15. Has difficulty in tracing.

Color Blindness

A relationship exists between *color blindness* and reading success in first grade. In most of the printed materials currently used for teaching children in kindergarten and first grade, extensive use is made of color. Reading readiness work teaches color words early; seat work involves use of the major colors; and teachers use colored chalk to give emphasis or differentiate. Children's books are filled with highly colored illustrations. Picture interpretation is extended by discussions of colors used; pictures are completed by coloring according to printed directions; and games are devised using color iden-tification. Many first-grade teachers have been observed dismissing children with such commands as, "Now, all who have on something *blue* may go next." In safety, *red, green,* and *yellow* are of primary importance; yet, to the color-blind child, all three of these colors may appear only as varying degrees of the same color. Older boys often have trouble with colors on maps, colors of game pieces, and printed descriptions of colors in scenes.

With approximately 5 percent of the boys in the schools being color blind, should some special precaution be taken to ensure their school success in the first grade? With this question in mind, Olson administered the AO H-R-R Pseudo-Isochromatic Plates individually to 275 boys in twenty-three first-grade classrooms in five selected ele-mentary schools. Twelve boys were found to be color blind. They were matched with twelve color-vision children based on Goodenough Intelligence Scale IQ scores and chronological ages. These twelve pairs were given the California Reading Achievement Test, Lower Primary, Form W, in the last month of their first-grade school year. On the vocabulary subsection, the t-test value of the difference in performance was significant at the .005 level of confidence in favor of the color-vision boys; on the comprehension subsection of the reading test, the t-test value of the difference in performance was significant at the .05 level of confidence in favor of the color-vision boys; and the value of the difference on the total test was significant at the .01 level of confidence. Olson found the incidence of color blindness to be 4.3 percent.[14]

Espinda found that 13.25 percent of the students in eleven classrooms of handicapped students were color blind while only 5.04 percent of the students in eleven regular classrooms had color-vision deficiencies. He concluded that color blindness was a factor in learning and behavioral problems, possibly resulting from the stress of coping with color as an important factor in classrooms.[15]

Schiffman has reported that when teachers are informed that boys in their rooms are color blind, those boys do statistically better in first-grade reading than color-blind boys in other first-grade rooms where the teachers have not been given this information.[16] This finding emphasizes the importance of teacher knowledge of color blindness to use as a guide for appropriate instruction on behalf of color-blind pupils.

Since each researcher has found that color blindness has a negative influence on the success of children in learning to read and being successful in school, to be aware of the students with color deficiencies in the classroom is important. Only a few minutes are required to identify the color-blind students. Teachers should also be alert to behaviors and comments signaling color confusion. The boy who colors an apple purple and says that he has colored it red should alert the teacher to a possible problem. Primary teachers, especially, should not overlook this additional possibility in eliminating all the factors that may be causing learning and reading difficulties.

Two tests for color blindness are (1) Dvorine Pseudo-Isochromatic Plates, Second Edition (Scientific Publishing Company, 2328 Entaw Place, Baltimore 17, Maryland) and (2) AO H-R-R Pseudoisochromatic Plates, Second Edition (American Optical Company, Vision Park, Southbridge, Massachusetts 01550).

Because teachers can test a whole class very quickly with either set of plates (twenty-five or thirty students in thirty to forty minutes), teachers can easily screen all children in the primary grades. The tests are valid, reliable, and easy to administer and interpret.

The color-blind children need to be identified. If the color plates are not immediately available, teachers can confirm their first judgments about children's understanding of color by asking them to do color matching, color naming, color sorting, or object arrangement by color patterns. This can be done quickly and informally.

If students are color blind, they need to be given special consideration in any work that calls for identifying, naming, or using colors. Teachers can offer subtle kinds of help in finding the right crayons, such as teaching the child to read color names on the crayon wrappers; they may compensate somewhat for such students by emphasizing auditory avenues to learning. The teachers' greatest need for the color-blind children is the *awareness* that they are color blind, an understanding of what being color blind means, and a few coping skills to enable the children to complete their reading tasks confidently without frustration caused by their inabilities to identify colors.[17]

Other Health Problems

Endocrine disturbances, especially thyroid problems, have in many cases been found to bear directly on difficulties in learning to read. *Hypothyroidism* manifests itself in such overt behavior as lack of effort, fatigue, and nonlearning. The detection of thyroid deficiency or any other medical problem is not within the province of the educator; neither is its treatment. Without help from the medical specialist, however, the teacher's effort to teach reading is apt to be unsuccessful.

To illustrate, Gerald was doing very poor work in the fourth grade when he was given a thorough physical examination. A basal metabolism test revealed an extremely underactive thyroid. He was given heavy dosage of thyroid extract and tested for enrollment in an eight-week remedial reading clinic. His reading skills were fairly evenly developed at easy second-grade level. His instruction during the eight-week summer school included thirty-seven two-hour sessions. He was taught all the developmental reading skills and strategies for second grade by reading and writing about his two major interests, bikes and tropical fish, and he began reading well from an easy third-grade book before the close of summer school.

Gerald's fifth-grade teacher the following year was an excellent, permissive, experienced teacher who used the detailed summer report as a basis for planning his reading in her room. He adjusted well and made further progress.

In a follow-up study five years later, Gerald's parents reported that in tenth grade he had no reading problems and that they were pleased with his progress in senior high school. He took thyroid extract for about three years, after which the family doctor had determined that it was no longer needed. He had been a member of the varsity football squad in his high school, and his physical stamina was assessed as "good now."

Joseph is another example of a child who had a variety of health problems. Joseph was in the second grade in a large city school. He was a small child for his seven years. He walked haltingly because of a congenital hip deformity. He had few friends. He was uninterested in his school work, even though his teacher made her lessons interesting and varied. At home he was not interested in active play and preferred to sit watching television both before and after school. His parents met with the teacher and principal about his failing school grades. They decided stricter demands should be placed on Joseph, both at home and at school. The stricter demands made no difference; the child's work became steadily worse. Finally, one day during recess, the teacher on duty found Joseph asleep behind one of the portable classrooms. This event caused the teacher and parents to decide that some action should be taken. A checkup by the family doctor revealed two serious problems—an abnormal thyroid that led to extreme lethargy and a low blood sugar condition that left the child continually tired and bothered by headaches. The label of "lazy" was quickly forgotten, a strict diet and medication for the thyroid condition were begun, and a careful schedule of play, work, and rest was established. Within weeks, Joseph was performing at grade level in his reading class and showed no further problems with school. He found several new friends and became a happy, active child at school and at home. After high school he entered college to study electrical engineering. He must still follow a strict diet and take certain medications, but he is a successful student who expects a satisfying career as an engineer.

Chemical imbalance, low vitality, underactive or overactive metabolism, and vitamin deficiency may affect reading as well as motor and speech activities. Slight, unrecognized birth injuries may account for a number of cases of undiagnosed reading difficulty.

Allergies

An allergic reaction is the body's adverse response to alien substances in the environment. Hay fever, some forms of hives, and asthma are common forms of *allergies*. Visible effects of allergic attacks include itching eyes and nose, runny nose, hives, sneezing, or throat constriction. Difficulty in breathing is usually the result of muscle spasms in bronchial walls that constrict the passages. Inhaling particles of plant pollen, animal dander, or dust causes such discomfort. Specific foods, tense situations, or house dust may generate hives, eczema, or gastrointestinal allergies. Sensitization that results from having been administered drugs for illnesses can cause individuals to become allergic to certain drugs.

Children whose allergies are chronic but not treated may find concentration on school work impossible. Outward signs of breathing discomfort, hearing loss, and general distress need to be understood by the children's teachers. These children need help, not admonishment. Some children's allergies may be seasonal with the presence of pollens, animal dander, or dust. Other children who are chronically affected have no seasonal respite.

Inventories and Interviews

An Interest Inventory

By talking privately with any pupil, the teacher can gain a great deal of personal information that can be useful when any question about the pupil's school success arises. In other words, the more one knows about a person, the more apt one is to be able to understand the person's behavior.

For the student who has difficulties with reading, the teacher may wish to conduct a more systematic inventory of the student's background and interests. The following suggestions are made for obtaining this type of information.

The teacher can complete part of an *interest inventory* on the basis of information he or she has already obtained from formal records and informal visits. When asking the pupil questions, the teacher should use short periods of time when both teacher and pupil can talk freely. If nothing particularly worthwhile is revealed, the inventory may not be of special use to the teacher in planning the remedial program. On the other hand, some information may be very helpful. For instance, what the pupil does after school, in the evening, and on weekends; the relationship with siblings and the kind of fun shared with the family; whether or not a great deal of time is spent with friends; special hobbies being developed; private lessons outside of school, such as tennis, art, piano; whether the pupil has collections or pets—all of these may reveal needed information. Habits of rest, sleep, play, and diet need to be investigated. Places where the pupil has been—a long train trip or a visit to an art museum—give facts about the background of experience. Experience stories can be dictated by the pupil and type-written by the teacher for reading practice. A collection of original stories based on these experiences may be very important to the pupil and may provide meaningful reading practice.

The pupil's knowledge of radio, television, and movie entertainment may add to the ability to write experience stories that will provide practice in reading. Interest in school, in the library, in what he or she wants to be when grown up, and other factors will be useful in extending reading skills.

The types of information to be sought in the compilation of an interest inventory include the answers to such questions as are suggested in figure 6.6.

Each teacher can obtain pertinent information from the pupils without a formal questionnaire, but he or she should write this information down while it is fresh in mind. Items revealed in such an interview may be useful in planning future remedial work in reading and writing.

Personality Data

The Incomplete Sentences Blank, College Form,[18] has been used as a measure of individuals' reactions and feelings about situations in everyday life. The instructions for this test read: "Complete these sentences to express *your real feelings*. Try to do every one. Be sure to make a complete sentence."[19]

Two purposes can be achieved in using this form with disabled readers. First, the blanks will reveal some of their feelings about the reading situation, and second, they may reveal other areas in which there are psychological problems affecting reading success.

If the student's ability to read and write is very low, the teacher may need to serve as the "secretary" and record responses. Unless this is done, the answers may be limited to what the child is able to write. The information may be limited or distorted as a result. Other teachers have found ways to use the cassette recorder, so that the child can complete the sentences orally. Still others have devised programs for the microcomputer, so that children can complete the sentences using the keyboard and printer.

Ruth

The test is reproduced here with answers given by Ruth, a sixteen-year-old girl who had not learned to read. She had been attending a reading clinic, and her clinician had established sufficient rapport to believe the answers were reliable. Because she could not read, the stems were read to her; she responded orally, and her answers were written for her. The sentences with her endings are:

1. I like . . . Max.
2. The happiest time . . . March 10—ten minutes to nine.
3. I want to know . . . if I ever can learn to read.
4. Back home . . . friends.
5. I regret . . . not learning to read.
6. At bedtime . . . I hit the hay.

Name _____ Age _____ Grade _____ Date _____

Parents name and address: _____

I. About *you*:

What do you usually do after school? In your spare time? In the evening? On Sunday? On Saturday?

What do you like best to do at home?

How many brothers and sisters do you have? How old are they? Do you play games with them? What are some of your favorite games?

Does your father or mother ever spend time with you? What do you do together?

II. About *your friends*:

Do your friends come to your house to see you? Would you rather go to their houses?

What do you play? Do you usually play whatever games they want to play?

Do you belong to any clubs?

III. About *your hobbies*:

Do you have a hobby? Tell me about it. What kinds of things do you like to make? Do you have a collection of any kind?

IV. More things about *you*:

Do you take any kind of special lessons outside of school? What kind? Would you rather take something else?

Do you have a pet? What is it? Tell me about feeding and caring for your _____?

What time do you usually go to bed at night?
What are you afraid of?
What time do you usually get up in the morning?

Do you like milk to drink?

Are there any things you don't like to eat? (Especially that your mother wants you *to eat*.)

V. Places *you have been*:

Have you ever been to a circus? Zoo? Farm? Ball game? Picnic? Concert? Camp? Museum?

Have you taken a boat trip?

Have you taken a train trip?

Have you taken an airplane trip?

Tell me about some trip you have taken.

VI. Ways *you* learn new things:

Do you have a transistor?
What do you listen to most?
What do you watch on television?

Do you go to movies? What movies have you seen lately? Tell me about one you liked.

Who do you go to movies with? Do you have a favorite movie actor or actress?

Do you like to read?
Do you ever read out loud to anyone? To whom?

Do you like to go to school?
What is your favorite subject?
What subject do you like least?

Do you have a library card?
Do you go to the library?
What are some books you have read recently?

Do you read the comics? What is your favorite comic strip? Do you see cartoons on TV on Saturday mornings?

What do you want to be when you grow up? Do you know what your parents want you to be when you grow up?

Figure 6.6. An interest inventory

172

7. Boys . . . fun!
8. The best . . . what can I do best? don't know.
9. What annoys me . . . a lot of things.
10. People . . . friends.
11. A mother . . . is a person that looks after you.
12. I feel . . . good.
13. My greatest fear . . . never learning to read.
14. In high school . . . fun.
15. I can't . . . read.
16. Sports . . . horseback riding, swimming.
17. When I was a child . . . had fun.
18. My nerves . . . ha! why?
19. Other people . . . just people.
20. I suffer . . . a lot on account of I can't read.
21. I failed . . . reading.
22. Reading . . . I wish I could.
23. My mind . . . Oh, Gad! nothing comes, I don't think.
24. The future . . . work.
25. I need . . . friends.
26. Marriage . . . fun.
27. I am best when . . . happy.
28. Sometimes . . . what do you mean? happy.
29. What pains me . . . a lot of things irritate me.
30. I hate . . . I don't know.
31. This school . . . isn't bad.
32. I am very . . . happy.
33. The only trouble . . . reading.
34. I wish . . . I could read.
35. My father . . . is a carpenter.
36. I secretly . . . nothing.
37. I . . . swim.
38. Dancing . . . some clubs where you can dance, dancing is fun.
39. My greatest worry is . . . Ha! one is reading; I want a letter from someone.
40. Most girls . . . like me.

Those answers that might have revealed some conflict with other people—items 7, 10, 11, 14, 19, 35, and 40—do not indicate any problem for this student. However, the answers to items 3, 5, 13, 15, 20, 21, 22, 33, 34, and 39 all relate to the reading failure. Certainly this shows genuine anxiety on the student's part about the failure in learning how to read. Alleviating such an anxiety might make for possible faster progress in reading in the future.

Making Connections 6.1: Using the Interest Inventory

Locate a child who would be willing to complete an interest inventory with you. You may wish to use the sample inventory shown in figure 6.6. You may find that you want to add certain questions or perhaps delete some, depending on the age of the child or circumstances unique to that particular youngster.

Complete the interview with the child. You may wish to take detailed notes, or you may find it more appropriate to record the session and transcribe the tape later.

When your information is ready for sharing, bring the record of your interview to class. In small groups, share your experience and the resulting data with others. Be sure to discuss how this information could be used in planning a reading program for the particular child.

Larry

Following is another observation of reading difficulties amid emotional problems. Larry was in the fourth grade. His reading ability was limited to easy second-grade level, although he had a Stanford-Binet IQ of 102. During a semester of individual tutoring in reading, the reading clinician obtained the following information:

About the Parents. Larry lived in a strict authoritarian household. His parents were trying very hard to teach him to be honest, fair, and just. They constantly applied excessive pressure to get what they considered to be acceptable behavior. Larry's father seemed to have a need to realize through his son what he, himself, wanted to do in life. Larry's psychological needs were not met at home because his father had such rigid notions of what Larry should do and be.

About the Five-Year-Old Brother. Larry expressed considerable hostility and jealousy toward his brother.

About the Teacher at School. The child had been referred to the school's child guidance department, and a written report was in the school file. The teacher had not read this report! While she expressed concern about the problem, she was doing nothing observable to solve it. Larry was often scolded in the classroom and was once required to write two hundred times, "I will respect my teacher." As soon as Larry's teacher saw evidence of his growth in reading with the reading tutor, she moved him up to the middle reading group and eliminated the lower reading group entirely.

From the Reading Tutor. Larry did make progress during the semester and gained a great deal of self-confidence. His sight vocabulary and his word-analysis skills improved, although he needed outside help with his psychological problems and further help with reading. One day Larry completed eight sentences of the incomplete sentences variety:

1. When I was little . . . I was bad.
2. Grownups think . . . right.
3. I hardly ever . . . am bad.
4. My father . . . is very good to me.
5. I am . . . a bad boy.
6. I used to . . . be bad but you are now.
7. When I get big . . . I will be a big man.
8. My mother . . . is a good cook.

The four items about himself all emphasize Larry's inadequacy. The answers about grownups make one think that these were learned responses that one must make! Grownups must think right, and one must say of one's father that he is very good.

When Larry was asked to draw a picture in which he put a house, a tree, and a person, he drew a very small girl in his house instead of a boy. Does this suggest that he feels he needs to be a girl so that he won't be so displeasing to his father? Is the diminutive size of the person (see drawing in figure 6.7) indicative of his feelings of insignificance and inadequacy?

An Interview about the Reading Process

When the teacher begins to gather information about the child's reading status, it is important to find out what is understood about the reading process and about the vocabulary used in reading instruction. The teacher may discover that the child has views about reading that contribute to poor learning and negative attitudes. Some children may view reading as a decoding act and focus almost entirely on naming words accurately. These readers may complain that reading is boring and no fun. They may well be right if they have never learned to see reading as a meaningful activity. Some children are puzzled about such questions as, "What is reading?" They have never been led to consider what reading is and how one goes about doing it. Frequently, they feel it is sounding or spelling out words; both ideas are destructive to the true nature of the reading act. The teacher may also inquire about such acts as skipping words or rereading passages. Both are strategies employed selectively by good readers, but many children see them as wrong and as behaviors they *never* exhibit. Some children, when asked who they know is a good reader, will select someone who is bigger, who "knows all the words," or who reads fast. Often such children have not learned what makes reading effective or what characteristics accurately describe the "good" reader. Other questions in a reading interview may focus on the child's knowledge of such terms as *syllable, word, sentence, line, sound, first,* and *last.* Failure to recognize the meanings of these and other words used by teachers in reading instruction may further confuse the child who is already having reading problems. The teacher may put together a list of questions that will yield information about the child's concepts of the reading process, or he or she may use prepared lists of questions developed explicitly for this purpose.[20]

Figure 6.7. Larry's drawing in the house-tree-person test

Parent Interviews

When parents and teachers work together for the educational well-being of children, the greatest possible academic gains can be expected. One way in which the significant adults in the lives of children can work together is through conferences or interviews.[21] If the teacher intends to conference with or interview parents, careful planning must precede the meeting. The teacher must prepare classroom information, work samples from the child, and reports from other school personnel to share with the parents. In addition, thoughtful questions must be prepared that will let the parents know what kinds of information will be most valuable in contributing to the solution of the child's reading problems. Most questions should be open ended so that the parents are invited to share the information that seems important to them. Parents can be helped to plan their part of a conference or interview through suggestions about the kinds of records and information they may need to share during the meeting.

After all information from school and home has been collected, the parents and teacher have the task of using that information to make plans for the child's learning. The teacher should be prepared to take the lead in this final phase of the conference or interview, but it is important that the ideas of the parents, who probably know the child best, be respected and incorporated into any plan of action that is prepared.

An example of a form a teacher might use as a guide for a parent interview may be found in appendix F.

Strategies that Yield Social and Psychological Data

A variety of techniques can help teachers to assess the social situations of children in their classrooms. The sociogram is one common, practical technique for obtaining information about interpersonal relationships among students. Bibliotherapy may be used as a technique to work toward more favorable social settings. It may also be used to help provide insights for children as they deal with a wide variety of difficult life situations.

The Sociogram

A *sociogram* is a chart showing the social interaction among the members of a group at a given time. Many teachers construct sociograms based on children's friendships so that they can take an objective look at the social status of all pupils. The popular students, the two who are always together but with no one else, the pupils who have no friends, and the one most children reject—are delineated for the teachers when the sociogram is finished.

There are several logical facts to be emphasized about the sociogram. It will, of course, not be shown or discussed with the students. Teachers never indicate to children who is the isolate or the reject, or naively urge popular children to be "nice" to unchosen ones. While the chart shows stars, isolates, and rejects, it does not in any way show what to do about them! If the teachers are apprised of some techniques to change the behavioral pattern, it can be a very valuable device. Naturally, choices made by children may be superficial, temporary, or fickle. A sociogram made in October may not tell the story in February. Nevertheless, as one index of pupil interaction, it is well worth the work involved in its construction. The following steps may help you in making a sociogram:

1. The students express two or three choices of friends or partners among their classmates. These choices will be most valid if there is some real purpose for making them. Sometimes the question the child will answer is simply, "Who do you consider to be your three best friends in this room?" or "Who do you want to have sit near you when a new seating chart is made?" After some discussion

of the question that is to be answered and the uses to be made of their choices, all pupils may be asked to write their names on one side of a three-by-five card and their three choices of classmates on the other side. The teachers need to make clear that they will make use of these preferences *as much as they can,* if this is to precede a new seating arrangement, for example. Sometimes a class activity is being planned in which committees will do projects or write research reports, or the teachers may plan small-group work in arithmetic. The teachers must also make clear that *no one* but them will see the cards with the choices on them.

2. If thirty children make three choices each, it is apparent that there will be a considerable amount of tabulating to be done. The choices can be tabulated on a large sheet of paper so that the total number of times that each child has been chosen can easily be seen. Such a tabulation pattern is suggested in figure 6.8. The names of all the children are to be listed both horizontally and vertically, and lines drawn so that the necessary squares for recording choices are provided. The totals at the bottom of each column become the data for making the sociogram. In most cases, if three choices are plotted, no distinction needs to be made between first, second, or third choice. However, only *first* choices should be plotted on a separate chart.

3. It may be necessary to begin more than one plotting of the sociogram. First draw some large concentric circles on the large sheet of paper and place the children's names outward from the center on the basis of number of choices. It may also be helpful to cut out small circles on which the girls' names are written and small hexagons on which the boys' names are written. These circles and hexagons can then be moved around on the master plan until their locations make possible the clearest drawing of lines. Careful study often helps in the discovery of small isolated groups, presence of cliques, and sometimes divisions strictly on ethnic group lines (see figure 6.9).

4. After the sociogram is complete, consider how (by assignment to working pairs or to small group projects, or by seating in quartets or at tables) a child who is an isolate might be grouped with one who might become friendly. Think of positive ways to give recognition to the shy, withdrawn, or silent child. Think of reasons for the rejection of the disliked child. According to Strickland:

Many times the evidence points to the fact that the isolate has become lost because of his inability to communicate with other children because he has a speech defect, comes from a foreign background, or uses speech in a manner different from that of other children. A child may be excluded by the children because he is "bossy" and overaggressive in his use of language, because he is inept in making contacts with people, or because he cannot fit into a group as a cooperative, participating member.[22]

A second-grade teacher made a sociogram of her thirty-one students based on the question, "Who do you consider to be your three best friends in the room?" Figure 6.8 shows the tabulation of their choices, and figure 6.9 is the completed sociogram based on this tabulation. The letter *A, B,* or *C* under each child's name indicates the reading

Chooser	Jack	Roger	Mary	David	Joan	Rose	Betty	Lupe	Greg	Sara	Dan	Jean	Rosa	Carol	Barbara	Grace	Jim	Laura	Marco	Anita	Larry	Dean	Bruce	Patsy	Donny	Ray	Kay	Glenn	Bill	Julian	Bobby
Jack									3																			2	1		
Roger																			2	1						3					
Mary					1				2																			3			
David									2															3	1						
Joan									1							2								3							
Rose							3								1									2							
Betty		3							1					2																	
Lupe					1										3									2							
Greg										2							3													1	
Sara			3		1									2																	
Dan		1														2								3							
Jean	2				3								1																		
Rosa												1			3									2							
Carol			3	1																				2							
Barbara		3															1							2							
Grace		3												2										1							
Jim									3															1							2
Laura														2	1										3						
Marco		2							3												1										
Anita																1					2	3									
Larry	2				1																3										
Dean																					2	3			1						
Bruce			3	2														1													
Patsy		2		3											1																
Donny															2	1					3										
Ray					3						1													2							
Kay							2			1														3							
Glenn		3																				2		1							
Bill	1	2							3																						
Julian									1	3																			2		
Bobby (Absent on day of vote)																															
Totals	2	5	1	3	2	4	7	2	4	4	0	5	2	3	7	1	2	2	2	0	4	2	1	6	8	4	2	1	2	1	1

(Column group label: "Chosen")

Figure 6.8. Sociogram tabulation: "Three Best Friends"

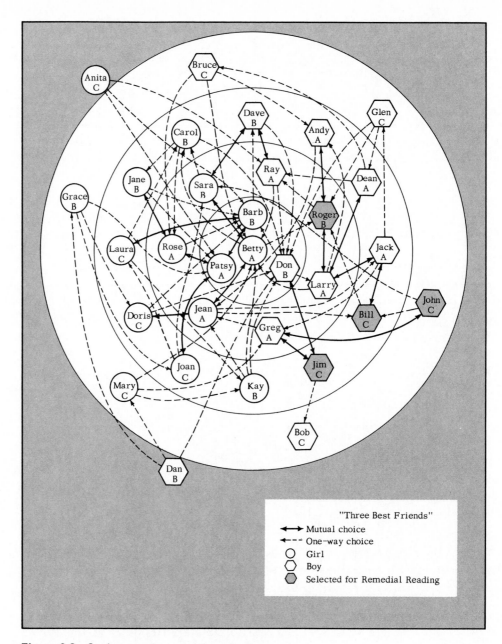

Figure 6.9. Sociogram of a second-grade class

group to which each was assigned at the time the chart was drawn. Roger, Jim, Bill, and Julian were designated by the teacher as the least successful in the reading program.

If children who are failing in reading are chosen by their peers, then this is one indication that their reading failure is not affecting their social interaction in the group. If they are on the fringe, are isolates, or rejects, the teachers may need to consider how a better interaction with the group might be achieved. In the sociogram, Roger was chosen five times, Bill three times, Jim twice, and Julian once.

Bibliotherapy

Shrodes defined *bibliotherapy* as "a process of interaction between the personality of the reader and imaginative literature which may engage his emotions and free them for conscious and productive use."[23]

Tews stated: "Bibliotherapy is a program of selected activity involving reading materials, planned, conducted, and controlled as treatment under the guidance of the physician for emotional and other problems."[24]

Literally, bibliotherapy is "treatment through books" or "healing through books." Books, that is, print materials, have different values for different people. If the right book can be selected at the right time, books may, for some people, provide the language and the ideas to clarify their personal problems.

If teachers were to entertain notions of recommending books for therapeutic purposes for their students, they should abide by these cautions:

1. Students *must* have freedom of choice in what they read.
2. Students should have *no* pressure to show results, such as book reports.
3. Teachers should proceed with caution.

Bibliotherapy is affected through the personality mechanisms of (1) identification, (2) catharsis, and (3) insights. Identification, catharsis, and insight must be present for a dynamic interaction between the reader and the books. First, the reader must identify with character elements of the story; share some characteristics such as age, sex, hopes, fears, problems. If the reader can identify with and admire the character, the reader can build self-image and increase the feeling of belonging. Sometimes when this personal identification is not possible, these positive effects can occur through hero-worship. *Identification,* then, is the recognition of commonalities between reader and characters.

Second, *catharsis* is the sharing of motivations, conflicts, and emotions of a character in a book. It is an active release of emotions, experienced either first-hand or vicariously. It goes beyond the simple recognition of commonalities and involves empathy (feeling as the character does). The readers relive *their* own past experiences. The generation of empathy is basic to catharsis.

Third, *insight* requires that after people see themselves in the behavior of the characters in the book, they get an awareness of their own motivations, needs, and problems. People need to see similarities and differences between themselves and fictional characters. Now, the reader considers a course of action to try to solve (overcome) the problem. This step requires the taking of some action to meet a need.

Personality changes occur through response to emotional experience, not through teaching and learning. Intellect is not a key factor in the therapeutic process. The personality change in bibliotherapy requires identification, catharsis, and insight. People overcome feelings of guilt, inadequacy, or inferiority by identifying these in characters, generalizing or seeing these traits as universals in human behavior; then, the catharsis is the ability to express "bad" feelings and to understand them. In adults this is likely achieved through talking; in children it is achieved through action (this is often play therapy). This must lead to *insight* in order for the reader to grow through to emotional maturity.

Roswell and Natchez have reported the case of Claude, age twelve, seventh grade, who felt that he was a failure and resorted to being a nuisance in class. His reading achievement was at least two years below grade level, although he had normal intelligence. After reading Hans Christian Andersen's life in *Stories to Remember,* Classmate Edition (high fourth-grade level),[25] Thomas Edison's life story in *Teen Age Tales,* Book 1 (fifth-grade level),[26] Dr. Fleming's struggle to discover penicillin, and Madame Curie's life story, both in *Doorways to Discovery* (seventh-grade level),[27] observable behavioral changes did take place.

Learning that Hans Christian Andersen was *the* Ugly Duckling; that Edison was considered dull and stupid by his classmates; that Dr. Fleming had the patience to wait nearly two decades for personal recognition for having discovered penicillin; and that Madame Curie's discovery of radium was a long and tedious process caused Claude to realize that perseverance wins in the face of failure and that he might really change his life. He did, according to his case file, make a three-year reading growth during one year and, when followed up in tenth grade, was still achieving well.

Not all students will respond to these same stories, nor is it expected that all teachers will be sufficiently analytically oriented to guide all students in this way. However, if a key is found that helps students unlock the world to them, they should be encouraged to take advantage of it.[28]

Remember that bibliotherapy does not include the use of didactic literature to drive home moral lessons. It simply takes advantage of good literature in which true-to-life people solve problems and conflicts and make adjustments to the realities of living.[29]

Recognizing cultural values, meeting and solving personal and human relations problems, and understanding people with physical limitations, all subjects to be found and discussed in good literature suitable for children, may help pupils to develop wholesome attitudes toward all kinds of differences when they become adults. Teachers will

---

Making Connections 6.2: Identifying Books for Use in Bibliotherapy

Bibliotherapy is a useful strategy to employ in helping a child to understand a problem and develop valid ways of dealing with it. Teachers need to know books well enough so that they can make suitable choices to recommend to children for specific purposes.

Identify some problem or situation that might confront a child who has a reading problem. Then, build a bibliography of books that might be used with such a child to help him or her understand the situation better. Besides the usual bibliographic information on each book, include a sentence or two summarizing the book and its potential for bibliotherapy.

If class members prepare sufficient copies of their bibliographies, sharing will permit each person to have the beginning of an extensive collection of books suitable for use in bibliotherapy.

---

find further suggestions in such books as *Reading Ladders to Human Relations*[30] and *The Bookfinder: A Guide to Children's Literature about the Needs and Problems of Youth Aged 2–15.*[31]

Other Language and Reading Assessments

Storytelling

Teachers may ask children to tell or retell stories in order to obtain more information about the students' understanding of stories. Relationships between children's understanding of the *structure of stories, story grammar, the goals, motivations, and feelings* of the characters, and overall comprehension abilities are becoming clearly established. When building a collection of data about a child's reading status, the teacher may ask the child to tell a story based on a picture or a wordless picture book and to retell a story that has been read. These tellings should be taped and transcribed for analysis. The teacher may look to see whether the child includes all of the parts of a story in the telling. Evidence of the child's perception of the goals of the characters and the child's understanding of the feelings of the characters may be noted. When the child seems to take no note of goals and feelings should also be noted. Children who have trouble with these tasks may well be failing to comprehend relationships within the stories, even though they may be able to answer simple recall questions.

Two transcriptions of stories based on the poster shown in the picture on page 184 are included here for study and comparison.[32]

David Woodward

The child may be asked to create a story about an intriguing picture, and the tape recorded story can be transcribed and evaluated later.

Story 1

Um . . . like these boys have two boys have um like a big bird. And um they're flying over like China or something like that. It's like a dream come true. And the bird's like a friend of theirs. It's like everybody's pointing to them and everything including the officers. . . . One thing they've got a big pet. . . . They're having a good time for one thing. . . . Oh, they're going over a city or small this small town. There's lots and lots of houses and lots of cars. . . . They're curious about the town. A small town. The bird is their friend, and he's taking them for a ride or something. And that's all.

Story 2

One day in Japan these two little kids they liked to go on adventures. Fun adventures too. One day they found a rock. It had a map to a cave. So one day they went out of the city, and they found this big cave. They went into the cave. They first found a whole bunch of string and bags and clothing. So they went farther and farther back into the cave. Suddenly they fell into these big old rocks. And then they felt furry feathers on top of them. So they climb on top. They hook something on this needle and they feel something walk. So they come out. They fly in the air and they see their city. And suddenly the bird they saw. They started to say, "The bird, the bird, the bird of the great white kingdom." And everybody started to point. And suddenly they turned him with the string. The guy with the big bag, he threw a rock down there and hit somebody. And suddenly somebody started to see the big bird. The big bird started to fly towards down towards the city. Everybody got afraid. Suddenly they went to the capital city and then they went down towards the sculpture of . . . Indian kingdom. So they flew down and they come there and all the people start to look at the bird. And the people that looked at the bird the bird started to peck at them. And suddenly they flew away. They never saw them again. The end.

Analysis of these stories might begin with questions such as:

1. Does the child include the parts of a story: introduction, introduction and resolution of one or more problems, and conclusion? Which parts are included? Omitted? Or, does the child simply list objects or describe the picture?
2. How literate is the story? Does the child use words and expressions that are typical of written stories?
3. Does the child express the goals of the characters? Do the characters' feelings and goals seem related?
4. How is time managed in the story?
5. How does the child link events? *Cohesive ties* are the linguistic structures that the child uses to make the parts of the story hold together.
6. Does the child make inferences or go beyond the material presented to her or him?
7. How fluent is the speaker? (Note that *fluency* does not always signal a well-constructed story. Nor is length a valid indicator of the understanding of story structure.)
8. Does the child use evaluative language as the story is told?

The Writing Sample

The teacher may ask children to prepare *writing samples* as part of the collection of information about language and reading development. The children may be asked to write on a teacher-identified topic, to tell or retell a story, or to write on a subject of their own choosing. The teacher will be able to observe how well each child has mastered the mechanics of writing and spelling. The child's ability to tell a story in writing may be evaluated and compared with oral storytelling capabilities.

The teacher may use a *story frame* for a relatively quick analysis of written stories.[33] Story frames may be constructed in outline form.

  I. Introduction
     A. Characters _____
     B. Setting and time _____

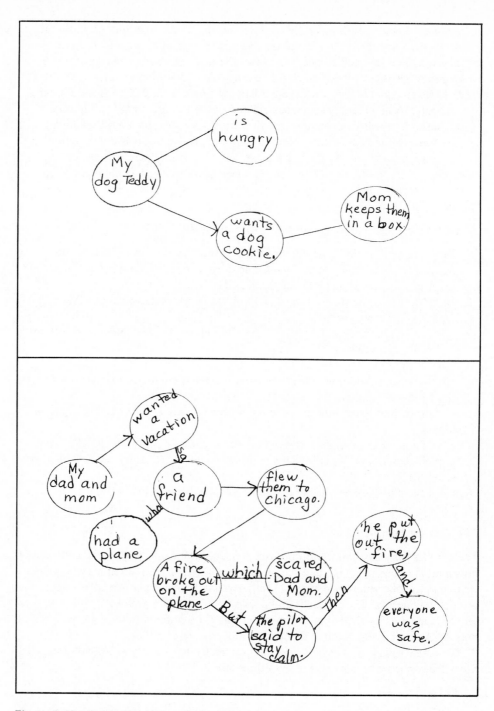

Figure 6.10. Diagrams of two written stories

II. Episode One
  A. Problem _____
  B. Goal _____
  C. Feelings _____
  D. Attempt _____
  E. Result _____
III. Repeated Episodes (Optional)
IV. Resolution

In order to determine whether stories are complete, the teacher may diagram them. Two very simple stories are diagrammed in figure 6.10 to demonstrate an undeveloped narrative and a short but complete one.

The technique of *holistic scoring* is a valuable one.[34] Writing samples may be sorted into three, four, or five sets, depending on the degree of differentiation desired. For example, stories might be sorted into "very good," "better than average," "poorer than average," or "very poor" categories. Some planning of criteria for each category should occur prior to the sorting. If the stories can be sorted by more than one person, the validity of the technique is improved.

Following are two writing samples by elementary school children. What comments would you make about these samples if you were evaluating them? Think of both positive comments and suggestions for improvement.

Story 1

Once there lived a farmer THaT had loTs of animals and there were pigs. And there were cows and horses and a dog and a cat.

Story 2

My name is Adam Lopez. I like different sports. My favorites are ballbase, football, swimming, and gymnastics. I play on a little league team. I have been on this team for 2 years. The name of my team is the Dodgers. My number is 3. I play infield. I like pitcher the most.

Cloze Procedure

The term *cloze* from the word *closure* explains the tendency of a thinking individual to anticipate the completion of a not-quite-finished pattern. Closure, as an idea, is a term used by Gestalt psychologists.

Closure is the ability of the readers—or the listeners, for that matter—to determine by anticipating contextually the word or concept that is needed immediately.

Weaver and Kingston found that the ability of students to write in every *n*th word in a passage correlated significantly with scores on vocabulary and comprehension sections of the *Diagnostic Reading Test*.[35]

The cloze procedure does not require special expertise in test construction. It merely presents the readers with a series of contextually interrelated blanks in a passage. A passage is prepared with every *n*th word missing with a blank of standard length substituted. Students read the passage and write in the missing words. It follows that the better the passage is understood by the readers, the more likely they will be to guess what words are missing. Schneyer found that cloze tests have adequate validity for evaluating reading comprehension for most general uses.[36]

Research to date suggests that the most valid and reliable cloze test for measuring passage difficulty is one in which:

1. An every *n*th mechanical mutilation system is used.
2. Not more than 20 words out of every 100 is deleted.
3. Passage length is at least 250 words.

4. Deletion ratios of 1:10 and 1:12 in longer passages may be valid for certain purposes.
5. At least 50 words are deleted in order to insure adequate sampling of passages.
6. The exact word deleted is indicated as the most useful and efficient scoring criteria.
7. Other scoring systems (synonym, form class) provide less interscorer reliability and require substantially more time.
8. The separate scoring of form classes or content and function words may provide specific information for specialized purposes.[37]

Taylor believed that the cloze procedure was a very useful tool in measuring general understanding of written material. Factors that affect comprehension—general language facility, specific knowledge, native ability to learn, specialized vocabulary, motivation, and ability to attend—are all being evaluated by cloze tests in which all types of words are deleted.[38]

Bormuth found cloze tests to be valid, reliable, and flexible measures of the comprehension of the passage being read.[39]

Tonjes found that the cloze procedure, using lexical deletions of nouns and verbs, and synonym scoring criteria, was a valid way to measure factual comprehension of an entire story. She recommended that the cloze procedure be used to supplement standardized tests of comprehension.[40]

When children's cloze tests are scored, the results can be converted to reading levels based on Bormuth's table:[41]

Independent level	over 57 percent
Instructional level	44 percent to 56 percent
Frustration level	43 percent or less

The *cloze procedure* is an important means for assessing and teaching comprehension, though the latter purpose is not discussed here. For children to understand how to work with a cloze test is important. Several practice sessions should be provided in which the cloze is done orally, completed using familiar material, done in groups or pairs so that ideas may be shared, and discussed thoroughly after each exercise. Then children may be ready to complete passages as tests. Two sample exercises are provided here, one for first graders and one for children in seventh grade.

A. The first-grade teachers can provide their reading groups a kind of comprehension test using the cloze procedure by duplicating a story like the one following:

Directions: Read the sentences, decide which word is missing, and write it on the blank space.

Mother said, "Dick, will you go to the store for me?"
"Yes, _____ ," said _____ , "What do you want me to _____ ?"
"I need a loaf of _____ ," _____ Mother. _____ ran to the store.

He got a loaf of _____ .
Dick was soon _____ .
Mother said, "Thank you, _____ . You are a good _____ ."
Dick went out to _____ .

B. The following exercise is of seventh-grade difficulty:

Directions: In this exercise you will use context clues to think accurately and to supply the missing word to give the meaning. Read the selection all the way through before filling in the blanks. You will need only *one* word for each blank.

FROM THE CLUTCHES OF DEATH

In France, about seventy-five years ago, a desperate woman brought her young (1) _____ into the laboratory of Louis Pasteur. The boy (2) _____ been badly bitten by a mad dog, and a terrible death from (3) _____ was certain to follow.

Pasteur was a (4) _____ . He had saved the silk industry of France from (5) _____ by working out a method for prevention of two diseases of (6) _____ . He had invented a process for preserving (7) _____ by killing the bacteria contained in it and chilling it. And he (8) _____ discovered a vaccine which protected chickens against virulent (9) _____ of chicken cholera, and another which protected both animals and men from the feared (10) _____ of anthrax. Pasteur had also developed a (11) _____ which would usually prevent rabies in animals (12) _____ by mad dogs. But the vaccine had never been (13) _____ on man. It would be a daring experiment, but the (14) _____ had been bitten so badly that he would surely (15) _____ unless quick action were taken. Pasteur (16) _____ the risk. He tried his vaccine on a human being for the first (17) _____ . The boy lived! Thus, a rabies vaccine was (18) _____ to the world.

Today, Louis Pasteur (19) _____ considered one of the greatest scientists of all time. Some of his (20) _____ made possible the control of diseases that (21) _____ cost millions of lives.

B Key (Grade level 7.0)

1. *son,* boy, child
2. *had*
3. *rabies*
4. *scientist,* doctor
5. *ruin,* destruction, disaster, bankruptcy, failure, extinction
6. *silkworms*
7. *food,* milk
8. *had,* also, then, alone
9. *attacks,* cases
10. *disease,* sickness
11. *vaccine,* serum
12. *bitten*
13. *tried,* used, tested
14. *boy,* child, patient
15. *die,* perish
16. *took*
17. *time*
18. *given,* known, introduced, presented, shown
19. *is*
20. *experiments,* works, vaccines, discoveries
21. *had,* would('ve), might, could('ve), once, normally[42]

Anecdotal Records

A most useful teaching technique for gathering data about a reader over a period of time is the keeping of *anecdotal records*. The teacher should keep a notepad available to make notes about reading behaviors that are observed. Care must be taken to make records of actual events and behaviors and to avoid recording opinions and conclusions. If anecdotal records are kept faithfully over a period of time, growth can be identified, patterns of behaviors can be detected, the child's responses to various kinds of materials and techniques can be clarified, and language samples can be preserved for later study. These kinds of records can add information to the study of a reader's problems that formal testing cannot be expected to contribute or can serve to clarify responses given during testing that are puzzling to the teacher.

When anecdotal records are kept, date each notation and, to the extent possible, note the conditions under which the observation was made. In the busy life of the classroom, the teacher cannot trust that each incident and its surrounding circumstances will be clearly remembered.

Observation

Classroom life is immensely complex. The teacher is constantly responding to demands from many sources. It is a rare luxury to have time to observe carefully a single child over a period of several minutes. However, if such observation time can be planned and the teacher can be free to record exactly what a child does over time, especially as it relates to reading and writing activities, much useful information can be obtained, providing new insights into a child's difficulties, learning patterns, and avoidance strategies.[43]

The daily schedule will need to be examined in order to find short periods of time when the teacher may be an observer. Perhaps, if self-selection is a part of the daily schedule, the teacher can be freed to watch and make notes. Other possibilities are to observe while someone else is working with the children or to ask another person to be the observer while the teacher continues with the usual class schedule. However the time for observation may be arranged, the teacher will want to make sure that the information recorded is the actual behavior of the child, not an interpretation or an opinion.

Video Recording

In many schools the teacher will find that equipment is available to make *video recordings* of instructional events. These are valuable for study and analysis, since they preserve all forms of teacher-pupil interaction.

Reading Problems in Special Education

Table 6.2 is a summary chart that may be useful in helping teachers to recognize that some of the students with problems in reading in the regular classroom have concomitant problems that can be analyzed and perhaps alleviated by the department of special education.

Summary

The classroom teacher makes ongoing efforts to obtain information about the pupils with reading difficulties. This information could be categorized as pertaining to intelligence, health, interests, concepts about reading, social and psychological status, other language and reading data, and general information obtained through anecdotal records and observation of behavior. When causal factors are identified, the teacher should have the opportunity to discuss their ramifications with the school psychologist, school social worker, diagnostician, or principal.

For Further Reading

Baumann, James F. "Using Cloze Tests to Make Grouping and Placement Decisions." In *Reading Assessment: An Instructional Decision-Making Perspective,* 176–89. Columbus, Ohio: Merrill Publishing Co., 1988. These pages deal with issues and procedures related to determining reading levels and placing students based on cloze testing.

Harp, Bill. "When the Principal Asks: 'Why Are You Doing Piagetian Task Testing When You Have Given Basal Placement Tests?'" *Reading Teacher* 41 (November 1987): 212–14. The point is made that preoperational children are at risk, or at best, under great cognitive strain, when required to do formal reading, despite adequate basal placement scores.

Harris, Albert J., and Edward R. Sipay. "Correlates of Reading Disability 2: Neurological, Physiological, and Physical Factors." In *How to Increase Reading Ability.* 8th ed., 266–99. New York: Longman, Inc., 1985. Data on a variety of neurological disabilities and vision and hearing defects are provided.

Jalongo, Mary R. "Bibliotherapy: Literature to Promote Socioemotional Growth." *Reading Teacher* 36 (April 1983): 796–802. This article provides some of the research background for bibliotherapy along with detailed suggestions for using the technique with children.

Marshall, Nancy. "Using Story Grammar to Assess Reading Comprehension." *Reading Teacher* 36 (March 1983): 616–20. Here the teacher may find practical suggestions for using story grammar in reading assessment.

Marzano, Robert J., et al. "Observing and Interviewing." In *Reading Diagnosis and Instruction: Theory into Practice,* 65–69. Englewood Cliffs, N.J.: Prentice-Hall, 1987. Besides a discussion of interviewing and observation techniques, several suggested forms are provided for teacher use.

Mitchell, Sara. "The Interest Inventory: An Antacid to Negative Reading Attitudes." *New Mexico Journal of Reading* 2 (Spring 1982): 10–12. The writer provides techniques to prevent a "deadlock of opinions at the classroom door." Very practical suggestions are included.

TABLE 6.2. When Is a Reading Problem a Problem for the Department of Special Education?

Special Education	*The "In-Between Area" of Reading Problems that Are Problems in Special Education*	*Remedial Reading*
Areas of exceptionality	Reading problems in special education	Programs in remedial and corrective reading

The mentally retarded
The intellectually gifted
The physically handicapped
  Hearing handicapped
  Visually handicapped
  Crippled
  Convulsive disorders
  Speech problems
  Heart conditions
Emotionally disturbed
Brain damaged
Neurologically handicapped
	Teaching reading to the brain-injured child
	Teaching reading using sight-saving materials with visually handicapped
	Neurological problems
	  Strephosymbolia
	  Hyperactivity
	Motor handicapped
	  Cerebral palsied
	  Congenital anomalies
	
	Lacking abilities in *selected* primary mental abilities, i.e., the child with very low scores on block design and object assembly on WISC[a]
	Convulsive disorders:
	  Petit mal seizures may prevent consistent, sequential learning in regular classroom
		Ten to 15 percent of the school population exhibit reading problems in various forms from mild to severe.
		Two-thirds to three-fourths of all these cases can be provided for in regular classes and are not legitimately called *special education.*
		Many of the remaining one-fourth to one-third are included in the "in-between area" as outlined.

[a]A child may earn scaled scores on all other subtests indicating normal or above general intelligence and still earn only very low scores on using blocks to build designs from models or in putting puzzles together.

Novoa, Loriana M., and Philip J. Lazarus. "Test Review: Test of Language Development-Primary (TOLD-P)." *Reading Teacher* 41 (February 1988): 592–95. The reviewers give a generally positive report and detailed discussion of this test. Matters of standardization, reliability, and validity are addressed.

Pappas, Christine C., and Elga Brown. "Young Children Learning Story Discourse: Three Case Studies." *Elementary School Journal* 87 (March 1987): 455–66. These abstracts provide techniques for story analysis. An excellent bibliography accompanies the report.

Paramour, Sally, and Andrew Wilkinson. "The Disruption of the Probable: Narrative Writing in Children Seven to Thirteen." *Language Arts* 62 (April 1985): 391–403. Three groups of children, ages seven, ten, and thirteen, were asked to produce narratives. Their stories are analyzed in detail, and a taxonomy of story development is provided.

Pertz, Doris L., and Lillian R. Putnam. "An Examination of the Relationship between Nutrition and Learning." *Reading Teacher* 35 (March 1982): 702–6. The article points out both direct and indirect relationships between diet and learning, citing several studies. There is an extended bibliography.

Searls, Evelyn F. *How to Use WISC-R Scores in Reading/Learning Disability Diagnosis.* Newark, Del.: International Reading Association, 1985. This IRA publication is rich with information about the WISC-R. It describes each subtest along with its interpretation and relationship to reading. WISC-R patterns and profiles are provided and discussed.

Taylor, Barbara, Larry Harris, and P. David Pearson. "Assessing Motivation to Read." In *Reading Difficulties: Instruction and Assessment,* 57–69. New York: Random House, 1988. A clear distinction between assessing attitudes and assessing student interests is made. The material includes models of forms.

Notes

1. Sandra McCormick, *Remedial and Clinical Reading Instruction* (Columbus, Ohio: Merrill Publishing Co., 1987), 59.
2. *Federal Register,* 29 December, 1977.
3. Eldon Ekwall and James Shanker, *Diagnosis and Remediation of the Disabled Reader,* 2d ed. (Boston: Allyn and Bacon, 1983), 252.
4. Guy L. Bond et al., *Reading Difficulties: Their Diagnosis and Correction,* 6th ed. (New York: Prentice-Hall, 1989), 39.
5. Louis M. Terman and Maude Merrill, *Stanford-Binet Scales,* rev. form (Boston: Houghton Mifflin Co., 1960); David Wechsler, *Wechsler-Bellevue Intelligence Scale for Children* (New York: Psychological Corp., 1974).
6. Roger Farr, "Reading Tests and Teachers: Use of Tests in Evaluation," in *Reading Diagnosis and Evaluation,* ed. Dorothy L. DeBoer (Newark, Del.: International Reading Association, 1970), 52.
7. *System of Multicultural Pluralistic Assessment* (New York: Psychological Corp., 1978).
8. Guy L. Bond and Leo J. Brueckner, *The Diagnosis and Treatment of Learning Difficulties* (New York: Appleton-Century-Crofts, 1955), 34.
9. R. M. Goldman, M. Friscoe, and R. W. Woodcock, *Goldman-Friscoe-Woodcock Test of Auditory Discrimination* (Circle Pines, Minn.: American Guidance Service, 1970).
10. Karen L. Anderson, "Does the Low Achiever in Your Classroom Have Fluctuating Hearing Loss?" *New Mexico Journal of Reading* 7 (Fall 1986): 5–9.
11. *Keystone Telebinocular Visual Survey,* Revised 1974 (Keystone View Division, Mast Development Co., 2210 E. 12th St., Davenport, Iowa).
12. *The Orthorater* (Rochester, N.Y.: Bausch and Lomb Optical Co.).
13. T. H. Eames, *Eames Eye Test* (Yonkers, N.Y.: World Book Co., 1941).
14. Arleen L. Olson, "An Experimental Study of the Relationship between Color Blindness and Reading Achievement in the First Grade" (Master's thesis, University of New Mexico, 1963), 58, 68–69.
15. Stanley Espinda, "Color Vision Deficiency: A Learning Disability," *Journal of Learning Disabilities* 61 (March 1973): 42–45.
16. G. B. Schiffman, *The Effect of Color Blindness upon Achievement of Elementary School Males,* Experimental Research Series Report No. 106 (Towson, Md.: Board of Education, 1963).
17. Zelda Maggart, "Color Blindness and Reading," *New Mexico Journal of Reading* 3 (Fall 1983): 18–21.
18. Julian B. Potter, *Incomplete Sentences Blank,* College Form. Copyright 1950, The Psychological Corporation, New York. All Rights Reserved. Reproduced by Permission.
19. Ibid., 1.

20. Marie Clay, *The Early Detection of Reading Difficulties: A Diagnostic Survey with Recovery Procedures,* 3d ed. (Auckland, New Zealand: Heinemann Educational Books, 1985); Bess Altwerger and Yetta Goodman, "Print Awareness in Preschool Children: A Working Paper," a study of the development of literacy in preschool children (Tucson: University of Arizona, Program in Language and Literacy, Arizona Center for Research and Development, June, 1981); and Carolyn Burke in *Reading Comprehension: An Instructional Videotape Service Resource Guide,* ed. B. F. Farr and D. J. Strickler (Bloomington, Ind.: Indiana University Press, 1980), 71.

21. Eldon E. Ekwall and James L. Shanker, "Diagnosis and Remediation through the Use of Interviews," in *Diagnosis and Remediation of the Disabled Reader,* 2d ed. (Boston: Allyn and Bacon, 1983), 412–42.

22. Ruth Strickland, *Language Arts in the Elementary School* (Boston: D.C. Heath, 1957), 136.

23. Caroline Schrodes, "Bibliotherapy: An Application of Psychoanalytic Theory." *American Imago* 17 (Fall 1960): 311–19.

24. R. M. Tews, "Introduction," *Library Trends* 11 (October 1962): 97–105.

25. Margaret Keating, "The Boy of Odense," in *Stories to Remember,* Classmate Edition, ed. Guy L. Bond and Marie C. Cuddy (Chicago: Lyons and Carnahan, 1953), 37–55.

26. Joseph George Cohen and Will Scarlet, "The Wizard of Menlo Park," in *Teen Age Tales,* Book 1, 3d ed., ed. Ruth Strang and Ralph Roberts (Boston: D.C. Heath, 1966), 93–102.

27. Irmengarde Eberle, "Penicillin—the Life Saver," in *Doorways to Discovery,* ed. David Russell and Mabel Snedaker (Boston: Ginn and Co., 1956), 340–48; idem, "Marie Curie," ibid., 167–73.

28. Florence G. Roswell and Gladys Natchez, *Reading Disability: A Human Approach to Learning,* 3d ed. (New York: Basic Books, 1977), 68–76.

29. Karel Rose, *Teaching Language Arts to Children* (New York: Harcourt Brace Jovanovich, Inc., 1982), 245.

30. Eileen Tway, ed., *Reading Ladders to Human Relations* (Urbana, Ill.: NCTE, 1981).

31. Sharon S. Dreyer, *The Bookfinder: A Guide to Children's Literature about the Needs and Problems of Youth Aged 2–15* (Circle Pines, Minn.: American Guidance Service, 1977, 1981).

32. Stories collected by Richard VanDongen, Carol Westby, and Zelda Maggart, University of New Mexico, 1985.

33. For further ideas and suggestions, see M. Dianne Bergenske, "The Missing Link in Narrative Story Mapping," *Reading Teacher* 41 (December 1987): 333–35; and Evelyn T. Cudd and Leslie L. Roberts, "Using Story Frames to Develop Reading Comprehension in a 1st Grade Classroom," *Reading Teacher* 41 (October 1987): 74–79.

34. Peter B. Mosenthal, Randie L. Davidson-Mosenthal, and Antonia K. Collela, "Two Determinants of Teachers' Holistic Scoring: Prior Knowledge and Ideology Type," *Elementary School Journal* 88 (September 1987): 39–49.

35. W. W. Weaver and A. J. Kingston, "A Factor Analysis of Cloze Procedure and Other Measures of Reading and Language Ability," *Journal of Communication* 13 (1963): 253.

36. Wesley J. Schneyer, "Use of the Cloze Procedure for Improving Reading Comprehension," *Reading Teacher* 19 (December 1965): 174.

37. Thomas C. Potter, "Readability and Reading Comprehension," in *A Taxonomy of Cloze Research* (Englewood, Calif.: Southwest Regional Laboratory for Educational Research and Development, 1968), 39–40.

38. Wilson L. Taylor, "Cloze Readability Scores as Indices of Individual Differences in Comprehension and Aptitude," *Journal of Applied Psychology* 16 (February 1957): 19.

39. John Bormuth, "Cloze as a Measure of Readability," in *Reading as an Intellectual Activity*, IRA Conference Report No. 8 (1963), 134.
40. Marian Tonjes, "Evaluation of Comprehension and Vocabulary Gains of Tenth Grade Students Enrolled in a Developmental Reading Program" (Master's thesis, University of New Mexico, 1969), 30–40.
41. J. R. Bormuth, "The Cloze Readability Procedure," in *Readability in 1968*, ed. J. R. Bormuth, (Champaign, Ill.: NCTE, 1968).
42. Tonjes, "Evaluation of Comprehension," 61, 68.
43. Courtney B. Cazden, "Contexts for Literacy: In the Mind and in the Classroom," *Journal of Reading Behavior* 14, no. 4 (1982): 413–28.

7
Planning Work with the Underachieving Child

Vocabulary

corrective instruction
basal approach
systems approach
Wisconsin Design
theme approach
web
readability
Fry Readability Graph
Raygor Readability
    Estimator
lesson plan
behavioral objectives
evaluation of learning
high-interest, low-
    vocabulary books
trade books
big books
predictable books
picture books
wordless picture books
drill
record keeping

Questions

1. What advantages and what disadvantages do you see for using the basal approach to corrective instruction? The systems approach? (**Inference**)
2. What do you see as potential strengths and weaknesses of a theme approach to corrective reading? (**Inference**)
3. What information is needed if the teacher is to plan an effective corrective program using a theme? (**Recall**)
4. Explain how to use the Fry Readability Graph. (**Recall**)
5. Compare big books and predictable books. (**Critical**)
6. What will be the role of drill in your classroom? (**Application**)

Introduction

If the teachers administer informal tests as presented in chapters 3 and 4, they will have determined the present functional levels of reading of the disabled readers. The cardinal principle in helping these students is to go back to where they are in learning sequential, developmental strategies and skills. Sufficiently easy levels must have been identified in order to establish security and build confidence. The students' work of the entire day must be planned at this level.

The teachers will gain additional information about their disabled readers by utilizing data from a variety of formal tests, making sure that the students are enjoying the best health possible, assessing oral language and written language abilities, gaining insights into the students' attitudes toward themselves and others, finding out the children's interests and goals, and obtaining knowledge of the social organization of the classroom. Finally, the teacher will have established contact with the parents of the children to facilitate the sharing of information, to provide the parents with continuing information about how children grow and learn, and to provide the children with learning opportunities whether at school or at home.

Managing Corrective Instruction

Managing *corrective instruction* in classrooms is dependent on the teachers' abilities and willingness to convince the students that the work that they are going to do is important, worthwhile, and relevant. The teachers must create an atmosphere that values learning and recognizes the integrity of every child. Teacher attitudes and classroom climate are basic ingredients in managing this learning situation effectively. The children must sense that *it is all right to be different* because every child in each classroom *is* different. Many interesting plans and activities as well as individual tasks *must* teach the child that all children in *one* classroom do not need to do the *same* things in the *same* amount of time in the *same* way.

Basal Approach to Corrective Instruction

If the basic principles of corrective instruction are followed, the great majority of underachievers will improve their reading ability and their attitudes toward self, reading, and others under the tutelage of their teachers. There are many approaches for accomplishing these important tasks. Typically, the corrective work would be developmental and would revolve around basal readers, workbooks, work sheets, and other materials such as tutorial software for the microcomputer that would provide direct instruction on the skills and subskills of reading at the needed levels. The corrective readers would complete the same kinds of assignments as children making expected progress in the classrooms. The lessons would simply be taught at lower levels in order to meet the instructional-level requirements of the students. The detailed steps of the directed reading lesson are provided in appendix D.

The basal materials chosen should be a series not used in any previous grade for regular group instruction. The graded series of readers provides the teacher with well-planned, sequentially developed materials for building all the missing word-recognition skills. If the teacher's demeanor has been persuasive and optimistic, and the child is convinced that he or she is going to learn to read, beginning at the instructional level in a series of readers and making progress as fast as possible may be the most satisfactory way for the busy classroom teacher to proceed. Much excellent, usable material is available to the teacher in the teacher's manuals and the workbooks that accompany the readers.

Teachers need sources of reading material that offer a controlled vocabulary load and that are of interest to older children. With these sources, when motivation based on interest is present, limited reading power will not preclude getting the material read. Appendix B will be useful for finding materials.

Publishing companies make detailed teacher's manuals available for their texts. These manuals should be studied carefully when the corresponding reader is being taught. Teacher's manuals are as completely detailed as manuals of directions that explain how to put a toy together or how to do a do-it-yourself job. While teacher's manuals need not be adhered to inflexibly, they contain a myriad of suggestions for teaching the directed reading lesson with all its follow-up. These manuals contain a great deal of information for the teacher about the philosophy of the reading series—the "why" of the methodology employed. They provide many suggestions to the teacher for taking care of individual differences within groups and for extra teaching of any missing skills. Building concepts is provided for in the sequential development of sight vocabulary and through suggestions for teaching what a particular word means in a stated context.

Systems Approach to Corrective Instruction

Instead of using the basal approach, teachers might choose a *systems approach* to the mastery of skills and subskills. Checklists of reading skills to be mastered to ensure that all students develop mature reading habits became commonplace during the 1970s. Administrators sometimes hold high hopes that if teachers teach and test all the skills sufficiently, the reading deficiencies in their schools will somehow be removed. Because of this, long lists of skills, outlined in minutely detailed subskills, are prepared so that teachers can complete checklists of all the skills mastered, those taught but not mastered, and those not yet learned. There are many educators who would question whether a sequenced hierarchy of skills exists that can be defended as the one most likely to produce successful readers. Even more educators seriously question the value of placing relentless effort on mastering subskills at the expense of many other facets of the total reading program. For these reasons, there may be some doubt as to the value of identifying 275 skills or 435 skills that must be taught to complete a commercial reading system.

Diagnostic prescriptive reading programs designed to teach the necessary skills for competent reading appeared in some profusion on the market in the 1960s and 1970s. They provided preassessment tests, lessons to teach to all students' weaknesses, as well as posttests. These tests were criterion-referenced since they were specifically designed to measure the success of teaching specific subject matter.

Fairly detailed record keeping will be necessary if students are to progress through series of exercises at individual rates. Some of the programs available to teach skills include:

1. *Criterion Reading* (New York: Random House). This program develops competency in many reading skills.
2. *Fountain Valley Teacher Support System in Reading* (Huntington Beach, Calif.: Richard L. Zweig Associates). This program has 77 tests on tapes and measures 277 skills.
3. *Prescriptive Reading Inventory* (Monterey, Calif.: CTB/McGraw-Hill). This program develops competency in 150 reading skills.
4. *The Wisconsin Design for Reading Skill Development* (Minneapolis, Minn.: Interpretive Scoring Systems).

The Wisconsin Design for Reading Skill Development states as its purposes: (1) to identify and describe behaviorally the skills that appear to be essential to competence in reading, (2) to assess individual pupil's skill development status, (3) to manage instruction of children with different skill development needs, and (4) to monitor each pupil's progress. The program goes on to say that teachers must have an organized approach to teaching if they are to guide effectively children's development of reading skills. The program provides "a skill-centered base for an elementary school reading program, means for focusing on individual's skill development, and a management system for both pupils and instructional materials."[1]

The four major components of the *Wisconsin Design* are: (1) word attack; (2) comprehension; (3) study skills; and (4) self-directed, interpretive, and creative reading. The six steps in its use are outlined for teachers as: (1) prepare, (2) pretest, (3) record, (4) instruct, (5) posttest, and (6) report/reward. The record card for the comprehension skills for all levels A through G is reproduced in figure 7.1. While the record card reproduced shows spaces for scoring exercises A1 through D6, the reverse side of the card provides scoring space for E1 through G8.

Theme Approach to Corrective Reading

Most teachers have an understanding of the management of a developmental basal reader program, and most systems approaches are unique but quite specific in their organization and management. In this chapter a theme approach capitalizing on the interests, values, and needs of the students will be presented. A further reason for emphasizing the theme approach to corrective instruction is that many children who are disabled readers have unpleasant memories of basal materials and need fresh starts to learning.

Getting Ready

Jim Stein was planning his reading program for his fourth-grade classroom in a small city. He knew that he would have basal readers in his classroom with the accompanying workbooks and skill sheets. However, his principal indicated that she would allow each teacher to decide how the basal materials would be used. Jim had been given his class

WISCONSIN DESIGN FOR READING SKILL DEVELOPMENT

© 1977 - The Board of Regents of the
University of Wisconsin System

COMPREHENSION
KEY TO STRANDS

W — Word Parts   T — Central Thought

C — Context   R — Relationships/
                                        Conclusions
D — Detail
                                   S — Sequence
P — Paraphrase

Circle: Mark (or punch) for skill
         application

Hole: Notch for 80% or above
        performance

> Notch when all skills applied

PC: Performance Category

NOTE: Skill marked **i** is assessed
       individually

LEVEL A:

Topic: Pictures
Relationships
First/Last Event

APPLIED All Level A Skills

LEVEL B:

- 1 D — Detail
- 2 T — Topic: With Organizer
- 3 R — Outcomes
- 4 S — Before
- 5 S — After

APPLIED All Level B Skills

LEVEL C:

- 1 D — Detail: Negatives
- 2 P — Paraphrase: Negatives
- 3 T — Topic: Without Organizer
- 4 R — Conclusions: One Relationship
- 5 S — Before/After

APPLIED All Level C Skills

LEVEL D:

- 1 C — Direct Clues
- 2 D — Detail: Passives
- 3 P — Paraphrase: Passives
- 4 T — Topic: Relevant Information
- 5 R — Cause-Effect
- 6 S — Calendar Markers

APPLIED All Level D Skills

WISCONSIN DESIGN FOR READING SKILL DEVELOPMENT

PUPIL NAME

SCHOOL   UNIT/GRADE

SKILLS	BRK-IN %C	PC	DATE	POST %C	PC	DATE
A1						
A2						
A3						
B1						
B2						
B3						
B4						
B5						
C1						
C2						
C3						
C4						
C5						
D1						
D2						
D3						
D4						
D5						
D6						

MCBEE® SYSTEMS · ATHENS, OHIO 250913X

APPLIED All Level G Skills

LEVEL G:

- 8 S — Implied/Stated Events
- 7 R — Conclusions: Modification (i)
- 6 R — Conclusions: Supported/Unsupported
- 5 T — Central Thought: Generation
- 4 P — Paraphrase: Restatements
- 3 C — Uncommon Meanings
- 2 W — Word Roots
- 1 W — Combining Forms

APPLIED All Level F Skills

LEVEL F:

- 6 S — Implicit Cues
- 5 R — Conclusions: Indirect Relationships
- 4 T — Central Thought: Without Organizer
- 3 P — Paraphrase: Prepositions
- 2 C — Indirect Clues: Application
- 1 W — Suffixes

LEVEL E:

W	C	D	P	T	R	S
1	2	3	4	5	6	7

- Prefixes
- Direct Clues: Application
- Detail: Clauses
- Paraphrase: Complex Sentences
- Central Thought: With Organizer
- Conclusions: Direct Relationships
- Explicit Cues

APPLIED All Level E Skills

Figure 7.1. Record card for the *Wisconsin Design for Reading Skill Comprehension* list, indicating the estimated reading level of each student. Four children appeared to be reading well below grade level. They were Rosie, whose instructional level was judged to be at second-reader level; Teddie, with an instructional level of easy first-reader material, Jorge, whose instructional level was thought to be second reader; and Evelyn, who was considered to be a nonreader.

Diagnosis

Jim decided to adopt a theme approach for working with these four children. This approach would allow him to integrate the language arts with other areas of the curriculum. He would also be able to utilize the interests of the children, which would hopefully stimulate their motivation to read and write. He planned to extend the approach to the whole class of twenty-seven students by the beginning of the second semester. Once all the children were working on themes, there would be less emphasis on ability groups in the classroom.

When school began, all the children were asked to fill out an interest inventory and an Incomplete Sentences Blank. Anyone who wished help with the task could request that Mr. Stein read the questions and sentence starters and record the answers. Teddie, Jorge, and Evelyn requested and received his help. Over the first few days of school, each child in the class wrote a story; participated in the oral reading of several stories (each succeeding one of greater difficulty); completed one to three cloze tests, depending on when the frustration level was reached; identified the child each would most like to work with on a project; completed the informal reading inventory during small blocks of free time; and told a story based on an interesting picture shared by the teacher. After Mr. Stein had given careful directions about how the task was to be done, each child recorded his or her story on a cassette tape. The ten children about whom the teacher had the greatest concerns completed the San Diego Quick Assessment for comparative data. Jim then supplemented the test results that he had gathered with frequent anecdotal records of children's language, behaviors, choices, and strategies for completing tasks.

When the children were not present, Jim studied the cumulative folders to obtain standardized test data for each child. He also noted the IQ scores of those students who had had individual intelligence tests; only eight had such scores. He also searched the records for any evidence of health problems or comments from previous teachers that might aid in planning the current year.

Within the first two weeks of school, Jim managed to talk at least briefly with all of the parents or guardians of the children except for three who were away on personal or business matters and one who could not be contacted. Some of the conversations were held when parents came to deliver or pick up their children; others were telephone calls made after school hours.

At the end of three weeks, Jim had a large amount of information on each child in the room. He developed a form that he thought would allow him to organize the information for rapid retrieval when he needed it for planning lessons. Jim's form and the information he gathered on Rosie, Teddie, Jorge, and Evelyn are presented in figures 7.2 and 7.3.

Pupil's Name Rosie K._____ Date 9/14/_____
READING TESTS

IRI- Oral: Word Recognition 3rd_____ Comprehension 2nd_____

IRI- Silent: Comprehension 2nd_____ } Instructional level
IRI- Capacity Level 4th_____ } 2nd on San Diego

Standardized Tests: CTBS 3.1 grade score, 3rd stanine
end of → 3rd gr. Other 1_____

Reading Interview Thinks you must not skip words; reading is words.
Cloze Test Instructional level - 1st_____

Informal reading from reading series (instructional level)

  Book used Toothless Dragon 1² Result Independent

  Book used Tricky Troll 2¹ Result Instructional

  Book used Whispering Ghosts 3¹ Result Frustration

Evaluation of writing sample Sentences repetitive - "I like school. I like reading," etc. No punctuation.

Oral language: Anecdotal information Has not asked me a question. Vocabulary appears limited - no interesting adjectives - often refers to "that thing".
Story telling Parts of story are there, but they are unconnected. Little evaluative language.
ADDITIONAL CASE HISTORY INFORMATION

Intelligence No record Interest inventory (Special interests)
_____ monsters
Sociogram Chose Ann, animals - especially big ones
a popular girl.
Health factors: Personality data Responses suggest

  Vision corrected - wears she is jealous of older sisters.
  glasses
  Hearing OK_____ Says she likes to read.

  Neurological } no Parent comments Mother says she
  record of never reads at home. Mother
  Endocrine } problem wants ways to help her.

Comments of Teachers
1st - hard worker, Anecdotal information Stays in at
but slow to read recess when I let her to
2nd - comprehension problems clean her desk. Likes art.

Figure 7.2. Summaries of data on Rosie and Teddie

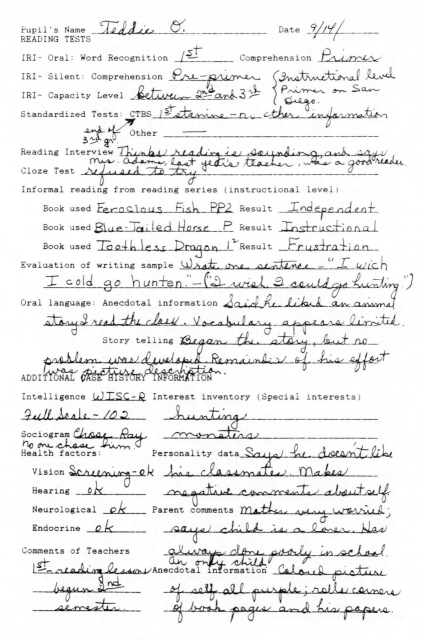

Pupil's Name *Teddie O.* _____ Date *9/14/* ____
READING TESTS

IRI- Oral: Word Recognition *1st* ____ Comprehension *Primer*

IRI- Silent: Comprehension *Pre-primer* { *Instructional level*

IRI- Capacity Level *Between 2nd and 3rd* { *Primer on San Diego.*

Standardized Tests: CTBS *1st stanine - no other information*

end of 3rd gr. Other _____

Reading Interview *Thinks reading is sounding, and says Mrs. Adams, last year's teacher, was a good reader.*

Cloze Test *refused to try* _____

Informal reading from reading series (instructional level)

    Book used *Ferocious Fish PP2* Result *Independent*

    Book used *Blue-Tailed Horse P* Result *Instructional*

    Book used *Toothless Dragon 1²* Result *Frustration*

Evaluation of writing sample *Wrote one sentence - "I wich I cold go hunten" - ("I wish I could go hunting.")*

Oral language: Anecdotal information *Said he liked an animal story I read the class. Vocabulary appears limited.*

    Story telling *Began the story, but no problem was developed. Remainder of his effort was picture description.*

ADDITIONAL CASE HISTORY INFORMATION

Intelligence *WISC-R* Interest inventory (Special interests)

Full Scale - 102   *hunting* _____

Sociogram *Chose Ray*   *monsters* _____
No one chose him

Health factors: Personality data *Says he doesn't like*

    Vision *Screening-ok*   *his classmates. Makes*

    Hearing *ok*   *negative comments about self.*

    Neurological *ok* Parent comments *Mother very worried;*

    Endocrine *ok*   *says child is a loner. Has*

Comments of Teachers   *always done poorly in school.*
                        An only child
1st reading lessons Anecdotal information *Colored picture*
begun 2nd   *of self all purple; rolls corners*
semester   *of book pages and his papers.*

Figure 7.2. Continued

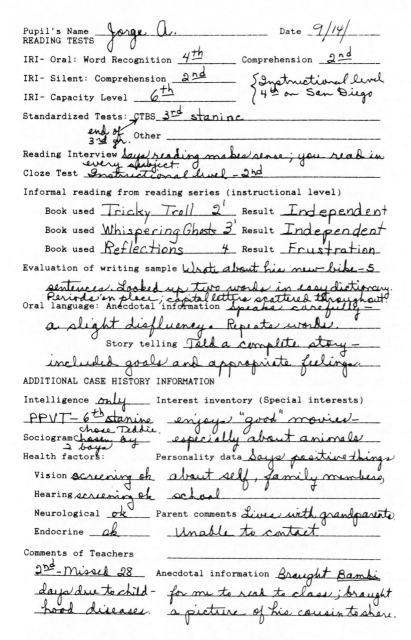

Pupil's Name _Jorge A._____ Date _9/14/___
READING TESTS

IRI- Oral: Word Recognition _4th_____ Comprehension _2nd____

IRI- Silent: Comprehension _2nd_____ } Instructional level
IRI- Capacity Level _6th_____ } 4th on San Diego

Standardized Tests: CTBS _3rd stanine_____
            end of
            3rd gr. Other _____

Reading Interview _Says reading makes sense; you read in_
Cloze Test _every subject._
            _Instructional level - 2nd_____

Informal reading from reading series (instructional level)

　　Book used _Tricky Troll 2'_ Result _Independent_

　　Book used _Whispering Ghosts 3'_ Result _Independent_

　　Book used _Reflections   4_ Result _Frustration_

Evaluation of writing sample _Wrote about his new bike - 5_
sentences. Looked up two words in easy dictionary.
Periods in place; capital letters scattered throughout.
Oral language: Anecdotal information _Speaks carefully -_
a slight disfluency. Repeats words.

　　　　Story telling _Told a complete story -_
included goals and appropriate feelings.

ADDITIONAL CASE HISTORY INFORMATION

Intelligence _only___ Interest inventory (Special interests)
PPVT - 6th stanine _enjoys "good" movies -_
　　　chose Teddie.
Sociogram _chosen by_ _especially about animals_
　　　2 boys
Health factors:　　Personality data _Says positive things_
　Vision _screening ok_ _about self, family members,_
　Hearing _screening ok_ _school_
　Neurological _ok___ Parent comments _Lives with grandparents_
　Endocrine _ok___ _Unable to contact_

Comments of Teachers _____
　2nd - Missed 28 Anecdotal information _Brought Bambi_
　days due to child- _for me to read to class; brought_
　hood diseases. _a picture of his cousin to share._

Figure 7.3. Summaries of data on Jorge and Evelyn

Pupil's Name _Evelyn N._____ Date _9/14/___
READING TESTS

IRI- Oral: Word Recognition ___—___   Comprehension ___—___

IRI- Silent: Comprehension ___—___   *Unable to read easiest*

IRI- Capacity Level _2nd_____   *pg. on IRI. Named 5*
words on pre-primer

Standardized Tests: CTBS _1st stanine_   *list on SDQ A*

end of 3rd gr. Other _____

Reading Interview _Says reading is what you do in school._
many "I don't knows"

Cloze Test _Couldn't complete_____

Informal reading from reading series (instructional level)

    Book used _Runaway Monkey PP!_ Result _Frustration_

    Book used _____ Result _____

    Book used _____ Result _____

Evaluation of writing sample _Wrote first and last names;_
wrote letters in mixed order when I dictated

Oral language: Anecdotal information _Mixes Spanish and_
English words in conversation. Often says, "What
do you say?" when searching for a word.
    Story telling _Named objects in picture_

_____

ADDITIONAL CASE HISTORY INFORMATION

Intelligence _No scores available_ Interest inventory (Special interests)

Sociogram _Chose Rosie. Not chosen_ _Likes caring for little brother._
Likes monster shows on TV

Health factors: Personality data _Says she doesn't know_

    Vision _has glasses_ _how to read because people will_

    Hearing _slight loss in L. ear_ _laugh at her. She's ashamed of glasses._

    Neurological _OK_ Parent comments _Mother has trouble_

    Endocrine _OK_ _getting her to wear glasses_

Comments of Teachers _Wants special help for her reading._

2nd - moved to this school mid-year. Anecdotal information _Draws pictures_
Read one pre-primer. _of monsters. Selects picture_
books for SSR

Figure 7.3. Continued

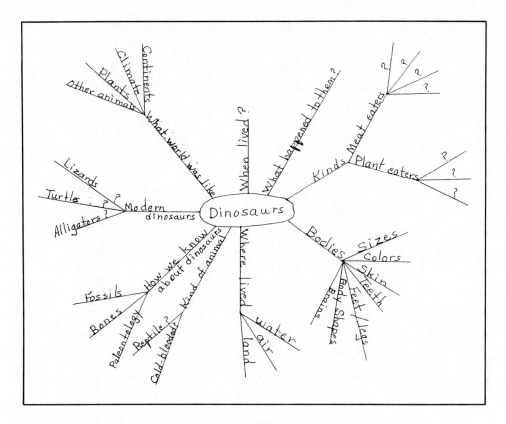

Figure 7.4. Web prepared by teacher and children

Planning with the Children Based on Diagnostic Information

Mr. Stein studied the information that he had obtained on Rosie, Teddie, Jorge, and Evelyn, and met with them early the next week. He commented that all four children indicated that they were interested in monsters. (The theme could center around any topic of child interest that the teacher felt comfortable in presenting.) He mentioned that dinosaurs were monsters of long ago. Perhaps they would like to start the year by learning about the huge beasts. The children greeted the idea enthusiastically. The teacher placed a large sheet of newsprint on the table, and as the children mentioned ideas about dinosaurs, he formed a *web* that they would use as a reference throughout the study. When many ideas had been mentioned and recorded, Mr. Stein drew a box around the web. He invited the children to think of ways of finding out about various aspects of dinosaurs or activities that they could do related to the theme. The original web and the framed web with activity suggestions around the edge may be found in figures 7.4 and 7.5. After the children had gone home, the teacher reproduced the

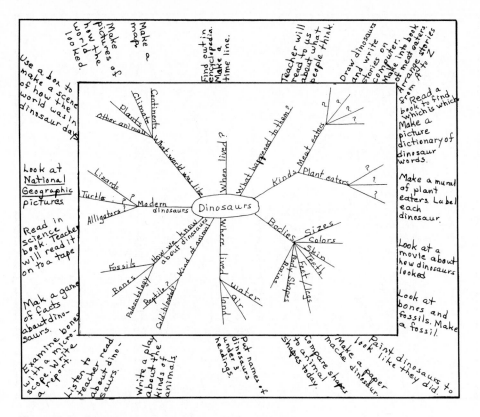

Figure 7.5. Activities suggested to accompany web

completed web and added still another frame around the outer edge. In this space he noted strategies and skills that each of the four children could learn in carrying out the activities. To identify the needed strategies and skills, he referred to his record sheets on the four children, to other detailed notes he had made, and to the basal manuals for the reading levels of each of the children. He would not be able to meet all of their needs during the development of this one theme, but there would be several other themes during the course of the year in which language arts strategies and skills could be developed and practiced. Figure 7.6 shows the completed web that served as Jim Stein's guide for the theme on dinosaurs.

Locating Materials for the Theme

Over the next days, Mr. Stein gathered a wide variety of materials that his four students might be able to use in their study of dinosaurs. He searched his own materials collection for any usable resources. The librarian located many books, filmstrips, pictures, and models for the children. A simple word-processing program was brought

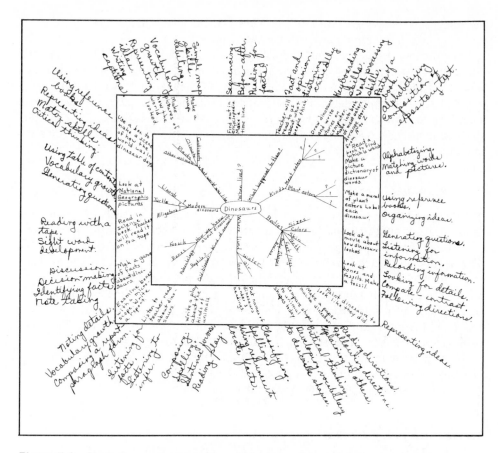

Figure 7.6. Strategies and skills that could be learned from the dinosaur theme

into the classroom so that the children could write stories and books that looked "professional." Mr. Stein was quite aware of the low reading levels of the four children. Many of the assembled materials were very easy to read. Some were more difficult, and they would be read to the children. Some of the more difficult books had excellent illustrations that the children could use well. Jim had time to read onto a tape three of the more valuable books that were too difficult for the children to read. The teacher also located a rock hound in the community who had a collection of dinosaur bones and fossil footprints that he would be pleased to explain and share with the children.

Estimating Readability of Materials

Mr. Stein needed a tool to help him *estimate* the difficulty of the materials he selected for the four children. He decided to apply a *readability* formula to his selections, keeping in mind the strengths and limitations of such formulas. A readability formula is based on a limited number of text characteristics, often the length of sentences, the number of syllables in words, and rare words in the passage to be evaluated. The formula provides no help in determining how easy the reading will be for an individual reader whose prior knowledge, command of the language of the text, and motivation for reading are unspecified. Keeping these limitations in mind, the teacher decided that a formula would provide useful insights about the difficulty of the materials that he was considering for use with the children. He also planned to attend to the general coherence and clarity of the texts as further checks on readability. After some consideration, Mr. Stein decided to utilize either the *Fry Readability Graph* or the *Raygor Readability Estimator.*

Fry's Readability Graph

By applying the easy-to-use formula in figure 7.7 to any book, teachers can find the book's level of difficulty, and thus not be limited to those books listed in appendix B.

In using Fry's graph (figure 7.7) for *estimating* readability, one need only count the total number of syllables in one hundred running words in each of three passages. Then count the number of sentences in the same passages and compute the average for the three. The average number of syllables in one hundred words and the average number of sentences in one hundred words provide the necessary information for an entry from the *x* and the *y* axes to find a point located in one of the grade-level areas. This is an estimate of the reader level or level of difficulty of that particular book.

If the point obtained falls in the gray area on the graph, the level of difficulty of that specific passage is probably not measured well by this graph.

Following are examples of the use of the graph:

Book Title	Syllables per 100 Words	Sentences per 100 Words	Reader Level
Squanto and the Pilgrims	125	15	
	116	13	
	137	13	
AVERAGE	126	13.5	Second grade
Danger Below	124	11	
(*Deep Sea Adventures Series*)	127	8	
	121	8	
AVERAGE	124	9	Fourth grade
The Mystery of Morgan Castle	124	12	
	132	14	
	133	11	
AVERAGE	130	12	Third grade

FRY'S READABILITY GRAPH

EXTENDED THROUGH PREPRIMER LEVEL

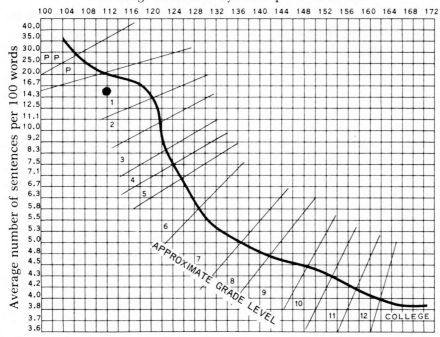

Figure 7.7. Fry's Readability Graph extended through preprimer level. From George Maginnis, "The Reading Graph and Informal Reading Inventories," *Reading Teacher* 22 (March 1969): 518.

This method of estimating readability is easily applied and should be very helpful to teachers who do not have at hand information about the level of difficulty of available books.

Raygor Readability Estimator

Raygor devised a readability estimate using a graph like the Fry Readability Graph, but substituting the number of words of six or more letters (long words) instead of the number of syllables.[2]

The directions for the use of the Raygor Estimator are:

1. Use three one-hundred-word passages.
2. Count the number of sentences in each passage, estimating to the nearest tenth.
3. Count the words of six or more letters in each passage.
4. Find the arithmetic average of the three counts for both number of sentences and number of long words.
5. Plot the point on the graph.

Baldwin and Kaufman have reproduced the graph in the *Journal of Reading* in their article reporting on the validity of the Raygor Estimator.[3]

A slide rule type of estimate maker is available for quickly assessing reading grade levels from Twin Oaks Publishing Co., Inc., 134 Mason Street, Rehoboth, Massachusetts 02769.

One may also obtain microcomputer software for determining readability. Such software programs measure only the surface features of text in the same way that hand-done readability checks do. The user must also take time to enter the text onto a disk, which can be time consuming.

Lesson Planning

As Jim Stein planned with the children the activities that they would do, he was faced with the school requirement that he have prepared *lesson plans* at all times. He realized that it would be difficult to prepare traditional lesson plans, although at times he might be able to use plans for the directed reading lesson found in appendix D of this text. After some study, he devised a plan that would meet the needs of the children and yet accommodate his required accountability to the principal.

Each lesson needed clearly stated objectives. The teacher had to state in the lesson plan what the student would do and the level of performance that the teacher would expect as a measure of achievement. Goals that are measurable in terms of student behavior are called *behavioral objectives.* For example, if Evelyn were to dictate a story about two dinosaurs to a sixth grader who came to help Mr. Stein, she might be expected to compose six sentences that would describe an introduction, a problem to be resolved, and a conclusion. If she composed the story of six sentences with the necessary parts, she would be judged to have met the objective.

A behavioral objective meets three criteria: (1) it indicates what the learner will do; (2) it states how the achievement of the objective will be measured; and (3) it establishes the minimum level of acceptable performance. Contrast the following nonbehavioral objectives with behavioral ones:

Nonbehavioral Objectives	*Behavioral Objectives*
1. Make a list of several pairs of words usually associated together: cow-calf; cup-saucer; shirt-tie.	1. When the teacher gives one of a pair of associated words, the student will be able to respond *every time* with the other word of the pair: knife-fork.
2. Arrange the list of given events in the sequence in which they appeared in the story.	2. After the story has been read, the five events will be presented to the students in a mixed-up order, and each student will number them in the correct order in which they appeared in the story.

The daily lesson plan *may* include:

1. An objective for the lesson, stated behaviorally.
2. Directed reading at the independent or instructional levels.
3. A writing experience in which the child organizes his or her thoughts in print, edits earlier writing, or prepares earlier writing to be read by others.
4. Work on a strategy or skill that may be embedded in an oral language, reading, or writing activity.
5. Specific materials to be used.
6. The conditions under which the learning will take place.
7. An evaluation of the success of the lesson; other pertinent comments about the child and the lesson may be included.

A satisfactory format for lesson plans is presented in table 7.1. Within this format, behavioral objectives are stated, materials are identified, and activities and evaluations are given. The plan may be prepared for an individual or for a small group of children. The sample plan in table 7.1 was designed to provide different learning experiences for Rosie, Teddie, Jorge, and Evelyn. The teacher could prepare more than one objective and activity for each child if time to accomplish them were available.

Teachers should recognize that there are many different lesson plan formats. Each teacher should select or develop a format that suits the needs of teacher and students. Some school systems will provide a standard lesson plan form for all teachers in the system. Whatever the format, the critical idea to remember is that the lesson plan is simply a tool to facilitate the planning of the school day and is of value only as it helps the teacher to accomplish needed planning and organization.

Evaluation of Learning

At different times during the study of the theme and certainly at its end, Mr. Stein will need to consider the evaluation of student learning. If he has tape recorded each child's reading at the beginning of the theme work, a comparison with a tape made at its conclusion will allow him to note changes in word recognition, fluency, and other oral reading behaviors. He may have completed a careful evaluation of each child's writing (see chapter 6) early in the year. A recent writing sample may be evaluated by the same means for evidence of growth. His anecdotal records will suggest growth in study skills, behaviors crucial to taking responsibility for one's own learning, and self-management skills. Children may be asked to self-evaluate orally. If their reading and writing skills are more developed, they may write their self-evaluations. A display of all the projects related to the theme could be prepared by the children for display and explanation to the rest of the class, another class, or the parents. The children could revisit their web to determine whether they dealt with the different aspects of it and whether they had completed the different activities they had planned. Finally, Mr. Stein should examine his more-detailed web, noting evidence of growth in the strategies and skills that he had identified as possible learning areas.

TABLE 7.1. Lesson Plan Format

Objective	Name of Material	Activity	Evaluation
Rosie When Rosie finishes the paragraph she is writing, she will locate and correct all punctuation errors.	An original passage of factual material about dinosaur teeth.	Rosie is writing a paragraph entitled "The Teeth of Dinosaurs."	Rosie found all four punctuation errors. She was visibly pleased.
Teddie After looking at a picture book of dinosaurs, Teddie will enter five words in his dictionary.	Picture book of dinosaurs; his own dinosaur dictionary.	Teddie will enjoy the picture book and will write five words in his own dictionary.	Teddie found four words for his dictionary. He needed help to locate a fifth one. Then he decided to illustrate them.
Jorge After a brief discussion of the article and a chance to read it silently, Jorge will be able to read it orally, meeting the criteria for the instructional level.	An article on fossils in an easy encyclopedia.	Jorge will talk over the article and note new words, then read the article silently and orally.	Jorge met the criteria for the instructional level.
Evelyn Given the book Evelyn wrote about the sizes of dinosaurs, she will be able to read the book with no word-recognition errors.	A book she has written and bound for the book table.	Evelyn will show her latest book to her mother, explaining her time line and drawings. Then she will read the book.	Evelyn was able to read the book with no word-recognition errors. Her mother was pleased. Evelyn could name words that her mother pointed out.

Supporting Corrective Instruction

The remainder of this chapter will be devoted to a discussion of materials that Jim Stein or any other teacher might find useful in planning for teaching, and to a discussion of some questions that teachers often ask when working with themes as an approach to reading and writing for disabled readers.

Materials

Today's teachers are fortunate to have many materials to use in planning corrective reading programs. Available materials include a variety of books: high-interest, low-vocabulary materials; trade (library) books on a wide range of topics and at a variety of reading levels; big books and predictable books for younger readers; picture books and wordless picture books; and textbooks in the sciences and social sciences. Micro-computer software is being produced as rapidly as it can be evaluated and fitted into the curriculum. Both computer and traditional board games abound. Teachers can also call on resource persons in their communities. Finally, teachers can use visual aids, realia, documents, maps and charts, films and video recordings, and a variety of concrete materials.

Reading Materials with a High-Interest Level but Low-Vocabulary Level

Many series of readers that are not prepared as basic readers are now on the market. The severely controlled vocabularies of these books make them much more usable with underachievers than many books one might choose from library shelves to fit children's reading abilities. A detailed bibliography of such series of specially prepared materials will be found by individual titles in appendix B.

Trade Books

A careful inspection of the school's library shelves will reveal books that have been written with young readers or disabled readers in mind. Some of these books are in series and are identified as the "easy" books about various topics. The vocabulary is usually kept simple, and the sentences are short. Frequently, good pictures instead of new or difficult vocabulary serve to clarify concepts the authors want to introduce.

Teachers will find that growing numbers of trade books are now sold along with taped readings of the stories. Sometimes four or more copies of the book are packaged with the tape. Children may listen to the tape of a story and follow in the book. After hearing the tape several times, they may be able to read along with the tape. Teachers may use listening centers for this activity; the children wear head sets and listen to the story without disturbing the rest of the class.

Big Books

Big books are oversize copies of popular titles that a group of children may share together with the teacher. The pictures and print are large enough to be seen by a small group seated around the book. Many folktales have been prepared as big books, while many other titles are found as big books only. Examples of big books are:

1. *The Big Toe, Mrs. Wishy-washy,* and *The Farm Concert* from The Wright Group, 10949 Technology Place, San Diego, California 92127
2. *The Ugly Duckling, Peter Rabbit,* and *Paul Bunyon* from Milliken Publishing Company, 1100 Research Boulevard, St. Louis, Missouri 63132–0579

Big books tend to be rather expensive. Some teachers have solved that problem by making their own. They make or find colorful pictures and carefully letter the text. Children are pleased with them. Sometimes teachers and children cooperate in creating big books. The children may illustrate stories prepared by the teacher.

Making Connections 7.1: Getting Children and Trade Books Together

Teachers are finding more and more ways to use trade books (library books) in their reading programs. Two particularly useful categories of trade books for children with reading problems are the high-interest, low-vocabulary books and the predictable books. Work with your instructor in planning to carry out one of the experiences described below.

1. Using references in this chapter and in appendix B or suggestions from your instructor, identify and locate at least three high-interest, low-vocabulary books. Evaluate the books carefully. Check to see how all are alike and how they differ. Make a list of what you see as strengths and weaknesses of each book. Then select one that you can share with a child. You may take turns reading the book, the child may do all the reading, or you may do most of the reading. What you do will depend largely on the reading ability of the child with whom you work. You may find that the child's comments and questions, if carefully recorded, will provide you with special insights. Share your evaluations of the high-interest, low-vocabulary books you examined. Also plan to share with peers your experience in reading one book with a child.

2. This chapter lists some predictable books. Your instructor or a librarian can help you to identify many more titles. Examine several of these books to draw your own conclusions about their predictable language. Plan to share the books and your conclusions with class members. Before the time set for sharing, read one of the books with a child. Note carefully how or if the child identifies the predictable nature of the language. Observe what happens when you read the story together. Does the child then try to read the book alone? Does the child preserve the meaning (if not the actual language) of the author? When you share this experience with your class, discuss the experience of reading a predictable book with a child, as well as your observations of several predictable books.

Predictable Books

Predictable books are a special group of trade books that are easy to read because the structure of the text makes the words highly predictable.[4] Careful examination of a variety of trade books will yield quite a collection of predictable books. Once such a book has been read with the child, it is likely that the child can then read the book alone. A few predictable books are listed here. Others can be identified by the school librarian.

Cameron, Polly. *I Can't Said the Ant.* Coward, McCann and Geoghegan, 1961.
Emberly, Barbara, and Ed Emberly. *One Wide River to Cross.* Scholastic Press, 1966.
Gàg, Wanda. *Millions of Cats.* Coward, 1928.
Higgins, Don. *Papa's Going to Buy Me a Mockingbird.* Seabury Press, 1968.
Joslin, Sesyle. *What Did You Say Dear?* Scholastic Press, 1958.

Martin, Bill. *Brown Bear, Brown Bear, What Do You See?* Holt, Rinehart and Winston, 1967.

Martin, Bill. *Instant Readers.* Holt, Rinehart and Winston, 1970. (Series)

Martin, Bill, and Peggy Brogan. *Sounds of Language.* Holt, Rinehart and Winston, 1972–73. (Series)

Picture Books

Picture books serve a unique role in the education of disabled readers. Children who have poor reading strategies and skills can gain much information about their world from such books. Those children who are trying to improve their reading ability will find that picture books often function in the manner of predictable books. The pictures make determining the print on the page predictable.

Wordless picture books encourage storytelling. The development of story grammar appears to be linked to success in reading comprehension. Children may tell their stories on tape for others to listen to as the pages are turned. Their stories may also be transcribed and written to be read in conjunction with looking at the pictures. If several children tell the same story for recording and transcribing, children may compare the various stories and come to see the creative possibilities of language.

Reading Material of Elementary-Level Difficulty for the Middle School Content Program

Middle school general science teachers need to be alert for materials that can be read and studied by students who function on only a third- or fourth-grade reading level. One recently published set of texts is *Ideas and Investigations in Science:*

1. Harry Wong, Leonard Bernstein, and Edward Shevick, *Ideas and Investigations in Science: Life Science* (Englewood Cliffs, N.J.: Prentice-Hall, 1978).
2. Malvin Dolmatz and Harry Wong, *Ideas and Investigations in Science: Physical Science,* 2d ed. (Englewood Cliffs, N.J.: Prentice-Hall, 1977).
3. Leonard Bernstein and Harry Wong, *Ideas and Investigations in Science: Earth Science,* 2d ed. (Englewood Cliffs, N.J.: Prentice-Hall, 1979).

These materials are available in separate unit booklets or in combined textbooks with laboratory data books and teacher's manuals. Each investigation is carefully sequenced, and the directions are very easy to follow.

Examples of other useful materials are:

1. John F. Mongillo, et al., *Reading about Science* (New York: McGraw-Hill, 1981). Many science concepts are presented in short articles with comprehension questions. Levels A–G cover difficulty levels 2.5 to 6.6.
2. Nila B. Smith, *Be a Better Reader,* 5th ed. (Englewood Cliffs, N.J.: Prentice-Hall). Reading skills in social studies, science, mathematics, and literature are covered. Grades 4–12.
3. Larry Berliner and Susan Berliner, *Reading Skills for Standardized Testing* (Maplewood, N.J.: Hammond, Inc., 1983). These materials (Levels A–E) are designed to help older students learn test-taking skills.

Microcomputers

As the teacher organizes the classroom, plans must be developed for the use of a modern teaching tool, the microcomputer. The daily schedule should be developed in such a way that every child will have opportunities to have experiences with a variety of programs. Much computer time should be spent with simulation, problem solving, interactive literature, and word-processing programs. However, the teacher may find that some "skill and drill" programs may also be helpful.[5]

A careful evaluation of any microcomputer program should be made before it is introduced into the classroom. The teacher may find that not all programs are suitable for all students. Some of the criteria that might be used to evaluate programs are:

1. Is this the most effective way to teach this particular skill or concept?
2. Does the program encourage a variety of responses?
3. How much teaching is required before the child can work independently?
4. How legible and readable is the print on the screen?
5. Does the computer experience encourage the child to continue learning about the subject in other ways?
6. Is there a record-keeping system that will help the teacher to evaluate what the child has accomplished?[6]

Games and Devices

If children are going to play games, teachers should keep in mind three criteria:

1. The primary emphasis must be on *learning a skill* needed in reading. In the case of *Vowel Dominoes,* every time the child plays a domino, a decision identifying the short vowel sound is made.[7]
2. The *mechanics of the game* must not be such that little time is spent on learning the skill needed in reading. If the child bounces a ball each time that he or she says a word and gets much more interested in bouncing the ball than g in saying the word, perhaps that game should be discarded.
3. The *fun of the game should center around the reading skill* rather than being something that the child enjoys apart from reading. In other words, the thing rewarded must be the learning of a reading skill. In playing *Go-Fish,* winning the largest number of books so as to win the game is the reward. In order to win each book of three cards alike, however, the child is practicing "hearing" the initial sound.[8]

Commercially prepared devices, homemade games, and work exercises that can be prepared by the teachers to be used over and over and that meet these criteria should be collected and filed in materials centers of all elementary schools.

Many games are available commercially through textbook publishing companies, variety stores, department stores, and drugstores. Some are more useful than others, although all teachers must make their evaluations and try to build up a stock of games

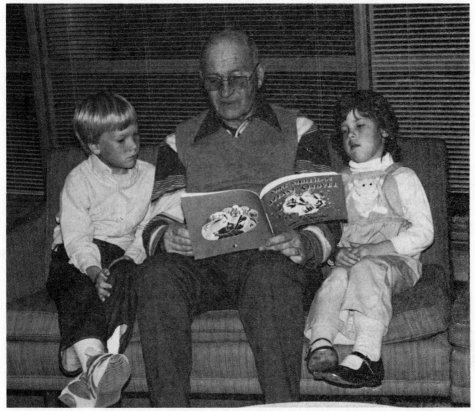

David Woodward

Teachers who are concerned about providing children with more opportunities for book experiences than the teacher can manage welcome community persons who volunteer to read to children.

that can be used by small groups or individuals during unsupervised work periods within the school day. The following list is only illustrative of those known to the authors of this text:

1. *Alphabet Acrobatics* (Palo Alto, Calif.: Sullivan Associates, 1972). The kit provides a big book showing children how to make their bodies look like letter shapes. It emphasizes the role of motor learning in learning to read.

2. E. W. Dolch, *Word Learning Games* (Champaign, Ill.: Garrard Publishing Co.). Games available include *Phonic Lotto, Group Word Teaching Game, Group Sounding Game, Take, The Syllable Game,* and *What the Letters Say.* Two consumable booklets are available in which children can practice recognizing the Dolch words in short sentences. The booklets may be cut up, laminated, and used in learning centers as permanent learning materials.

3. *Gold Cup Games* (Bomar, 622 Rodier Drive, Glendale, Calif. 91201, 1972). The games are independent activities in which up to six children can participate at one time. The purpose is to reinforce reading and language skills. Individual games are entitled *Horse Trail Ride, Bicycle Rally, Motor Cycle Motocross,* and *Dune Buggy Rally.*

4. Lift-up puzzle games (Elgin, Ill.: The Child's World, 1972). These little puzzle booklets are in three series: *Guess Who, What and Where,* and *What and Which.* The individual puzzle booklets in the *What and Where* series are *What Belongs Where, What's Part of What, What Goes with What,* and *Going through the Tunnel.*

5. *Little Brown Bear* (Learning Associates, Inc., P.O. Box 561167, Miami, Fla. 33156). Publishes a variety of games aimed at improving decoding skills. One of the games is *Tick-Tack-Go,* a vowel game. Some games give practice with the skills taught in related books.

6. Milton Bradley Company, 43 Cross Street, Springfield, Mass. 01103. Games include *Picture Word Builder, Sentence Builder, Phonic Drill Cards, Phonetic Quizmo, Dial 'n Spell, Concentration,* and *Vowel Wheels.*

7. *Monster Hunt* (Allied Educational Council, Distribution Center, Box 78, Galien, Mich. 49113). *Monster Hunt* assesses ten levels of phonic or structural abilities: beginning consonants, short vowels, consonant clusters, long vowels and final *e,* long vowel digraphs, reinfluenced vowels, irregular double vowels and diphthongs, syllabication, prefixes, suffixes, and affixes.

8. *The New Phonics We Use Learning Games Kits* (Chicago: Rand McNally). Kit one—ten supplementary, small-group learning games—primary grades; kit two—ten supplementary games adding some more difficult phonic skills—intermediate grades. The kits must be purchased in their entirety, which makes them very expensive. If the kit can be housed in the school learning center and made available to many teachers, the purchase may be worthwhile.

9. Parker and Sons Publishing Co., 241 E. Fourth St., Los Angeles, Calif. 90013. Games include: *Spill 'n Spell* and *Play 'n Talk.*

10. *Reading Laboratory 1: Word Games* (Chicago: Science Research Associates, Inc.). Contains forty-four word games, a phonics survey test, a pupil's workbook, teacher's guide, and progress tests.

11. *Reading Wheel: Consonants and Vowels* (Boston, Mass.: Teaching Resources Corp., 1974). An attractive version of the phonics wheel using pictures and individual words provides an activity for one or two children at a time with each wheel.

12. The Remedial Education Press (Kingsbury Center, 2138 Bancroft Place, N.W., Washington, D.C. 20008). The games are: *Go-Fish, Series 1,* and *Go-Fish, Series 2, Vowel Dominoes, Build It,* and *Affixo.*

13. *Sullivan Reading Games* (Palo Alto, Calif.: Behavioral Research Laboratories). The games reinforce the decoding concepts taught in the Sullivan Reading Program. The ten games are available only as a set. Again, if the box is housed in the school learning center where it is available to many teachers, the purchase may be worthwhile.

14. *Teach Key Reading and Spelling* (Box 9905, St. Paul, Minn.) *Teach Key:* four volumes, each containing twenty-four colorful word and picture cards.

Other Teaching Resources

The variety of instructional resources is limited primarily by the imagination of the teacher. Only a few possibilities will be discussed here.

The classroom, in order to be a literate environment, should be rich with magazines; newspapers (those intended for children as well as regular city dailies); pamphlets from government agencies, chambers of commerce, national parks, and even some businesses; books written and bound by children and their teacher; and maps, globes, and charts. The actual materials will differ somewhat with the age of the children, but the printed materials in the classroom should represent a broad spectrum of what is available.

Realia must not be neglected. Children are quick to profit from concrete materials. The school librarian should be encouraged to accumulate a variety of real materials—tools, costumes, toys, and objects from homes and workplaces. This collection should represent varied times and places. Teachers may want to build their own collections of such materials. A collection of hats of many kinds, coins, buttons, stamps, tools, writing implements, kitchen tools, containers, postcards from around the world, period clothing, and measuring tools may provide rich learning experiences for children of all ages. Searching for such materials and composing the collections can become a valuable experience for teachers and their students.

Yard sales and flea markets may be lucrative hunting grounds. If parents know that you are collecting certain kinds of materials, they will often have contributions to make. In some communities museums are willing to present suitcase exhibits of clothing and objects characteristic of a particular time. Children are invited to wear the clothes and to experiment with the objects and tools.

Films, filmstrips, and other audiovisual resources should not be neglected. A film that can be stopped at certain points may allow children to predict or to generate alternative endings. The class may be encouraged to write the ideas as well as discuss them. Captions may be prepared for filmstrips, or the script may be prepared for a movie made by the class. All are language opportunities.

The teacher must not neglect a vital resource in any community—persons who can contribute to classroom learning. A father has just returned from a tour of duty in Spain, a mother has taken a course in weaving, or a grandparent can help the children to make quilt blocks or birdhouses. Each of these is an opportunity to encourage children to learn from others and to broaden their knowledge bases.

The classroom is more than books and papers. It must be a place in which children have opportunities to learn from multiple resources. This is especially true if the teacher plans to use themes as an approach to learning.

Where Can the Teacher Find Resources?

These commercially prepared handbooks will be useful:

1. Lou A. Burmeister, *Words—From Print to Meaning: Classroom Activities for Building Sight Vocabulary, for Using Context Clues, Morphology, and Phonics* (Reading, Mass.: Addison Wesley, 1975).
2. Paul C. Burns and Betty D. Roe, *Reading Activities for Today's Schools* (Chicago: Rand McNally, 1979).
3. Dolores Durkin, *Strategies for Identifying Words,* 2d ed. (Boston: Allyn and Bacon, 1980).
4. Peter Edwards, *Reading Problems: Identification and Treatment* (London: Heinemann Educational Books, 1978).
5. Eldon E. Ekwall, *Locating and Correcting Reading Difficulties,* 4th ed. (Columbus: Merrill Publishing Co., 1985).
6. Arthur Heilman, *Phonics in Proper Perspective,* 5th ed. (Columbus: Merrill Publishing Co., 1985).
7. Selma E. Herr, *Learning Activities for Reading,* 4th ed. (Dubuque, Iowa: Wm. C. Brown Co. Publishers, 1982).
8. Josephine Ives, Laura Bursuk, and Sumner Ives, *Word Identification Techniques* (Chicago: Rand McNally, 1979).
9. Dale D. Johnson and P. David Pearson, *Teaching Reading Vocabulary* (New York: Holt, Rinehart and Winston, 1978).
10. Harry Miller, Cindy Thompson, and Dana Holloway, *Teacher's Kaleidoscope of Reading Activities* (New York: University Press of America, 1985).
11. Lee Ann Rinsky and Barbara Griffith, *Teaching Word Attack Skills,* 3d ed. (Dubuque, Iowa: Gorsuch Scarisbrick, 1984).
12. David H. Russell and Elizabeth F. Russell, *Listening Aids through the Grades,* 2d ed., edited by Dorothy Grant Hennings (New York: Teachers College Press, 1979).
13. David H. Russell, Etta Karp, and Anne Marie Mueser, *Reading Aids through the Grades,* 4th ed. (New York: Teachers College Press, 1981).
14. Delwyn G. Schubert and Theodore Torgerson, *Improving the Reading Program,* 4th ed. (Dubuque, Iowa: Wm. C. Brown Co. Publishers, 1976).
15. Carl B. Smith and Peggy G. Elliott, *Reading Activities for Middle and Secondary Schools: A Handbook for Teachers,* 2d ed. (New York: Holt, Rinehart and Winston, 1986).
16. Nila B. Smith, *One Hundred Ways of Teaching Silent Reading* (Darby, Pa.: Darby Books, 1981).
17. Evelyn B. Spache, *Reading Activities for Child Improvement,* 3d ed. (Boston: Allyn and Bacon, 1981).
18. Jeannette Veatch et al., *Key Words to Reading: The Language Experience Approach Begins,* 2d ed. (Columbus: Merrill Publishing Co., 1979).

What about Drill?

Some teachers who have tried to do corrective reading with children have assumed that *what the children need is drill and more drill.* They have used the same general method and have employed the same materials and have aimed at the same goal as in their regular class teaching. The results of relying upon more drill and nothing but more drill have usually been disappointing. This is not to say that there is no place for drill, but *effective drill is never mere repetition;* drill is effective only when there is *understanding* of what is being drilled and where the *learners see need and purpose for the drill.*

Effective drill is repetition where the conditions of learning have been considered and are appropriate. Some of these conditions of learning are:

1. Practice periods should be short and spirited.
2. Drill should be individualized and *at the point of error.* This means that the drill for children who cannot succeed very well is different from that for children who succeed very well, and the topic that they drill on is that which they missed.
3. Drill should involve the use of ideas and, in reading, should use context. The first-grade teacher teaching the sight word *said* calls attention to the word in meaningful context in the sentences of a dictated story. Each sentence changes only slightly from the sentences just preceding it. By turns, several children read the story of their recent cooking experience.

   > Rubin *said,* "Put in the flour."
   > Jean *said,* "Put in the salt."
   > Jamie *said,* "Put in the baking powder."
   > Coleen *said,* "Now, put in the shortening."
   > Everybody *said,* "Yum, yum, good!"

   The drill is in context with respect to the word *said,* and the pupils should be thinking as they read.
4. Practice must be motivated. Too many motives in school are artificial. Learners work for grades. Reading teachers are competing for the pupils' interest, which may be centered in many other activities at school. For young children, immediate goals are much better than distant goals. They need to experience success. Marks that signify *hope* rather than *despair* ought to be given, especially to the poorest in the class. If the children are to keep on working, they must feel that they are successful; otherwise they have no reason to continue to work.
5. Knowledge of results helps the students to define *success and failure for them.* Immediate knowledge of results will help them to know whether they are succeeding. Success is rewarding. Success brings personal satisfaction; with failure, the mere fact of having failed is in itself a form of punishment.

Drill, based on these criteria, will be very useful in corrective reading.

What about Record Keeping?

Although record keeping should be reduced to a minimum, keeping records of past performances as a standard of comparison for future performance is very necessary. In addition, the teacher needs samples of the pupil's work and other information for parent conferences or in planning new ventures in reading.

Keeping anecdotes as the events happen is possible if the teachers write notes to themselves in the margins of the daily assignment book, the class schedule book, or in a loose-leaf notebook. Later, these anecdotes should be placed in the pupil's cumulative folder as a part of a running record of what the teacher knows about the child.

The teacher should start a simple one-page record of each disabled reader. Interest inventories, sociograms, test results, and grade cards become part of the file of useful information from which pertinent data can be extracted.

Pretesting, teaching, and posttesting afford excellent opportunities for small assignments to become tangible measures of progress. The important consideration here is that progress at the first-grade reader level is commendable even if the student is in junior high school. The measure of progress is the important thing.

A concise record of pertinent information can be summarized on a single page (such as was illustrated in figures 7.2 and 7.3). Using all the information gained through interest inventories, personality inventories, health data, family data, school history, and methods of evaluating intelligence, the teacher will be able to organize a summary. By accommodating new information as it is obtained through the school year, the teacher is enabled to adjust the pupil's reading program as often as necessary.

If the students are beginning corrective instruction, the teacher should be observant while working with them, making mental notes of conversation, behavior, and reactions to all subjects discussed. These should be recorded briefly in a daily log. They usually should not be recorded in the presence of the pupils. Having this kind of information

---

Making Connections 7.2: Teachers' Record Keeping Systems

It is important to be aware of a variety of means for lesson planning and classroom record keeping. There are almost as many ways of doing these tasks as there are teachers! Each teacher needs to develop an effective system that is comfortable and practical.

Interview a classroom teacher to find out how lesson plans are developed and classroom records maintained. Perhaps the teacher will be able to let you bring blank forms back to your class to share with other students. Ask to see not only the unused forms but also plan books and records that have actually been written and used.

If each class member brings back information as well as actual lesson plans and record systems, the class should have a collective store of practical information to help in thinking about classroom organization and management.

Writing a Summary Report for a Student Who Has Had Special Instruction

I. *Personal data*

Student _____   Date _____

Grade in school _____   Parents _____

Age _____   Address _____

Present Reading level _____   Dates of lessons _____

School semester _____   Number of lessons _____

II. *Introductory statement.* Summarize generally the child's background reading experiences. First recognition of problem, first diagnosis, first remedial instruction, improvement or lack of it. Affective factors related to attendance, punctuality, general disposition, moods, personal evaluation of self as expressed in conversation.

III. *Personality data.* Describe personality factors pertinent to the reading or attendance at lessons. Omit superficial comments like "He's a nice boy."

IV. *Reading Progress.* The arrangement of topics should be adapted to the work you did with your client.

   1. Writing experiences completed.
   2. Books, pamphlets, magazines, or newspaper articles read.
   3. Vocabulary skills. If you followed a commerically prepared set of lessons, give specific bibliographical information. If you planned your own, outline in detail.
   4. Phonic and Structural Skills. Be specific about which skills were practiced.
   5. Other kinds of language experiences.
   6. Summary of progress.

V. Recommendations. What will be most helpful to the child in ensuing semesters?

VI. Your report needs to be signed and should generally be countersigned by your supervisor.

_____   _____
Date   Reading Clinician

_____   _____
Date   Reading Supervisor

Figure 7.8. Suggested outline for a summary report

will help the teacher to guide daily conversation, obtain further information, and utilize interests of the pupils. A diary record of the materials used in corrective reading, including pages covered and books used, should also be kept.

If the teacher has kept a daily log of the work completed and new case history information acquired, the completion of a summary report can be condensed from this information. An outline for the summary report appears in figure 7.8.

Focusing on the Learner

Planning Use of the Student's Time

Teachers must take advantage of every opportunity to check the progress of the students, to encourage them in their efforts, and to make sure that they understand what they are expected to do before they begin work.

In contrast with the usual procedure of having directed silent reading before oral reading, these students may need to read orally much of the story material they use for independent seat work later.

Underachievers need to do a great deal of oral reading. Part of this can be done with a student-tutor if this can be arranged in the classroom, but the teacher needs to hear enough of this oral practice to note difficulties and to plan the seat work and other learning experiences that will overcome obstacles to progress. It is especially important to listen with undivided attention while the student reads so that teacher and student can enjoy the story together. The student may read into a cassette or tape recorder, and the teacher can listen later.

Also in oral reading, the teacher can be alert to the need for sharing the oral reading by taking turns by pages, for example, or by interjecting questions to keep interest up when the reading may seem difficult to the students.

The students should read the directions for their work to the teacher before they begin to work alone. They should have a list of tasks in mind that they can do as time permits so that they need not wait for further instructions. *The work should be corrected as quickly as possible after it is finished*. Types of exercises for which a glance down the page will reveal mistakes or shortcomings should be used.

Checking-up time for all children just before recess or dismissal should be routine, and thus certain children are not singled out as the only ones who have need for this. If several children have assignments to be checked at times such as this, attention is not directed to the underachievers.

These pupils must have time to read aloud to the teacher. If it is not feasible to do this as a "reading group" in the daily schedule, it must be arranged at some other time. While not the most desirable plan, asking the children to come fifteen minutes earlier in the morning or to stay a few minutes after school may work out smoothly if the teacher makes the period a happy, optimistic one. An independent work period for all students in the room may provide an opportunity to do some planning with the underachievers.

Planning is very important. Setting up realistic goals is a must, and deliberately making time to check regularly with the underachievers throughout the day will be rewarding over a period of time.

If the teachers look upon their classrooms as laboratories where few children need to do exactly the same things, and where the underachievers need do nothing as outlined in the proposed state course of study, there will be time to do many things from which they can profit.

"I don't see why my Audrey doesn't get the special help she needs in reading."

Figure 7.9. Miss Emmy (Reprinted by permission of *The Oklahoma Teacher.*)

What Should We Teach?

Don't teach what can't or won't be learned.

A junior high school boy came to his counselor almost in tears. "I have an exam tomorrow in English," he said, "and we will be asked to define and give an example of seven kinds of pronouns. I don't even understand the explanations in the textbook." The kinds of pronouns are relative, demonstrative, possessive, indefinite, personal, intensive, and reflexive. Since most of you would flunk the test, why inflict it on a twelve-year-old boy?[9]

Certainly teachers can change priorities. First things can be put first instead of being second, third, fourth, or twentieth. But what priorities?

1. If you are doing some old things that don't work, discard those and try something new.
2. Try some things that may not work, a necessary condition for any innovative program.
3. Study what works and what doesn't work.

Summary

In this chapter many problems that classroom teachers must face when disregarding the grade levels on their classroom doors and allowing students to work all day at individual levels of achievement are discussed. A detailed strategy for the theme approach to corrective reading is presented.

Many types of instructional materials are discussed. However, the teacher must remember that materials of instruction do *not* instruct. Learner responses to materials of instruction can be limited, cursory, or very fruitful. One can skim over the surface or study in depth. Trying to "cover the ground" is usually not helpful. Many a child has gone through a book without much of the book going through the child. One can read the lines, read between the lines, or read beyond the lines.

For Further Reading

Blanchard, Jay S., George E. Mason, and Dan Daniel. *Computer Applications in Reading,* 3d ed. Newark, Del.: International Reading Association, 1987. This is a comprehensive statement on the interface between reading and computers.

Cianciolo, Patricia Jean. "Use Wordless Picture Books to Teach Reading, Visual Literacy and to Study Literature." In *Jump Over the Moon,* edited by Pamela P. Barron and Jennifer Q. Burley, 139–44. New York: Holt, Rinehart and Winston, 1984. The author proposes the use of wordless picture books to encourage visual literacy, the understanding of literal and figurative language, and an awareness of literary style.

Combs, Martha. "Modeling the Reading Process with Enlarged Texts." *Reading Teacher* 40 (January 1987): 422–26. Big books allow children to see text as it is read and as comments are made, which gives them insight into the reading process.

Duffelmeyer, Frederick A. "Estimating Readability with a Computer: Beware the Aura of Precision." *Reading Teacher* 38 (January 1985): 392–94. Computers make determining readability levels easy. They do not make such determinations accurate. They are still just estimates.

Hansen, Jane. *When Writers Read.* Portsmouth, N.H.: Heinemann Educational Books, 1987. This book emphasizes the close relationship between writing and reading. In twenty-two chapters the author touches on almost every phase of the literacy process.

Samuels, S. Jay, and P. David Pearson, eds. *Changing School Reading Programs.* Newark, Del.: International Reading Association, 1988. The authors suggest principles for change, provide models for change, and review the Metcalf Project.

Scott, Diana, and Jeanne Barker. "Guidelines for Selecting and Evaluating Reading Software: Improving the Decision Making Process." *Reading Teacher* 40 (May 1987): 884–87. Samples of various types of software are named. The strength of the article is the "Sample Evaluation Checklist" for software.

Wong-Kam, Jo Ann, and Kathryn H. Au. "Improving a 4th Grader's Reading and Writing: Three Principles." *Reading Teacher* 41 (April 1988): 768–72. The writers suggest that children should be helped to focus on the purposes of literacy and then should be given chances to apply their literacy skills.

Zakaluk, Beverley L., and S. Jay Samuels. *Readability: Its Past, Present, and Future.* Newark, Del.: International Reading Association, 1988. This is the most current statement about the status of readability. It features extensive bibliographies.

Notes

1. *The Wisconsin Design for Reading Skill Development: Overview* (Minneapolis: National Computer Systems, Inc., 1977).

2. Alton L. Raygor, "The Raygor Readability Estimate: A Quick and Easy Way to Determine Difficulty," in *Reading: Theory, Research and Practice,* ed. P. David Pearson, Twenty-Sixth Yearbook of the National Reading Conference (Clemson, S.C.: National Reading Conference, 1977), 259–63.

3. R. Scott Baldwin and Rhonda Kaufman, "A Concurrent Validity Study of the Raygor Readability Estimate," *Journal of Reading* 23 (November 1979): 148–53.

4. Connie A. Bridge, Peter N. Winograd, and Darlene Haley, "Using Predictable Materials vs. Preprimers to Teach Beginning Sight Words," *Reading Teacher* 36 (May 1983): 884–91.

5. Ernest Balajthy, "Reinforcement and Drill by Microcomputer," *Reading Teacher* 37 (February 1984): 490–94; John O. Green, "Computers, Kids, and Writing: An Interview with Donald Graves," *Classroom Computer Learning* 4 (March 1984): 20–24.

6. I. C. H. Smith, *Microcomputers in Education* (New York: John Wiley and Sons, 1982), 28; Marc Tucker, "Computer in Schools: A Plan in Time Saves Nine," *Theory into Practice* 22 (Autumn 1983): 313–20.

7. *Vowel Dominoes* (Washington, D.C.: Remedial Education Press).

8. *Go-Fish* (Washington, D.C.: Remedial Education Press).

9. Edgar Dale, "How Do We Provide Access to Excellence?" *Apropos,* a publication of the Center on Educational Media and Materials for the Handicapped (Summer 1974).

8
Scheduling Time for Corrective Reading

Vocabulary

theme approach
unit method
learning laboratory
course of study
curriculum guide
"average student"
reading as a developmental
    process
problem-solving approach
integration of curriculum
learning materials center
"separate-subjects"
curriculum
planning time
informal room arrangement
creative opportunities for
    learning
easy oral reading practice
Children's Catalog
Standard Catalog for High
    School Libraries
"fun reading"
directed reading lessons
reading using committees
time blocks
case studies
bilingual
nonlingual

Questions

1. What role does the course of study or curriculum guide have in planning the daily life of the classroom? (**Inference**)
2. What are the steps in theme or unit development? (**Recall**)
3. Develop a web on the theme *horses* or *summer holidays*. (**Application**)
4. Describe a learning laboratory that you might create as your classroom. (**Application**)
5. What values may teachers derive from reading *case studies* of corrective readers? (**Critical**)

Introduction

If the school as an institution really exists for the education of all children and youth, then the students who need corrective reading must be given time *during the school day* for this purpose. They deserve their fair share of the teacher's direct attention for instruction from which they can profit.

Even those children who receive reading instruction from special education teachers and special reading instructors must have help with reading in the regular classroom as a part of the ongoing instructional program. These special programs are designed to supplement and support—but never to replace—the regular instructional program.

Instructional Resources for the Classroom Teacher

Finding time and keeping a positive, constructive attitude require a commonsense evaluation of instructional resources for the classroom teacher: (1) the place of the course of study in teaching; (2) the *theme approach,* often called the *unit method* or problem approach, to teaching; (3) the classroom, very flexibly managed as a *learning laboratory;* (4) the development of a center for instructional materials in the school; (5) suggestions for "making time" for corrective reading; and (6) organizing the elementary school day in large blocks of time.

Following this discussion, case studies are presented of three students, in fourth, eighth, and twelfth grades, respectively, who were helped throughout the school day to improve their developmental reading skills.

The Course of Study or Curriculum Guide

An often-heard but *misleading idea* voiced in teachers' groups is that teaching has to follow a rather rigid, inflexible pattern outlined in the state *course of study* or the school *curriculum guide.* Too many times this apparently generates a slavish endeavor to force all students through precisely cut and well-established patterns as they progress through any particular grade in school. The disabled readers will be unable to perform satisfactorily if held to such an inflexible standard.

A course of study or curriculum guide is a valuable document. It makes possible some kind of standard for judging the achievement of the *"average" children* in a given grade. It permits teachers to arrive at some judgment about what is adequate achievement for children who are six, eight, or ten years old. This comparative expectation of children at various ages is worthwhile and important. *But,* teachers must recognize the course of study or curriculum guide for exactly what it is: an outline of materials that the *average* students may logically be expected to utilize. *Average,* in this frame of reference, is that statistically hypothetical median performance above and below which half of any unselected class of students will probably perform. When given an achievement test battery, only a relatively small percentage of children in any given class actually perform *at the grade level* to which they are assigned.

Beyond this philosophical basis, the course of study is only as useful or as meaningful as the classroom teachers can make it. One of the basic purposes of formal education is the transmission of the cultural heritage. In this respect, the course of study or curriculum guide provides more or less generally uniform education for students as they progress through school. It makes possible more satisfactory school adjustment when students transfer from one school to another or from one part of the country to another.

Teachers must recognize that there are many ways to meet the requirements established by a curriculum guide or course of study. The instructional strategies, the means by which children are given opportunities to learn, may be chosen by teachers to fit the needs of their students.

Poor readers can find a place in the classroom when teachers view them as persons of competence and dignity. Even the poorest reader has skills and talents to offer to others. If the school day is organized at least in part around themes, there will always be learning opportunities for poor readers and appropriate and relevant literacy tasks in which they can engage. All readers must learn reading and writing as *developmental processes,* beginning each year where they left off the previous year. The disabled readers are not exceptions. They need the same opportunities to continue in the fall the learning that was in progress the previous spring.

No single textbook can ever accommodate the range of reading abilities in a class. The teachers must be continuously alert for new and additional ways to plan learning experiences that are not dependent upon the single textbook in any content area.

The theme approach to teaching, which is closely associated with the unit method or *problem-solving approach,* lends itself to the *integration of curriculum.* When children engage in the study of a theme that they were involved in choosing, elements of science, social studies, math, and the arts can be integrated into the activities. The key elements in the theme approach are oral language, reading, and writing; they serve to unite all the others. The theme approach is heavily dependent upon the *learning materials center* in the school for a great variety of print and nonprint materials that teachers will need in order to manage their classrooms as *learning laboratories* in which children read, hypothesize, compare, create, compute, explore, test, ponder, evaluate, reflect, and wonder.

The Theme Approach to Learning

The theme approach, the curricular organization of subject matter into problems to be solved or projects to be developed, was discussed at length in chapter 7. Developing a theme is an evolving process by which a series of learning experiences that interrelate are developed. The purpose of the theme approach is to integrate the learning experiences around a central idea. This is to be contrasted with the teaching of a *separate-subjects curriculum,* where the learning may be compartmentalized and unrelated.

The theme, or unit, develops through five stages: first, the orientation to, or introduction of, the topic; second, the teacher-pupil planning, which may develop out of a webbing experience[1] (see figure 8.1); third, obtaining and organizing information; fourth, sharing information; and fifth, the culminating activity.

How do we know that
dinosaurs ever lived?

What kinds of fossil
remains are there?

Where have dinosaurs been
found?

When did dinosaurs live?

What do fossils tell us?

What did dinosaurs eat?

Were they meat eaters or
plant eaters?

Did dinosaurs fight each
other?

Did they eat each other

What did dinosaurs eat?

What were dinosaurs like?

What happened to the
dinosaurs?

What did dinosaurs look
like?

How big were they?

Were they all four-legged?

How smart were they?

Why do we think they were
not smart?

What was the size of the
dinosaur's brain?

Why don't we have
dinosaurs today?

Why did they die out?

Find at least four reasons
why the dinosaurs
disappeared.

Figure 8.1. A different web for a dinosaur unit

Since reading and writing are likely to be the key activities in obtaining information in the third stage, it becomes important to plan for many levels of ability. Teachers should have skillfully directed the pupil-teacher planning periods so that comprehensive lists of questions and tasks have been formulated, and have made available reading material suitable for all pupils so that all can read something, answer some of the questions, record their ideas, and carry out a variety of activities. Teachers need to find reading materials that typically encompass a range of achievement from three levels below the grade being taught to three levels above it. This is a difficult task for many themes and must be systematically and jointly worked on over long periods of time by school faculties. It should be the goal of every school to house its own library in the learning materials center. The resources of state traveling libraries and public libraries should also be explored. Many children can bring worthwhile books and references from home to contribute to the theme or unit under study. Teachers and children may also prepare their own books of useful information.

A web for a dinosaur theme was developed in detail in chapter 7. A different web on the same theme is presented here in figure 8.1. Note that an endless variety of webs on any given theme or to initiate any unit could be prepared, depending on the interests, purposes, and ages of the children.

The Classroom as a Learning Laboratory

The classroom must become a learning laboratory where students can experiment with a wide variety of learning aids that will lead them to make discoveries of meanings and ideas, to work out solutions, and to gain insights. Adequate equipment and materials must be provided if the classroom is to become a learning laboratory.

In a learning laboratory there are jobs to do for which pupils see real purposes; there are tasks that will satisfy some fairly immediate need in solving other problems so that a kind of chain reaction to the solving of problems evolves; jobs that are easy and jobs that are difficult; tasks that individuals can do, as well as those that groups of pupils work together to complete; jobs demanding cooperation, sharing, and planning, as well as jobs of reading, writing, and answering teachers' questions.

In a learning laboratory, where students are actively participating in the learning process, a great deal of oral communication takes place—listening to explanations, giving instructions, asking questions to clarify instructions, reporting, conversing, and discussing. A clear understanding of a purpose, before starting work, can prevent the waste of unlimited amounts of time after beginning.

Planning time is an activity that needs a generally increased emphasis in the classroom. A detailed, well-structured planning period early in the day should give each pupil a feeling of definite tasks to be accomplished throughout the day. Planning also needs to be done during the day with individuals and small groups as needs emerge. The teacher usually will conduct the planning session, but the objectives for getting work done must be defined in terms of the abilities of the pupils.

Planning requires a great deal of time and conversation. Then, pupils need to express clearly in their own words what their personal objectives are.

Informal room arrangement is essential in creating an atmosphere of a working, active laboratory. Movable desks, separation into small groups, interest centers, ongoing projects, interesting things to catch one's eye and to be observed, and freedom to talk in connection with one's work—all are an integral part of the learning laboratory.

The learning laboratory has another basic criterion. There is no minimum or maximum level of performance set as a standard for the whole group for the year. In this classroom where learning is an active, participating process, problem solving, creative thinking, memory work, and drill can be engaged in at all levels, from that of readiness

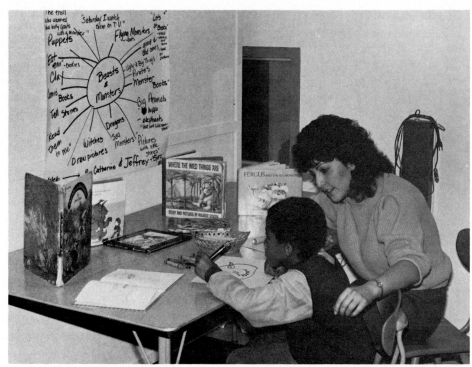

David Woodward

When the teacher and child develop a web around a theme, they identify many topics to explore that will encourage meaningful reading and writing activities.

for reading to generally mature reading habits with the discussion of problems of interest far above the traditional grade placement where the student is enrolled. Teachers must keep in mind that some students may be much farther advanced academically at the beginning of the year than others in the same class will be at the end of the year.

The Learning Materials Center

The solution to the problem of providing a variety of materials of instruction in the school seems to be most attainable through the *learning materials center*. A learning materials center housed in one central place within each separate building is a functional unit of the larger curriculum laboratory of the whole school system. A learning materials center should house the following: a good, well-stocked library; extensive audiovisual aids; maps, globes, and charts for social science and science teaching; all of the apparatus needed for extensive teaching of general science throughout the elementary or junior high school; art and industrial art materials and equipment to be drawn on loan by classrooms; music listening rooms with audio equipment; film and filmstrip viewing rooms; committee and conference rooms; and three-dimensional materials for making arithmetic meaningful.

Schools without libraries place teachers in the same position as that in which any tradesperson would be without tools. There is no way to learn to read except by reading; reading can be made pleasurable to the pupils only when the choice of material fits their needs, interests, and levels of reading abilities. The school library should contain a minimum total number of volumes equal to ten times the student enrollment.

Scheduling Time for Corrective Reading

When will time be found for doing the corrective or remedial teaching with the students? The most important thing, probably, is that the teachers will save the students' time by not having them do tasks at which they will not be successful. In other words, the students will save time by not trying to do something that they cannot do anyway, thus leaving them free to do things that they can do. If they work on spelling words that are too difficult and memorize a list of words all week so that they can write them on Friday but forget them by Monday, if they sit frustrated while others complete textbook assignments, or if they sit looking at the workbook without knowing what to write on the blanks in the sentences, they are using time that they could spend doing their special assignments. In other words, if the teachers would stop the students from doing the frustrating things, that time would be saved for tasks at which they could succeed.

Very short periods should be used all day long, although poor readers working on a task related to a theme may be able to sustain themselves for longer periods of time. The teacher may take three minutes in going from one activity to another with other groups to go over a page of seat work covering a reading lesson with an individual reader, or may save three minutes before dismissal for a brief period to summarize something or to drill on word recognition, word attack, or vocabulary. The teacher should find five minutes to listen to the pupil read the beginning of a story orally. This will help the child to become interested in the content of the story so that he or she will want to finish reading it silently. The student's assignment needs to be very specific and of the type that can be checked quickly and easily. The student should be praised for successful efforts. Peer teachers can do reading tasks with the one who needs help.

Teachers need to build, in succeeding years, an ever-greater repertoire of *creative opportunities for learning* that can be planned quickly with individuals either on the chalkboard or at their seats.

Examples of creative seat work might be the following assignments (teacher to child):

1. You told me that your father and your uncles were going to butcher a hog last Saturday and that you were going to help. Could you write me a story that would tell me what happened? I'm sure you began early in the morning. Did it take a long time? How did you and your brother help? If you will begin writing, I'll help you put all your ideas into a good story.
2. You know that the opposite of "up" is "down." "In" is the opposite of "out." Make two columns on your paper, and write all the pairs of words you can think of that are opposites. You may use the wall dictionary for spelling or ask a friend.
3. Make a seek-and-find puzzle. Put all the words for the colors in it.

The teachers may use commercially prepared seat work for the very disabled individuals and the very small groups that are doing corrective reading. They should confer with specialists whenever possible for additional suggestions.

One of the activities badly needed by most retarded readers is a great deal of *easy oral reading practice.* (Appendix B is a bibliography of appropriate books.) Listening to the children read aloud is something that other adults can do if they know the story being read and if they have empathy with the children. The listener must be genuinely interested in the content being read and must discuss it carefully with the reader. Aides, volunteer mothers, interested senior high school students, members of grandparent clubs, and the student's own peers will all be effectively used in classrooms when differentiated staffing is more clearly understood. Peers of differing reading abilities working on common interests may be very helpful to each other.

Good readers within the classroom can act as "helping teachers" by listening to oral reading practice of individuals or small groups. The teacher needs to exercise judgment in providing capable pupil-teachers and adequate working space so that other children's work is not disrupted.

A program of corrective reading instruction in the regular classroom has many advantages:

1. The regular teacher, if alert, can spot problems that can be prevented or corrected at their inception. Most children whose retardation in reading stems from absence from school, change of school, or interim environmental problems can be helped through intelligent classroom procedure. Helping the children before their difficulties become too acute can do much to lessen the number and the seriousness of the reading problems with which schools are faced today.
2. The regular teacher can plan a balanced "all day program" to enable the students to spend more time on reading, if indicated, but reading fitted to their levels of attainment and the interests being pursued.
3. The regular teacher, having an awareness of the pupils' new achievements in gaining reading power, can plan opportunities for the pupils to put their reading to use throughout the day.
4. The regular teacher is in a position to plan for some prevention and correction for all those who are working below their capacity. Many borderline or "fairly good" readers who could not be included in a special teacher's caseload have minor difficulties or "gaps" in learning.
5. The regular classroom teacher can plan for children to work independently in available periods during the day. Children can also work together or help each other. Games, devices, and seat-work exercises can be used.
6. The regular classroom teacher, having considerable opportunity to know the children, their interests, aptitudes, abilities, and limitations, and to find their needs, can utilize the children's other abilities throughout the day, which may provide the needed stimulus, the ego satisfaction, or source material for reading lessons to raise their reader levels.
7. The regular teacher can use an abundance of vocabulary-controlled reading material in subject areas so that the individual's reading assignments all day long fit the instructional level of reading. It is vitally important that reading be

integrated with the total school curriculum. Reading is not a subject to be taught as such, but a necessary tool to be used constantly in the learning process.

8. A contract plan between teacher and students making explicit the students' objectives for the day in behavioral terms may be useful with several members of the class or with all members for certain subjects or assignments.

9. Fifth- or sixth-grade students can be brought in to teach first-, second-, or third-grade students, under the watchful eye of the regular teachers. Some schools have arranged such opportunities on schedules like twenty minutes three times a week. The older children can listen to the younger ones practice oral reading, they can read to the younger children, or they can do word-recognition exercises if the teachers are careful to make sure that the words are in the younger children's sight vocabularies. Volunteer mothers, teacher aides, or high school or college students can be valuable support to teachers with large numbers of children. Classroom teachers do not have enough time to provide a sufficient amount of easy oral reading practice for the bottom 40 percent of the class. (The staggered day is another way for primary teachers to get more individual time with children. Half of the class report from 8:30 until 2:30, and the other half report from 9:30 until 3:30. Much more individualizing can go on with twelve to fifteen youngsters the first and last hours than can go on with up to thirty youngsters the remainder of the day.)

Corrective Teaching in the School Day

Adequate reading instruction in the schools necessitates both special teachers for clinical cases and good corrective teaching for those who will respond to proper practices in classroom remedial teaching. Attention is focused here only on specific suggestions for the classroom teachers, relative to finding time in the school day for remedial teaching.

1. Allow the children to work independently of usual reading groups for skills work in reading, spelling, and language. Excuse the children from academic assignments too difficult for them, and extend their time for completing work at their own levels. Or, involve children in learning that is organized around a theme, using reading materials at appropriate levels.

2. Start the remedial teaching at a level that is sufficiently easy to give confidence and ensure success. It is better to select material a half-year easier than necessary and build confidence than to select material above the instructional levels.

3. Make use of very short periods of time. Stop at a child's desk for two- or three-minute periods when you may be able to encourage him or her to keep on working. Check to see that what is being done is correct.

4. Include commercially prepared materials for worthwhile seat work to keep the learner profitably employed while the rest of the class does something else. Some of the pupil's time should be spent in writing stories, being read to, preparing personal dictionaries or word files, illustrating stories, and working at listening-reading centers.

5. Select books with controlled vocabulary easy enough to be "fun reading" for all the children, and have them read aloud to other children. If two or three children are all reading at about the same level, they can have shared oral reading. Be sure that these books are easy enough. (See appendix B for a list of books with controlled vocabularies.)
6. Work on the attitudes of the students and others with whom they associate to get more understanding of the problem and of the need for working constructively to solve it. These may be termed psychological aspects of the problem that the teachers work on during the day as an integral part of helping all children to grow and develop:
   a. Help the child to accept his or her situation.
   b. Help the child's parents to understand the situation and accept it (see chapter 13).
   c. Help the entire class to understand the many individual differences in people.
   d. Keep trying to locate causes of the difficulty, and be sure to get results of vision, hearing, and physical examinations.
   e. Assume that what you try will work, and then be willing to discontinue it if it does not work.

Tables 8.1 and 8.2 may be helpful in pointing up alternative ways of organizing instructional time for reading instruction. Table 8.1 suggests a plan in which the students in the class may be divided into three reading groups. Each group will spend about forty minutes in independent constructive activities, so the teacher needs to plan several learning experiences that can be completed during that time. The teacher will work with each of the three groups in turn in *directed reading lessons*.

Table 8.2 suggests the use of small groups or *committees* as learning groups. These small groups may be formed on the basis of interests or other needs. The teacher will spend time with one group each day but will also find time to observe and interact with other groups and individuals. Dated records will be made of the observations; in the records the teacher may include verbatim use of language, notations about the needs of learners, and observations of what children have learned. The record may also contain suggestions about needed changes in the learning environment, requests from children, and materials and supplies needed for the next day.

Using Blocks of Time

Many teachers find that breaking the school day into a few large *blocks of time* allows for more integration of subject matter and for more efficient use of time. One time block early in the day needs to be set aside for group planning. During this class meeting, the plans for the day are developed and perhaps recorded on a chart so that they can be referred to when needed. Other, shorter planning times may be needed, but the morning planning time must not be missed. Teachers may count on the planning session as a time for the application of language skills as students listen to the teacher and one another, as they agree on a workable plan for the day, and as they record it and read it together.

TABLE 8.1. Division of Time for Directed Reading Lessons in Three Reading Groups

Time Period	Group I	Group II	Group III
9:00–9:20	Exercises related to directed reading: 1. Workbooks 2. Questions on chalkboard to answer 3. Mimeographed seat work 4. Practice reading orally in pairs or small groups 5. Draw original pictures	Free time reading activity: 1. Games 2. Seat-work exercises 3. Dramatizations 4. Library books 5. Work related to other subjects 6. Microcomputer games, problem-solving software, interactive stories	Reading group with teacher
9:20–9:40	Free time reading activity: 1. Games 2. Seat-work exercises 3. Dramatizations 4. Library books 5. Work related to other subjects 6. Microcomputer games, problem-solving software, interactive stories	Reading group with teacher	Exercises related to directed reading: 1. Workbooks 2. Questions on chalkboard to answer 3. Mimeographed seat work 4. Practice reading orally in pairs or small groups 5. Draw original pictures
9:40–10:00	Reading group with teacher	Exercises related to directed reading: 1. Workbooks 2. Questions on chalkboard to answer 3. Mimeographed seat work 4. Practice reading orally in pairs or small groups 5. Draw original pictures	Free time reading activity: 1. Games 2. Seat-work exercises 3. Dramatizations 4. Library books 5. Work related to other subjects 6. Microcomputer games, problem-solving software, interactive stories

The teacher may designate a large block of time in the morning for language arts. During this time, all aspects of language development—reading, writing, spelling, and oral language—will receive attention. No effort should be made to compartmentalize the different forms of language; instead, they are used as tools as children explore stories, write and tell their own tales, engage in drama experiences, consult references on topics of interest or ones that have been assigned, practice skills that are timely, and share experiences with one another.

TABLE 8.2. Time Organization for Reading/Language Arts Using a Committee Structure

---

Time Period 9:15–10:15

Committee I	Children in this committee will be sharing stories that they have read silently. The theme will have been identified earlier as "dogs." The children, of varying reading abilities, will read the stories they have chosen orally. The last twenty minutes of the committee time will be spent illustrating the stories with chalk and paper and writing a brief summary of the day's work for the teacher.
Committee II	This group of children, of varying reading abilities, will spend time with the teacher learning encyclopedia reference skills that will be needed in two weeks for a unit to be initiated in social studies. The teacher will provide a variety of experiences both in learning the new skills and in practicing them.
Committee III	These children will have a bookmaking experience. Each child, prior to this committee cycle, will have written a book to be bound. A parent, who has book binding knowledge and has planned with the teacher, will be the resource person for this group. The children will display their books at the end of the day as their "report" of the group's work.
Committee IV	This group of children will be spending their committee time in the school's microcomputer lab playing a variety of reading games. The teacher has reserved the lab for the same time each day this week so that a different group may work with the lab director on the games. The last ten minutes will be saved for the children to write a brief report about their experiences and their reaction to them. The report will be posted in their classroom.
Committee V	This group will spend their committee time reading a story and preparing to role-play it later in the day for the rest of the class. A sixth-grade student will serve as the resource person for this group. As each group works on this task, the teacher will provide a different story to be prepared for presentation.

Note: The rotations through the various committee tasks are planned to last for a week. In the beginning, to ensure success of committee work, the committees might meet for only twenty minutes. Or, the teacher may focus on one committee per day and still allow time to observe the students, to talk with individuals, and to gather data for planning future committee cycles. Each child is able to do all of the activities each week; at the end of each activity each child has some responsibility for helping the group to think through and summarize the completed learning experience.

Other large blocks of time may be devoted to math and science and to social studies. Some teachers design even larger time blocks in which the distinctions between these content areas and the language arts tend to blur. Such time periods are usually organized around large units designed to permit students to explore the theme at appropriate levels of difficulty without concern for information that is usually associated with particular content areas. When learning opportunities occur at many levels, the teacher has opportunities to help children with a variety of needs—those who are capable of functioning well beyond the level of most of their classmates, the bilingual and bidialectal children, those who have learning difficulties, and those with physical problems such as vision or hearing.

At the end of the day, the teacher allows another time block during which children can reflect on the learning experiences that have occurred, can evaluate the plans made that morning, and can look forward to tomorrow.

Making Connections 8.1: Finding Out about
Classroom Organization for Reading

Achieving a satisfactory organizational plan for reading in the classroom is one of the most demanding tasks for the teacher. Good plans do not *just* happen. They are planned thoughtfully and are adjusted as children's needs change.

Plan to do one of the following activities, depending on whether you are now teaching.

1. If you have not taught, gain permission from at least three teachers to interview them concerning their plans for managing reading instruction. Take rather complete notes on their responses. If you feel comfortable enough to do so, you might ask what they see as strengths of their system. You might also ask if they are thinking of possible changes, and why these changes seem important.

   Bring all of your information to class to share with other class members. You should have quite a range of possible plans of organization, as well as strengths and weaknesses of them.

2. If you are teaching or have taught, write out your organizational plan for reading instruction. Pay particular attention to that part of the plan that addresses the needs of the poorer readers in the room. Ask another teacher in your building, who is willing to share with you, what his or her plan for reading instruction is like. Compare your two plans. Try to critique both plans in terms of their strengths and weaknesses.

   Plan to share the plans and your critique with class members. The group should produce quite a variety of plans, along with their accompanying critiques.

Case Studies

The following three case studies are examples of how classroom teachers at different grade levels have attempted to effect a corrective reading program for students in (1) the fourth grade, (2) the eighth grade, and (3) the twelfth grade. These case descriptions show, further, that the program was made effective throughout much of the school day.

Planning Work All Day for Jimmy in the Fourth Grade

Jimmy was a nonreader at the beginning of his fourth-grade year. He could not read the arithmetic problems, do research in social studies or science, spell or write anything that could be read, or read in the lowest reading group. It was no wonder that he was a behavior problem, causing general annoyances all day long by shooting pins, throwing spitballs, and kicking girls! It was no wonder that he sat staring out the window and never seemed to be aware when the class changed from one subject to another. The reader may wonder how Jimmy passed the first three grades with this condition. The cumulative record did not show that any diagnostic reading tests had ever been administered.

There was no doubt in the fourth-grade teacher's mind that Jimmy needed attention, and although he was low in all subjects and seldom said anything, his California Test of Mental Maturity results of the year before had shown him to have normal intelligence—an IQ of 92. Vision and hearing were also normal.

The teacher concluded that he must be able to learn to read, and she was challenged to find a way to teach him. She began by observing him throughout the day. The observation showed the following: He did nothing constructive, but just sat during all activities, even art. An interest in learning anything seemed to be nonexistent. He appeared to be very uninterested in his teacher, also. He never paid any attention to her directions or suggestions even when they were given to him individually. It was evident that his past failures had grown into a pattern of failure acceptance.

Had this child no ambition for himself? He did not seem particularly unhappy. In his home, personal development and ambition were apparently not greatly stimulated. His father was a laborer; a brother who recently graduated from high school was staying at home and was unemployed. Jimmy had one school friend, a very poor student in another fourth grade in the school. When together, they were constantly in mischief.

At the beginning of the fourth-grade year, Jimmy's teacher gave several informal reading tests to determine Jimmy's reading level—what he knew, what his difficulties were, and where to begin his instruction. He knew thirty-six Dolch Basic Sight Words. He failed to identify some of the initial consonant sounds and knew only a few blends. He had not learned hard and soft sounds of *c* and *g*. His strategies of predicting and confirming were totally absent. He could not write in cursive writing or spell. This evidence indicated definitely that any scores recorded on standardized reading tests were meaningless. To determine what reader he could read as his instructional level (that is, with 95 percent accuracy in mechanics and 75 percent comprehension as determined by answers to questions asked by the teacher), the teacher had him attempt to read a preprimer. He made too many errors. The instructional level at which he would progress best in learning to read would be at the beginning of a reading series— a first preprimer.

His capacity level for reading, determined by the Bond-Tinker formula—number of years in school times IQ plus 1.0,[2] was the seventh month of third grade $(3 \times .92 + 1.0 = 3.76)$.

In summary, the fourth-grade teacher was faced with a nonreader with normal intelligence, no foreign language handicap, a potential behavior problem, and a very passive attitude toward reading.

Accepting this challenging problem, the teacher:

1. Went back willingly and ungrudgingly to this child's level. She found very easy library books, since Jimmy resented the idea of reading preprimers.
2. Removed *competition* with other fourth graders and initiated a system of rewards for improvements made on his past records.

3. Removed all pressure of trying to get "grade-level work" out of the child at any time during the day.
4. Initiated and taught an individualized program in "how to read."
5. Provided kinds of activities the child could do throughout the entire day.
6. Located a great variety of materials that would interest the child and that could be completed and checked while the room activity continued for the thirty-three other youngsters.
7. Continued looking for *reasons why* the child failed in reading, but began reteaching without wasting any time, making sure that the child's reading was successful this time.

The teacher began by trying to do all these things. In the beginning, she gained his confidence and cooperation, found it quite easy to find two or three minutes at different times during the day to stop by his desk to see if his work sheets, writing exercises, or matching games were being done correctly.

The teacher's day was so organized that she had a thirty-minute work period for the class during the morning that all children used for "catch-up" time, free reading, or study. Jimmy could always be checked on during this period. This time period also provided a much-needed opportunity for the teacher to conference with any of her thirty-four students, to check on knowledge of basic sight words, to sample a new book where the level of difficulty was questionable, or to discuss other little problems that arose.

Jimmy's day was organized, eventually, to follow a schedule somewhat like this: He arrived at school with his morning studies already planned the previous afternoon; he read orally to another fourth-grade child for twenty minutes; he reviewed his growing file of sight vocabulary cards; he did seat-work exercises related to the oral reading he had just completed and to his word file; he wrote simple sentences and stories and on occasion a simple "book." Then he worked on the classroom microcomputer using the Houghton Mifflin Microcourse, "A Comprehensive Skills Program—Reading."[3] Initially, he worked with the software on word-attack skills. He became the classroom *expert* on the operation of the microcomputer; he was able to help other students "boot it up" and could explain how to handle the floppy discs so they would not become damaged. Jimmy had been doing a great deal of sound-tracing, based on what his teacher had read about the Fernald Method[4] and the Harris Visual-Motor Method.[5]

In arithmetic, where Jimmy was also achieving at a very low level, he was in a group of six children who constituted a separate class within the room.

Social studies was more difficult to encompass. He saw movies, went on a field trip, and was included in the total group during the teacher-pupil planning sessions. He drew a fairly detailed map (from copy) that was used on the bulletin board; he collected pictures (from copies of *Saturday Evening Post, Look, Life, National Geographic, Time,* and *Newsweek* magazines provided by the teacher); he made a scrapbook, and the teacher wrote brief explanations for him to read from context. On two occasions, a capable fourth-grade girl wrote summaries that were typed by the teacher and given to Jimmy for reading material. When studying about Mexico, Jimmy read an easy picture book to a reading partner after he had sampled it with the teacher.

Science is possible for fourth-grade children without relying primarily on reading. Jimmy gathered lists of needed equipment for science experiments. He did an experiment with an empty tin can with a screw-type lid that was placed on a hot plate with some water in it. The following story of what happened was planned with Jimmy and made possible his reading about the experiment. He carefully typed the story using the word-processing program on the classroom microcomputer.

Air Pressure

Here is a can.
We put water in the can.
Then we put the can on the stove.
The water boiled.
Steam came out.
Steam pushed some of the air out.
We put the lid on the can.
Then we took the can off the stove.
The can cooled.
Now, there is little air inside the can.
The can collapses.
The air outside pushes in the sides of the can.

Jimmy

Jimmy's teacher made him feel that he was a needed and wanted member of the class and, at the same time, provided activities for him that were instructional and interesting.

The teacher can have available many games and devices. As time permits, one child who knows a game well can play it with one or more other children who need practice. Jimmy learned to play *Take*,[6] matching *initial* sounds. He learned to play both *Go-Fish*, beginning sounds, and *Go-Fish*, blends.[7] He learned to play *Phonetic Quizmo*,[8] Bingo,[9] using Dolch Basic Sight Words, and Bingo,[10] using phrase cards based on phrases that he learned to recognize quickly. He used short flash-card drills in game situations with another child on words that the teacher was anxious for him to habituate.

Reading games, as such, are of value only if they are teaching children a skill or ability. Lots of easy reading practice is of more value if the child is interested in reading independently as quickly as possible. By the time the fourth-grade year was half over, Jimmy had read twenty easy, predictable books to another child or to someone in the family. He then was quite proud of himself because his teacher entered the title of each book on the class's reading chart showing the number of books read. His twenty books showed his rocket approaching the moon far ahead of many other children in the room (see figure 8.2).

The teacher recognized the importance of Jimmy's learning as quickly as possible the 220 Dolch Basic Sight Word List so that he would know the most common service words in children's reading. During the semester, he improved in his ability to recall these. In September, he knew 36; on November 1, he knew 60; on January 15, he knew 85; and in February, 110. His graph of progress continued throughout the year. Jimmy's teacher reinforced his progress by using visuals such as bar graphs.

Moon

Roll Over!

Go Tell Aunt Rhody

The Judge

Someone Is Eating the Sun

The Haunted House

I Was Walking Down the Road

Pancakes for Breakfast

The Fox Went Out One Chilly Night

When I First Came to This Land

A Treeful of Pigs

Where in the World Is Henry?

Figure 8.2. Jimmy's rocket moves closer to the moon by using predictable books.

The teacher gained confidence in her ability to keep Jimmy progressing. She felt that her entire array of teaching skills was improving by experimenting with new ways of meeting individual needs. Jimmy was doing well at primer level by midyear. His attitudes had improved to the point where he did his work without prompting; he gained confidence in his teacher's interest in helping him. He seemed to feel that he had become a genuine working member of the class, and he worked and played better with the other children.

The teacher found that Jimmy's mother was most willing to listen to him read at home those things that he had already read at school. In a home visit, the teacher explained to the mother that Jimmy did have normal intelligence (a happy relief for parents, always) but that he could not read and would need to start from the beginning in the reading process. The mother volunteered that perhaps Jimmy needed a physical examination to see why he was somewhat listless and indifferent. The teacher emphasized the need for such an examination and encouraged the mother to make an appointment right away. The teacher took time to send the mother short informal notes to tell her when Jimmy had done something especially well on a given day. The mother needed this encouragement as much as Jimmy did.

Peter, an Eighth Grader

Pete was an easygoing fifteen-year-old in the eighth grade. He got along smoothly and graciously with his peers.

Pete's cumulative folder indicated that most of his previous teachers had labeled him as a "lazy" boy who took no interest in his work. (The reading teacher knew, however, that there is no such thing as a "lazy" boy, but some boys, for reasons that need investigation, act in such a way that teachers call them "lazy.")

Pete had repeated two grades, the third and the fifth, and seemed to be getting nowhere after he entered junior high school. Several other boys had dropped out of school as soon as they had become sixteen, so the fact that Pete was interested in learning, attended school regularly, and responded intelligently in his general behavior prompted his reading teacher to offer needed extra help.

Pete was *bilingual*. He spoke Spanish a great deal outside of school. Because his parents relied almost entirely on Spanish for communication, Peter probably did his thinking in Spanish. Because he had never learned to read and write Spanish, however, he was severely limited in the amount of Spanish he knew. His Spanish vocabulary was limited to meeting the needs of casual conversation and work assignments around the house. Because Pete never learned to read English well and had little comprehension of what he did in English, he might be thought of more correctly as *nonlingual* than bilingual in terms of the language performance expected by the school.

Pete's intelligence had been tested with a group intelligence test and was recorded in his cumulative folder as an IQ of 82. But the teacher had read that IQ scores on a group intelligence test earned by the bottom 40 percent of the class are entirely unreliable.[11] In addition, Pete had a language handicap, so the IQ score was of little help in his case.

Pete was able to pronounce many words if given enough time to analyze them, but he could not supply meanings for them. When the teacher showed interest in helping Pete, he asked for almost constant help, and the teacher had to repeat short assignments or instructions many times.

When a hearing problem was suspected, Pete was referred to the school nurse who said that, even though she found a very slight loss in one ear, it was not to be considered serious enough to affect his schoolwork.

When the teacher tested from a series of readers for Pete's instructional level of reading, he read the words well enough at the fifth-grade level, but he could not answer questions to indicate comprehension of ideas until he read from the second level, third reader.

Pete knew all the 220 Dolch Basic Sight Words, although he made half a dozen substitutions, which he corrected himself. He was given the Inventory of Phonic Skills, Level 3, and had no difficulty except for a few vowel errors.

The reading teacher was also Pete's general science teacher for one period every day. In eighth-grade reading class, SRA Laboratories were used three days a week, and the teacher was able to call Pete to her classroom when she had her "free" period on some days. In addition, by talking with several of his teachers and the school principal, she was able to exercise considerable influence over much of Pete's school day. His program evolved in a pattern somewhat as follows:

1. The teacher called Pete to her room three days a week during her free period and used this time for administering tests—the Woodcock Reading Mastery Tests,[12] vocabulary tests she designed for measuring his ability with multiple meanings of common words, synonyms, homonyms, antonyms, prepositions, and oral reading abilities. Much of the need here proved to be that of teaching a much broader knowledge of English as a second language.

2. The reading teacher arranged for Pete to use the *Reading for Understanding, SRA Laboratory,*[13] rather than the graded series of laboratories. He needed to start with the lowest level to be sure that he could read and could always get meaning in context. The record of his SRA work was kept on graphs in his Student Record Book.

3. The teacher planned carefully for Pete to do work closely related to each chapter in the eighth-grade science book, which was her guide for subject matter material to be covered. The teacher found reading materials in third-, fourth-, and fifth-grade science books related to the topics being discussed in class. She then prepared questions, always easy at first, such as filling in blanks, matching words with definitions, making lists of terms, giving reasons "why" when clearly stated in easy books. She made sure Pete had opportunities for first-hand experiences with concepts that seemed unfamiliar to him. In this way, Pete was able to answer seat-work exercises just like the other students in the class.

4. Since Pete needed help primarily with story problems in arithmetic, the mathematics teacher was willing, *after he was alerted,* to assign Pete to work with a cooperative partner when such problems were to be read and worked, either as silent seat work or as a group work assignment in class.

   The history teacher learned that the *Children's Catalog*[14] and the *Standard Catalog for High School Libraries*[15] were invaluable for searching out books on specific topics related to all the units in American history. A few books and many stories in readers or in nonfiction collections were available on a third-to-fourth-grade reader level.

5. The first book that Pete read for "fun reading" was *Secret Island,*[16] followed by *Rescue*[17] and *Flying to the Moon.*[18] Each was read with the teacher. Pete particularly liked the books because they contained many suggestions of related activities that extended the ideas and made words more meaningful. He then read *2-B and the Rock 'n Roll Band,*[19] which he enjoyed so much that he obtained permission to read it to both the second- and third-grade boys. Reading *The Missing Aircraft*[20] was a more difficult task, since the reading level was high and the ideas were more complex. He persisted, however, and his reading improved noticeably as he read through the book.

George, a Twelfth Grader

George, nineteen years old, lived with his mother and three brothers and was a senior in high school. In spite of a severe reading disability all through school, he had expressed an ambition to go to college, to major in physical education, and to become an athletic trainer. Cultural deprivation offered at least a partial explanation for George's meager vocabulary and limited experience. His physical examination revealed no visual, auditory, or neurological handicapping conditions.

George volunteered for remedial instruction in reading when he learned that one of his teachers was enrolled in a corrective reading class and needed a "case" to work with for a semester.

George had been given an intelligence test, but because it had been a group intelligence test involving reading, the teacher suspected that the recorded IQ score of 82 was entirely unreliable.

When the 220 Dolch Basic Sight Word Test was administered as a recall test, George made thirty-three mistakes, many of which were middle-vowel substitutions. George was not aware of roots, prefixes, and suffixes as clues to word pronunciations, and he did not know their separate meanings. He placed fifth-grade level in the placement test of the *Reading for Understanding, SRA Laboratory.*

As a measure of George's capacity level for reading, the teacher found that he understood the material in the twelfth-grade textbooks quite well when the teacher read it aloud to him.

Early in the semester, George was selected to complete a special short-training course as the athletic trainer to help the high school coach. He completed the course and demonstrated aptitude for successfully carrying out this assignment. The teacher found a book called *Treatment and Prevention of Athletic Injuries*[21] that contained many illustrations and elementary reading. With some help, George succeeded in reading this book. He was highly motivated, and he reread and explained the text to the remedial reading teacher. George then read *Baseball Bonus Kid*[22] in the *Signal Book Series* independently. He also enjoyed books from the *Sportellers Series,* especially *Strike Two*[23] and *Foul Play.*[24]

The high school teaching staff gave its complete cooperation in helping George to successfully carry out his remedial program. When staff personnel who were George's teachers were informed about his reading problems and his level of aspiration, they were very willing to use suggestions in their respective subjects. George's first period in the day was spent in supervised study. His remedial teacher kept this study hall, so the period was utilized in checking on the work sheets done the previous day in all classes, and in making plans about what George would do that day. He usually read orally fifteen minutes of this first period from one of the *Teen-Age Tales* books.[25] Special arrangements were made for George during his English period. He did exercises with such useful materials as *Vocabulary Building Exercises for the Young Adult*[26] and the *TR Reading Comprehension Series.*[27]

The reading teacher recognized the great need for expanding George's English vocabulary, and she prepared many exercises involving idiomatic and slang expressions, multiple meanings of common words, synonyms, homonyms, antonyms, fifty common prepositions in the English language, and figures of speech.

Summary

In this chapter an attempt has been made to alleviate any anxiety that teachers may feel about permitting the students to do the work they can do rather than forcing them to continue with work that is too difficult. The teachers must understand the place of the course of study in teaching and must have adequate materials available in order to convert the classroom into a learning laboratory. Reports of classroom teachers demonstrate that faculty cooperation can enable students at elementary, middle school, and senior high school levels to begin to overcome their reading disabilities.

For Further Reading

Allen, JoBeth, et al. "Studying Change: Teachers Who Become Researchers." *Language Arts* 65 (April 1988): 379–87. The five authors identify the elements in the change process for teachers. This is an important article for teachers wanting to change their ways of working in the classroom.

Beck, Judith S. "A Problem Solving Framework for Managing Poor Readers in Classrooms." *Reading Teacher* 41 (April 1988): 774–79. Managing poor readers in the classroom is not as easy as it is made to seem. Practical and realistic ideas are presented for helping poor readers to function in the classroom.

Gamby, Gert. "Talking Books and Taped Books: Materials for Instruction." *Reading Teacher* 36 (January 1983): 366–69. The author distinguishes talking books (taped at normal speed) from taped books (recorded at slower speed). Their differing uses in the classroom are discussed.

Loughlin, Catherine, and Mavis Martin. *Supporting Literacy: Developing Effective Learning Environments.* New York: Teachers College Press, 1987. Dedicated to the memory of Marie Hughes, this volume presents an exhaustive examination of the classroom environment as a strategy for promoting literacy.

Loughlin, Catherine, and Joseph Suina. *The Learning Environment: An Instructional Strategy.* New York: Teachers College Press, 1982. Recently translated into Spanish, this text is an important tool for organizing an effective learning environment. Aspects of promoting literacy are also developed.

Nevi, Charles N. "Cross-Age Tutoring: Why Does It Help the Tutors?" *Reading Teacher* 36 (May 1983): 892–98. When teachers are developing ways to help all the readers in their classrooms, they should not neglect the idea of cross-age tutors. Everyone wins!

Smith, Frank. *Essays into Literacy.* Exeter, N.H.: Heinemann Educational Books, 1983. Some of Smith's most famous essays are presented in this book. An especially important one is, "Twelve Easy Ways to Make Learning to Read Difficult."

Notes

1. The center pages of any issue of *The Web,* published by the Ohio State University Press, provide examples of webs organized around themes and emphasize the use of children's books.
2. Guy L. Bond et al., *Reading Difficulties: Their Diagnosis and Correction,* 6th ed. (Englewood Cliffs, N.J.: Prentice-Hall, 1989), 41–42.
3. Houghton Mifflin Minicourse, *A Comprehensive Skills Program—Reading* (Hanover, N.H.: Houghton Mifflin Co., 1984).
4. Grace Fernald, *Remedial Techniques in Basic School Subjects* (New York: McGraw-Hill, Inc., 1971), 21–82.
5. Albert J. Harris and Edward R. Sipay, *How to Increase Reading Ability,* 7th ed. (New York: Longman, 1980), 409–11.
6. *Take* (Champaign, Ill.: Garrard Press).
7. *Go-Fish* (Washington, D.C.: Remedial Education Center).
8. *Phonetic Quizmo* (Springfield, Mass.: Milton Bradley Co.).
9. *Group Word Teaching Game* (Champaign, Ill.: Garrard Press).
10. Modeled after *Group Word Teaching Game.*
11. Bond et al., *Reading Difficulties,* 39.
12. R. Woodcock, *Woodcock Reading Mastery Tests* (Circle Pines, Minn.: American Guidance Service, 1973).
13. *Reading for Understanding, SRA Laboratory* (Chicago: Science Research Associates, Inc.).
14. *Children's Catalog,* 14th ed. (New York: H. W. Wilson Co., 1981).
15. *Standard Catalog for High School Libraries,* 11th ed. (New York: H. W. Wilson Co., 1977).
16. Edward Ramsbottom and Joan Redmayne, *Secret Island* (Cleveland: Modern Curriculum Press, 1983).
17. ———, *Rescue* (Cleveland: Modern Curriculum Press, 1983).
18. ———, *Flying to the Moon* (Cleveland: Modern Curriculum Press, 1983).
19. Sherry Paul and Bob Miller, *2-B and the Rock 'n Roll Band* (Cleveland: Modern Curriculum Press, 1981).
20. Ben Butterworth and Bill Stockdale, *The Missing Aircraft* (Belmont, Calif.: Pitman Learning, 1977). A book from the Jim Hunter Series.
21. Joseph P. Dolan, *Treatment and Prevention of Athletic Injuries* (Danville, Ill.: The Interstate, 1955).
22. Steve Gelman, *Baseball Bonus Kid* (Garden City, N.Y.: Doubleday, 1961).
23. George Shea, *Strike Two* (Belmont, Calif.: Pitman Learning, 1981).

24. Dick O'Connor, *Foul Play* (Belmont, Calif.: Pitman Learning, 1981).

25. Ruth Strang and Ralph Roberts, eds., *Teen-Age Tales,* Levels A, B, 1–6 (Boston: D. C. Heath, 1966).

26. Dorothy McCarr, *Vocabulary Building Exercises for the Young Adult* (Beaverton, Oreg.: Dormac, Inc., 1983).

27. *TR Reading Comprehension Series* (Hingham, Mass.: Teaching Resources, 1983).

9
Teaching Word Recognition

Vocabulary

word-recognition strategies
and skills
rapid word identification
mediated word
identification
stock of sight words
environmental print
"bubbles"
functional print
dictated stories
high-frequency words
language-experience
approach
rebus
theme
Dolch Basic Sight Words
Stone's Word List
Fry Basic Word List
wordless picture book
predictable books
taped books
bookmaking

Questions

1. Why is it important for the reader to learn a stock of sight words as quickly as possible? (**Recall**)
2. What are the advantages of rapid sight-word recognition over mediated word recognition? (**Inference**)
3. Describe how you plan to help children in your classroom to acquire a collection of words that can be recognized at sight. (**Application**)
4. Identify and describe the word-recognition skills and strategies. Do the same for the structural-analysis skills and strategies. (**Recall**)
5. Differentiate between structural analysis and phonics skills and strategies. (**Critical**)
6. What is important to teach the child about the dictionary for word identification? (**Recall**)
7. What advantages and disadvantages do you see in using the microcomputer for word-recognition activities? (**Inference**)

Vocabulary

picture clues
context clues
prior knowledge
cloze procedure
structural analysis and
    syllabication
affixes
combining forms
compound words
contractions
CVC-CVCe contrasts
homonyms
synonyms
antonyms
consonant substitution
silent letters
blend
consonant digraph
location skills and strategies
alphabetical order
pronunciation skills and
    strategies
meaning skills and
    strategies

Introduction

Word-recognition strategies and skills are those abilities that students need in order to make predictions about print and to confirm or reject them, unlocking words independently and rapidly as they read. From the earliest experiences with print, the children should be taught to utilize the knowledge they possess and the information suggested by the print, as well as their knowledge of syntax, to make astute hypotheses about the words that they are likely to meet on the page. However, the mechanical aspects of *rapid word identification* in reading separate the beginning or disabled readers from the mature readers. Mature readers go directly from print to meaning, making the visual process a small part of the task in comparison to the manipulation of ideas, which is the reason for reading. Beginning and disabled readers must *mediate* what words are. This is a process that requires time, effort, and much practice.

The beginning readers must memorize a bank of sight words as rapidly as possible. The more words the readers have in their banks, the more readily they can move from print to meaning in reading. One of the teacher's first tasks is to help the children to acquire a small vocabulary of sight words. Disabled readers also need to develop a sight-word bank as rapidly as possible.

While memorizing a stock of sight words to begin reading is satisfactory, the students must acquire many additional skills if they are to grow in the ability to read independently. Picture clues are useful as long as the students are reading well-illustrated materials. When there are no illustrations to carry a story theme, the students must rely on other skills. Five of these skills are:

1. Learning a basic sight vocabulary.
2. Using meaning or context clues contained in the reading.
3. Using structural analysis clues: looking at word parts.
4. Using phonic clues: breaking the word into parts for sounding.
5. Using the dictionary.

Learning a Stock of Sight Words

An early task in learning to read or in overcoming reading difficulties is to develop a stock of sight words. Fortunately, the teacher has many means for helping children to learn the needed sight words. The teacher will need to make some decisions about which strategies and materials to use in accomplishing this necessary task. Most strategies and materials will give children opportunities to make and confirm or reject predictions about the words that they see in print.

Environmental Print

Environmental print is a term used to refer to the words observed in the community outside the classroom. Settings for such print include billboards, street signs, labels on food products, and names of stores. Environmental print may also refer to the print the teacher uses in the classroom to organize, manage, and instruct students. Both

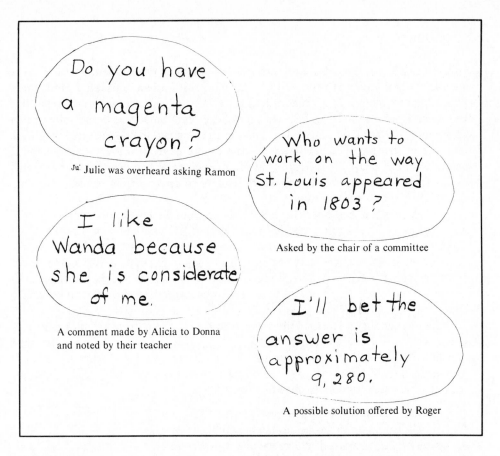

Figure 9.1. Typical comments of children recorded by a teacher for temporary display in the classroom

types are valuable as vehicles for teaching word recognition, as well as for demonstrating the importance and pervasiveness of print.

When children enter school, they usually come with some concepts about print and its meaning. Frequently, they can read signs such as "Stop," "Railroad Crossing," names of food products purchased in stores, names of favorite fast-food outlets, service station signs, and labels on T-shirts and other clothing items. The teacher needs to acknowledge this recognition of labels and signs. Children may begin the year by making books of labels from cans, boxes, fast-food containers, greeting cards, and other such sources of environmental print. The teacher may indicate that the children are going to learn more about reading, thus validating that what the children already know is a legitimate form of reading.

The teacher will find many functional uses for print in the classroom environment. "Bubbles" containing records of children's talk in the classroom are often helpful. Teachers who use the bubbles (see figure 9.1) often cut out many blank ones all the same size and shape. Then, recording and displaying interesting language is an easy

---

TASK CARD FOR MAKING BUTTER

These are the steps in completing this task.

1. Gather a box of cream, a spoon, the mixer, the salt box, and a bowl to use.

2. Follow the recipe over the table to make the butter.

3. When the butter is made, get the box of crackers from under the sink. Spread butter on the crackers and enjoy eating them. Taste the buttermilk that is left.

4. Wash all dishes and put them away. Put away the salt and crackers.

Making a Book

Choose a sheet of colored paper.
Fold it in half.
Put in 8 white sheets.
Staple the book together
Skip the title page and write your story. Put a picture on each page.
Last, write the title page.
Put the book on the old table.

Our Report
It was easy to make butter, but we made it too salty, especially with salty crackers. We washed the dishes real clean.

My Book
I got red paper.
I wrote about fish.
Fish are easy to draw.
I hope people liek it.   Jody

Figure 9.2. Task cards prepared by teachers, and reports written by children.

---

task. The teacher may note names of the speakers on the backs. When a child has several bubbles, the teacher may bind them into a booklet for the child to read and share with others. Signs providing needed information and notes to children are additional types of functional print in the classroom. Task cards and reports of small-group work prepared by the children (examples appear in figure 9.2) are other significant ways to make print important to students. Finally, the teacher should display the dictated stories of groups and individuals, or labels might indicate where materials may be found. All of these materials must be changed frequently so that there are always new items for children to read. The important message is that the print in the environment works for the children and can provide information, directions, enjoyment, and records for their use.

When working with disabled readers, the use of *functional print* is important because it provides for the students practical and relevant reasons to read. The teacher does not have to comment on the value of learning to read. The print speaks for itself. The students learn that in order to function in the classroom environment, they must read. This is made easier by the obvious contexts in which the print appears. A sign posted by the paint brushes and easel is obviously related to the work to be done there and not to the care of the hamster! The step-by-step directions often augmented by pictures (rebuses) along with a mixing bowl, measuring tools, flour, chocolate, and sugar are clearly aimed at making brownies, not completing a map for social studies!

As children grow in their ability to understand environmental print, whether in the classroom or in the larger community, they grow in the confidence that they need to deal successfully with print in other settings. They also develop an increasing number of sight words and high-frequency words that will serve them well in other settings.

Moving from Speech to Print

As children associate spoken words with written words, they learn to recognize their own names and the names of classmates and names on labels in the room; in general, they become word conscious. Such sentences expressed orally as "Howarya?" become "How are you?" as three separate words. The fisherman's question, "Ketchuninny?" becomes in its deep structure: "Are you catching any fish?" Beginning readers have to learn how spoken sounds are divided up into words—where a word begins and where it ends.

Dictated Stories

Most children begin to add to their first sight vocabulary by reading language-experience stories that they have *dictated*. The teacher needs to spend sufficient time discussing orally an experience or topic familiar to and interesting for the children. Then the teacher writes the sentences that the students dictate to tell the story in sequence.

If teachers are *aware* of the children's environments and life experiences, they can build stories using whatever language the children bring to school. If the first stories can be *personal* to the children, so much the better. An example is illustrated in figure 9.3.

In this story, five *high-frequency* words, *is, I, go, to,* and *the,* appear. Since all the nouns will be familiar to George, he will probably read this story with ease.

Language Experiences

The reading and writing that the students do may grow out of the exploration of the theme that is the focus of the student or the small group. Some of the writing, especially among the younger children, may sound a bit like "primerese," but if the writing and the related reading are personal work, motivation is likely to be high. Even the reading of resource material in order to find out more about the *theme* (topic) is important to the children. Of course, the teacher will need to devise a workable system for filing new words and reviewing them in meaningful ways, if they are likely to appear in later reading and writing.

Language experience requires that the teacher and children explore the topic (*theme*) orally before attempting to write and read about it. The oral experiences may be stimulated by some types of concrete experiences. At this time the teacher is careful to model new words and phrases, providing the students with opportunities to link concepts and language.

My name is George.

I am 7.

I go to school

I ride the bus.

Figure 9.3. Sample of children's personal stories

After one or more oral experiences, the teacher may encourage the children to record their experiences and ideas. If the students are young or having serious reading and writing difficulties, the teacher may take dictation so that the children may have the satisfaction of seeing their words written down.

The Balloons
We went to see the balloons.
They were very big.
They were red and yellow.
They were blue and green.
One looked like a big fish.
They went up in the sky.
We liked to see the balloons go up.

The *language-experience approach* to reading is an approach in which the learners' experiences are recorded for them to read later. This is a meaningful approach to beginning reading in which the children's own experiences and explorations and the children's personal language become the vehicles in learning to read. In this approach, meaning is the starting place, the emphasis, and the result of reading the prepared story. Instead of choosing characters in beginning reading books, children learn to read words that they've used in retelling their own personal experiences. This causes the content and choice of words to be unique to the children's cultural and experience background. It is believed that this approach to reading the written word relates spoken language more closely to written language. Children can initially learn several dozen sight words by this approach if the teachers are careful to provide repetition on commonly used words and to use a "selecting out" process that causes children to center attention on words to be remembered.

The very high frequency of a few basic words indicates a need to help children to learn these words as early as possible in their reading program. In the language-experience approach, these words can be taught in context with nouns and verbs familiar in the experiences of the learners so that reading can always be meaningful and purposeful. It must be emphasized that children should not be presented words in isolation and expected to retain them. The words need to be used orally in meaningful ways and then the oral form translated to writing.

Sight-Word Lists

When teachers encourage children to dictate or write their own stories to be placed on charts or bound into books for reading and rereading, to have one or more basic sight-word lists available may be helpful. Teachers may consult these lists to find the words the children have written that have particularly high utility. They may also use the lists to make choices of words to include in stories and other chart materials.

There are several lists that teachers might use as guides to the most important words to be learned first as sight words. Among them is Stone's list, which appears in figure 9.4. Other lists are the 220 words in the Dolch Basic Sight Word Test[1] (given in chapter 3) and the first 300 of the Fry Basic Word List.[2]

Other Ways to Develop Sight Vocabulary

The teacher needs a variety of means to help children develop rapid recognition of sight vocabulary. Young readers may lose motivation to continue learning if practice activities are limited in variety or are devoid of meaningful context. The teacher should encourage the use of rebuses and games as well as a variety of activities with books.

Rebus Reading

Rebuses are symbols, usually pictures, that represent words. Road signs, when the words are not used and symbols replace them, are rebuses. While rebuses may be geometric or abstract, only the pictorial rebus will be discussed here.

O'Donnell used the rebus in the preprimers of the Harper and Row reading series. She justified it in this way:

> The rebus may be used to represent words that have high interest value; so, without imposing upon the pupil the task of learning to read those words, the author is able to write interesting stories of high quality. . . . The use of rebuses makes possible a wider use of the child's speaking vocabulary.[3]

Woodcock taught five children to read twenty rebuses and compared the results with teaching the corresponding twenty words to five comparable children. His results were strongly in favor of introducing reading through the use of the rebus.[4]

With the rebus, the child can (1) give more attention to the meaning of the passage; (2) avoid some of the frustration of abstract symbols in lines of print; (3) bypass part of the traditional readiness programs; and (4) give more attention to left-to-right direction and visual motor perceptual training that may be helpful. Figure 9.5 is a story about the cat and her kittens told by using a rebus.

Children may be encouraged to create their own rebuses when they write in order to expand the vocabulary that they are able to use independently. Disabled readers may also find rebuses an alternative to struggling with seemingly endless spelling difficulties. This short-term remedy may contribute to a more measured approach to the mastery of needed spellings.

a	dog	I	not	the
after	doll	in	now	then
am	down	into	oh	they
and	father	is	on	this
are	find	it	one	three
of	for	jump	out	to
away	fun	kitten	play	too
baby	funny	laughed	rabbit	two
ball	get	like	ran	up
big	girl	little	red	want
blue	go	look	ride	was
bow-wow	good	make	run	we
boy	good-bye	may	said	went
came	had	me	saw	what
can	have	milk	school	where
car	he	morning	see	who
cat	help	mother	she	will
color	here	my	some	with
come	home	new	something	yes
did	house	no	stop	you

Figure 9.4. One hundred important words for prebook, preprimer, and early primer reading (Clarence R. Stone, *Progress in Primary Reading,* Manchester, Mo.: Webster Publishing Company, 1950).

Wordless Picture Books

During the past decade a number of illustrated books without words have appeared. *A Boy, A Dog, and A Frog* should elicit a good conversation from most any nonreader if the teacher provides the setting and takes the time to enjoy the story. Wordless picture books may stimulate original stories that the students will want to read because they will be their own. *Go Tell Aunt Rhody* can provide both conversation and the opportunity to sing the song that they have heard and to create new verses to add to it.

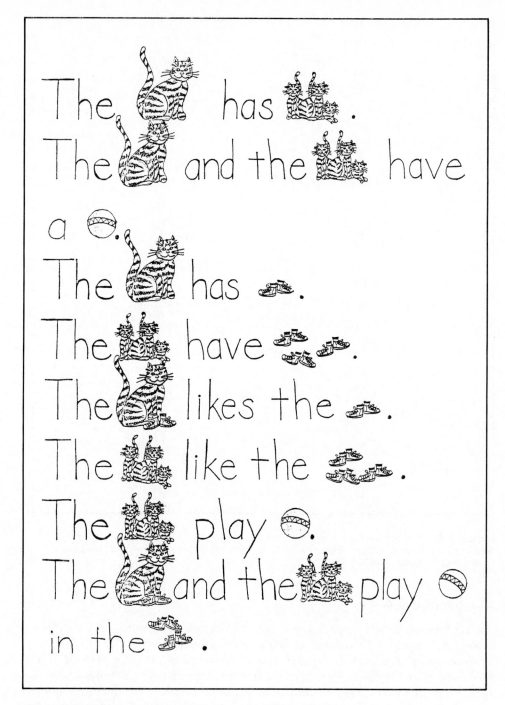

Figure 9.5. Rebus example prepared by Jean Martin, graduate student, University of New Mexico, Albuquerque, 1979.

The teacher must be alert to the child who simply describes the pictures and seems to make few connections between them. The teacher may need to model the use of connectives so that the pages link together in a flow of narrative parts—the introduction with characters and setting, the introduction of a problem or conflict, the resolution of the conflict, and finally the end. If the teacher is working with children who demonstrate this difficulty, he or she should select wordless picture books with pronounced narrative organizations, not books that consist of a series of interesting but unrelated pictures.

Weaver noted that wordless picture books encourage authorship.[5] Sentences dictated about each page may be clipped or taped at the bottom so that the young author or other classmates may enjoy the pictures and the accompanying story.

A few examples from the many dozens of available wordless picture books are:

Aliki, *Go Tell Aunt Rhody* (New York: Macmillan, 1974).
Anno, Mitsumasa, *Anno's Journey* (New York: Collins-World, 1978).
dePaola, Tomie, *The Hunter and the Animals* (New York: Holiday House, 1981).
Krahn, Fernando, *The Great Ape* (New York: Viking Press, 1978).
Mayer, Mercer, *A Boy, A Dog, and A Frog* (New York: Dial Press, 1967).
Mayer, Mercer, *One Frog Too Many* (New York: Dial Press, 1975).
Spier, Peter, *Noah's Ark* (New York: Doubleday, 1977).
Van Soelen, Philip, *A Cricket in the Grass* (New York: Scribners, 1981).

The reading teacher can use this concept by encouraging the students to draw a series of pictures to tell a story and then to compose the sentences that the story tells. When these sentences are written in manuscript below the pictures, the children will have their own stories, which they can read, reread, or share with others.

The teacher can focus the children's attention on meaning, sequencing, prediction, and seeing relationships, since the problem of word recognition is avoided.[6] For children who have focused heavily on word naming, wordless picture books may be especially useful, since the reader must attend to meaning to make sense.

Predictable Books

In chapter 7, *predictable books* were discussed as material that quickly allows a child to read independently. Predictable books are written so that the words are likely to be identified from the repetitive patterns, the sentence meanings, and the pictures. Once the children have heard the story, they are likely to be able to read it over and over to themselves. In fact, they will probably find enjoyment in doing so. If the teacher's goal is to promote the rapid recognition of sight words, the many rereadings of predictable books will surely help. Word-recognition practice will be associated with positive feelings about reading and with comprehension of a familiar story. The school librarian can supply a list of predictable books to help teachers build classroom collections.

Making Connections 9.1: Using Wordless Picture Books

Teachers are beginning to appreciate the value of wordless picture books in helping children learn to read or improve their reading. These books may be used to help children to sequence events, to find the parts of a story (beginning, problem, resolution, end); to study the goals, plans, feelings of characters; and to enjoy dictating, writing, and reading again and again their own stories.

A few wordless picture books are mentioned in this chapter. If you work with a librarian, you can learn the names of many more books of this type.

Select a wordless picture book that you especially enjoy. Share it with at least two children in separate sessions. After discussing the pictures in the book, have each child either write or dictate a story based on the pictures. You will probably get the most complete story if the child dictates or if you record the story on tape and transcribe it later.

After the stories have been written, dictated, or transcribed, have the children read their own and perhaps the story written by another child. Make this an enjoyable experience, encouraging the children to feel proud of their efforts at authorship.

You will want to examine the children's stories to see whether they maintained understandable story lines, whether the important parts of a story were present, whether the children kept the characters clearly identified through the use of pronouns, and whether they made their stories fit the pictured situation. You may see clear differences in the abilities of the children.

Bring the book, the stories, and your analyses to class to share with others. Discuss how these stories could help children to practice basic sight vocabulary as well as to learn more about the structure of stories.

Taped Books

A growing number of books is now published with accompanying records or cassette tapes of the story being read clearly and interestingly. Frequently, multiple copies of the book in paperback form with the tape or record come in a kit. As many as six to ten children may hear the book read, or a single child may enjoy the story alone. If a listening center equipped with earphones is available, the listeners may enjoy the reading of the story while the rest of the students go about their tasks undisturbed.

Listening to tapes or records of books while following along gives children an excellent way to practice word recognition in a meaningful setting. Since the children may listen again and again, the needed repetition of sight words is gained with enjoyment.

If the children are working with themes, the teacher may read some books and reference materials onto tapes so that children with reading difficulties may participate in information gathering. The greatest value in terms of word recognition will be obtained if the children are provided with the texts so that they may follow the taped readings. If the materials are reread, the children may read along with the tape for additional practice.

Bookmaking

When children make books, they have real and personally interesting reasons for learning words. They have many ideas to express, and the words with which they express them are frequently the words the teacher is anxious for them to learn. The teacher needs to keep a constant supply of various materials that may be used in making and binding books. The children should be encouraged to experiment with different materials and with different ways of producing both the contents of the book and its binding. It is helpful if a typewriter is available to the children as well as all sorts of pens, pencils, and markers. Some classrooms may be fortunate enough to have a microcomputer with a printer. With these tools children can write their stories and immediately have attractive printed copies to read and bind into books. Paper, glue, cardboard, laminating materials, fabrics, and sewing supplies should be readily available for binding.

Children may write books together, telling the story of a group experience or emphasizing some aspect of a theme being studied. Groups of children may have experiences such as cooking, making birdhouses, or sailing boats, but each child should also write an individual book. Some children want to write alone, basing their stories on what is important to them. Teachers should also write and bind books. They are powerful models for young writers.

In classrooms where book writing and binding are ongoing activities, children's own books are very popular during quiet reading times. Students read their own books and books made by their classmates. A large amount of enjoyable practice on basic sight words is gained, since the children use these words over and over in their writing.

Games

Teachers often think of games as a means to practice sight words. Studies have shown that games do indeed help children to learn or retain vocabulary. Games in which children are active may be particularly helpful.[7] Teachers should study games carefully to make sure that they provide for as much practice as possible and that the words are presented in meaningful settings. Make sure that the words in the games chosen for the class are words that the children need to learn. Games that allow children to use words creatively are to be preferred over those in which players must follow set rules.

David Woodward

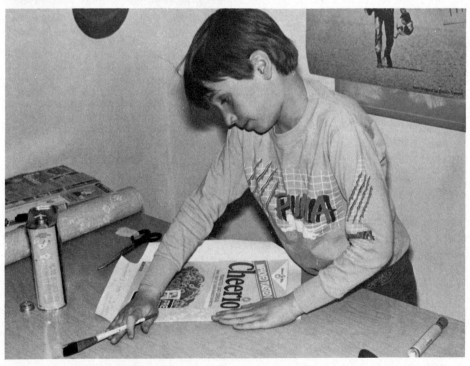

David Woodward

Writing books and binding them are recognized as important aspects of literacy development.

David Woodward

And when the book is finished, there is great satisfaction in sharing it with one's mother when she visits school.

Many games are available, and more are being produced each year. A few games were suggested in chapter 7. Teachers may also ask children to make games for the class. One group of teachers gave each student a piece of cardboard two feet square at the beginning of the year. The first homework assignment was to develop a reading game for the classroom. As children brought in their completed games, each game was laminated. The classrooms had a generous supply of games for the year, and the children had the satisfaction of having made a useful contribution.

Context Clues: Anticipation and Reconstruction of Meaning

The reader's ability to derive meaning from written language is primarily dependent upon how rich an experiential or conceptual background the reader brings to the passages being read. The reader should be predicting what is going to happen next, continually testing hypotheses to see if his or her predictions were correct, and confirming or rejecting the ideas by the concepts that they reveal through reading. Just as the young children expand their oral language syntax and vocabulary by repeated cycles of sampling, hypothesis testing, receiving immediate feedback and reinforcement, and recycling new hypotheses about language usage, so the ones who are ready and have need to do so will exercise the same cycle of activity in learning to read print.

Children need guidance in predicting and confirming strategies. This is especially true with children whose word-recognition focus has been limited to "sounding out" words. Useful techniques derived from the concept of predicting and confirming include:

1. Actively using one's background or prior knowledge to make predictions about what is currently being read.
2. Anticipating what a word is from the meaning of the phrase or sentence containing the word.
3. Anticipating the meaning of a sentence as a whole to help arrive at a meaning for a new word.
4. Learning techniques of minimizing alternatives in word identification to transfer from the spoken language to the reading setting.

Picture clues may be profitably used by children as they read.[8] They may tell what the whole sentence says. Pictures at the top of the page may give a clue to the new words in the reading material and may help evaluate the accuracy of the other word-recognition practices being used.

Context clues may help the reader to derive the meaning of the word from the setting in which it is used. Meaning is so dependent upon context that all new words should be presented in meaningful context. Use of context to confirm meaning is an excellent check on the accuracy of all the other word-recognition techniques.

The children's abilities to use picture clues effectively, their abilities to decipher context clues, and their abilities to anticipate what will come next—all three are dependent upon the storehouse of known concepts they already have. Their total backgrounds of experience make them able to cope with these clues as they appear. For those with limited conceptual backgrounds, the teachers will be most helpful by finding as many concrete ways as possible to help them expand their stock of word meanings.

The ability to predict what is coming next in the line of print can be taught. In children's context reading, the word, or even the entire next sentence, can be predicted many times from the reading already done. This partially explains the success of the cloze procedure in measuring comprehension in silent reading. When every nth word is deleted, the use of redundant words and syntax, the repetition of the same idea in different ways, and the restatement of fact make it possible for children to supply the missing word with considerable accuracy if they are attending to the thought as they move through the lines of print. Smith pointed out that the context itself is redundant. That is, it contains "prior knowledge, which reduces the alternative number of possibilities that a . . . word can be."[9]

Types of Context Clues

Several types of context clues can be directly taught to children. They will be remembered and used if they are pointed out in meaningful lessons that the students are doing.

Direct Explanation

The new word or concept is explained in a sentence:

1. A *chauffeur* is a man or woman who drives an automobile for a living.
2. A nest of young pheasants is called a *nide*.
3. The action of manufacturing food in the leaves of green plants is called *photosynthesis*.

Background of Experience

The meaning of the unknown word can be deduced from the students' backgrounds of experience (*prior knowledge*):

1. Mother said that the old man with a hump on his back who lived down the street had *kyphosis*.
2. While a large number of cattle driven together is called a herd, a large number of whales is called a *pod,* and a large number of lions is called a *pride.*

Comparison and Contrast

Relating the meaning of a new word to a known word opposite in meaning may clarify a concept:

1. Sheep and deer are small animals, but the whale, the largest living mammal, is *enormous.*
2. Gayle was shy and retiring, but her sister Helen was *effervescent* and *gregarious.*

The Synonym Clue

The new concept may be followed by a synonym or restatement of meaning:

1. The *cacique,* the person of highest authority in the village, asked all the men to come to the kiva.
2. We stayed in the *lobby,* a small waiting room in front of the doctor's office.

A Summary Clue

This is the use of a general term to encompass the description given:

1. His eyes were dull, his feet were sore, and his back ached; he was *exhausted.*
2. A child diagnosed as *dyslexic* probably has failed in school, lacks adequate oral language achievement, demonstrates persistent failure, and oftentimes has other family members with the same symptoms.

Previous-Experience Clue

This clue is dependent upon the student's use of prior knowledge to transfer:

1. The *zebra* looks very much like a horse, except he is covered with black and white stripes.
2. The station attendant said to stay on the *main artery,* and they knew that he meant the principal route.

Reflection of a Mood

The "tone" of the general situation provides a clue:

1. When the football team won a 7–0 victory, the *exuberance* of the crowd was uncontrollable.
2. We watched the *anguished* expressions on the people's faces as they saw the burning house collapse.

Recognizing Antecedents

Readers must recognize the antecedents of pronouns as they read:

1. Jane put the *scrapbook* on the top shelf so that *it* would not be lost.
2. The *dog that* caught and killed the rat was very valuable.

Directional (Structure) Words

There are words that indicate continuing, concluding, reversing, or illustrating action in the sentence:

1. I can't go skating with you today. *Moreover,* the ice is too thin. (continuing)
2. *As a result* of this study, we will shorten the lunch period by ten minutes. (concluding)
3. He was very tired; *nevertheless* he kept on working for several hours. (reversing)
4. Tom's doctor told him *specifically* that he must leave eggs and butter out of his diet. (illustrating)

These examples illustrate several types of clues that students need to be aware of. They will be able to find others as they read critically in their texts. When *no clues* to meaning are given, students must be encouraged to use the dictionary.

Cloze Procedure

The *cloze procedure* is usually associated with the testing or teaching of comprehension skills. However, it can be used to facilitate word recognition, through the use of context clues. The teacher can develop cloze sheets in which words that the children need to learn are omitted. Passages can be prepared that contain words that the children need to learn or need to practice in context. It may be useful to develop cloze passages in which certain kinds of words—prepositions, adjectives, verbs, and so on—are deleted. The children may need to attend to several prepositions, for instance, that have been especially troublesome. It may also be desirable to have children generate sets of synonyms that could fit the blanks. More opportunities for word recognition would thus be created.

At least initially, the teacher may wish to use highly predictable materials for creating cloze lessons. Well-known jingles and rhymes, material from predictable books, and stories written by the children are readily available sources that will provide enjoyable opportunities for word-recognition practice.

Examples of cloze activities may be found in chapter 10.

Using Structural-Analysis Clues: Looking at Word Parts

Structural analysis of words includes the study of derived and inflected forms and compound words. Students need a knowledge of root words and affixes so they will be able to understand the changes in word forms, sound, accent, and spelling. Knowing what a syllable is and some generalizations about syllables in words will be useful. Teachers need knowledge of structural analysis so that they will easily recognize when the readers need that kind of information.

The Syllable

A *syllable* is a word or part of a word that has only *one* vowel sound. A one-syllable word may have two vowels, but only one vowel is sounded. A polysyllabic word has as many syllables as it has separate vowel sounds. Teachers can help children to hear how many sounds (syllables) there are in a word by counting (pen–1; cil–2); or by clapping as the teacher pronounces by syllables; or by saying the word in separated sections. Thus, by listening and counting, the teachers and the learners can tell how many syllables are in words such as these: bookcase, countryside, paper, rule, notebook, pen, chalkboard.

Syllabication

Following are some generalizations about dividing words into syllables. They need to be stated cautiously to keep students aware of exceptions. Students will usually learn such rules and be able to retrieve and apply them most easily if they have been guided to discover them through the use of meaningful vocabulary items. The timing of learning opportunities is important, also; the information should be given when the child has the greatest need for it. If, in pursuing some aspect of an interesting theme, the child needs specific input about a syllabication rule, learning is likely to take place. The teacher will increase the chances of the student continuing to use the information if the child is also given a strategy for retrieving the rule if it is forgotten.

TABLE 9.1. Syllabication of VCV Words

VCV Words in which the Consonant Begins the Second Syllable			VCV Words in which the Consonant Remains with the Preceding Syllable		
fa *tal*	be *gin*	to *tal*	*shiv* er	*tax* i	*rap* id
pa *per*	sa *ble*	a *muse*	*nov* el	*ex* ert	*trav* el
de *lay*	ti *ger*	po *lite*	*com* et	*per* il	*mon* ey
e *ver*	gro *cer*	a *corn*	*sol* id	*rob* in	*mim* ic

1. In a polysyllabic word where there are two consonants between two vowels, the syllables will usually divide between the two consonants, unless the first vowel has a long sound. (If the readers are already aware that the vowel will have a long sound, they can probably pronounce the word and so do not need to worry about the generalization.) VCCV indicates letter order—vowel-consonant-consonant-vowel:

   VCCV words: mon key   ob ject   per fect   mis take
   VCCV words with the first vowel sound long: *se* cret   *mi* crobe
   "Twin consonants" between the separated vowels are also a part of this generalization: but ter   cab bage   lad der   cot tage
   skim ming   bal loon   com mon   cop per

2. When there is one consonant between two vowels in a polysyllabic word, the consonant usually goes with the second vowel if the preceding vowel has a long sound, and with the first vowel if the first vowel has a short sound. If the consonant between the two vowels is either *x* or *v*, this letter usually remains with the preceding vowel to form the syllable. VCV indicates letter order—vowel-consonant-vowel—in table 9.1.

3. Syllables are classified as open or closed. Open syllables are those that end with a vowel sound; closed syllables are those that end with a consonant sound:
   Open syllables: *se* cret   *po* nies   *ti* ger   *sto* ries   *fa* mous
   Closed syllables: *sun* set   *mon* key   *but* ter   *rab* bit   *cir* cle

4. Prefixes and suffixes are usually separate syllables:
   un fair   *re* paid   *dis* play   *mis* take   *in* active
   hope *less*   pay *ment*   like *ly*   work *ing*   mo *tion*

5. Usually *ed* added to a word does not constitute a separate syllable. However, when *ed* is added to a word that ends with a *t* or a *d,* the *ed* constitutes a separate syllable:
   bolt *ed*   bud *ded*   mend *ed*   plant *ed*   hint *ed*   need *ed*

6. Polysyllabic words ending in a consonant and *le* usually form the final syllable with the consonant plus *le*. For example:
   an *kle*   ap *ple*   arti *cle*   bat *tle*   cir *cle*   bee *tle*   Bi *ble*
   nes *tle*   no *ble*   tan *gle*   sta *ble*   tri *ple*   sam *ple*   ket *tle*

TABLE 9.2. Common Prefixes

Prefix	Meaning	Examples
un	not	unassuming, uncertain, unlimited, unconscious
mis	badly/wrongly	misbehave, misconduct, mismanage, misjudge
fore	before	forehead, forethought, forecast, foremost
co, com, con	together	cooperate, compact, consolidate, coeducate
dis	not	disagreeable, disobey, disorganize, discolor
re	again	react, rearrange, rebuilt, redistribute
sub	under	submarine, submerge, subdivide, subterranean
trans	across	transgress, transport, transact, transatlantic
im	not	improper, impossible, imperfect, improbable
in	not	inadequate, infinite, insignificant, incomplete

TABLE 9.3. Common Suffixes

Suffix	Meaning	Examples
ful	filled with	wonderful, thoughtful
ness	state of being	sickness, weariness
less	without	doubtless, tasteless
ly	like	laughingly, curiously
er, ist	one who performs	builder, flier, geologist, druggist

7. When a word is composed of two complete words, that is, a compound word, it is divided between the two words that make up the compound. For example:
   some where   bird house   school yard   air plane   cow boy   milk man
8. Syllables usually do not break between consonant blend letters or special two-letter combinations:
   lea *ther*   bro *ther*   chil *dr*en   an *gry*
9. When each of two adjacent vowels in a word forms a separate syllable, the word divides between the two vowels:
   gi *a*nt   cre *ate*   li *ons*   fi *at*   Su *ez*

Affixes

Affixes added to root words may be either prefixes or suffixes. A syllable at the beginning of a word that modifies its meaning is a *prefix*. A *suffix* is a letter or a syllable added to the end of a word to modify its meaning. Some common prefixes and suffixes are defined and illustrated in table 9.2 and table 9.3.

   Ten of the most frequently occurring prefixes with their meanings and examples are given in table 9.2

TABLE 9.4. Combined Words

Word	Word Parts	Meaning	Literal Meaning
biology	*bio*	life	study of living things
	logy	study	
zoology	*zoo*	animals	study of animal life
	logy	study	
biography	*bio*	life	write about life
	graph(y)	write	
geography	*geo*	earth	write about the earth
	graph(y)	write	
photograph	*photo*	light	write in the light
	graph	write	
thermometer	*therm(o)*	heat	measure the heat
	meter	measure	
pentagon	*penta*	five	having five angles (sides)
	gon	angle	
polygon	*poly*	many	having many sides
	gon	angle	
synonym	*syn(o)*	equal	an equal name
	nym	name	
telephone	*tele*	far	sound from far away
	phone	sound	
diameter	*dia*	through	to measure through
	meter	measure	

Suffixes may be either inflected forms or derived forms. The inflected forms are the word endings needed because of grammatical changes such as number, case, gender, or tense; examples are dog-dogs, work-worked, it-its. Derived forms are syllables added to give the root word a new meaning: brave-bravery, amuse-amusement, trick-trickster. The most common inflectional endings are *s, ed, ing, er, est.* Suffixes that are derived forms may have more than one meaning, and learners must be aware of this. Some of the common ones are given in table 9.3. For the greatest learning, students need to meet affixes in context, rather than in isolated drill.

Combining Forms

Combining forms are those linguistic entities that occur in compound words and are distinguished from affixes by their ability to be the root of a word when used with an affix: *cephal,* meaning "head," and *cephalic,* meaning "of or relating to the head." Combining forms are generally derived from Greek or Latin. Each comes to us *with* and *retains* its meaning. Knowing the meanings of these combining forms will help students to gather meaning from context efficiently (see table 9.4). Children will often meet such words as they pursue aspects of themes or units from content areas.

Compound Words

Early in their reading experiences, children begin to meet *compound words*. English abounds in compound words, and new words entering the language are likely to be compounds. Rinsky and Griffith estimated that 60 percent of the new words are compounds.[10]

Children usually read compound words easily if they know the two root words from which the compound is made. However, the teacher must not assume that the child knows the meaning of the compound because the meanings of the roots are known. The new word may have a slightly different meaning, such as *doghouse,* made from *dog* and *house,* or a very different meaning from the roots, such as *overdrawn,* made from *over* and *drawn.* The teacher should take time to talk about how the compound words that the children meet are formed, what the meanings of the roots are, and what the compound word itself means.

Children may be interested in making collections of compound words that they find in their reading. They may cut compound words from magazines and newspapers. They may design their own games in which the object is to form pairs of words that become compound words.

Contractions

English uses many *contractions,* and the number of contractions appears to be growing. Children are exposed to many oral contractions that may be confusing when reading begins. Children are surprised and confused to find that *gonna* and *hafta* are not words, since they hear them spoken frequently. Teachers and children need to take time to talk about these oral forms that do not appear in print except as individual words.

Children need help in dealing with standard contracted forms. One cannot assume that because the child can read *can* and *not* that *can't* will be readily known. The child needs to see the teacher remove the letters that are to be dropped and then see the letters replaced by the apostrophe. Sentences containing the full and contracted forms should be compared.

John *did not* go to town.
John *didn't* go to town.

Some contractions look quite different from the words they replace. For example, *I'd* may be a replacement for *I would* and *I had.* These contractions that bear little resemblance to the full forms need to be discussed and used in a variety of sentences until the children become familiar with them. Children need to practice changing contractions into the full forms. They also need to change pairs of words into contractions.

Practice in Structural Analysis

Practice in structural analysis may be planned to occur in a variety of ways. Children who write and read interesting materials will have multiple contacts in context with the varied aspects of structural analysis. If the teacher is aware of the needs of individual learners, information about an unknown or misunderstood aspect of structural analysis can be supplied at the point of need.

However, if the teacher decides that individual children need additional practice with one or more aspects of structural analysis, workbook pages and well-prepared practice sheets may be given. They should be corrected as soon as they are completed so that the child can be helped immediately to understand any errors that were made. Teachers will also find basal reader manuals replete with suggestions for teaching structural-analysis strategies and skills. Teachers should also have references in their personal or school professional libraries to provide additional suggestions. Three books giving suggestions for helping children to learn structural analysis strategies and skills are:

Durkin, Dolores. *Strategies for Identifying Words.* 2d ed. Boston: Allyn and Bacon, 1981.
Johns, Jerry L. *Handbook for Remediation of Reading Difficulties.* Englewood Cliffs, N.J.: Prentice-Hall, 1986.
McCormick, Sandra. *Remedial and Clinical Reading Instruction,* 267–79. Columbus, Ohio: Merrill Publishing Co., 1987.

Special Categories of Words

Certain categories of words may require special attention by teachers as students write and read during the school day. While many children may work out such difficulties alone, students with reading problems may need extra help. Meaningful drill is often appropriate, followed by the application of what has been practiced in meaningful contexts. Four categories of such words are given here along with suggestions for instruction.

CVC-CVCe Contrasts

The student should pronounce, use in sentences, and learn to spell words like the following:

hop	strip	can	tap
hopping	stripping	canning	tapping
hope	stripe	cane	tape
hoping	striping	caning	taping

Homonyms

Homonyms occur frequently in English and require attention by the teacher to make clear the different spellings and meanings. Children may enjoy "collecting" homonyms for bulletin boards, wall dictionaries, private collections, and homemade games. Some trade books also feature the humor to be found in confusing the spellings and meanings of homonyms. Two of these books are:

Gwynne, Fred. *A Chocolate Moose for Dinner.* New York: E. P. Dutton, 1973.
Gwynne, Fred. *The King Who Rained.* New York: Windmill, 1970.

Common homonyms used for spelling and writing in stories include:

aisle-isle	great-grate	profit-prophet
ant-aunt	groan-grown	rein-rain-reign
beach-beech	heal-heel	sew-sow-so
meat-meet	cereal-serial	cite-sight-site
dear-deer	dew-due	vain-vane-vein
mail-male	shone-shown	pear-pare-pair
knew-new	in-inn	cent-scent-sent
hour-our	pain-pane	right-write-rite
fair-fare	foul-fowl	road-rowed-rode

Synonyms

Children may be introduced to synonyms through cloze activities in which *synonyms* are accepted in the blanks. Encouraging children to write and to select precise language also encourages thought about synonyms for nouns, verbs, adjectives, and adverbs, as well as the composition of more interesting stories and expository writings. For *ghost* the child might write *spook* or *phantom,* and *cry* could be recorded as *weep* or *whimper.* Many good children's dictionaries are available. Two children's thesauruses are:

In Other Words: A Beginning Thesaurus. Andrew Schiller and William A. Jenkins. Glenview, Ill.: Scott, Foresman, 1986. Suited for upper elementary reading levels.
In Other Words: A Junior Thesaurus. Andrew Schiller and William A. Jenkins. Glenview, Ill.: Scott, Foresman, 1982. Suited for late primary reading levels.

Antonyms

Practice may be given in naming *antonyms* by encouraging children to make posters illustrating opposites such as *friendly* and *menacing* or *vacant* and *occupied.* Children may look for pictures that contrast meanings in magazines. Examples of antonyms may be found in readers and content texts. Antonyms are often found in dictionaries and thesauruses as well. Examples of antonyms for naming, writing, and reading are:

hard-easy	small-large	buy-sell
full-empty	tall-short	early-late
fast-slow	shut-open	summer-winter
noisy-quiet	sunny-cloudy	before-afterward
bold-timid	halt-advance	capture-free

Using Phonic Clues

The use of phonics to decode words is a *last resort.* The student should have learned to look carefully at the word to see if he or she understands its meaning in the rest of the sentence, if he or she can identify parts of the word and put the parts together to arrive at a meaning, or if he or she can discover the meaning in an illustration on the page. Then, if these efforts have failed, the learner should use phonics to pronounce the word, in combination with *any* other clues the reader has obtained. Any teaching of phonic information out of context should be followed immediately by an opportunity to apply what has been learned in a meaningful setting.

The phonic elements are single consonants, consonant combinations, single vowels, vowel combinations, vowel-consonant combinations, and the schwa. The phonic elements may provide the key to pronunciation so the readers can get quickly to meaning. The only purpose phonics serves in *reading* is to help the readers go from print to meaning immediately. A breakdown of all the phonic elements in English is presented in chapter 3. If teachers are confident about supplying the phonic elements when the learners need them, there will be no specific order in which these need to be taught. To help the readers understand how the phoneme is *sounded* in a given context is more appropriate.

There are those who are overconcerned with the matter of teaching the phonic skills so that children can "break down and pronounce" words. The emphasis should be much more on reading and approximating what the authors had in mind when they put the ideas on paper.

Some steps for teaching consonant and consonant-blend sounds are given in table 9.5. Most children will hear and remember the phonic elements easily if teachers have pictures and provide oral language lessons.

Young children will enjoy practice in using and hearing repetition of different consonant sounds:

C	c:	The cat, the cow, and the camel can come in.
Ch	ch:	The charming children chased the chickens.
D	d:	Daisy did the dirty dishes.
E	e:	Elsie the elephant eats everything.
F	f:	Funny Phillip fell over the footstool.
G	g:	There goes the girl with her gaggle of geese.
H	h:	Harry hung his hat on a hook in the hall.
J	j:	Jack and Jill enjoyed the jar of jam.
K	k:	The kangaroo kicked the copper kettle.
L	l:	Louise liked the lovely lemonade.
M	m:	The monkeys made more money than the men.
N	n:	The nine noisy nestlings never nestled in the nest.
P	p:	Pat put the pony in the pasture.
R	r:	Ruth and Robert ran around the red roses.
S	s:	Sally sells seashells by the seashore.
Sh	sh:	Sharon shouted as she sheared the sheep.
T	t:	Tom took the toys to the table.
Th	th:	Thelma thinks that they're thin things.
V	v:	Verna arranged a vase of violets.
W	w:	Willie works in the west wing of the warehouse.
Wh	wh:	What a whale of a whistle!

Older children may enjoy such tongue twisters as "Peter Piper," which usually emphasize one beginning consonant. They may even enjoy composing tongue twisters to try on one another.

TABLE 9.5. Steps in Teaching a Consonant or Consonant-Blend Sound

Steps	*For the Letter "b"*	*For the Blend "fl"*
1. Provide realia or pictures that are nouns beginning with the sound. Elicit from the learner that the nouns all begin with the same sound.	ball, box, boy, bear, bicycle, balloon	flag, fly, flower, flute, flame
2. Ask the learner to think of words that begin with the same sound.	basket, baby, buffalo, banana, butterfly, bird	flat, flash, fleet, float, flock
3. Ask the learner to look at a short list of words and underline all the words that begin with the designated sound.	ball balloon dog baby boy cowboy pig box	flag drown play flame flash flock trip fly
4. Say several words, and ask the learner to indicate which ones begin with the designated sound.	boy, toy, pig, big, box, pack, back, bell, fell, banana, baby	flash, trash, flock, grass, float, flick, flag, clash
5. Give the learner a list of words to be changed to new words beginning with the designated sound.	change: *at* to *bat* *ox* to *box* *all* to *ball* *ill* to *bill* *and* to *band*	change: *ash* to *flash* *oat* to *float* *at* to *flat* *lame* to *flame* *lock* to *flock*
6. Ask the learner to identify the ending sound of the word.	cab, mob, rib, hub	does not apply to the consonant-blend sounds; however, it does apply to the consonant digraphs: *ch, ck, gh, ng, nk, ph, sh, th*
7. Ask the learner to use the new sound in figuring out new words in context.	*Bill* came *back* to the *bank.* The *beds* were *built* of *boxes.*	The *flag* is *flying.* The *flower* was on the *floor.* The *fly flitted* away.

Teaching New Words through Consonant Substitutions

The suggestions that follow are examples of the types of phonic information that children may need. Frequently, such skills and strategies may be learned in the context of interesting reading and writing activities connected with themes or units that children are developing. On occasion, the teacher may need to isolate certain types of information so that children may identify the learning task clearly. However, whatever has been learned must immediately be applied to meaningful and relevant material.

Initial Consonant Substitutions

In primary reading, children have much opportunity to discover new words for themselves after they have already learned the necessary skills to do so.

The language that follows gives children practice in initial consonant substitutions:

Take *b* away from boy; put in *t* and you have
toy.
Take *s* away from sing; put in *fl* and you have
fling.
Take *t* away from tore; put in *sh* and you have
shore.

With this skill, using sight words the children already know, they can:

Take *t* from *Tom* and *oy* from boy and discover
toy.
Take *fl* from *fly* and *ing* from *sing* and discover
fling.
Take *sh* from *show* and *ore* from *tore* and
discover *shore.*
Take *ch* from *children* and *ance* from *dance*
and discover *chance.*

Final Consonant Substitutions

In the same way, children practice the substitution exercise with final sounds:

from bo*y*	from su*n*	from ca*p*	from fi*t*	from pe*t*
to bo*x*	to su*p*	to ca*n*	to fi*x*	to pe*n*
to bo*g*	to su*b*	to ca*t*	to fi*n*	to pe*g*
to Bo*b*	to su*m*	to ca*b*	to fi*ll*	to pe*p*

Medial Consonant Substitutions

Vowel substitutions in one-syllable words constitute the same type of practice:

from p*i*t	from f*i*ll	from p*i*n	from p*e*g	from p*o*p
to p*e*t	to f*e*ll	to p*e*n	to p*i*g	to p*u*p
to p*u*t	to f*a*ll	to p*a*n	to p*u*g	to p*e*p
to p*o*t	to f*u*ll	to p*u*n		to p*i*p
to p*a*t				

Initial Consonant Additions

Consonants or consonant blends can be affixed to phonograms:

ill	and	end
will	band	mend
hill	hand	bend
spill	stand	blend
still		spend

Final Consonant Additions

Affixes can be added to change endings:

for	see	go	she
ford	seed	gob	shed
form	seek	God	shep
fort	seem	got	sheep
	seep		

Hearing Sounds

The letter *g* represents two sounds. The hard sound of *g* is heard in *go* and *game;* the soft, or *j*, sound is heard in *gem* and *giant*. More words used in beginning reading instruction begin with the hard sound of *g*. In consonant-blend sounds, the *g* has the hard sound. Two groups of words are given below: words in which *g* is followed by *e, i*, or *y*, and words in which *g* is followed by any other letter.

Words in which *g* sounds like *j:*

giant	generous	judge
giraffe	George	cabbage
germ	gentle	orange
gypsy	general	large

Words in which *g* has the hard sound:

game	gallon	glass
program	good	gold
gas	goose	gutter
grit	green	glad

The letter *c* also represents two sounds. The letter *c* has the *k* sound in words like *cat, cold, cut*, and when it is used in consonant blends, such as *clean, cream*, and *crumb*. The letter *c* has the *s* sound in *cent, cider*, and *cycle*. Two groups of words follow: words in which *c* is followed by *e, i*, or *y*, and words in which *c* is followed by other letters.

Words in which *c* sounds like *s:*

cent	city	circle
cedar	cycle	bicycle
ceiling	decide	celery
mice	cigar	cymbal

Words in which *c* has the *k* sound:

call	come	color
coat	catch	crow
client	cuff	crocodile
acre	alcohol	dedicate

Teachers need to be aware that the commonly made *ul* sound is not a representation of the *l* sound at the beginning of a word. They also need to be aware that the *l* on word beginnings is not exactly the same as the *l* on word endings:

little   lake   laugh   wall   bill   cupful

When *r* appears in words, it, too, has a different sound at the end of a word than it has at the beginning. *R* also produces different sounds when combined with vowels.

Making Connections 9.2: Structural-Analysis Skills in Basal Readers— Scope and Sequence

To know what structural-analysis skills are being presented in basal readers is useful. It may be helpful to know which ones are presented in the primary grades and which are usually reserved for the upper elementary grades or even the middle school years.

The members of your class should divide themselves so that one or more persons can work with the teacher's manuals at the various grade levels from preprimer through eighth reader. Select one or more series, as your instructor directs, to study thoroughly.

Make a list of the structural-analysis skills taught at your particular level. If you are evaluating more than one series, you will probably want to keep the two lists separate. Look to see not only what skills are taught but also how many lessons are suggested for each skill. Study the lessons to see how the textbook authors expect the teacher to develop the skills.

When all class members have their analyses prepared, the class should be able to develop a scope and sequence chart for structural analysis for one or more series of readers. A scope and sequence chart shows all the skills that are to be taught and the grades at which they are to be taught or reviewed.

Can you see some advantages or strengths of a scope and sequence chart? What are some of its disadvantages or weaknesses? What can you say about the structural-analysis skills expected to be taught across a complete basal reader series?

Silent Letters

1. The letter *g* is silent before *m* and *n:* gnat, gnu, sign, diaphragm.
2. The letter *h* may be silent before any vowel or when preceded by *r:* rhyme, rhinoceros, honest, herb.
3. The letters *gh* are silent after *a, i,* or *o:* high, eight, bought, caught.
4. The letter *k* is silent before *n:* knock, know, knife, knee.
5. The letter *l* is silent before *k, d,* or *m:* talk, would, calm, salmon.
6. The letter *p* is silent before *s, t,* or *n:* psalm, pneumonia, ptomaine.
7. The letter *t* is silent following *s* or *f:* listen, often, thistle, soften.
8. The letter *w* is silent before *r:* wrist, write, wren, wrong.

Teaching Blends

Techniques for teaching the *cl* blend (see table 9.5) include:

1. Hold up such articles as clothespin, cloth, clay, clown, clock, or clip. Elicit from the children that they all begin with the sound *cl*.
2. Underline the *cl* blend in a series of words (words in the child's reading vocabulary): *clean, climb, clothes, clap, clown, clock.*
3. Say a list of words, and ask the children to raise their hands when the word begins with *cl*.
4. Give the children a list of words to be changed to *cl* words:

lip	*cl*ip	flash	*cl*ash
lean	*cl*ean	rub	*cl*ub
bean	*cl*ean	slap	*cl*ap

5. Use the blend sound that is known to figure out new words:

clean⎯⎯⎯→	clog⎯⎯⎯→	climb
flash⎯⎯⎯→	flap⎯⎯⎯→	flask
bland⎯⎯⎯→	blush⎯⎯⎯→	blunder

The objectives of the child in mastering blends are: (1) to hear clearly the blended sound of the two or more consonants, and (2) to distinguish the different blended sounds from single consonant sounds in phonograms.

A *consonant digraph* is a combination of two letters that result in a new (single) speech sound. The new sound is not the separated consonants blended together but is a new sound.

The consonant digraphs are: *th* in *this* and *thimble; sh; ch* in *choir, chef,* and *chicken; ph; gh; ng;* and *nk.*

Using the Dictionary

For purposes of finding words needed, determining proper pronunciation of words being used, and establishing meanings appropriate to the context in which the words are being used, all children must achieve proficiency in the effective use of the dictionary. Second-grade students who read at or above grade level should be developing many of the dictionary skills outlined in this section. Much time will be devoted to teaching dictionary skills in both fourth and fifth grade because children will not all acquire the skills when they are taught, and the teachers must provide for much reteaching and review.

The teachers will need to provide for teaching and reteaching these skills in the third, fourth, and fifth grades because *all* children need the opportunity to learn a skill *when* it is useful, meaningful, and relevant to their needs. Presentation of new skills to small groups has a place in present classroom organization, but the teachers must have some way of measuring *all* children's successes in learning and *using* skills.

There should be an effectively programmed, self-motivating set of exercises that could be completed individually by students whenever they are ready to learn these dictionary skills. Then such a program could be completed by any student, whether seven or seventeen years old, when knowing dictionary skills would be meaningful and relevant to him or her:

Three such programs are:

1. *Lessons for Self-Instruction.* These programmed materials teach dictionary skills. California Test Bureau, 5916 Hollywood Blvd., Los Angeles, California 90029.
2. The Macmillan *Beginning Dictionary,* edited by William D. Halsey, is accompanied by the *School Dictionary Practice Book*. New York: Macmillan Co., 1985.
3. *Using the Dictionary.* This is a set of six 32-page booklets for reading levels one through six. The booklets cover the major dictionary skills of the elementary school. Scholastic Inc., P.O. Box 7501, 2931 McCarty St., Jefferson City, Missouri 65102.

Several dictionaries are available for students in the elementary school, and classrooms should be provided with sufficient copies of a variety of dictionaries so that all children can have easy access to them. The dictionaries should span the range of reading levels in the classroom. This is necessary in order to make dictionary use possible for all the children and to develop the dictionary habit.

A few of the elementary school dictionaries are:

Ginn Intermediate Dictionary. Lexington, Mass.: Ginn, 1986. Has 57,000 entries. For grades six through nine.

Heyward, Linda. *The Sesame Street Dictionary.* New York: Random House, 1980. Based on "Sesame Street" characters; 1,300 entries.

Houghton Mifflin Primary Dictionary. Boston: Houghton Mifflin, 1986. For grades one and two. Words are defined in sentences. Has a skills workbook.

Jenkins, William A., and Andrew Schiller. *My First Picture Dictionary.* Glenview, Ill.: Scott, Foresman, 1982. Introduces 914 words, arranged by categories. Includes a skills workbook.

Scott, Foresman Beginning Dictionary. Edited by E. L. Thorndike and Clarence Barnhart. Glenview, Ill.: Scott, Foresman, 1983. Has 25,000 main entries.

Webster's Elementary Dictionary. Columbus, Ohio: Ginn, 1986. For grades three through six; 32,000 entries.

The skills and strategies needed for dictionary usage have been classified as location, pronunciation, and meaning skills, and are outlined here. This chapter includes some additional exercises and some important techniques to help children with comprehension in reading.

Location Skills and Strategies

In order to find words quickly in the dictionary, children need to know how entries are made and how many forms of a word are included in the dictionary. If the children are looking for *reporting* and there is no entry for this word, they must know that *reporting* is derived from *report* and that they must look for the *report* entry. Six needed *location skills* are:

1. Ability to arrange words in alphabetical order: by initial letter, by second letter, and by third and fourth letters.
2. Ability to find words quickly in an alphabetical list.
3. Ability to open the dictionary quickly to the section in which the word is to be found, to the proper third or fourth of the book.
4. Ability to use the two guide words at the top of the page.
5. Ability to think of the names of letters immediately preceding and immediately following the letter being located.
6. Ability to use special sections of the dictionary; for example, sections on pronunciation, medical terms, slang expressions, musical terms, and foreign words and phrases.

Activities to Help Children Learn Alphabetical Order

To fix *alphabetical order,* the teachers may use a number of different activities, according to the needs of the children.

1. Alphabetical order may begin with only part of the alphabet.
   a. Put these words in alphabetical order:
      face, green, dog, cow, elephant, box, apple
      1. _____ 2. _____ 3. _____ 4. _____
      5. _____ 6. _____ 7. _____
   b. Arrange the names of the children in alphabetical order as they will appear on the program for our play, "Building a House in the Arctic."
   c. Write in the missing words in alphabetical order. Choose one from the box for each line:
      1. animal 2. _____ 3. fox 4. _____
      5. milk 6. _____ 7. _____

      | boy |
      | study |
      | penny |
      | hill |

    d. Arrange all the words in the box in alphabetical order:

1. _____

2. _____

3. _____

4. _____

5. _____

6. _____

7. _____

8. _____

> store
> house
> city
> boxes
> zoo
> yesterday
> puppy
> friend

2. Alphabetical order can later include the entire alphabet.

    a. Some words below appear in alphabetical order. Choose (from the words in the box) the necessary words to complete a list of twenty-six words in alphabetical order:

1. after	10. _____	19. straw	zest	donkey
2. baby	11. kind	20. turkey	camel	Indian
3. _____	12. _____	21. _____	lake	uncle
4. _____	13. mouse	22. _____	orange	pony
5. _____	14. nest	23. _____	rabbit	water
6. friends	15. _____	24. xylophone	yesterday	jello
7. goats	16. _____	25. _____	hill	vest
8. _____	17. quickly	26. _____	evergreen	
9. _____	18. _____			

    b. The teachers can provide the students with lists of twenty-six words and ask them to arrange the lists in alphabetical order.

    c. Students can arrange all the first names or the surnames of the class members in alphabetical order.

3. Arranging alphabetical lists by second letters in words:

Arrange all of the "c" words in your theme dictionary of "car" words in alphabetical order.

chrome   carburetor   combustion

Activities to Help Children Learn about Guide Words

1. Guide words

First part of the dictionary is A–G.

Second part of the dictionary is H–P.

Third part of the dictionary is Q–Z.

In which part will you find:

a. mathematics   c. favorite   e. question
b. weather   d. arithmetic   f. mood

2. Guide words
   The guide words on one page of the dictionary are *storehouse* and *strain.*
   Do these words come (1) before this page, (2) on this page, or (3) after this
   page?

   a. _____ stony   c. _____ strike   e. _____ stork
   b. _____ straight   d. _____ stub   f. _____ spy

Pronunciation Skills and Strategies

Twelve pronunciation skills and strategies are detailed below:

1. Ability to use the pronunciation key at the bottom of each page.
2. Ability to use the full pronunciation key in the front of the dictionary.
3. Ability to use and interpret accent marks, both primary and secondary.
4. Ability to select the proper heteronyms; for example, rec'ord or re cord', ob'ject or ob ject'.
5. Ability to identify silent letters in words pronounced.
6. Ability to recognize differences between spelling and pronunciation (phoneme-grapheme relationship).
7. Ability to use phonetic spelling for pronunciation.
8. Ability to discriminate vowel sounds.
9. Ability to use diacritical marks as an aid in pronunciation.
10. Understanding of the way syllables are marked in dictionaries.
11. Ability to identify unstressed syllables in words.
12. Arriving at pronunciation and recognizing it as correct.

Exercises to develop pronunciation skills and strategies should utilize the pupils' interests and learning experiences as much as possible. When children ask questions about pronunciation keys or when they make errors that can be corrected by providing specific information are ideal times to teach pronunciation techniques. Three specific suggestions include:

1. The pronunciation key can provide for the comparison of sounds. If the teachers give the stimulus word *role*, the children can respond with $\bar{o}$ as in *go* and *open*. The children will use the pronunciation key in their dictionaries. If the teachers say *much-mush,* the children can respond with "*much* ends with *ch; mush* ends with *sh.*"

   If the teachers say "long *a*" or "short *e*," the children can give the appropriate words from the key.
2. After some familiarity with the key, pupils may be challenged by this exercise. Look at the picture and the phonetic spelling, then spell the word correctly. If the children are in doubt, encourage them to use the dictionary. They should avoid misspelling if possible. (See figure 9.6.)

kabᶦij   eᶦzəl   erth′ werm¹

Figure 9.6. Exercises in pronunciation skills

3. The dictionary tells you three things about a word's pronunciation and spelling:
   a. How to divide it into syllables
   b. Which syllable to stress or accent
   c. Pronunciation by respelling

Look up these words. Copy them in syllables and put in the accent. Copy the respelling to show the pronunciation.

Words	Syllables	Respelling with Marks
1. separate	sep-a-rate	sep′ə rāt
2. examination	ex-am-i-na-tion	eg-zam′i nā′sh ən
3. refinement		
4. understanding		
5. appreciate		

Meaning Skills and Strategies

Ten *meaning skills and strategies* in using the dictionary are:

1. Learning meanings of new words by reading simple definitions.
2. Using pictures and meanings in the dictionary to arrive at meanings.
3. Using an illustrative sentence to arrive at meanings.
4. Using two different meanings for the same word.
5. Approximating real-life sizes by using dictionary pictures and explanatory clues.
6. Selecting the specific meaning for a given context.

7. Understanding special meanings: idioms, slang expressions, and other figures of speech.
8. Using the concept of root word.
9. Interpreting multiple meanings of words.
10. Knowing when meaning has been satisfied through dictionary usage.

Two possible activities might be:

1. Mark the words in the reading you are doing about tropical fruits for which you do not know the meanings. Find each word in the dictionary. Then write a new sentence to illustrate the meaning of each word.
2. Using your dictionary, write the meaning of the word *play* as it is used in each of the following sentences:
   a. Children like to *play* during recess.
      Definition of play: (fun, sport, action to amuse oneself)
   b. She will *play* the piano at noon today.
      Definition of play: (have fun; do something in sport; perform)
   c. He will *play* a leading part in the game.
      Definition of play: (to take part in)
   d. The children gave a *play* at the end of the unit.
      Definition of play: (a story acted on a stage)
   e. John's dog will *play* tricks.
      Definition of play: (act)
   f. We watched the sunlight *play* on the leaves.
      Definition of play: (make light, quick movements)
   g. Let's *play* that the big paper box is a boat.
      Definition of play: (make believe; pretend in fun)
   h. Tom made the winning *play* in the checker game.
      Definition of play: (a turn, act, or move in a game)
   i. Don't *play* with your pencils.
      Definition of play: (act carelessly; do foolish things)
   j. Our team will *play* the other sixth grade.
      Definition of play: (compete against)

Using the Microcomputer as an Aid in Teaching Word-Recognition

The microcomputer offers the teacher several possible ways to help students with word recognition. There are numerous "skill-drill" types of programs similar to pages found in many workbooks and ditto packages. The teacher must decide whether such programs have utility for the children or whether students can gain as much from more conventional presentations if such practice is needed at all. Advantages of microcomputer programs are that they can be used as many times as the child wishes to run them and that they respond with no impatience to the child's efforts.

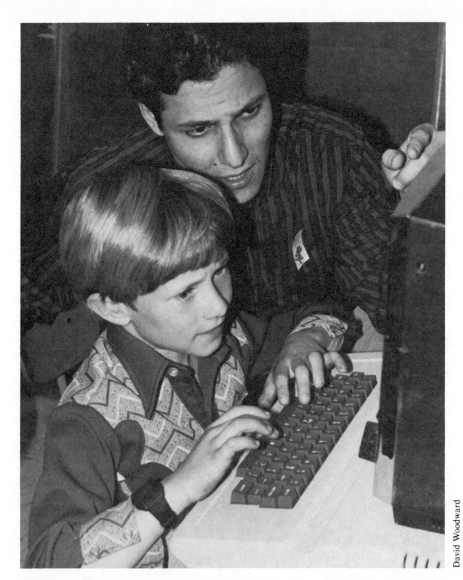

David Woodward

The intensity with which teachers and children work with the microcomputer may make the literacy aspects of the program even more valuable.

A variety of many new software games is available to help the child develop word-recognition abilities. These may be quite attractive to the children. They should be evaluated by the same standards that are used to assess the quality of regular games. The teacher will need to decide whether all the skills practiced in playing the available games are necessary to learn to read.[11] Games that emphasize thinking strategies in addition to the skills of reading may be the most desirable ones.

Word-processing programs that allow children to write their own stories and print them out with printers that produce hard copy for bookmaking may be the most useful tools for promoting word recognition. As with writing using more conventional tools, the child writes the words he or she needs in meaningful and personally relevant settings. If a microcomputer is available, the teacher should take full advantage of at least one word-processing program for the young writers and readers.

Finally, teachers should be cautioned to evaluate programs carefully before purchasing them. Many programs have not been carefully reviewed. Thus, it becomes the classroom teacher's responsibility to make critical decisions. Developing or locating a checklist to guide in evaluation of various kinds of programs may be helpful.[12] The teacher may also invite children to provide feedback on their reactions to programs being tried in the classroom.

Summary

Helps for teachers in teaching word-recognition skills and strategies to students have been presented in this chapter. Learning a meaningful stock of sight words through the use of language experiences was discussed. Language experiences could include using environmental print, dictated stories, rebus, wordless picture books, predictable and taped books, and bookmaking. The use of context clues, both those derived from pictures and from print, was stressed as a meaningful approach to word recognition. Aspects of structural and phonic analysis were outlined for teachers. A section on the use of the dictionary was included. Many of the word-recognition skills and strategies can be learned while children are studying a variety of themes or units. The chapter ended with a discussion of the use of the computer as an aid to word recognition. The use of word-processing programs by children was identified as an important way to encourage word recognition.

For Further Reading

Bridge, Connie A., Peter Winograd, and Darlene Haley. "Using Predictable Materials vs. Preprimers to Teach Beginning Sight Words." *Reading Teacher* 36 (May 1983): 84–91. The authors found predictable materials to be superior to preprimers in teaching beginning word recognition.

Ekwall, Eldon E. *Locating and Correcting Reading Difficulties.* 4th ed. Columbus, Ohio: Merrill Publishing Co., 1985. This author presents many ideas for teaching word recognition and for dealing with the problems that children have in recognizing words.

Flatley, Joannis K., and Adele D. Rutland. "Using Wordless Picture Books to Teach Linguistically/Culturally Different Students." *Reading Teacher* 40 (December 1986): 276–81. The article describes and illustrates strategies for teaching reading with wordless picture books.

Harris, Albert J., and Edward R. Sipay. "Developing Word-Recognition Skills and Dealing with Word-Recognition Problems." In *How to Increase Reading Ability.* 8th ed., 364–443. New York: Longman, Inc., 1985. A comprehensive review of the problems of word recognition and their remediation.

Heald-Taylor, Gail. "Predictable Literature Selections and Activities for Language Arts Instruction." *Reading Teacher* 41 (October 1987): 6–12. A list of predictable books, categorized from most predictable to least predictable, is provided.

Johns, Jerry L. "Recognizing Words and Building Vocabulary." In *Handbook for Remediation of Reading Difficulties,* 57–117. Englewood Cliffs, N.J.: Prentice-Hall, 1986. A wealth of suggestions for facilitating word recognition. Section 3 includes several useful lists and a lengthy review of materials.

Johnson, Dale, and P. David Pearson, *Teaching Reading Vocabulary.* 2d ed. New York: Holt, Rinehart and Winston, 1984. Provides much useful information and varied instructional strategies for developing vocabulary.

Loughlin, Catherine, and Mavis Martin. "The Functional Use of Print." In *Supporting Literacy: Developing Effective Learning Environments*, 63–79. New York: Teachers College Press, 1987. The authors discuss many ways of making the classroom environment "print rich."

Marzano, Robert J., and Jana S. Marzano. *A Cluster Approach to Elementary Vocabulary Instruction.* Newark, Del.: International Reading Association, 1988. The authors present a theory that organizes vocabulary building for children. The appendix presents lengthy lists of clustered vocabulary. This is a very helpful reference.

Miller, Harry, Cindy Thompson, and Dona Holloway. *Teacher's Kaleidoscope of Reading Activities.* New York: University Press of America, 1985. This book provides detailed instructions to the teacher for making a great assortment of aids to word identification, as well as for teaching other areas of reading.

Smith, Frank. "The Role of Prediction in Reading." In *Essays into Literacy: Selected Papers and Some Afterthoughts,* 26–34. London: Heinemann Educational Books, 1983. This is a concise statement of the theoretical aspects of the brain activity of prediction as basic to the reading process.

Weaver, Constance. "How Does Context Aid in Word Identification?" In *Reading Process and Practice: From Socio-Psycholinguistics to Whole Language,* 84–112. Portsmouth, N.H.: Heinemann Educational Books, 1988. The author considers context within and beyond the sentence as well as the cues that operate to aid in word identification.

Notes

1. E. W. Dolch, *Dolch Basic Sight Word Test* (Champaign, Ill.: Garrard Press, 1942).
2. Edward Fry, "The Instant Words," a 600-word basic vocabulary, graded according to frequency and approximate grade level of difficulty. These are found in Fry's book *Elementary Reading Instruction* (New York: McGraw-Hill, Inc., 1977), 73.
3. Mabel O'Donnell, *Teacher's Manual for the Pre-primer Program, The Harper and Row Basic Reading Program* (New York: Harper and Row, 1966), 21.
4. Richard W. Woodcock, *Rebuses as a Medium in Beginning Reading Instruction* (Nashville, Tenn.: Institute on Mental Retardation and Intellectual Development, George Peabody College for Teachers, 1968). Supported by Grant HD 973 from the National Institute of Child Health and Human Development.
5. Constance Weaver, *Reading Process and Practice: From Socio-Psycholinguistics to Whole Language* (Portsmouth, N.H.: Heinemann Educational Books, 1988), 248.
6. Patricia Cunningham et al., *Reading in Elementary Classrooms: Strategies and Observations* (New York: Longman, 1983), 13–14.

7. Dolores P. Dickerson, "A Study of Use of Games to Reinforce Sight Vocabulary," *Reading Teacher* 36 (October 1982): 46–49.

8. Karl Koenke, "Pictures in Reading Materials: What Do We Know About Them?" *Reading Teacher* 40 (May 1987): 902–5.

9. Frank Smith, *Understanding Reading* (New York: Holt, Rinehart and Winston, 1971), 7.

10. Lee Ann Rinsky and Barbara Griffith, *Teaching Word Attack Skills* (Dubuque, Iowa: Gorsuch Scarisbrick, Publishers, 1978), 61.

11. Ernest Balajthy, "Reinforcement and Drill by Microcomputer," *Reading Teacher* 37 (February 1984): 490–94.

12. Jay S. Blanchard, George E. Mason, and Dan Daniel, *Computer Applications in Reading,* 3d ed. (Newark, Del.: International Reading Association, 1987), 49–54.

10
Teaching Reading Comprehension

Chapter Outline

Vocabulary

comprehension as a brain
  activity
world model
world knowledge
prior knowledge
schemata
interaction with text
predictions
experience in
  comprehension
language in comprehension
function of comprehension
cognitive levels of
  comprehension
chunking
anaphora
cohesive ties
organization of text
direct teaching of
  comprehension
generalization
skimming
levels of questioning
writing techniques
context
scaffolding
function words
figurative language
journal writing
cloze procedure as a
  teaching technique
easy oral reading practice
trade books

Questions

1. Write a set of statements describing the reading process. **(Recall; Inference)**
2. Why is the building of schemata so important in comprehension? **(Inference)**
3. What are two ways of analyzing comprehension? **(Recall)** How does each contribute to teaching comprehension? **(Inference)**
4. What are the levels at which questions should be asked? Give examples of questions at each level. **(Recall; Application)**
5. What is the purpose of scaffolding? **(Recall)**
6. How is an understanding of function words and figurative language important to comprehension? **(Recall)**
7. What is important about lots of easy practice? **(Recall)** How would you plan for it in your classroom? **(Application)**

Introduction

A primary concern of teachers is helping students to develop meaningful concepts as they read. Unless the pupils learn to synthesize meanings as they read through the lines of print, they are wasting their time. For most readers, there is a positive relationship between the ability to handle the mechanics of reading and the ability to understand and interpret the ideas they read. Some children pronounce words well and comprehend little, while others glean much from the print but have great difficulty with fluent pronunciation.

In this chapter, perspectives for understanding are presented along with a discussion of the strategies and skills of comprehension, strategies for teaching, and materials for helping children learn to comprehend print.

Comprehension in Reading

All teachers would agree that the primary reason for reading anything is to understand it. Without that purpose, there would be little reason for reading. In recent years reading researchers and teachers have come to realize that reading comprehension is derived from a basic *activity of the brain*—the continuing effort to make sense of the environment by building a personal model of the world, replete with cognitive, affective, and motor elements. Any text that is being read is part of that *world model*. The basis of that ever-expanding model is the individual's world knowledge, the prior experience unique to that person. Since every individual's prior knowledge is unique, the mental model created by each person is also unique. What each reader brings to the reading of a text is the total of his or her prior knowledge organized as a model of the world. The text stimulates relevant aspects of the reader's model of the world. New knowledge, new ways of organizing or integrating prior knowledge, and new attitudes and perspectives result. The reader may then say that comprehension has taken place.

Items of world or *prior knowledge* are organized in the brain into groupings that may be manipulated, altered, or expanded. These groupings are called *schemata*. Individuals have a seemingly endless number of schemata for everything from cars, desserts, deserts, football games, and the color *red* to France, money, snow, and big cats. These schemata are changed and expanded as the individual has new experiences. Throughout life they continue to grow, as suggested by the schema for dogs explored in figure 10.1. The more schemata the reader has and the more complex they are, the more world or prior knowledge the person can bring to the reading event, resulting in greater comprehension. As schemata become more numerous and more complex, they will come to overlap. Thus, the schema for dogs may overlap with the schema for camels in a schema of "animals that work for humans."

World knowledge organized into schemata, *interaction with text,* and the resulting comprehension seem to operate in a circular manner. The more world knowledge the reader has, the greater the comprehension resulting from interaction with text is likely to be. The new understandings are apt to result in expanded schemata that will be operative in the next interaction with text. Figure 10.2 suggests this circular process.

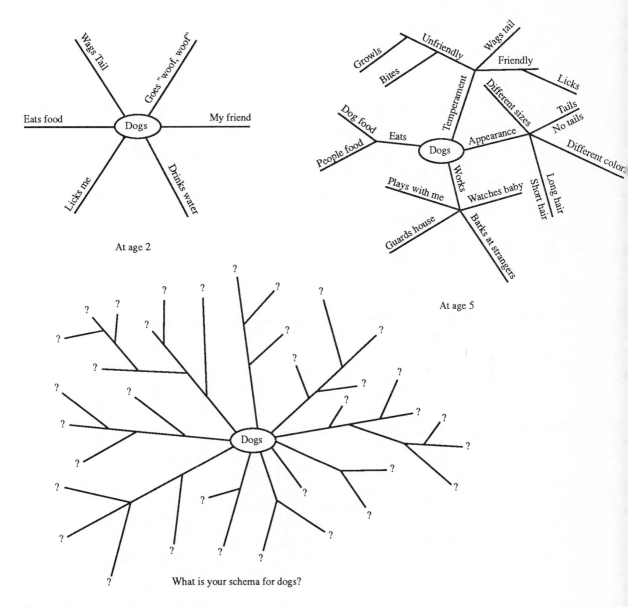

Figure 10.1. The growth of a schema

Comprehension requires the application at appropriate times of many reading strategies and skills. The reader must have developed efficient word-recognition abilities to facilitate making and confirming *predictions* about the print on the page, a rich store of world knowledge organized into schemata, and the vocabulary with which to label and manipulate the available schemata and their components. The reader must also have knowledge of the ways in which text is organized. The structure of sentences and

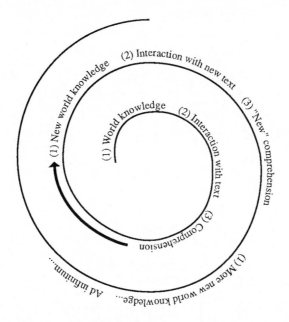

Figure 10.2. Growth of schemata is continuous

paragraphs must be familiar enough so that the reader can use it as an aid to comprehension. The reader must also understand the structure of larger units—stories, poems, chapters in content textbooks, novels and other genre—as a factor in comprehension of the entire text.

Experience Essential to Comprehension

Experience is essential for comprehension. For younger children, personal, meaningful experiences mediated by language are essential to reading comprehension. Adults in the home and at school have an obligation to work together to provide the mediated experiences, the raw material of schemata. Thus, when particular ideas are confronted in reading, the readers will be able to draw on their personal experiences to bring meaning to the print and to use the print to expand their meanings (schemata). As children grow older, they are better able to profit from the experiences of others, either those they are told about, those they experience through television, or those they read about. They still need the opportunity to share these experiences with others through language, art, music, or other avenues of expression.

Randy and Harold were reading a story about a bear who raided trash barrels in a campsite in a state park. They were especially interested in the foods that the bear seemed to prefer. Randy remembered that his family had left some watermelon rinds on the ground near his family's mountain cabin. The family was surprised to look out the window and see a young bear lying on his stomach munching the rinds. The bear was apparently unconcerned about the people peeking out the window. After eating all the rinds, he wandered away. Randy speculated that the bear in the park probably wanted watermelon rinds, too. Harold said, "I never knew bears liked to eat watermelon! I thought they ate animals and bugs and even bit people."

Randy was able to use what had probably been a significant experience for him to bring personal meaning to what was read. His friend Harold used the text and Randy's experience to expand his schema for bears.

Language Essential to Comprehension

This text has emphasized the importance of enriched oral *language* competence before reading. Horn cautioned us, decades ago, about the language needs of reading-disabled students:

> . . . with the exception of a few special types, most of the so-called reading disabilities may more properly be ascribed to disability in language. The full significance of this fact for the teaching of reading has not always been appreciated. As a result, the more technical and peripheral aspects of reading, such as phonics, eye movements, and mechanical drills, have loomed overlarge both in research and in practice, as compared with the vastly greater importance of the central thought processes. Yet it is clear that very little improvement may be expected from formal drill in reading unless at the same time provision is made for the enrichment of experience, the development of language abilities, and the improvement of thinking.[1]

In 1984, Adams presented similar ideas. In an interview he stated:

> I take the word *self* to mean a personal model of language. That is, the way children make sense of themselves and their place within their world by using language to express themselves and explore their own identity. . . . Expressive discourse differs from other kinds of discourse in that it is highly personal, particular to the person doing the speaking. . . . In making sense of new information, the expressive is fundamental to learners of any age. When I am trying to cope with concepts that are new to me, I have to explore them, come to terms with them, by talking about them in my own personal language, before I am ready to cope with them in the language of the . . . textbook.[2]

Comprehension Strategies and Skills

Comprehension is an active process in which the reader is actively involved in bringing appropriate prior knowledge to the reading task and in formulating new ideas as a result of reading. The reader cannot derive the *same* meanings from the text that the author tried to encode (unless the reader and writer are the same person), since the two persons have had different experiences and have somewhat different ways of talking about those experiences. The author's words simply serve as stimuli for the reader's personal meanings.

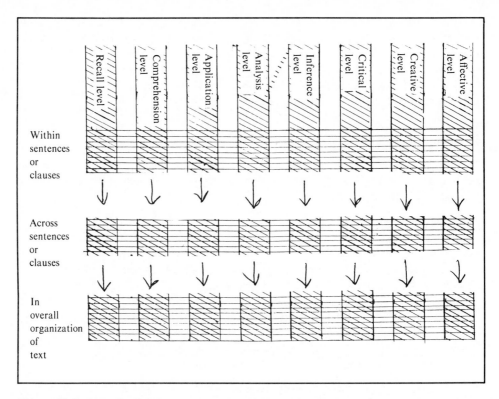

Figure 10.3. Interplay of two ways of analyzing comprehension. Each of the eight *levels* of comprehension can be dealt with in each of the three functions. Such interplay may enable teachers to analyze more effectively how children are understanding and assimilating new information.

Comprehension is apparently a holistic process. This conception of comprehension contrasts with the earlier belief that it consisted of a set of discrete skills. In order to talk about reading comprehension, we must separate it into smaller units, but the reader does not make those divisions during the act of reading. In any discussion of types of comprehension, we must keep in mind, then, that such segmenting is for the purpose of studying the comprehension act and is not descriptive of the actual process.

Comprehension may be analyzed by studying its *function* (1) within sentences or clauses, (2) across sentences or clauses, and (3) in the overall organization of a text.[3]

Comprehension during reading may also be studied by considering levels derived from the taxonomies of Bloom[4] and Krathwohl.[5] The recall (literal) level would be followed by comprehension, application, analysis, and inference. Finally, critical, creative, and affective levels of comprehension may be identified in this way of segmenting comprehension.

These two different ways of looking at comprehension may be integrated to show the relationships between them. Figure 10.3 suggests how comprehension levels based on units of language, and levels based on *cognitive* and *affective* domains could be meshed to provide a structure for teachers as they plan ways to help children improve their comprehension abilities.

The teacher must also be aware of the role of metacognition,[6] the ability to consider one's own thinking, as a comprehension strategy. Children who are helped to think about their own thinking and understanding will be able to monitor when they are comprehending and when they are losing meaning. Teachers can provide children with specific techniques to further this ability.

Comprehension within the Sentence or Clause

Comprehension within the sentence or clause must focus on the relationships of the words in that language unit. For children to know the formal names for different words in the unit (for example, *noun* or *adverb*) is not necessary; children who are acquainted with the language have that knowledge at an intuitive level.

Teachers can help children to focus on meaning at this level with questions designed to elicit relationships between the words. Children may find that the words tend to group themselves into smaller units, including subjects, predicates, and phrases. Irwin referred to the grouping of words within sentences or clauses as *chunking*.[7] When teachers encourage children to write frequently, the children face the task of composing sentences in which the chosen words bear the desired relationships to one another. The increased awareness of relationships between words that is learned in writing appears to generate a heightened sensitivity in reading as well. Cloze activities draw attention to comprehension at various levels, including the within-sentence level.

Teachers may also use questions and discussions to make the children aware of meanings beyond the recall level within the sentence unit and of attempts by the author to shape opinions and feelings. Other questions, open-ended and without specific answers, may guide children to comprehend at the critical, creative, and affective levels.

Comprehension across Sentences or Clauses

Attention to comprehension across sentences and clauses must focus on the means by which they are linked together for different purposes and the linguistic techniques that are employed to relate ideas expressed in one clause or sentence to an earlier or later clause or sentence. Two linguistic devices that children will meet frequently and that accomplish these tasks are *anaphora* and *cohesive ties*.

Anaphora

Anaphora is a linguistic means of transferring meaning from one sentence to another.[8] Two examples of anaphora are:

George gave the balloon to two-year-old *Billy*.
His little brother wanted it very much.

We watched the *mare* nuzzle her week-old *colt*.
She wanted *it* to follow *her*.

Teachers need to be alert to anaphora in the reading that children do. They may need to ask questions to make sure that the children understand such relationships. Referents and antecedents are sometimes widely separated and may be more difficult for them to understand, as are backward relationships.[9] An example of a backward relationship is:

> Since John had already been *there,* he did not
> wish to return to the *cave.*

Cohesive Ties

Cohesive ties are words or groups of words that link one clause or sentence to another. They also have an important role in conveying relationships between sentences and clauses. Time sequences, cause and effect, and coordinate and subordinate relationships may be expressed. Function words are used to express cohesive ties. For example:

> He came right back *because* the library was
> closed.
> We canceled the trip *after* it rained.
> She held up her hand *until* the presiding officer
> recognized her.

Function words are discussed in greater detail later in this chapter.

The teacher will need to ask questions at the various levels from recall to evaluation and also in the affective domain to help children understand relationships across sentences and clauses and in larger units such as paragraphs. Children may be guided to formulate their own questions, which will help to reveal relationships across linguistic units.

The Overall Organization of a Text

An understanding of the *organization of the text* being read is an important factor in comprehension. Each type of text, whether it is a narrative, material from a social studies text, or the story problems in arithmetic, has its own characteristic organization. A knowledge of the structure of the particular type of text being read facilitates predictability. The reader knows what to expect next and may even be able to predict the language that will be used. Teachers should point out to children the distinctive characteristics of the various types of writing that they meet. Eventually, the students should be able to identify the types of texts and their patterns of organization.

Expository text, the type found in content textbooks, is more difficult to read than narrative (which makes up most of the selections in basals as well as many popular trade or library books). Narratives follow essentially a single pattern, though some stories may contain more cycles of problems and resolutions than others. Expository text, on the other hand, may take different forms in different content areas. Students must learn not only the vocabulary and concepts in the subject matter texts but also the common organizational patterns to be anticipated there if they are to comprehend satisfactorily. The problem of writing patterns in subject matter texts will be discussed further in chapter 11.

Direct Teaching of Comprehension

A variety of comprehension strategies and skills has been discussed. However, the teacher needs to have direct means of teaching comprehension. The teacher must be able to model and explain the steps in the thinking process through which the reader must go in order to achieve comprehension.

The *direct teaching of comprehension* may be very important when working with disabled readers. These students often focus attention on decoding while ignoring the meaningful aspects of reading. Many poor readers *fail to expect* reading to "make sense." As a consequence of these attitudes and expectations, the teacher will often find it necessary to implement direct teaching of comprehension.

Gersten and Carnine proposed a set of steps for direct teaching of comprehension.[10] These include teaching the particular strategy or skill step by step, working for mastery at each step, implementing correction strategies when errors are made, providing organized practice with increasing amounts of direction being given to the learners, reviewing, and anticipating at what points errors are likely to be made so that potential errors can be prevented. Teachers are advised to follow these systematic steps to assure full understanding of the skill or strategy as well as its application.

Skills that May Require Direct Teaching

Smith has proposed twelve types of comprehension skills and strategies, at the literal level as well as at the higher levels of thinking.[11] The following skills and strategies may need direct teaching to be sure that children, especially children with reading problems, master them:

1. Understanding and remembering details or facts. The ability to do this has value, but it is probably overused in many classrooms.
2. Finding the main idea in the paragraph.
3. Understanding sequences of time, place, idea, or events.
4. Following directions.
5. Reading for implied meanings, and drawing inferences.
6. Reading to understand characterization and setting.
7. Sensing relationships in time, place, cause and effect.
8. Reading to anticipate outcomes.
9. Recognizing the author's mood or tone.
10. Comparing and contrasting.
11. Forming generalizations.
12. Skimming.

Activities and Materials for the Direct Teaching of Smith's List of Comprehension Skills and Strategies

A few examples of commercial materials and activities that could be developed around themes are suggested here for use in the direct teaching of comprehension.

1. *Understanding and remembering details or facts.*
   The example in figure 10.4 asks the reader to note important details. The second example in figure 10.5 asks the reader to eliminate irrelevant details.

• Read the following paragraphs, and pay close attention. Below the paragraphs are some unfinished sentences with three possible endings. Print an X beside the best ending.

People in the western part of the United States are quite used to seeing large, dried bushes rolling along a plain or by the side of a road. These bushes are called *tumbleweeds*. The tumbleweed is a type of plant found on North American plains and prairies.

One of the best known tumbleweeds in the United States is called the Russian thistle. This spiny plant is round and bushy. It grows to be two feet high or more.

The main stem of the tumbleweed is pale green and has many white branches shooting out from it. On these branches are the tumbleweed's flat, egg-shaped leaves. In the fall, when the seeds of the tumbleweed are ripe, the leaves wither and the stem of the plant breaks off at ground level.

The dried plant is then carried along by the wind for many miles until it is stopped by a barbed-wire fence or until it falls into a gully. In this way, the tumbleweed is able to scatter its seeds over the plain.

1. The tumbleweed is a

_____ Russian weed.

_____ type of plant.

_____ prairie dog.

2. You would probably see tumbleweeds if you lived

_____ in a forest.

_____ on the western plains.

_____ near the ocean.

3. The tumbleweed's stem breaks off

_____ in the summer.

_____ in the spring.

_____ in the fall.

4. A tumbleweed dries up and is "tumbled" about by the wind to

_____ attract honeybees.

_____ scatter its seeds.

_____ fall into a gully.

Figure 10.4. Noting important details. From William K. Durr, Jean M. LaPere, and Ruth H. Brown, *Practice Book for Passports* (Boston: Houghton Mifflin, 1976), 59.

The recent work of August, Flavell, and Clift suggested that poor readers have much greater difficulty in separating main ideas from details in paragraphs or stories.[12]

Teachers might help children to find the important facts in writing by teaching them to edit the writing that they do or to edit the writing of others. The students would be taught to identify important details and to identify irrelevant or distracting material.

2. *The main idea in the paragraph.*
Read the paragraphs in figure 10.6. Circle the letter in front of the sentence opposite each paragraph that gives the correct answer.

Read each paragraph. The first sentence in each paragraph tells the main idea. Draw a line through any other sentence that does not give details about the main idea. You will draw a line through two sentences in 2.

1. There was not enough light each day. This was because the sun ran too fast across the heavens. The people needed more light to finish their work. ~~The dogs were barking at the moon.~~ There was not enough light for plants to grow.

2. Maui's mother was a clever worker. The sun made the hills light and warm. His mother took bark from trees and made tapa cloth. She pounded the bark and made thin strips. Maui ran across the heavens. She pasted the strips together. They dried and became tapa cloth.

Figure 10.5. Finding irrelevant details. Adapted from Theodore Clymer, Gloria Keil, and Robert B. Ruddell, *Skilpack for How It Is Nowadays,* Reading 720, Rainbow Edition (Lexington, Mass.: Ginn, Xerox Corporation, 1979, 1976), 137.

3. *Understanding sequences of time, place, ideas, or events.*
   Exercises appear in student workbooks requiring the students to arrange ideas in numerical order or to decide what happened first, second, third, and so on. In the exercise in figure 10.7, the reader must decide which of two *events* occurred first or last.

Teachers who work with themes will find that the planning of the work with the children will provide opportunities for sequencing the activities to be done and listing persons who will work together, the materials that they will use, and the ideas that they will consider. When these plans are posted, the children have ready reference materials. The comprehension tasks will be the same as those addressed in workbooks and skill sheets, but they will have the advantage of being personally meaningful.

4. *Ability to follow directions.*
   When students follow the directions on task cards or write out plans for the tasks that they hope to accomplish, they are learning the steps in *following directions.* Games in the classroom provide highly motivating lessons in following directions. Some teachers ask children to make games. When the child must develop directions for someone else to follow, a sensitivity to the importance and logical nature of directions is acquired. These activities can be the focus of a directed lesson in comprehension.

5. *Reading for implied meanings, and drawing inferences.*
   Children will probably be most motivated to work on this task in the context of their activities related to themes. However, teachers may wish to organize directed lessons around text or workbook materials. The important idea to remember is that when such materials are used, they should not be filled out alone by the children. Rather, the students should be guided through the lesson, as suggested by Gersten and Carnine.[13]

Unit 3

1.   Mushrooms don't grow on trees. If you see mushrooms stuck between the branches, you know they were put there. Most likely it was the work of a red squirrel. Red squirrels like mushrooms. They like to put them in trees. They they have food to eat in the winter.

1. The story mainly tells:

   (A) **Why there are mushrooms in trees**

   (B) **Why squirrels like mushrooms**

   (C) **Where to grow mushrooms**

2.   Most dead birds are never found. Some may be covered by leaves or dirt. Others are eaten by animals. Still other dead birds may fall into the water or other places where they can't be found. We find only about two of every hundred dead birds.

2. The story mainly tells:

   (A) **Why we don't see many dead birds**

   (B) **Why animals eat dead birds**

   (C) **Why birds die**

3.   Polar bears grow very big as they get old. When they are grown up, polar bears weigh about a thousand pounds. When polar bears are born, they weigh only one pound. Wouldn't it be something if older people weighed a thousand times more than they did at birth?

3. The story mainly tells:

   (A) **How big polar bears grow to be**

   (B) **How small polar bears are**

   (C) **How people are like polar bears**

4.   It's a salty world in which we live. There is salt in the ocean. There is salt in the earth. There is salt inside of you—in your blood, sweat, and even in your tears. It's a good thing too. Without salt you couldn't live.

4. The story mainly tells:

   (A) **How salty the world is**

   (B) **What salt is like**

   (C) **Why people use salt**

5.   How long can a cactus go without water? There is one type of cactus plant that lives for four years without water. When it finally rains, this plant makes up for lost time. It stores up to two tons of water!

5. The story mainly tells:

   (A) **Where cactus plants live**

   (B) **How big cactus plants are**

   (C) **How long some cactuses go without water**

Figure 10.6. Finding the main idea. From Richard A. Boning, *Getting the Main Idea,* Book C, Unit 3. Copyright 1982 by Barnell Loft Ltd., 958 Church Street, Baldwin, Long Island, New York 11510. Used with permission.

The following activity is an example of a directed lesson involving reading for implied meanings:

Read the story.[14]

Old Ironsides has tall masts and many sails. A long time ago, it was used in a war at sea.

Old Ironsides was built at a *shipyard* in Boston in 1794. It is made of wood. But people called it "Old Ironsides" because its sides were very hard, like *iron.* Today, Old Ironsides is open to the *public.* All people can go on it and see what ships were like many years ago.

Owney became the greatest dog traveler of all time. The dog was a pet of the post office. It went everywhere on the mail trains. After visiting post offices in America, it went across the sea. The Emperor of Japan gave the dog a medal. Owney finally returned to New York with more than 200 medals!

True or False

1. The scene above took place after Owney was allowed to travel on trains.

2. The ruler of Japan gave Owney a medal after the dog traveled across the sea.

Figure 10.7. Understanding sequences. From Richard A. Boning, *Detecting the Sequence,* 3d. ed., Book D, Unit 9. Copyright 1982 by Barnell Loft Ltd., 958 Church Street, Baldwin, Long Island, New York 11510. Used with permission.

Circle the words that best complete each sentence.

Old Ironsides is a _____ .
   building (ship) city
Iron is a _____ .
   (metal) cloth color
A *shipyard* is _____.
   a place where ships sail   a place to play games
        (a place where ships are built)
The *public* means _____ .
   (all people) sailors builders

6. *Reading to understand characterization and setting.*
   Much attention needs to be given to an understanding of the characters in narratives—of their feelings and motivations as they attempt to reach their goals. Some children who are limited in the understanding of their own feelings, motivations, and goals find it difficult to understand those of other persons as well as those of characters in stories. Teachers need to take every opportunity to discuss these aspects of stories with students.

Workbook exercises may be used to teach this aspect of comprehension. They will be most valuable if they are used for direct teaching, with the teacher helping the children to locate the cues in the passages that suggest feelings, motivations, and goals of story characters.

7. *Sensing relationships in time, place, cause, and effect.*
   Teachers would be well advised to give the same kind of detailed attention to these elements of narrative (time, place, cause, effect) as was suggested for the understanding of characterization and setting. Children frequently do not grasp these relationships and must be systematically guided to do so. Teachers need to talk them through stories, noting the words that signal time, place, cause, and effect. They may even make diagrams that link these elements with the feelings, motivations, and goals of characters.

Typical of a prepared activity that might be used in direct teaching is this section of a workbook page:
The sentences on the left tell what the children are doing. The sentences on the right tell what will happen because of their work. Match the sentences. Write each number on the line in front of the words that tell what will happen.[15]

1. The children are cleaning up the block.
2. The children are planting seeds.
3. On one day a week, cars cannot drive down the street.
4. The children are painting on the wall of one building.
5. The children are gathering bottles from all the people.

 _4_ The children will have a nice picture to look at.
 _5_ There will be no broken glass on the street.
 _3_ Children can play in the street.
 _1_ The block will look clean and nice.
 _2_ Flowers will grow.

8. *Reading to anticipate outcomes.*
   When teachers read to children, occasionally it is useful to stop short of the end of the story and ask children to predict the ending. Children's ideas may be noted on a chart or the chalkboard. The children may also list with their possible outcomes the clues that led them to those conclusions. Then the story may be finished. A valuable discussion may follow in which the group searches for clues about the author's story plan. Such lessons will help children as they plan their own story endings.

Developmentally, as children learn about the structure of stories, they attend first to the beginnings. Later they begin to formulate endings. At first these may be very brief; often endings take the form of simply, "The end." When teachers do directed teaching such as the activity just suggested, children may be helped in developing endings for their own stories.

9. *Recognizing the author's mood or tone.*

A good reader senses the author's mood or tone. This ability to respond to the writer's feelings is important to the reader. The author's purpose, mood, and general outlook need to be understood by the reader whether these are stated directly or subtly implied.

Tennyson reveals a great deal about how he feels about a brook in the last four stanzas of his poem:

The Brook

I steal by lawns and grassy plots,
I slide by hazel covers;
I move the sweet forget-me-nots
That grow for happy lovers.

I slip, I slide, I gloom, I glance,
Among my skimming swallows;
I make the netted sunbeams dance
Against my sandy shallows.

I murmur under moon and stars
In brambly wildernesses;
I linger by my shingly bars,
I loiter round my cresses;

And out again I curve and flow
To join the brimming river;
For men may come and men may go,
But I go on forever.[16]

10. *Comparing and contrasting.*

GEESE AND AIRPLANES

Often fifty or sixty geese, hissing and honking in their excitement, fly southward together in the fall of the year. As they soar upward into the air, they gradually form a wedge, or huge "V", in the sky. Usually at the point of the wedge is a fearless old gander that leads the flight. Faithfully each year he pilots the flock to the South, where the geese spend the winter. Early in the spring, he brings them back to the northern wilderness. There, concealed by the tall reeds of a lake, the geese make their nests and raise their young.

During their long flight the geese must have places to rest and to recover their strength. Many little lakes hidden deep in the forest are used by the geese as resting and feeding stations. The pilot-gander always seems to know where each of the lakes is. He stops briefly so that his flock can rest and eat, just as the pilot of an airplane stops to rest and eat.

When pilots fly planes in a group, they form a wedge. The airplanes soar far upward into the sky and look much like silver geese flying fearlessly in calm or cloudy weather.

Flying in a V-shaped wedge helps the planes in many ways. The plane that flies ahead of the others leads the way safely. The pilot of each plane has a clear view before him. This would not be true if the planes flew in a straight line.

The strong wind made by the powerful thrust of the planes' jet engines stirs up waves in the air. By flying in a wedge, each plane can stay out of the strong wind that is stirred up by the airplanes ahead of it.

Put *G* before statements that are true about flying geese.
Put *A* before statements that are true about flying airplanes.
Put *A* and *G* before statements that are true of both geese and planes.

_____ They often fly in a wedge.

_____ In a wedge, each one is out of the wind wave made by the others.

_____ The one at the point of the wedge is the leader.

_____ They look like silver.

_____ The thrust of the jet engines stirs up a strong wind.

_____ While in a wedge, each one has a clear view.

_____ They stop for rest and food.

_____ They nest in northern lakes.[17]

11. *Formulating generalized statements.*

A generalization is a statement or principle that encompasses the common characteristics of a chain of ideas or individual statements. Generalizations can be developed with children through an inductive method of teaching. By analyzing their own experiences, and stating concepts that are meaningful and useful to them, they can organize the descriptive data that they have to formulate generalized statements.

Very young children can discuss with the teachers the products provided by the cow for us to use. The cow gives milk; the cow provides butter and cheese; the cow provides meat; the cow gives us leather, tallow for candles, buttons, and even jello. From such a list, we can generalize that the cow is a very useful animal to people.

Teachers are asking their students to generalize when they use such informal questions as:
"How is this like what we did yesterday?"
"What would happen if . . . ?"
"Now do the experiment again, and see if the same thing happens."

Successful people often seem to have similar qualities. Two of these qualities are *determination* and *courage*. Read the following article about Dr. Frederick Banting. Look for details in the article that demonstrate these qualities. Write the details under the headings below.

DR. FREDERICK BANTING

Dr. Frederick Banting was determined to help people suffering from diabetes. One day, while preparing for a lecture at his university, Dr. Banting thought of a new way to treat this disease. Although he was told that others had tried this method and failed, he was convinced that it could work. He continued to request help until he was given a laboratory in which he could prove his idea.

Later, he resigned his job at the university and gave up his medical career in order to give complete attention to his laboratory work. After eight months of steadfast labor, he discovered insulin. Insulin has helped to save the lives of many diabetics.[18]

Determination _____

_____

_____

_____

Courage _____

_____

_____

12. *Skimming.*

    Skimming is a skill that can be developed to a high degree and used profitably
    in all kinds of reading. Skimming enables people to quickly select those items
    that they are interested in reading and to reject those that they are not. Most of
    us use skimming regularly in selecting those parts of the daily newspaper we
    want to read more closely. Teachers need to point out to students that skimming
    is only to grasp general significance and not to learn details or factual
    information. Skimming requires that the reader cover a large quantity of
    reading material without "reading the words"—perhaps moving down the
    middle of the column of print rather than following lines of print from left to
    right across the column.

    Students are using skimming wisely when they can:

    a. Look through a table of contents to see on what page a specific chapter
       begins.
    b. Skim the article in the encyclopedia about Edna Ferber to see which of her
       novels was published in 1958.
    c. Skim through the ending of the story to see whether the lost puppy was
       rescued or came back home.
    d. Skim through the story to find the part that describes what kind of person
       the old peddler was.

Strategies for Teaching Comprehension

Many students have an inadequate sense of organization; they are unable to make the
parts of the lesson fit together or "fall into place" as key ideas, subordinate ideas, and
details. Because they lack skill in synthesizing meanings, they are unable to evaluate
or interpret the content as they read.

Teachers may use many teaching strategies that help students with the problems of
comprehension. Teachers should:

1. Plan to assign stories to be read that coincide with children's experiences. If
   stories must be read that contain ideas foreign to the experiences of the readers,
   then plan ways for the children to obtain the background information and
   language.
2. Use different *levels of questioning* to cause students to think about and use
   what they read: literal level, interpretive level, and applied or evaluative level.
3. Point out to students the techniques that writers use to clarify meanings.
4. Encourage the students to use the context at the sentence and paragraph levels;
   they should also make use of the general context in which the material was
   written.[19]

5. Use scaffolding as a strategy in which the experienced language user (the teacher) guides the novice (the child) through unfamiliar language tasks.[20]
6. Point out those function words that signal meaning.
7. For all students, but especially those with either meager vocabularies or a foreign language background, spend considerable time with figurative language and the unusual facets of English.
8. Teachers may use journal writing to encourage children to use print to express their own ideas.
9. Use the cloze procedure as a means of leading students to anticipate meanings and to think ahead about what the writers are thinking.
10. Plan time to have oral conference sessions in which the teacher can listen to the students and then question *how* they read to learn.
11. Since the only way students become competent readers is to *read, read,* and *read,* provide a great deal of meaningful, oral reading. In corrective reading, teachers need to find more time for oral reading.
12. Make sure that students understand the close relationship between writing and reading.

Developing good comprehension skills is not a matter of a lesson or two or a single strategy. The teacher will need to utilize teaching techniques such as those in the list just given continuously if the goal of reading comprehension is to be met.

Encourage Experience and Language

It is generally accepted that children will write and read best about those topics with which they have the greatest familiarity. At least initially, children should have the opportunity to begin their literacy tasks dealing with familiar experiences, concepts, and language. Despite this general assumption, all too many children begin reading and writing dealing with books that contain words that represent concepts that are totally foreign to the beginners' experiences.

Making Connections 10.1: Developing Meaningful Experiences with Children

Select a story from a basal reader that contains a concept that children might not understand. Make a careful plan about how you would introduce the concept to children through a concrete experience. Brainstorm a vocabulary list that you might use with the children during the activity. Decide how you would move from the activity to the story in the basal reader.

Prepare to share your proposed plans with others in your class. Ask for input from others on the value of the plan for developing the concept in question.

In order to encourage children to read for meaning, it is important for the teacher to begin with reading material that refers to familiar concepts; the children's own dictated stories and books will probably be the best materials. As the children move into prepared texts, the teacher must be alert to words and stories that deal with unfamiliar ideas and that require schemata the children do not possess. If the teacher thinks that some stories containing strange concepts are necessary, they should build the required concepts before reading begins. Build these ideas through first-hand experiences with appropriate accompanying language when possible. Films, pictures, guest speakers, charts, and field trips are examples of possible substitutes, usually not as effective as building *real* experiences, but certainly better than no attempt to build background.

Actually making butter as butter was churned in the past is far more meaningful than seeing a movie about how it was done or hearing someone explain the process. Experiencing the tired arm muscles from turning the churn, watching the butter separate from the whey, squeezing the last drops of whey from the lump of soft butter with a wooden paddle, and spreading the smooth substance on slices of bread and eating them can never be equalled by words and pictures. As the children have such experiences, the teacher must be alert to provide the important language. In the butter-making experience, the teacher might introduce the words *churn, cream, butter, salted, paddle, whey, buttermilk,* and *fresh* in the context of the experience. Later the words could be included in stories the children write. These words should be meaningful now in a story about making butter.

Levels of Questioning

Bloom and others provided in their taxonomy a hierarchy of questioning.[21] They categorized levels of operation from simplest to most complex: memory, comprehension (translation, interpretation), application, analysis, synthesis, and evaluation. Teachers need to challenge students with all levels of questions to keep them thinking, understanding cause and effect, and thinking beyond the convergent levels of right and wrong.

With students who have failed to learn to read in the usual progression, teachers may need to teach the students how to understand the simplest kinds of questions. The students must become adept at both reading the words and thinking what the words are saying to them.

Teachers can easily identify three levels of understanding—the literal, the interpretive, and the applied or evaluative one. Each builds on the previous level.

The *literal level* produces knowledge of what the authors said. However, it is quite possible for students to identify what the authors said, and even memorize and repeat it in class, without understanding what the authors meant when they wrote it.

The *interpretive level* is using what the authors said in order to derive meaning from the writing. The readers must find relationships among the statements in the material they have read. When they understand these relationships, they can derive meanings.

The *applied level* is using what the authors said (literal) and what the authors meant to convey by what they said (interpretive) and applying it in some new situation to solve a problem.

Examples of the various levels include:

1. Recalling details in a narrative—requires literal meaning.
2. Predicting outcomes—requires some interpretation.
3. Associating personal experience with reading content—requires application or evaluative skill.

Questioning is an integral part of comprehension. Considerable time is devoted in reading methods courses and workshops on comprehension to the preparation of suitable questions that set the stage for reading and that evaluate understanding of what is read. Questioning and answering strategies have other powerful uses. The careful selection of questions undergirds the correct use of scaffolding, the interpretation of figurative language, the use of the cloze procedure as a thinking activity, the interpretation of the writing techniques of authors, and the clarification for children of the relationships between reading and writing.

Specific Strategies for Improving Answers to Questions

Many poor readers have trouble answering questions that require inferencing abilities. Holmes wrote that answering inference questions requires strategies similar to problem solving, identifying the relevant problem, bringing to bear relative information in an active struggle for a solution, and carefully analyzing solutions until a satisfactory one is found.[22] Since so many poor readers have struggled with inference questions, she proposed the following steps that can be taught to children:

1. Read the material and the related inference question.
2. Develop tentative hypotheses as answers.
3. Identify important words that support or do not support the hypotheses.
4. Compare the student-generated hypotheses and the key words. The comparison can be done by answering yes/no questions.
5. Select the hypothesis that fits all the key words. This is the most likely answer.[23]

Children appear to be able to answer questions better when they have had experience in generating questions about material that they have read. The strategies for generating answers appear to be strengthened by the thinking required to ask questions. Walker[24] suggested a specific technique for use with children in the fourth grade and beyond. The teacher begins the activity by modeling the development of questions. Then the children read a selection and develop questions. After they have written the questions, they answer them and compare their work with the teacher's questions.

Cohen found that even primary-grade children could improve their ability to answer questions by learning to generate questions of their own.[25] Children seemed most able to generate literal-level questions, but the research did not show that they could improve in their ability to ask themselves higher-level questions and transfer this ability to answer questions on work sheets and tests.

Writing Techniques that Authors Use

Writers for children use techniques that will help children to pick out meanings of new words within the context of what they are reading. Such techniques have been described by Artley and McCullough.[26] They include:

1. A brief explanation of the word can be given in parentheses or in a footnote:
   The *cacique* ordered an inquisition of the intruders who came into the village. (The *cacique* is the chief, or person of the highest authority, in the village.)
2. A clause or phrase that explains the meaning of the word can be inserted in the sentence:
   At certain times during the year in the northern skies one can see the *aurora borealis,* a colorful display of flickering, shifting lights.
   Moss, grass, and flowers grow in the *tundra,* the treeless plains found in Arctic regions.
3. A synonym or substitute phrase is used to indicate the meaning:
   shrimp, a small shellfish
   the lobby, a small waiting room
   the cacique, the chief of the tribe
4. A new word is *emphasized* by using italics, quotation marks, or boldface type to call attention to it:
   The farmer uses a machine called a *combine* to harvest the wheat.
   Pioneer farmers used a "cradle," a scythe with a wooden frame attached, to harvest the grain.
   Farmers who shared their crops with the landowner were called **sharecroppers.**
5. A direct explanation of the word can be presented in a full sentence:
   In the hot desert, the man makes his garden in an oasis. An oasis is a green spot where there is a water supply.
   The nomads of the desert are coming to the trading center. Nomads are people who constantly move about and who have no settled home.

Using Context

Teachers must encourage children to use the *context* of the sentence or paragraph to predict what unknown words might be. The teacher may ask questions such as,"What word would make sense there?" or "Read on to the end of the sentence. Now what should the word be?" If this prompting technique is used enough, children will begin to rely on the context on their own to make the text make sense.

Smith reminded teachers, *"The more nonvisual information you have when you read, the less visual information you need."*[27] The term "nonvisual information" has been referred to earlier as prior or world knowledge. This is a strong argument for presenting meaningful text and for utilization of context. Context frequently gives meaning to words, as in these sentences:

Jack played with the *top* on the floor.
His mother screwed the *top* on the jar.
Ralph said, "I will *top* off the tank at the filling station."

There are larger contexts than the sentence or the page to which the teacher and children must attend. The setting for reading provides a context, whether it is in the cozy reading corner of the classroom, in the supermarket, or in the doctor's office. Where we read dictates to some extent how we comprehend. Who the reader is and what the reader has experienced also provide a context that influences comprehension. Sometimes experiences support comprehension; other experiences may be the cause of misunderstanding if prior knowledge and the text are in disagreement. Teachers need to be aware of these larger contexts and to use them when possible in designing effective opportunities for comprehension.

Scaffolding Techniques

When persons competent in some skill help novices to acquire a skill with suggestions, supportive questions, or even a helping hand, the skilled person is providing *scaffolding* for the learner. When the young child tackles the problem of climbing a short ladder, the helpful adult makes suggestions about how to start the climb, holds the ladder steady for the child, and provides verbal feedback about each successful step. As the child starts to read, the adult may point to the left side of the page to suggest where to look, may provide cues or questions to encourage the child's word recognition, may even read the sentence with the proper inflection to help the child to perceive the meaning, and may help the child to connect the picture with the words.

Much scaffolding is done almost intuitively by adults who are interested in helping children to master more difficult tasks than they might otherwise be able to learn. However, teachers may intentionally provide scaffolding for children through the lessons they plan and the questions and comments they design.[28] Teachers who deliberately use scaffolding techniques with disabled readers provide the students with strategies for asking questions to guide comprehension, for facilitating word recognition, and for using the cues in print such as punctuation marks. If these supports are given long enough and often enough, the child can learn to "talk" through many reading problems that are encountered. Teachers must remember that scaffolding is intended to help the learners accomplish their goals; it is not intended as a technique to enable adults to impose their purposes on the learners.[29]

Function Words that Signal Meaning

Words that have no referents are called *function* or *structure* words. It is estimated that there are no more than three hundred such words in everyday English, but they make up nearly half of all the words in elementary reading context. Because of this, they need to be mastered as sight words as early as possible in the reading process. They are termed *markers* for the type of structural element they precede:

Noun markers: *a, the, some, three*
Verb markers: *am, are, is, had*
Phrase markers: *up, down, out, above*
Clause markers: *if, until, because, how*
Question markers: *who, why, how, when*

These structure, or service, words help the reader to anticipate meanings that nouns or verbs carry in a given sentence structure.

Some of these function words may also be key words appearing in content reading. In content reading these words alert the student to paragraph content and are helpful in the organization of the content being read. For instance, if in a long paragraph or in a series of short ones the words or phrases *first, in the second place,* or *fourth and finally* appear, these are clues to items being listed that the reader should be able to sort out easily. If chronology is a key factor in the paragraph or essay, the words or phrases *in the first place, next, after a short while, then,* and *in the end* are clues to the progress of movement of the writing. In other reading, emphasizing contrast with words such as *both . . . and, neither . . . nor, on the one hand . . . on the other hand, nevertheless,* and *in spite of* will be important.

The teacher must not assume that the roles and meanings of function words are learned automatically. As children read material in which function words occur, the teacher needs to discuss with the students how these words make text cohesive and contribute to meaning. Readers will find that function words signal cause and effect (*because* and *since*), time and sequence (*finally, then,* and *at last*), coordinate relationships (*and*), condition (*if* and *although*), subordinate relationships (*because*), contrast (*whereas* and *while*), and parallels (*therefore* and *accordingly*).[30] Children, especially those with reading problems, need repeated opportunities to work with sentences containing the sample of function words just identified and many others.

Figurative Language and Other Facets of English

In Jean Craighead George's *Julie of the Wolves,* sentences like the following are found:

A flower twisted in the wind. (p. 8)
The wolf groomed his chest with his tongue.
(p. 10)
The sun slid slowly down the sky, hung still for
a moment, then started up again.
It was midnight. (p. 43)
Her eyes roamed the street. (p. 164)[31]

Louise Fitzhugh used some figurative expressions in her book *The Long Secret:*

Beth Ellen was so overcome by shyness, a
timidity so powerful it *turned her mind to
dough.* (p. 33)
She felt *nailed to the floor.* (p. 54)
Mama Jenkins smiled a *beautiful hippo smile.*
(p. 83)[32]

Figures of speech are used in writing to add beauty and color and to extend sensory images. Because most children hear these expressions all their lives, they begin using them in their own speech at an early age. They appear in all writing and must be understood by readers. Slang expressions, idioms, and unusual words can create problems for students who have reading difficulties. Because understanding these facets of English presents problems for all students learning English as a second language, chapter 14 is devoted to teaching the linguistically and culturally different child.

Six useful articles in professional journals that contain suggestions for teachers are:

Leona M. Forrester, "Idiomagic!" *Elementary English* 51 (January 1974): 125–27.
Linda G. Geller, "Exploring Metaphor in Language Development and Learning," *Language Arts* 61 (February 1984): 151–61.
Estelle K. Lorenz, "Excuse Me, But Your Idiom Is Showing," *Reading Teacher* 31 (October 1977): 24–27.
John E. Readence, R. Scott Baldwin, and Robert J. Rickelman, "Instructional Insights into Metaphors and Similes," *Journal of Reading* 27 (November 1983): 109–12.
Joanne M. Rogacki, "Poetry in Motion," *Language Arts* 61 (March 1984): 261–64.
Eleanore S. Tyson and Lee Mountain, "A Riddle or Pun Makes Learning Words Fun," *Reading Teacher* 36 (November 1982): pp. 170–72.

A list of trade books that could provide enjoyment of figurative language may be found in *Learning to Read Naturally* by Margaret G. Jewell and Miles V. Zintz (Dubuque, Iowa: Kendall/Hunt Publishing Co., 1986), pages 244–45.

Journal Writing

Many teachers find that *journal writing* is a significant tool for encouraging children to record their ideas. Children of all ages may enjoy writing in journals. To remember, however, that what is written in a journal is personal writing and should not be subject to correction by the teacher is important. If the children agree to share their journals with their teacher, the teacher may write responses to the ideas that the students have recorded. With these responses, the teacher will be able to model spellings, punctuation, letter forms, spacing, and other mechanical features of writing. Sample pages from a journal containing the writing of a kindergarten child and his teacher's responses are shown in figure 10.8.

The journal is more than just an opportunity for the child to continue to grow in writing. It becomes an often-read book. The author who is also the reader has many opportunities to read easily comprehended material and to practice reading the words that were chosen to express ideas.

Using the Cloze Procedure as a Teaching Technique

The cloze procedure as a *testing* technique was discussed in chapter 6. Many references to the cloze procedure describe it as a testing device. However, it may be used as a *teaching* technique. Sentences with blank spaces in which the children are asked to write the words that best complete the thought, or sentences in which the children think

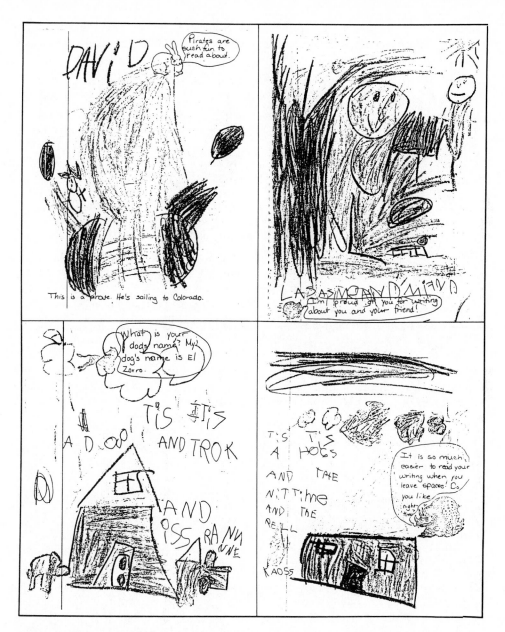

Figure 10.8 David's journal pages show his progress over four months from dictation to writing with spaces between words.

of a synonym for the underlined word are types of exercises that develop skill in the use of the cloze technique. Sample cloze activities one might do with elementary school students follow:

Directions: Write the word that is missing in the following sentences:

1. He lives _____ the city.
2. Come to the party _____ me.
3. Sometimes on Sunday, we go _____the zoo.

Complete the following sentences using words that describe:

1. The baby chickens were _____ and _____ .
2. The afternoon clouds were _____ and _____ .

Read the sentences all the way through. Decide what words are missing and write them in the blanks. After everyone has filled the blanks, talk about the possible words that could have been used for each blank.

The teacher asked three _____ boys to go to the _____ and bring back several _____ about goldfish and other _____ that could live in _____ tank. The children were _____ because they were sure _____ they were going to _____ some new pets in _____ classroom. When the boys _____ , they brought several colorful _____ , which all the children _____ . Then the teacher said, " _____ , when you arrive at _____ , you will have a _____ ." He would not tell _____ children what it would _____ . Everyone went home excited, _____ what the surprise would _____ .

Even before children can read, teachers can read familiar rhymes and stories to them, leaving out endings or other known words. For instance, the teacher might say:

Jack and Jill
Went up the _____
To get a pail of _____ .
Jack fell down
And broke his _____
And Jill came tumbling _____ .

When children are comfortable with such activities and they have begun to read, the teacher may print similar, known poems and rhymes for the children to read, filling in the blanks. Later, longer pieces of print may be presented on which children work together to fill in the blanks. They may even try to generate long lists of words that would make sense in the blanks. If the children used the sentence, "The boys walked silently to the _____ house," they would be able to fill in the blank with many different words that would help to create entirely different pictures of the house—*tiny, haunted, tall, deserted, brick.* Children may enjoy drawing pictures to represent the houses that they have described.

Making Connections 10.2: Locating Figurative Language

Figurative language occurs frequently in materials written for children. Surveying some basal readers at different levels to see how much figurative language is actually being used may be helpful.

Select basals at the first-, third-, and sixth-grade levels from a single publishing company. Examine at least four or five stories at each level, listing the figurative language. Then think about these points:

1. Compare the amount of figurative language you found in texts across the three grade levels.
2. Are different types of figurative language introduced at different levels?
3. Select three examples at each grade level. How would you plan to teach children the meanings of these examples?

In your class share your findings with your peers. You may wish to compare your findings across different publishing companies.

Helping Students to Analyze Their Reading Situations

Strang suggested that teachers sit down with students individually and encourage them to *talk about* the miscues they have made, to tell why they chose the specific answers they did, and to analyze the students' thinking in arriving at the answers they chose.[33]

Standardized tests do not help to explain how the students read—how the process works for them—or what reading problems they have when reading tasks are presented. Two students may get exactly the same score on a standardized test, but their levels of comprehension of the paragraph or their maturity in thinking about the reading material may not be at all equal. Strang suggested working individually with students in this way:

> Read the following paragraph aloud as you usually read orally. While the student reads, the teacher records errors by whatever method he usually uses. He also observes phrasing, intonation, stress, and pauses that indicate the student's understanding of the language structure of the selection. It is easy to detect word-by-word reading, mechanical division of sentences into parts of phrases and clauses and other evidence of failure to read in thought units. . . . Performance may cover a range from colorless monotone to the richness of feeling and significance that a great actor gives to every line.[34]

The teacher can observe whether the student approaches reading with enjoyment, indifference, dislike, anxiety, resistance, or hostility.

Classroom teachers need to remember that formal diagnosis can be time consuming and is usually done by people other than those who expect to work daily with the students. Such formal diagnosis does, occasionally, overemphasize some single problem in learning to read when the real cause is a whole cluster of problems. Since the people who do the diagnosis may not communicate directly with the teachers who work with the students, the diagnosis itself will be inadequate unless the teachers make many astute observations about the students in the reading situations—judging their total *effect* in the reading situation and analyzing the nature of their successful and unsuccessful responses to questions for meaning.

Easy Oral Reading Practice

The way that all children become accomplished readers is by having hours and hours of reading practice. The way to learn to read is to *read, read, read!* Those students who do not have mastery over a large stock of sight words must read these common words over and over in interesting contexts until they have overlearned them. Because meaning is the center of all reading activity, reading context is much preferred over studying words in isolation, as in flash card drill.

While it is difficult for the teacher to find time, all children need as much oral reading practice as possible. However, when the children do read aloud, they must have an audience; this means that if the teacher asks them to read aloud, then the teacher must be prepared to give attention to the reading being done. Teachers may manage the classroom in many ways so that there is time for individual oral reading practice. Other children can be pupil-teachers if the regular teacher plans carefully with them how to read in pairs; older brothers and sisters who read well may be able to listen to children read; volunteer parents are one of the richest sources of interested adults who can give undivided attention to children for a few minutes two or three times a week; teacher aides, student teachers, and senior high school volunteers are other possible listeners. Placing a tape recorder in a quiet corner and stationing one student with it who can operate it makes it possible to ask children to record their oral reading exercise for the teacher to hear and evaluate at a later time.

Appendix B contains an extensive bibliography of books prepared to meet the teachers' needs for easy oral reading materials for all students.

Uniting Reading and Writing

Children need to see the close relationships between reading and writing. There should be many opportunities to write stories and books and to read what has been written to teachers, other children, brothers and sisters, and parents. The children can learn that by writing they convey their meanings to the readers of their work. As readers they learn what writers must do to make their efforts understandable.

> Writing is the discovery process *a la* language. . . . Writers use language to unlock meaning. They do not follow a blueprint, but rather find their ideas developing as they express them. . . . Children learning the written form of language ought to be producing it as well as reading it. They should be reading *and* writing. They should be aware of someone reading their writing, and that what they are reading is someone's writing.[35]

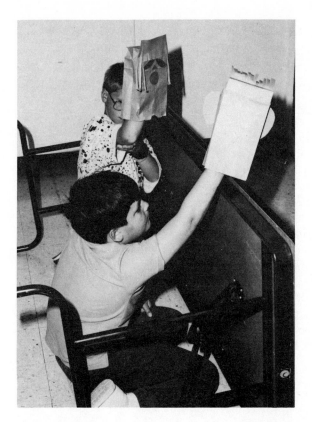

For independent work, two boys wrote a play, made quick paper bag puppets, turned a table on its side for a stage. . . .

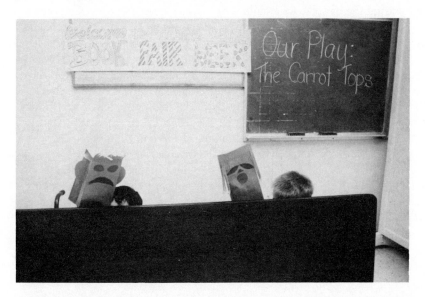

. . . and presented their efforts to their class. Their work involved oral language, writing, and reading.

Hansen noted that:

> The members of the writing community rejoice in each other's
> accomplishments. . . . We share and others share with us. We want to learn,
> and through sharing we know what others know. . . . Writers know they don't
> know everything. They use writing to help them explore and learn about topics
> and concerns of interest to them.[36]

Children need many concrete experiences demonstrating the relationships between reading and writing. Teachers should stress that what has been read has obviously been written and that authors and readers are interacting in trying to share experiences and ideas. But children need to have experiences with these concepts. In chapter 9 suggestions that would encourage understanding of the relationships between reading and writing included (1) using dictated stories and language experiences, (2) writing rebus stories for others to read, (3) making books, (4) gathering and utilizing environmental print, and (5) using the computer to compose stories to be printed for others to read. Other suggestions for integrating the related language behaviors of reading and writing were covered earlier in this chapter in our discussion of teaching strategies for reading comprehension. Teachers may encourage the study of authors' techniques, they may employ scaffolding strategies to help readers understand what writers are trying to say, and they may teach children to be critical consumers of writing, whether it is found in basals, in trade books, or in the books written by their peers.

Materials for Teaching Comprehension

The classroom teacher has access to many materials that can be used to teach comprehension. One of the most common is, of course, the *basal reader*. Much can be accomplished by using the basal to help children learn the varied skills of comprehension, including such diverse tasks as finding main ideas, reading to identify facts and opinions, sequencing parts of a story, and identifying cause-and-effect sequences. Teachers must be aware that problems may arise from following the basal without questioning the stories to be read or the skill activities to be completed. Stories must be analyzed for their appropriateness for the children who will read them. Some selections simply will have no realistic connections with the lives of the children. Either these stories may be omitted, or the teacher will need to prepare activities that will familiarize the children with the concepts and language to be introduced in the text. A careful analysis of the questions to be asked by the teacher may reveal that most of them are low-level, factual questions. The teacher may need to prepare new questions that require the children to think at higher levels and to exert critical reading skills. The teacher may also need to develop careful plans to provide scaffolding for readers who are having difficulties with ideas or words.

Other Practice Materials

Many commercial materials are available to help children practice comprehension skills. Teachers need to study the materials carefully before giving them to the children to make sure that the stories or articles are suitable for the readers' experiences, decoding abilities, and comprehension needs.

A few examples of materials prepared to promote growth of comprehension skills are given in appendix G: Instructional Materials for Word Identification and Comprehension.

Trade Books

The teacher should have a rich variety of *trade books,* including wordless picture books, predictable books, picture story books, short books for reading in one sitting, and chapter books. As many topics as possible should be represented at a variety of levels of difficulty. The books should be attractively displayed; children are more likely to select books if the front covers are displayed than if they are shelved as in the library. Books should be included in interest and learning centers to provide opportunities for children to explore topics conveniently. Children who can select books on topics of interest at levels at which they can read comfortably will have few comprehension problems.

Books Written by Children

The trade book collection in the room needs to be supplemented by books that have been written by the children themselves (and their teachers). These may well be the most cherished books in the room. They are sure to be excellent means for promoting comprehension since they will be about known topics and reflect the interests of the children. If blank pages are included at the ends of the books, readers may be encouraged to write positive reactions and suggestions.

Microcomputer Programs

Various kinds of microcomputer programs may be used to further comprehension. Some are designed to give practice in specific skills very much as certain workbooks and practice sheets do. Simulation games may be useful in encouraging children to read critically, to follow directions, and to respond to sequences of events. They also encourage risk taking and making predictions, which are critical to reading. Word-processing programs encourage writing, and when a printer is available, books may be produced from the children's efforts.

Some representative microcomputer programs are:

1. *The Bank Street Writer,* (Broadway, N.Y.: Scholastic, Inc.). This word-processing program is suitable for young students as well as adults.
2. Edward Fry and Lawrence Carrillo, *Reading Comprehension Tutor Program* (Wilmington, Del.: BLS). This software is designed for reading levels three to six.

3. *The Oregon Trail* (American Peripherals, 122 Bangor St., Lindenhurst, N.Y. 11757), and *The Lemonade Stand,* (Minnesota Educational Computing Consortium—MECC, 3490 Lexington Avenue, St. Paul, Minn. 55112). These are examples of simulation games that promote risk taking, problem solving, and alternative solutions, all critical to reading comprehension.

4. *Reading Comprehension* (Chatsworth, Calif.: Opportunities for Learning). There are ten programs for elementary levels and beyond.

5. *Reading: Tutorial Comprehension.* (Westminster, Md.: Random House). This tutorial program is suited to reading levels two to four and encompasses several of the subskills of reading comprehension.

6. *Story Tree* (Broadway, N.Y.: Scholastic, Inc.). Children at all levels can write and read their own stories.

7. *Trickster Coyote* (Pleasantville, N.Y.: Reader's Digest Services, Inc.). The two games are based on the coyote as the native American trickster. They are for ages eight and up.

Summary

This chapter has been organized around three aspects of teaching comprehension: an understanding of what is included in instruction in comprehension in reading, strategies for helping children learn to comprehend better, and suggestions about materials for the classroom that the teacher and children can use to improve comprehension abilities.

Suggestions for teaching comprehension have been organized for comprehension at different text levels and for different levels of thinking. Suggestions have also been made for teaching comprehension in the context of themes as well as through the use of basal readers and workbooks.

Levels of questioning, writing techniques for aiding comprehension, awareness of signal words that control meanings, the cloze procedure, understanding figurative language, and provisions for easy reading practice are among the strategies that teachers will find useful. Teachers who are familiar with these strategies will be able to draw upon them rather spontaneously throughout the day to help students develop skills for working independently.

For Further Reading

Alvermann, Donna E., Deborah R. Dillon, and David G. O'Brien. *Using Discussion to Promote Reading Comprehension.* Newark, Del.: International Reading Association, 1987. The authors define discussion and its role in comprehension. Then they provide strategies for its use and evaluation.

Anderson, Richard C., et al. *Do Errors on Classroom Reading Tasks Slow Growth in Reading?* Technical Report No. 404, Center for the Study of Reading. Champaign, Ill.: University of Illinois at Urbana—Champaign, 1987. The authors review many studies on the topic. They find that oral reading errors can have a positive effect on comprehension.

Baumann, James F. "Anaphora in Basal Reader Selections: How Frequently Do They Occur?" *Journal of Reading Behavior* 19, no. 2 (1987): 141–57. Among the findings reported in this article are (1) that anaphora occur more frequently in narrative text, (2) that the number of anaphora does not appear to be related to the grade level of the text, and (3) that the anaphora differ as a function of the publishers of basal readers.

Costa, Arthur. *Developing Minds: A Resource Book for Teaching Thinking.* Washington, D.C.: Association for Supervision and Curriculum Development, 1985. This is a compendium on the teaching of thinking. After defining thinking, the author presents strategies and programs for its development.

Gardner, Michael, and Martha Smith. "Does Perspective Taking Ability Contribute to Reading Comprehension?" *Journal of Reading* 30 (January 1987): 333–36. The authors conclude that perspective taking is related to reading comprehension, especially at the inferential level.

Heimlich, Joan, and Susan D. Pittelman. *Semantic Mapping: Classroom Applications.* Newark, Del.: International Reading Association, 1986. Semantic mapping is proposed as a comprehension strategy at all grade levels. Several examples of semantic maps are provided.

Irwin, Judith, ed. *Understanding and Teaching Cohesion Comprehension.* Newark, Del.: International Reading Association, 1986. The book's three parts are: (1) what is cohesion, (2) research on cohesion, and (3) teaching cohesion comprehension.

Johnston, Peter H. *Reading Comprehension Assessment: A Cognitive Basis.* Newark, Del.: International Reading Association, 1983. The author presents a variety of methods of assessing comprehension, as well as suggestions for new directions in comprehension assessment.

Pearson, P. David, and Dale Johnson. *Teaching Reading Comprehension.* New York: Holt, Rinehart and Winston, 1978. An older reference, but one with valuable suggestions and strategies.

Reutzel, D. Ray. "Story Maps Improve Comprehension." *Reading Teacher* 39 (January 1985): 400–404. The writer suggests using story maps to help readers to comprehend relationships among story elements. Three examples of story maps are provided.

Smith, Frank. *Reading without Nonsense.* 2d ed. New York: Teachers College Press, 1985. This is a basic text for an understanding of the reading process. Comprehension is basic to that process.

Temple, Charles, et al. *The Beginnings of Writing.* 2d ed. Boston: Allyn and Bacon, 1988. This is an important book on the teaching of writing. Writing and reading are interdependent language processes. Writing appears to facilitate reading comprehension.

Weaver, Constance. *Reading Process and Practice.* Portsmouth, N.H.: Heinemann Educational Books, 1988. The author clarifies the various aspects of the reading process and the teaching of reading from a socio-psycholinguistic viewpoint. Whole language is identified as the most appropriate approach to reading instruction.

Wells, Gordon. *The Meaning Makers: Children Learning Language and Using Language to Learn.* Portsmouth, N.H.: Heinemann Educational Books, 1986. The author reports a major study of several children in family settings learning to make meaning with spoken language and later with written language. Meaning is central to all language use.

Wham, Mary Ann. "Metacognition and Classroom Instruction." *Reading Horizons* 27 (January 1987): 95–102. The author proposes that the processes involved in metacognition may be more important than the products. Students should not have to consciously identify comprehension strategies, but should focus on meaning, which is certain to require the use of various comprehension strategies.

Whitney, Paul. "Psychological Theories of Elaborative Inferences: Implications for Schema-Theoretic Views of Comprehension." *Reading Research Quarterly* 22 (Summer 1987): 299–310. In this article research is reviewed concerning how elaborative inferences are made. The activation of knowledge permitting elaborative inferences appears to be more dynamic than anticipated.

Notes

1. Ernest Horn, *Methods of Instruction in the Social Studies* (New York: Charles Scribner's Sons, 1937), 156.
2. Anthony Adams, "Talk and Learning in the Classroom: An Interview with Anthony Adams," *Language Arts* 61 (February 1984): 119–20.
3. Judith W. Irwin, *Teaching Reading Comprehension Processes* (Englewood Cliffs, N.J.: Prentice-Hall, 1986), 3–5.
4. Benjamin S. Bloom, ed., *Taxonomy of Educational Objectives—Handbook I: Cognitive Domain* (New York: Longman, Green, 1956).
5. David R. Krathwohl et al., *Taxonomy of Educational Objectives—Handbook II: Affective Domain* (New York: David McKay, 1964).
6. Steven R. Yussen, "The Role of Metacognition in Contemporary Theories of Cognitive Development," in *Metacognition, Cognition, and Human Performance, Vol. I, Theoretical Perspectives,* ed. D. L. Forrest-Pressley, G. E. MacKinnon, and T. Gary Waller (New York: Academic Press, 1985), 253–83.
7. Irwin, *Teaching Reading Comprehension Processes,* 29–30.
8. Miles V. Zintz and Zelda R. Maggart, *The Reading Process: The Teacher and the Learner,* 5th ed. (Dubuque, Iowa: William C. Brown Co. Publishers, 1988), 310.
9. Irwin, *Teaching Reading Comprehension Processes,* 29–30.
10. Russell Gersten and Douglas Carnine, "Direct Instruction in Reading Comprehension," *Educational Leadership* 43 (April 1986): 71.
11. Helen K. Smith, "Sequence in Comprehension," *Sequential Development of Reading Abilities,* Supplementary Monograph, no. 90, ed. Helen Robinson (Chicago: University of Chicago Press, 1960), 51–56.
12. Diane L. August, John H. Flavell, and Renee Clift, "Comparison of Comprehension Monitoring of Skilled and Less Skilled Readers," *Reading Research Quarterly* 20 (Fall 1984): 39–53.
13. Gersten and Carnine, "Direct Instruction," 72–77.
14. Robert B. Ruddell, Anne L. Ryle, and Martha Shogren, *Workbook for Moon Magic* (Boston: Allyn and Bacon, 1978), 53.
15. Ibid., 11.
16. Alfred Tennyson, "The Brook," in *Bobbs Merrill Readers: Fifth Reader,* ed. Clara Baker and Edna Baker (Indianapolis, Ind.: Bobbs Merrill, 1924), 426–27.
17. William S. Gray, Marion Monroe, and A. Sterl Artley, *Basic Reading Skills for Junior High School Use* (Glenview, Ill.: Scott, Foresman, 1957), 126.
18. Renni Fetterolf, Bernice Golden, and Ralph Weintraub, *Skillbook for Moments* (New York: American Book Co., 1977), 122. Litton Educational Publications, Inc., copyright.
19. Kathy Pezdek, "Arguments for a Constructive Approach to Comprehension and Memory," in *Reading and Understanding,* ed. Joseph Danks and Kathy Pezdek (Newark, Del.: International Reading Association, 1980), 40–73; Argiro L. Morgan, "Context: the Web of Meaning," *Language Arts* 60 (March 1983): 305–14.

20. Arthur N. Applebee and Judith A. Langer, "Instructional Scaffolding: Reading and Writing as Natural Language Activities," *Language Arts* 60 (February 1983): 168.

21. Benjamin S. Bloom et al., *Taxonomy of Educational Objectives, The Classification of Educational Goals, Handbook I: Cognitive Domain* (New York: David McKay Co., Inc., 1956).

22. Betty C. Holmes, "A Confirmation Strategy for Improving Poor Readers' Ability to Answer Inferential Questions," *Reading Teacher* 37 (November 1983): 144–45.

23. Ibid., 145–46.

24. Barbara J. Walker, *Diagnostic Teaching of Reading* (Columbus, Ohio: Merrill Publishing Co., 1988), 65–66.

25. Ruth Cohen, "Self-Generated Questions as an Aid to Reading Comprehension," *Reading Teacher* 36 (April 1983): 770–75.

26. A. S. Artley, "Teaching Word Meaning through Content," *Elementary English Review* 20 (1943): 68–74; Constance M. McCullough, "The Recognition of Context Clues in Reading," *Elementary English Review* 22 (1945): 1–5.

27. Frank Smith, *Reading without Nonsense,* 2d ed. (New York: Teachers College Press, 1985), 14.

28. Applebee and Langer, "Instructional Scaffolding," 168–75.

29. Dennis Searle, "Scaffolding: Who's Building Whose Building?" *Language Arts* 61 (September 1984): 480–83.

30. Marion D. Jenkinson, "Increasing Reading Power in the Social Studies," *Corrective Reading in the High School Classroom,* ed. Alan Robinson and Sidney Rauch (Newark, Del.: International Reading Association, 1966), 76.

31. Jean Craighead George, *Julie of the Wolves* (New York: Harper and Row, 1972).

32. Louise Fitzhugh, *The Long Secret* (New York: Harper and Row, 1965).

33. Ruth Strang, *Diagnostic Teaching of Reading* (New York: McGraw-Hill, Inc., 1964), 137.

34. Strang, *Diagnostic Teaching of Reading,* 66.

35. Suzanne L. Holt and JoAnne L. Vacca, "Reading with a Sense of Writer: Writing with a Sense of Reader," *Language Arts* 58 (November/December 1981): 937–40.

36. Jane Hansen, *When Writers Read* (Portsmouth, N.H.: Heinemann Educational Books, 1987), 15.

11
Study Strategies and Skills, and Content Fields Reading

Vocabulary

study strategies and skills
locational strategies and
   skills
reference materials
card catalog
taped books
talking books
concrete materials
alphabetical order
organizational strategies
   and skills
outlining
note taking
underlining
gloss
advance organizer
structured overview
study guide
guide-o-rama
summarizing

Questions

1. What is meant by study strategies and skills?
   (Recall)
2. What are the locational strategies and skills that
   children need? **(Recall)** How would you help a
   remedial reader to acquire each? **(Application)**
3. Identify the differences among glosses, advance
   organizers, structured overviews, and study
   guides. **(Inference)**
4. What is included in interpretive skills? **(Recall)**
5. What steps would you take to teach your middle-
   grade students to follow directions? **(Application)**
6. How will you prepare your students to take tests
   in your classroom? **(Application)**
7. Compare narrative and expository texts.
   (Evaluation)
8. What are the kinds of vocabulary that may be
   troublesome in content reading? **(Recall)**
9. Describe how you will plan to make reading
   content texts easier in your classroom.
   (Application)

Vocabulary

sequencing
interpretive strategies and
    skills
presenting information
directions
remembering
test taking
narrative text
expository text
text superstructures
text organizational patterns
SQ3R
specialized vocabulary
technical vocabulary
critical reading
advertising
propaganda
integration of reading and
    writing
global method

Introduction

Children who have reading problems frequently receive some form of special instruction. Some children attend Chapter I classes or are taught in a special education setting for a part of the day. A few have private tutoring or specialized instruction away from school. In the classroom, these children are allowed to read from readers at their instructional levels rather than being required to read grade-level texts.

The students who receive special attention for their reading programs are expected to study mathematics, social studies, science, and other school subjects. They are usually given grade-level texts for these subjects, regardless of their actual reading abilities. Obviously, they experience difficulties in using the textbooks and often cease making any effort to complete assignments.

The responsibility of the classroom teacher is to plan the student's *entire* instructional program so that success can be experienced. The teacher must plan not only for a reading program that will promote learning but also for an adjusted academic curriculum that takes into account the student's reading strengths and problems. Texts and other materials must be available at several levels above and below the grade being taught because the range in reading abilities in any classroom is normally several years.

Study strategies and skills are not so much *something* to be taught as they are *ways* of teaching, if the teacher accepts the philosophy that the teaching of a particular subject is synonymous with the study of that subject. When the subject is taught, the students increase their knowledge of that content area. The instruction also provides the students with knowledge of how to study the particular content. This knowledge may be useful in the study of other subject matter, supporting the students' needs to become independent learners.

Slow readers, disabled readers, and even nonreaders can achieve *something* in the content areas if the teachers are willing to set *different goals,* provide them with *different study guide sheets,* and develop a *different method of evaluation* at the end of the unit of work.

The teacher should be aware that content field texts pose some special problems for readers. The material is usually expository; basal readers contain mostly narratives. The vocabulary of social studies, mathematics, and science texts is studded with technical and specialized vocabulary items that often represent unfamiliar concepts. Specialized study skills are needed by the student, since content texts have different patterns of organization depending on the subject. All of these problems need careful attention for the student who may still be struggling with basic sight vocabulary.

This chapter is devoted to a discussion of study skills that need special attention if the disabled readers are to be successful and to the consideration of their problems in reading in the content fields. Methods for helping remedial readers with these difficulties will be suggested, along with the identification of suitable types of materials.

Study Strategies and Skills

Study strategies and skills can be set apart from other reading strategies and skills by describing them as "deliberate procedures for retaining and applying what is read."[1] All children need at least some help in learning desirable study strategies and skills. Even good readers need some guidance, but children with reading problems require careful, step-by-step teaching. The teacher should consider skills in locating information; organizing facts after they are found; interpreting visual information such as that found on maps, graphs, charts, and pictures; and applying what has been learned. The students should also have help with learning to follow written directions, to organize information so that it can be remembered, and to take tests successfully.

The assessment of a child's mastery of study strategies and skills can best be accomplished by observing the completion of a task requiring their application. When a child notes the copyright date or takes notes for a report, the teacher can infer mastery of that particular skill more surely than when the child completes a ditto sheet or workbook page on the skill. Rogers noted that many public schools have developed study skills lists that are often rigid and mechanical. It is important to remember that these behaviors are supposed to be secondary to pursuing a topic or activity of interest. They are simply a means to the end of increasing the efficiency with which students can learn from printed materials.[2]

Locational Strategies and Skills

The effort that must go into teaching *locational strategies and skills* increases with time, for the sheer quantity of knowledge continues to grow amazingly, and the techniques for knowledge retrieval are becoming ever more sophisticated and complex. The students in today's schools will spend most of their adult lives in a world of electronic information retrieval; teachers must at least address simple forms of this system that are currently available, as well as teach more conventional strategies and skills such as dictionary use and making the most of an index.

Using Reference Materials

Social studies and science units are often planned to include the use of *reference materials* for locating information. Some typical references are encyclopedias, almanacs, dictionaries, nonfiction trade books, magazines, and newspapers. These materials may be much too difficult for remedial readers unless special care is taken. The school should make sure that sets of encyclopedias and other reference materials at different levels of difficulty are available to students. Some simple encyclopedias are written at the third- to fifth-reader levels of difficulty; their articles are richly illustrated. An example of a good encyclopedia for children is *World Book*.[3] The articles begin at the fourth-grade level and become more difficult after the first few paragraphs. These encyclopedias are more useful to struggling readers than are the more difficult sets. The children can be helped to locate information in an encyclopedia or other reference and to read it by predicting what information is likely to be presented, by learning to study the pictures and captions carefully, and by reading headings and the beginning sentences of paragraphs.

Dictionaries are available from primary levels upward. (See chapter 9 for a brief list of children's dictionaries.) Each class should have a variety of dictionaries at different levels. Of course, trade books range in difficulty from simple picture books to difficult references on most topics. Teachers can make sure that magazines and newspapers at a variety of levels are available to children. Magazines and newspapers especially for school children represent the easier levels. Regular city newspapers and magazines such as *National Geographic* or *Natural History* represent more difficult reading for elementary children.

Some teachers read parts of reference articles that will be needed in units on cassette tapes so that students who need the help can listen as well as attempt the reading. Other teachers mark the most critical information so that a child has a manageable reading task. Still others organize children in pairs that cross reading abilities so that one child in each group is able to read the reference materials to the other.

Children need help in selecting the right kind of reference book for a particular task. The teacher should examine the various reference materials with the class, discussing when one should refer to a dictionary, an encyclopedia, a trade book, an atlas, or other material. Particularly with struggling readers who have had fewer experiences with these materials than most children, the teacher should continue helping students to decide which reference is suitable for what task.

Using Book Parts

Children must use book parts efficiently in order to make the best use of references. The parts of a book that children should learn about include:

1. Title page, including author, publisher, copyright
2. Table of contents
3. Indexes
4. Chapter headings
5. Side headings
6. Footnotes, endnotes, sidenotes
7. References at ends of chapters
8. Glossaries
9. Questions

Children will grow in the knowledge of these aids if the teacher models their use and refers to them by their names and if meaningful activities are planned that emphasize their value. The teacher should label book parts accurately, saying, "Look in the index," and not "Look in the back of the book." Teachers should know their instructional materials well enough so that they can point out book parts that are new or may cause confusion.

Using the Library

Children are feeling the effects of the information explosion when they go to their libraries in search of information. On most subjects they can choose from a wide variety of books. Even in an elementary school library, children need to be able to locate entries in the *card catalog* or to use the computerized visual displays of library holdings that are rapidly replacing the catalog.

The student with reading problems will find either locational task difficult. The teacher or the librarian must assist in the reading task and then help the student to locate the needed material. It may be helpful for the teacher to prepare large catalog cards for teaching the child what information is critical and what notations may be less vital in finding materials. Some of the words will need to be practiced enough times for the child to recall them. Beyond practice activities of these kinds, the child needs repeated opportunities to visit the library and find materials. Some teachers have paired good readers with poor readers to make library visits more successful.

Some collections in the library may be shelved or stored according to a variety of schemes. For example, fiction is often alphabetized by authors' last names. Children will need alphabetizing skills to locate these books. Encyclopedias and similar references are usually housed separately near a study area. Newspapers and magazines have their own display systems; some libraries store back issues on microfiche. Many school librarians shelve paperbacks simply by authors' last names, regardless of whether they are fiction or nonfiction. Where materials are stored in the library and how they are organized must be made clear to children, or they will not elect to consult or select them.

Using Tapes, Records, and Talking Books

Many books are sold with accompanying tapes or records that permit children to hear the books read while following along. Frequently, the books are sold in sets so that several children can hear and read at once. The teacher may be able to find taped books that will fit units that are being taught. If reference materials that children will use to obtain information are not on tapes, the teacher or someone else who reads well may make tapes. These can be displayed with the matching books. By using tapes, poor readers can be exposed to content appropriate for their ages and grades rather than being forced to read overly simplified books that contribute little to the extension of their knowledge.

Talking books are becoming popular with good readers, both children and adults. They are readily available for times when one cannot conveniently read, as when driving a car. Many of these tapes will be equally valuable for students with reading problems.

Many books that are on tapes are also on records. Probably tapes are easier to use and cheaper to replace when damaged, but some schools are equipped only for records. Teachers will need to teach children how to care for records so that they will last as long as possible. Unless tapes and players are of very high quality, records may provide better reproductions of musical scores accompanying some story records.

Finding Information Outside the Library

The experience of finding information extends beyond the library. The child should view the environment as a potential source of important information. Slow readers can learn as much from the environment as good readers can. *Concrete materials* and first-hand experiences are rich sources of multisensory experiences that cannot be replicated with words. All readers can learn to ask thoughtful questions, make predictions, assume alternate viewpoints, and draw conclusions. Real experiences related to units being taught will provide valuable insights. The child who actually weaves a small mat can appreciate the work of a Navajo weaver or a pioneer mother in ways not possible if books are the only sources of information. The teacher may bring such experiences and reading together by having the child write about the experiences or by recording as the child dictates.

Reading skills will not limit the poor readers when interviews with knowledgeable persons are planned for gathering information. These children can ask good questions, tape record responses or take simple notes, and present what was learned orally to the class.

Learning Alphabetical Order

The location of information is frequently dependent on the child's knowledge of *alphabetical order*. Since many slow readers have trouble remembering the order of letters long after their more successful peers have that information mastered, it will be helpful to have the alphabet displayed in order near encyclopedia sets and other references that are alphabetized. Children with reading problems may profit from alphabetizing activities such as getting in line based on first or last names, placing a collection of books in order based on authors' last names, or ordering collections of word cards alphabetically. They may enjoy trying to open the dictionary to a particular letter such as *S* or *M* without peeking.

Children may enjoy making a list of how alphabetical order is used in locating information. The list might include:

1. Words in the dictionary
2. Entries in encyclopedias
3. Cards in the card catalog
4. Volumes in the set of encyclopedias
5. Place names in the atlas index
6. Entries in an index
7. Arrangement of items in a glossary
8. Entries in a bibliography
9. Names in a telephone book

As the list grows, the children can begin to appreciate alphabetical order as a means of organizing information and the need to master the skills related to alphabetical order.

Ekwall and Shanker noted that a rather large number of upper-grade children are still confused about letter names and how to make or distinguish the letter forms.[4] Confusion about letters at this level almost always indicates a severe reading problem. While trying to remediate the problem that these boys and girls are experiencing, the teacher may support their learning by helping them to locate information and to participate in content classes through the use of taped books, films and filmstrips, records, pictures, and similar materials. These children may function as productive members of committees where locational tasks are divided up and their responsibility does not involve reading.

Organizational Strategies and Skills

When children have located information, they then need *organizational skills* to make the data manageable. This group of skills includes outlining; note taking; underlining; using glosses, advance organizers, and study guides; summarizing; and sequencing. A number of these skills can be introduced in the primary grades, even kindergarten. Young children can work with simple materials (including pictures) to take notes, make outlines, and sequence events. Children who have had these experiences early often find the organizational skills required in later school years to be easier to master since they have already developed concepts about such tasks as outlining and are ready to refine them and develop appropriate mechanics and forms.

Slow readers need special support from teachers as they try to learn organizational skills. Some of the strategies that are used with younger children may be appropriate as long as the children do not view them as demeaning.

Outlining

Outlining instruction may begin as a modified sequencing activity. After a trip to the anthropology museum, the children might draw pictures and label their drawings. Then the teacher can caption a large paper with the title "The Trip to the Museum." The children begin to paste their pictures in order. When the record is finished, the teacher notes that the class has created a simple outline of the trip. The record is chronological. The children are helped to find that they could record the labels that they wrote for the pictures, creating a sentence outline. If this kind of activity is carried out many times, the children will begin to gain a concept of what an outline is and how it is made. Only after they can complete the task easily is it necessary to include the mechanical aspects of the outline, the Roman numerals, capital letters, and numbers.

A web may be transferred into an outline. After the web is completed, the teacher may write the title on the chalkboard. The major branches of the web become the major headings of the outline. Branches on the web become the subheadings, and the outermost branches will become the sub-subheadings. Children will come to see that well-made webs and outlines are simply different ways of arranging material to show the relationships among ideas.

Dupuis and Askov reminded teachers that skills like outlining *do have to be taught*.[5] On occasion a teacher will assign children to make outlines or take notes with no previous instruction. Unless the teacher checks the assignment carefully, he or she may have no idea that the students do not know how to do the task.

Note Taking

A teacher took his first-grade class on a trip to a ranch. Before they left the classroom, each child was equipped with a miniature, homemade clipboard with a pencil attached with a string. Each child was to take notes about what was seen and heard on the trip. Since it was early in the year, few of the children could write much, so most of them drew pictures of what they experienced. When the children returned to the room, they were able to talk at length about the experience from their "notes." The group had learned the value of *note taking,* even though few words had been written.

Children may want to know why they should take notes. Tonjes and Zintz suggested three purposes: (1) to organize information, (2) to hold the attention, and (3) to study material for exams.[6] Teachers need to emphasize that notes do serve these purposes by building into theme or unit planning note taking experiences to meet each of the objectives.

The slow readers have at least three kinds of problems with which to cope when they attempt to take notes based on written materials. First, they may not be able to read the selection and may have the most trouble with the words that are critical in recalling the information. Technical and specialized vocabulary may prove the most difficult, yet the most important, to read. Because they are likely to spend so much time with the decoding problems, the slow readers may not know much about what they read. If comprehension has not occurred, then note taking will be useless since the readers will not be able to identify what is important and worth remembering. Finally, the children will face all the problems of trying to write, framing ideas, organizing the page of notes, spelling words, and managing the necessary mechanics. Teachers can help these children by talking them through note-taking exercises many times. They can read with them, talk about how to make decisions about selecting facts and ideas to record, and guide the writing of the notes. When these children are asked to work independently, they should be able to read the material, and they should be able to record the ideas without frustration. Children can have successful experiences with note taking if instructional-level materials are chosen and if the task has been rehearsed with the teacher. The following points may also be useful to remember when working with slow readers who are learning to take notes:

1. It is the process and progress that are important. The form chosen for the notes—words or phrases, whole sentences, outlining, paragraphs—is important only in that it should match the writer's needs.
2. Notes are meant to remind the writer. They should not be graded or otherwise red-penciled.
3. Note taking should have genuine purposes; it should not be busy work and must not be used as a punishment.

4. Children should be encouraged to rely not only on print as a source of notes, but should also study pictures, graphs, charts, and other information sources in the selection to be read.
5. It may be helpful to prepare *with* the children a chart that will serve as a step-by-step guide for note taking and place it where the students are likely to be doing this kind of work.

Underlining

Underlining, marking the key ideas or sentences in a passage, is a valuable instructional tool for students of all ages and reading abilities. It may be even more valuable for slow readers, since they are relieved of the task of writing. Since students cannot mark in textbooks and references, the teacher will need to duplicate the materials they will use. Even with this limitation, the activity is worthwhile since it (1) presents important words and phrases in their original context, (2) highlights those key concepts in sequence, (3) forces the student to read a passage more than once, and (4) teaches selective comprehension.[7] Poostay suggested these steps for teaching underlining:

1. Select and pre-identify the key concepts, words, and phrases.
2. Make a copy of the material with your underlinings for each student.
3. Tell the students to point to your underlinings as you read only what is underlined aloud. Do not read the entire selection.
4. Discuss why each word or phrase was underlined.
5. Read the underlinings again, having the students predict the content from the underlinings.
6. Have the students read the original passage.
7. Have the students recall the material without the underlinings, then with the underlinings.
8. In later lessons, ask the children to do their own underlinings.[8]

With slow readers it is important to select material that is at the instructional level and to repeat the steps identified by Poostay several times.

Using Glosses, Advance Organizers, Structured Overviews, and Study Guides

The teachers of remedial readers should have available as many techniques as possible for helping children to make sense of text. Glosses, advance organizers, structured overviews, study guides, and a variety of techniques of similar natures may be most useful. They help children to know what is coming in the print that they are reading, and they explain vocabulary or extend concepts.

"Gloss notations are marginal notes written to direct readers' attention while they read"[9] They may focus on either the content being read or on the process of reading. *Glosses* are written on strips of paper that are laid by the page of print. The usefulness of glosses for remedial readers lies in the ability of the teacher to make them fit the needs of individuals. The teacher can concentrate on vocabulary or skills known to be needed by the students.

Advance organizers, based on the theoretical work of Ausubel,[10] are passages prepared to introduce later material to be read. They prepare the reader by providing an organizing structure to aid in comprehension. The reader recalls better when there is a framework for remembering or for grouping ideas. Remembering is not as efficient when the reader tries to store lists of apparently unrelated ideas.

Making good advance organizers is difficult, especially when the reading abilities of the students are below grade level. The teacher must find simple ways to explain or call attention to sometimes complex ideas in the material to be read. For the teacher to read the advance organizer with the children to preclude reading problems is best. Tonjes and Zintz suggested the following steps for a teacher to follow in preparing advance organizers:

1. Read the chapter carefully, noticing the major ideas.
2. Reorder these ideas into a hierarchy that will show their relationship to each other or from superordinate (most general) to subordinate (most specific).
3. Write a 50- to 300-word passage showing this relationship or order, for the reader to understand while reading the chapter.
4. Go over the written organizer with the students before they read the chapter, making sure that they understand the purpose and interrelationships.[11]

Structured overviews, prepared *with* the children and cognitive maps prepared by the teacher before meeting with the class are diagrams that demonstrate the relationships that exist between related ideas. Also called *graphic organizers*[12] and *webs,* these graphic displays have appeal for remedial readers since the amount of print on them is limited. A teacher developed the structured overview shown in figure 11.1 with three children who were interested in learning about the cat family. The relationships that were shown were used by the three children to develop their plans for dividing the tasks while they studied the cat family.

Study guides, called *guide-o-ramas* by Wood and Mateja,[13] are lists of questions, comments, and suggested tasks that provide a *written tutor* for readers. A study guide is more than just a list of questions to be answered. Its items should stimulate thinking through questions written at different levels, encourage conceptual thinking, and guide the student to see the relationships between ideas. The study guide is meant to be used during reading or as a follow-up lesson. Wood and Mateja suggested that the study guide should be attractively designed to stimulate student interest.[14] Slow readers may find a study guide useful because it will direct them to the most critical elements in the material that they must read. The guide must be written in such a way that it does not add to the reading burden the children already carry.

Summarizing

Summaries become important in classrooms where children are expected to obtain ideas from several sources. Thoughtful, selective reading is necessary to write a summary. The assignment of summary writing will require reading comprehension. Harris and Sipay noted that each language-experience story that is written is a summary of an

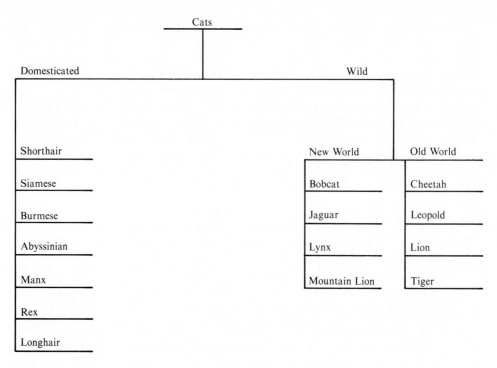

Figure 11.1. Structured overview to guide the study of the cat family

experience.[15] Children whose early school lessons have included the writing of many personal stories should be able to move easily into writing summaries of the experiences of others that they find in their reading. Some children will not have had the earlier opportunities to write about their own experiences. These children will require careful instruction, perhaps working first with note taking and underlining before attempting summarizing. Teachers whose students simply copy material from the reference books should examine the children's ability to identify critical ideas and compose summary paragraphs, not accuse them of copying. Copying can be the only strategy available to a child who must write a summary but does not know how.

Winograd studied the summarization skills of eighth-grade students who understood, in general, the tasks in summarization. He found, however, that poor readers had difficulties with discerning important information and with transforming the ideas in the original text into summary statements.[16] Remedial readers may be helped to concentrate on the ideas to be summarized by having the writing task delayed or eliminated. The child may do best at the task by dictating the summary and perhaps later copying it. If the child works in a group, the other members may find the poor readers' ideas to be valuable contributions to their summarizing task, but another group member will do the writing.

Taylor's investigations have led him to the belief that students generally do poorly at summarizing.[17] He indicated that there are three stages to summarizing—reading, analyzing, and writing. Poor readers tend to go directly from reading to writing. Good readers and trained persons insert the analyzing step, which may include second or third readings to make sure that the intent of the writer is captured. Apparently, teachers can promote summarizing skills by insisting that the middle step, analyzing, not be skipped. The second and third readings could be useful to slow readers not only for helping them to become certain of the author's meaning but also to improve their fluency on a single passage.

Sequencing

Sequencing is closely related to outlining, but it has broader implications. Very young children generally learn to think sequentially and to recall sequences of activities in their own lives. Children must be able to perform this metacognitive activity before they can understand sequences in the lives of others, in print, and in places and events of long ago and far away. Sequence has a relationship to cause-and-effect thinking. This relationship is involved with understanding one's own plans and goals and, eventually, the plans and goals of others.[18] These understandings are essential to the understanding of characters in story and the actions of people recorded in subject area texts.

Teachers should be sure to call children's attention to the sequence of events in material that they read. For some children who find difficulty with this task, the teacher may need to help the child to sequence the events in the classroom and in life outside the classroom on a daily basis. It may also help to talk about step-by-step directions for making a toy or constructing a gift. The child must learn that you cannot put the pin through the pinwheel and into the stick until the paper has been folded, for example.

Interpretive Strategies and Skills

Most school textbooks contain maps, charts, tables, pictures, graphs, and other types of visual aids.[19] Each child needs to learn to make good use of these tools for learning. Learning how to use these visual aids should begin early in the elementary school years with children making them as summaries of their own experiences. Primary-grade children often graph the birthdays of classmates by months and their attendance daily as the teacher takes the role. Charts of schoolroom tasks and who will do them are typical in classrooms. Students may make tables that show the amount of candy that has been sold by class members or the weight of the various foods consumed by the hamster. Children enjoy drawing pictures. The teacher needs to be sure that each child explains about what has been drawn and points out important details to the observers. When the production of visual aids in the classroom is a normal part of the school day and they are discussed and referred to when needed, the same sorts of learning tools in published materials will be accepted positively.

The teacher needs to be aware that the visual aids in texts may be considerably more complex than those produced by children. Care must be taken to explain legends, to clarify meanings of symbols, and to discuss the information that can be obtained. When children do not understand and have not learned of their importance, the tendency is for the reader to glance briefly at visual aids and then skip them. With older

Figure 11.2. *The Small Society* by Brickman. Used with the permission of the Washington Star Syndicate, Inc.

boys and girls, reference to maps, charts, graphs, and other aids may be made in glosses and study guides that are prepared for reading chapters in texts.

Kirkman proposed that attention be directed to graphic aids in text during the previewing stage of reading in which the material to be read is skimmed for a sense of the overall organization. At this time the teacher would focus student attention on the important aspects of the text and on any visual aids that would increase comprehension.[20] If slow readers are helped to understand these learning tools, they may find them inviting; the amount of reading to be done is usually less than the explanations in the text.

Reading and *interpreting* cartoons and comic strips can keep students actively thinking and using the communication abilities that they have, even though little reading may be necessary. The Small Society carries a message for the person who thinks about issues (figure 11.2); and Hi and Lois must evaluate important principles of child growth and development through briefly written anecdotes (figure 11.3). Ted Key tells a story without words in the Hazel cartoon (figure 11.4).

Strategies and Skills in Presenting Information

For children to gather a lot of information on a topic, to take notes and make an outline, but then be unable to prepare a written or oral report that meets the teacher's expectations is not unusual. Children need as much help at learning how to make reports and give talks as they do with the information-gathering process. When children copy extensively from references, the teacher has a good indication that they do not know how to move from collections of information to putting ideas into their own words.

Some teachers will take a class through the entire process by having them gather data, organize notes and outlines, and dictate a report that will be written on the chalkboard. Class members experience the transition from gathering the ideas written by others to expressing those ideas as personal examples of understanding. Children see

Figure 11.3. Hi and Lois. Used with the permission of the King Features Syndicate.

Figure 11.4. Hazel. Used with the permission of the King Features Syndicate.

how major points on an outline become paragraphs fleshed out by the outline's supporting details. They learn how to prepare footnotes or other forms of citation. Together they experience creating an attractive opening paragraph and a summarizing closing one. The slow readers in the group may need extended help of this kind to grasp the necessary organization. Their reading and writing skills will probably be the troublesome ones; their abilities to think about the task and to perform the cognitive tasks may be as strong as those of the rest of the class. For some students with severely impaired reading and writing skills, the tape recorder can be used. The report may be given orally and later typed by the class "secretary."

Children also need practice in giving oral reports. Almost every adult can remember some unpleasant experience with an oral report in school—a time when you hoped the floor would swallow you or you felt sadness for another student's misery. These experiences need not happen if children from the first are encouraged to share experiences in front of their classmates. Later, children will begin to share the experiences of others based on their reading. Reports can be made more formal if the older students work from an outline so that certain points that were preplanned can be made. The child can be given chances to rehearse with the teacher or a close friend. These efforts will not be "graded" since grading has a terrifying effect on many students. Children should be allowed to experiment with group presentations such as panel discussions, skits, and audiovisual productions. Slow readers may be quite successful at oral presentations, when the problems with decoding print are removed. These children have an opportunity to achieve success in the same way as their classmates if the teacher makes sure that they have prepared and rehearsed adequately.

Following Directions

Almost every teacher complains at one time or another about students who cannot follow directions. According to Harris and Sipay:

> In former times, children learned mainly by watching and imitating their elders. In modern life, people must rely more and more on printed directions and manuals of procedure. . . . Practice in reading and following directions is best provided in relation to activities that children wish to carry out or skills that they want to learn.[21]

In a society in which being able to follow printed directions is essential, its children should have every possible chance to practice this skill. Teachers must take every classroom opportunity to have children follow directions. If a new piece of equipment is purchased, the children should help to read the directions and assemble it. If a pet is purchased and a set of directions for its care comes with the animal, the class should assume responsibility for reading and carrying out the directions. Sometimes teachers may need to contrive activities, even work sheets, for practicing following directions, but the best learning opportunities come out of real experiences. Following recipes in classroom cooking experiences, attending to construction steps in building some much-needed bookcases, and interpreting the guidelines in making a gift are all real reasons for reading and following directions.

For children who have problems, the teacher might:

1. Supplement the written directions with pictures or rebuses in place of some of the words.
2. Have the children read the directions, followed by an oral statement of the steps to be taken.
3. Limit the number of steps in a set of directions, and increase the number as the children's skills grow.
4. Play games and sing familiar songs that require following directions. Finger plays may be useful in this respect, too.
5. Work on varied sequencing activities; directions are simply a specialized kind of sequence.
6. Encourage the child to work on the microcomputer. The microcomputer proceeds based on the directions that the user gives it.
7. Rewrite complex directions using simpler words, smaller steps, and examples.

Helping Students to Remember

One topic that is almost never dealt with in school is learning how to *remember*. Eventually, most people develop some personalized strategies that seem to work, but rarely are these shared with children. If one were to ask a group of adults how they would learn the names of the fifty states, the answers would include alphabetizing, associating the names with other ideas, learning groups of states located in the same geographical area, ordering the names from shortest to longest, listing them in the order the person has visited them, and saying them in random order as they were thought of. The more useful remembering techniques should be practiced in the classroom.

Children should see note taking and underlining as study strategies designed to help the person remember. They should learn that making a list reminds one to accomplish certain tasks. They should know that mnemonic devices (such as the famous string around the finger) are legitimate means of remembering.

In general ways, the teacher may take certain steps to make remembering more likely. Otto, McMenemy, and Smith made several suggestions:

1. Secure the learner's cooperation.
2. Offer material at the learner's level.
3. Reinforce success.
4. Keep tasks and materials meaningful.
5. Encourage pupils to discover relationships for themselves.
6. Provide spaced practice.[22]

Tonjes and Zintz offered these suggestions to teachers who want to help their students remember:

1. Teach students that they must always have a purpose for reading.
2. Students should work to grasp the author's organization. Outlining may help.
3. Make notes about important points. Students should know that writing facilitates memory.
4. Students should practice summarizing, including only important ideas.
5. Encourage students to discuss what has been read.
6. Students who apply what has been read will remember it better.[23]

Test Taking

Test taking is a challenge to almost all students. It is particularly burdensome for the slow readers in the class. The teacher may work to have these children excused from some testing, but inevitably they will have to participate. The tests they do take may be especially important to them, since these tests may be used to help determine special placements or eligibility for special services.

Children can be prepared to do their best on the tests that they must take. Going into the testing session having studied and prepared to the best of one's ability offers reassurance. The teacher can describe to the children what to expect—the physical setting, how one will respond (essay, marking circles for machine scoring, and so forth), the time frame, how scores will be reported, and what the value of the test might be for the individual.

Finley and Seaton[24] suggested that students should be instructed in the patterns of texts in science and social studies. When these patterns are understood, the students should be able to create questions over the text material most likely to be tested. Such a strategy would need to be used many times with different content materials in order for the students to be able to predict likely questions.

Rubin suggested the following test-taking principles:

1. Plan to do well; have a positive attitude.
2. Get enough rest before the test.
3. Be well prepared.
4. View a test as an opportunity to learn.
5. Look over the whole test before you begin.
6. Know how much time you have to work.
7. Concentrate on the test.
8. Read instructions carefully.
9. Begin with questions that you are sure of.
10. If answers are not known, make intelligent guesses.
11. After answering questions that you are sure of, work on those items that count the most.
12. Go over all the answers before the time is up.
13. When (if) the test is returned, learn from the results.[25]

Reading in the Content Fields

The teacher's responsibilities for instructing students in reading in the content fields fall into two categories: (1) general skills instruction and (2) instruction in specific content areas such as social studies or mathematics.

General Strategies and Skills in Content Fields Reading

There are at least five areas of general skills that must be addressed by the classroom teacher. These areas are reading *expository text* as opposed to *narrative text,* using appropriate study strategies, learning a large amount of vocabulary, developing critical reading skills and employing reading and writing as interrelated forms of language. Each of these areas represents particular problems for the boys and girls with reading difficulties.

Narrative versus Expository Text

When children work in their basal readers, nearly all of the selections that they read are narrative in nature. They are stories with beginnings, one or more problems that must be resolved, and endings.[26] By the time the children have left the primary grades, they have heard or read hundreds of selections based on this organization.

Making Connections 11.1: Finding Out What Children Know about Study Strategies and Skills

Before you plan lessons to use with children, it is important to know what they already know. Over several months with a group of children, a teacher becomes very good at predicting the knowledge the children have.

To interview a group of three or four middle-grade students to gain a sense of what they know about study skills may be helpful. Plan with a teacher, who will let you "borrow" some students, to include at least one or two children who are slow readers.

Develop a list of questions based on the outline of the study strategies and skills at the beginning of this chapter to find out what the children know and can do in relation to the various topics. Your questions might include:

1. If you needed to find out about a topic, perhaps locomotives, what kinds of references would you use? How would you find "locomotives" in the encyclopedia?
2. Have you ever made an outline? How did you do it?
3. Tell me how you go about taking notes. Do they help you to remember what you have read? In what ways?
4. When you have to remember ideas that you have read, how do you do it?

You will want to develop questions in addition to these.

When you have conducted your interview, share your findings with peers who have also interviewed students. What conclusions can you draw from the collective information the children have given you?

When children begin to have reading assignments in content area textbooks, they meet a variety of other organizational patterns. Their history texts will usually be organized chronologically, their science books will have chapters devoted to concepts such as microscopic life or the solar system, and their mathematics books will use a particular quantitative concept as an organizer. The children who read their third-grade readers well may struggle with their third-grade textbooks. Children who have problems with reading narrative may be overwhelmed by their content area texts.

Part of the problem is the difference between narrative and expository text. The following lists provide a brief comparison of the two forms:

Narrative Text	*Expository Text*
Characters are central to story.	People are incidental to text.
Agent oriented.	Subject matter oriented.
Located in a time, indicated by verb tense.	Time is not focal.
Chronological ordering.	Logical ordering.
Strong story grammar.	Weak story grammar if at all.
Lower loading of content words.	Density of concepts.[27]

Alvermann and Boothby asked fourth graders to identify narrative and expository texts and found that children at that age could do so reliably.[28] The children were unable to say why they could tell the two types of text apart but indicated that they thought expository text was harder to read, had harder words, and was less interesting than narrative.

Recent work on expository text organization has led to identification of text *super-structures.* Three basic kinds of expository writing are exploratory, informative, and scientific.[29] Students should be taught to identify each type in their textbooks and other expository materials. Such identification will improve comprehension because the readers will be able to use knowledge of text superstructures in predicting and confirming strategies.

Teachers must also help children to recognize the ways in which social studies, science, literature, and math texts are structured. Each will be related to a text super-structure type. Finley and Seaton identified the following *organizational patterns* in social studies: cause-effect, sequence, and comparison-contrast. In science the patterns include definition, sequence in a process, analysis, classification, and cause-effect (problem-solution). They identified sequence (narration), example, description, and comparison-contrast as the common text organizational patterns in literature.[30]

It is important for the teacher to talk with children about the differences in the way print is organized in their various texts. The slow reader will be aided by any personalized help that can be given by a peer tutor; a parent or grandparent volunteer; the teacher during brief conferences; and well-planned, easy study guides and questions. The teacher may be able to find library books that will contain similar facts and ideas embedded in narrative forms. Underlining those parts of the child's text that contain the most significant information also may be helpful. The teacher may guide the child to read the first sentence of a paragraph or section and then predict the kind of information that is likely to be found in it. The follow-up reading will be for the purpose of confirming the prediction. This predicting/confirming strategy may help the child to identify a structure in expository text that will make reading easier.

Study Strategies

The best-known study strategy is surely *SQ3R,* which was developed by Francis Robinson in 1941.[31] The SQ3R formula was designed to promote long-term memory of what has been studied and learned. The steps are S—survey, Q—question, R—read, R—recite, and R—review. The strategy was later revised to include a fourth R: reflect. A number of strategies, some suited to reading in particular content areas, have been developed from it. Variations include SQRQCQ for mathematics.[32] PQRST for science,[33] and REAP for processing information by reading, encoding, annotating, and pondering.[34]

A consistent study strategy should be taught to remedial readers. To suggest a variety of strategies could well be confusing. The teacher should work with the child until the strategy is well learned. A card taped to the desk or other study site may serve as a reminder of the requisite steps. It is important to remember that the strategy will not work if the material to be read is too difficult. Successful study will depend on instructional level materials *and* a well-learned strategy such as SQ3R.

Vocabulary

Three kinds of vocabulary problems await the disabled reader when reading content field materials. The first is part of the general reading problem—lack of mastery of the basic sight vocabulary. Not only is the child troubled by the specialized words that abound in the text, but even *through, where, tried,* and other common words cause difficulty. The child with this level of difficulty will be much more successful with taped books, filmstrips, and greatly simplified texts while the mastery of basic sight words is attempted.

Many words that have common meanings are also used in *specialized* ways in content fields. These words may be particularly troublesome to remedial readers, who have basically one definition for each word.

An example of such a word is *bank.* The child has gone with Dad or Mom to the bank since infancy. In science class the teacher talks about water running down the *bank,* washing away the soil. Then, in a story, the child reads that an airplane *banks* when it makes a wide turn. Another example might be the word *blocks.* They have been familiar toys for years. But the social studies book discusses city *blocks,* and the physical education teacher says that Bill *blocks* the other players better than anyone else.

Teachers need to identify such words in texts and make sure that children apply the appropriate meaning. The words need to be discussed and written in sentences that will provide the needed contrasts in meanings. Children may enjoy selecting a word and making sentences using as many different meanings as possible.

Textbooks also have a variety of *technical* terms that children must learn to identify and relate to meanings. One third-grade social studies text that is representative of such materials contains the following sentences:

> President Roosevelt knew that having more *national forests* was a good thing.
> But he thought it was an answer to only part of the problem of *conservation.*
> The President asked the *governors* of the states to come to a meeting. . . . He
> wanted all the people to use *natural resources* with care.[35]

Children who read such passages with comprehension must have had some experiences with the concepts represented by the technical terms. If the teacher wishes all children to understand such material, it will be necessary to plan activities that allow children to conserve, to visit a national forest at least in a film, and to talk about our natural resources. Since many remedial readers are children who have had few relevant experiences, building concepts related to technical terms is critical.

A student teacher planned a unit on the desert and its plants and animals. To his surprise, he found that the five children whom he was to teach had never been out of their city; two had never been farther than two miles from home. From the teacher's description of a desert, the children thought it was a bit like a nearby parking lot. The teacher made arrangements to take the children to an arid area about thirty miles from the school. The children were excited about the trip but were able to control their enthusiasm to attend to what the teacher was telling them. He introduced several technical terms related to deserts. The children went on the trip prepared to see a sand dune, a blow-out, a blue-tailed lizard, and a dry wash. They returned able to talk knowingly about all of these concepts and more. The unit proceeded successfully, with the children building a diorama of "their" desert. The student teacher knew that his unit would have been another unsuccessful experience for these unsuccessful students without this first-hand knowledge.

Critical Reading

Remedial readers tend to be very uncritical readers because they are engrossed in the decoding task and hardly expect print to mean much. However, unless teachers make them aware of the fact that print is not always true, correct, or straightforward, they may become victims of the very skill they are trying so hard to master.

At the very least, teachers should help remedial readers to understand that:

1. Untrue statements appear in print.
2. Writers can bias readers' attitudes and opinions.
3. *When* a text is written may have some bearing on its current accuracy.
4. Some texts make racist and sexist statements.
5. Advertising must be read with care to see what it is that the writer wants the reader to do.
6. Propaganda must be treated as an attempt to influence readers' thinking.
7. Some authors are more qualified to write on a particular subject than are others.

The teacher can prepare exercises or buy workbooks or masters that can be used with children to give them practice with critical reading skills. However, the best materials are probably the children's textbooks and materials out of the environment, such as *advertisements,* slogans, biographies of authors, copyright dates, and *propaganda* materials. Some computer games will also encourage critical reading and thinking. The teacher should examine such software carefully to make sure the children will understand and be able to identify the point that is being made.

Integrating Writing and Reading

Complete issues of professional journals have been devoted to teaching writing in the elementary school. Some of the articles pertain to *integrating reading and writing* in the content fields. Books, workshops, college courses, institutes, and in-service training programs featuring the teaching of writing have multiplied in every state.[36]

If teachers employ a webbing approach to curriculum, writing and reading are sure to be significant parts of mediating what is usually considered social studies and science content. If differing subject matter is taught in separate time periods, teachers can still make increased use of the interactive powers of writing and reading.

The language-experience approach can be employed. Children can have direct experience with subject matter content through such activities as field trips, interviews, realia, or role-playing. Indirect experiences obtained from reading, viewing films, and listening to guest speakers may also be the source of language experiences. After the input phase, the children should have opportunities to share, discuss, and evaluate ideas.

Then, writing may be a productive activity in which ideas are presented, evaluated, and summarized. Writing will encourage children to combine data in new ways, to think new thoughts, and to create new knowledge.

Sullivan suggested the label *global method* for the language-experience approach in the content areas. The focus of the global method is content, with language arts strategies and skills as byproducts.[37]

Cunningham and Cunningham stressed that content area lessons that include reading and writing increase student learning and also increase the ability to learn. The reading lesson should include helping children to identify what is already known before reading begins, setting purposes for reading, completing purposeful reading, and identifying what has been learned. The writing lesson that follows within one to two days should include models of what is expected of the children, guided practice, and feedback oriented toward future improvement. Strategies that may improve reading and writing include charting in matrix form what is known and what needs to be learned; preparing webs, outlines, and time lines; and sharing of the writing that is done.[38]

Reading in Specific Content Areas

Each of the elementary school subjects has textbooks that are organized to present its subject matter as authentically as possible. It is important for the teacher to examine these materials to see how they are written, where the organizational differences are and how these will affect the students, what aids for reading are present, and what concepts will have to be developed. Reading in subject matter areas is generally more difficult than the reading done in organized reading classes. Such reading requires special vocabulary, comprehension of concepts, and organizing and evaluating. It also requires the ability to locate and read maps, graphs, and charts, and the ability to use their content in further reading of the text. Fay listed the following difficulties that students encounter when reading in the content areas:

1. There is an unduly heavy load of facts and concepts.
2. The variations in typographical arrangement from one area to another may confuse the pupil.
3. All too frequently the materials are uninteresting to the pupils.
4. The ease of readability of materials is often considerably less than that of basic readers.
5. Many writers tend to assume greater background than pupils possess.
6. All this emphasizes the need for carefully fitting materials to pupils and for carefully organizing instruction for reading such materials.[39]

Mathematics

The difficulties of reading in mathematics are many. Nolan listed these potential sources of trouble:

1. The writing in mathematics books is terse, with a lack of redundancy.
2. Writing in mathematics texts is dense and requires slow, careful reading.
3. Mathematical symbols do not bear a grapheme-phoneme correspondence.

4. The student must employ left-right, right-left, up, down, and diagonal eye movements in reading and solving problems.
5. Mathematics has both a specialized and a technical vocabulary.[40]

Any one of these problems could seem grave for remedial readers. The teacher must spend much time helping these students learn to interpret the reading in mathematics. Talking children through pages in the text and being sure that needed vocabulary and symbols are thoroughly learned are two important techniques. Threadgill-Sowder et al. stated that the solution of word problems is one of the most sophisticated of all mathematical tasks because the solver must use so many reading skills.[41] They noted that many children who can read well and can compute cannot solve story problems. Kresse supported their position, noting that in a study of sixth graders, 95 percent could read the words in the problems, and 92 percent knew what the problem was asking them to find, but only 36 percent knew how to work the problem.[42]

Kresse proposed modeling the problem-solving task by talking the children through five steps: (1) surveying the task by reading the problem and making needed sketches, (2) asking the important questions related to "what it is that it wants me to find," (3) reading pertinent parts of the problem again, (4) working the problem, and (5) checking your reasoning.[43] She proposed going through these steps so many times that they become automatic.

Aaron discussed the areas of difficulty in reading in mathematics: (1) vocabulary, (2) concepts necessary to understand mathematical ideas, (3) knowing *how to read* in mathematics with respect to speed of comprehending the problem, (4) ability to read the variety of types of mathematical stimuli, print, equations, charts, and tables, and (5) interpreting appropriate symbols and abbreviations in mathematics.[44] Aaron also made suggestions for students about how to read problems in mathematics:

1. Read the problem quickly to get an overview.
2. Reread the problem, this time at a slower rate, to determine what facts are given.
3. Think of the specific question to be answered.
4. Think of the order in which the facts are to be used in answering the question raised in the problem.
5. Think of the operations required for solving the problem.
6. Estimate an answer that seems reasonable.
7. Work the problem by performing the appropriate operation.
8. Compare the answer with the estimated answer.
9. Go back to the first step if the answer seems unreasonable.[45]

Radebaugh suggested that children's literature can be the source of mathematics insights and problems.[46] She listed many books that could be used to develop counting, geometric knowledge, number concepts, addition, the history of our number system, money, large numbers, multiplication, and fractions. These materials could well be attractive to slow readers, much easier to read, and less likely to stimulate negative attitudes.

Social Studies

Blake suggested that the skills required to read the social studies texts fall into three categories—technical and specialized vocabulary development, comprehension skills, and study skills.[47] The major comprehension skills to be developed include cause and effect, comparison and contrast, sequence, fact versus opinion, and graphic patterns. The study strategies and skills include many already discussed, including establishing a purpose for reading, using the parts of the textbook, organizing information, note taking, and using the rate skills of skimming and scanning.

Children with poor reading strategies and skills will find many of the required tasks listed in the previous paragraph very difficult to master. They may find more success in learning social studies content with trade books. The school librarian can help the classroom teacher to identify a collection of books at varied reading levels on most social studies unit topics. The teacher may also send for the annual list "Notable Children's Trade Books in the Field of Social Studies" from the Children's Book Council, 67 Irving Place, New York, New York 10003.

Cunningham, Cunningham, and Arthur suggested additional ways to help slow readers with social studies reading tasks.[48] They suggested having children work in small groups with one child reading the text. The reading is stopped frequently, and all children engage in discussion to identify main ideas and supporting details. Poor readers can learn from listening in this setting. They also suggested that the teacher gather slower readers together and read the assignment to them. The children are then asked to translate what has been read, that is, to put it in their own words. At this point, children have an opportunity to express their ideas in writing, as was suggested earlier in this chapter. Finally, they suggested that the elementary classroom should emphasize nontext resources in the social studies; these resources would include many first-hand experiences.

Science

The final example of an elementary school content field that may pose serious reading problems for poor readers is science. Science texts are rich with technical and specialized vocabulary. It is important that students have as many real experiences as may be arranged to make these words and the concepts that they represent come alive. If this is not done, children may have the feeling that they are trying to read a foreign language in their science texts. In addition to the complex vocabulary, Weidler noted that science books are characterized by cause-and-effect writing and causal chaining patterns in which one action causes another, which in turn causes another. The writing is filled with passive forms and embedded sentences that also contribute to increasing the difficulty of reading.[49]

Smith analyzed fifty-two science texts, sixty social studies texts, forty-nine mathematics texts, and forty-five literature texts to find out about the special writing patterns in the content fields.[50] From these she identified unique patterns of writing for which students can develop special reading skills and abilities. In science, students need to identify the following:

1. *The classification pattern.* A major heading, living things, will have two subheadings: plants and animals. Animals can be subdivided into vertebrates and invertebrates. Once the students are aware of the form (pattern) in which the content will be presented, they can adapt their reading style to that pattern.
2. *Explanation of a technical process.* The explanation of a process is usually accompanied by diagrams that must be read carefully and concomitantly with the text.
3. *Instructions for an experiment.* This pattern usually requires the ability to follow precise directions. However, in order for the experiment to be successful, the readers must make all the correct observations and decisions at each step of the way.
4. *Detailed statement-of-fact pattern.* This pattern requires "intensive" reading, sorting out numerous "facts," selecting the main idea, and relating the subordinate ideas.
5. *The descriptive problem-solving pattern.* This pattern requires that the students identify each successive problem and be sure that they grasp its solution before going on to the next.
6. *Abbreviations and equations.* Students need to recognize special symbols and abbreviations as they appear in context in addition to the word symbol—for example, the symbol for "degree" in Fahrenheit (F) and Centigrade (C) scales.

To help readers, Cunningham, Cunningham, and Arthur recommended walking children through the science lesson pointing out pictures, graphics, headings, and special vocabulary. The children are invited to make predictions and to read to confirm predictions.[51] This strategy gives even the poorest readers many clues as to what the reading is all about.

Smardo has developed a long list of trade books that children may read to help them develop or expand science concepts. The topics range from rainbows and insects to evaporation and seasons.[52] With the cooperation of the school librarian, science reading could be done almost entirely with trade books. Since they are available at so many levels of difficulty, every reader should be able to find something to read.

Barrow, Kristo, and Andrew proposed that science be carried out using the language-experience approach. Children in science classes have experiences of various kinds. These experiences would be followed by drawing and writing times. This approach would allow even the slowest readers to have important science experiences and to process those experiences through talking, drawing, and writing.[53]

Martin and Miller suggested that teachers employ the art of storytelling in science instruction. They commented that children need "to make associations and to see relationships among the facts they are studying."[54] Noting that the "history of science

---

Making Connections 11.2: Examining Content Textbooks

Select one mathematics, one social studies, and one science textbook at a single grade level. Select just five pages from each text. They may be consecutive or widely separated pages. Study each of these pages in detail in order to make a list of reading difficulties that a child might encounter. You will probably want to keep the problems you identify for each content area separate or code them for identification on a single list.

1. What problems seem to be common to all three texts?
2. What problems are unique to each subject area?
3. What did the authors do to try to make the reading tasks as easy as possible?
4. What would you do as the teacher to make reading these pages as worthwhile as possible for students?

You will want to share your findings and conclusions with others in your class who have also completed the assignment.

---

is very much a story of changing perspectives,"[55] they have written that science teaching appears to fit the narrative mode well. These writers also commented on science textbooks and the nature of science teaching in elementary schools:

> The science books adopted in most schools transmit a body of knowledge with little attention to the bodies for whom that knowledge is intended. The very nature of such texts is unscientific. Static, linear, and nonparticipatory, they stand in stark contrast to the dynamic, cyclic, and directly involving mode of science that is so inviting to young children. These texts offer children no stories, no connections between forms and forces, between observers and observed. Without this profound connectivity which is the lifeblood of science, the body of scientific knowledge can be reduced to a corpse. Through a storytelling mode, scientific knowledge can be kept alive for children.[56]

Summary

This chapter presented information on two closely related topics: study strategies and skills, and reading in the content fields. Suggestions have been made for teaching study strategies and skills related to locating, organizing, interpreting, and presenting content. In addition, the specific topics of following directions, remembering, and test taking were discussed. When children prepare to read content texts, they are faced with some general problems, including reading the less-familiar expository text form, employing study strategies such as SQ3R, learning specialized and technical vocabulary, reading critically, and integrating writing and reading. Finally, there are problems specific to reading content in such areas as mathematics, social studies, and science. Suggestions were given for helping children to do this type of reading more satisfactorily.

For Further Reading

Amlund, Jeanne T., Janet Gaffney, and Raymond W. Kulhavy. "Map Feature Content and Text Recall of Good and Poor Readers." *Journal of Reading Behavior* 17, no. 4 (1985): 317–30. In this study, good readers recalled more map features than poor readers in fifth and sixth grades, even when the features were represented in different ways. Information on the map was recalled better than information in text.

Anderson, Thomas H. "Study Strategies and Adjunct Aids." In *Theoretical Issues in Reading Comprehension,* edited by Rand J. Spiro, Bertram C. Bruce, and William F. Brewer. Hillsdale, N.J.: Lawrence Erlbaum Associates, Publishers, 1980. The author presents a summary of major studies of study strategies and skills. These studies examine topics such as note taking, imaging, and advance organizers.

Dupuis, Mary M., ed. *Reading in the Content Areas: Research for Teachers.* Newark, Del.: International Reading Association, 1984. The book contains suggestions for reading in each of the major content areas. Each chapter has an extensive bibliography.

Earle, Richard. *Teaching Reading and Mathematics.* Newark, Del.: International Reading Association, 1976. This is one of a series of booklets addressing reading in particular content areas. This one has not been updated in over a decade.

Gentile, Lance M. *Using Sports and Physical Education to Strengthen Reading Skills.* Newark, Del.: International Reading Association, 1980. One of a series on reading in special curriculum areas, this booklet contains a number of important ways to link reading and physical education.

Graham, Kenneth G., and H. Alan Robinson. *Study Skills Handbook: A Guide for All Teachers.* Newark, Del.: International Reading Association, 1984. A wide variety of topics associated with study skills is addressed in a succinct and usable manner.

Konopak, Bonnie, and Nancy Williams. "Using the Keyword Method to Help Young Readers Learn Content Material." *Reading Teacher* 41 (March 1988): 682–87. A method is proposed in which new information is associated with a concrete image so that it can be recalled later.

Lunstrum, John P., and Bob L. Taylor. *Teaching Reading in the Social Studies.* Newark, Del.: International Reading Association, 1978. Another one of the booklets in the series on reading in the content fields, this work contains many excellent ideas despite its copyright date.

Piccolo, Jo Anne. "Expository Text Structure: Teaching and Learning Strategies." *Reading Teacher* 40 (May 1987): 838–47. Expository text structures are identified and described. The article suggests several teaching strategies along with model organizers for various kinds of paragraphs.

Rinehart, Steven, Steven Stahl, and Lawrence Erickson. "Some Effects of Summarization Training on Reading and Studying." *Reading Research Quarterly* 21 (Fall 1986): 422–36. This study involved sixth graders who were able to improve recall of major, but not minor, information in paragraphs by using summarization techniques.

Singer, Harry, and Thomas W. Bean. "Three Models for Helping Teachers to Help Students Learn from Text." In *Changing School Reading Programs,* edited by S. Jay Samuels and P. David Pearson. Newark, Del.: International Reading Association, 1988. The intern, inservice, and evolutionary models are discussed and diagrammed. This article might be especially useful for teacher trainers or for those who conduct in-service training.

Stock, Patricia L. "Writing Across the Curriculum." *Theory into Practice* 25 (Spring 1986): 97–101. When children write across the curriculum, teachers are able to engage students in subject matter from their points of view. Stock proposes a model of writing across the curriculum.

Thelen, Judith. *Improving Reading in Science.* 2d ed. Newark, Del.: International Reading Association, 1984. In this booklet, the author provides an update on some important ways to make reading of science materials easier and more profitable for students.

Notes

1. Douglas B. Rogers, "Assessing Study Skills," *Journal of Reading* 27 (January 1984): 346.
2. Ibid., 352.
3. *World Book Encyclopedia* (Chicago: Field Enterprises Educational Corporation, 1988).
4. Eldon E. Ekwall and James L. Shanker, *Diagnosis and Remediation of the Disabled Reader,* 2d ed. (Boston: Allyn and Bacon, 1983), 81.
5. Mary M. Dupuis and Eunice N. Askov, *Content Area Reading* (Englewood Cliffs, N.J.: Prentice-Hall, 1982), 229.
6. Marian J. Tonjes and Miles V. Zintz, *Teaching Reading/Thinking/Study Skills in Content Classrooms,* 2d ed. (Dubuque, Iowa: Wm. C. Brown Co. Publishers, 1987), 226.
7. Edward J. Poostay, "Show Me Your Underlines: A Strategy to Teach Comprehension," *Reading Teacher* 37 (May 1984): 829.
8. Ibid., 828–29.
9. Donald J. Richgels and Ruth Hansen, "Gloss: Helping Students Apply Both Skills and Strategies in Reading Content Texts," *Journal of Reading* 27 (January 1984): 312.
10. David P. Ausubel, "Use of Advance Organizers in the Learning and Retention of Meaningful Verbal Material," *Journal of Educational Psychology* 51 (1960): 267–72.
11. Tonjes and Zintz, *Teaching Reading/Thinking/Study Skills in Content Classrooms,* 295–96.
12. Richard A. Earle and Richard F. Barron, "An Approach to Teaching Vocabulary in Content Subjects," in *Research in Reading in the Content Areas: Second Year Report,* ed. Harold L. Herber and Richard F. Barron (Syracuse, N.Y.: Reading and Language Arts Center, Syracuse University, 1973).
13. Karen D. Wood and John A. Mateja, "Adapting Secondary Level Strategies for Use in Elementary Classrooms," *Reading Teacher* 36 (February 1983): 494.
14. Ibid., 495.
15. Albert J. Harris and Edward R. Sipay, *How to Increase Reading Ability,* 8th ed. (New York: Longman, 1985), 518.
16. Peter N. Winograd, "Strategic Difficulties in Summarizing Text," *Reading Research Quarterly* 19 (Summer 1984): 400–425.
17. Karl K. Taylor, "Teaching Summarization Skills," *Journal of Reading* 27 (February 1984): 389.

18. Bertram C. Bruce, "Plans and Social Actions," in *Theoretical Issues in Reading Comprehension,* ed. Rand S. Spiro, Bertram C. Bruce, and William F. Brewer (Hillsdale, N.J.: Lawrence Erlbaum Assoc., 1980), 367–84.

19. Sandra J. Berkowitz, "Effects of Instruction in Text Organization on Sixth-Grade Students' Memory for Expository Writing," *Reading Research Quarterly* 21 (Spring 1986): 161–78.

20. Pamela K. Kirkman, "Preparing Students for an Information Society: A Study Skills Approach," *Contemporary Issues in Reading* 1 (Fall 1985): 89.

21. Albert J. Harris and Edward R. Sipay, *How to Increase Reading Ability,* 7th ed. (New York: Longman, 1980), 21.

22. Wayne Otto, Richard A. McMenemy, and Richard J. Smith, *Corrective and Remedial Teaching,* 2d ed. (Boston: Houghton Mifflin Co., 1973), 56–58.

23. Tonjes and Zintz, *Teaching Reading/Thinking/Study Skills in Content Classrooms,* 248–49.

24. Claudia D. Finley and Martha N. Seaton, "Using Text Patterns and Question Prediction to Study for Tests," *Journal of Reading* 31 (November 1987): 124–32.

25. Dorothy Rubin, *Diagnosis and Correction in Reading Instruction* (New York: Holt, Rinehart and Winston, 1982), 277–78.

26. Jill S. Bartoli, "Metaphor, Mind, and Meaning: The Narrative Mind in Action," *Language Arts* 62 (April 1985): 332–42.

27. Carolyn E. Kent, "A Linguist Compares Narrative and Expository Prose," *Journal of Reading* 28 (December 1984): 232–36.

28. Donna E. Alvermann and Paula R. Boothby, "Text Differences: Children's Perceptions at the Transition Stage in Reading," *Reading Teacher* 36 (December 1982): 298–302.

29. Suzanne B. Hoskins, "Text Superstructures," *Journal of Reading* 29 (March 1986): 539.

30. Finley and Seaton, "Using Text Patterns," 125.

31. Francis P. Robinson, *Effective Study* (New York: Harper and Row, 1946), 28–33.

32. Leo Fay, "Reading Study Skills: Math and Science," in *Reading and Inquiry,* ed. J. A. Figurel (Newark, Del.: International Reading Association, 1965), 93.

33. George Spache, *Toward Better Reading* (Champaign, Ill.: Garrard Press, 1963), 94.

34. Marilyn Eanet and Anthony Manzo, "REAP, A Strategy for Improving Reading/ Writing/Study Skills," *Journal of Reading* 19 (May 1976): 647–52.

35. V. Phillips Weaver, *People and Resources,* Teacher's Edition (Morristown, N.J.: Silver Burdett Co., 1979), 98–99.

36. Edward B. Jenkinson, "Learning to Write/Writing to Learn," *Phi Delta Kappan* 69 (June 1988): 712–17.

37. Joanna Sullivan, "The Global Method: Language Experience in the Content Areas," *Reading Teacher* 39 (March 1986): 664–68.

38. Patricia M. Cunningham and James W. Cunningham, "Content Area Reading-Writing Lessons," *Reading Teacher* 40 (February 1987): 506–12.

39. Leo C. Fay, "What Research Has to Say about Reading in the Content Areas," *Reading Teacher* 8 (1954): 68–72.

40. James F. Nolan, "Reading in the Content Areas of Mathematics," in *Reading in the Content Areas: Research for Teachers* (Newark, Del.: International Reading Association, 1984), 28–29.

41. Judith Threadgill-Sowder et al., "A Case against Telegraphing Math Story Problems for Poor Readers," *Reading Teacher* 37 (April 1984): 746.

42. Elaine C. Kresse, "Using Reading as a Thinking Process to Solve Math Story Problems," *Journal of Reading* 27 (April 1984): 598.

43. Ibid., 599–600.

44. I. E. Aaron, "Reading in Mathematics," *Journal of Reading* 8 (May 1965): 391–95, 401.

45. Ibid., 394.

46. Muriel R. Radebaugh, "Using Children's Literature to Teach Mathematics," *Reading Teacher* 34 (May 1981): 902.

47. S. Blake, *Teaching Reading Skills through Social Studies and Science Materials* (Brooklyn: New York City Board of Education, Division of High Schools, 1975).

48. James W. Cunningham, Patricia M. Cunningham, and Sharon V. Arthur, *Middle and Secondary School Reading* (New York: Longman, 1981), 86–87.

49. Sarah D. Weidler, "Reading in the Content Area of Science," in *Reading in the Content Areas: Research for Teachers,* 54–55.

50. Nila B. Smith, "Patterns of Writing in Different Subject Areas," in *Elementary Reading Instruction, Selected Materials,* 2d ed., ed. Althea Beery, Thomas C. Barrett, and Wm. R. Powell (Boston: Allyn and Bacon, 1974), 460–71. Reprinted from *Journal of Reading* 8 (October and November 1964): 31–36, 97–102.

51. Cunningham, Cunningham, and Arthur, *Middle and Secondary School Reading,* 82.

52. Frances A. Smardo, "Using Children's Literature to Clarify Science Concepts in Early Childhood Programs," *Reading Teacher* 36 (December 1982): 267.

53. Lloyd H. Barrow, Janice V. Kristo, and Barbara Andrew, "Building Bridges Between Science and Reading," *Reading Teacher* 38 (November 1984): 188–92.

54. Kathleen Martin and Etta Miller, "Storytelling and Science," *Language Arts* 65 (March 1988): 255.

55. Ibid., 258.

56. Ibid., 259.

12
Attitudes of Teachers toward Students Who Fail

Vocabulary

empowerment
child advocate
involvement in own learning
acceptance
causal approach
achievement differences
middle-class values
success
negative self-image

Questions

1. What does it mean to accept a child completely? **(Inference)**
2. How does good teaching increase the range of differences in a class as the school year progresses? **(Inference)**
3. What does *success* mean to you? How could your definition of success pose problems for you in the classroom unless you understand the issues involved? **(Application; Evaluation)**
4. What kind of things can a teacher do to prevent the growth of negative self-image? **(Application)**
5. Make a list of the ways that adults may reward children for not learning. **(Application)**
6. After studying Axline's eight basic principles, make definite suggestions about carrying out each in the classroom. **(Application)**

Introduction

A frequently observed attitude of teachers toward those students who are not successful in achieving the expected norms is that of blaming the students in negative ways for their lack of success. Perhaps this is the expected attitude, since the alternative would be for the teachers to question their own teaching abilities, which would, in turn, immediately cause them to be defensive about their own shortcomings. But if children present themselves at school for the purpose of learning and fail to meet the expectations of the adults around them, who is really accountable for the results?

The first chapter of this text opened with a focus on the affective domain in children's lives. Teachers were reminded that if corrective reading instruction is to be successful, it is critical that teachers *empower* students to feel good about themselves.[1] Children who feel a sense of control over their own lives can take greater risks in order to be successful in learning. Teachers were also reminded that one role that they must play is that of *child advocate*. Being a child advocate requires a teacher to plan for successful learning opportunities for all of their pupils as well as to work for each child's right to an education. Finally, teachers were reminded that children must be *involved* in the planning of their own learning experiences if they are to have self-confidence and a healthy sense of control over their own lives and learning.

If the professional staff of the school has failed to empower children, if it has failed to serve as child advocates, if it has failed to involve children in their own learning, if it has failed to accommodate the individual differences in achievement that are *normally* found in larger numbers of people, who, then, has failed—the school system, the classroom teachers, or the children? Has the curriculum as outlined for the teachers prescribed the teaching of subject matter to the exclusion of consideration for those individual students who need a special opportunity to learn? This chapter will direct the reader's thinking toward the attitude of the teachers toward the students, the learning process, and the reading standards of the schools.

Making Connections 12.1: Who Is a Child Advocate?

Search newspapers and magazines for articles about persons whom you would consider to be child advocates. You will find that they represent many professions and positions in life.

Collect the articles that you can find, and bring them to class on the day designated by the instructor. As class members share their articles, note the positions of the persons, the actions that were taken, and the problems they overcame that made them advocates for children. The class should prepare a summary statement of what was discovered about advocacy.

Acceptance: Positive and Negative

The most important single step in working successfully with students who are under-achieving is to create a feeling of complete *acceptance* by the teacher. The teacher's manner and speech must not betray superficial attempts at acceptance. For all students who enter the classroom, it is the teacher's first and foremost obligation to accept them, to make them feel that they belong to the group, and to give them opportunity to win socially approved status and recognition as members of that group. Occasionally students who cannot do any particular academic tasks or meet any prescribed academic standards will be assigned to an intermediate-grade classroom. In order for the students to feel that they are accepted by their teacher, the teacher must see that they are provided with tasks that they can usually do *successfully.* Specifically with respect to reading, this means that the teacher must make sure that the pupils have reading material that is *sufficiently easy for their instructional levels* and, if they have no instructional levels, teachers must recognize that fact and meet it objectively in planning assignments for them. The students will sense the empathic response of their teacher most by what the teacher *does* in recognizing what the students can do. If the teacher really "accepts" the students and envisions their growth toward self-realization, the teacher will analyze the present reading status and plan specifically and sequentially to build better reading skills, make a concerted effort to develop a long-range plan, and keep honest and objective records of results.

If students in the intermediate or upper grades have little reading ability, the teacher may say, "Because I teach by the unit method, they get along very well. They work with others on committees, and they do good work in construction activities and drawing." The teacher should not feel secure in the belief that certain students make their only contribution to the group by the use of their hands. It is probably unfair to confine *any* student by such a narrow expectation. The basic problem rests in seeking reasons why they find reading very difficult. This necessitates accurate testing of their learning abilities to determine the degree to which they are mentally retarded, candidates for remedial reading, or a composite of the two.

If students are not able to do *any* academic work or are seriously educationally retarded, for them to have some tutoring outside of the classroom may be the most desirable course. On the other hand, if they are *not* mentally retarded, they should *not* be put in a classroom of educable mentally retarded students. In actual practice, a much greater number of these reading disability cases are totally dependent upon regular classroom teachers than are provided for in other ways.

Suppose you are a fourth-grade teacher and a child who moves into your school district is assigned to your classroom. The first day you discover that the child is

1. Unable to spell any of the fourth-grade words correctly on the pretest in spelling.
2. Unable to read orally from the story in the fourth-grade reader or a library book of similar difficulty unless you pronounce every third or fourth word (which he or she seems to expect).
3. Unable to complete any independent writing about the theme the class is studying.

When and how will you proceed? A *causal approach* (taking into account the origins of problems) can accept any of these answers only as rationalizations:

1. "I'm too busy already. How can I do anything about this when I've got thirty others who can all do fourth-grade work?"
2. "I'll let him listen and pick up what he can from the others."
3. "Put her back into the third grade until she learns how to do the work that the fourth grade is doing."
4. "I'll make her take her books home and study at night; then I'll keep her in to finish her written work."
5. "Perhaps she will do especially well in arithmetic. Everyone is good at something."

None of these answers indicates that the teacher is attacking the *problem* in order to meet the student's learning needs. What the teacher must do is obvious: Find out what the student can do, *start where he or she is,* and try to teach the student something.

Need for Empathy

Empathy means to genuinely "accept the child where he or she is" and to communicate a sincere feeling for the child. The child may have had daily experience of hostility, resignation, and despair, and may not believe that the teacher wants to be empathic.

Smith reported comments made by parents in reporting behaviors of teachers toward reading problems in their classrooms. Smith interviewed scores of parents concerning the history of their children's reading failures. Teachers were reported to have reacted as follows:

"She scolded him continuously because he was unable to read."
"Teacher screamed at him when he tried to read and couldn't."
"The teacher continuously subjected him to embarrassment before the other children by referring to his lack of ability to read."
"The teacher complained constantly because he didn't get busy and learn to read."
"The teacher kept him after school because he couldn't read."
"The teacher often made him stand in front of the class for long periods because he couldn't read."[2]

Preston reported an investigation in which she drew the conclusion that 78 percent of the teachers studied could not refrain from expressing their annoyance at slow, stumbling readers.[3]

After Tommy had come for a few remedial reading lessons, his clinician called his regular fourth-grade classroom teacher to discuss his developmental reading skills and to find out what the teacher felt would be helpful ways in which they might work together. The teacher said, "Of course, there really isn't much that I can teach them in reading. They've already had all the reading skills by the end of third grade. We just work on comprehension a little bit."

She did not offer to make any adjustments in Tommy's schedule at school, suggesting that she really planned for him to do what other children in the fourth grade did each day.

Sally completed books A, B, and C in SRA[4] during her first-grade school year. At the beginning of second grade, she appeared to have forgotten the content of the three books, demonstrating no phonics sense. In grade two, she did books A, B, C, and D and was working in book E at the end of the school year. Sally herself wanted to read desperately, but it was obvious even to her that she wasn't learning "any words to read with." Her mother arranged for summer tutoring. During one of her early lessons, Sally told her clinician, "I sure don't want to begin over again with book A next year." When tested in April, she was well informed about phonics, sounded each phoneme in isolation, and pronounced the word "time" as "Timmy"! During one of her early tutoring lessons in June, while playing *Go-Fish,* she said, "I'll have your *ju* as in *gate.*"

Sally's avenue to learning is obviously not in the auditory channel. Two years in phonics had netted practically nothing. She still did a little bit of reversing and could not tell the difference between *where, when, what, who, there, then, that, these,* and *three* as sight words. She sounded slowly through each word, wanted very much to read, and was self-conscious about having to guess. Only seven years of age, she had started school *young* because she was given an individual intelligence test and was found to be a bright child.

When George got his report card at the end of the year, he read: "At the mother's insistence, he is being promoted on probation. I know that George is not ready for fifth grade, and George knows that he is not ready for fifth grade, but at the mother's insistence, he is being promoted on probation." This was followed by other negative statements. Later, George told his father: "You know I'm smart, and Mother knows I'm smart, and Mrs. Zintz thinks I am, but that's not what counts. I don't get the grades."

Teachers should recognize and provide for achievement *"differences"* all through the students' school lives. Children see clearly that some run faster than others, some plan more wisely, some grow fatter or taller, and some *read better.* When they settle down to schoolwork they need purposes that are personal to them, and their efforts ought to be inner-directed to an increasing degree as they continue through school.[5] This is possible only if assignments are differentiated.

Differences Are Normal

The teachers who help students at various levels will understand that with good teaching the range of differences in their rooms increases as the year progresses. Hence, they *will not aim to make the group more alike,* but will welcome the natural development that makes them more different. They will not try to bring the poor ones up to grade level in academic achievement while they neglect the gifted; rather, they will anticipate that the gifted will continue to learn rapidly at their capacity, the slow at their rate of development, and that the spread will increase as it properly should.

Education within a democratic culture must provide for equality of individual opportunity in accord with inborn capacity so that an individual will not be deprived of educational advantages because of race, religion, age, geographical location, physical, social, or economic conditions, and the group will not be deprived of the possible services and contributions of any individual.[6]

Wang expressed similar ideas in 1980:

When the instructional program is designed to accommodate the individual differences of all students in the class, differences in the placement and learning progress of individual students are expected and even assumed by the teacher, students, and parents. In such classes no special labeling is needed to differentiate one child from another, and momentary problems in learning are not viewed as failures, but as occasions for further teaching.[7]

The students who cannot read well will find themselves in many school situations attempting a fixed curriculum, forced to go to school in the first place, and then expected to conform to a pattern that defeats them. There is an old Greek legend concerning the bed of Procrustes that is analogous to the situation in which such children find themselves. According to the legend, Procrustes and his men were robbers who extracted a toll from all who wished to pass the fording place that they controlled. When a traveler was given lodging on one of Procrustes' famous beds, Procrustes had an ingenious way of fitting the bed to the sleeper. If the guest was too long, his legs were cut off to make him fit; if he was too short, ropes tied to his head and feet stretched him until he fit the bed.

The inflexible school program, too often observed, says that children should achieve a fixed standard—a standard set from outside the children that does not take into consideration what they are actually able to do. Such a fixed curriculum and social promotion practices place considerable pressure on the children who fail. This pressure is observed in the behavior of the peer group, the organization of the school, and the expectations of the parents and community that the child move along in a lockstep pattern through the traditional grades in the public school. The school is not making use of what it knows about child growth and development if more effort goes into forcing the students to fit the pattern than goes into tailoring the learning experiences to fit them. Much is said concerning the attainment of standards prescribed by a course of study. This, far too often, means that school authorities are conveying to the students that they disapprove of them because they do not measure up to what is wanted or what is considered adequate. Buckingham said:

There are no misfit children. There are misfit textbooks, misfit teachers, and misfit courses of study. But by the very nature of things there can be no misfit children. The child is what education is for. One might as well say that a man does not fit his trousers as to say that a child does not fit the school.[8]

Teachers and parents need to understand and accept the rate of each child's ability to learn. If there is indication that what the child is doing is at the maximum rate of growth, it must be accepted and no more expected. Much difficulty comes from pressuring children to achieve beyond their ability. This pressure to achieve comes, of course, from both parents and teachers.

The concept of flexible standards of attainment for children is a most significant one, not only to believe and give lip service to, but definitely to internalize.

The Teacher's Attitudes toward Failure

As pointed out elsewhere, sociologists recognize three major socioeconomic strata or classes. These have been termed *upper, middle,* and *lower.* Each of these social classes has a way of life that is distinctly its own and is different from that of the other two. Children from the lower class have a value system that works best for them in their everyday life. Immediate rewards, low level of aspiration, live today and face tomorrow when it comes, earning money today is better than getting ready to earn more tomorrow—all are values adhered to by the lower class.

In middle-class life, education is very important. The lower middle class values education for the ways in which it encourages social mobility to the next social class. This social group sees its opportunity to improve its status and to acquire more and more of the artifacts and value patterns of the upper middle class through hard work, climbing the ladder of success, and acquiring higher education.

The major drives of middle-class teachers are achievement and early success, work for "work's sake," getting education, being responsible, and shaping one's own destiny. There is nothing wrong if teachers hold these values for themselves if these values represent a means for achieving their goals in life. It is extremely important, however, for them to see these values for what they are: those by which they live their own lives, not divinely mandated values that cover the ambitions of all the students whom they teach.

How aware are the teachers, for example, that the students may be expected to learn a completely different set of behaviors if they try to achieve these goals? How aware are the teachers that many children have never been taught to value these goals? How aware are the teachers that children may originate in vastly different cultures where the teachers' values are in direct conflict with the harmonious life of their social group?

More pertinent to the present discussion, however, is: How aware are the teachers of what attempting to achieve these values does to the children who cannot meet them? What about the children who face constant failure and whose egos are shattered until they have little feeling of personal worth?

Teachers have been conditioned to work in a social order where failure is unacceptable, where hard work brings rewards to most people, where "pollyannaish" promises are often given in the hope that, with this encouragement, success will come. A very high value has been placed on being able to conform. If teachers make single assignments to entire classes, they convey the notion that they think everyone should conform to an already fixed, arbitrary standard. Not to conform is to be disapproved, rejected, inadequate, unacceptable.

What Is Success?

Unless people critically appraise their own systems of values, they are apt to think that *success* for each of the students they teach is the same level of achievement that was success for them. Furthermore, this level of achievement that they remember as success is only as they remember it now in retrospect after perhaps a decade.

An understanding of all the individual differences found among children forces school philosophy to accept the logical fact that success, per se, is different for different people. "Success" for the so-called normal children cannot be narrowly defined as "success" for the bright children, and an entirely new concept of "success" is necessary for the slow learners. At the same time, the need for success is acknowledged by the mental hygienist as basic to good mental health.

Combs, Avila, and Purkey wrote:

> With a positive view of self one can dare, be open to experience, confront the world openly and with certainty. Negative views of self may lock a person in a vicious circle in which efforts to deal with life are always too little, too late, or inappropriate.[9]

Deutsch investigated the existence of special problems in educating black children in a large urban area. He analyzed social and behavioral factors as they related to the perception of self, frustration, tolerance, group membership, and the rate of learning. The effect of social stress on motivation, personal aspiration, and the concept of self suggested an urgent need for understanding of the value conflicts between the middle-class teacher and the lower-class child. Before the children leave the elementary school, Deutsch reported, they have learned that the larger society views them as inferior and expects an inferior performance from them. A *negative self-image* relates strongly to the fact of being black. Observers keeping diaries during the study recorded that teachers often directed derogatory remarks toward individual children.

> The most frequent such remark was to call a child "stupid," and as a result, the teacher, and through the teacher, the school played a role in reinforcing the negative self-image of the child, and contributed a negative reason for learning.[10]

Deutsch emphasized over and over again the role of the social scientist in the study of these racial-class problems. The social psychologist or the cultural anthropologist should study extensively the dynamic relationships among environmental and social circumstances and personality and intellectual performance.

An Ounce of Prevention

Teachers must approach their classrooms at the beginning of the school year ready to ignore the grade numbers posted on the doors. They must accept all children in terms of their abilities to perform at that time. (If the principal assigns them to your room, they *belong,* whether or not they can read anything!) Teachers must carefully assess exactly where all children are in a developmental reading program and teach them at that level. They must insist on mastery, unit by unit, before putting the children in more advanced work. Teachers must overcome any "we-must-hurry-and-cover-the-ground" attitude.

The teachers must help the children to face their problems squarely, to set attainable goals, and to keep tangible records of their progress. Tangible evidence rests in seeing a box of new words or phrases grow, an attractive bulletin board of books read, a graph of speed and comprehension scores, or a graph of sight words learned on different testing dates. The teachers should try to:

1. Help the children to build a positive attitude toward themselves and toward reading. (If needed, toward adults, too.)
2. Reward them at each step of the way in the right direction.
3. Accept and appreciate them as people. Some teachers may think of slow learners as nuisances and would prefer to be rid of them. They take a fatalistic attitude toward retardation in reading.
4. Let them talk—encourage them to express themselves.
5. Help them to see that reading must be fun. It cannot be fun if the books are all too hard.

Be Consistent throughout the Day

Many teachers feel that there is much pressure to complete a prescribed course of study for their specific grade level. They recognize that it will not be possible to do the prescribed work with disabled readers. Yet, at the same time they do not completely accept the level of work that these children could do successfully throughout the school day.

Mrs. Wall teaches third grade. Sandy came as a "repeater" from another third grade, yet he was unable to read beyond the preprimer level. Mrs. Wall recognized the need to "begin over again" in the reading process and arranged for Sandy to work both with three older boys who had reading difficulty and entirely alone for as much time as she could devote to an extra reading group for just Sandy. She planned the time he would need to work alone carefully. She had already analyzed his miscues on an informal reading inventory, noting the strategies that Sandy employed and the ones that were missing for both comprehension and word recognition. She also had had the boy read the words on the San Diego Quick Assessment and noted the types of mistakes that he made. Because Sandy had concomitant problems that might be physical, neurological, or psychological, Mrs. Wall referred him to the school's guidance clinic. In discussing Sandy's schoolwork with her supervisor, however, Mrs. Wall showed the supervisor regular third-grade arithmetic papers, language papers, spelling papers, and penmanship practice lessons.

The point for emphasis is that children who cannot *read* a basic sight vocabulary certainly cannot write or spell it for any useful purpose. Neither can they perform "story" problems in arithmetic. To "go only halfway" in accepting the children at their levels in a reading group and then not give them opportunity during the rest of the school day to put to work the new skills that they have learned is pointless.

Making Connections 12.2: What Does "Success" Mean?

Frequently, teachers and students are failing to communicate, yet neither knows it. Because the communication breakdown is not identified, further misunderstandings result. It is most important that teachers and students listen carefully to each other to hear not just the words but what the actual meanings are that are being verbalized.

To get a feeling of the different perceptions that teachers and students have about success, and particularly success in becoming readers, talk with a teacher and a student about the meaning of the word *success*. You may want to ask a child questions similar to these:

1. Whom do you know who is a successful reader? What makes this person successful?
2. Are you a successful student? Reader? Why?
3. Do your parents and teacher think you are a successful reader? Why do you think so?
4. How do you know a successful reader/student from an unsuccessful one?
5. How do you think teachers feel about successful readers? Unsuccessful ones?
6. How important is it to be a successful reader?

You might ask a teacher questions similar to these:

1. How do you identify successful readers in your class?
2. What behaviors characterize unsuccessful readers?
3. Do you and your students always agree on what behaviors contribute to success in reading and in the classroom?
4. Who is the most successful reader in your class this year? What criteria did you use for making your choice?
5. How important is it for the child to be successful in reading?

After you have completed your conversations, make lists of critical words and phrases that each person used to identify success. In what ways did the two people agree? Disagree? What could a teacher do to understand these different perceptions and to talk about them with children? Could such a discussion become a valuable learning experience for all in the classroom? How?

When you share your lists, interpretations, and ideas in class with other students, you should become more sensitive to the ways in which teachers and students often fail to understand each other.

Emphasis on Reading

Earp raised the question as to whether reading is *overemphasized* in the schools.[11] Certainly parents and teachers are apt to cite failure to learn to read as the school's number one problem. Title I Programs, the Right to Read Program, and special federal grant programs all emphasize the emotional climate attached to reading success in school. So the children who fail to acquire the needed skills learn to see themselves as failures, see leaving school as an escape, and reflect overt behavior that their parents and teachers are prone to evaluate negatively. Whole-group objectives—to have everyone read a certain book, know a standard vocabulary, turn in the expected assignment—are diametrically opposed to the individualized learning styles of the students in school. But if the pressures were removed, and if learning opportunities were available and their values understood, with great variations in terms of time for expected mastery, students themselves might find learning to read a desirable objective *from their own point of view,* and the school might find its program much more successful. The teachers who worked with Michael (see chapter 15) during his first four years in the elementary school were able to demonstrate this possibility, at least in some measure.

Reward for Not Learning

Attitudes in children that cause them to accept an antisocial or negative reward for not learning may be generated through failure. If somebody usually nags or gets excited when the child does not learn, the child may value this as a reward for keeping right on not learning. If the child's inability to do the work forces an adult to give that child a great deal of attention, the child has a reward for not learning.

Jack was such a boy. He probably gained satisfaction from coming every morning to the reading clinic where he had the undivided attention of a reading clinician for a fifty-minute period. Back in his fourth-grade room, he was one of thirty-five children expected to read textbooks of fourth-grade difficulty. His reader level in the reading clinic had progressed over a period of one and a half years from preprimer to second level, second grade. While Jack was in fourth grade, however, the reading in the clinic at hard second-grade level seemed to be on a plateau. When Jack's reading did not improve over a relatively long period of time, his clinician arranged a conference with the fourth-grade teacher. The clinician asked how the clinic might best help Jack so that he could make better progress in the fourth grade during the day. The fourth-grade teacher asked if the clinician might each day have Jack read the story in his fourth-grade reader that the rest of the children read while he was gone. She said that Jack was expected to do the pages in his workbook when he got to school, but he had not read the story. Since the exercises in the workbook were geared to a reader level two years beyond Jack, and since he was attempting to do the exercises without having read the related story in the reader, Jack found coming to the clinic a welcome escape from a rather impossible situation. If he did not learn to read, he could continue to attend the clinic and thus avoid a school situation with which he was unable to cope. He had a rather tangible reward in the enjoyment of his hour of clinical reading, and if he did not learn to read well, it might go on indefinitely. This is a kind of negative reward that usually greatly puzzles the teachers. When children feel that they are not accepted as they are or when they feel that adults do not accept their inability to perform or that the performance of other children more nearly fits what adults had expected, the children may subconsciously refuse to learn.

Occasionally children in the primary grades find out that their slightly younger siblings can read better than they can or at least can read with greater confidence. They go to great lengths to think of all the reasons why they should not read; they think of many other things that they prefer to do instead of reading; or they merely state objectively, "I can't read." They seek for themselves a multitude of pleasurable activities, none of which involves reading.

Concerning the idea that children learn "not to read" the same as they learn "to read," Stroud had this to say:

> It is understandable . . . if the pupil who puts in a year in not learning to read, and who to boot is the object of invidious comparisons or of guilt-producing behavior at home, does not show up next year filled with enthusiasm for his reading lesson. . . . Given more failure the second year, more trips to school by the mother who "can't see why . . . ," more "helps" from mother or father, and we can see how escape from reading actually becomes rewarding. As these avoiding reactions are rewarded we have exactly the conditions required for learning *not* to read . . . the task has been made needlessly hard. What he really needs by this time is a reconstruction of his personality.[12]

Bettelheim has written concisely and lucidly about the problem of children having motivation to fail instead of to succeed in an article, "The Decision to Fail."[13]

One of the serious problems in school is that of allowing children to "sit through" weeks and weeks of school attendance without developmental learning taking place. Classroom teachers need to be more accepting of, and much less defensive about, this fact. When adequately accepting and less defensive, they will ask for and demand outside help for problems that are not amenable to the limited individual instruction that they can provide. Such children, for whom the school is not offering successful instruction, *might be excluded* from the school. At least in this way their problem will not be "unrecognized," and once it is made clear that the child needs special help, most communities can provide it.

Terry is a case in point. Terry was referred to the educational clinic in the spring of his eighth-grade year. His parents had been notified by the principal that the school would be glad to give him an eighth-grade diploma if the parents would promise *not* to enroll him in the ninth grade in high school. With this "threat," the parents could no longer remain complacent as they had up to this time. They took the problem to their minister, who made inquiries and found a reading clinic for a diagnostic examination for the boy. The fact that special arrangements were made and that the boy learned in fifteen months of tutoring to read well at the sixth-grade level indicates that the school would have done a big favor both to the boy and to his parents if it had excluded him five years earlier when he enrolled in fifth grade as a nonreader. As it was, the school allowed him to sit through one year each in fifth and sixth grades and two years each in seventh and eighth grades as a nonreader, and then asked that he

When Michael Cooper of the Los Angeles Lakers demonstrates his interest in books by reading to children in a summer program, positive affective responses toward print are sure to result.
Used with the permission of the *Albuquerque Journal* and Michael Cooper.

not come back! Many referrals to reading clinics come from ministers, school nurses, and social workers instead of from classroom teachers themselves, who should be calling for help with difficult problems.

Cultivating Positive Affective Responses

If teachers learn to put *feelings* first, they will try to be open, warm, nonthreatening, and nonpunitive partners in the learning process. They will perform in the role of facilitators of learning; not as authoritarians exacting work from others. Clarification of one's values in relation to the values of others becomes a primary problem in such a facilitating relationship. While the teachers may value punctuality, excellent grades, future rewards for hard work, and the nonwasting of time, the students in their classes may never have had these same values emphasized in their experiences of living. At least those values, or some of them, may not have been emphasized for the students by those for whom they cared most.

In relation to this objective acceptance of all people in the teachers' classrooms as fully functioning, worthwhile individuals, there are some commonsense guidance principles that the classroom teachers should bear in mind and probably reread frequently until they feel that they practice them most of the time.

Basic Counseling Principles for Classroom Teachers

1. Confident teachers do not need to seem authoritative to children. Try to cultivate a more "we're equals" kind of atmosphere. Naturally, if teachers are mature adults, the children are not going to take advantage of their kindnesses. If they do, then the teachers must help them to achieve more mature behavior in an atmosphere of mutual respect.
2. Learn to listen. Learn when to allow periods of silence. Learn how to accept long pauses while children are thinking through something that they can explain to you if you give them time. Some specifics might be:
   (a) Be sure you do not talk more than your half of the time.
   (b) Do *not* interrupt students even if you think they are off the subject.
   (c) Pause long enough before answering to see whether the students will add anything else.
3. Watch for and try to interpret nonverbal clues. Are the students especially fidgety today? Are they acting inattentive most of the time? Could they be really worried about something else that they face that day? Are they talking faster or in voices that are higher-pitched than usual—or are they unusually quiet today?
4. When they make statements, whether you agree or not, learn to make neutral statements that reflect their feelings so that they can think through their thoughts and respond further. For example: "How did you feel when he said that?" "Is this really *your* idea?" "How do you feel when this happens?" "Do you care very much what he does?" "Were you really glad about that, or didn't it make much difference?" Empathic expressions like these may help the students to clarify and interpret their thinking.
5. Do not show rejection or negative feelings. Be patient, nonthreatening, and use *no* sarcasm.
6. Do not make false promises. What happens to students will result much more from their behavior than from yours.
7. Questions that can be answered "yes" or "no" may get little language out of the students. *What, how, why, which,* and words like these to start the question may get you much more information.
8. Be careful about moralistic admonishments. Focus on behaviors that are unacceptable, not on the persons. The teacher should try to think through: "Why did they do this?" "Why have they failed?" "What did I do that turned them off that time?"

Axline's Therapeutic Principles

Axline outlined eight basic principles used by a psychotherapist and expressed the belief that teachers could become much more therapeutic in their relationships with children than they have been in the past. Worked at sincerely, consistently, and honestly, these principles have much to offer the teacher-student relationship:

1. The therapist must develop a warm, friendly relationship with the children.
2. The therapist accepts the child exactly as he or she is.

3. The therapist establishes an environment in which the child is free to express his or her feelings completely.
4. The therapist recognizes the child's feelings and *reflects* them back in such a way that the child gains insight into his or her behavior.
5. The therapist has a deep respect for the child's ability to solve his or her own problems if given the opportunity to do so.
6. The therapist remains largely nondirective—the child leading the way in discussing or acting out his or her difficulties.
7. The therapy is a gradual process and cannot be hurried.
8. The therapist establishes only those limitations that are necessary to anchor the therapy to the world of reality and to make the child aware of his or her responsibility in the relationship.[14]

Axline explained:

When a teacher respects the dignity of a child, whether the child is six or sixteen, and treats the child with understanding, kindness, and constructive help, the teacher is developing in the student an ability to look within the self for the answers to his or her problems, and to become responsible as an independent individual in his or her own right.

It is the relationship that exists between the teacher and students that is the important thing. The teacher's responses must meet the real needs of the children and not just the material needs—reading, writing, and arithmetic.[15]

Bibliotherapy, using books to help persons to cope with their problems, may be useful for some teachers in improving their affective responses to children. Rubin suggested using bibliotherapy in "preventive and ameliorative" ways.[16] She described ways to link bibliotherapy with role-playing, problem solving, drawing, and discussion.

Summary

Children need to be empowered to learn by the teacher and the school. They also need to be involved in planning their own learning, which contributes to the sense of empowerment. The teacher must expect to become a child advocate in order to support learning in the classroom.

Acceptance of the students has been described in this chapter as the genuine willingness of the teachers to analyze the levels at which the students can work and to *permit* them to grow from that level.

Empathy for children requires understanding of their frustrations about their failures, and an empathic response to the children includes alleviating anxiety and sequential development of missing skills.

Smith and Preston reported negative attitudes of teachers toward children who are unsuccessful in reading. Teachers need to reevaluate their own attitudes toward success and failure—what is approved and what is disapproved—and to evaluate objectively the status of the underachievers.

Finally, it was pointed out that children can learn "not to learn" if their school situation offers more rewards for not progressing than for continuing to grow up. This is one of the areas where it is most necessary for teachers to be sensitive to the thinking, feeling, and behavior of children.

For Further Reading

Axline, Virginia Mae. *Play Therapy*. Boston: Houghton Mifflin Co., 1947, 1969. This is the original and most authoritative statement on play therapy. Axline also wrote *Dibs*, the story of a little boy who underwent play therapy. This book is definitely worth reading.

Beck, Judith S. "A Problem Solving Framework for Managing Poor Readers in Classrooms." *Reading Teacher* 41 (April 1988): 774–79. Children should expect the best of reading instruction. This article gives specific suggestions for helping children to change nonproductive behaviors.

Combs, Arthur W., Donald L. Avila, and William W. Purkey. *Helping Relationships*. 2d ed. Boston: Allyn and Bacon, 1978. This is an important book about interpersonal relationships, specifically *helping* relationships. Every teacher should read it.

Gentile, Lance M., and Merna M. McMillan. *Stress and Reading Difficulties*. Newark, Del.: International Reading Association, 1987. This booklet addresses research, assessment, and intervention in helping children to cope with stress. The role of the teacher is part of the consideration in managing stress.

Gentile, Lance M., and Merna M. McMillan. "Stress and Reading Difficulties: Teaching Students Self Regulating Skills." *Reading Teacher* 41 (November 1987): 170–78. Specific suggestions are made for coping with *fight* and *flight* behaviors in relation to reading. The roles of the teacher and parents are emphasized.

Notes

1. Jim Cummins, "Empowering Minority Students: A Framework for Intervention," *Harvard Educational Review* 56 (February 1986): 18–36.
2. Nila B. Smith, "Teachers' Responsibility to Retarded Readers," *Education* 77 (May 1957): 548.
3. Ibid., citing Mary I. Preston, "Reading Failure and the Child's Security," *American Journal of Orthopsychiatry* 10 (April 1940): 239–52.
4. Donald Rasmussen and Lynn Goldberg, *Basic Reading Series* (Chicago: Science Research Associates, 1965).
5. Alice R. Eldredge, "An Investigation to Determine the Relationships among Self-Concept, Locus of Control, and Reading Achievement," *Reading World* 21 (October 1981): 59–64.
6. Arthur B. Moehlman, *School Administration* (Chicago: Houghton Mifflin Co., 1940), 127.
7. Margaret C. Wang, "Adaptive Instruction: Building on Diversity," *Theory into Practice* 19 (Spring 1980): 123.
8. B. R. Buckingham, *Research for Teachers* (Chicago: Silver Burdett and Co., 1926), 299.
9. Arthur Combs, Donald L. Avila, and William W. Purkey, *Helping Relationships,* 2d ed. (Boston: Allyn and Bacon, 1978), 85.

10. Martin Deutsch, *Minority Group and Class Status as Related to Social and Personality Factors in Scholastic Achievement,* Monograph No. 2 (Ithaca, N.Y.: The Society for Applied Anthropology, Cornell University, 1960).
11. N. Wesley Earp, "Challenge to Schools: Reading Is Overemphasized," *Reading Teacher* 27 (March 1974): 562–65.
12. James B. Stroud, *Psychology in Education,* (New York: Longman, Green and Co., 1956), 127.
13. Bruno Bettelheim, "The Decision to Fail," in *Conflict in the Classroom: The Education of Emotionally Disturbed Children,* ed. Nicholas Long, William C. Morse, and Ruth Newman (Belmont, Calif.: Wadsworth Publishing Co., 1965), 435–46.
14. Virginia Mae Axline, *Play Therapy* (Boston: Houghton Mifflin Co., 1947, 1969), 75–76.
15. Ibid., 156–57.
16. Dorothy Rubin, *Diagnosis and Correction in Reading Instruction* (New York: Holt, Rinehart and Winston, 1982), 335.

13
Working Cooperatively with Parents

Vocabulary

mainstreaming
regular education initiative
values
socioeconomic status
reading environment
parents as models
parent-teacher conference
parent interview
P.L. 94-142
Parent Advisory Council
    (PAC)
home visits
advocacy

Questions

1. How would you describe the responsibility shared by parents and teachers for the education of children? (**Inference**)
2. What are some valid reasons why parents should not teach their children to read? (**Recall**)
3. What advice would you give to the parents of your students about helping their children with reading? (**Application**)
4. Why should teachers be sensitive to the feelings that can be a factor in parent-teacher relations? (**Inference**)
5. Make a list of guidelines that you would follow in conducting parent-teacher conferences. (**Application**)
6. What roles might parents play in the classroom? (**Recall**)
7. What does it mean to be in the role of child advocate? (**Inference**)

Introduction

A great deal of the variation in student achievement scores is caused by family-related factors. Clearly, then, focusing only on the child at school overlooks a dynamic family interaction that supports or fails to support the school program. The development of children is dependent upon a process of parent-teacher sharing and interacting. When one stops to realize that a teacher can influence children for only one year while parents may have considerable influence for nearly twenty years, one sees why parents must be teaching partners.[1]

Parents and Teacher Share a Responsibility

The need for school personnel to emphasize the relationship of parent and teacher as one of *equals* working together on mutual concerns was well stated by Kelly:

> No matter what level of expertise I possess, you know your own child, his needs and feelings, his reactions to success and failure, his good and bad points, better than I ever will. In our own separate ways we are responsible for his social, emotional, and educational growth, and interested in his welfare and his progress toward maturity. Let us, therefore, as equal partners in the instructional process, find ways that we can work together to help this child in both school and home contexts, to learn and enjoy learning to the best of his abilities.[2]

Demands for Close Parent-Teacher Cooperation

Mainstreaming, as a recent thrust in education, demands the close cooperation of parents and the school in program planning for all children. The definition of mainstreaming by Houck and Sherman is pertinent here:

> Mainstreaming is the integration of eligible handicapped children and normal peers based upon individually determined educational needs which necessitates the shared responsibility for planning and programming by regular and special education administrative and instructional personnel. Key words are *eligible* and *shared responsibility*. The rationale for mainstreaming is praiseworthy. Handicapped children should not be isolated if they *need not* be. Integration provides better opportunity for acceptance and understanding. Mainstreaming deemphasizes the labeling of individuals. Legal mandates for equal protection support some mainstreaming. Perhaps mainstreaming will help insure that each child does have a well-worked-out individualized plan for his education.[3]

The current *regular education initiative*,[4] which will result in the placement of more children with learning difficulties in the regular classroom for most or all of the school day, will also demand close cooperation between teachers and parents. Some children will experience problems that can be managed only by continuous communication between home and school.

Values in Conflict

When children have learning difficulties in school, the teacher must bear in mind that the parents play the most crucial role in the total life experience of their children. Reading success is dependent upon all the other facets of the children's lives: motivation, level of aspiration, values rooted in socioeconomic background, and the expressed attitudes that children hear at home about the value of education.

For students from the lowest socioeconomic level or most culturally deprived homes, teachers are their greatest hope for achieving mature reading interests and habits as a basis for adding to their *values* and improving their economic status.

Specifically, for example, over half of the children come to the public schools from homes and neighborhoods of lower *socioeconomic status* while teachers have universally internalized middle-class socioeconomic values. Some of the conflicts in these sets of values can be stated in this way:

Lower-class Environment Values	*Middle-class Values*
Living in the present	Living for the future
Immediate rewards	Anticipating future rewards
Quit school and get work	Graduate and get a better job
Work today; get paid today; enjoy the reward now	Save for a rainy day
No expectation of rising in the class system	Upward mobility to climb the ladder of success

While teachers are certainly as tolerant as any group, they must recognize social stratification as it operates in American society.

Since mobility in the social classes requires drive and directed purpose as well as willingness to forego immediate pleasures for greater future gain, lower-lower-class members have values in conflict with striving, and few will be motivated to try. Many upper-lower-class members have been unsuccessful when they have aspired to social mobility.

Middle-class parents may exert too much pressure for success. It is, perhaps, safe to generalize that parents from the middle class, socioeconomically speaking, *expect* success of all their children because they themselves were successful in school.[5]

The children who have parents who graduated from college will likely be expected to attend college. However, reading problems in school may set in motion a whole chain reaction of emotional responses rooted in child-parent conflicts, sibling jealousies, or sibling comparisons. Without remediation or counseling to restructure personalities, the conflicts may never be resolved.

Sally came for some remedial reading instruction the year she was in the sixth grade. She profited greatly from study of phonic analysis, structural analysis, word study, prefixes, roots, suffixes, and speed-of-comprehension exercises. Recently, when her name appeared on the senior high school honor roll list, the clinician remarked to a teacher friend, "I'm delighted to see her name on the honor roll. I taught her remedial reading in sixth grade." The teacher, uninitiated in the nature of remedial reading, said, "Oh, no. You couldn't have. She has always been very bright." The clinician remembered the mother's anxiety six years before when she had worried that the child's reading difficulty might preclude effective use of her good intelligence.

Charlene came for some reading tests because her parents recognized her inability to read and the fact that her little sisters were reading better than she was. Charlene was in the sixth grade and told the reading tutor that she was reading the regular sixth-grade reader at school. After making an informal analysis, the tutor selected an easy second reader that Charlene could read adequately.

When her tutor established her capacity for reading achievement at or above her grade level, her tutor assured her that she was an intelligent girl. Charlene said, "You mean I'm not dumb?" Later she explained, "Wait till I can read! I'll show Mary. She said I was in the dumb group and that I was the dumbest one in it!" With help to achieve reading success, Charlene also may meet her parents' aspiration that she attend college successfully.

Working with parents necessitates an understanding of the way that parents feel, how they think about schools and teachers, how completely they can be convinced that their children can profit by the school's program, and whether they feel that too much success in school will eventually mean less and less acceptance of the way of life at home by the children.

Parent-teacher conferences in an environment in which an unhurried, constructive exchange of views can take place are necessary if the children's academic, social, and emotional growth is to be discussed and evaluated fairly. Parents may wonder about the extent to which they need to try to teach their children; they surely want to know in what ways they can contribute constructively to their children's greater success; they may sense rejection of their children by the teachers; and the parents may reject teachers because of their past experience. This chapter will discuss these problems and give suggestions for structuring parent interviews.

Ways Parents Help Their Children with Reading

Should Parents Try to Teach Reading?

Many parents wonder whether they should teach their child to read. Sometimes they feel that they must supplement the teacher's work by helping their child to do exercises at night. But most teachers agree that, in general, parents should *not* try to teach their children to read. That does not mean that parents should avoid answering children's questions about print, reading to their sons and daughters, and providing books and other elements of an *environment* that stimulates literacy.

Parents have many responsibilities toward their children; making sure that they learn to read and write is just one of them. Teacher-parent cooperation will help to define areas of responsibility in relation to literacy development.

The teacher-pupil relationship is not as emotionally charged as the parent-child relationship. Wollner pointed out that it is much better for the child's morale if correcting is done by one who is not as emotionally involved as the parent. The children are able to progress best in an "atmosphere of friendly impersonality."[6] Wollner also pointed out that:

> Parents, when they try to be teachers, tend to focus their main attention on the outcome and to view the errors as stumbling blocks. Reading clinics focus their main attention on the learner and his individual way of learning; they view the errors as sign posts to help them to design correct instruction.[7]

As the teachers become fully aware of the role that parents play in their children's education, they are able to teach most effectively. This point deserves special emphasis because too often teachers ignore parents, keep them away from the schools, or do not make an effort to cooperate or work with them. This minimizes any parent-school relationship, and it is harmful to the children since the teacher-parent relationship is reflected in the child-parent relationship.

Keeping in mind the influence that parents have on their children, one becomes aware of the myriad problems that can arise when the child does *not* make progress in learning to read. A very normal reaction of parents is "if the school won't do it, we will." That the teaching is more complicated and requires more skill than this has often been stated, and the only way this problem can be handled is by continuing contact between teachers and parents. This communication must involve more than progress reports on the children. It must also be an education program for the adults. This will require both time and effort on the part of classroom teachers.

Ways Parents Should Help

Be Sure Children Are in an Optimum State of Physical Health

Parents can cooperate with the school psychologist and the family doctor to make sure that the child is in an optimum state of physical health with respect to hearing, vision, and other physical or psychological factors. Parents can make sure that the child's physical needs are adequately taken care of. It may mean adequate rest for a child. It may mean prohibiting the watching of television until midnight. It is not hard to understand why a child's behavior at school is not conducive to learning if he or she has had insufficient sleep and rest. It may also mean planning a diet that provides adequate nutrition and stresses healthful foods.

Parents are usually anxious to cooperate with the school in obtaining hearing and vision screening examinations for their children. Teachers need to be aware of community social agencies that are available to provide these services for children from families in low socioeconomic groups. The teachers must feel responsible for discovering many of these problems and referring them to the principal, the school nurse, the school psychologist, or the school social worker.

Children Need to Feel Secure and Confident

Mental health, a basic need, is so important that it should be discussed separately. Harris and Sipay wrote:

> Any child outdistanced by other children is apt to be disturbed by lack of progress. At first he is likely to try harder. If his efforts are misdirected and fail to bring improvement, eventually a strong feeling of frustration develops. . . . He generally builds up a strong dislike for reading and takes every opportunity to avoid it. . . . His parents are likely to show strong disappointment because of poor report cards and may nag, threaten, or punish him. This in turn tends to intensify his emotional difficulties and increase his dislike for school.[8]

Harris and Sipay summarized several studies of family reactions to reading disability in their children and made the following points:

1. Severe reading disability was often the cause of family emotional problems.
2. Parental denial of the reading problem is a basic form of protection against the pain of addressing reality.
3. Another parent reaction is to blame someone outside the family for the reading problem.
4. Families may need therapy in order to avoid making the reading problem worse and to develop positive ways of dealing with the difficulty.[9]

Sometimes teachers have difficulty hiding their anxiety about a particular child's failure to read. Understandably, parents, who are even more emotionally involved with their own children, would have an extremely hard time hiding their anxiety.

One of the principles that teachers and parents must be aware of is that just as children grow physically at their own paces, so they develop their reading skills at their own paces. This means that all children will not be ready to start reading at the same time, nor will they progress at the same speed. That this is a difficult concept for parents to grasp is not surprising, since teachers sometimes ignore it in their teaching. Parents need to realize that children's emotional and physical health affect their growth in reading.

Children Who Live in a Reading Environment Learn More Easily

Parents can surround children with books. Children should be surrounded with books at home as well as at school. School boards should spend a great deal of money on books for children. There is an economic factor for parents; they must learn how to purchase as many good books as their budget will allow and then rely upon libraries to supply the rest. Parents can read to children. Children need to be read to even after they begin to read for themselves. Reading is a way of sharing experiences, and the things read can be talked about. This further enhances language skill. Reading to children gives adults mutual experiences with children, and this is desirable.

Parents need to be aware that they are powerful *models* for their children. They should not only encourage their children to read and to read with them. They should also be readers in their own right, letting their children see them reading and enjoying a variety of printed materials.

Parents can also point out other aspects of the environment where print is important. Letters that are sent and received, lists that are made and followed, directions that appear on cans and boxes of food products, and notes left for family members are all forms of print that can be significant in the lives of children. Print in the environment is now recognized as a significant factor in learning to read. Parents need to be apprised of its value.

Parents Need to Understand the Methods of Teaching that the Teacher Uses

It would help parents if they were aware of some of the methods that are used in teaching reading today. Probably this knowledge would enable them to be more enthusiastic and less critical about the teaching of reading. They need to understand the "whole thought" method and the word-recognition techniques. Phonics is taught today, but it is taught differently. Oral reading is not synonymous with general reading skill, and it certainly should not be considered as the result. Today many different comprehension strategies and skills are taught to increase reading ability. Certainly drill in itself is not a way to increase reading skill. The necessity for parents to obtain the correct information about the teaching and development of reading cannot be overemphasized. One such teaching technique for parents to use is discussed in the following article by Kenneth Topping: "Paired Reading: A Powerful Technique for Parent Use," *Reading Teacher* 40 (March 1987): 608–14.

Children Can Be Encouraged to Read Aloud to Parents

Finally, parents can encourage the child to read aloud to them. Teachers should ask children to take books home to read aloud to their parents. This should be done when the teachers are sure that the child will be able to read well; thus, reading to the parents will be rewarding. As a rule, it should be done in such a way that parents will listen to the child read, so that they will praise good reading, and so that they will not expect the child to sound out words. They will not expect to supplement the teaching of phonics, but will supply any words with which the child needs help. Their primary motive will be to enjoy the story with the child.

Parent Responses to Technology

Today's parents know that their children are bombarded by ideas and language from several technological sources. Many children are participants in video games at home and in commercial game rooms. Children often view television for many hours each week. Television may well serve as baby-sitter for thousands of latchkey children.[10] Radios are frequently constant companions, being carried to and from school and even between classes in middle schools and high schools. Less frequently, children have access to computers at home as well as at school.

Demos suggested that parents should plan to utilize the technological communication devices to their children's advantage:

1. Use television as a tool for language development, discussion, and inquiry. Listen to the desirable language, incorporate it in your conversation, and encourage children to use it.
2. Collect books, articles, and newspaper accounts related to programs viewed on television. Read and discuss these materials with the children.
3. Obtain copies of suitable popular songs so that the children can read the words as they sing along. Unusual words and repeated uses of sight words will be found in the lyrics.
4. Facilitate comprehension by watching television for varied purposes—to summarize, to critique, to note details.
5. Encourage children to write letters to television stations that include comments, both favorable and unfavorable, about programs.
6. Provide a variety of programs for children to use on the computer. These should range from games, simulations, interactive novels, and skill-and-drill programs to word-processing and problem-solving software.[11]

Developing Constructive Attitudes

Exerting undue pressure on the child who is having difficulty in reading is perhaps the cardinal mistake that parents make. Scolding him and telling him that he *must* learn to read may cause him to become so tense and worried that he will be unable to make use of learning in reading to which he has been exposed, and such a condition may even be so severe that it prevents new learning from taking place.[12]

Making Connections 13.1: Interviewing Teachers about Working with Parents

One way to help yourself feel confident about working with parents is to have as much information about successful parent-teacher interaction strategies as possible.

Arrange to interview at least two teachers about how they work with parents. Pay particular attention to the strengths they see in such cooperation, the varied strategies they use, and the problems that they have experienced. Make notes of the points that are made, or gain permission and tape record the meetings.

Bring your information back to your class for a general discussion of strategies for working *with* parents. You should have a good list of practical suggestions at the end of the discussion.

Feelings Experienced by Parents, Children, and Teachers

Wollner stated that "release from home pressures . . . that surround . . . the subject of reading is one factor essential to the progress of each pupil."[13] She also pointed out one of the reasons why the release is so important, "Release from pressure is a protective measure; that is, it is intended to protect and preserve the essential qualities of the parent-child relationship."[14]

Removal of pressures was also emphasized by Bliesmer:

If a child is having trouble a lot of his day is spent in frustration . . . he needs to be able to get away from this.

If he's forced to spend hour after hour, at homework, the home is no longer the place of security which it should be for the child; and he has no opportunity to escape.[15]

Parents simply must realize what the frustrated children experience day after day at school and become cognizant that they must not put them through the same thing at home.

Lieben reported that in a graduate class of seventeen experienced teachers and five psychologists, all "clearly reflected hostile, negative attitudes toward the parents of the poor achievers."[16] She went on to say that "there was little recognition of the feelings that parents might be experiencing when children consistently perform below normal."[17] Lieben also reported that teachers often put too much stock in the adage "Find the disturbed child, and you find the disturbed parent." " 'Overanxious,' 'over-ambitious,' and 'rejecting' are terms too loosely used to describe parents of children who are failing to progress academically in expected ways."[18] The relationships between parents, their children, and their children's school progress are far too complicated to make such generalizations.

When teachers have feelings about parents similar to those just discussed, the situation becomes worse because whatever the teacher says to parents will be reflected in the child-parent relationship. Lieben observed that the following happens:

The mother knows something is wrong, but she has only vague generalizations about the causes and is told there's little which she can do. She then either gives up on the child or gets mad at him for not trying harder.[19]

Teachers must realize that most parents do the best they can for their children, and the mistakes that they make are not intentional.

. . . the mother of a child delayed in reading does the very best she can within the limits of her understanding, capacities and the exigencies of the everyday living. Few parents fail their children willingly, and most parents suffer pangs of guilt over their real or imagined failures.[20]

Redl and Wattenberg described the special roles in which teachers and parents cast each other that may prevent them from achieving cooperation and understanding.[21] For example, one such role is that in which the teachers feel that the parents should be called to school and told what to do. Another example of casting parents in special roles is where parents' clubs are thought of and tolerated as necessary evils. In another, the teachers think of the parents as powerful and punishing adults; probably this is the way they see their own parents. In this case, the teachers will be shy and timid and lack confidence, and they may feel persuaded to say what they think the parents would like to hear.

A fourth such special role is that in which parents are of a low or very different economic status or of a much different background of experience.[22] This often brings classroom teachers to such confusion in their own thinking that they wonder how to "handle" parents, how to "conquer and outwit the enemy." As long as the teacher must think in terms of *handling* parents, it is hardly possible to work with them confidently in solving mutual problems.

A fifth role was proposed by Iverson who questioned the idea that parent-teacher interaction is always good.[23] The results of her study suggested that home-school contacts stimulate achievement of younger children but inhibit growth in reading abilities in older children. Teachers should help parents to time their contacts with the school.

Parents also often cast teachers in specific roles. For example, parents think of Johnnie's teacher as the same old ogre who taught them a generation ago.[24] A specific role is one in which parents resent and resist the authority of the school and see in the teacher the symbol of school authority. These parents are apt to be defensive just because they come to the school.

Parents may be in awe of the school, accepting its decisions and mandates without question. Wolf wrote of such parents:

> They would not have dreamed of questioning a decision made by their child's teacher. Public education was sacrosanct. They were so grateful for the opportunities their child had for formal education. They would not think of questioning any decision made by school people.[25]

A specific role is one in which parents fear they will not measure up to the teachers' standards. They have an unrealistic set of arbitrary standards for themselves and their children. Fear of failure thus is a threat to their security.

Bringing Parents to the School

> Many parents have had a history of dehumanizing and disillusioning experiences with the school. Their feelings of alienation and powerlessness are reinforced by society, which blames the home and parents for the difficulties children experience.[26]

Ferreiro and Teberosky made it clear that normally there is no evil intent on the part of teachers. They wrote: "We are not referring to the conscious intentions of teachers as particular individuals but to the social role of the educational system."[27]

The school is fortunate if it has sufficient space for a room that can be set aside as an open room for parents to come at any time. If the room has a coffee pot, some reading material, displays of children's work on the bulletin boards, and information about coming events, many parents who would like to talk about the education of their child are apt to find their way to such a room. Then, if teachers use their coffee-break time or arrange other special conference times, they may be able to listen to parents and learn a great deal about what they are thinking.

Suggestions for Parent-Teacher Cooperation

After teachers have begun to view parents as partners in the education of children, they must identify a variety of ways to make that partnership effective. Five suggestions to implement this cooperation are: (1) suggestions for the parent-teacher conference, (2) suggestions for working with parents in the interview situation, (3) using written materials with parents, (4) home visits, and (5) parents as resources in the classroom. Each of these suggestions will be discussed below.

Suggestions for Parent-Teacher Conferences

Keeping parents informed is essential to building positive, cooperative attitudes. Hastily written notes for children to carry home, telephone calls at times convenient for the parent, and brief home visits are ways of keeping two-way lines of communication open. Some teachers find that weekly or monthly newsletters telling about class experiences, explaining teaching methods, and suggesting at-home learning activities are good communication tools.

The best practice in reporting children's progress to their parents must come through two-way communication. This is to say that there must be some time and some way that the teacher can discuss in a face-to-face situation with the parents the progress in academic work and social development that the children are making, and the parents can say in that same face-to-face situation what they are thinking. Then, in this same conversational atmosphere, teachers and parents can work out any semantic differences, and while they may not agree, at least they will have a greater degree of understanding of each other's opinions. Such a conversation can give them a great deal of mutual support in accomplishing their respective goals with the children. The semantic differences that may stem from the teachers' overuse of professional jargon that does not seem meaningful to the parents can be overcome if parents are sufficiently at ease to raise questions.[28]

One of the best ways to begin helping children who are having difficulty in reading is to have a *parent-teacher conference.* Here, if the parents seem uncooperative and resistant, the teacher must not take the behavior at face value but should try to determine *why* the parents are acting as they are. If the teacher can be honest and concerned about the problem, there should not be difficulty in working with the parents. The teacher should look upon the parents as people who can help to diagnose and correct the child's reading difficulties. It is all right for the teacher not to have all the answers to the problem; together, the teacher and the parents should be able to work out possible solutions.

Suggestions for Working with Parents in the Interview Situation

Teachers may find that the *interview* is an effective technique for obtaining useful data for working with remedial readers. To be selective in interviewing parents will probably be necessary because the process requires a significant amount of time to plan the interview, conduct it, and evaluate the information obtained.[29]

1. Meet the parents (both together, if at all possible) early in the school year to talk about their child.
2. Give the parents an opportunity to talk first. Inquire about their ideas concerning the cause of the child's difficulty.
3. Evaluate parents' comments during the interview, and begin tactfully to:
   a. Restore their confidence in the child (if loss of confidence is indicated).
   b. Alleviate any indicated guilt feelings or concerns about mental deficiency.
   c. Reassure parents if they depreciate the current methods of teaching reading.
   d. Explain the harmful effects of comparing siblings, nagging, blaming, scolding, and applying other pressures, if any of these is indicated.
4. Give an honest, sincere appraisal of the remedial situation as you have found it up to the time of the interview.
5. Share with the parents all objective information you have.
   a. Samples of the child's schoolwork.
   b. Standard test scores in achievement tests.
   c. Information of a meaningful nature concerning intelligence and achievement tests. Classification of test scores as high, above average, average, below average, dull normal, retarded are more accurate than exact IQ scores. Percentile ranks can be interpreted to parents in a very meaningful manner to give them an understanding of the child's rank in a group. The IQ score of 110, for example, can be understood if it is interpreted as a percentile of 73 if the parents understand that their child has done better on that specific test at that specific time than 73 out of 100 children of the same age in the general population who have taken the test. Teachers can clarify scores with parents.
   d. Anecdotal records that describe child behavior in specific situations.
6. Suggest, if necessary, that the parents' responsibilities to their children include:
   a. Providing for the child's psychological needs: love, security, belonging, recognition, response from others, and new experience.
   b. Providing for the child's physical needs: assurance of adequate sleep and rest, diet and exercise, vision, hearing, and coordination. If handicaps are present that cannot be corrected, the best possible adjustment to the limitation should be made.
   c. Developing individual responsibility, a healthy attitude toward growing up and achieving independence; and developing habit patterns commensurate with achieving these goals.
7. Emphasize that learning to read is a developmental process that requires a long time and much practice. *Never* promise that a remedial problem can be eliminated within a specified amount of time. Reading teachers do not work miracles. Growth in reading is usually not phenomenal. It is gradual and should

be expected to show only step-by-step improvement through the school year. The teacher hopes this improvement will be consistent but can never be sure that long periods of plateaus showing little growth will not occur. The teacher must help the parents to understand that the children will *never* move to higher levels of reading until they register success at each level of difficulty preceding the next higher level.

Kroth has written succinctly about the nature of positive teacher-parent interaction:

1. The teacher obtains as much information from parents as is necessary to plan educational programs for the children;
2. The teacher provides the parents with the information they need to work cooperatively with the teacher toward common goals for the children; and
3. Cooperative planning between teachers and parents may prevent, alleviate, or solve many problems that arise during the school year.

Teachers and parents who recognize their roles as complementary and not supplementary, who approach their interactions enthusiastically and not apprehensively, and who view their relationship as a partnership will usually be rewarded with happy, achieving children and warm personal feelings of mutual respect.[30]

The greatest difficulty is in getting that first, positive contact between teachers and parents to take place. Since the school is the institution offering service to the parents, one might surmise that it is the responsibility of the teachers to initiate this contact. Many teachers either lack the confidence or are reluctant to give the time necessary to take the first step.

Using Written Materials with Parents

When *P.L. 94-142* and other similar legislation were enacted, it was specified that parents must be involved in the education of their children. The *Parent Advisory Council (PAC)* that is part of Chapter I reading programs is an example of required parent involvement. Frequently, the parent must read and comprehend information about the diagnosis and placement of a child. Roit and Pfohl reported that much of this written material is difficult to read and is far above the reading capabilities of many parents.[31] It is important that teachers read over these materials *with* parents, clarifying terms and explaining what is happening to their children. Teachers must be astute in determining how much help parents may need. Too much help may be interpreted as patronizing; too little leaves parents confused, suspicious, and helpless.

Meetings with Parents

Plans for parents' involvement at school necessitate understanding of values in the home, cultural expectations, community mores, and special problems of working parents with very young children.

Making Connections 13.2: Getting Ready for Parent Conferences

One of the important jobs of the teacher is conducting parent conferences. An effective parent conference does not "just happen." It requires careful planning and conscientious follow-up. In fact, there are at least three phases in a conference cycle. First, the teacher must gather together examples of the child's work and other materials or records to be shared with the parents. Careful notes need to be made concerning information to be discussed. A tentative agenda needs to be prepared. The second phase is the conference itself. The teacher is responsible for seeing that important topics are discussed, that the child's strengths along with areas for growth are identified, and that notes are made of the interaction. Finally, the teacher must follow up on suggestions or other agreements that were made at the conference.

One way to prepare to conduct a parent conference is to role-play this teacher responsibility with a peer. Find another member of your class to team with you. Prepare a paragraph describing the child that you will be discussing. Then after deciding who will be the "parent" and who the "teacher," role-play the meeting. Ask your audience to critique your practice conference. You may want to carry out the task more than once, making use of the feedback from class members each time. You might also vary the routine by having both "parents" attend the conference with the "teacher."

When parents say to the teachers, "I think Bill is behind in his reading. Is there anything I can do at home to help him?" they would probably like to have some specific, helpful suggestions. Professor Alma Harrington considered this question to be important enough to warrant her teaching an evening course for parents, "Helping Children with Reading in the Home," at the State University of New York, Buffalo. Such a course usually meets for two hours once a week, over a six-week period.

Criscuolo described such a reading course for parents taught by two reading teachers in the New Haven public schools. Their course met twice a week for ten weeks in high school buildings.[32]

Hunter proposed that school faculties use staff meeting time occasionally to role-play parent conferences. Teachers might learn better to listen to the words and feelings of parents with an atypical problem. They might become more adept at reflecting feelings and probing for better explanations from parents: "Let me see if I understand you now, . . . " "Help me to understand what you meant when you said . . . " or any other forms of neutral responses.[33]

Suedmeyer reported the results of a remedial program for thirty-two fourth graders when the parents of the children were involved in programs to gain awareness and understanding of their children's problems. The parents were assigned to one of four subgroups: One group attended a weekly seminar for six weeks and was given supplemental instruction to enable group members to participate in the tutoring sessions; a second group was given the instruction for participating in tutoring but did not attend

David Woodward

When a teacher makes a home visit, insights into the life of the child are sure to be obtained. The child profits from being able to explain her work to both her parents and the teacher.

weekly seminars; a third group observed the tutoring of their children and participated in ways possible without instruction; and the fourth group did not participate and served as a control. Posttesting did not highlight any significant differences among the four groups. Suedmeyer suggested, however, that the understanding and the ability to verbalize their children's problems achieved by the first two groups would indicate that further investigation over a longer time period might be worthwhile. The overt indications of personal interest on the part of the parents and their suggesting to other parents that they inquire about the service also suggest that further evaluation of the procedure is warranted.[34]

References for Parents

Many books, booklets, and magazine articles have been prepared to give parents advice about working with their children. They vary widely in quality and usefulness. A sampling of such materials is presented here as a resource for teachers as they work with parents.

Boehnlein, Mary. *When Your Child Has Problems in Reading*. Cleveland, Ohio: Cleveland State University, 1979.
Butler, Dorothy. *Babies Need Books*. New York: Atheneum, 1982.
Butler, Dorothy. *Cushla and Her Books*. Boston: The Horn Book, Inc., 1979.
Ervin, Jane. *Reading with Your Child: Number One Priority*. Boston: Allyn and Bacon, 1981.
Lamme, Linda L. *Growing Up Reading*. Washington, D.C.: Acropolis Books, 1985.

Larrick, Nancy. *A Parent's Guide to Children's Literature,* 5th ed. New York: Bantam Books, 1983.

Reed, Arthea J. S. *Comics to Classics: A Parent's Guide to Books for Teens and Preteens.* Newark, Del.: International Reading Association, 1988.

White, Dorothy. *Books before Five.* Portsmouth, N.H.: Heinemann Educational Books, 1984.

Home Visits

Teachers need to approach *home visits* with an optimistic attitude. Such visits should be flexibly planned so that the time may be as short as is comfortable or extended if parents have interest or questions. Bringing samples of children's work is an excellent means of opening conversation. A major purpose of home visits is to get information *from* parents. Be sure that they have ample opportunity to talk. Be a good listener.

Parents as Resources in the Classroom

Some parents find satisfaction in working in the classroom as support to the teacher. They can be helpful in listening to children read and supplying words that are not known. Some parents may be able to make notes about the reading of individuals for the teacher's use. Other parents may prefer to work with small groups in various kinds of assignments and activities, from completing work sheets to bookmaking. Still others may enjoy making games and other instructional materials and learning how they will be used in the classroom. Parents who can type may take dictation as children write books.

If parents are to work with children who have learning difficulties, they must recognize the frustration-tolerance levels of their children and accept and respect them. *Some* parents are able to enjoy:

1. Listening to their children read. Tell the children the words that they are not able to pronounce as they read.
2. Talking about a story read. (What was interesting, unusual, or different; if the child or parent liked it, why?)
3. Reading together, taking turns page by page.
4. Playing word games, for example, *Concentration,* with a pack of sight-word cards.
5. Reading directions in a do-it-yourself kit and assembling something for the learners.

Fortunate are the teachers who learn early in the school year about any "special skills" that some of the parents have. Anyone who makes really good *tortillas* will usually be flattered to be asked to come to school and show the children how *tortillas* are made. Then they can enjoy watching the children eating them. Someone who knows how to do folk dances from other countries may be happy to demonstrate and perhaps teach them to the children. Even a young parent whose memories of his primary school years are not pleasant may be glad to come to school to repair the cage that holds small animals.

Some parents will have traveled, bringing back interesting objects and materials that could make faraway places more real to schoolbound children. Some will have hobbies ranging from rock collecting to knitting and candle making. Such activities will prove to be learning opportunities for children. Other parents may be fine story readers or tellers who can hold children spellbound. It may be possible for some parents to take small groups of children to their homes to cook, build birdhouses, or practice fly casting. Whatever talents parents and other community members may have, teachers should be aware of these and plan ways to use them in the instructional program.

The Advocacy Role

Advocacy means that parents will have strong support and encouragement in asking for optimum education for their children. The conceptual bases for parent advocacy lie in (1) the legal aspect as provided in P.L. 94-142 and supporting court cases; (2) the logical theoretical concept that parents have always been team members at any level or in any phase of their child's program; (3) the research aspect, which shows that parental activity in such areas as motor skills, language development, academic progress, and social skills yields favorable results; and (4) the moral and ethical responsibility to support parents' rights for optimal educational facility for all children. This advocacy approach is a continuing interaction between parents and teachers as partners in assuring appropriate services for handicapped students.[35] Wolf wrote that advocacy groups should be in contact with one another, as well as with school boards, legislators, and school personnel.[36]

McLoughlin, McLoughlin, and Stewart have summarized the positive and negative behaviors concerning advocacy in the interaction of professionals and parents. They further detailed some of the professional responses to disagreements with parents. Examples of these responses are in table 13.1. Parents must be communicated with frequently, actively involved in the educational process of their children, and continually guided in their search for their legal, moral, and ethical rights.

TABLE 13.1. Professional Responses to Disagreements with Parents

Advocate Behavior	*Nonadvocate Behavior*
1. Stays with parents and encourages them not to give up. Keeps trying to communicate.	1. Basically tells parents that they are on their own.
2. Does not take criticisms or rejections of recommendations as personal affronts.	2. Turns red, loses composure, talks loudly and in an angry tone.
3. Continues to suggest and explore alternatives with parents.	3. Gets defensive and slows down the communication process. Gets fidgety and shows impatience.
4. Continues to clarify committee recommendations and provides as much information as possible.	4. Quotes regulations or school policies in attempts to intimidate parents and solve the problem to the satisfaction of self.
5. Stays cool and calm while working on the problem.	

James A. McLoughlin, Robert McLoughlin, and William Stewart, "Advocacy for Parents of the Handicapped: A Professional Responsibility and Challenge," *Learning Disability Quarterly* 2 (Summer 1979): 55.

Summary

In discussing children's work with parents, teachers should accept in principle that the parents will have considerable and unique information to share. In the areas of behavior, physical health, and possible handicapping conditions, the teachers and parents can share information and exchange opinions about working with the children. In one area of operation the teachers should express themselves clearly, however; they should be able to help the parents to understand the nature of the learning process with respect, specifically, to the teaching of reading. In this particular area—reading in the primary grades, when to teach phonics, how much phonics to teach, size of the child's basic sight vocabulary, present reader level in a reading book—the classroom teacher should share his or her background of knowledge and approach to the teaching of reading so that the parents can expect whatever adjustments are necessary in accommodating their children in the classroom.

Teachers must see children's problems objectively and not become defensive about not having all the answers. If the teacher has assigned Charlene, described earlier in this chapter, to a sixth-grade reading book, he has made a mistake that must be faced realistically and corrected. Teachers need *never* answer parents' comments about their children's failures with superficial responses: "He's doing quite well lately," or "Don't be worried; he's getting along all right." If the parents say that the child needs easier material and the teacher has not checked to find out, an informal reading inventory is indicated to find out about missing skills.

There are ways that parents can and must help their children, including participating in the school program; but these do not include the teaching of the "how-to-read" skills. Suggestions for conducting profitable parent-teacher conferences and interviews about the child's reading, and a list of books about children's reading were included in this chapter.

For Further Reading

Boehnlein, Mary Maher, and Beth H. Hager. *Children, Parents, and Reading.* Newark, Del.: International Reading Association, 1985. The authors have assembled an extensive annotated bibliography of books and articles concerning the parents' role in reading. The book also contains a list of children's magazines.

Childrey, Jr., John A. "Home Remedies for Reluctant Readers." In *Motivating Reluctant Readers.* Edited by Alfred J. Ciani. Newark, Del.: International Reading Association, 1981. Elaborates on areas such as modeling reading, using the library, developing areas of interest, and gifts of reading.

Dreher, Mariam J. "Making Standardized Achievement Test Performance More Understandable for Parents." *Reading Improvement* 22 (Summer 1985): 98–101. The author suggests that teachers discuss tests at parent conferences, define test terminology in lay language, provide examples of test items, and encourage the comparison of the child's performance with past performance.

Fredericks, Anthony D., and David Taylor. *Parent Programs in Reading: Guidelines for Success.* Newark, Del.: International Reading Association, 1985. This is a complete guide for involving parents with the school reading program. Several sample checklists and evaluation instruments are provided.

Greaney, Vincent. "Parental Influences on Reading." *Reading Teacher* 39 (April 1986): 813–18. The author examines aspects of the home environment, citing research to support his points. He notes the effects on reading of age, gender, and the child's position in the sibling order.

Hanson, Shirley, and Michael Sporakowski. "Single Parent Families." *Family Relations* 35 (January 1986): 3–8. In 1984 single parents headed 25.7 percent of all families. This fact has significance for many aspects of children's lives, including school.

Heath, Shirley Brice. *Ways with Words: Language, Life, and Work in Communities and Classrooms.* Cambridge: Cambridge University Press, 1983. This is the report of an *important* study of communities and their interface with schools and literacy.

Kroth, Roger, and Richard Simpson. *Parent Conferences as a Teaching Strategy.* Denver: Love Publishing Co., 1977. This is a practical guide for conducting effective parent conferences. It is grounded in sound theory.

McLaughlin, Milbrey, and Patrick Shields. "Involving Low-Income Parents in the Schools: A Role for Policy?" *Phi Delta Kappan* 69 (October 1987): 156–60. We can no longer afford to ignore low-income parents in the education of their children. Professionals must meet the need by trying new strategies for involving them.

Shields, Portia H., Jessica Gordon, and David Dupree. "Influence of Parent Practices upon the Reading Achievement of Good and Poor Readers." *Journal of Negro Education* 52, no. 4 (1983): 436–45. Low-income parents do try to help their children to learn to read. Parents of good readers can serve as models to help other parents to support the reading of their children more effectively.

Taylor, Denny, and Dorothy Strickland. *Family Storybook Reading.* Portsmouth, N.H.: Heinemann Educational Books, 1986. The authors answer parents' questions about how to read to children, how to make reading to children contribute to their learning to read, where to find books, and how to select good books.

Notes

1. Ira J. Gordon, "The Effects of Parent Involvement on Schooling," in *Partners: Parents and Schools,* ed. Ronald S. Brandt (Alexandria, Va.: Association for Supervision and Curriculum Development, 1979), 4–5.

2. Edward J. Kelly, *Parent-Teacher Interaction* (Seattle, Wash.: Special Child Publications, Bernie Straub Publishing Co., 1974), 143.

3. Cherry Houck and Ann Sherman, "The Mainstreaming Current Flows Two Ways," *Academic Therapy* 15 (November 1979): 133–40.

4. Daniel P. Hallahan et al., "Questions about the Regular Education Initiative," *Journal of Learning Disabilities* 21 (January 1988): 3.

5. Dorothy J. McGinnis and Dorothy E. Smith, *Analyzing and Treating Reading Problems* (New York: Macmillan, 1982), 163.

6. Mary Wollner, "Should Parents Coddle Their Retarded Readers?" *Education* 80 (March 1960): 431.

7. Ibid., 432.

8. Albert J. Harris and Edward R. Sipay, *How to Increase Reading Ability,* 8th ed. (New York: Longman, 1985), 317.

9. Ibid., 317–18.

10. Ellen Gray and Peter Coolsen, "How Do Kids Really Feel about Being Home Alone?" *Children Today* 16 (July–August 1987): 30–32; and Bryan E. Robinson, Bobbie H. Rowland, and Mick Coleman, "Taking Action for Latchkey Children and Their Families," *Family Relations* 35 (October 1986): 473–77.

11. Elene S. Demos, "Technological Resources for Parents," *Reading Horizons* 28 (January 1988): 85–92.

12. Guy L. Bond et al., *Reading Difficulties: Their Diagnosis and Correction,* 6th ed. (Englewood Cliffs, N.J.: Prentice-Hall, 1989), 76–78.

13. Wollner, "Should Parents Coddle Their Retarded Readers?" 430.

14. Ibid.

15. Emery Bliesmer, "Some Notes on Helping Children with Reading Difficulties," *Education* 77 (May 1957): 551–54.

16. Beatrice Lieben, "Attitudes, Platitudes, and Conferences in Teacher-Parent Relations Involving the Child with a Reading Problem," *Elementary School Journal* 58 (February 1958): 279–86.

17. Ibid., 280.

18. Ibid., 281.

19. Ibid., 280.

20. Ibid., 282.

21. Fritz Redl and William W. Wattenberg, *Mental Hygiene in Teaching,* 2d. ed. (New York: Harcourt, Brace, 1959), 452–76.

22. McGinnis and Smith, *Analyzing and Treating Reading Problems,* 163.

23. Barbara K. Iverson et al., "Parent-Teacher Contacts and Student Learning," *Journal of Educational Research* 74 (July–August 1981): 394–96.

24. Hope J. Leichter, "Families as Environments for Literacy," in *Awakening to Literacy,* ed. Hillel Goelman, Antoinette Oberg, and Frank Smith (Portsmouth, N.H.: Heinemann Educational Books, 1984), 45–46.

25. Joan S. Wolf, "Parents as Partners in Exceptional Education," *Theory into Practice* 21 (Spring 1982): 77.

26. Shirley C. Samuels, "Johnny's Mother Isn't Interested," *Today's Education* 62 (February 1973): 37.

27. Emilia Ferreiro and Ana Teberosky, *Literacy before Schooling.* (Exeter, N.H.: Heinemann Educational Books, 1982), 4.

28. Robert M. Wilson and Craig J. Cleland, *Diagnostic and Remedial Reading for Classroom and Clinic,* 5th ed. (Columbus: Merrill Publishing Co., 1985), 372–73.

29. Eldon K. Ekwall and James L. Shanker, *Diagnosis and Remediation of the Disabled Reader,* 2d ed. (Boston: Allyn and Bacon, 1983), 412–13.

30. Roger Kroth, *Communicating with Parents of Exceptional Children* (Denver: Love Publishing Co., 1973), 9–10.

31. Marsha L. Roit and William Pfohl, "The Readability of P.L. 94–142 Parent Materials: Are Parents Truly Informed?" *Exceptional Children* 50 (April 1984): 504.

32. Nicholas Criscuolo, "Reaching Unreachable Parents," *Journal of Reading* 17 (January 1974): 285–87.

33. Madeline Hunter, "Staff Meeting: Madeline Hunter Discusses Parent Conferences," *Instructor* 83 (February 1974): 18.

34. Joan Ann Suedmeyer, "Reading Remediation, Parent Group Meetings and Reading Performance of Fourth Grade Children," *Dissertation Abstracts International,* vol. 32 (Ann Arbor, Mich.: University Microfilms, 1972), 4256A–57A.
35. James A. McLoughlin, Robert McLoughlin, and William Stewart, "Advocacy for Parents of the Handicapped: A Professional Responsibility and Challenge," *Learning Disability Quarterly* 2 (Summer 1979): 51–57; 62.
36. Wolf, "Parents as Partners," 78.

14
Teaching Children with Limited English Proficiency in the Regular Classroom

Vocabulary

limited English proficiency
affective environment
empowerment
language structure
discourse analysis
dialectology
bidialectal
standard English
natural approach
affective filter
total physical response
BICS
CALP
think tank model
common underlying
   proficiency
theme approach
intellectual kits
peer tutoring
cultural relevance

Questions

1. Why does teaching limited-English-proficiency children begin with their affective lives? **(Inference)**
2. What are the four ways of describing language? **(Recall)**
3. Describe the meaning of the term *dialectology*. Why is an understanding of dialectology important for teachers? **(Inference)**
4. Describe the natural approach. **(Recall)**
5. Compare and contrast *BICS* and *CALP*. **(Evaluation)**
6. What are elements of the theme approach that would help you to work with limited-English-proficiency children in your class? **(Application)**
7. Describe what is meant by culturally relevant materials. **(Recall)**

Introduction

An adult with severely *limited English proficiency* is described below:

Marco, a Spanish-American twenty-year-old who was enrolled in Job Corps, came to a university reading clinic. Though he wanted to learn to read very much, the best efforts of his tutor produced few results. After four weeks he could write his name and recognize a few words, such as *stop,* from the environment. An interview was part of an effort to get to the heart of his problem. He was the son of a migrant worker in the Texas-Oklahoma-Kansas corridor. He remembered first grade, his kind teacher, and a book about a family that he learned to read. But his own family soon moved on, and he remembered no other kindly teachers or books that he could read. He dropped out of school in sixth grade and drifted until he enrolled in Job Corps at nineteen. The interviewer questioned him about the book he had learned to read and, on a chance, showed him an old copy of *We Look and See,*[1] the first of the Dick and Jane preprimers. His eyes lit up, and he took the book, thumbing through its pages fondly. A few of the words were identified for him, and he proceeded to piece together several of the simple stories. He was given the book, and he took it with him as though it were a treasure. Such an irrelevant book for this man, but it represented his own brief period of success in school!

Although learning English is, of course, a necessity for everyone in an English-speaking country, in a pluralistic society it is not the only priority. Children who are learning English as a second language have a first language that is very much a part of their system of meanings and ways of learning. The goal of teaching English as a second language is to help children "adopt a positive attitude to their bilingualism and wherever possible help them maintain and deepen their knowledge of their mother tongue."[2]

According to Irving:

> The . . . teacher must remember that in a social context, although it is possible not to speak, it is impossible not to communicate. Learning to communicate in a new culture means learning *what* to say (words, phrases, meaning, structure), *who* to say it to (role perception, status hierarchies), *who you are* (self-concept), *how* to say it (affective components, nonverbal cues, intonation, and stress), *why* you say it (intentions, values, assumptions, attitudes), *when* you say it (time), and *where* you say it. We learn all these things in our native language without thinking about the complexity of the issues involved. But when we are teaching students to communicate in a second language, we must first be aware ourselves and then make our students aware of the complexities of communicating interculturally.[3]

One cannot *not* communicate. If you say nothing when you were expected to respond, you have communicated something. A telephone call that does not come may communicate as much as it would if it had come, if you were really expecting it. An incessant talker may say little about the subject but be telling the listener a great deal about himself or herself as a person.

Coping

Helping students to experience success in school depends more on the *affective environment* than on cognitive abilities. In order to be advocates for children, we need to legitimize their current behaviors, negotiate with students in planning lessons, and then offer positive reinforcement for learning. This *empowerment* of the individual will have ramifications in the process of learning to read as well as in the child's development in other areas. In the classroom, teachers will need (1) to recognize that evaluation of the child's current achievement may require different materials or experiences in the curriculum and (2) to negotiate with the child what he or she might learn, how best to work on learning it, and how to measure the success of the learning.

The Affective Life of the Child

Before we think about teaching English as a new language, or any subject matter for that matter, to the students, we must be prepared to respond to the student's needs, attitudes, and feelings. One needs to have and maintain a strong ego, to feel good about oneself, and to have and retain confidence.

The teacher's first effort needs to be directed toward the student and must give consideration to:

> Who is this person who needs special help with learning to converse in
> the English language?
> Has the child tried to learn the language elsewhere?
> How fluently does he or she now use it?
> How large is the student's English speaking vocabulary?
> Has this person already learned some negative behaviors that will affect
> retention of the content that you are planning to teach?
> Does the child feel like a failure?
> Does he or she manifest anxiety in the classroom situation?
> Is the student willing to take risks and to make mistakes?

What are the child's interests, likes, and dislikes? If these students express no special interests, we need to encourage them to develop some. Do they admire either of their parents very much? Have the children tell about events in their own lives: games, television shows, or pets of special interest. Watching the child play such games as *Old Maid, Concentration, King's Corners, Uno,* or *Dominoes* with peers may be a way to evaluate the child's concentration and willingness to take risks in a situation where knowledge of language may be less necessary. How well is the learner accepted by peers? Perhaps a sociogram that maps choices of three friends will reveal something about acceptance. Does the student enjoy comics or cartoons in newspapers and magazines?

Building Positive Relationships

Giving consideration to the affective domain in the child's life, we seek to build positive relationships. The components of this approach may involve new vocabulary for some teachers: (1) *empowering* the student, (2) being an *advocate* for the student, (3) allowing the learner to *negotiate* about his or her assignments, and (4) *legitimizing* the behavior and the expression of the learner. (See chapter 1.)

1. Teachers must *empower* the students to feel good about themselves.[4] The learners need to have confidence and strong egos in order to feel free to take risks in anticipating meaning in the use of language. Can they help to plan their course of study? Are they willing to write what they master in oral language?
2. The teacher's role includes the responsibility of being an *advocate* for the child. The teacher must be willing to make whatever adjustments are necessary in the generally inflexible school curriculum to provide successful learning experiences for any student who needs such adjustment.

The Structure of the English Language

Goodman summarized five principles from linguistics that teachers should know and use:

1. By the time they come to school, children have already achieved virtual mastery over the oral language of their community. In the language-experience approach, new emphasis must be given to preserving the *real* language of the child—his or her grammar, phrasing, vocabulary—instead of the teacher's style of language or that of the preprimer he is trying to learn to read.
2. Language is systematic. Words have to be arranged in an acceptable pattern within a language system in order to carry meaning. The system of language is its grammar. (Word lists, flash cards, and phonic charts isolate elements from their meaningful grammatical contexts.) The child senses, deep within the self, the grammar of his or her language—that is, understanding of the ideas expressed in sentences in that language.
3. A language is a family of mutually understood dialects. Each speaker of a language speaks one or more of these dialects. Dialects can and do differ in sounds (phonemes), inflections (word endings), grammar, intonation, vocabulary, and idioms.
4. Language is constantly changing. The child with a dialect has the same kind of language resource as any other child. The teacher should not confuse this student by correcting him or her when what the student has read is consonant with his or her own dialect.

5. Though English uses an alphabetic writing system, the oral and written systems have considerable irregularity in phoneme-grapheme correspondence. The reading program must be personalized to make it relevant to the learner or groups of learners.[5]

Ways to Describe Language

Language has phonology, morphology, syntax, and semantics. *Phonology* is the study of the distinct sounds of the language. The alphabet is an imperfect representation of the English phonemes. So, we have forty-four phonemes represented by twenty-six letters. Phonemes combine into meaningful sound units called *morphemes,* which may be words or parts of words. Morphology is the study of these smallest meaningful units of language. The morphemes that are especially important in elementary school are compound words, inflectional endings, prefixes, suffixes, and Greek and Latin combining forms. *Syntax* is often thought of as the grammar of the language. More precisely, it is the set of rules governing how morphemes are combined into sentences. *Semantics* is the study of meanings communicated through language. Table 14.1 is a diagram that details these four facets of language.

Phonology

The phonology (sound) of words includes the following features:

1. There are forty-four separate phonemes in English but only twenty-six letters in the alphabet.
2. Many times we rely on context to determine which meaning of a word is being used. The part of speech of the word may tell us what meaning to attach.
3. One phonemic difference can completely change the meaning in a pair of words. When two words have only one phonemic difference, they are said to be a minimal pair. Teachers have traditionally taught children a great deal of "phonics" distinguishing minimal pairs; for example, the final sounds: pi*ck*-pi*g,* ma*p*-ma*t.*
4. Accent patterns change meanings phonemically. A *black bird* is not necessarily a *blackbird;* nor is the *green house* necessarily a *greenhouse.*
5. The phoneme-grapheme relationships are confusing in English because some consonants have more than one sound and the five vowel letters have many sounds.
6. The suprasegmentals of stress, pitch, and juncture convey phonemic differences:
   Did you buy the *book?*
   Did you *buy* the book?
   Did *you* buy the book?
   Was that the *greenhouse?*
   Was that the *Green* house?
   Was that the *green* house?

TABLE 14.1. The Structure of Language

Phonology	Morphology	Syntax	Semantics
Phonology is the study of the distinctive sounds of language.	Morphology is the study of the smallest meaningful units of language, called *morphemes,* which are mainly words or parts of words. Morphemes especially important in elementary school teaching are:	Syntax is often thought of as the grammar of a language. More precisely, it is the set of rules governing how morphemes are combined into sentences.	Semantics is the study of the meanings communicated through language.
1. There are 44 distinctive sounds, called *phonemes,* in the English language. (Sources differ: 40, 44, 45, 47.) The alphabet is an imperfect representation of those sounds.	1. Compound words. 2. Inflectional endings *er, est, ed, ing, s, es.* 3. Prefixes and suffixes. 4. The common Greek and Latin combining forms.	1. Word order, an important distinctive feature of English, is an aspect of syntax (a *pocket watch* is not the same as a *watch pocket*).	1. English is a language with a rich vocabulary, or lexicon, which has many words borrowed from other languages.
2. Phonemes combine into distinctive meaningful units, called *morphemes,* which are words or parts of words.		2. Basic ("kernel") sentence patterns: a. Noun— transitive verb—object b. Noun—linking verb—predicate noun or adjective c. Noun—verb— prepositional phrase	2. The listener or the reader must rely on context clues; meanings depend upon context.
3. Minimal pairs are two words with only one phonemic difference, which changes meaning (pick-pig, map-mat, big-pig, big-bag).		3. Transformations: a. Negative statements b. *Or* changes c. Expansions d. *There* changes e. Question changes f. Passive changes g. Combined kernel sentences h. *Until, if, because* changes i. Tense changes	3. The language contains many figures of speech, idiomatic expressions, and slang expressions.
4. Stress and juncture (called *suprasegmentals)* are also distinctive features of English, comparable to phonemes, which change meaning. (*You* bought that. You *bought* that. You bought *that.* A blue bird is not necessarily a bluebird.)			4. The vocabulary contains antonyms, heteronyms, homographs, homonyms, synonyms.
5. The phoneme-grapheme relationships are often confusing in English because the same sound may have many variant spellings, and different sounds may have the same spellings.			5. Suprasegmentals, which are phonemic, are also semantic in communicating meaning changes.

Miles V. Zintz and Zelda R. Maggart, *The Reading Process: The Teacher and the Learner,* 5th ed. (Dubuque, Iowa: Wm. C. Brown, 1988), 75.

Morphology

The morphology (structure) of words includes the following features:

1. Teaching of compound words.
2. Teaching inflectional endings *er, est, ed, ing, s, es.*
3. Teaching prefixes and suffixes.
4. Teaching contractions.
5. Teaching the common Greek and Latin combining forms.
6. Teaching the dictionary skills for reading and writing.

Syntax

Syntax is the grammar of the language. Grammar is the set of rules governing the use of the language so that people can communicate meaningfully with each other.

1. Generally, native speakers have no difficulty mastering language syntax that they hear from their models as they grow up. If they hear nonstandard English, they will learn to speak nonstandard English.
2. The language is quite arbitrary in following a specific, prescribed structure. One can say, "The pencil is brown," but one cannot say, "The is pencil brown."
3. The basic sentence patterns of children are:
   a. Noun—transitive verb—object
   b. Noun—linking verb—predicate noun or adjective
   c. Noun—verb—prepositional phrase
4. Sentences can be *transformed* to discuss an idea in different ways. Meanings become more complicated when the passive voice is used instead of the active voice.

Semantics

Teachers must build on *the oral language base* that the children have. Yet, ways are not available to determine that base for all children. The children may know the meaning of the sentence when you say, "The boy *cries*." But if you change *cries* to a noun in "The *cries* of the boy were heard," do they know? They may understand, "We are going to the *circus*," but that is not the same *circus* in "We saw the *circus* clown." They may understand, "Put it on the *table*," but not, "*Table* the motion" or "Look in the *table* of numbers." The readers bring preconceived predictions to the reading; they read by following what they see and what they expect to see.

The beginning readers learn to zero in on the most helpful clue, which is usually the initial consonant. The reading process may then break down into three steps:

1. Predict;
2. Sample and select; and
3. Test it out.

In decoding the word *lead,* for example, when the linguistic form carries the information, "it is a noun and refers to a metal," the word is pronounced *led;* when it conveys the information, "it is a verb and refers to guiding or direction," it is pronounced *leed*—but both words are spelled alike. Consider the linguistic forms of *mist* and *missed.* I *missed* the exit and could not get off the expressway. Or, the dense morning *mist* hid the house from view.[6]

Transformational grammar has two *levels* of syntactical structure: a surface level and a deep structure level. The *surface* level is that which is directly observed in the words themselves—"on the surface," so to speak. *Deep structure* is the meaning, or interpretation, level. The deep structure level of language must be developed if students are to use language accurately and wisely.

Bowen's example of two sentences with the same *pattern* on the surface clearly requires two very different interpretations:

Mary is *anxious* to paint.
Mary is *difficult* to paint.

In one case, Mary wants to do the painting herself; in the other, Mary is the subject of someone else's painting.[7]

Rutherford also illustrated the differences in meaning in many pairs of sentences that look on the surface to follow the same pattern:

1. What he wants is *more* of your business.
   What he wants is *none* of your business.
2. It was a moving *train.*
   It was a moving *experience.*
3. Who's the person you want to (want ta) call? (You make the call.)
   Who's the person you want to (wanna) call? (The person calls you.)[8]

The sentence "I had Mary for lunch and made sandwiches" is clear in its deep structure. If one judged only on the surface language, it suggests that the speaker is a cannibal.[9]

Goldfield made some significant statements about "reading for meaning" and its dependence on semantics:

Strictly speaking, one doesn't "get" meaning from print. Rather, he "gives" or "produces" a meaning. For example, ask students to explain "The chicken is too hot to eat." Responses could vary: too stove-hot to eat; too spicy to eat; a stolen chicken; or even a chicken who is too overcome by the sun to eat its feed.[10]

Efficient readers realize that words are not things they point to—the menu is not the meal. They understand that there are not written facts, only statements about facts. With this in mind, the able reader will not react to words as though they were, indeed, life facts.[11]

. . . semantic awareness alerts the student that there is no one, exact meaning to words or phrases. It compels the reader to define terms with specific examples, and repeatedly demonstrates that most of the meaning is not in words but in people.[12]

Discourse Analysis

Another way to study language is to attend to units larger than words or sentences. This study, *discourse analysis,* provides the means for analysis of both oral and written texts and the settings in which they are produced.[13]

> Because the analyst is investigating the use of language in context by a speaker/writer, he is more concerned with the relationship between the speaker and the utterance, on the particular occasion of use, than with the potential relationship of one sentence to another, regardless of their use.[14]

Two important characteristics of discourse or text as related to reading are:

1. Cohesion—those strategies that speakers have to bind parts of texts together. The interpretation of some element in the discourse is dependent on that of another.[15] Elements that are cohesive include substitution, ellipsis, pronominalization, conjunctions, and lexical cohesion.[16]

Substitution	This copy is blurred. I need a clear *one.*
Ellipsis	This is a tasty pie. I've never *tasted better.*
Pronominalization	Bill chose Sue to work, and *he* put *her* to work stapling booklets.
Conjunctions	Sam wanted a winesap apple *because* he remembered the ones from his parents' tree on the farm.
Lexical cohesion	The *Coral Sea* is one of this country's older carriers.

2. Inference—the process that the reader (hearer) must go through to get from the literal meaning of what is written (or said) to what the writer (speaker) intended to convey.[17] The reader or listener must fill in one or more gaps to arrive at the intended meaning.
   The children swished down the hill on their
   sleds.
   They picked up speed as they went over the
   frozen snow.

   The reader must infer that sleds are used for traveling over snow and that speed is related to going downhill and to slick surfaces. Poor readers are frequently troubled by the need to make inferences as they read. Teachers need to help children to identify texts that require readers to infer meaning and to talk through the steps in thinking that may be required to make sense of the material.

Dialectology: Language Problems of Bidialectal Children

Many black children feel that our society has rejected them. Many feel that it has rejected them because they are black. Black children soon acquire a poor self-concept. They interpret blackness, poor self-concept, and so forth as inferiority.

Many black children speak a nonstandard dialect of English that differs, in varying degrees among blacks, from *standard English*. For six-year-olds in school, nonstandard English sets up the same types of interference that a second language does to learning to read in standard English and to obtaining cognitive learning in standard English. Many teachers believe that the language spoken by these children is inferior and lacks complete grammatical construction and lexical form. This is not true. Their morphology and verb structure constitute a complete grammar. The black children may have a very great number of words in their speech that substitute for words ordinarily used in standard English. If the teachers are aware—know about the substitution of words or phrases for words commonly used in their own speech—no serious language problems need exist between the teachers and children. One language is not inferior, another superior; the two dialects of the language are just different.

When the teachers reject the children's language as "careless"—that is, "bad"—the children will likely feel that they are being rejected as people. In rejecting them, the teachers must also be rejecting those who mean the most to them, their immediate families. If the teachers continually say, "Don't say it like that, say it like this," the children interpret this as a rejection of them through their ways of behaving.

The black children, especially of the inner-city poor, have a number of reasons other than language to believe that the teachers' values and life-style have little in common with theirs.

The absence of a father in many black families has a debilitating effect on boys. Aggressiveness is likely to be valued more than intellectualism. The readiness of these children for beginning school is different. Ghetto elementary schools need more black male teachers.

According to Labov:

> One of the most extraordinary failures in the history of American Education is the failure of the public school system to teach black children in the urban ghettos to read. The fact of reading failure is so general, and so widespread, that no one school system, no one method, and no one teacher can be considered responsible.[18]

Labov illustrated the phonological problems of the *"r*-lessness," the *"l*-lessness," the difficulties with consonant clusters, and the weak final consonants. The *r* is absent in pronouncing *guard* as *god,* or *nor* more like *gnaw.* Without *l, toll* becomes *toe, help* becomes *hep*, and *tool* becomes *too.* Words ending with *st, ft, nt,* or *ld* usually lose the last consonant: *fast* becomes *fas; don't* becomes *don.* Weakened final consonants cause *seat* or *seed* to become *see; poor, poke,* or *pope* to become *poo'.*

Labov suggested that teachers:

1. Distinguish carefully between dialectic differences in pronunciation and errors in reading.
2. It may help to spend more time on the grammar of the language to help some children understand the two ways in which the language is spoken.
3. Extra auditory perception instruction may be helpful in teaching children to hear and make distinctions in standard and nonstandard speech.

4. Work on the premise that children can learn to read standard English texts in a nonstandard pronunciation. The teachers need to know the language of the children—both its lexical and grammatical forms—as well as standard English . . . and the differences between the two.
5. The teachers need to determine that the children "know" both differences in *meaning* and in *sound* if they think *cold* and *coal* are both *col.*[19]

Stewart reminded us that the black children may be able to set up their own sound-spelling correspondences—a system different from that of the speakers of standard English—but that allows them effective word identification. For example, they will likely substitute *f* and *v* for two sounds of *th,* so that they learn to use *f* or *v* for *th* when *th* appears other than at the beginning of the word. Thus, they are able to read *bref* for *breath* and *brev* for *breathe.*[20]

Educators have often been blinded by their ethnocentric and egocentric ways of viewing education problems. Thus, when large numbers of speakers of nonstandard English failed to learn to read, our immediate assumption was "faulty language." We might more logically have blamed instructional methods and materials. Myers cautioned about the need to respect cognitive styles and learning preferences:

> The holistic world view of African culture has special significance . . . affective/cognitive separations are artificial for them . . . intellectual stimulation, teacher/student rapport, and personal, physical and environmental well-being all come together as mandatory concerns for the best learning situation.[21]

The teachers must believe that, for certain dialect speakers, the sentence "The dog, he look funny" is an accurate and meaningful translation of the printed words "The dog looks funny." This is a meaningful realization of a standard English sentence for a nonstandard speaker. The insertion of "he" and the omission of "s" from "looks" have traditionally been considered word-recognition errors. We now know that they are not reading errors for certain dialect speakers. The teachers must recognize they are not errors.[22]

The bidialectal children must be permitted to read standard material in their own dialects. Likewise, they will learn to read more readily if their first language-experience stories are written in the dialect of the language that they speak. Cramer wrote:

> The language experience approach is predicated upon the notion that reading can be most meaningfully taught when the reading materials accurately reflect the child's own experience as described by his language. The language of instruction then must be that which proceeds from the wealth of linguistic, conceptual and perceptual experience of the child.
>
> The language experience approach is an ideal means of overcoming the instructional problem created for the divergent speaker (the bidialectal child) by the mismatch between his language and the language of beginning reading materials. The language experience reading avoids the necessity of writing reading textbooks in dialect; it asserts that the child's nonstandard dialect is ideal for initiating him into the mysteries of reading written language.[23]

Making Connections 14.1: Experiencing Another Language

Though we may verbalize how we would function in a setting in which we do not know the language, many teachers have had few such first-hand experiences. In completing this assignment, you will have an opportunity to explore some of the feelings that accompany such an experience.

Arrange with your instructor to spend at least an hour and preferably longer in a setting where the language in use is unknown to you. It will be a better experience if you are not able to be a passive observer, but must actually try to communicate and to understand the meanings of others. You may need to be creative to find a setting. A few suggestions are an ethnic club such as a German Club in a community, a meeting of a specific group of foreign students at your college or university, perhaps a family that will enjoy helping you with the experience, a classroom conducted in another language, or a preschool where small children are speaking another language.

After your experience, come to class prepared to talk about what you learned and how you felt during the visit. Share the strategies you used to communicate when language was denied to you. Then apply what you learned during this experience to the life of children in the classroom who speak little or no English. You should be a more sensitive teacher because of this experience.

Methodology for Teaching Students with Limited English Proficiency

The Natural Approach

In the past decade, one method of teaching that has been widely accepted by English-as-a-second-language (ESL) specialists is the *"natural approach"* to language learning. The natural approach encompasses three major facets:

1. Knowledge about how language is acquired;
2. Provision of maximum input of learning stimuli to the learner, which is *always comprehensible* to her or him;
3. Low-anxiety environment in which the child's *affect* is always positive and where the non-English-speaker feels that success is likely. (We protect the child's ego or self-esteem and *prevent* failure.)

Krashen and Terrell emphasized that the *comprehensible input* (item 2 above) and low anxiety resulting from the teacher's skillful *affective filter* (item 3 above) are the two most significant factors in language learning.[24] About the first point, language acquisition, Terrell wrote:

Language acquisition refers to the unconscious absorption of general principles of grammar through real experiences of communication using the second language (L-2). It is the basis for most first language ability and with respect to L-2 is commonly known as "picking up the language."[25]

Dulay and Burt differentiated between meaningful messages for the boys and girls and what may be the teacher's lesson plan:

Perhaps the most important characteristic of a natural communication situation that is most overlooked in language classrooms is that the attention of the speaker and hearer is on the *message* or the content of the verbal exchange rather than on its form. Yet, most language teaching materials focus on the structures to be taught, often with the result that the message of the sentences taught, if there is one, is meaningless for both teachers and children.[26]

Natural language learning requires that the children take an *active role* in communication and that they are willing to take calculated risks in interacting verbally with others. Further, they need to be able to *negotiate* with others about the language to be presented. This means that useful language must respond to the question: Who says what, to whom, and for what purpose? Negotiation means that the children have choices about the time, the manner, and the extent to which they will initiate language responses or conversation in their interactions with others.

Brian Gray has helped teachers to develop and expand *concentrated* encounters with children. The encounter is any meaningful situation in which language context is developed, expanded, and shared by the teacher and children. Probing and modeling strategies enable teachers to maximize language development. Gray gave "saddling a horse" and "making toast" as two examples of context in the real-life experiences of the boys and girls with whom he works.[27]

As one who works with aborigine children in the Northern Territory of Australia, Gray has asked teachers to move *from* the inflexible *textbook content* planned by experts from far away *to* children's learning contexts worked out by the children with the help of their teacher. The ESL program of twenty years ago that failed to produce the desired results was designed by someone who decided what to teach and when to teach it, was used by teachers who were asked to follow a guidebook, and often was *not mastered* by the children who were not invited to express an opinion about its content. Gray suggested that we start by *empowering* the children to express their feelings about what content is important, interesting, or necessary to them, and encourage them to talk about it. Children will talk when or because they want or need to talk. In this way, children negotiate their own language development. Then the only methodology the teacher needs is that of *facilitating effective interaction* to get language out of the children that can be used for talking, writing, and reading. *Concentrated encounters* become significant when the teacher finds out what language, in the child's current circumstances, is important to him or her and serves a need. Once the teacher finds this out, he can then negotiate topics of conversation of intrinsic interest to the boys and girls.

Developing Listening Fluency

Asher has contributed two very significant notions to the teaching of English as a second language.[28] First, he found that learners of new languages need *time* to hear the language before trying to respond by using it. He recommended that language lessons continue for weeks with the teacher using the language and the learners demonstrating understanding of it without speaking it. The idea is that the mind needs to hear the rhythm, the suprasegmentals, and the intonation of the language for some time before the learner needs or is ready to try to imitate it.

The Total Physical Response

The second contribution of Asher has been termed the *total physical response*. Total physical response is a point of view that in the beginning all the new language learning should be *to understand spoken commands* and to exercise these commands—but the method does not require speaking any language. For example, the teacher says, "Stand up." Those who are directed to do so stand up. The teacher says, "Turn around twice," and everyone in the group turns around twice. The learner executes the command but the child is not required to say anything.[29]

These two concepts—that we should give the learner ample time to get ready to speak the language before demanding oral responses and that the first learning in the new language should be language to which the child or learner can respond through physical activity to show understanding—are very important concepts in the natural approach to language learning.

The Interdependence of Literacy in Two Languages

Jim Cummins, at the Ontario Institute for Studies in Education, has made some significant contributions to understanding how the student learns a second language. According to Cummins, the use of either of two languages, under positive conditions, promotes the development of proficiency in both languages. He differentiated two levels at which boys and girls use the language and the significance of this difference. And he has concluded, with support from other researchers, that boys and girls need five to seven years in school undergirded by the use of their first language to give them enough time to master the second language sufficiently to use it for regular academic work. These items are explained below:

There are two diametrically different conceptions about the learning of two languages. One notion is that learning a second language is sure to detract from greater mastery of the first language; the other notion is that the two languages, in long-term memory in the brain, complement each other. The first point of view is that if one learns two languages, they constitute two separate linguistic systems in the brain. Thus, one has a separate underlying proficiency for each language. This implies that the more one is stimulated to develop one language, the more the other language will be diminished. So, if the second-language learners continue to have instruction in language one, they will be less efficient in the learning of language two. While this common assumption is widely believed, *it is not true*. (See figure 14.1.) During the last two decades of bilingual instruction in the public schools, *no* evidence has been found to support

Unilingual   Bilingual

Figure 14.1. The Think Tank Model utilizes and builds on knowledge of both languages. Some people believe, as shown in the center picture, that one has a "given" quantity of language ability. Anyone who tries to develop two languages will have less capacity for each. This has been called the balance effect theory. In the picture at the right, the think tank model shows that L1 and L2 develop in one language area in the brain. Both languages combined can nurture greater language ability. If the students master vocabulary, grammar, and concepts in one language, they need only to learn the word equivalents in a second language and can then function well in both. Adapted from Jim Cummins, *Bilingualism and Minority Language Children* (Toronto, Ontario: Ontario Institute for Studies in Education, 1981), 27–32. Used with permission).

this model.[30] This point of view has been working against adequate education of Spanish-American children in New Mexico and Texas for generations.

Cummins supported a model of bilingualism that he called the *common underlying proficiency.* The cognitive/academic proficiency gained in language one is equally useful in language two if the learner knows the labels in both languages. This means that the literacy skills in the two languages are interdependent. This model tells us that the use of either language in meaningful contexts promotes the development of proficiency in both languages if there is adequate exposure to the second language to apply all the concepts learned in the first language.

The Acronyms BICS and CALP

The teacher must help the new language learner to develop enough sophistication to succeed in the regular classroom and to achieve on a par with his or her age-mates. Cummins has explained that two aspects to the language program are important. First, there are the *basic interpersonal communicative skills* (BICS), which include all the language needed for the interpersonal communication during the day. Greetings, talk about the weather, personal questions that teachers must ask to complete their records, directions, and general commands and responses constitute basic interpersonal communicative skills. These few hundred most common expressions (What's your name? How old are you? What did you do yesterday?) were the primary content of the early ESL drill books.

But another corpus of language that is needed to insure success in academic subjects is *cognitive/academic language proficiency* (CALP). Cognitive/academic language proficiency is the dimension of language related to achievement in school. Understanding concepts of time, measurement, and distance in mathematics; understanding metaphor, simile, and idiom in literature; and knowing the meanings of the concepts of latitude, altitude, the equator, and the life zones of the earth are all examples of this cognitive/academic language.[31]

How Long Does It Take?

If one accepts the distinction presented in the terms *CALP* and *BICS,* then one must think seriously about the levels at which boys and girls are to be *admitted to* and *terminated from* bilingual programs in the schools. In the transitional programs, the directors tend to move children back to the mainstreamed classes, without additional help, as early as possible.

Clearly, transferring boys and girls out of the bilingual programs must not be based only on measuring their basic interpersonal ability to converse. Such "natural communication" is not sufficient to determine the student's ability to compete with peers in mathematics and social studies achievement. However, Cummins believed that most bilingual programs are apt to focus on the differences in BICS in language one and BICS in language two and not to pay nearly enough attention to CALP in language one and CALP in language two.[32]

Chamot, writing for the National Clearing House for Bilingual Education, said:

Recent Canadian research shows that whereas the LEP (Limited English Proficient) child requires only about *two* years to reach native speaker proficiency in BICS, it takes *five* to *seven* years to reach a CALP level comparable to the native speaker.[33]

Harris, in Australia, also emphasized the need for long periods of instruction to master this language as it is used in textbooks.[34]

From the learning point of view, dangers are inherent in the concept of drill books that prescribe what to do each day. The review of Gray's approach suggests that teachers must know something about language acquisition; how to create rich, learning environments in classrooms; and how to give boys and girls freedom to learn what they want and need to learn.

Using the Learning Environment

According to Loughlin and Suina:

The learning environment can be a powerful teaching instrument at the disposal of the teacher. Thus, teachers can predict behavior in classroom settings. They can teach through the environment and its materials. Teachers can easily arrange and position learning materials so the materials themselves play an active role in the teaching-learning process. A carefully arranged learning environment will permit the teacher more time for direct interaction with students. Materials in the environment stimulate learning by awakening curiosity, providing information, and promoting conversation. The child's environment must be viewed from the child's eye level and not from the teacher's.[35]

Accepting Krashen's point of view that the major function of the elementary classroom is to provide a high level of intake for language acquisition and Loughlin and Suina's viewpoint that a carefully planned learning environment in the classroom can provide the access to a high level of intake for language acquisition, we recommend:

1. Teacher behaviors that will generate a relatively low level of anxiety in the affective filter in the child;
2. Learning centers and questioning strategies that will make use of the local environment both in and out of the classroom; and
3. That each teacher build an effective language program that maximizes language acquisition for LEPs.

The Theme Approach to Improved Language Learning

In previous chapters we have discussed the use of the *theme approach* to developing interesting content reading for those students who should read much better than they do. Now we are recommending that same strategy for the child who has limited English abilities. We believe that this strategy fits the point of view supported in empowering the child, serving as an advocate for the individual who needs support, and freeing the child to learn in a positive atmosphere.

The theme approach follows naturally from the description of the natural approach and the use of the total physical response. The example given of Gray and a group of small children making toast and talking about and riding a horse represent typical activities of the theme approach.

At the Elementary Level

A book by Ventriglia utilizes this approach to help classroom teachers guide the learning of a new language.[36] The book is directed at children in the primary and elementary grades who must master a new language. Some of her generalizations are:

1. Children learn language as a conveyor of meanings rather than as a system of syntactic rules.
2. Children need to learn language so they can communicate in social situations. Conversations are the building blocks of language learning.
3. Teachers need to make language learning lessons out of what is going on in the environment.
4. Topics that serve best for bridging words into concepts may include such items as eating ice cream, going to the grocery store, *having* a picnic, *buying* new shoes, *visiting* a farm, *going* to the zoo, or *riding* in a car.

5. Creative conversations provide time for clarification, repetition, imitation, and searching for vocabulary.
6. Time is required to develop listening comprehension. If the child isn't ready to respond, give him more time to get ready.

At a More Advanced Level of Language Learning

A book by Lee[37] also utilizes this approach to help older students develop the ability to generate conversations and to *bridge* words and phrases into sentence concepts. The book, *My Turn,* consists of two distinct parts, a book of suggestions for student *one* and a book of suggestions for student *two.* The presentation requires that the students open up a conversation about a topic, share what information they have, and then ask each other questions to expand their communication. The two students have different bits of information they can pool. Their activity ends with them composing a conversation.

At the close of each lesson in Lee's book, a conversation as native speakers of English might deal with the same topic is presented. The object is to cause the learners to explore the topic (utilizing the learner's own need, desire, or motivation) to learn both about the subject and to develop spontaneous conversation in his new language.

The text enables the learners to explore and extend their own language capabilities. It places responsibility on the learners and requires the meaningful use of language. Twenty-five themes are utilized: one's family, good health, buying and selling, classifying things, food, shelter, and clothing.

The comparisons of conversations of native speakers with that of the learners enables the learners to see ways to expand their own language growth. However, the conversations of native speakers were *not* designed to be memorized by the learners.

At All Levels of Language Learning—Using Lots of Free Reading Choices

Appendix B of this text contains a bibliography of books for corrective reading. These books with high-interest level and low-vocabulary load may be very useful in encouraging students with Limited English Proficiency to read. A study by Elley and Mangubhai illustrates this extensive reading strategy.

Elley and Mangubhai[38] experimented with a reading program for teaching English as a second language to Fiji Island children. They hypothesized that repeated exposure to high-interest illustrated storybooks in the target language would produce rapid learning of that new language. They delineated factors in language learning that cause learning of a second language to be increased: (1) strong motivation, (2) emphasis on meaning, (3) increased exposure to the language, (4) attention to the redundancy in the language and the awareness of the suprasegmentals that add meaning, and (5) the quality of good models (pp. 54–55).

First, Elley and Mangubhai decided to contrast their extended reading experience with the already established practice in the schools of drilling on patterns as taught in an oral English syllabus, which provided for extensive oral practice. They judged this

When the teacher arranges for a helpful adult to work in the classroom for a time each day with a limited English proficiency child, greater progress can be expected.

practice not to be genuine communication; the repetitions were contrived and often monotonous, the exposure was minimal and carefully controlled, and many of the teachers were themselves teaching in their second language.

These authors selected a sample of 380 boys and girls in classes four and five in eight Fijian rural schools and provided in each classroom 250 high-interest, low-vocabulary storybooks in English. Generally these classrooms had very few books for pupil selection for reading. The sixteen participating teachers used either a usual SSR program or a Shared Book Experience Approach. A control group of 234 boys and girls was taught by the traditional oral language drills. The control method put little emphasis on reading.

Posttests after eight months showed that the pupils who were exposed to many stories progressed in reading and listening comprehension at twice the normal rate. At the end of the following year, according to Elley and Mangubhai, the gains had increased further and spread to related language skills.

> . . . the critical factors which brought about the substantial improvements
> were related to greater and repeated exposure to print in high-interest
> contexts, in conditions where pupils were striving for meaning, and receiving
> sufficient support to achieve it regularly. These features were common in the
> experimental groups and absent in the controls. (p. 66)

This study strongly supports the provision of a wide range of suitable, well-illustrated, high-interest storybooks for children with limited English proficiency and a plan for scheduling time to insure that students read them.

Illustrative Strategies that Follow from a Theme Approach

A theme approach enables the teacher to observe the boys and girls and to select from their interests, attitudes, and motivations specific units of work around which to develop themes. Then through the webbing strategy, the teacher and students can build simple outlines to which they can add many concepts as they are learned. The topics that follow are natural developments from theme approaches.

Learning Nouns to Read With

Language learning begins by mastering the names of many objects and materials to talk about. This can easily begin with building short units of categories of words. A book, *Words to Use,* contains helpful material.[39] Teachers will be able to motivate minimal conversations by using some topics selected from this list:

1. The world we live in (space, the world, light, fire, water)
2. Living things (flowers, trees, animals, birds, fish, insects)
3. Being alive (things we do, things we need)
4. How we view the world (the five senses, classifying things)
5. Living together (communication, transportation, production)
6. Using words for sentence building

Titles of picture dictionaries were given in chapter 9, Teaching Word Recognition.

Activities that Promote Situational English

These activities are means to developing meaningful conversation. Each conversation may well be centered on a specific theme; for example:

1. Greetings and introductions in polite social conversation
2. Identifying people by occupations
3. Learning about community helpers
4. Mastering the use of *who, which, what, when, where,* and *why*
5. Talking about family, relatives, and friends
6. Going shopping; going to the doctor; eating in a restaurant

Language-Experience Reading

The theme approach is a whole-language approach and provides many opportunities for the teacher and the boys and girls to record their experiences through dictating, writing, and recording stories, and by chart reading and bookmaking.

Intellectual Kits to Expand Language Learning

Kits can be used with a small group of children as means of helping them to learn concepts.[40] *Kits* are collections of objects that are relevant in the children's environment. Working with these objects helps identify concepts, extend vocabulary, and permit teacher questions. The teacher can build on the child's response and attempt to extend it.

The adult serves as a language model. The teacher models by labeling, explaining, comparing, and speculating about the objects in the kit. The child is taught to distinguish different objects by color, shape, size, form, and texture. Teachers may be able to extend these differences to include taste and smell.

Teachers will do well to collect, sort and organize kits with such articles as the following:

bottles	candles	jars	nuts
boxes	cards	jewelry	pencils
brushes	chains	magnets	pliers
buttons	gloves	nails	combs
corks	cups	dolls	plastic fruit
scissors	seeds	shells	springs

Lessons with kits can be designed to provide materials to promote conversations and questions that confront the child in learning about his or her world.

Peer Tutoring

Since teachers have groups of children too large for the necessary individual attention they need, all teachers would do well to identify those in their classrooms who can capably help others for short periods during the school day. Children can be paired for playing games with a partner; carrying messages outside the classroom with a partner; or working jigsaw puzzles with a partner. Teachers will find many ways that children of the same age, as well as children from more advanced levels, can be helpful.

Using Culturally Relevant Pictures

For children from very different cultures, the textbooks that they will use most of the time will contain pictures of typical middle-class Americans. We need to give credence to the people in the children's families and to the environment from which they have come. A picture of Aunt Rose shearing sheep is a good example. (See figure 14.2.)

Using Songs and Chants

Internalizing the rhythm of the language and becoming attuned to the rhyme can be aided by the learning of songs that contain much repetition, finger plays, and many singing games.

Folk songs with many verses and the opportunity for boys and girls to have lots of listening time should help second-language learners to develop the suprasegmentals of English (pitch, intonation, and stress) to enhance their facility in the use of the language.

Tapes should be available for cassettes so that small groups or individuals have readily available good listening already planned for them. Tom Glazer's *Eye Winker, Tom Tinker, Chin Chopper: Fifty Musical Fingerplays with Piano Accompaniments and Guitar Chords* (New York: Doubleday and Co., Inc., 1973) will be very useful. The teacher may be able to sing the many verses of these songs on the cassette tape and

Aunt Rose begins shearing the sheep in April.

My Aunt Rose has a middle-sized flock of sheep.

Thousands more are sold for income in the fall.

In October, it is time to get the sheep ready for winter.

Figure 14.2. Using culturally relevant pictures will demonstrate to the student that his or her culture is valued.

have them available for children's use; if the teacher is unable to record the songs personally, any friend who sings well can make a set of tapes for the class.

Two other books that may be useful are *Jazz Chants for Children: Rhythms of American English through Chants, Songs, and Poems* by Carolyn Graham (New York: Oxford University Press, 1979); and *Wee Sing and Play: Musical Games and Rhymes for Children* by Pamela Conn Beall and Susan Hagen Nipp (Los Angeles: Price/Stern/Sloan Publishers, Inc., 1983).

Book Choices to Enrich Language

All of the following kinds of connected print should be available in the classroom:[41]

   Picture books (wordless picture books). These are books without words
      in which the story plot is carried by pictures alone.

Making Connections 14.2: *Studying Children's Storytelling*

The child's mastery of story structure seems to be an important element in the reading process. Teachers should devote much time to reading and telling stories and letting children do likewise. Teachers should also learn to analyze a child's storytelling performance.

Ask a child to tell you a story. You may ask him or her to work from a wordless picture book, an interesting picture, or from some personal experience. Tape the child's efforts.

Bring your tape to your class to share with two or three other students. Listen for the parts of the story and for how the child connects the parts or moves from one part to another. Does the story make sense without having the picture book or picture in front of you? (This means you are concerned with the clarity of expression and its content independence.) Identify the vocabulary that lends interest and clarity to the story. Does the child tell a story or simply name objects or events?

If three or more people listen to that many stories, you will begin to get a sense of the range of ability in the development of a child's sense of story. The teacher should remember that, for the ESL child, stories across cultures may differ in structure. The child's *good* story may not be the teacher's model of a well-constructed story.

Picture story books. Books in which the pictures play an integral part in telling the story.

Predictable books. Books especially written so that children can anticipate quite accurately what is coming next.

Books of both fiction and nonfiction.

Jingles, rhymes, jokes, riddles, and puzzles.

Basal readers.

Magazines. Examples are *Sesame Street, Zoo Nooz,* and *Highlights.*

Newspapers for children.

The relations between utterances and texts become acute when children are first confronted with printed books . . . children are familiar with using the spoken utterance as one cue among others. Children come to school . . . only to be confronted with an exemplar of written text, the reader, which is an autonomous representation of meaning. Ideally, the printed reader depends on no cues other than linguistic cues; it represents no intentions other than those represented in the text; it is addressed to no one in particular; its author is essentially anonymous; and its meaning is precisely that represented by the sentence meaning. . . . Children familiar with the use of textlike language through hearing printed stories obviously confront less of a hurdle than those for whom both reading and that form of language are novel.[42]

Hearing many stories, then, has at least two important purposes: (1) to find out the structures of stories and (2) to sense the formality and abstractness of text as compared to utterance.

The teacher would do well to spend time each school day reading and telling stories to children. Children should also have opportunities to tell stories so that they may grow in their understanding of how the elements of stories combine into wholes. As teachers listen to their students tell stories, they can gain important insights into the children's understanding of story structures.

The teacher should have books and materials in the classroom that facilitate storytelling and reading. Books of many kinds are appropriate. Wordless picture books may be particularly helpful if children are encouraged to spin tales based on them. Tape recorders encourage children to preserve their stories. (Teachers may analyze them later in an effort to understand children's concepts of stories.) Action figures, such as zoo or farm animal sets, collections of human figures, doll houses, farms, and villages may all stimulate storytelling. "Show and tell" times can be beneficial if they are made into storytelling sessions.

Stories from a variety of cultures should be included to acknowledge each child's culture and to provide experiences with the stories from other cultures.

Children's Written Work

There are several means by which the classroom teacher can obtain written expression from children that conveys how well they read, how well they can think about and use what they read, and also how they feel about the material read and how they feel about the job of reading.

Teachers often obtain from children early in the year an original paragraph describing a summer vacation incident. Since children usually need to be helped to delineate specifics and describe them in concrete terms, teachers should help them to delimit their topic and *not use* such global titles as "What I Did Last Summer" or "My Summer Vacation." Instead, topics might be "When I Ate Too Much Watermelon" or "My Big Fish I Almost Caught."

More valid information about children's reading-related writing abilities may be obtained by asking them to write about an interesting picture. The teacher might say, "Write the best *story* you can about this picture." The directions suggest that you do not want a list or a description; however, do not discuss or plan the story with them.

While the teacher may want to note the children's uses of writing mechanics, it is their attempts to structure their stories that will be more directly related to reading instruction. Some children will only name objects in the picture, describe it, or grasp fleeting scraps of the plot. For example, one child recorded about a picture of a movie being filmed:

> This picture here, it is a film about a winter storm. Seems to me like the boy
> and the girl are trying to get home or they are lost.

Then the child lapsed back into naming other people and objects in the picture.

Other children may be able to record parts or all of a story, showing a better grasp of the grammar of a story. Finally, some children may be able to relate stories containing great detail, while at the same time demonstrating a relative mastery of the mechanics of writing. Westby related the ability to create a story to the ability to comprehend stories when she wrote:

> The child's comprehension of a story is based upon the story he has read or heard, not the story the adult thinks the child has read or heard. That is, a child's comprehension of a story is dependent upon the child's interpretation of the story. Story comprehension, as measured by adult standards, is only possible when a child has a narrative schema for stories.[43]

Children can only write or tell stories for which they have the necessary schema. Children who cannot demonstrate this knowledge are likely to have difficulty understanding stories in their readers. They will be limited in their ability to predict what is apt to be coming next, since they do not know what *should* happen next in a story.

Measuring Knowledge of English Usage

Measuring instruments for determining children's understanding of verbal concepts in English will be useful to the classroom teachers for both second-language and culturally different students.

Vocabulary Development

> One of the most fundamental problems relates to the matter of vocabulary. . . . This relates to the inability to distinguish between shades of meaning as expressed by words.[44]

Because reading is the ability to bring meaning to the printed symbols out of the background of experience, vocabulary growth is dependent upon real and vicarious experiences of the children.

The greatest single barrier to understanding is language.[45] The policy in American schools has been to censor rather ruthlessly any language other than English. The children must speak English on the playground and on the street, and they must read English books. This insistence on English usage may cause the children to think of their own parents as inferior, disapproved of, and old-fashioned. The social customs of their parents—in the preferred foods in their diet, their style of dress, their leisure-time activities, and certain deep-seated religious practices—add to the children's great inner conflict when they are forced to choose between the strongly motivated goals of the school and their desire to defend and uphold their parents' tradition.[46]

It would be helpful if the teachers:

1. Knew something of the language of the child's parents.
2. Knew something of the cultural practices and cultural contributions of the foreign culture.
3. Had tact, common sense, and sympathetic understanding.

4. Would visit the home not once, but many times.
5. Would explain the basic purposes of the school and clarify erroneous ideas brought home by the child.
6. Would show genuine appreciation for the worthwhile values of the culture of the parents.[47]

Understanding English as the Language of the School

The teaching of English as a second language encompasses these three facets: (1) the memorization of, and drill on, the common speech utterances of the second language; (2) the extension of vocabulary in the second language beyond the initial levels required in such common utterances; and (3) the reading and writing of the second language.

Teachers can measure the extension of vocabulary in the language by investigating semantic difficulties as found in common idiomatic expressions, multiple meanings of common words, simple analogies, and opposites. Test exercises, measuring these abilities, indicated that Indian and Spanish-American children were significantly handicapped in comparison with Anglo children with whom their performances were compared. Fourth-grade Anglo children with unilingual backgrounds performed significantly better statistically on all these tests than did Indian and Spanish-speaking sixth-grade children enrolled in public school classes.

The following sections outline activities that will help children to understand the use of idioms, slang expressions, multiple meanings, simple analogies, antonyms, similes and metaphors, and compound words.

Idioms

1. Understanding the idiom in the English language. Following are idioms found in context in the school readers:
   a. Mother will *piece out* the supper.
   b. Tom knew he was *saved by a hair*.
   c. His plan *fell through*.
   d. "O.K.," he retorted, *"Don't bite my head off."*
   e. He won't be *worth his salt* for a long time to come.
   f. Mr. Bird chuckled, "Now I've *let the cat out of the bag."*

Student workbooks contain exercises to give some practice in identifying proper meanings for idiomatic expressions. Foerster has suggested using idioms as motivation to get students interested in their language. Because idioms carry a meaning other than the literal one, when taken literally the meaning can be good humor. She illustrated this with "I'd like to have you for dinner" and "Mother told you to get off the phone."[48] Foerster suggested:
   a. Drawing pictures to illustrate an idiom and then letting the class guess which idiom it is, using such idioms as "He's a big wheel," "He flew off the handle," or "It was a hair-raising experience."

   b. Pantomiming idioms, playing a charades-like game using such idioms as "You turn me on," "He kicked the bucket," or "He's got a chip on his shoulder."
   c. Classifying idioms:
      (1) Idioms that involve color: "I'm in the red," "He's awfully blue."
      (2) Idioms that include parts of the body: "Lend me your ear," "She has a sharp tongue," or "He has a nose for news."
      (3) Idioms dealing with animals: "He's a fat cat," "She's no spring chicken," or "Quit horsing around."
      (4) Idioms relating to food: "He's the salt of the earth," "She's in a pickle," or "I'm in a stew."

Edwards tested the relative level of difficulty of reading material containing idiomatic expressions and the same material rewritten with literal meanings. He was concerned only with those idioms that are common, widely used, accepted standard English, such as "fly in the ointment," "crow about something," or "steal the show." He found that the group reading passages rewritten in literal English performed significantly better than the group reading passages that contained idiomatic language. Edwards emphasized the need for finding appropriate ways to develop better understanding of idiomatic language for all junior high school students, but especially for those from minority groups who lack knowledge about the cultural background in the books they are expected to read.[49]

Slang Expressions

   2. Understanding commonly used slang expressions in the English language.
      a. Mr. Jones really *cramps my style*.
      b. When everyone else quit, I was *stuck with the job*.
      c. He is great for *talking through his hat*.
      d. It's about time to quit fooling around and *talk turkey*.
      e. Tom likes to *pull your leg* every chance he gets.

These slang expressions will surely be baffling if translated in a completely literal way.

Multiple Meanings

   3. Understanding multiple meanings of the same English word. The word *run,* for example, has some seventy-five uses in the elementary school dictionary, such as:[50]
      a. The boy will *run* a race.
      b. The disease has *run* its course.
      c. The fence *runs* east and west.
      d. The man *runs* a garage.
      e. The boy has *run* a splinter in his finger.
      f. She will *run* out of money.
      g. He will *run* up a bill.

Figures 14.3 and 14.4 illustrate how boys and girls may be encouraged to draw pictures to show multiple meanings of common words.

4. Lack of adequate word meanings for words heard. Children often misunderstand words completely when they attempt to use them orally in sentences.[51]

a.	*blot*	Where blood comes. (*clot*)
b.	*spool*	A place where there is water. (*pool*)
c.	*habit*	We habit be quiet. (*had better*)
d.	*rack*	When we go fast we rack the car. (*wreck*)
e.	*won*	The Indians have a wigwon. (*wigwam*)
f.	*tasks*	They cut the tasks of the elephant. (*tusks*)
g.	*bushel*	The name of a big bush.
h.	*climate*	The natives climate the trees to get coconuts. (*climbed up*)
i.	*oyster*	A kind of bird in the zoo. (*ostrich*)

Simple Analogies

5. Understanding simple analogies. Some simple analogies readily understood by Anglo fourth graders may give much difficulty to all those for whom English is a second language.
   a. Water is to drink as bread is to *eat*.
   b. Cowboy is to horse as pilot is to *plane*.
   c. Tree is to trunk as flower is to *stem*.

Antonyms

6. Understanding antonyms.

Similes and Metaphors

7. Understanding figurative language.
   The simile expresses a comparison between two persons or things. It uses *like* or *as* to make the comparison. For people for whom English is the vernacular, these comparisons become everyday expressions through usage. For the children learning English as a second language, however, such expressions need to be specifically taught. "Brave as a lion," "cross as a bear," "sharp as a tack," or "clean as a whistle" are common expressions.
   Other examples include:
   a. The bad old shoemaker was *as sly as a fox*.
   b. A fox hid behind a log and kept *as still as a mouse*.
   c. The dog scampered off *as quick as a wink*.
   d. In her new dress, Judy looked *as pretty as a picture*.
   e. The cook's roast lamb was *tough as shoe leather*.

Lap

Baby sat in mother's <u>lap</u>.

The waves <u>lap</u> against the shore.

The dog will <u>lap</u> up all the milk in the pan.

The track men ran another <u>lap</u> around the track.

Figure 14.3. Multiple meanings for the word *lap*

Figure 14.4. Multiple meanings for the word *light*

Making Connections 14.3: Examining Instructional Materials

Some instructional materials are prepared specifically for children who speak another language and are learning English. These are often referred to as ESL (English as a second language) materials. Other materials are prepared in the first language of the children.

Locate a collection of these materials, whether in the public schools or in your university or college library. Select three books or other instructional items that particularly interest you. Examine them carefully, paying attention to the language used, the content, and the illustrations.

After you have studied the materials and evaluated them, bring them and your ideas to share with your class. This activity should allow students to see quite a variety of instructional materials and hear them discussed. Students should become aware of the commercial materials that are available for working with bilingual and ESL children.

Compound Words

8. Compound words
   The following exercise was designed to help children put two words together to build a compound word.[52] The students are to identify the root words in compounds as meaning units by putting together the two italicized words:
   Father said, "I can't *work* in any *room* in this house. I need a _____ of my own."
   The *bed* was *spread* with a fine old woolen cover. "I'm proud of this _____ ," said Mrs. Page.
   The *side* of the *hill* was covered with beautiful purple flowers. They made the whole _____ look blue.
   "A *crow* eats my seeds when I'm not around to *scare* it off," said Woody.
   "I'll make a _____ ."

A sixth-grade teacher who found that many students in his class were limited in depth of knowledge of English searched through workbooks for basal readers and compiled a collection of exercises that were appropriate for teaching many facets of the language.

Specific exercises covered in children's workbooks included: using different meanings; differentiating various meanings of words; opposite meaning words; using related words; selecting the correct definition; homonyms; context clues; cause and effect; matching definitions; word perception; selecting appropriate meanings; categorizing words; synonyms; figurative language; interpreting figurative language; perceiving part-whole relationships; comprehending sentence meaning; paraphrasing; forming sensory images; emotional reactions; matching morals and fables; simple analogies; connotations; comparing and contrasting; generalizing; understanding idioms; and sensory impressions.

Motivation to Learn a New Language

Learning language seems to require stimulation from others and considerable reinforcement (feedback) from others. Consider the following:[53]

1. *Stimulation.* Young children are literally surrounded by stimulation from parents, other adults, siblings, the TV, the radio, and the record player. The language that youngsters hear will likely be the natural language of a wide variety of speakers.
2. *Identification.* Young children identify with the adult who gives them the intensive care that they need. Identification with the adult leads to a strong motivation to imitate what the adult does.
3. *External reinforcement.* The caring adults are very likely to reward young children for their language attempts. The more adults or older siblings there are in the environment, the more the child is praised, asked to say a new word again, and given tangible rewards for "trying to talk."
4. *Conveying information.* Very early, children are trying to ask for their needs to be met and to communicate information about their environment. Children's insatiable curiosity can frustrate the parent who tires of "What's that?" or "Why?"
5. *Self-reinforcement.* Children start talking to themselves by verbalizing the rhythm of adult speech, using much repetition.

Summary

Language and culture create barriers to understanding concepts taught in the school. Teachers are cautioned *not* to confuse language differences or cultural barriers with lack of innate intelligence. Many bright children fail because of lack of facility with English or because of meager backgrounds of experience.

Many types of exercises are available to teachers for developing better understanding of the facets of English—idioms, figures of speech, opposites, synonyms, homonyms, and prepositions. It is recommended that teachers search for specific helps in the commercially prepared workbooks for students and that they develop new materials experimentally and compile varieties of helpful exercises.

With young children, we know that an informal approach in a carefully planned, rich learning environment with a low anxiety level is a good way to extend and enrich language. This is just as true for children learning English as a new language, or learning a greater depth of English as a second language, as it is for native speakers of English.

Some of the key ideas cited from ESL specialists are these:

1. Children need a rich, comprehensible input of meaningful language.[54]
2. Children work and learn best under states of low anxiety.[55]
3. Children need to be taught in rich, well-arranged learning environments.[56]
4. Improving oral language competence may improve reading ability.[57]
5. Children profit most from the content of language that focuses on the needs and interests of the group.[58]

6. Promotion of the first language of the LEP child will significantly benefit the student's intellectual functioning.[59]
7. The *quality of the interaction* that children experience with adults is *more important* than whether the language of the home is the same as the language of the school.
8. Students with limited English proficiency need at least five to seven years of instruction in the language to master that language sufficiently to be able to read textbooks effectively.[60]

For Further Reading

Anderson, Billie V., and John G. Barnitz. "Cross-Cultural Schemata and Reading Comprehension Instruction." *Journal of Reading* 28 (November 1984): 102–8.

Bromley, Karen D'Angelo. "Teaching Idioms." *Reading Teacher* 38 (December 1984): 272–76.

Cummins, Jim. *Bilingualism and Minority Language Children.* Language and Literacy Series. Ontario, Canada: Ontario Institute for Studies in Education, 1981.

Cummins, Jim. "Empowering Minority Students: A Framework for Intervention." *Harvard Educational Review* 56, no. 1 (February 1986).

Elley, Warwick B., and Francis Mangubhai. "The Impact of Reading on Second Language Learning." *Reading Research Quarterly* 19 (Fall 1983): 53–67.

Flatley, Joannis Kelly, and Adele Ducharme Rutland. "Using Wordless Picture Books to Teach Linguistically/Culturally Different Students." *Reading Teacher* 40 (December 1986): 276–81.

Gonzales, Phillip C. "How to Begin Language Instruction for Non-English Speaking Students." *Language Arts* 58 (February 1981): 175–80.

Goodman, Jesse, and Kate Melcher. "Culture at a Distance: An Anthroliterary Approach to Cross-Cultural Education." *Journal of Reading* 28 (December 1984): 200–207.

Hough, Ruth A., Joanne R. Nurss, and D. Scott Enright. "Story Reading with Limited English Speaking Children in the Regular Classroom." *Reading Teacher* 39 (February 1986): 510–14.

Jalongo, Mary Rench, and Karen D'Angelo Bromley. "Developing Linguistic Competence through Song Picture Books." *Reading Teacher* 37 (May 1984): 840–45.

Krashen, Stephen D., and Tracy D. Terrell. *The Natural Approach: Language Acquisition in the Classroom.* San Francisco: The Alemany Press, 1983.

Minkoff, Dorothy. "Game Activities for Practicing English as a Second Language." *Journal of Reading* 28 (October 1984): 40–42.

Perez, Eustolia. "Oral Language Competence Improves Reading Skills of Mexican American Third Graders." *Reading Teacher* 35 (October 1981): 24–27.

Saville-Troike, Muriel. *A Guide to Culture in the Classroom.* Rosslyn, Va.: National Clearing House for Bilingual Education, 1978.

Ventriglia, Linda. *Conversations of Miguel and Maria: How Children Learn a Second Language.* Reading, Mass.: Addison-Wesley Publishing Co., 1982.

West, Betsy E. "The New Arrivals from Southeast Asia." *Childhood Education* 60 (November–December 1983): 84–89.

Yelden, Janice. *Communicative Language Teaching: Principles and Practice.* Language and Literacy series. Toronto: Ontario Institute for Studies in Education, 1981.

Notes

1. William S. Gray et al., *The New We Look and See* (Atlanta: Scott, Foresman, 1956).
2. Hilary Hester, "Peer Interaction in Learning English as a Second Language," *Theory into Practice* 23, no. 3 (Summer 1984): 208.
3. Kathy Irving, "Cross-Cultural Awareness and the English-as-a-Second-Language Classroom," *Theory into Practice* 23, no. 2 (Spring 1984): 141.
4. Jim Cummins, "Empowering Minority Students: A Framework for Intervention," *Harvard Educational Review* 56, no. 1 (February 1986).
5. Kenneth Goodman, "Linguistic Insights Teachers Can Apply," *Education* 88 (May 1968): 313–16.
6. Josephine Piekarz Ives, "Linguistic Principles and Reading Practices in the Elementary School," in *Reading and Realism*, ed. J. Allen Figurel (Newark, Del.: International Reading Association, 1969), 88–93.
7. J. Donald Bowen, "The Structure of Language," in *Linguistics in School Programs,* 69th Yearbook, NSSE, ed. Herman G. Richey (Chicago: University of Chicago Press, 1970), 46.
8. William E. Rutherford, "Deep and Surface Structure, and the Language Drill," *TESOL Quarterly* 2 (June 1968): 71–79.
9. Ibid., p. 76.
10. Ben Goldfield, "Semantics: An Aid to Comprehension," *Journal of Reading* 16 (January 1973): 311.
11. Ibid., 313.
12. Ibid.
13. Gilliam Brown and George Yule, *Discourse Analysis* (Cambridge: Cambridge University Press, 1983), 1–4.
14. Ibid., 27.
15. Ibid., 191.
16. Peter Freebody and Richard C. Anderson, "Effects of Vocabulary Difficulty, Text Cohesion, and Schema Availability on Reading Comprehension," *Reading Research Quarterly* 18 (Spring 1983): 280–81.
17. Brown and Yule, *Discourse Analysis,* 256.
18. William Labov, "Language Characteristics of Specific Groups: Blacks," in *Reading for the Disadvantaged: Problems of Linguistically Different Learners,* ed. Thomas D. Horn (New York: Harcourt, Brace, 1970), 139.
19. Ibid., 156–57.
20. William Stewart, "On the Use of Negro Dialect in the Teaching of Reading," in *Teaching Black Children to Read,* ed. Joan Baratz and Roger Shuy (New York: Harcourt, Brace, 1970), 178.
21. Linda James Myers, "The Nature of Pluralism and the African American Case," *Theory into Practice* 20 (Winter 1981): 5.
22. Ronald L. Cramer, "Dialectology—A Case for Language Experience," *Reading Teacher* 25 (October 1971): 33–39.
23. Ibid., 37–38.
24. Stephen D. Krashen and Tracy D. Terrell, *The Natural Approach: Language Acquisition in the Classroom* (San Francisco: Alemany Press, 1983).
25. Tracy D. Terrell, "A Natural Approach to Second Language Acquisition and Learning," *Modern Language Journal* 61 (November 1977): 325–37.

26. Heidi Dulay and Marina Burt, "Should We Teach Children Syntax?" *Language Learning* 23, no. 2 (1973): 257.

27. Brian Gray, "Helping Children to Become Language Learners in the Classroom" (Brisbane, Australia: Meanjin Reading Council, 1983), photocopy.

28. James J. Asher, "The Total Physical Response Approach to Second Language Learning," *Modern Language Journal* 53 (January 1969): 3–17.

29. James J. Asher and B. Price, "The Learning Strategy of the Total Physical Response: Some Age Differences," *Child Development* 38 (1967): 1219–27; and James J. Asher, "The Learning Strategy of the Total Physical Response: A Review," *Modern Language Journal* 50 (1966): 79–84.

30. Jim Cummins, *Bilingualism and Minority Language Children,* Language and Literacy series (Ontario, Canada: Ontario Institute for Studies in Education, 1981), 27–32.

31. Jim Cummins, "The Entrance and Exit Fallacy in Bilingual Education," *NABE Journal* 4 (Spring 1980): 25–59.

32. Ibid., 49–51.

33. Anna Uhl Chamot, "Applications of Second Language Acquisition Research to the Bilingual Classroom," *National Clearing House for Bilingual Education,* no. 8 (September 1981): 6.

34. Stephen Harris, "More Haste Less Speed: Time and Timing for Language Programs in Northern Territory Aboriginal Bilingual Education," *Aboriginal Child at School* 8 (August/September 1980): 37.

35. Catherine E. Loughlin and Joseph H. Suina, *The Learning Environment: An Instructional Strategy* (New York: Teachers College Press, 1982), 5–18.

36. Linda Ventriglia, *Conversations of Miguel and Maria: How Children Learn English as a Second Language* (Reading, Mass.: Addison-Wesley Publishing Co., 1982).

37. Nancy Lee, *My Turn* (Wilmington, Del.: Dawn Press, 1983).

38. Warwick B. Elley and Francis Mangubhai, "The Impact of Reading on Second Language Learning," *Reading Research Quarterly* 19, no. 1 (Fall 1983): 53–67.

39. Patrick Drysdale, *Words to Use: A Primary Thesaurus* (Toronto, Canada: Gage Educational Publishing Ltd., 1971).

40. We have borrowed this suggestion from Professor Halene Weaver, Adjunct Professor, University of New Mexico.

41. Margaret Greer and Miles V. Zintz, *Learning to Read Naturally* (Dubuque, Iowa: Kendall/Hunt Publishing Co., 1986), 166.

42. David R. Olson, "From Utterance to Text: The Basis of Language in Speech and Writing," in *Thought and Language/Language and Reading,* ed. Maryanne Wolf, Mark K. McQuillan, and Eugene Radwin (Cambridge, Mass.: Harvard Educational Review, 1980), 103.

43. Carol Westby, "Children's Narrative Development: Cognitive and Linguistic Aspects" (Paper presented at the Conference on Language, Learning, and Reading Disabilities: A New Decade, at Hunter College, New York, 22–23 May 1980).

44. Loyd S. Tireman, "The Bilingual Child and His Reading Vocabulary," *Elementary English* 32 (January 1955): 34.

45. Loyd S. Tireman, "School Problems Created by the Homes of Foreign Speaking Children," *California Journal of Elementary Education* 8 (May 1940): 234–38.

46. Ibid., 236.

47. Ibid., 236–38.

48. Leona M. Foerster, "Idiomagic," *Elementary English* 51 (January 1974): 125–27.

49. Peter Edwards, "The Effect of Idioms on Children's Reading and Understanding of Prose," in *Teachers, Tangibles, Techniques: Comprehension of Content in Reading,* ed. Bonnie Smith Schulwitz (Newark, Del.: International Reading Association, 1975), 37–46.

50. Ernest Horn, "Language and Meaning," in *The Psychology of Learning,* 41st Yearbook, Part II, NSSE (Chicago: University of Chicago Press, 1942), 298–99.

51. Tireman, "The Bilingual Child," 33–35.

52. William S. Gray et al., *Think and Do Book to Accompany Just Imagine,* Curriculum Foundation Series (Chicago: Scott, Foresman, 1954), 11.

53. Arthur Wingfield, E. Hugh Rudorf, and Richard T. Graham, "Why Should the Child Want to Learn to Read?" in *Applied Linguistics,* ed. R. F. Shafer (Newark, Del.: International Reading Association, 1978).

54. Krashen and Terrell, *The Natural Approach.*

55. Heidi Dulay, Marina Burt, and Stephen Krashen, *Language Two* (New York: Oxford University Press, 1982), 261–69.

56. Catherine Loughlin and Joseph Suina, *The Learning Environment: An Instructional Strategy* (New York: Teachers College Press, 1982).

57. Eustolia Perez, "Oral Language Competence Improves Reading Skills of Mexican American Third Graders," *Reading Teacher* 35 (October 1981): 24–27.

58. Brian Gray, "Helping Children to Become Language Learners in the Classroom" (Brisbane, Australia: Meanjin Reading Council, 1983), photocopy.

59. Cummins, *Bilingualism and Minority Children;* Elizabeth Peal and Wallace Lambert, "The Relationship of Bilingualism to Intelligence," Psychological Monographs: General and Applied, No. 76: 1–23 (Washington: American Psychological Association, 1962); and Paul Rosier and Lillian Vorik, "Rock Point Community School: An Example of a Navajo-English Bilingual Elementary Program," *TESOL Quarterly* 13 (September 1978): 263–69.

60. Harris, "More Haste Less Speed: Time and Timing for Language Programs."

15
Meeting the Challenge of Severe Reading and Writing Disabilities

Vocabulary

learning disabilities

neurological impairment

hypothyroidism

hyperthyroidism

dyslexia

neurological impress
method

Fernald Kinesthetic Tracing
Technique

VAKT

Hegge, Kirk, and Kirk
"Grapho-Vocal" Method

Gillingham-Stillman
remedial training

VAK

repeated readings

assisted reading

echo reading

language experience

modeling

big books

predictable books

sandpaper letters

shadow reading

hyperactivity

disinhibited child

perseveration

drug therapy

operant conditioning

Questions

1. Compare the Fernald; Hegge, Kirk, and Kirk; and Gillingham-Stillman techniques. (**Inference**)
2. Describe the techniques that are variants of the neurological impress method. (**Recall**)
3. How are the teacher's reading and writing activities related to those of the students? (**Inference**)
4. How would you plan to manage students who are hyperactive, who perseverate, and who are disinhibited? (**Application**)
5. What should the teacher know about the use of drugs to manage behavior and support learning? (**Recall**)
6. How would you plan to help a student with perceptual difficulties? (**Application**)

Introduction

Occasionally children will appear in your classroom who look alert, are as vocal as the others, think when you ask for opinions orally, and are warm, creative, imaginative human beings—everything good—until that moment when you ask everyone in the class to read or to write.

School is not particularly well organized to accommodate these youngsters—although the truth is that if we give them their own time schedules about undertaking most of the tasks of the elementary school, they will learn to master them.

In an interview about the problem of being a child in our society, Hughes said:

> But do we ask why the children didn't find something intriguing about reading, some time, in some grade? That is the point the public school should be interested in. Why weren't they in a situation, sometime, where someone had a book that they WANTED . . . NEEDED to read . . . the dictionary, the encyclopedia, some resource for something truly meaningful. This just shows us the sterility of the concrete, imposed sequence of skills, the sterility of the experiences we are offering to the children.[1]

Educators must look at not only methods of teaching reading but also classroom organizational practices that will facilitate learning and minimize feelings of failure and inadequacy. Otherwise, children who are capable of reading may not learn to read.

Michael, a Reluctant Reader

Michael could not read when he enrolled in first grade. Fortunately, he was enrolled in an open classroom where many interesting activities went on all the time. There was a skills center, which Michael ignored; a reading center, where he thumbed through pages of books; a games center; a science center, where he studied, observed, and asked questions every day about the displays; and a listening center, but Michael was not much interested in that. The teacher had made more space available by having a few tables instead of individual desks; a rug in one corner of the room provided a place where everyone could meet to discuss topics and to plan for the day. There Michael talked well—he talked to all his peers and could explain clearly many things to the adults around him.

Michael's teacher tried to help all the children to set their own limits for study; to know what is expected in social behavior and interaction; to be able to perform the skills they accepted as their assignments; and to be sufficiently motivated to want to be successful at whatever they undertook. The teacher knew that discipline used in its negative sense usually means that inadequate planning has been done; bad behavior is caused *by* something, and when disruptions occurred or other inappropriate behavior took place, she asked the group to help decide how to correct the problem.

Michael learned that school was a happy, interesting, accepting place, but learned nothing about reading and writing. His experiences were extended so that his vocabulary was growing, and his ability to ask questions was improving. His teacher was aware that almost all of the skills taught in reading workbooks can, in some degree, be developed in oral language lessons. For example, students can:

1. Determine the central idea in a discussion as well as they can in a written paragraph.
2. Put ideas in sequential order, whether the message is oral or written.
3. Put things in categories; classify and order by sizes and shapes and colors. These can be done with concrete objects, and learning is going on.
4. Detect whether the key idea in simple sentences tells who, where, what, when, or how. These can also be developed orally to some extent.
5. Extend word meanings; choose words that describe more exactly; study word opposites, synonyms, and homonyms.

Michael passed through the second-grade year continuing to feel that he was an important part of his class—extending his interest and curiosity, exercising personal choice, increasing his personal involvement, experiencing some successes other than reading and writing; becoming ever more aware of some of the things that he did well, and accepting praise when it was earned.

When Michael came to the third grade, he was beginning to feel the pressures of his peers, his parents, his school principal, and any others who knew that he did not want to face the task of reading. They were becoming alarmed that Michael might never learn to read, which is not surprising. However, the important message here is that he was given two years of positive school attendance without the pressures causing him to devalue his personality, destroy his ego, or make him feel like a failure. By third grade Michael was almost nine years old and he was mature enough to accept the fact that he would have to learn how to overcome the aversion he displayed toward reading— carefully done, facing it would not destroy him.

Michael attempted to write the alphabet when he entered third grade. He wrote all the letters to *T,* and they were all in capitals except *i, j, l,* and *r.* The letter *j* was reversed. When asked if he knew any words, he wrote in quite immature manuscript: *no, yes, bed, mom, book, look.*

During that year, he became interested in the *Go-Fish* game and became skilled at winning it. The teacher tried unsuccessfully to get him to dictate stories that could be classified as language-experience stories. Instead, she resorted to sentences, which evolved as little books of three-by-five cards held together by notebook rings. The first was *Michael Can* and included sentences with occasional rebuses. The stories followed this sequence:

Michael Can
Michael can go.
Michael can run and jump.
Michael can go to the store.
Michael can go to the store with his mother.
Can Michael see a red car?
Can Michael see a yellow car?

Michael Went
Michael went to the store.
Michael went to get some candy.
Mother said, "Yes, Michael went to get some candy."
Mother said, "Yes, Michael went to the stupid school."
(Michael could soon read these stories without help.)

Michael Can
Look Mother.
"I can jump up and down," said Michael.
"Yes, Michael can jump up and down," said mother.
"Can you look up and down?" said mother.
"Yes, Mother, I can."
"I can look up and down."
"I can jump up and down."
"I can, I can, I can," said Michael.

Michael Came
Michael came today.
Michael came in a yellow car.
Michael came in the yellow car.
Mother said, "Michael came with me."
Michael said, "I came with Mother."

Michael Likes
Michael likes to chew gum.
Michael likes to eat candy.
Michael likes to play.
Michael likes to play Go-Fish.
Michael likes television.
Michael likes to fish.
Michael likes to go to the store.

Then Michael was asked more directly about reading books, and he responded freely. "No! That is a no-no!" However, he was presented with the fairy tales that contain a great deal of repetition, which he had already heard many times. He read all the stories in *I Know a Story* (Harper and Row). All the time, a minimum of writing was required of Michael. He must always put the correct heading on his paper and then write a sentence or two. He was given help with the words so that he would write them correctly. His writing sentences from dictation gradually increased until he was able to do five. Some of his writing practice is included here (figure 15.1).

The next book Michael read from was *Blue Dog and Other Stories* (Lyons and Carnahan). He read other individual stories from other first- and second-grade readers, but the teacher often read every other page. Since it was evident that following the

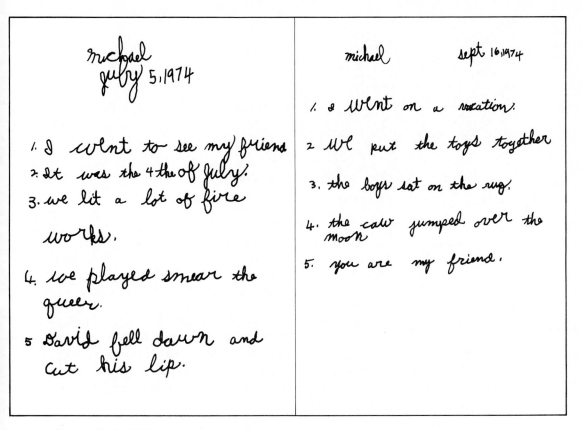

Figure 15.1. Michael's writing practice

lines was difficult, one three-by-five card was used to screen out all lines above the one being read, and another was used to screen out all lines below the one being read. Eventually he advanced to the use of a three-by-five card with a small slot cut out of the middle so that he could move it down the page himself and see only one line at a time (see figure 15.2). His willingness to attempt to read longer passages increased after this.

Michael finished the fourth grade. He still found reading done by others fascinating; but he still rejected the idea that he could read what he wanted to learn independently. However, by the end of his fourth-grade year, he was able to read (alternating with his teacher) with some fluency and complete enjoyment the story "The Twelve Sillies" in *It Happened One Day,* second-grade level (Harper and Row). He had mastered the Dolch Basic Sight Words but did them better in isolation than in a line of print. When he was offered a reward of one dollar for instant recognition of all 220 words, he worked diligently on those in the questionable column for about a week and won his dollar. Knowing the words was not of great importance to him, but he was proud to win in competition with his teacher.

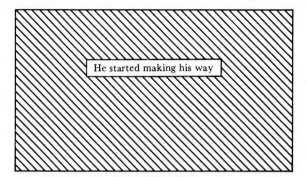

He started making his way

Figure 15.2. The card screens out all but the line being read.

The positive aspects of Michael's program at this point were that he still had a positive image of himself. He knew that he could be *all right* even though he rejected reading; he recognized that there are certain school assignments in fourth grade that are just not acceptable to anyone without extensive reading and writing; and he was not overcome with failure or defeated by his lack of this facility. Because of these positive feelings about himself and the aid he received from helpful teachers, Michael made good growth, albeit a couple of years late. Given the time to overcome his visual, motor, perceptual, neurological, or whatever problems he has, he may be successful in school. If he had encountered negative experiences along the way and developed serious emotional overtones to failure in reading, his remediation might have been more difficult.

Learning Disabilities in Regular and Special Classes

Peggy was a sixteen-year-old who had attended a reading clinic two hours a day for several months. In her developmental skills she had progressed to the reading level where she had learned the rules of syllabication so that she could state them in "figuring out" polysyllabic words. One day her clinician wrote the word *photograph* on the chalkboard. Peggy recited:

> There are three separated vowels so there are probably three syllables. *T* goes with the second *o* and *ph* says *f*. *Gr* stays together and says *grr* and *ph* says *f* at the end. The *o's* are open syllables so they are long. (Pause) *fo-to-graf* (Each syllable pronounced correctly) (Pause) *fo-to-graf*. I don't know what the word is.

Even though she recognized all three of the syllables and pronounced them correctly in isolation, Peggy could not integrate them to produce the word *photograph*. She could not make the association even though the word had appeared in her reading lesson several times the day before and the photographs being read about were some she had taken with her own camera!

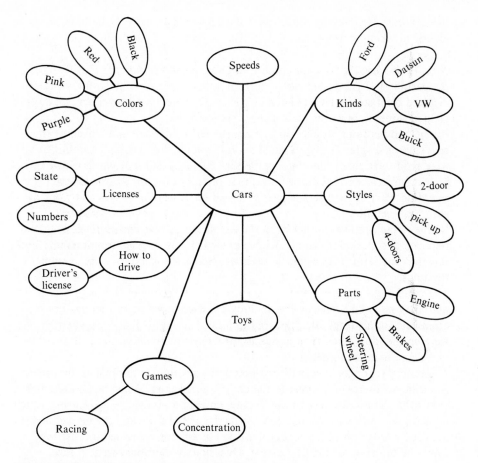

Figure 15.3. Web of ideas related to the theme—cars

Richie, a younger child with severe learning problems, came to a reading clinic at age eight. He had experienced two falls, which doctors said had caused some neurological damage. During Richie's initial evaluation, he was able to write his first name and the first two letters of his last name. He read four Dolch words: *can, is, big,* and *my.* He demonstrated knowledge of all single consonant sounds, but did not appear to be able to use that information to blend words. He had no sense of anticipating meaning. He was totally unable to use prediction as a strategy. His attention span was short for writing and reading tasks—two or three minutes at the most.

Richie began a reading program organized around a theme of interest to him—cars. The web that he and his tutor made is shown in figure 15.3. Several activities grew from this web, which was printed on a large sheet of paper for easy reference.

1. Richie and his teacher made a list of the kinds of cars they found in a parking lot near the clinic. From the list they made a picture graph. Then a story was written. The teacher underlined four words for Richie to learn. These were printed on cards that were matched to the words in the story. Richie added

these words: *car, pickup, look,* and *I.* These words along with the four words he identified when he was tested formed the beginning of an alphabetized shoe box of words.

2. Next Richie used a Polaroid camera to photograph several cars that he liked in the parking lot. He pasted the pictures in a book he had bound, and wrote or dictated brief stories about each. This activity, which lasted over several days, yielded three more words for his shoe box word file.

3. Richie and his tutor took a trip to a nearby car dealership and looked at the new cars on display. They obtained several colorful advertising pamphlets that were read to Richie when they met again. Richie found four words in them that he wanted to learn. The tutor found that review of the words was essential for retention. Part of each session was reserved for rereading stories and working with the word file.

4. Richie wrote a thank-you letter to the car dealer. It was one sentence long and required two working sessions. Richie knew few letter forms from memory and reversed any letter that could be reversed. Some of his letters were examples of rotations.

5. The child and his tutor made a concentration-type game of car pictures, pasting matching pairs on three- by five-inch cards. Richie played this game very well, often beating his tutor. He appeared to have a strong memory for where cards were on the table, even though intense practice was required to recall word forms and names consistently.

6. The school year was filled with reading activities similar to the ones described. A variety of topics of interest to the child was selected. When he had about fifty words that he usually recognized, Richie entered a plateau period during which he had great difficulty adding new words. By the end of the year he had about a hundred words in his reading vocabulary. His writing remained inconsistent from one tutoring session to the next. Occasionally he would write a few reversals, but usually he was generally no longer troubled by letter formation difficulties. His attention span for listening to stories had increased to the point that he would have liked for most of the sessions to have been spent in that way.

One hears more and more today about children who have brain damage or *neurological impairment.* Teachers must be cautioned that such terms are medical, and they must be very careful not to apply these labels if the pupils' problems have not been diagnosed medically. Also, since it is difficult for parents to accept such a diagnosis when it really exists, the teacher will only create undue anxiety if such terms are applied to specific pupils without medical diagnosis. Nevertheless, if some children have failed to make progress after the teacher has tried a variety of teaching methods, the parents should then be urged to seek medical help.

Many precedents have already been established in this regard. *Hypothyroidism* and *hyperthyroidism* have long been treated; their relationship to reading has been reported in the literature, for example, by Harris and Sipay:

Marked thyroid deficiency is usually accompanied by obesity and mental sluggishness; an overactive thyroid gland may cause loss of weight, fatigue, and nervous irritability. . . . Among the poor readers seen by the writers, the frequency of endocrine deviations has been greater than in the normal child population. . . . Many of these children have shown marked improvement in mental alertness, effort, and learning ability after appropriate endocrine treatment.[2]

The reader is referred also to the case of Betty (see chapter 2).

Learning disability affects boys rather than girls approximately 4:1. The disability is evidenced more often in symbolic written language than in numerical symbolization, as indicated by the frequently higher level of performance in computational areas of arithmetic. Science, too, can be presented graphically rather than verbally and is often a stronger subject for dyslexics than are history and the language arts. Some authorities believe that perception is intact for individual letters but becomes faulty in the Gestalt of words (word wholes). Some believe the symbolic abilities are impaired so that while the child with specific learning disability may have conceptual strengths, he cannot come up with proper symbolic designations (height for tallness; summer for hot weather). Rabinovitch and Ingram[3] interpreted this problem of translating perceptions into symbols as conceptual deficiency in orientation. On the other hand, perception may be distorted in certain ways so that faulty concepts arise from faulty percepts. Nevertheless, the children with specific learning disabilities have difficulty with the printed page, whether they read it (receptive) or whether they must perform it in writing (expressive). It is most noticeable in inferior handwriting, with irregularly shaped and poorly spaced characters (see example under the heading "Accommodation in the Classroom" later in this chapter), and in spelling, in which the errors are erratic and bizarre, with frequent reversals of letter shapes and letter order.

The distractible, hyperactive students require a neutral environment, devoid of unnecessary stimuli of sight and sound. If their seats can be placed in the front of the room, a bit separated from others, and/or comfortably confined by a three-panel screen or carrel, they may be able to function more efficiently. There should be no pictures or displays in this corner of the room to distract their attention. The teachers should avoid such clothing accessories as jingling jewelry or cluttery ornaments. Noise level should be reduced as much as possible. The teachers need to structure their lessons very carefully. They should give short, precise directions, refrain from allowing alternative choices, and speak in well-modulated voices, without overtones of anxiety.

Every new process should be broken down into previously learned components, adding only one new element to be associated with those that are familiar. In other words, learning is a step-by-step process, each new insight building on previously achieved concepts. Memory is not an indication of insight. Insight must be achieved first; then overlearning is desirable until the response by the students becomes automatic. Some children with dyslexia have an amazing rote or "inventory" memory that deceives teachers and parents about their capabilities. But this memory must never be substituted for insight, because the learner cannot make use of what he or she knows without "thinking processes."

Making Connections 15.1: Finding Out about Learning Disabled Children

Arrange with your instructor to interview a special education teacher of learning disabled children. When you meet for the conversation, indicate to the teacher that you would like to talk about *one* child who has been diagnosed as learning disabled. Take careful notes on the characteristics of the child that the teacher identifies and of the program of instruction that is described.

After all members of your class have completed their interviews, share the information you have obtained in class. Note the variety of characteristics that teachers identified. Look to see what is common and what is different about their instructional programs.

Understanding of *numerical* concepts of *more* and *less, bigger* and *smaller*, and so on can be checked in simple arithmetic problems.

Spatial concepts of *adjacent to, above, under, left,* and *right* can be tested through the directed placement of concrete objects.

Temporal concepts of *before, after,* and *until* can be observed by having the student follow instructions dependent upon those key words.

Working with Learning Disabled Students

Rawson's data demonstrate that *dyslexic* students, competently diagnosed between the ages of six and twelve, have the *same* chance as do nondyslexic students for success in later educational achievement.[4]

Rawson reported a follow-up study of fifty-six boys with developmental language disability enrolled in the School in Rose Valley, 1930–47. Twenty of these boys were diagnosed as definitely dyslexic.

A closer look at individual records of the 20 boys adjudged dyslexic in childhood shows two boys who were not college graduates; four who had by 1964–1965 achieved bachelor's degrees only; four who had each added one year of graduate study; one who had a law degree, one a graduate degree in divinity, and three others, already with master's degrees, who were doctoral candidates; five already with doctorates, one of them with two years' post-doctoral study and another with a Ph.D. in addition to his M.D. This seems, indeed, an encouragingly good record to have been made by a group of true dyslexics, some of them with severe initial handicaps. Could one conjecture that a disability, when it is not insuperable, may act as a spur to achievement? Some research in motivation and learning points in that direction.[5]

Diagnostic criteria used by Rawson included:

1. The initial failure of the boy to try to read.
2. Ways the boy failed to measure up in language achievement.
3. Persistence of characteristic spelling inadequacies.
4. Many family histories contain reference to other family members with the same or similar symptoms.[6]

Orton defined the problem in 1928:

Our concept of strephosymbolia as a physiological variant rather than a general mental defect naturally gives a decidedly better prognosis, and there is not only good theoretical basis for the belief that the disability can be corrected and the children taught to read, but there is also to be derived from the theory a path of attack for such retraining.[7]

Mrs. Orton reaffirmed the use of her husband's definition in 1966:

Whether or not our theory is right, I do not know, but I do know that the methods of retraining which we have derived from that viewpoint have worked. I do not claim them to be a panacea for reading troubles of all sorts, but I do feel that we understand the blockade which occurs so frequently in children with good minds and which results in the characteristic reading disability of the strephosymbolic type of childhood.[8]

Richek, List, and Lerner reminded teachers that the National Advisory Committee on Dyslexia and Related Reading Disorders could not reach agreement on a definition for dyslexia in 1969. However, the committee indicated that severely disabled readers' "characteristics include a lack of prerequisite skills, a failure to appreciate what reading is about (lack of cognitive clarity), inadequate language development, and learning styles that inhibit reading growth."[9]

Englebardt reported the difficulty in securing needed services for children with severe learning problems in school.

Many educators and most parents refuse to recognize the problem. . . . They keep pushing, cajoling, even threatening the youngster, in an attempt to make him pass courses . . . refusing to recognize that maybe he can't do the work.

If the problem is brain damage or emotional disturbance, then special education should be started before the child's self-esteem is completely destroyed.[10]

At the Adams School for Exceptional Children in New York City, Englebardt reported that more than 80 percent of the students who take an academic course go on to college, while 90 percent of those taking occupational courses are able to get and hold productive jobs. These are the youngsters, he says, who would have been classified as "uneducable" ten years ago.

A number of programs planned to help children are available. Fernald,[11] Hegge, Kirk, and Kirk,[12] Ellingson,[13] and de Hirsch, et al.[14] recommend prereading training to develop gross motor skills, eye-hand coordination, laterality, directionality, time-space relationships, and perception of form. Visual perception and discrimination, auditory perception and ability to scrutinize word forms are important prereading activities.

Other programs have been designed to provide exposure to fluent language on a repeated basis. Originally called the *neurological impress method,*[15] it has been modified and variously labeled.[16]

There has also been an emphasis on exposure to print, on the total development of language, and on the role of the teacher as a language model.

The Fernald Kinesthetic Tracing Technique

This method begins by asking the children what words they would like to learn how to read. Their initial words may build such a sentence as "I live in Albuquerque." They are encouraged to compose their own stories, and the vocabulary is not controlled. They learn to write from memory each word used in their stories. They read their written copies and then within twenty-four hours are presented with a typewritten copy to ensure learning to read print. Either manuscript or cursive writing may be used. The kinesthetic method develops through four stages:

Tracing

The teacher writes the word for the student in large print. The student traces with the middle and index fingers over the teacher's writing *and* pronounces the word in syllables as it is traced, repeating it until he or she can write it without error. The child then attempts to write it in his or her story. If the word is misspelled, the student goes back to tracing. In this stage, finger contact is important, writing from memory to put the word in the story is significant, and the child pronounces the word by syllables as he or she writes it. The teacher writes the words on large uniform strips of paper for filing alphabetically as they are learned. The student then learns alphabetical order through practice from the beginning.

Writing without Tracing

Depending on the individual, after a student has learned about one hundred words, he or she looks at the new word, pronounces it in syllables, and writes it from memory without tracing. This is similar to the visual-motor method described by Harris. The child's stock of sight words can be filed alphabetically on three- by five-inch cards.

Recognition in Print

The student becomes able to study the word in print, is told what it says, pronounces it in syllables, and writes it from memory. To keep a file of every new word is no longer necessary. Book reading can now be introduced. The child knows 150 words and can *begin* to read in a more difficult book than a preprimer.

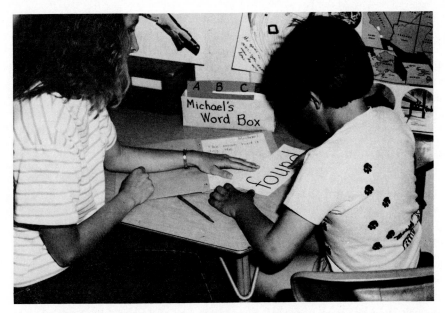

Michael's teacher is using the Fernald VAKT approach to teaching him to read. Michael is at the tracing stage in his learning.

Word Analysis

Word-attack skills are developed through techniques that teach the child to decipher new words through parts of "old" ones and through learning structural-analysis skills sequentially.

For the psychoneurologically impaired child learning to read, every device that helps firmly establish a concept or process should be used. These include filmstrips, tape recorders, tachistoscopes, and slide projectors. All the modalities of learning need to be involved to reinforce new learnings. *Visual, auditory, kinesthetic,* and *tactile* (*VAKT*) channels should be strengthened. Programmed workbooks are valuable because of their sequential structure and immediate feedback of correct response. New programs that rely minimally on reading can be incorporated into the curriculum, but the reading process should never be discouraged.

The VAKT approach is particularly emphasized in reading. The student sees the word, hears it pronounced, then writes it or traces it as he or she pronounces it slowly. Tactile memory is employed when three-dimensional letters can be traced. These can be made of wood to which sandpaper is applied. Pipecleaner letters are also satisfactory surfaces for tracing.

The Fernald Technique was designed to be used with one learner at a time. Some modifications for working with small groups of children have been proposed, making the technique more practical for teachers.[17] A classroom is known to the authors in which third- to fifth-grade children who had serious reading problems were instructed in how the method would be carried out and how they were to function. The children were then given notebooks for their stories.

Each constructed an alphabetical card file. The teacher provided words on the cards as individuals requested them and typed each child's writing each evening. Time was provided to individuals for reading and rereading their stories and reviewing their card files. Children in the group withdrew from the intensive tracing technique at various times as they felt that they could remember the words without that support. The children and their teacher were able to make the method succeed when no more than seven children were working at one time.

The Hegge, Kirk, and Kirk "Grapho-Vocal" Method

This is a method of teaching word recognition in which the students "sound out," pronounce, and write each word. They pronounce words entirely phonetically (synthetically) and later write the words from dictation. As the teacher pronounces words for spelling, the students must sound the parts (analytically). The drills are designed primarily for:

1. Those of primary reader level.
2. Those with whom usual methods of teaching have failed or do not seem to yield results.
3. Those who know the initial consonant sounds or who will be taught these before using the drills.
4. Those needing help in auditory discrimination in word structure.

The drill book is divided into the following four sections:

Section I presents introductory sounds including short vowels, long vowels, double vowels, vowel-consonant teams, and some word endings. The drill is usually presented in these steps:

1. Sound the words letter by letter.
2. Blend the sounds together.
3. Pronounce the words.
4. Write the words as a spelling lesson.

The first of the four parts of lesson one follows:

s a t	m a t	r a t	b a t	c a t	f a t
c a p	s a p	m a p	t a p	l a p	r a p
a m	r a m	S a m	h a m	d a m	j a m
r a g	b a g	t a g	w a g	h a g	l a g
c a n	m a n	r a n	t a n	f a n	p a n
s a d	m a d	h a d	l a d	p a d	d a d

Section II presents many vowel-consonant combinations of sounds. With some pupils, to discontinue book reading all through Section I of the drills may be desirable. Book reading at grade level two or three may be started when the pupils are ready for Section II drills. In transferring to story reading, the teacher must pronounce all nonphonetic words for the pupils.

Section III presents advanced sounds including vowel combinations and variants, prefixes and suffixes, and some "family" roots. The manual suggests that when Section III is reached, emphasis should be placed on reading for meaning, evaluation of ideas in print, and developing vocabulary.

Section IV presents supplementary exercises and exceptions to configurations previously taught.

While these drills are designed as a specific reading method for a few pupils with special difficulties, they are often useful with some other students who need extra individual teaching to develop adequate auditory abilities for reading, writing, and spelling.

Gillingham-Stillman Remedial Training for Children with Specific Disabilities

For those students who have a great deal of difficulty in sequencing letters in words, Gillingham and Stillman suggested:

1. When this method is begun, it is to be followed very precisely and no use should be made of reading in any way until after this method is well established.
2. One begins with the names and sounds of the letters and builds words.
3. The learner reads only "phonic" words at first.

Gillingham and Stillman believed that all children would profit from an alphabetic approach; that knowing the names and sounds of the letters facilitates reading and spelling for all children. This method uses visual, tracing, and auditory skills in an integrated fashion. The first task is to teach all the letters.

The first group of letters taught is: *a b h k p i f j m t.*

This makes possible building and teaching the following words:

at	bat	fat	mat	hat	pat
it	bit	fit		hit	pit
am	jam	tam	ham		
ap	map	tap			
ab	jab				
ip	hip	tip			
ib	bib	fib			
im	him	Jim	Kim	Tim	

The writing procedure follows these five steps:

1. The teacher makes the letter.
2. The student traces the letter.
3. The student copies it.
4. The student writes it without copy.
5. The student writes the word but turns away so that he or she cannot see what he is writing.

Gillingham and Stillman described a four-point process in practicing the writing exercise:

The teacher writes and pronounces the word: for example, *bat*.

The children:

1. Repeat *bat*.
2. Spell "b–a–t."
3. Write the word and spell as they write "b–a–t."
4. Read *bat*.

While learning the letters in Group 1, they read only words and sentences built from the letters taught up to that point. The teacher gradually adds phonemes in this order:

g	o	r	l	n	th (this)
u	ch (chin)		c	e	s
sh (ship)		d	w	wh	y
v	z				

Teachers who expect to use the Gillingham-Stillman method would need to study the manual carefully.

The Gillingham-Stillman method was designed to be used with one learner at a time. Therefore, it is suitable for only special learning settings where the focus can be individualized. Slingerland developed a classroom modification of the technique to be used as a preventive or early remedial measure with specific language disability (SLD) or specific developmental dyslexic children in the primary grades. It is a classroom adaptation of the Orton and Gillingham approach to reading, writing, and spelling.[18] The method is supported by extensive testing and detailed teacher's manuals. It continues the *visual-auditory-kinesthetic (VAK)* methodology of Gillingham-Stillman.

Other Techniques that Have Worked

Ellingson reported an anecdote about a boy who, after deliberate, synthetic teaching, learned all the parts of the word *until*. Yet, he could never recognize the word quickly in print. Ellingson's report follows:

> Finally, he said to his teacher, "If I could just *see* an 'until,' I know I could remember it." What was necessary to complete the boy's mastery of the word was an associative method. The boy was instructed to draw, from within himself, his idea of the word—to make a picture to go with a sentence using the word. The boy then carefully drew a picture of a herd of cows, pastureland, a fence with a gate, and a farmhouse in the distance, with the cows going through the gate toward the farmhouse. He then wrote the sentence, "I will wait until the cows come home." For this boy, with this word, "until the cows come home" provided the needed association and visual memory that firmly "set" it in his mind. From then on, whenever he came across the word, no matter how different or complicated the context, he would

look at it and say, "Oh, yes, that's until—until the cows come home." This achievement is not inconsequential. The child had used all of his avenues of learning—then added association and was able to read, write, spell, and comprehend the word "until."[19]

If the student is willing, new approaches can be tried, such as one suggested by Harold and Harriett Blau, designed to block the visual channel when learning a new word.[20] The word is pronounced and spelled as it is traced on the pupil's back. The student does not look at the word until he has spelled it (by arranging three-dimensional letters in proper sequence) along with the teacher during the tracing experience. Finally, they look at it, write it on paper or on the chalkboard, and then record it on a card to keep in the vocabulary file.

Ravenette, in *Dimensions of Reading Difficulties,* cites the case of a fourteen-year-old boy who was referred to a child guidance center for help with his reading. His reading ability was comparable to that of third graders.

> On one occasion . . . he was reading from a book geared to the older
> backward reader and was confronted with the following sentence: "Tugboat
> Annie was liked by all the people in the docks." He got as far as the word *was*
> and then stopped with a puzzled look. The sentence was rewritten, "All the
> people in the docks liked Tugboat Annie," and this was read unhesitatingly. He
> was asked about the difficulty and his reply was to the effect that the word
> "liked" in the original sentence did not seem to make sense, so he did not go
> on. Using the idea of different linguistic codes, we can say that the sentence in
> its first form was using elaborate language, expressing an idea using the
> passive mood. The idea presented in the second form used the active mood, a
> form which is more common in the restricted code.[21]

For this boy, the linguistic form and therefore the thought it communicated was unusual, and inhibited his ability to read this specific sentence with meaning. Ravenette discussed this example in relation to the sociological and family dimension of poor readers who come from homes in low socioeconomic settings, where the family shows little interest in reading, where many mothers have full-time jobs, and where school gets little encouragement. *However,* this problem of children's ability to understand more *elaborate* as well as *restricted* language needs very badly to be explored for children with psychoneurological learning disabilities.

Neurological Impress Method

The neurological impress method (NIM) was designed to increase reading efficiency, fluency, and comprehension by having the child and the teacher read pages simultaneously. As many pages as possible were to be read so that the child would gain a sense of what fluent discourse should sound like. There are several variations on that method that the reading teacher might wish to study and have available for use. Samuels[22] and Chomsky[23] suggested techniques that are called the *method of repeated readings.* The child reads and rereads short passages until they can be read fluently in Samuels' technique. Then all the short passages can be read as a single, longer unit. Chomsky has children listen to taped stories until they can be read fluently. Holdaway commented on the debate about whether *memorizing* materials is reading:

> Clearly, the extent to which memory for the text contributes to a "reading" varies widely from individual to individual, from stage to stage, and from time to time. To some extent it is dependent on the number of repetitions, the recency of those repetitions, and the place of that particular "story" in the total range of material for which some recall through familiarity is available . . . . it is in the area of confirmation and self-correction that memory for text plays the most essential role in early reading. . . . *The most important aspect of memory for text in early reading is not the exact recall of word items learned by heart but the proper assurance of the reader through his own language system that he is operating successfully.*[24]

Kann found that repeated readings resulted in improved fluency, comprehension, attitudes, and motivation of disabled readers.[25] O'Shea, Sindelar, and O'Shea linked *repeated readings* and attentional cues to improved reading fluency and comprehension.[26] Carbo taped entire books for eight elementary school students who had serious reading problems. The students listened to the books and read when they felt that they could be successful. Follow-up lessons with games and activities, excluding phonics, were provided for each child.[27]

Other labels for similar methods include *assisted reading,*[28] *echo reading,* and *impress.*[29] The variations among all these methods are in their details, since they are all based on immersion of the reader in fluent discourse. Many researchers and practitioners working with these techniques have shown good results. What seems to be lacking is a neurological explanation of why the methods work.

Language-Based Techniques

Much has been written about reading to children, immersing them in the sound of language, and familiarizing them with the literary nature of print as opposed to the informal characteristics of speech.[30] Butler reported a dramatic immersion program in *Cushla and Her Books* that helped transform a severely handicapped child into one performing better than her peers.[31]

Reading is one facet of total language development, having intimate connections to listening, speaking, and writing with overall umbrellas of experiences and thinking. Allen provided an extensive guide for carrying out such a unified, or *language-experience,* program.[32] Dionisio described a program for sixth graders in which they wrote, conferenced about their writing, and read not only what they had already written but also materials that provided more opportunities for writing. Eight guidelines were provided for implementing such a program:

1. Develop your own personal background.
2. Assess the students' perceptions of writing.
3. Explore possible topics, audiences, and purposes for writing.
4. Model writing behaviors (for teacher).
5. Choose the first topic.
6. Circulate and respond to the content.

7. Provide materials—books, writing references, writing materials.
8. Adhere to cautions, realizing that writing takes time; writing is controlled by the writer; and technical editing comes after content is developed.[33]

Holt and Vacca reminded teachers:

Children learning the written form of language ought to be producing it as well as reading it. They should be reading *and* writing. They should be aware of someone reading their writing, and that what they are reading is someone's writing.[34]

The adult is a powerful *model* for children. If we want children to read and write, we need to be seen doing those language activities also. If some reading problems that eventually become serious are initially attitudinal and motivational, then teachers and parents need to be faithful to their own reading and writing. It might be worth noting that few youths in our society have to be persuaded to learn to drive cars; the power of the adult model is clearly demonstrated!

A young teacher provided that kind of powerful model for her students when she wrote:[35]

> *BRUTALITY*
> Words swim inside
> My ink pen,
> Happily perfecting
> Their backstroke,
> Wading through the
> Sweet blue-black
> And floating
> contentedly
> On their little backs.
> But I
> (My mind having
> grown restless)
> Selfishly
> Pluck out the plug
> And watch the
> bewildered little
> Creatures
> Be sucked onto
> The vast, blank page
> Where they
> Dry and crystallize
> Unable to voice
> Their tiny cries
> Of protest.
> —*Opal A. Evans*

Besides the model that she provided for taking risks with writing, the author provided some exciting uses of metaphorical language.

One has only to study the titles of articles appearing in various professional publications for teachers to note the emphasis on teacher modeling of reading and writing for children with varied abilities.[36] These models are especially powerful for children with reading problems, for the models can replace much of the nagging that many of these children must endure, provided the children find ways in which they can identify with the teacher.

Teachers should remember that *big books* and *predictable books,* discussed earlier, may help severely disabled readers to develop insights about the reading process and the predictability of print. These children may find reading such books several times helpful so that the mechanics are under control and they can focus on meaning.

Techniques to Explore with Younger Reluctant Readers

1. Letters can be cut out of relatively fine *sandpaper* so that children who have difficulty remembering size, shape, or form of letters can trace them with their fingers—preferably when they are spelling words (see figure 15.4).
2. *Shadow reading* is described by Frostig as that situation in which the teacher and child both read aloud. When the child is getting along quite well, the teacher lowers his or her voice so that the child carries the responsibility; when the child does not know the words, the teacher goes on reading, and they get through difficult sections until the child can again read successfully.[37] This is sometimes identified as the "impress method."[38]
3. Auto mechanics, practical arts, and shop classes can be motivation for learning to read. Motivation to read better is likely to be sharpened when students realize the need to read manuals, specifications, directions, and plans. Here the names of tools, how they are used, for what purposes, how they are maintained in good condition—all of this—is clearly important to the future skilled worker.[39]

   The teachers should remember that many of the words used in industrial arts are used in other contexts also, and this understanding can serve as reinforcement to the slow learners; as an example, the word *chisel* is a tool but also is a word used to denote swindling or cheating. There is a relationship, too, between the learning of symbols on drawings, blueprints, and diagrams, and the use of and need for both the understanding of mathematical symbols and of reading maps and charts.[40] For seriously retarded readers, the following is suggested:

   An excellent kind of beginning reading material is the description of a process that they have already learned. They can dictate the directions, the teacher writes what they say, has it typed, and returns it to them as part of a shop manual for them to read and study. Being thoroughly familiar with the subject and having expressed it in their own vocabulary and sentence structure, they can read it more easily than the printed material for their grade.[41]

4. Beyond providing the younger children with markers with just one line exposed at a time, teachers may find, though very rarely, that older students will adjust to the reading task easier if the lines are shortened into meaningful phrases.

Figure 15.4. Sandpaper letter samples

1. witch   watch   Which is   ?

2. track   truck   Which is   ?

3. spoon   spin   Which is   ?

Figure 15.5. Word-recognition exercises

This process makes *short lines,* which is one of its objectives, but it also divides the print into *meaningful phrases*—separated on different lines. The following paragraph is taken from *The Mystery of Morgan Castle:*

The man took Gabby
into the basement
of Morgan Castle.
The other two men
were watching them
when they came in.

Gabby saw
Miss Wellington and Bill
on the other side
of the room.
They seemed
to be all right.[42]

5. Associating vowel sounds and letters—as the letter affects the meaning of a word—can be a worthwhile, fun game for children in interest centers:

What do you cook in, a *pat* or a *pot*?
What do you sleep on, a *cot* or a *cut*?
Do you ride in a *track* or a *truck*?
Do you put the food in a *dish* or a *dash*?
Do you run a *rice* or a *race*?
Do you bake in an *oven* or an *even*?
This is good practice done *orally* for those needing to improve auditory discriminating ability. For children hearing various dialects of English, different problems arise in hearing vowel sounds. Later, word-recognition exercises can be designed to discriminate the words in print (see figure 15.5).

Needs of Older Students

Teenagers who read three or more grades below their grade level need two ingredients in their reading program. They require *practice* with oral and silent reading, and they must experience *success*.

The goals of the secondary reading program are comprehension and independence. These goals are achieved by developing familiarity with our written language. Following are some exercises that have been found to be effective in teaching teenagers who are deficient in skills:

1. Practice: silent reading in materials at individual's independent reading levels.
2. Practice: oral reading in materials at individual's instructional level on a one-to-one basis with the teacher (or another adult).
3. Cloze procedure exercises using short passages at the independent and instructional levels to develop skills in predicting and anticipating.
4. Multiple meanings exercises compiled from various sources to increase vocabulary flexibility (see figures 14.3 and 14.4).
5. Writing articles for the school newspaper where the main idea is summarized in the title and stated in the first sentence of a paragraph.
6. Writing telegrams: take a message and reduce it to very basic information.
7. Elaboration: Take a telegraph message and elaborate, using as many descriptive words as you can think of. This can also be nonsensical, but whether it is sense or nonsense, it can be fun.
8. Newspaper and magazine ads: Read them, find the fact and the opinion. Evaluate the propaganda involved. Then write and design your own ads.
9. Reading to follow directions:
   a. Read the auto driver's manual for passing the test to get a driver's license.
   b. Write down the directions for making a macramé purse (or some other project of interest), and then teach this to another student.
10. Commercial games for relaxation—and familiarity with written words:
    a. Spill and Spell.
    b. Dolch Group Word Game (Bingo).
    c. Scrabble.
    d. Word wheels: one smaller circle superimposed on a larger one and fastened wth a brad creates word wheels to practice substitutions with initial consonants, blends, prefixes, and suffixes (see figure 15.6).
11. Learning to fill out job applications, driver's license forms, resumes, and other real-world writing requirements.
12. Using computer software, including tutorials, simulations, and word processors.
13. Read a story aloud to a small group of teenagers. Of course, the stories have to be carefully chosen; for example, "The Lady or the Tiger." Students may make inferences and draw conclusions in writing or orally.

The remainder of the suggestions never replace numbers one and two. One-to-one instruction is essential. During this time phonics instruction, word analysis, and use of context clues are taught as each need arises. Phonics instruction is not very effective

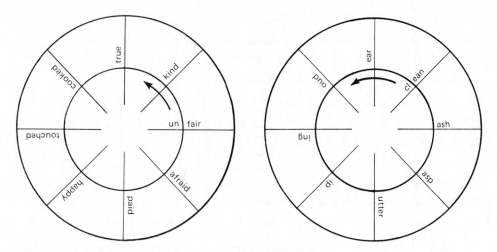

Figure 15.6. Word wheels

if it is isolated or continued over a very long period of time. If these kinds of exercises can be continued and teenagers do experience success, they really can *learn how to learn* and that is what the teacher's job is all about.

Unusual Behaviors that Distress Teachers

The occasional students who (1) distract easily, (2) are hyperactive all day long, (3) are continually interrupting the class, talking about irrelevant topics, or (4) perseverate, are sure to create many difficult classroom situations for their teachers. Professional help, through the services of the school psychologist, is necessary for many of these children. The following suggestions may help the teachers adjust to the children until such help is available.

1. The children who distract easily often need alert redirection and a favorable seating location in the classroom. The teacher's objective is to provide a seating arrangement that minimizes distracting stimuli and puts the child in a good working location without complete isolation. The least distraction may result from seating the children in an "up front" corner near the chalkboard, in a side corner partially screened by an easel, a movable chalkboard, or a bookcase, or near a shy, quiet child. Greatest distractions come beside the teacher's desk, near the door, or near an obstreperous peer (see figure 15.7).

    The teacher may retain a calm atmosphere in the room by (1) having materials ready on time so that the children do not have undirected waiting periods, (2) establishing routines so that the children know what to do next and make these transitions with a minimum of interruption, and (3) lending a child

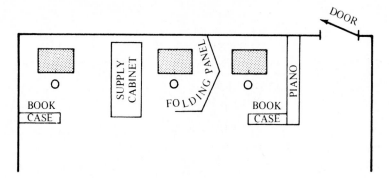

Figure 15.7. Use of carrels in a classroom

support, perhaps by standing in close proximity, putting a hand gently on his or her shoulder, or by speaking quietly after such difficult transitions as seeing a movie or returning from a strenuous game at recess. The teacher's presence may have a quieting effect on overstimulation.

2. The children who are *hyperactive* need sympathetic understanding rather than censure and punishment. If they *feel* that they cannot sit still, it will not help much to make them do so; if they are constantly playing with a toy, pencil, ruler, eraser, or knife, they may be able to concentrate better on what the teacher is saying with something in their hands than if it is taken away; if ten minutes is as long as they can sit still, they should be permitted a "change" at the end of that time.

   The teacher can try (1) giving the hyperactive pupils tasks of short duration, (2) giving them tasks that they are *sure* to do successfully, and (3) keeping their frustrations at a minimum by being sure that directions are understood, the work is not too difficult, and the environment has a minimum of distractions.

3. The *disinhibited child*—the child who interrupts the whole class with irrelevant information—cannot be permitted to continue to talk and, as rapidly as possible, must learn to wait until an appropriate time to express his or her thoughts. The child exhibits this behavior when continually interrupting and asking irrelevant questions in the middle of a class discussion. In the middle of a discussion of a directed reading lesson, the child may ask loudly, "What kind of soup will we have for lunch?" Obviously the group cannot change its activity and permit an endless "sharing period" to go on. The teacher can say firmly, "Not right now, John, in just a few minutes." However, this carries a promise that the teacher will give John his opportunity in a few minutes. By then he may have forgotten. It does seem best to encourage him to wait short periods, and then increasingly longer ones, until he can "share" only when the others do. Luxford[43] suggested that older pupils be given a little notebook, and when they interrupt, they are told to make a note of what they wanted to say in the notebook. Then at a later time, they may talk from their notes. This practice has a curing effect because the difficulty of writing is so great that soon the pupils remember not to interrupt, but do not bother to write anything down and continue quietly with their work.

4. The pupils who persist in continuing a response, a line of activity, or other inappropriate repetition are said to *perseverate.* If the teacher is getting the wrong response repeatedly to a word-recognition exercise, it would be well to change the subject radically enough to force a new pattern of thought. Dubnoff and others stated that perseveration is one of the most common distinguishing symptoms of children with neurological impairments. They recommend that the perseveration may be broken by:

Picture cues, that is, matching a word to the picture it represents; or color cues, that is, recognizing different *colors* of beginning letters.[43]

Johnson and Myklebust illustrated perseveration in an older child:

A twelve-year-old boy when asked to write the alphabet wrote the letters in proper sequence but with three "e's." When asked why he had written them, he replied, "I got started and couldn't stop." This boy often wrote the words "see" or "three" with either three or four "e's" instead of two.[44]

Accommodation in the Classroom

Classroom organization can help to accommodate children with specific learning disabilities:

1. *Each classroom should be planned* so that furniture could be rearranged so as to make two or three carrels (enclosed desk space) where children could be seated in relatively isolated, quiet, "protected" places to work. In the traditional classroom this is not difficult to do with bookcases, a piano, if there happens to be one in the room, or folding panels. The diagram in figure 15.7 shows how one teacher made three carrels along one side of the classroom.

   In the modular style of buildings being built today, it will be necessary to organize "quiet" areas in other ways. But the hyperactive, distractible child needs help in order to concentrate and make progress.

   The carrels are useful for other children, too, and should also be available to them. Not only the inattentive children but also the ambitious children who write scholarly reports can profitably work there occasionally. Work that distracts others, reading aloud or telling stories to record them on a tape recorder, or other kinds of language activities that require "office space" or "conference room" space to best carry on the activity can be done in these cloistered areas.

2. *Admitting children to the regular classroom for short periods of time each day* is an important step in helping them to adjust to staying for longer periods. If a child can conform for half an hour in a large group of children, he or she should be accommodated for that period of time. Normally, the child will want to stay with peers. Normally, too, he or she wants to lengthen the attention span. If this does not happen, the help of a counselor, psychologist, or resource teacher is needed. Hopefully, the half hour can be extended to an hour, and progressively

the child learns to adjust to a half day in the room. The important point is that if the child is excluded altogether from the classroom, no opportunity to begin making this adjustment gradually is provided.

3. Encourage parents to discuss the use of *drug therapy* with their family physician for the child who is hyperactive, disinhibited, a constant talker in the classroom, or who in other ways continually interrupts classroom routine. The administration of drugs is strictly a medical problem. Numbers of both physicians and parents do not look favorably upon this practice, yet it is the teacher's responsibility to try to accommodate the child in the classroom. For some children the behavior is so marked that after half an hour of a tutoring session, competent clinicians can safely record in their log, "Bruce must not have had his medicine today; his behavior was just like it always is when his mother forgets."

Sally Williams, California School Nurses Association, testifying before the Government Operations Subcommittee of the U.S. House of Representatives on the Right to Private Inquiry on the Use of Various Behavior Modification Drugs on Elementary School Pupils said that:

> . . . about two percent of the pupils with normal or above normal intelligence were unable to achieve acceptably in reading, spelling, and mathematics. Parents, teachers, and school nurses agreed that this pupil tended to have these characteristics. "The child was extremely hyperactive, as though he had 'springs inside,' had a very short attention span, could not write his full name, was excessively distractible, and had no impulse control."
>
> Mrs. Williams noted that the literature is filled with documented case studies showing that such pupils, carefully identified by psychological and medical evaluation have been significantly helped by amphetamines and Ritalin.[45]

Carpenter wrote:

> Learning disabilities vary greatly among students. What helps one child will not necessarily help another, even though the problems are similar. . . . proper medication can calm the overactive child and cause a dramatic improvement in behavior and learning ability.
>
> But . . . medication can also properly make more alert a listless daydreamer by increasing his attention span and improving his ability to concentrate.
>
> . . . medication can also be used to improve significantly short attention span, poor concentration, distractibility, handwriting and printing, visual perception and fidgetness.
>
> . . . medication can also reduce tempers, mood swings, hostility, and certain types of headaches, stomach aches and sleep problems.[46]

However, Divoky presented another side to the argument.[47] She stated that the widespread habit of grossly labeling children is sure to be more harmful than helpful. Creating misleading expectations is sure to lead to an inadequate prognosis of behavior.

Figure 15.8. Cursive writing before letter separation

Figure 15.9. Cursive writing with letter separation

> Unfortunately, there is little agreement either in medicine or in education as to the criteria which would be used to identify children with minimal brain dysfunction or learning disabilities. The disabilities presented by these children are extremely heterogeneous and the search for commonality in symptoms, pathology or etiology has, so far, been fruitless. . . . General terms such as minimal brain dysfunction and undefined learning disabilities have no consistent meaning and no value as a basis either for the development or application of effective methods.[48]

Classroom teachers have to make sure that labeling boys and girls as having learning disabilities does not become an "easy cop-out" for not teaching these children.

4. *Teachers must be constantly alert to specific methodologies* that help children to overcome whatever specific problem they face presently. Westeen reported that a fourth-grade boy had great difficulty separating his letters in cursive writing. It was hardly readable, as is illustrated in figure 15.8.

One day she gave him paper ruled in one-half inch squares and instructed him that only one letter went into each square (see figure 15.9). She demonstrated carefully and worked with Tom while he started. Amazingly, his first paper written on this lined paper was very well done and, after using the lined paper for a period of time, he separated his letters very satisfactorily in cursive writing.[49]

5. *Operant Conditioning.* Bandura reported a remedial reading case treated by operant conditioning. The three elements in operant conditioning in psychotherapy are: (1) reinforcing through the use of tangible rewards, in enjoyable activities, in praise, and in special attention; (2) making reinforcement

conditional on achieving desired behavior correctly timed, and behavior that is predictable; and (3) being able later to elicit the desired behavior.[50]

These principles were applied to a fourteen-year-old delinquent boy who, in addition to a history of aggressive, destructive behavior, always received failing school grades and read at second-grade level. He was judged at school to be uneducable, incorrigible, and mentally retarded.

In remedial reading therapy, he received points for each new word mastered; these points could be exchanged for tangible rewards, such as phonograph records, for small sums of money, or for other requests. In four and one-half months, his reading level progressed from second to fourth grade, he received passing grades in all subjects, and his aggressive, destructive behavior stopped. The tangible rewards that helped obtain these desirable results had cost a total of $20.31 for all the items received in exchange for points.

Behavior modification became a very popular technique for discussion in educational circles a decade ago. While it is less discussed as a "new" or unusual methodology for changing behavior today, it is certainly being used by many teachers. Certain modification techniques are more appropriate than others, but many of the expected ends of behavior modification have been in vogue for some time. A few of these are:

a. *Praise.* Generally speaking, praise is given easily enough by some people, but not nearly often enough. Both children and teachers should be given much more praise than they get. Ignoring people's undesirable behavior and commenting only on the good behavior that one sees pays dividends.

b. *Modeling.* Children need models to imitate. And they do modify their behaviors to try to conform to the model of someone they respect or might want to emulate. Young children can model behaviors of older children, their teachers, or other adults.

c. *Token reinforcement.* Technically, this behavior involves the systematic giving of rewards for desired behavior. Tangible rewards with which we are familiar, or social rewards such as earning extra playtime or an opportunity to spend a dinner hour with the teacher, have both worked in appropriate circumstances.

   If they are to use behavior modification as a technique of behavior control, then teachers need adequate preparation and discipline in the technique they are using. Under proper circumstances this technique can strengthen students' self-control and expand their skills.[51]

6. *Amplifying sound.* Johnson, in an article entitled "Treatment Approaches to Dyslexia," discussed the possibility of amplifying the sound for some children who have auditory perceptual problems:

Occasionally, we give children portable, binaural amplifiers to use during brief periods of instruction. When the sound is amplified through the headsets, many can perceive units within words that they cannot detect under ordinary listening conditions. A seventh-grade boy improved substantially in spelling when he decided to wear the amplifier while the teacher dictated words in class.[52]

Making Connections 15.2: Examining Perceptual Handicaps

For this activity you can use figure 15.12 in this chapter, or you can select any other picture that contains hidden pictures.

Hunt the hidden pictures with as many children as you can find to work with. Complete the task with each child individually. Keep notes about each child's performance. Plan to share with your class what you learned about the variety of perceptual abilities among children with whom you worked. Note especially any comments children made and the nonverbal messages they were sending during the task.

Teachers and parents need to keep alert to breakthroughs in technology for improvement of aids for the hearing impaired.

7. *Restating instructions before starting work.* Zedler worked with a group of children diagnosed as neurologically impaired.[53] The teachers tried to improve the auditory comprehension of these children by requiring them to repeat their oral instructions before responding. This helped the teacher to "see whether or not the child understood what was said to him, it reinforced auditory retention and recall, and it provided feedback for constructing a response."

8. *Managing diet.* Many studies have been conducted concerning diets, allergies, food additives, and "junk foods" for children.[54] The results of the studies frequently offer conflicting advice. Teachers and parents should look at children's responses to foods individually and base their decisions on the actual behaviors of children. Some children do respond better to instruction if sugar intake is limited, if foods with specific additives are eliminated, or if "junk foods" are denied or severely limited. If teachers and parents keep careful records and communicate about what each is doing in experimenting with foods and instruction, the best learning situation for the child will be identified.

Visual Motor Exercises

Perceptual disabilities in reading may be improved by having the students pay attention to letter details. This can be accomplished by supplying missing letters or filling in disconnected letters. Exercises in left-to-right direction can be devised. Outlining, stenciling, finding hidden pictures, and coloring first letters or difficult letters in heavy crayon are all beneficial activities. Sequencing can be practiced in copying and reproducing from memory.

Exercises in figures 15.10, 15.11, and 15.12 illustrate:

1. Finding the missing parts in pictures.
2. Finding the right "other half" of the picture.
3. Finding many hidden pictures of objects in the large picture.

Figure 15.10. What important part is missing?

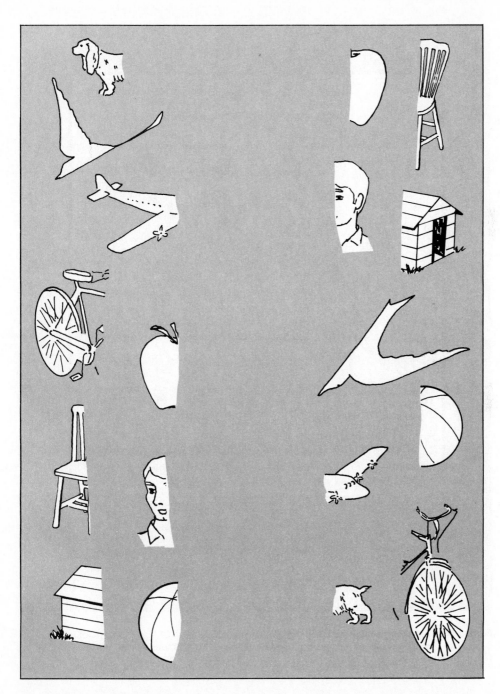

Figure 15.11. Draw a line from half of the picture in the first column to the half of the picture in the second column.

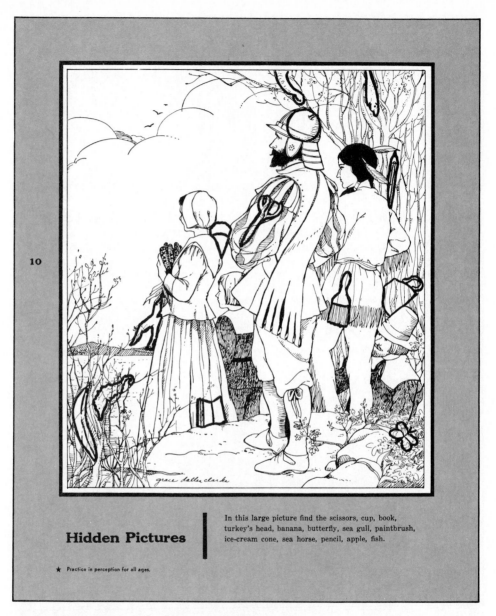

10

Hidden Pictures

In this large picture find the scissors, cup, book, turkey's head, banana, butterfly, sea gull, paintbrush, ice-cream cone, sea horse, pencil, apple, fish.

★ Practice in perception for all ages.

Figure 15.12. Hidden pictures. Copyright 1970 Highlights for Children, Inc., Columbus, Ohio. The "Hidden Pictures" page appears in each month's issue of *Highlights for Children*. Reprinted by permission. (The bold lines have been added by the authors.)

In Conclusion

The text has presented a need for the teacher to understand both the individual student and the procedures for assessing his or her abilities and strategy and skill deficiencies, and planning for his or her growth in reading. Understanding the student as a person requires some knowledge of the student's language background and language ability, learning difficulties if they exist, and home and adults who most influence his or her learning. Teachers must be competent to use the informal reading inventory, informal tests of word recognition, and tests of comprehension. They must know where to look beyond the classroom when they need special help. Finally, the teacher must be able to plan the range of skills that students are not using so that they will be able to complete the schoolwork expected of them. This concluding statement asks the reader to think philosophically about the student and his or her reading.

The brief case studies of Lester and John that follow represent two very different but fairly common types of readers found in regular classes. They need teachers who can first respond to them in affective ways and then program for them the needed cognitive skills.

Lester was referred to the reading center because he made many mistakes in his oral reading, and his writing was so badly spelled that his teacher could not read it. He was eight years old and finishing the second grade. His clever, well-thought-out story (figure 15.13) is fine, but his spelling is hardly the expected standard English spelling! For example: *eche* for *each; siad* for *said; are* for *our; how* for *who; bos* for *does; lost* for *lots; jumt,* with the *j* backwards, for *jumped; win* for *when; thow* for *through;* and *tiy* for *tie* suggest that he is listening carefully to what he thinks the word sounds like and then is trying to record that. Of course, reversals are giving him problems, too. One hopes that he will receive some help with the directional difficulty before he becomes discouraged and loses his creative imagination for writing his own stories.

A translation may help for parts of Lester's story;

> Once upon a time there lived a frog and a
> mouse. One day they met. And they had a
> fight. Each said, "I'm better."
> The mouse said, "Why don't we do our best
> at things and then see who does best and he is
> the winner."
> So the mouse jumped and the frog jumped
> and lots of things.
> When they were through, it was a tie.

John was in a special seventh-grade language arts class. He had no independent skills in reading and writing. However, as the story in figure 15.13 will make quite clear, he was informed about many of the activities going on in his neighborhood. The story was dictated to a seventh-grade peer who possessed grade-level skills, but the

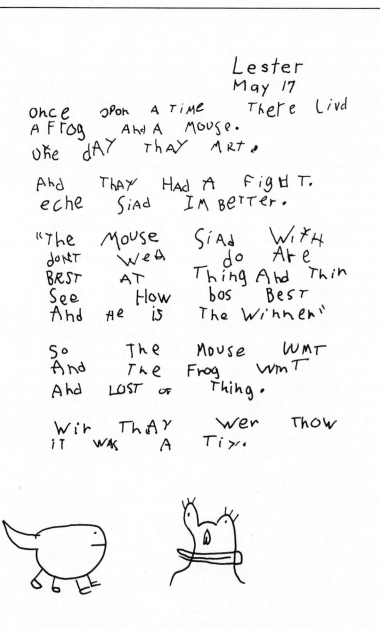

Lester
May 17

Once opon a time There Livd
A Frog And A Mouse.
One dAy They Mrt.

And They Had A FighT.
eche Siad IM BeTTer.

"The Mouse Siad WiTH
doNT Wea do ATe
BRST AT Thing And Thin
See How bos BesT
Ahd He is The WinneR"

So The Mouse WMT
And The Frog WMT
And LOST oF Thing.

Wir ThAy wer Thow
iT WAs A Tiy.

Figure 15.13. Lester's story

A Junkie on the Loose

The junkie was a heroin addict. He had escaped from prison and he did not have any money to buy heroin. He broke into a house and stole a television, stereo, and some money that was hidden. He sold the television and the stereo and got $200.00. He bought $200.00 worth of heroin and it would last him for three days. After three days passed, he broke into a grocery store and stole the money and some food because he was very hungry. He got $12,000.00 from the store. He bought himself a car, and rented an apartment and he bought more heroin. He still had some money left so he went to a concert and he almost got busted. One day, he was driving real fast, the pig stopped him and found some heroin on him. They took him to city hall. Then they found out that he had robbed the store and broke into the house. Then they took him back to prison and he was sentenced for 25 years.

*John
2/16
4th period*

Figure 15.14. John's story, as dictated

story was entirely John's. Also, he could read it amazingly accurately when he saw it in typewritten form. And he was delighted and motivated to prepare another one when his teacher had copies made for his entire class (figure 15.14). Not only had he "written" a story, but also it was "published."

Numerous writers have conveyed to teachers the need to reflect objectively on their responsibilities in teaching all of the students and accept the range of results in achievement. McCullough asked her readers to take an *eclectic* position in teaching reading and utilize all of the suggestions that they find to be helpful. She recommended a balance of silent reading, oral reading, word-recognition practice, and comprehension. Meier wrote of four myths that cause some people to expect the impossible of the classroom teachers. These myths themselves defy all that is known about the normal growth and development of children. Individual differences, readiness to master a task, motivation, and the psychological and physical well-being of the students in any given classroom have predetermined a wide range in achievement. All members of a given class will not read meaningfully at the *same level;* some are "ready" for the tasks of formal reading long before others; and it is not possible to master the skills of reading in isolation from thinking, problem-solving activities in subject matter fields. Further, Meier reminded us that "the good old days" were not really as good as they seem in retrospect. Vickery offered some excellent suggestions about the conditions under which students will learn best. And finally, Johnson chided us about the apathy we nurture when we are willing to be passive observers in front of the television set.

Much of the knowledge we now have about the teaching of reading has been developed by a curious and—in terms of the lives of children—wasteful pattern of extremes. We learned a great deal about oral reading by having too much of it, about silent reading by neglecting oral, about extensive reading by neglecting intensive, about sight vocabulary by neglecting phonics, about phonics and speed by neglecting comprehension. We are now involved in a great controversy over the relative virtues of a developmental program with systematic instruction and an individualized program with incidental instruction.

One would think that it should finally have dawned on us that all of these practices have value and that the sensible, most efficient program encompasses them all.[55]

Brighton has said that today's teachers are expected to be all things to all people, at all times, for all reasons, on all occasions that appear to be even remotely related to the school.[56]

Meier explained that the public-at-large generally still accepts four myths about reading instruction in school, and because they believe these myths they do not understand why we need new approaches to school organization to meet all of the needs of all the children.[57]

1. Schools used to teach children how to read in the "good old days."
2. The success of the schools can be measured by their capacity to bring everyone up to "grade level" in reading.
3. The best way to have everyone read at grade level is to start teaching reading as early as possible.
4. Schools should concentrate on nothing but reading skills until they are mastered.

Meier urged teachers to try to dispel these myths and to try to demonstrate for parents any new innovations that work in their classrooms. She explained that children have to read about *something*. If they do not *know* about anything, if they do not *care* about anything, if they do not *think* problems through, and if they do not relate knowing, caring, thinking, and *reading,* then what will they ever do with all the discrete little reading skills teachers work so hard to teach.[58]

And according to Vickery:

1. The child learns best in an environment where he is rewarded, his differences accepted, and his humanness respected.
2. The child will learn best if the teacher knows that word recognition is much more than phoneme-grapheme relationships.
3. The child will learn best if the teacher carefully analyzes the prerequisite skills with the child that he needs for that lesson.
4. The child will learn best when the teacher uses language cues in both word recognition and achieving meaning.
5. The child will learn best when the teacher utilizes and develops the auditory-perceptual base for language.
6. The child will learn best when the teacher asks worthwhile questions.
7. The child will learn best when the teacher focuses positively on helping the child to organize and use culturally-appropriate experiences or those experiences common to all human existence.
8. The child will learn best when the teacher does diagnostic teaching.
9. Finally, the child learns best how to read when he reads.[59]

Nicholas Johnson expressed his apprehension about television media causing the viewer to be mentally unresponsive and to develop vacuous attitudes and behaviors:

> Very few of the American people are performing at more than five percent of their capacity—their capacity to perceive, to produce, to understand, to create, to relate to others, to experience joy. Of all the tragedies confronting an American of the 1970s; this one may well be the most sad. I believe that television—which provides most of the people of this country with their principal source of education, entertainment, information and opinion—bears perhaps more responsibility for this state of the nation than any other single institution.[60]

Summary

The primary task of the corrective reading teacher is the teaching that meaning is the first requisite in the process. The readers must find the sentences and the paragraphs that they are reading interesting and meaningful. Any teaching of phonic or structural skills as a word-analysis process must be subordinated to a reading experience that is important to the students. Short, motivated phonics lessons can be interesting if they are making worthwhile reading material easier to decode and understand.

> Too many students have cracked the symbol-sound code and yet remained reading cripples. Although they read so someone else could understand the message, they themselves fail to understand what they read either orally or silently. For instance, after pronouncing, "The cat sat on a mat," a first grader drew a picture of the cat and the mat widely separated. Certainly the words had meaning for him or he could not have pictured the cat or the mat; but the sentence had no meaning. A fifth grader read a paragraph correctly and answered the question, "What did you read?" with "I don't know." A seventh grader answered the question, "How fast did the boat go?" with "It didn't say," although it plainly did. Obviously, cracking the code had not allowed these children to attach meaning to what they read aloud.[61]

Rather than intensifying remedial effort to develop prescribed reading ability in primary school children who have learning disabilities or demonstrate no interest in learning to read, responding to their interests and extending their intellects in many areas orally may be more productive in the long run. This is not to say that all reading activities will be delayed; but rather that those reading activities needed with all the work the children are doing will be continued and utilized to try to develop a need for and encourage an interest in reading.

Older students must keep meaning as the primary focus of their remedial work. They need to see any special instruction as directed to their interests, present activities, and even future career goals.

The classroom teachers can organize the school day into flexibly arranged blocks of time during which students complete tasks for which they have a purpose and sufficient reading power. The teachers should remember:

1. Start where the student is.
2. Respect the individual.
3. Success may be its own motivation.
4. Specific lessons need to be related to a unified whole so that learning is cumulative, integrated, and purposeful.
5. A few children have special problems and need continued observation and planning.
6. The environment must be restructured for those who have experienced serious disapproval, rejection, or failure.
7. No one method works for all students—what awakens interest in some or convinces them that they can learn may not elicit such a response in others.
8. As long as the pupils are enrolled, a search for the best ways to "reach" them must continue.

For Further Reading

Bialystok, Ellen, and John Mitterer. "Metalinguistic Differences among Three Kinds of Readers." *Journal of Educational Psychology* 79, no. 2 (1987): 147–53. The researchers identified two populations of disabled readers and found that two different metalinguistic skills were the sources of their difficulties.

Bond, Guy L., et al. "Treating the Extremely Disabled Reader." In *Reading Difficulties: Their Diagnosis and Correction.* 6th ed., 201–17. Englewood Cliffs, N.J.: Prentice-Hall, 1989. This is a helpful chapter in a textbook devoted to basic approaches to severe disability.

Ekwall, Eldon E., and James L. Shanker. "Diagnosis and Remediation of the Severe Reading Disabilities." In *Diagnosis and Remediation of the Disabled Reader.* 2d ed., 313–41. Boston: Allyn and Bacon, 1985. This is a lengthy chapter in a textbook that deals with diverse aspects of the treatment of severe reading problems.

Fernald, Grace. *Remedial Techniques in Basic School Subjects.* New York: McGraw-Hill, 1971. This is a classic text in the field of remediation of severe disabilities.

Gillingham, Anna, and Bessie Stillman. *Remedial Training for Children with Specific Disability in Reading, Spelling, and Penmanship.* Cambridge, Mass.: Educators Publishing Service, 1966. Another classic text in severe reading disability, this work is based on the theories of Samuel Orton.

Loughlin, Catherine, and Joseph Suina. *The Learning Environment: An Instructional Strategy.* New York: Teachers College Press, 1982. This book gives many practical ideas based on sound theories for designing workable, literate environments for classrooms.

Manzo, Anthony V. "Psychologically Induced Dyslexia and Learning Disabilities." *Reading Teacher* 40 (January 1987): 408–13. The author suggests that emotional problems may be a neglected cause of learning disabilities.

Moskowitz, Fern C. "Success Strategies: Help for Struggling Students." *Learning* 17 (July–August 1988): 46–47. In chart format, the author presents specific suggestions for dealing with children who can't stick to tasks, organize time and space, deal with information heard, control visual-motor difficulties, understand spoken language, or memorize.

Reading Teacher 41 (April 1988). This whole issue is devoted to working with poor readers.

Samuels, S. Jay. "Information Processing Abilities and Reading." *Journal of Learning Disabilities* 20 (January 1987): 18–22. Based on the information-processing model of reading, the view presented is that lack of automaticity in decoding leads to processing meaningless units of print.

Searls, Evelyn. *How to Use the WISC-R Scores in Reading/Learning Disability Diagnosis.* Newark, Del.: International Reading Association, 1985. The author presents numerous connections between WISC-R scores and strengths and weaknesses in reading.

Notes

1. Mavis Martin, "A Talk with Marie Hughes," *Insights into Open Education* 11 (March 1979): 8.
2. Albert J. Harris and Edward Sipay, *How to Increase Reading Ability,* 8th ed. (New York: Longman, 1985), 297.
3. R. D. Rabinovitch and W. Ingram, "Neuropsychiatric Considerations in Reading Retardation," *Reading Teacher* 15 (May 1962): 433–38.
4. Margaret B. Rawson, *Developmental Language Disability: Adult Accomplishments of Dyslexic Boys* (Baltimore: Johns Hopkins Press, 1968), 81.
5. Ibid., 76.
6. Ibid.
7. S. T. Orton, "Specific Reading Disability—Strephosymbolia," *Journal of the American Medical Association* 90 (1928): 1095–99.
8. J. L. Orton, "Word-Blindness in School Children and Other Papers on Strephosymbolia" (Specific Language Disability, Dyslexia), 1925–1946, Monograph No. 2 (Pomfret, Conn.: Orton Society, 1966).
9. Margaret Richek, Lynn List, and Janet Lerner, *Reading Problems: Diagnosis and Remediation* (Englewood Cliffs, N.J.: Prentice-Hall, 1983), 160–61.
10. Stanley L. Englebardt, "Disturbed Children: Reaching the Unreachables," *Think* 36 (July/August 1970): 24–26.
11. Grace Fernald, *Remedial Techniques in Basic School Subjects* (New York: McGraw-Hill, Inc., 1943, 1971).
12. Thorlief Hegge, Samuel Kirk, and Winifred Kirk, *Remedial Reading Drills* (Ann Arbor, Mich.: George Wahr, 1940).
13. Careth Ellingson, *The Shadow Children: A Book about Children's Disorders* (Chicago: Topaz Books, 1967); *Winter Haven Testing and Training Materials* (Winter Haven, Fla.: Winter Haven Lions Research Foundation, 1963).
14. Katrina de Hirsch et al., *Predicting Reading Failure* (New York: Harper and Row, 1966).
15. R. G. Heckelman, "Using the Neurological Impress Remedial Technique," *Academic Therapy Quarterly* 1 (1966): 235–39.

16. Albert J. Harris and Edward R. Sipay, *How to Increase Reading Ability,* 8th ed. (New York: Longman, 1985), 413–14; Dorothy J. McGinnis and Dorothy E. Smith, *Analyzing and Treating Reading Problems* (New York: Macmillan, 1982), 307–8; Robert Kann, "The Method of Repeated Readings: Expanding the Neurological Impress Method for Use with Disabled Readers," *Journal of Learning Disabilities* 16 (February 1983): 90–92.

17. Serena Niensted, "A Group Use of the Fernald Technique," *Education Digest* 33 (May 1968): 52–54.

18. Beth H. Slingerland, *A Multi-Sensory Approach to Language Arts for Specific Language Disability Children, A Guide for Primary Teachers* (Cambridge, Mass.: Educators Publishing Service, 1971), xv.

19. Ellingson, *The Shadow Children,* 88–90.

20. Harold Blau and Harriett Blau, "A Theory of Learning to Read," *Reading Teacher* 22 (November 1968): 126–29, 144.

21. A. T. Ravenette, *Dimensions of Reading Difficulties* (Elmsford, N.Y.: Pergamon Press, 1968), 42–43.

22. S. J. Samuels, "The Method of Repeated Readings," *Reading Teacher* 32 (1979): 403–8.

23. C. Chomsky, "When You Still Can't Read in Third Grade: After Decoding, What?" in *What Research Has to Say about Reading Instruction,* ed. S. J. Samuels (Newark, Del.: International Reading Association, 1978).

24. Don Holdaway, *The Foundations of Literacy* (Sydney, Australia: Ashton, Scholastic, 1979), 126–27.

25. Kann, "Method of Repeated Readings," 90–92.

26. Lawrence O'Shea, Paul Sindelar, and Dorothy O'Shea, "The Effects of Repeated Readings and Attentional Cues on Reading Fluency and Comprehension," *Journal of Reading Behavior* 17, no. 2 (1985): 129–42.

27. Marie Carbo, "Teaching Reading with Talking Books," *Reading Teacher* 32 (December 1978): 267–73.

28. Kenneth Hoskisson, "The Many Facets of Assisted Reading," *Elementary English* 52 (March 1975): 312–15.

29. Mary W. Strong and Elaine Yurek, "An Individualized Remedial Reading Program Using Neurological Impress," *Reading Improvement* 23 (Spring 1986): 27–31.

30. Andee Rubin, "A Theoretical Taxonomy of the Differences between Oral and Written Language," in *Theoretical Issues in Reading Comprehension,* ed. Rand J. Spiro, Bertram C. Bruce, and Wm. F. Brewer (Hillsdale, N.J.: Lawrence Erlbaum Associates, 1980), 411–38.

31. Dorothy Butler, *Cushla and Her Books* (Boston: The Horn Book, 1979).

32. Roach Van Allen, *Language Experiences in Communication* (Boston: Houghton Mifflin, 1976).

33. Marie Dionisio, "Write? Isn't This Reading Class?" *Reading Teacher* 36 (April 1983): 749.

34. Suzanne L. Holt and JoAnne L. Vacca, "Reading with a Sense of Writer: Writing with a Sense of Reader," *Language Arts* 58 (November/December 1981): 939.

35. O. A. Evans, prepared as part of a student teaching assignment, University of New Mexico, Albuquerque, N.M., December 1984.

36. Dianne W. Hampton, "Hey, Teacher, What Did You Write!" *Language Arts* 60 (March 1983): 341–43; Kathleen Matthews, "Are You Willing to Be the Kind of Writer You Want Your Students to Be?" *Learning* 12 (April/May 1984): 42–45; Nina Middelsen,

"Teacher as Partner in the Writing Process," *Language Arts* 61 (November 1984): 704–11; Jane Hansen, *When Writers Read* (Portsmouth, N.H.: Heinemann Educational Books, 1987).

37. Marianne Frostig, *Selection and Adaptation of Reading Methods* (San Rafael, Calif.: Academic Therapy Publications, 1973), 69.

38. Kenneth Langford, Kenneth Slade, and Allyson Barnett, "An Examination of Impress Techniques in Remedial Reading," *Academic Therapy* 9 (Spring 1974): 309–19.

39. Ruth Strang and Donald Lindquist, *The Administrator and the Improvement of Reading* (New York: Appleton-Century Crofts, 1960), 81.

40. Ibid.

41. Ibid., 81–82.

42. John Rambeau and Nancy Rambeau, *The Mystery of Morgan Castle* (San Francisco: Field Education Publications, 1962), 54. University of New Mexico, 1965), 35–43.

43. Belle Dubnoff, George Fargo, and Donald Weiss, "Aspects of Perceptual Training with Brain Injured and Emotionally Disturbed Children as Related to Reading," in *Twenty-Fifth Yearbook,* Claremont College Reading Conference (Claremont, Calif.: Claremont University College, 1961).

44. Doris J. Johnson and Helmer R. Myklebust, *Learning Disabilities* (New York: Grune and Stratton, 1967), 302.

45. "School Nurses Back Medicine for Pupil Control," *NEA Reporter* 9, no. 8 (23 October 1970).

46. Robert D. Carpenter, M.D., *Why Can't I Learn?* (Glendale, Calif.: Regal Books Division, G/L Publications, 1972), p. 2 of the author's preface.

47. Diane Divoky, "Education's Latest Victim: the LD Kid," *Learning* 3 (October 1974): 20–25.

48. Ibid., 25.

49. Miriam Westeen, fourth-grade teacher, Gallup-McKinley County Public Schools, Gallup, New Mexico, 1970.

50. Albert Bandura, "Behavior Psychotherapy," *Scientific American* 216 (March 1967): 81, reporting on a study by A. W. Staats and W. Butterfield, "Treatment of Non-Reading in a Culturally Deprived Juvenile Delinquent: An Application of Reinforcement Principles," *Child Development* 36 (1963): 925–42.

51. Bertram S. Brown, M.D., "Behavior Modification: What It Is and Isn't," *Today's Education* 65 (January/February 1976): 67–69.

52. Doris J. Johnson, "Treatment Approaches to Dyslexia," in *Reading Disability and Perception,* ed. George D. Spache (Newark, Del.: International Reading Association, 1969), 100.

53. Empress Zedler, "Management of Reading in the Educational Program of Pupils with Neurologically Based Learning Problems," George D. Spache, ed., *Reading Disability and Perception* (Newark, Del.: International Reading Association, 1969): 106.

54. Jeffrey A. Mattes, "The Feingold Diet: A Current Reappraisal," *Journal of Learning Disabilities* 16 (June/July 1983): 319–23; D. J. Rapp, "Does Diet Affect Hyperactivity?" *Journal of Learning Disabilities* 11 (1978): 56–62; F. J. Stare, E. M. Whalen, and M. Sheridon, "Diet and Hyperactivity: Is There a Relationship?" *Pediatrics* 66 (1980): 521–25.

55. Constance M. McCullough, "Individualized Reading," *NEA Journal* 47 (March 1958): 163.

56. Howard Brighton, *Utilizing Teacher Aides in Differentiated Staffing* (Midland, Mich.: Pendleton Publishing Co., 1972), 17.

57. Deborah M. Meier, "Poor Readers—I: Children with Problems," *Today's Education* 63 (October 1974): 32–36.

58. Ibid., 36.

59. Verna Vickery, "A Note of Encouragement: Can We Teach Reading?" *New Mexico School Review* 50, no. 4 (Fall 1974): 43.

60. *How to Talk Back to Your Television Set* (New York: Bantam Books, 1970), 7.

61. Serena Niensted, "Meaninglessness for Beginning Readers," *Reading Teacher* 23 (November 1969): 112.

APPENDIX A

Books for Teachers of Corrective Reading

Allen, Roach Van. *Language Experiences in Communication.* Boston: Houghton Mifflin, 1976.

Askov, Eunice, and Wayne Otto. *Meeting the Challenge: Corrective Reading Instruction in the Classroom.* Columbus: Merrill Publishing Co., 1985.

Baumann, James F. *Reading Assessment: An Instructional Decision-Making Perspective.* Columbus: Merrill Publishing Co., 1988.

Bond, Guy L., et al. *Reading Difficulties: Their Diagnosis and Correction.* 6th ed. Englewood Cliffs, N.J.: Prentice-Hall, 1989.

Bowren, Fay F., and Miles V. Zintz. *Teaching Reading in Adult Basic Education.* Dubuque, Iowa: Wm. C. Brown Co. Publishers, 1977.

Burmeister, Lou E. *Reading Strategies for Middle and Secondary School Teachers.* 2d ed. Reading, Mass.: Addison Wesley, 1978.

Carroll, John B., and Jeanne S. Chall. *Toward a Literate Society.* New York: McGraw-Hill, Inc., 1975.

Cazden, Courtney, Vera John, and Dell Hymes, eds. *Functions of Language in the Classroom.* Prospect Heights, Ill.: Waveland Press, 1985.

Clay, Marie M. *The Early Detection of Reading Difficulties: A Diagnostic Survey with Recovery Procedures.* 3d ed. Auckland, New Zealand: Heinemann Educational Books, 1985.

Ekwall, Eldon E. *Locating and Correcting Reading Difficulties.* 4th ed. Columbus: Merrill Publishing Co., 1985.

Ekwall, Eldon E., and James L. Shanker. *Diagnosis and Remediation of the Disabled Reader.* 2d ed. Boston: Allyn and Bacon, 1985.

Fernald, Grace. *Remedial Techniques in Basic School Subjects.* New York: McGraw-Hill, Inc., 1971.

Gearheart, B. R. *Learning Disabilities: Educational Strategies.* 4th ed. St. Louis: C. V. Mosby, 1985.

Glazer, Susan, and Lyndon Searfoss. *Reading Diagnosis and Instruction.* Englewood Cliffs, N.J.: Prentice-Hall, 1988.

Goodman, Kenneth. *What's Whole in Whole Language?* Portsmouth, N.H.: Heinemann Educational Books, 1986.

Guszak, Frank. *Diagnostic Reading Instruction in the Elementary School.* 3d ed. New York: Harper and Row, 1985.

Hall, Mary Anne. *Teaching Reading as a Language Experience*. 2d ed. Columbus: Merrill Publishing Co., 1981.

Harris, Albert J., and E. R. Sipay. *How to Increase Reading Ability*. 8th ed. New York: Longman, 1985.

Herr, Selma. *Learning Activities for Reading*. 4th ed. Dubuque, Iowa: Wm. C. Brown Co. Publishers, 1982.

Johns, Jerry L. *Handbook for Remediation of Reading Difficulties*. Englewood Cliffs, N.J.: Prentice-Hall, 1986.

Kroth, Roger L. *Communicating with Parents of Exceptional Children: Improving Parent-Teacher Relationships*. 2d ed. Denver: Love Publishing Co., 1985.

LaPray, Margaret. *Teaching Children to Become Independent Readers*. New York: Center for Applied Research in Education, 1972.

McGinnis, Dorothy J., and Dorothy E. Smith. *Analyzing and Treating Reading Problems*. New York: Macmillan Co., 1982.

O'Brien, Carmen A. *Teaching the Language-Different Child to Read*. Tucson: Communication Skills, 1983.

Richek, Margaret, Lynne List, and Janet Lerner. *Reading Problems*. 2d ed. Englewood Cliffs, N.J.: Prentice-Hall, 1989.

Roswell, Florence, and Gladys Natchez. *Reading Disability: Diagnosis and Treatment*. 3d ed. New York: Basic Books, 1980.

Rubin, Dorothy. *Diagnosis and Correction in Reading Instruction*. New York: Holt, Rinehart and Winston, 1982.

Rupley, William H., and Timothy R. Blair. *Reading Diagnosis and Remediation*. 2d ed. Chicago: Rand McNally, 1983.

Silvaroli, Nicholas. *Classroom Reading Inventory*. 4th ed. Dubuque, Iowa: Wm. C. Brown Co. Publishers, 1982.

Smith, Frank. *Reading without Nonsense*. 2d ed. New York: Teachers College Press, 1985.

Taylor, Barbara, Larry Harris, and P. David Pearson. *Reading Difficulties: Instruction and Assessment*. New York: Random House, 1988.

Tonjes, Marian J., and Miles V. Zintz. *Teaching Reading/Thinking/Study Skills in Content Classrooms*. 2d ed. Dubuque, Iowa: Wm. C. Brown Co. Publishers, 1987.

Turnbull, Ann P., and Jane B. Schulz. *Mainstreaming Handicapped Students: A Guide for the Classroom Teacher*. 2d ed. Boston: Allyn and Bacon, 1983.

Walker, Barbara J. *Diagnostic Teaching of Reading*. Columbus: Merrill Publishing Co., 1988.

Weaver, Constance. *Reading Process and Practice from Socio-Psycholinguistics to Whole Language*. Portsmouth, N.H.: Heinemann Educational Books, 1988.

A Bibliography of Books for Corrective Reading

These are books recommended for pupils who read below their assigned grade level; they combine *high-interest level* and *low-vocabulary load*. Some of these materials are no longer in print. However, they may often be found in school libraries and book storage rooms and may prove very useful with corrective readers.

1. **Action**

   Scholastic Book Services, 904 Sylvan Ave., Englewood Cliffs, N.J. 07632. For severely retarded readers in secondary schools. Reading levels 2.0–4.0. They are available in kits; each kit contains four copies of five titles. Ditto masters and cassettes are also available.

   Action Libraries I and IA—reading levels 2.0–2.4;
   Action Libraries II and IIA—reading levels 2.5–2.9;
   Action Libraries III and IIIA—reading levels 3.0–3.4;
   Action Libraries IV and IVA—reading levels 3.5–3.9;
   Double Action Library I—reading levels 3.0–3.4;
   Double Action Library II—reading levels 3.5–3.9.

2. **Adapted Classics**

   Globe Book Company, Inc., 175 Fifth Ave., New York, N.Y. 10010. There are many titles in the series—clothbound and well illustrated. Teaching aids and testing materials are provided in the books. The following are representative of the entire list:

TITLE	READING LEVEL
Prince and the Pauper	4–5
Robin Hood	4–5
Swiss Family Robinson	4–5
Tom Sawyer	4–5
20,000 Leagues under the Sea	4–5

3. **Animal Adventure Series**

   Benefic Press, 10300 W. Roosevelt Road, Westchester, Ill. 60153. Preprimary to grade three. Record or cassette available for each book.

TITLE	READING LEVEL	INTEREST LEVEL
Becky, the Rabbit	PP	1–3
Squeaky, the Squirrel	PP	1–3
Doc, the Dog	PP	1–3

Pat, the Parakeet	PP	1–3
Kate, the Cat	PP	1–3
Gomer, the Gosling	P	1–3
Skippy, the Skunk	P	1–3
Sandy, the Swallow	P	1–3
Sally, the Screech Owl	1	1–4
Pudgy, the Beaver	1	1–4
Hamilton, the Hamster	1	1–4
Horace, the Horse	1	1–4

4. **Beginner Books**

Random House, Inc., 201 E. 50th St., New York, N.Y. 10022. Regular and special library bindings are available. Reader level is based on the Spache Readability Formula.

TITLE	GRADE READING LEVEL	NUMBER OF DIFFERENT WORDS
The Cat in the Hat	2.1	223
The Cat in the Hat Comes Back	2.0	253
A Fly Went By	2.1	180
The Big Jump and Other Stories	2.4	216
A Big Ball of String	2.5	215
Sam and the Firefly	2.0	200
You Will Go to the Moon	1.8	181
Cowboy Andy	1.8	226
The Whales Go By	1.8	183
Stop That Ball!	1.9	201
Bennett Cerf's Book of Laughs	2.1	237
Ann Can Fly	2.0	210
One Fish, Two Fish, Red Fish, Blue Fish	1.7	276
The King's Wish and Other Stories	2.0	198
Bennett Cerf's Book of Riddles	2.2	194
Green Eggs and Ham	1.9	50
Put Me in the Zoo	1.5	100
Are You My Mother?	1.7	100
Go, Dog, Go!	1.5	75

5. **Better Reading Series**

By John F. Rambeau and Nancy Rambeau. Educational Guidelines Co., A Division of The Economy Co., Oklahoma City, Okla.

TITLE	GRADE READING LEVEL
The Jinx Boat	2
Explore	3
Venture	4
Quest	5
Las Caras de Chico	3
On Polecat Mountain	5
Moneywise	5
Teacher's Guide	

6. **Blue Bug Books**
   By Virginia Poulet. Children's Press, 1224 W. Van Buren St., Chicago, Ill. 60607.
   Talking-picture books for preschool to grade three. Thirty-two pages.

   Blue Bug's Circus
   Blue Bug's Surprise
   Blue Bug Finds a Friend
   Blue Bug's Vegetable Garden

7. **Box Car Children Books, The** See *Pilot Books* (listing no. 43)
   By Gertrude Warner. Pilot Books, Albert Whitman, 506 West Lake Street, Chicago, Ill.
   60637. Mystery stories about the four Alden children—Jessie, Henry, Violet, and Benny.

8. **Butternut Bill Series**
   By Edith McCall. Benefic Press, 10300 W. Roosevelt Road, Westchester, Ill. 60153.
   Carefully controlled vocabularies. An LP record (33⅓-rpm) is available with each book in
   the series. Sight Sound Sets (five books and one record) are also available.

TITLE	READING LEVEL	WORD COUNT	PAGES
Butternut Bill	PP	35	48
Butternut Bill and the Bee Tree	PP	58	48
Butternut Bill and the Big Catfish	PP	51	48
Butternut Bill and the Bear	P	43	64
Butternut Bill and the Little River	P	64	64
Butternut Bill and the Big Pumpkin	P	64	64
Butternut Bill and His Friends	1	158	64
Butternut Bill and the Train	1		64

9. **Button Family Adventure Series**
   By Edith McCall. Benefic Press, 10300 W. Roosevelt Road, Westchester, Ill. 60153.

TITLE	READING LEVEL	INTEREST LEVEL	WORD COUNT
Buttons at the Zoo	PP	PP–2	30
Buttons Takes a Boat Ride	P	P–2	75
Buttons and the Pet Parade	P	P–2	80
Buttons and the Boy Scouts	2	2–4	281
Buttons and the Little League	3	3–5	340
Teacher's Manual for the Series			

10. **Checkered Flag Series, The**
    By Henry A. Bamman and Robert J. Whitehead. San Francisco: Field Educational
    Publications, Inc. Study exercises in each book teach reading for specific details, recall of
    a main idea, character identification, word usage, discussion and critical thinking, and
    word meanings. Audio-visual kit with each title includes color filmstrip, LP record, and
    magnetic tape.

TITLE	GRADE LEVEL
Wheels	2.4
Riddler	2.5
Bearcat	2.5

Smashup	2.6
Scramble	3.0
Flea	3.5
Grand Prix	4.0
500	4.5
Teacher's Guide for the Series	

11. **Childhood of Famous Americans Series, The**

Bobbs-Merrill Co., Inc., 4300 W. 62nd St., Indianapolis, Ind. 46268. The reader level of all the books in this series is about fourth grade. The 1974 Publishers Trade List Annual showed 216 books available in this series. Newer titles include:

Dwight D. Eisenhower: Young Military Leader, by Wilma Hudson
Carl Sandburg: Young Singing Poet, by Grace Hathaway Melin
David Sarnoff: Radio and TV Boy, by Elisabeth P. Myers
Frederick Douglass: Boy Champion of Human Rights, by Elisabeth P. Myers
Harry S. Truman: Missouri Farm Boy, by Wilma J. Hudson
J. C. Penney: Golden Rule Boy, by Wilma J. Hudson
Langston Hughes: Young Black Poet, by Montrew Dunham
Louis Armstrong: Young Music Maker, by Dharathula H. Millender
Lyndon B. Johnson: Young Texan, by Thomas F. Barton
Mahalia Jackson: Young Gospel Singer, by Montrew Dunham
Pearl S. Buck: Literary Girl, by Elisabeth P. Myers
Older titles in the series include: *Abe Lincoln, Booker T. Washington, Sacagawea, Clara Barton, John F. Kennedy, Henry Ford, Babe Ruth, and Davy Crockett.*

12. **Contact**

Prepared by the editors of Scholastic Scope. Scholastic Book Services, 904 Sylvan Ave., Englewood Cliffs, N.J. 07632. Interest level for the secondary school student; reading level third to sixth grade. Units are organized around themes with the general objective of all units to teach better communication skills.

TITLE	RECOMMENDED FOR GRADE LEVELS
Drugs: Insights and Illusions	9–12
Environment: Earth in Crisis	9–12
The Future: Can We Shape It?	9–12
Getting Together: Problems We Face	8–10
Imagination: World of Inner Space	7–8
Law: You, The Police and Justice	9–12
Loyalties: Whose Side Are You On?	9–12
Maturity: Growing Up Strong	8–10
Prejudice: The Invisible Wall	9–12

Materials for *Contact* include log books for writing, long-playing records of teenage interviews, posters for stimulating discussion, and teachers' guides.

13. **Cowboy Sam Series**
By Edna Walker Chandler. Benefic Press, 10300 W. Roosevelt Road, Westchester, Ill. 60153.

TITLE	READING LEVEL	INTEREST LEVEL	WORD COUNT
Cowboy Sam and Flop	1	1–4	149
*Cowboy Sam and Shorty**	1	1–4	158
Cowboy Sam and Freddy	1	1–4	237
Cowboy Sam and Sally	2	2–5	356
*Cowboy Sam and the Fair**	2	2–5	278
Cowboy Sam and the Rodeo	2	2–5	333
Cowboy Sam and the Airplane	3	3–6	431
*Cowboy Sam and the Indians**	3	3–6	421
Cowboy Sam and the Rustlers	3	3–6	485
Teacher's Manual for Series			

*Workbooks available

14. **Crossroads**
James Olson and Lawrence Swinburne, Eds. Noble and Noble Publishers, 1 Dag Hammerskjold Plaza, 245 E. 47th St., New York, N.Y. 10017. Level of difficulty—grades four through nine.

LEVEL ONE: Four student paperbacks, four 12-inch 33⅓-rpm records, a student activity book, a teacher's manual, and a library of twelve additional paperbacks. The four student books are: *With It, Solo, Against All Odds,* and *Beyond Tomorrow.*
LEVEL TWO: Four student paperbacks, four twelve-inch 33⅓-rpm records, a student activity book, a teacher's manual, and a library of twelve additional paperbacks. The four student books are: *Love's Blues; Me, Myself, and I; Dreamer of Dreams;* and *He Who Dares.*
LEVEL THREE: Four student paperbacks, four twelve-inch 33⅓-rpm records, a student activity book, a teacher's guide, and a library of twelve additional paperbacks. The four student books are: *Tomorrow Won't Wait, Breaking Loose, In Other's Eyes,* and *Playing It Cool.* This was designed to be a highly motivating, nongraded program for junior and senior high school use; readability levels fourth to ninth grades. It is an attempt to be *relevant* to teenagers. The workbooks provide opportunity for critical thinking and for composition and writing practice.

15. **Dan Frontier Series**
By William J. Hurley. Benefic Press, 10300 West Roosevelt Road, Westchester, Ill. 60153.

TITLE	READING LEVEL	INTEREST LEVEL	WORD COUNT
Dan Frontier	PP	PP–2	57
Dan Frontier and the New House	PP	PP–2	44
Dan Frontier and the Big Cat	P	P–3	86
Dan Frontier Goes Hunting	P	P–3	86
Dan Frontier, Trapper	1	1–4	142

Dan Frontier with the Indians	1	1–4	131
Dan Frontier and the Wagon Train	2	2–5	278
Dan Frontier Scouts with the Army	2	2–5	227
Dan Frontier, Sheriff	3	3–6	323
Dan Frontier Goes Exploring	3	3–6	276
Dan Frontier Goes to Congress	4	4–7	
Teacher's Manual for Series			

16. **Discovery, Short Introductory Biographies**
Mary C. Austin, Consultant. Garrard Publishing Co., Champaign, Ill. 61820. Sixty-five titles in series. Reading level, grade three; interest level, grades two through five. Selected titles of recent books include:

Rachel Carson, Who Loved the Sea
Martha Washington, First Lady of the Land
Jim Beckwourth, Black Trapper and Indian Chief
Robert H. Goddard, Space Pioneer

17. **Dolch Four-Step Program**
Garrard Publishing Company, Champaign, Ill. 61820.

First Reading Books: Reading level, grade one; interest level, grades one through four. Vocabulary: easier half of the 220 Basic Sight Words, the 95 most common nouns. Set of sixteen books includes:

Dog Pals
I Like Cats
Once There Was a Bear
Some Are Small

Basic Vocabulary Books: Reading level, grade two; interest level, grades one through six. Vocabulary: 220 Basic Sight Words, the 95 most common nouns. Set of sixteen books includes:

Bear Stories
Circus Stories
Folk Stories
Navajo Stories

Folklore of the World Books: Reading level, grade three; interest level, grades two through eight. Vocabulary: The Storytellers' vocabulary, 684 words. Set of twelve books includes:

Stories from Alaska
Stories from France
Stories from Japan
Stories from Russia

Pleasure Reading Books: Reading level, grade four; interest level, grades three through eight. Vocabulary: First 1,000 words for children's reading. There are thirteen books in this set, all good for remedial reading. Among them are:

Aesop's Stories
Andersen Stories
Far East Stories
Robinson Crusoe

18. **Doubleday Signal Books**

Doubleday & Company, School and Library Division, Garden City, N.Y. 11530. There are more than seventy books in this series. The stories have high interest for teenagers; written in vocabulary and style suited to fourth-grade reading level. Prepared especially for reluctant readers in junior and senior high school. Newer titles include:

The Day the World Went Away, by Anne Schraff
High School Dropout, by John Clarke
I Was a Black Panther, by Chuck Moore
Loner, by Constance Kwolek
Mighty Hard Road: The Story of Cesar Chavez, by James Terzian and Kathryn Cramer
Motorcycle Racer, by John P. Covington
Nat Dunlap: Junior "Medic," by Evelyn Fiore
The Otis Redding Story, by Jane Schiesel
Shirley Chisholm, by Susan Brownmiller

19. **Easy Reading Books**

Children's Press, 1224 W. Van Buren St., Chicago, Ill. 60607. Available in multiple-copy sets with cassette and resource cards.

Benje
Birds in the Sky
Chicken Little Count to Ten
Lucky and the Giant
Martin Luther King, Jr.
Mystery of the Roll Top Desk
Seven Diving Ducks
We're Very Good Friends, My Brother and I

20. **Fast Mystery Series, 1984**

Pitman Learning, Inc., 6 Davis Drive, Belmont, Calif. 94002. Contains twelve books by various authors. Intended for middle schoolers and beyond, but written at elementary reading levels.

21. **Fastback Romance Series, 1984**

Pitman Learning, Inc., 6 Davis Drive, Belmont, Calif. 94002. Contains twelve books by various authors. Intended for middle schoolers and beyond. Reading levels are elementary.

22. **Field Literature Program, K–6**

Henry Bamman, Helen Huus, and Robert Whitehead. Field Educational Publications, Inc., 2400 Hanover St., Palo Alto, Calif. 94304. Excellent selection of children's literature, beautifully illustrated.

TITLE	GRADE LEVEL
Apple Trees	PP
Gingerbread	P
Toadstools	1
Roller Skates	2
Sailboats	3
Windowpanes	4
Fox Eyes	5
Seabirds	6

23. **Follett Beginning-to-Read Books**
    Follett Publishing Co., 1010 W. Washington Blvd., Chicago, Ill. 60607.

    END OF GRADE ONE LEVEL:
    Big Bug, Little Bug
    Big New School
    The Elf in the Singing Tree
    Gertie the Duck
    Have You Seen My Brother?
    Jiffy, Miss Boo and Mr. Roo
    Just Follow Me
    Little Quack
    Nobody Listens to Andrew
    Sad Mrs. Sam Sack
    Too Many Dogs
    The Wee, Little Man

    MIDDLE GRADE TWO LEVEL:
    Barefoot Boy
    Big Bad Bear
    The Boy Who Wouldn't Say His Name
    The Dog Who Came to Dinner
    The Dog Who Took the Train
    Linda's Air Mail Letter
    Mabel, the Whale
    The No Bark Dog
    When the Wild Ducks Came
    Crocodiles Have Big Teeth All Day

    END OF GRADE TWO LEVEL:
    Beginning to Read Riddles and Jokes
    Benny and the Bear
    A Day on the Big O
    A Frog Sandwich: Riddles and Jokes
    Gingerbread Children
    The Ice Cream Cone
    Sparky's Fireman
    A Uniform for Harry
    Ride, Willy, Ride

24. **Follett Just Beginning-to-Read Books**
    By Margaret Hillert. Follett Publishing Company, 1010 W. Washington Blvd., Chicago, Ill. 60607.

    PREPRIMER LEVEL:
    The Birthday Car
    Circus Fun
    The Funny Baby
    The Little Runaway
    The Magic Beans
    Snow Baby

The Three Bears
The Three Goats
The Three Little Pigs
The Yellow Boat
Cinderella at the Ball
A House for Little Red

25. **The Galaxy 5 Series, 1979**
Pitman Learning, Inc., 6 Davis Drive, Belmont, Calif., 94002. Reading difficulty is third reader; skill builders included.

Goodbye to Earth
On the Red World
Vacation in Space
Dead Man
Where No Star Shines
King of the Stars

26. **Helicopter Adventure Series**
By Selma Wassermann and Jack Wassermann. Westchester, Ill.: Benefic Press. Any grade level one through six.

TITLE	READING LEVEL
Chopper Malone and the New Pilot	Primer
Chopper Malone and Susie	Primer
Chopper Malone and the Big Snow	Grade 1
Chopper Malone and Trouble at Sea	Grade 1
Chopper Malone and the Mountain Rescue	Grade 2
Chopper Malone and the Skylarks	Grade 3
Teacher's Guide	

27. **Hip Pocket Series**
Biographies of celebrities. Developmental levels: 4–12; remedial levels: 7–12. Cassettes, workbooks, teacher's guide. About third grade level on the Spache formula. (Mankato, Minn.: Creative Education, Inc.)

Diana Ross
Bill Cosby
Shirley Chisholm
Geraldo Rivera
Johnny Bench

28. **Impact** For reluctant readers, grades seven through nine.
Charlotte Brooks, ed. Holt, Rinehart and Winston, Inc., 383 Madison Ave., New York, N.Y. 10017. Teacher's guides and twelve-inch LP records.

LEVEL I:
I've Got a Name
At Your Own Risk
Cities
Larger than Life

LEVEL II:
Unknown Worlds
Conflict
Sight Lines
Search for America

LEVEL III:
Turning Point
I (Me)
Nobody but Yourself
On Edge

29. **Instant Readers, The**

By Bill Martin and Peggy Brogan. Holt, Rinehart and Winston, Inc., 383 Madison Ave., New York, N.Y. 10017. Three levels, primary grades. Listening, reading and listening, reading. Books and cassettes. Guitar accompaniment on cassettes by Al Caiola.

30. **Jim Forest Readers, The**

By John F. Rambeau and Nancy Rambeau. San Francisco: Field Educational Publications, Inc. Teacher's manual provides suggestions for skill development and the first four books have accompanying workbooks for remedial reading use.

TITLE	READING LEVEL
Jim Forest and Ranger Don	1.7
Jim Forest and the Trapper	1.7
Jim Forest and the Ghost Town	1.8
Jim Forest and the Bandits	1.9
Jim Forest and the Lightning	1.9
Jim Forest and the Phantom Crater	2.0
Jim Forest and the Mystery Hunter	2.2
Jim Forest and the Plane Crash	2.4
Jim Forest and Dead Man's Peak	2.6
Jim Forest and the Flood	2.8
Jim Forest and Lone Wolf Gulch	3.1
Jim Forest and Woodman's Ridge	3.2
Teacher's Manual	

31. **Jim Hunter Books**

Ben Butterworth and Bill Stockdale. A twelve-book series. Increases in length (thirty-two to eighty pages) and in reading level (grade 1 to grade 3): Belmont, Calif.: Pitman Learning.

Danger in the Mountains
Jim and the Sun Goddess
The Sniper at Zimba
The Temple of Mantos
Teacher's guide

32. **Keytext**

The Economy Company, 1901 West Walnut St., Oklahoma City, Okla. 73125. This is a basal reading program for students reading below grade level:

Puddlejumpers and *Castlebuilders*, Level 1 for use in grade 2
Summerdaze and *Streetsongs*, Level 2 for use in grade 3
Thundercover and *Turnstyles*, Level 3 for use in grade 4
Daystreaming and *Bootstraps*, Level 4 for use in grade 5
Worldwind and *Forerunners*, Level 5 for use in grade 6

33. **Learning to Read While Reading to Learn Series**

By Jo Stanchfield, S. I. Hayakawa, Ralph Kellogg, and Frank Hutchinson. San Rafael, Calif.: Leswing Press.

TITLE	READING LEVEL
A Peculiar Lawnmower	Grades 4–6
Pedro's Secret	Grades 4–6
Dognappers	Grades 4–6
Loud and Clear	Grades 4–6
Operation Phoenix	Grades 4–6
Hundred Milers	Grades 7–8
Deadline for Tim	Grades 7–8
The Vanishing Pirate	Grades 7–8

34. **Monster Books**

Bowman, 4563 Colorado Boulevard, Los Angeles, Calif. 90039. Easy to read. Relevant interest for middle grades and junior high. Presently twenty-four titles, including:

Monster Looks for a Friend
Monster Gets a Job
Lady Monster Has a Plan

35. **Morgan Bay Mystery Series**

By John F. Rambeau and Nancy Rambeau. San Francisco: Field Educational Publications, Inc.

TITLE	READING LEVEL
The Mystery of Morgan Castle	2.3
The Mystery of Marble Angel	2.6
The Mystery of Midnight Visitor	3.2
The Mystery of the Missing Marlin	3.5
The Mystery of the Musical Ghost	3.5
The Mystery of the Monks' Island	3.7
The Mystery of the Marauder's Gold	3.9
The Mystery of the Myrmidon's Journey	4.1
Teacher's Manual	

36. **Mystery Adventure Series**
Henry A. Bamman, Benefic Press, 10300 W. Roosevelt Road, Westchester, Ill. 60153.
Written at fourth- to ninth-grade interest level.

TITLE	READING LEVEL
Mystery Adventure at Cave Four	3
Mystery Adventure at Longcliff Inn	5
Mystery Adventure of the Indian Burial Ground	4
Mystery Adventure of the Jeweled Bell	2
Mystery Adventure of the Smuggled Treasure	6
Mystery Adventure of the Talking Statues	2

37. **Nature and Science Series**
Raintree Publishers, 310 West Wisconsin Ave., Milwaukee, Wis. 53203.

TITLE	READING LEVEL
Read about Animals series—14 titles	3
Read about Science series—15 titles	3
Nature Close-Ups series—40 titles	3–4
Ask About series—10 titles	3–4
Life Cycles series—16 titles	1–2
Animals in the Wild series—26 titles	2–3
Look at Science series—10 titles	2
A Look Inside series—12 titles	3–4

38. **Owl Books, The**
Bill Martin, ed. Holt, Rinehart and Winston, Inc., 383 Madison Ave., New York 10017.

Kin/Der Owl Books (Preschool–grade 1)
Little Owl Books (K–2)
Young Owl Books (Grades 2–4)
Wise Owl Books (Grades 4–6)

39. **Pacemakers—Bestellers**
Bestellers I (ten titles), Bestellers II (ten titles), and Bestellers III (ten titles) are written at third-grade level or below using the Pacemaker Core Vocabulary of 1,821 words. They have an adult format and are stories of adventure, science fiction, and mystery. Available in sets (four copies of each of ten titles) with teacher's guides. Selected titles are:

Bestellers I:
The Candy Man
Diamonds in the Dirt
Night of the Kachina
The Time Trap

Bestellers II:
Escape from Tomorrow
Tiger, Lion, Hawk
Wind over Stonehenge
Wet Fire

Bestellers III:	*Counterfeit*
	Secret Spy
	Star Gold
	Village of Vampires

40. Pacemakers—True Adventure

An eleven-book series; reading level 2.0–2.5; interest level grade five–adult basic.

Tales of Escape
Tales of Flying
Tales of Rescue
Tales of Speed
Teacher's Guide

41. Pacemakers—Vocational Readers

A ten-book series; reading level about second grade; interest level grades seven through twelve. Each book has sixty-four pages. Tape cassettes of the stories are available.

I'll Try Tomorrow (Gardener)
The Other Side of the Counter (Short Order Cook)
Ready to Go (Auto Mechanic)
Until Joe Comes Back (Supermarket)
Teacher's Guide

42. Perfection Library

Perfection Form Company, 1984. Reading levels 1.5–3.5. Middle school interest level.

Kid Brother
The Day Dad Cried (about child abuse)
The Well-Kept Secret
Teacher Trouble
An Ended Friendship

43. Pilot Books

Albert Whitman, 506 West Lake Street, Chicago, Ill. 60637. The Box Car Children Books, by Gertrude Warner. Mystery stories about the four Alden children—Jessie, Henry, Violet, and Benny—are about third-grade reader level, with third-grade to sixth-grade interest.

Bus Station Mystery	*Mike's Mystery*
Mystery in the Sand	*Blue Bay Mystery*
Bicycle Mystery	*The Woodshed Mystery*
Tree House Mystery	*The Lighthouse Mystery*
Snowbound Mystery	*Mystery Behind the Wall*
Houseboat Mystery	*Caboose Mystery*
Schoolhouse Mystery	*Mountain Top Mystery*
Mystery Ranch	*The Yellow House Mystery*
Surprise Island	*The Box Car Children*

44. **Racing Wheels Readers**
    By Anabel Dean. Benefic Press, 10300 W. Roosevelt Road, Westchester, Ill. 60153. Each book is fourth- to twelfth-grade interest level. All books are eighty pages in length.

TITLE	READING LEVEL
Hot Rod	2
Destruction Derby	2
Drag Race	3
Stock Car Race	3
Road Race	4
Indy 500	4

45. **Ranger Don Series**
    Written by Robert Whitehead. Level of difficulty: grades one through three; interest level: grades one through six. Sold in learning kits, there are five copies of a book, one cassette, one filmstrip, one teacher's guide, five pupil activity cards, five evaluation cards, and five answer cards.

    Ranger Don
    Ranger Don and the Forest Fire
    Ranger Don and the Ghost Town
    Ranger Don and the Mountain Trail
    Ranger Don and the Wolverine

46. **Reading Incentive Program**
    Bowmar Publishing Co., 622 Rodier Drive, Glendale, Calif. 91201. The books listed below are written by Ed Radlauer and are available in single copy or in *sets*. A set includes ten copies (paperbound) of a reader, one seven-inch long-playing recorded narration, and one color filmstrip. There is also a teacher's manual. The level of difficulty of the reading material in all of these books is about fourth grade.

    Slot Car Racing
    Drag Racing
    The Mighty Midgets
    Motorcycles
    Karting
    Teen Fair
    Horses
    Surfing
    Drag Racing Funny Cars
    Dune Buggies
    Dune Buggy Racing
    Custom Cars
    Teacher's Manual

47. **Sailor Jack Series**
    By Selma Wassermann and Jack Wassermann. Benefic Press, 10300 W. Roosevelt Road, Westchester, Ill. 60153.

TITLE	READING LEVEL	INTEREST LEVEL	WORD COUNT
Sailor Jack	PP	PP–2	62
Sailor Jack and Bluebell's Dive	P	P–3	73

Sailor Jack and Bluebell	P	P–3	73
Sailor Jack and the Jet Plane	P	P–3	
Teacher's Guide			96

48. **Science Research Associates Pilot Libraries**

Science Research Associates, 259 E. Erie St., Chicago, Ill. 60611. Pilot Library selections are unaltered excerpts from carefully chosen juvenile books. Each *library* contains seventy-two selections (each twenty-four to thirty-two pages in length), of graded levels of difficulty. With each *library,* the teacher is furnished a handbook that provides a synopsis of each selection and questions for discussion. A student record book provides exercises for testing the student's comprehension.

Pilot Library IIa, Fourth grade
Pilot Library IIb, Fifth grade
Pilot Library IIc, Sixth grade
Pilot Library IIIa, Seventh grade
Pilot Library IIIb, Eighth grade

49. **Scope**

Prepared by the editors of Scholastic Scope, Scholastic Book Services, 904 Sylvan Ave., Englewood Cliffs, N.J. 07632. For grades seven through twelve language arts classes. Readability level fourth to sixth grade.

SCOPE I:
Seven Plays, edited to a fourth- to sixth-grade reader level, extensively illustrated, selected to motivate discussion and role-playing.
Twelve Angry Men and Other Plays
Appalachian Autumn and Other Plays
Requiem for a Heavyweight and Other Plays
No Time for Sergeants and Other Plays
Dino and Other Plays
Teacher, Teacher and Other Plays
The Winner and Other Plays

SCOPE II:
Visuals (visual masters and transparencies)
Reading Skills
Vocabulary Building
Observation Skills
Determining Sequence
Reasoning Skills
Vowel Crosswords
Consonant Crosswords
Language Usage Crosswords
Word Attack
Word Power
Word Meaning through Context
Puzzle Crostics
Getting Applications Right (filling in forms)
Building Reading Skills
Figurative Language
Career Crosswords

SCOPE III:
Wide World
Dimensions
Spotlight
Across and Down
Word Puzzles and Mysteries
Jobs in Your Future (Job skills)
Countdown (Study skills)
Trackdown (Language skills)
Sprint (Speed-reading skills)

50. **See How I Read Books, 1981**
Modern Curriculum Press, 13900 Prospect Rd., Cleveland, Ohio 44136. Six books at first- and second-reader levels.

Blossom Bird Finds a Family
Blossom Bird Goes South
Blossom Bird Falls in Love
2-B and the Rock 'N Roll Band
2-B and the Space Visitor
Finn the Foolish Fish

51. **See How It Grows Series, 1983**
Modern Curriculum Press, 13900 Prospect Rd., Cleveland, Ohio 44136. Includes twelve books at the first-reader level.

52. **See How It's Made Series, 1983**
Modern Curriculum Press, 13900 Prospect Rd., Cleveland, Ohio 44136. First-reader level difficulty.

Titles include:
The Bar of Chocolate
The Knife and Fork
The Glass Jug
Rubber

53. **Shapes around Us Reading Series**
By Frances Fox and Penrod Moss. Century Communications, Inc., San Francisco, Calif. Designed for primary reading levels. Most words are first-grade words, and the pictures and context should help with all others.

What Is Round?
What Has Four Sides?
What Has Three Sides?
What Comes in a Can?
What Comes in a Box?
What Shape Is It?

54. **Signal Books** *See Doubleday Signal Books* (listing no. 18)

55. **Sounds of Language Readers, The**
Revised, 1974. Grades K–8. By Bill Martin, Jr. and Peggy Brogan. Holt, Rinehart and Winston, Inc., 383 Madison Ave., New York, N.Y. 10017.

Listening and observing pictures
Reading and listening to the voice on the cassette
Reading the book alone

56. **Space Science Fiction Series**
By Henry A. Bamman, et al., Benefic Press, 10300 W. Roosevelt Road, Westchester, Ill. 60153. Each book is fourth- to twelfth-grade interest level. All books are seventy-two pages in length.

TITLE	GRADE LEVEL
Space Pirate	2
Milky Way	2
Bone People	3
Planet of the Whistlers	4
Ice-Men of Rime	5
Inviso Man	6

57. **The Specter Series, 1979**
Pitman Learning, Inc., 6 Davis Drive, Belmont, Calif. 94002. Reading difficulty is third reader; skill builders included.

Dreams
'57 T-Bird
A Deadly Game
The Actor
No Rent to Pay
Homecoming
The Ear
ZB4

58. **Sports Mystery Series**
By Evelyn Lunemann. Benefic Press, 10300 W. Roosevelt Road, Westchester, Ill. 60153. Each book is fourth- to twelfth-grade interest level. All books are seventy-two pages in length.

TITLE	READING LEVEL
Ten Feet Tall	2
No Turning Back	2
Fairway Danger	3
Tip Off	3
Pitcher's Choice	3
Face Off	4
Swimmer's Mark	4
Tennis Champ	4

59. **Spotlight on Literature**
Random House School Division, Department 469, 400 Hahn Road, Westminster, Md. 21157. Classics are rewritten.

Collections 1 and 2	Reading levels 3–4
Collections 3 and 4	Reading levels 4–5
Collections 5 and 6	Reading levels 5–6
Collections 7 and 8	Reading levels 6–7

60. **Sprint Libraries**
Scholastic Book Services, 904 Sylvan Ave., Englewood Cliffs, N.J. 07632. For severely retarded readers in secondary schools. Reading levels 1.5–4.0. Available in kits containing four copies each of five titles. Ditto masters and teacher's guide are also provided.

Sprint Starter: Libraries A and B (ten titles)
   The Haunted House—32 pp., reading level 1.5
   Kitchen Caper—32 pp., reading level 1.6
Sprint, Libraries I, IA, and IB
   The Prize—32 pp., reading level 2.0
   Karate Ace—32 pp., reading level 2.2
Sprint, Libraries II, IIA, and IIB
   Mystery on Elm Street—64 pp., reading level 2.6
   The Liquid Trap—64 pp., reading level 2.7
   The Homesteaders—64 pp., reading level 2.9
Sprint, Libraries III, IIIA, and IIIB—Reading levels 3.0–3.4
   The Mystery of the Jade Princess
   Sabatage Rock
   Sea Lab
   Star Jewel
   Strange Friends
   Dogs and Danger
   Pier 92
Sprint, Libraries IV, IVA, and IVB
   Ghost Town—96 pp., reading level 3.5
   Cartwheels—96 pp., reading level 3.9
   Skyhawks—96 pp., reading level 3.8

61. **Superstars, Creative Education Books**
By James T. Olsen. Children's Press, 1224 W. Van Buren St., Chicago, Ill. 60607. Grade level three through eight. More than sixty books in this series.

Evonne Goolagong: Superstar
Jackie Robinson: Superstar
Joe Namath: Superstar
Lee Trevino: Superstar
Muhammad Ali: Superstar
Roberto Clemente: Superstar
Vince Lombardi: Superstar

62. **Target Books**
Garrard Publishing Company, Champaign, Ill. 61820. Easy reading, high interest, mature format. Reading level, grades three through four: interest level five and up. Some titles are:

Adventures in Buckskin
Heroes of the Homerun
Jazz Greats
Women Who Dared to be Different

63. **Teen-Age Tales**
Ruth Strang et al., eds. D. C. Heath & Company, 125 Spring St., Lexington, Mass.
02173. The level of reading difficulty is about fifth or sixth grade. The interest appeal is
very good for adolescents. There are eight books in the series.

Teen-Age Tales: Books A, B, I, II, III, IV, V, and VI.

64. **Tom Logan Series**
By Edna Walker Chandler. Benefic Press, 10300 W. Roosevelt Road, Westchester, Ill.
60153.

TITLE	READING LEVEL	INTEREST LEVEL	PAGES
Pony Rider	PP	PP–2	48
Talking Wire	PP	PP–2	48
Track Boss	P	P–3	64
Cattle Drive	P	P–3	64
Secret Tunnel	1	1–4	64
Gold Train	1	1–4	64
Gold Nugget	2	2–5	96
Stage Coach Driver	3	3–6	96

65. **Treat Truck Series**
By Genevieve Gray, Sylvajean Harrington, Lee Harrington, and Sandra Altheide. Benefic
Press, 10300 W. Roosevelt Road, Westchester, Ill. 60153. Each book in the series is forty-
eight pages in length.

TITLE	READING LEVEL	INTEREST LEVEL
Mike and the Treat Truck	PP	PP–2
Treat Truck and the Fire	PP	PP–2
Treat Truck and the Dog Show	P	P–2
Treat Truck and the Big Rain	P	P–2
Treat Truck and the Parade	1	1–2
Treat Truck and the Lucky Lion	1	1–2
Treat Truck and the Storm	2	2–4
Treat Truck and the Bank Robbery	3	3–5

66. **True Books**
Children's Press, 1224 W. Van Buren St., Chicago, Ill. 60607. Each book contains forty-
eight pages; interest level, grades two through five.

True Book of Dinosaurs, by Mary Clark
True Book of the Mars Landing, by Leila Gemme
True Book of Metric Measurement, by June Behrens
True Book of Moonwalk Adventure, by Margaret Friskey

67. **Venture Books**

Leland Jacobs and John McInnes, Consultants. Garrard Publishing Co., Champaign, Ill. 61820. For first grade, there are thirty-two books of forty pages each, on four levels of difficulty. Illustrative titles are given.

LEVEL 1 (yellow cloth with green titles):
Bedtime for Bears
Count on Leo Lion
Dance to a Happy Song

LEVEL 2 (yellow cloth, black titles):
The Sleep-leaping Kangaroo
Pink, Pink
April Fool!

LEVEL 3 (yellow cloth, blue titles):
Too Fat to Fly
On with the Circus
No, No, No, and Yes

LEVEL 4 (blue cloth, red titles):
Willie's Whizmobile
Drat the Dragon
A Dog for Danny

For second grade, there are twenty books of sixty-four pages each, on four levels of difficulty.

LEVEL 1 (blue cloth, green titles):
That's How the Ball Bounces
Mrs. Twitter, the Animal Sitter

LEVEL 2 (blue cloth, black titles):
The Jelly Bean Contest
Hello, People

LEVEL 3 (blue cloth, blue titles):
Percy the Parrot Passes the Puck
The Chocolate Chip Mystery

LEVEL 4 (blue cloth, red titles):
Here Comes Mirium the Mixed-up Witch
You're Sure Silly, Billy

68. **Wonder Story Books**

By Miriam Huber and Mabel O'Donnell. Harper and Row, Publishers, 10 E. 53rd St., New York 10022. Although written for children in the primary grades, these books of old fairy tales are good reading in the intermediate grades also.

TITLE	READING LEVEL
Once upon a Time	Primer
I Know a Story	First Reader
It Happened One Day	Second Reader
After the Sun Sets	Third Reader

69. **World of Adventure Series**

By Henry A. Bamman and Robert Whitehead. Benefic Press, 10300 W. Roosevelt Road, Westchester, Ill. 60153. All of the following are fourth- to ninth-grade interest level.

TITLE	READING LEVEL
City Beneath the Sea	4
Fire on the Mountain	3
Flight to the South Pole	2
Hunting Grizzly Bears	3
Lost Uranium Mine	2
Sacred Well of Sacrifice	5
Search for Piranha	4
Viking Treasure	6

70. **Yearling Individualized Reading Program**

Noble and Noble, 1 Dag Hammerskjold Plaza, 245 E. 47th St., New York, N.Y. 10017.

LEVEL 3—for third grade—contains seventy-five books, two or three copies of each of thirty titles, and thirty-six teacher reference cards. Selected titles are:
Amelia Earhart, level 3.3
A Bear Called Paddington, level 4.1
Helen Keller, level 2.8
Charlotte's Web, level 3.5

LEVEL 4—for fourth grade—contains sixty-five books, two or three copies of each of twenty-five titles, and thirty-one teacher reference cards. Selected titles are:
All-of-a-Kind Family, level 4.0
Call Me Charley, level 3.3
Mystery of the Fat Cat, level 3.7
Story of Dr. Doolittle, level 3.8

LEVEL 5—for fifth grade—contains sixty-five books, two or three copies of each of twenty-five titles, and thirty-two teacher reference cards. Selected titles are:
Blue Ridge Bill, level 3.4
The Four Story Mistake, level 5.8
Roller Skates, level 4.7
The Secret Garden, level 5.5

LEVEL 6—for sixth grade—contains sixty-five books, two or three copies of each of twenty-five titles, and thirty-one teacher reference cards. Selected titles are:
The Black Cauldron, level 6.4
Edge of Two Worlds, level 3.7
The Singing Tree, level 4.6
The Wolves of Willoughby Chase, level 6.6

APPENDIX C

Selected Tests for Classroom Teachers

1. *Basic Achievement Skills Individual Screener,* 1983
   For all elementary reading levels. Tests reading, spelling, and mathematics. Psychological Corp.
2. *California Achievement Tests: Reading,* 1978 edition
   Level 11 for grades 1.0–1.9 tests phonic analysis, reading vocabulary, reading comprehension; Level 12 for grades 1.6–2.9 and Level 13 for grades 2.6–3.9 test phonic analysis, vocabulary, comprehension, and structural analysis; Levels 14–19 for grades 3.6–12.9 test vocabulary and comprehension. California Test Bureau.
3. *Doren Diagnostic Reading Test,* 1973 edition
   Diagnoses weaknesses in primary and intermediate grade word-recognition skills: letter recognition, beginning sounds, whole-word recognition, words within words, speech consonants, ending sounds, blending, rhyming, vowels, discriminate guessing, spelling sight words. A group test requires one to three hours depending upon group size and reading level. American Guidance Service. One form.
4. *Durrell Analysis of Reading Difficulty,* 1980 edition
   Tests oral and silent reading, listening comprehension, word analysis and word recognition, visual and auditory memory of words, spelling and handwriting. Individually administered. Requires forty to fifty minutes to administer but yields a valuable profile. Psychological Corp.
5. *Gates-MacGinitie Reading Tests,* 1978 edition
   Level A, grade 1; Level B, grade 2; Level C, grade 3; Level D, survey, grades 4–6; Level E, survey, grades 7–9; Level F, survey, grades 10–12. Two forms. Tests vocabulary and comprehension. Houghton Mifflin.
6. *Nelson Reading Skills Tests,* 1977 edition
   Level A, grades 3.0–4.5, requires sixty minutes working time; Level B, grades 4.5–6.0, requires thirty-six minutes working time; Level C, grades 7–9, requires thirty-six minutes working time. Two forms. Vocabulary and Comprehension. Houghton Mifflin.

7. *Nelson Reading Test,* 1962 edition
   Forms A and B, grades 3–9. Tests vocabulary and comprehension. Requires thirty minutes working time. Houghton Mifflin.

8. *Silent Reading Diagnostic Tests,* 1976 edition
   For students having difficulties in grades 3–6. Tests word recognition, words in context, syllabication, synthesis, beginning sounds, ending sounds. A group test. Rand McNally.

9. *Stanford Diagnostic Reading Test,* 1984 edition
   Red level, grades 1.5–4.5; Green level, grades 3.5–6.5; Brown level, grades 5.5–8.5; Blue level, grades 7.5–13.0. A group test. Psychological Corp.

10. *Stanford Diagnostic Reading Test,* 3d ed., 1984
    Red level, 1.8–4.8; Green level, 4.1–6.8; Brown level, 6.1–8.8; Blue level, 8.1–12.8. All levels test decoding and comprehension. Brown and Blue levels test vocabulary and rate of reading, also. Forms G and H. Psychological Corp.

Teaching the Directed Reading Lesson

A guided reading lesson usually follows five sequential steps. These are:

1. Motivating an interest in the lesson by:
    a. Studying the pictures that illustrate the story;
    b. Talking about new or unusual words in the story;
    c. Relating the ideas in the story to the background of experience of the class;
    d. Setting up a purpose for reading, that is, reading to find out something.
2. Teaching new vocabulary and reviewing words "that cause trouble" by:
    a. Presenting new words in meaningful ways;
    b. Practicing flash-card drills;
    c. Playing games that teach or give practice matching, comparing, arranging, and so on, the basic vocabulary.
3. Guiding the silent reading of the lesson by:
    a. Asking guide questions so that pupils read to find specific information;
    b. Completing the story section by section with attention to understanding the plot of the story;
    c. Checking pupils' understanding as indicated throughout the story.
4. Interpreting the story by:
    a. Reading orally conversation parts;
    b. Reading orally favorite parts;
    c. Retelling the ideas in the story in proper sequence;
    d. Reading sentences or paragraphs to answer specific questions or to evaluate pupils' opinions;
    e. Evaluating the happenings in the story with such questions as:
        (1) Would you have done what Bob did? or
        (2) Is this true or only imaginary?
5. Providing related activities (follow-up) by:
    a. Using seat-work exercises to give:
        (1) Further practice on vocabulary;
        (2) Attention to phonic and structural skills;
        (3) Comprehension checks.

  b. Extending the lesson through:
    (1) Free reading at the book table;
    (2) Searching encyclopedias for additional information;
    (3) Art work, writing, dramatization as related to the lesson;
    (4) Shared oral reading in small groups.

These steps are amplified in the following outline only for clarification. The story "The Five Brothers" in the second reader *Come Along*[1] has been selected for this purpose. This story of the five Chinese brothers has been divided into four teaching units. The first of these units is summarized as it might be taught to a reading group in second grade.

1. Motivation
    It is suggested that teachers and pupils study three pictures: the mother with her five grown sons; one man gathering fish from the bottom of the sea; and one man with his arm in the mouth of a ferocious crocodile. The teacher may elicit the responses that the family lives in China, that the brothers may be fishermen, and that each brother can do something remarkable.
2. New vocabulary[2]
    The new words are introduced in context by use of the chalkboard with class discussion:
    a. Mrs. Brown is Jack's mother.
       She is Bill's mother, too.
       Bill and Jack are *brothers*.
    b. We catch fish in the *sea*. (If the group does not pronounce "sea" quickly, the teacher may ask what word that begins with the sound "s" would make the sentence clear.)
    c. A crocodile has a very big *mouth*.
    d. Any box has a top.
       Does it have a *bottom*, too?
    e. Bill got the first prize.
       Jack got the *second* prize.
    f. The ball hit Freddy, but it didn't *hurt* him.
  Six other words are similarly presented.
3. Guided silent reading
    Now we are ready to begin reading the story about the five brothers. . . .
    Read these three pages to yourself. Find out what the remarkable things were about the first two brothers. If you come to a word you do not know, use the beginning sound of that word and the meaning of what you are reading to help you decide what the word is. If you need more help, use the sound of any other part you know in the word.[3]
4. Interpreting the story[4]
    What was the remarkable thing about the first brother?
    How did this help him?
    Did the people know what the first brother could do?
    What was the remarkable thing about the second brother?
    Why did the second brother work at the zoo?

Could anyone tell the brothers apart?

Is this a true story? (It is really a Chinese fairy tale.)

Read aloud the lines on page 154 that tell what the brothers could do and whether they told people about these things.

Read the lines on page 155 that tell what the first brother did while he held the sea in his mouth and how he did it.

Read the lines on page 156 that tell what was remarkable about the second brother.

5. Related activities[5]
   a. Word analysis and reading skills
      (1) Word recognition

brother	second	stretch
sea	fourth	burn
bottom	mouth	third

      (2) Initial consonant substitution

Take *s* from *sea*, substitute *t* and make *tea*.

Take *s* from *sea*, substitute *p* and make *pea*.

Take *m* from *mouth*, substitute *s* and make *south*.

Take *b* from *burn*, substitute *ch* and make *churn*.

      (3) Recognizing antecedents in sentences.

Go upstairs and get the *shoes. They* have already been wrapped.

      (4) Reading new sentences using new words.

      (5) Associating letters and sounds:

whine	when	whistle	whit
thine	that	the	
thin	thing	thick	
shine	shoe	she	shin

      (6) Choosing and writing the correct word:

He is my _____ .

  mother   brother   brown

There is water in the _____ of the well.

  bounce   balloon   bottom

      (7) Choosing the correct word:

learn	to find out about something
	to go to sleep
follow	to go before
	to come after

      (8) Using beginning sounds:

Which of these could you put on your head?

  good   hood   stood

Which one of these do you have on your feet?

  toes   foes   goes

b. Extending the lesson[6]
    (1) The lesson for Part One of "The Five Brothers" does not suggest any activity for this part. However, at the end of Part Two, it is suggested that the class may draw pictures to illustrate sentences:

        No. 3: It is brown.
                It is up in a tree.
                A bird made it.
                It has three babies in it.

    (2) At the end of the story of "The Five Brothers," it is suggested that individual pupils may wish to read *The True Book of Birds We Know* by Margaret Friskey.[7]

Notes

1. Paul McKee, et al., *Come Along,* revised, Teacher's Edition (Boston: Houghton Mifflin, 1957), 327–37.
2. Ibid., 328–29.
3. Ibid., 330.
4. Ibid., 330–31.
5. Ibid., 333–35.
6. Ibid., 348 and 367.
7. Margaret Friskey, *The True Book of Birds We Know* (Chicago: Children's Press, 1954).

The Informal Reading Inventory

Making an informal reading inventory (IRI) is a task that each teacher should accomplish. The passages may come from the children's readers, from trade books, from stories they write, or from stories made by the teacher. Care should be taken that all of the passages are either narrative or expository in form. The two formats require different reading abilities, and mixing them may confuse the results of the informal reading inventory. After passages are selected, assign a reading level to each one. Levels can be estimated by using Fry's Readability Graph. Then, questions must be prepared. The questions should be written at different levels of thinking. Questions about word meanings may also be asked. Finally, try out the IRI on several children to see whether the assigned reading levels and the questions are appropriate.

Passages from a teacher-made IRI are shown here to be used as a guide for constructing one for classroom use. In practice, the teacher would need one with several more levels than are provided in this sample.

First-Reader Level (Oral)

Motivating Statement: This story is about a child whose father went away on a trip. Let's find out what happens.

The Jet Airplane Trip
My father went on a jet airplane.
He went to a city far away.
He flew for three hours.
He had work to do in the city.
The work took one week.
It was very hard.
He had to talk to people and write what they
said.
I was glad when he came home.
He came down the steps and hugged my mom
and me.
He brought us both presents.

Questions:

1. From the child's story, what tells us that the father went to a city that was far away?
2. What were the two kinds of work the father had to do?
3. How do we know that the family was glad to be together again?
4. How many days was the father gone?
5. Where was the father just before he came down the steps and hugged the family?

Number of words	70	Summary:
Number of syllables	77	Word recognition
Number of sentences	10	Number of miscues _____

Summary:
  Word recognition
    Number of miscues   _____
    % accuracy   _____
    Level   _____
  Comprehension
    Number of errors   _____
    % accuracy   _____
    Level   _____
  Overall level   _____

First-Reader Level (Silent)

Motivating Statement: This story is about two children who went to play. Let's see what happened during the play time.

Playing on the Mesa
My friend and I went to the mesa to play.
Our moms knew we were going.
We didn't go far.
We could still see our houses.
First, we made a road for our toy cars.
A lizard ran on it.
We thought it was funny that a lizard ran on
our road.
We made our cars go on the road, too.
Then we made a parking lot.
We parked our cars in it.
All at once we stopped!
There was a noise—a buzz!
Then we saw the snake.
We took our cars and ran home as fast as we
could.

Questions:

1. Who knew the children were going to play on the mesa?
2. How did the children know they were not far from home?
3. Why do you think the children thought it was funny that the lizard ran on the road?
4. What made the children stop playing?
5. Why did the children run home as fast as they could?

Number of words	101	Summary:
Number of syllables	107	Comprehension
Number of sentences	14	Number of errors _____
		% accuracy _____
		Level _____

Second-Reader Level (Oral)

Motivating Statement: This is a story of a child whose big brother bought a snow-mobile. Let's see how he felt about it.

Steve's Snowmobile
My big brother's name is Steve.
Last year he decided to buy a snowmobile.
He saved his money until he had enough to buy
it.
He went to some stores.
He found the one he wanted.
When it began to snow, he took it up in the
mountains.
He rode it along the roads.
He didn't want to hurt the trees in the forest.
He didn't want to scare the animals, either.
Once the snowmobile went into a snow bank.
Steve was covered with snow.
When he got home, he told me about the fun he
had.
Someday I want a snowmobile, too.

Questions:

1. How did Steve get the money to pay for the snowmobile?
2. Where did Steve ride the snowmobile?
3. How do you know that Steve cared about the plants and animals in the forest?
4. What do you think a snow bank looks like?

5. What did the person who wrote the story decide about snowmobiles?

Number of words   <u>108</u>   Summary:
Number of syllables   <u>126</u>   Word recognition
Number of sentences   <u>14</u>

                       Word recognition
                           Number of miscues   _____
                           % accuracy   _____
                           Level   _____
                       Comprehension
                           Number of errors   _____
                           % accuracy   _____
                           Level   _____
                       Overall level   _____

Second-Reader Level (Silent)

Motivating Statement: This is a story about a girl who visited her friend and learned about other families.

Ann's Family
I went to visit my friend.
Her name is Ann, and she lives across the city.
Her grandfather and grandmother live with
them.
Her family is different from mine.
Grandmother stays at home and takes care of
the children.
They all live in an apartment.
Other families live in the building, too.
You can hear them laugh and talk.
All the families like each other.

At night Ann's family comes home.
They eat in the kitchen.
When I was there, they didn't have enough
chairs.
So Ann and I watched TV and ate.
At bedtime, Ann and I slept on the sofa.
She doesn't have her own room.
When I got home I told my mother that
families live in all sorts of ways.

Questions:

1. Who looked after Ann and the other children in the family?
2. Where did Ann's family live?
3. Why did Ann and her guest eat in front of the TV?
4. What is a sofa?
5. What did the writer mean when she told her mother that families live in all sorts of ways?

Number of words	124	Summary:	
Number of syllables	134	Comprehension	
Number of sentences	16	Number of errors	_____
		% accuracy	_____
		Level	_____

Third-Reader Level (Oral)

Motivating Statement: Have you ever lost a book? This is about a child who did. Let's see if it was found.

The Day I Lost My Library Book

I love to read books. I am lucky because our school has a good library, and we can check out three books each week. Ever since I was little, my mother has warned me to take good care of books, especially borrowed ones.

That Monday I checked out two mysteries and a thin joke book. By Friday I had read them and told the jokes to my friends.

When it was library time on Monday, I got the two mysteries out of my desk. But the joke book was missing. I thought my friends had taken it. They got mad when I accused them. I looked everywhere, but I couldn't find it. The teacher said we had to go to the library. She said I just wouldn't be able to check out more books until the joke book was found. I was so upset!

Then my spelling workbook fell out on the floor and the joke book fell out of the spelling workbook. I was very happy and I told my friends I was sorry I had accused them of taking it. So I got to check out more books after all.

Questions:

1. Why do you think losing a book was so upsetting to the writer?
2. What did the writer do when the book couldn't be found?
3. What did the teacher say would happen because the book was missing?
4. Why do you think the child missed the joke book in the desk?
5. What does *warned* mean?

		Summary:	
Number of words	192	Word recognition	
Number of syllables	235	Number of miscues	_____
Number of sentences	16	% accuracy	_____
		Level	_____
		Comprehension	
		Number of errors	_____
		% accuracy	_____
		Level	_____
		Overall level	_____

Third-Reader Level (Silent)

Motivating Statement: This story is about some neighbors who had a problem. Let's see what it was.

Neighbor Dogs

We have a little black poodle. He stays in the house most of the time. He loves to watch TV and sleep in my dad's special chair. When Dad arrives home, Teddy has to get out of the chair.

Our neighbors have a big, black German shepherd dog. He barks a lot and will try to attack anyone who goes in his yard. He is a good guard dog, and the neighbors are all glad he guards our houses.

One day Teddy got in the yard with the German shepherd and was attacked by the big dog. My mother and I couldn't help Teddy. The big dog's owner came out and got Teddy away.

Poor Teddy had a torn ear and a cut on his shoulder. We took him to the vet and got stitches in the cuts. Teddy cried a lot, but he got well. He still sleeps in my dad's chair. He knows not to go in the German shepherd's yard.

Questions:

1. Compare how the two dogs lived.
2. Why did the neighbors like the German shepherd?
3. What mistake did Teddy make?
4. Why do you think the writer and the mother couldn't help Teddy?
5. Why did Teddy cry after his trip to the vet?

		Summary:	
Number of words	165	Comprehension	
Number of syllables	193	Number of errors	_____
Number of sentences	15	% accuracy	_____
		Level	_____

Fourth-Reader Level (Oral)

Motivating Statement: As you read this story, decide if you would like to have been the child on the wild ride.

The Wild Ride

My grandfather told me a story about when he was a boy. He had a pony named Wee-Bob that he rode every day. One Friday his father sent him to the neighbor's house to ask Mr. Bell to come and help with some work.

My grandfather got on his pony and started up the road. The road lay beside the railroad track. In the pasture beside the road, horses and cows were eating grass.

As they came trotting along, Grandpa heard a train whistle. Soon the train was in sight. When a horse in the pasture neighed, the pony laid back his ears, stiffened himself, and began to run. For a short distance he ran in the road. Then, suddenly, he turned and ran in front of the train engine. Before the engineer could whistle, the pony crossed the train track, jumped over the fence, and landed in the pasture with the horses.

It all happened too fast for Grandpa to be scared. But when the pony landed in the pasture, Grandpa fell flat on the ground. He lay there and shook with fright. Then he thought of the exciting story he would tell when he got home.

Questions:

1. Where was the child going on his pony?
2. Why do you think the pony ran in front of the train?
3. Why do you think the rider was not scared until he fell on the ground?
4. Why didn't the engineer blow the whistle when the pony ran in front of the train?
5. What is a pasture?

Number of words	198	Summary:
Number of syllables	247	Word recognition
Number of sentences	16	Number of miscues _____
		% accuracy _____
		Level _____
		Comprehension
		Number of errors _____
		% accuracy _____
		Level _____
		Overall level _____

Fourth-Reader Level (Silent)

Motivating Statement: This is a story about a child who wanted to make a snowman. Let's find out what was unusual about the snowman.

Our Snowman

I wanted to build a snowman. I had wanted to for several days, but I just didn't know how to do it. Finally, Mom grew tired of my nagging, and she said, "Why don't you start with that very large old beach ball in the garage with our camping things."

So I got the beach ball. It was half white already. I pasted white paper over the green parts. Then, I searched for a smaller round object for the middle of the snowman. Mom had a round, white flower pot that I perched on top of the beach ball. I got a large styrofoam ball Mom gave me from her hobby-box for a head. I could stick pins in it, so I fastened on a paper carrot nose, a red pepper mouth, and two prunes for eyes. I added an old coat with the sleeves stiffened with newspapers. Last of all, I wrapped a scarf around its neck and pinned gloves on the ends of the sleeves. The snowman looked great!

Mom said, "That's a pretty good snowman for July 12!" Later we saw a man stop his car, laugh, and take a picture of our July snowman in the front yard.

Questions:

1. Why did the mother finally suggest a way to make the snowman?
2. What object was the snowman's head?
3. Why do you think the man laughed at the snowman?
4. Show me with your arms how large a beach ball would be.
5. What is styrofoam?

Number of words	202	Summary:
Number of syllables	243	Comprehension
Number of sentences	15	Number of errors _____
		% accuracy _____
		Level _____

Fifth-Reader Level (Oral)

Motivating Statement: Read to see whether you would like a pet named Cappy.

Cappy

I once had a pet duck named Cappy. When she hatched, she had a tuft of feathers on top of her head and looked like she was wearing a drum major's hat. She was very lively and followed me like a shadow.

She loved water and never got tired of swimming in the pond and would spend hours diving for food in the murky water. Then, suddenly, she would get out of the water, shake herself, and come running to me. I enjoyed her friendship so much.

In our pond were several turtles. Turtles are enemies of ducks and will grab them by a leg and drag them to the bottom of the pond. They had gotten a couple of my mother's ducks.

One day when Cappy was splashing in the water, she suddenly quacked loudly and disappeared. I was helpless to do anything. Just as suddenly, she came back to the surface and raced for the shore. I could see blood, and when I got to her, I could see that the turtle had torn her leg badly as she struggled to get free.

My mother bandaged her wound, and Cappy just sat around for several days. But she did get well and lived for many years. She limped badly, but I was so glad to have her that I didn't mind the comical way the feather cap bounced on her head.

Questions:

1. Why do you think the child named the duck "Cappy"?
2. Why did the child compare the duck to a shadow?
3. What makes water look murky?
4. Why do you think the child was helpless to do anything to help the duck when the turtle had her?
5. What does comical mean?

Number of words	234	Summary:
Number of syllables	293	Word recognition
Number of sentences	16	Number of miscues _____
		% accuracy _____
		Level _____
		Comprehension
		Number of errors _____
		% accuracy _____
		Level _____
		Overall level _____

Fifth-Reader Level (Silent)

Motivating Statement: Would it be scary to have eyes following you? This is about a child who had that experience.

The Eyes That Moved

When I was in fifth grade, my teacher, Mr. Cobb, took the class on a field trip to a natural history museum. It was a good trip. We saw dinosaur bones, rocks and minerals, and a volcano.

While we were looking at the dinosaur skeletons, I noticed that one skull on a shelf had eyes that moved. I looked down quickly, but when I looked back the eyes had followed me. Each time I moved, the eyes moved, too.

I was just about to tell my friend about the moving eyes when a lady came into the room calling, "Betty Jean! Betty Jean!" Then she burst out crying. She said that her daughter who was four had gotten away from her and that she was sure she would never find her.

Then I thought of those eyes behind the dinosaur skull. I slipped around behind the shelf where I wasn't supposed to go, and there was a little girl. I was sure it was the lost Betty Jean.

I took her hand, and the child followed me. I pointed to the crying woman and asked if that was her mother. The child answered by calling, "Mommy! Mommy."

Betty Jean and her mother were happy to find each other, and I was glad to know that those eyes really didn't belong to a dinosaur.

Questions:

1. What kinds of things did the children see in the museum?
2. What did the child notice that was strange about one dinosaur?
3. Why did the child go behind the shelf where visitors were not supposed to go?
4. Why do you think the little girl was hiding behind the dinosaur skull?
5. Why was the child who told the story glad that the dinosaur really didn't have eyes that moved?

Number of words   223   Summary:
Number of syllables   284   Comprehension
Number of sentences   17   Number of errors   _____
                                  % accuracy   _____
                                  Level   _____

Sixth-Reader Level (Oral)

Motivating Statement: Have you had something interesting happen on Thanksgiving Day? See what happened to this family's dinner.

Pumpkin Pie and Butter

It was Thanksgiving Day, and we had friends for dinner. My mother was busily putting the final touches on the dinner. We were going to eat turkey and dressing, potatoes and gravy, two vegetables, and salad and carrot sticks. Dessert was pumpkin pie, and Mother was whipping cream to go on it.

She had just turned on the mixer and put the beaters in the whipping cream when the peas boiled over. She took the peas from the stove and wiped up the mess. All this time the beaters were turning and turning the whipping cream.

When Mother got back to the bowl of whipping cream, she looked surprised and said, "Oh, my word! The mixer ran too long, and we have butter instead of whipped cream."

I looked in the bowl. Little yellow lumps were floating in thin-looking milk. Mother explained that that is how butter is made. Cream is whipped until butter forms. The thin-looking milk is buttermilk.

Mother didn't have any more whipping cream, and the food stores were closed. So we didn't have whipped cream for our pumpkin pie, but we did have homemade butter for our bread.

Questions:

1. What foods was the family serving for Thanksgiving dinner?
2. What happened that caused the whipping cream to turn to butter?
3. What is buttermilk?
4. What does it mean "to put the final touches" on dinner?
5. Why didn't Mother make more whipped cream when the first batch was ruined?

Number of words	192	Summary:
Number of syllables	241	Word recognition
Number of sentences	16	Number of miscues _____
		% accuracy _____
		Level _____
		Comprehension
		Number of errors _____
		% accuracy _____
		Level _____
		Overall level _____

Sixth-Reader Level (Silent)

Motivating Statement: Going to a fair is fun, unless something happens that you don't expect. Then it may not be fun at all.

Our State Fair Trip

I went with my younger brother to the State Fair when I was ten and he was eight. My mother didn't want us to go alone, but we begged, and finally she let us do it. We rode a city bus to the entrance, paid the entry fee, and entered the magic land.

We had been told to stay together whatever we did, and we had promised to obey. We bought cotton candy and ate it quickly. Then we went to see the horses, cattle, sheep, and pigs in the different animal barns. Soon my brother got tired, and I told him to sit under a cottonwood tree while I bought some soda pop. It took me about fifteen minutes to find a food stand and buy two medium cups of pop.

When I got back with the drinks, my brother wasn't there. I was frightened because we had made Mom a promise and had broken it. I looked everywhere, but I couldn't find my brother. Finally, I spotted a policeman. I shouted out my story, and he tried to calm me. He promised that he would find Teddy. He asked me questions about where I had left him and where I had gone. Then, he talked to someone on his walkie-talkie.

In a few minutes someone called him back. I was relieved because he had found my brother. The policeman explained that after I had bought the sodas, I had gotten turned around and gone to the wrong trees.

When we got to Teddy, he said, "You sure were gone a long time! I was worried. I didn't want to have to tell Mom that you got lost."

Questions:

1. Why did the boy call the fair the "magic land"?
2. Who was Teddy?
3. Where was the younger boy to wait?
4. Who really got lost? Why?
5. What does "medium" mean?

Number of words	279	Summary:
Number of syllables	357	Comprehension
Number of sentences	20	Number of errors _____
		% accuracy _____
		Level _____

Home Information Questionnaire

THE UNIVERSITY OF NEW MEXICO

MANZANITA CENTER

HOME INFORMATION QUESTIONNAIRE   Remedial Reading Program

_____   _____
Name of student   Date

The staff at Manzanita Center wants to provide the best possible reading program for your son/daughter. The information asked for below will be helpful in achieving that goal.

1. We are interested in your observations of your child's reading performance. Does he/she:
   a. Read orally? _____ Read silently? _____
   b. Move his/her lips when reading silently? _____
   c. Follow the line with finger or pointer? _____
   d. Hold book about 16 inches from the eyes? _____
   e. Appear relaxed when reading? _____
   f. Choose to read on his/her own? _____
   g. Talk to you about what he/she has read? _____
   h. Ask you to pronounce words? _____
   i. Become easily distracted when reading? _____

   Please attach any additional comments about your child's reading performance.

2. Good vision and hearing are important in learning to read.
   Has your child had a vision test? _____ When? _____
   Results? _____
   Has your child had a hearing test? _____ When? _____
   Results? _____
   Does your child: Blink constantly? _____ ; rub the eyes? _____ ;
   squint? _____ ; complain about not being able to see? _____ ;
   complain of headaches after reading? _____ ; have red eyes
   frequently? _____ ; wear his/her glasses when reading? _____ .

Does your child: Turn up the TV or radio abnormally loud? _____ ; talk loudly? _____ ; ask you to repeat statements? _____ ; have problems following directions? _____ ; fail to respond to what you say occasionally? _____ .

3. A student's health, both past and present, may be important to present reading performance. It may also be a factor in future achievement. Please give information about the items below. Please give approximate date that each occurred.

Childhood Diseases	Surgery	Accidents	Allergies

4. Reading is closely related to general speech and language development. It would be helpful to know the following:
   a. At about what age did your child begin to talk? _____
   b. At about what age did your child talk in sentences? _____
   c. Were there problems with making specific sounds? _____
      If so, which ones? _____
   d. What language or languages did your child learn to speak? _____
      _____
   e. At about what age did your child start noticing signs and asking to have them read?
      _____
   f. At about what age did your child start having books and stories read to him/her?
      _____

5. Emotions also seem to influence reading achievement.
   Does your child: Seem to worry about little things? _____ ; get nervous? _____ ; show nervous mannerisms (nail biting, complaining of stomachache, twisting hair, picking nose)? _____ ; cry easily? _____ ; make friends easily? _____ ; prefer to play alone? _____ ; prefer to play in a group? _____ ; act tolerant of others? _____ ; adjust to new situations easily? _____ .

6. Your child's attitude toward reading and school are important factors in his/her future reading success.
   Does your child: Like school? _____ ; like to read? _____ ; tell you what happens at school? _____ ; like the teacher(s)? _____ ; have a good attendance record? _____ .

7. Has anyone in the family tried to help your child with his/her reading? What kind of things were done to help? Do you feel the family efforts were helpful? (Please write comments on the back of this form.)

8. Why do you think your student is having reading problems?

_____

9. Have you talked with the school teacher(s) about the reading situation? What were the teacher's suggestions? Did the school suggest remedial help? _____

_____

10. Please add any other comments that could be helpful in planning a program for your child. (Use the back side of this form or attach your response.)

APPENDIX G

Instructional Materials for Word Identification and Comprehension

1. Anderson, Donald, *New Practice Readers,* 2d. ed., (New York: McGraw-Hill Book Co., 1978). Each book contains a series of short stories with accompanying vocabulary words and comprehension questions. The entire books are taped so that children may use them independently.

Book A	Grade 2	Book E	Grade 6
Book B	Grade 3	Book F	Grade 7
Book C	Grade 4	Book G	Grade 8
Book D	Grade 5		

2. *Barnell Loft Multiple Skills Series* (Baldwin, N.Y.: Barnell Loft, 1982). This series is designed for primary, intermediate, and middle-school levels.

3. Benner, Patricia Ann, and Virginia Law, *Troubleshooters I* (Boston: Houghton Mifflin, 1975). This program includes eight consumable workbooks to teach English language communication skills in junior and senior high school, and it is self-teaching, self-correcting, and self-directing. Titles: *Sound Out, Sound Off, Spelling Action, Word Attack, Word Mastery, Sentence Strength, Punctuation Power,* and *English Achievement.* Teacher's guides are included. Spirit Masters are also available.

4. Boning, Richard A., *Cloze Connections* (Baldwin, N.Y.: Barnell Loft, 1980). Materials are written at grade levels third through ninth.

5. Boning, Richard A., *Specific Skills Series* (Baldwin, N.Y.: Barnell Loft).
   Detecting the Sequence, Levels 1–6 and Adv., 1982
   Using the Context, Levels 1–6 and Adv., 1982
   Getting the Facts, Levels 1–6, 1982
   Working with Sounds, Levels 1–6 and Adv., 1982
   Drawing Conclusions, Levels 1–6, 1982
   Getting the Main Idea, Levels 1–6, 1982
   Locating the Answer, Levels 1–6 and Adv., 1982
   Following Directions, Levels 1–6 and Adv., 1982
   Using Guide Words, Levels 4–6 and Adv., 1974
   Identifying Inferences, Levels 1–8, 1988

Using an Index, Levels 3–6 and Adv., 1975
Syllabication, Levels 2–6 and Adv., 1975
Using a Table of Contents, Levels 1–6 and Adv., 1975
Understanding Questions, Levels 1–6 and Adv., 1975
These skills books provide exercises that focus on necessary subskills to improve reading with understanding. Pretests and posttests are provided. Many new exercise booklets are added to the list each year.

6. Boning, Richard A. *Supportive Reading Skills* (Baldwin, N.Y.: Barnell Loft). Titles include:
Recognizing Word Relationships, Intermediate
Understanding Word Groups, Level 3
Understanding Questions, Level 2
Interpreting Idioms, Level 3
Syllabication, Level 4
Mastering Multiple Meanings, Level 1
Reading Homographs, Level 3
Reading Homonyms, Level 3
Reading Heteronyms, Level 6
Discovering Word Patterns, Intermediate
Reading Schedules, Level 5
Reading Ads, Level 6
Using a Table of Contents, Level 5
Using an Index, Level 3
Learning to Alphabetize, Level 3
Using Guide Words, Level 6

7. *Building Reading Competencies* (Dobbs Ferry, N.Y.: Oceana Educational Communications, Inc., 1981). *Structural Analysis* was prepared for levels A through E, as were *Antonyms, Synonyms,* and *Analogies.*

8. Cohen, Lawrence H., *Neighborhood Stories* (Providence, R.I.: Jamestown Publishers, 1982). These materials are designed for the intermediate grades.

9. *Competency Press Cloze Booklets.* White Plains, N.Y.: Competency Press.
Competence in Cloze (Level C, Part 1). Grade levels 2.5–4.5.
Competence in Cloze (Level E, Part 1). Grade levels 3.5–5.5.
Reading and Writing through Cloze: A First Book. Grade levels 1.5–2.0.

10. *Developing a Sight Vocabulary.* (Baldwin, N.Y.: Barnell Loft, 1983). This same company developed *A Word Recognition Program,* 1982. The levels are: A1, first grade; A2, first grade; B, second grade; C, third grade; and D, fourth grade.

11. Durham, John, Lorenz Graham, Kirstin Hunter, Jean Merrill, and Elsa Grasser, *Directions* (Boston: Houghton Mifflin). Readability: Fourth-grade level measured by the Dale-Chall readability formula. There are two reading levels: Levels I and II. Each level contains two anthologies, six novelettes, teacher's guides, and two workbooks.

12. *Hits Pak* (San Juan Capistrano, Calif.: Modu Learn, Inc., 1976). This program designed by Matt Glavach uses popular songs to help upper elementary grade students to adults who need primary grade reading abilities.

13. Kelley, Sandra, project manager, *Spotlight on Reading* (New York: Random House, 1984). Each level contains stories followed by questions and covers eight skills: main idea, sequence, critical reading, story elements, inference, vocabulary, details, and charts, maps and globes. Level 2, 1.5–2.5; Level 3, 2.5–3.5; Level 4, 3.5–4.5; Level 5, 4.5–5.5; Level 6, 5.5–6.5; Level 7, 6.5–7.5; Level 8, 7.5–8.5.
14. Lapp, Diane, and James Flood, *Clues for Better Reading* (North Billerica, Mass.: Curriculum Associates, 1982). The kits are designed for grades 2–3, 4–6, and 7–9.
15. Liddle, William, *Reading for Concepts* (Manchester, Mo.: Webster Division, McGraw-Hill, 1977). A series of graded workbooks that include factual articles and worthwhile information, drawn from many academic disciplines. Test exercises cause students to think evaluatively about factual details, using context, drawing inferences, recognizing antecedents, finding key ideas, verifying information, and recognizing cause and effect. The readability levels of the books are roughly: Book A, 1.9; B, 2.5; C, 3.2; D, 3.9; E, 4.6; F, 5.2; G, 5.8; and H, 6.4. They are available in either hard or soft cover. Informal tests for placement at each level are available.
16. Markstein, Linda, and Louise Hirasawa, *The Classic Reading Skills Series* (New York: Newbury House Publishers). Cross-cultural material.
Developing Reading Skills: Beginning
Developing Reading Skills: Intermediate
Expanding Reading Skills: Intermediate
17. Potter, Dan, *Little Trolley Books* (Oklahoma City: Economy Co., 1977). The collection of books is meant for readers at the primary levels. Examples of titles are *Water, Water Everywhere; Columbus;* and *A Workday in the City.*
18. *Reader's Digest Reading Skill Builders* (Pleasantville, N.Y.: Educational Division, Reader's Digest Services, Inc.). The format is similar to *Reader's Digest.* There are two books for each reading level, grades 1–6. Levels A and B are for adult reading level and are somewhat easier than grade 3, but with the same format.
19. *Reading Comprehension Series,* Levels A–H (Bingham, Mass.: Teaching Resources Corp., 1983). This series is for elementary students.
20. Ribisl, Jean, and Paul Ribisl, *Consonant Capers* (Boston: Houghton Mifflin, 1975). This includes finger plays, stories, tongue twisters, riddles, activities, and games.
21. Smith, Nila B., *Be A Better Reader Series,* 5th ed. (Englewood Cliffs, N.J.: Prentice-Hall, Inc., 1984). The levels are planned for the middle grades through high school.

Glossary

Ability grouping A process by which classroom teachers subdivide their classes into small groups for efficient teaching. Many teachers provide several reading groups in their classes based on general reading ability.

Accountability The responsibility of educators to do their job—and to provide measurable results to show success of the educational endeavor.

Advance organizer A passage written as a clarifying structure to introduce material to be read later.

Advocacy Support and encouragement given by parents and teachers for the best possible education of children.

Affect A measure of a person's emotional response to any situation (feelings, interests, attitudes already learned). As contrasted with cognition (knowing and understanding), affect measures personal responses to whatever is read.

Affixes Prefixes and suffixes.

Ambidexterity Ability to use either hand for many activities usually done only with the right hand.

Ancillary services Related, or auxilliary services provided to insure that children's programs are most successfully augmented.

Anomaly Deviation from the common rule, or type or form; an abnormality.

Audiometer A device for testing hearing.

Auditory discrimination Ability to differentiate between different sounds, for example, *big* and *pig*.

Basal readers Carefully graded (sequenced) series of texts with workbooks. The detailed teacher's manual provides for teaching word-recognition and comprehension skills.

Basic sight vocabulary Those high-frequency words (*the, in, is, for, to*) that constitute about 65 percent of the words in primary reading and 50 percent of the words in the upper elementary grades.

Behavior modification A highly structured program in a planned environment in which the desired behavior (either social or academic) is immediately rewarded (reinforced). The concept of immediate feedback is to praise, reward, or reinforce desirable behavior and to ignore or not reward undesirable behavior.

Bibliotherapy Literally, "treatment with books." It is a strategy of asking clients to read books in which characters have kinds of problems or handicaps that may enable the readers to gain insights into their own problems. By reading about how others have managed, they may learn how to overcome difficulties.

Bilingualism The ability to use two languages. Some people hope this means literacy skills in two languages; there are many levels of bilingualism.

Blend Two or three consonant letters that retain the sound of each consonant when pronounced; *tr*ap; *spr*ing; *spl*endid.

Breve The arc placed over a vowel (ă) to indicate the short sound.

Capacity reading level The highest grade level at which the students understand at least 75 percent of the ideas in material read aloud by an examiner.

Chapter I Classes that are federally funded for students who read below grade level and come from lower socioeconomic groups.

Cloze technique A strategy of deleting every *n*th word in a passage (*n* may be any number from 5 to 12). Students develop the ability to anticipate meaning in print by being forced to make closure wherever words are deleted. Cloze can also be used in practice exercises to delete only nouns, prepositions, or other classes of words.

Cognition The process of perceiving or knowing.

Cohesion The linguistic elements that speakers use to connect parts of text. The meaning of one element of text depends on another element.

Configuration The general form or shape of a word.

Congenital From birth (existing at birth).

Content fields Organized bodies of knowledge commonly called mathematics, social science, and so forth. Reading is *one tool* for learning in content fields.

Context The linguistic, social, emotional, and physical settings in which language, written and spoken, is produced.

Context clue Identification of a new word in context by anticipation of its meaning from the other words and ideas.

Criterion A standard by which a test may be judged; a set of scores, ratings.

Criterion-referenced test A test that measures students' performances on criteria specifically set by the examiner. The criteria detail what will be mastered and the level of performance required on that specific test. Criterion-referenced tests may be contrasted with norm-referenced tests in which students' performances are compared to the general ability of large numbers of others who took the same test.

Decoding Changing the written message into a spoken message; understanding the relationship between the writing system and the more familiar sound system; the process of rendering written or printed symbols into speech.

Deep structure The underlying meaning or the semantic interpretation of the sentence—what the sentence really means. "I had Mary for lunch" means "I invited Mary to eat with me."

Diacritical marks Symbols that designate particular sounds of letters: ă, a, ä.

Diagnostic test A test designed to determine specific areas of weakness or strength; to determine the nature of weakness by finding, for example, some subtests in a given battery on which the client is unable to perform.

Dialect Any form of the language spoken by a large number, or a specific group, of people. Dialect differs from the standard form of the language.

Dialectology The study of variations in language production as they are influenced by social, regional, and temporal conditions.

Differential diagnosis The process of analyzing the nature of a given student's learning or behavior problem.

Digraph Two letters of the alphabet that form a single phoneme. There are consonant digraphs; *sh, th, ch, wh, ng, ph*. There are vowel digraphs: *ea, ai, oa*.

Diphthong Two vowels together that are glided to form a sound to which both contribute, as in b*oi*l and b*oy*. A glide from one vowel sound to another in the syllable as in c*ow* and f*oul*.

Directed reading A reading lesson, usually with a basal reader, including building motivation, teaching new words, guiding silent reading, discussing the story, and rereading parts orally or doing other follow-up work.

Discourse analysis The study of units of language, oral or written, that are larger than sentences and the settings in which the language samples are produced.

Dyslexia A label for the disorder in which students do not attain the communication skills of reading, writing, and spelling commensurate with their general learning (intellectual) abilities.

Empowerment Enabling the individual to assume an important role in making decisions affecting herself or himself.

Environmental print Print found apart from the usual sources in schools—books and related materials. May be in the classroom environment (announcements or assignments) or in the nonschool environment (street signs, store names, labels on products).

Etiology Pertaining to the causes of a disorder.

Expository text Discourse that is arranged logically or chronologically; usually found in subject area texts or reference materials.

Eyedness The preference or dominance of one eye in perceptual motor tasks.

Feedback Information that individuals receive from intrinsic or extrinsic sources supporting their decisions about the accuracy of their responses or understandings.

Free reading Independent reading for one's own pleasure or to obtain information.

Frustration level The lowest level at which the student fails to recognize more than five words in one-hundred words in context or comprehends less than 70 percent of the ideas read.

Gloss Notes written in the margins of texts that help a reader to focus on the content of what is being read or on the reading process. The notes may be written on strips of paper and laid beside the text.

Grade equivalent The grade level for which a given score is the estimated value. A 5.7 is the seventh month of fifth grade.

Grapheme A minimum unit of the writing system, as in the letter *b* or the digraph *ch*.

Grapheme-phoneme correspondence The relationship between the grapheme of writing and the phoneme of speech.

Hyperactivity A higher than normal level of activity that is chronic in nature and is often characterized by distractibility, emotional instability, poor social skills, and inability to adjust to environmental changes.

Idiom A phrase whose meaning is derived from sources other than the common definitions of its words. An idiom is based on connotative, rather than denotative, meanings.

Independent reading level On the IRI, the students score no less than 99 percent in word recognition and have no difficulties in understanding the context.

Individualized educational program (IEP) A curriculum plan for any child that includes objectives, methodology, specific curriculum changes, and any classroom adjustments. IEPs are required by P.L. 94–142 for all exceptional children.

Individualized reading A method of teaching reading based on self-seeking, self-selecting, and self-pacing in which the teacher plans individual conferences with students. The teacher keeps individual progress reports for students on the basis of these conferences.

Inference The process of obtaining the intended meanings in discourse. Requires deriving implied, rather than directly stated, ideas.

Informal reading inventory (IRI) A test in which the student reads from a series of passages, easy to more difficult, until he or she reaches the frustration level. By recording all miscues in word recognition and measuring comprehension, the teacher can determine independent, instructional, and frustration levels of reading. If the teacher uses the same series of paragraphs and reads to the student beyond the frustration level of reading, the highest level of hearing comprehension, or capacity level for reading, can also be estimated.

Instructional reading level On an IRI, the highest level at which the student scores 95 percent in word recognition and at least 75 percent in comprehension; the level at which the student can make progress in reading growth.

Intelligence quotient A ratio of mental ability (IQ) of an individual based on performance on an intelligence test and the chronological age.

Kinesics The term applied to what people do when they communicate through body movement or gesture such as a frown, a stern look, or a defiant posture.

Language A system of communication by means of spoken or written symbols.

Language-experience approach (LEA) A method of reading instruction in which learners dictate stories from their own experience. The stories are written by the teacher and used as the content of reading lessons.

Limited-English-proficiency (LEP) child The child with less than an adequate command of English for basic interpersonal communicative needs and/or cognitive academic language demands.

Look-say approach A method of beginning reading instruction in which teachers stress word recognition without intensive work in phonics in teaching an initial sight vocabulary.

Macron A diacritical mark (ă) to indicate, for example, that the long vowel sound is found in the word "mate."

Mainstreaming The process by which many exceptional children are integrated into the regular classroom setting for some part of, or for all of, the school day.

Miscue The unexpected response to written language so that the reader's pronunciation is at variance with the writer's words.

Morpheme The smallest unit of meaning in a language. *Girls* has two morphemes: *girl,* which has meaning by itself, and *s,* which is a bound morpheme that does not have meaning by itself.

Morphology The study of the structure of words, derivations, inflections, and the addition of prefixes and suffixes.

Myopia Nearsightedness.

Narrative A discourse form in which a story is told.

Nonreader The individual who cannot read even after considerable instruction.

Normal curve The symmetrical, bell-shaped curve of the normal distribution.

Norm-referenced test Any standardized test in which a given student's performance is compared with the performance of many others of similar age and educational achievement.

Ophthalmograph A device for photographing eye movements during reading.

Pacing Controlling the rate of reading; also, assigning materials to students at a rate that insures success at a given stage of reading development.

Percentile A point on a scale of scores in a distribution below which a given percent of scores occur. Thirty-eight percent of the scores fall below the 38th percentile.

Perseveration The persistence of an activity or a response after the stimulus or need is past.

Phoneme The smallest speech sound unit; the *f, a,* and *t* in *fat* are each phonemes.

Phonemics The study of language in terms of its sound elements: the phonemes.

Phonetics The study and classification of all the sounds in human communication.

Phonic analysis A process of "sounding out" words according to the letter-sound relationships.

Phonics The study of sound-letter relationships in reading and spelling.

Phonogram The consonant and vowel of a word ending such as "ill" or "ent" to which single consonants can be added to form words, as in *bill* and *sent.* Sometimes referred to as word families, *as, at, ap, an.*

Phonology The study of the sounds of the language.

Predictable book A book that is written so that the text is likely to be identified from the repetitive patterns, sentence meanings, and pictures.

Prefix A syllable before the root word that usually changes the meaning, as in *im*possible.

Profile A chart, or diagram, that shows an individual's relative position in the performance of several traits or tests— performances vary from trait to trait or test to test.

Random sample A scientific selection of a total population—operating on the principle that each one had equal chance of selection—without bias.

Range The distance between the highest and lowest measures of a distribution.

Rapport Mutually harmonious working relationships.

Readability The level of difficulty of a book or article as measured by any one of several readability formulas.

Reading expectancy The level at which given students would be expected to read as judged by their intellectual maturity.

Realia Real things as opposed to representations, or abstractions, from a time in history or from a geographical area.

Redundancy The duplication of information in a sentence. The duplication is provided by the syntax, number, gender, or verb forms.

Reinforcement The strengthening of a response by reward or satisfaction.

Retention Learning that permits later recall or recognition.

Reversals Producing symbols backwards: *b* for *d; n* for *u; how* for *who;* or one may reverse Arabic numbers: �घ for 6: ℮ for 9, the word *strephosymbolia* is sometimes used in referring to reversals.

Root A basic word form from which new words are developed by the addition of suffixes or prefixes.

Scaffolding The strategies that skilled persons use to help novices learn what *they* want to learn. Reading scaffolding might include pointing to the place to begin reading or helping to break a word into parts so that it can be pronounced.

Schema A dynamic data structure, in the mind, for representing the generalized concepts for understanding the environment; a building block of cognition.

Schwa An unaccented vowel. Written as an upside down *e,* it has the sound of *uh* as in *a*bout.

Self-concept The status of one's ego; the ability to accept oneself as one is. Also requires an understanding of oneself in relation to other people.

Semantics The study of meaning in words, phrases, thought units.

Sight word A word that is memorized and recognized as a unit.

Sinistral Innately left-handed. Opposed to dextral.

Skimming Very rapid reading through a selection for a specific purpose.

Standard deviation A measure of variability of scores around an average. The closer the scores cluster around the average, the smaller is the standard deviation.

Standard score Statistically manipulated scores converted from raw scores for ease of interpretation.

Standardized test A systematic sample of performance obtained under prescribed conditions, scored according to definite rules, and capable of evaluation by reference to normative information. Validity and reliability are established for standardized tests.

Stanine One of the steps in a nine-point scale of normalized standard scores with a mean of 5 and a standard deviation of 2.

Strabismus Squint or cross-eye.

Strephosymbolia Literally, twisted symbols, as in the reversing of *was* and *saw* or *left* and *felt.*

Structural analysis Analysis of words by affixes, roots, syllabication, or their compound parts.

Structured overview A diagram or outline prepared with the learners to show the relationships existing between related ideas; a cognitive map.

Study skills Techniques and strategies that readers apply to the acquisition, retention, and application of information and concepts.

Suffixes Affixes at the ends of words: *ing, ful, ness, ment*. Derivational suffixes change the part of speech and the meaning: *ment, ism;* inflectional suffixes do not change the part of speech or the meaning: *ing, ed.*

Supplementary reading Reading assigned to reinforce, or add to, some learned ability in reading or any other subject.

Surface structure The observed phoneme-grapheme representation of the sentence.

Survey test A standardized test that measures general achievement in a subject or area.

Syllabication Division of words into syllables, as *com for ta ble.*

Syndrome A constellation of symptoms of a given condition.

Synonym A word that has the same, or nearly the same, meaning as another word, as *happy—pleased.*

Syntax The grammar of the language, that is, the rules by which sentence structure is regulated.

Tachistoscope A device in which exposure time is controlled to permit flashing words, letters, numbers, or figures on a screen.

Tactile Pertaining to the sense of touch.

Taxonomy A classification for systematically labeling and organizing characteristics in a given field; Bloom's taxonomy for cognition: knowledge, comprehension, application, analysis, synthesis, and evaluation.

Text A verbal record of communication; written material; the theme of a discourse.

Trade books The books provided in the school library for general information, research, and pleasure. Not part of any basal reading series.

Validity The extent to which a test serves the purpose for which it is used.

Visual discrimination Recognizing likenesses and differences in symbols, words, and phrases. One discriminates *b* from *d; horse* from *house.*

Visual memory span The number of items that can be recalled after seeing them presented.

Visual perception Receiving images and interpreting them through the sense of sight.

Vowel In the alphabet, *a, e, i, o, u,* and sometimes *w* and *y.*

Vowel digraph Two vowels together with only one vowel sound, as in cr*ea*m.

Webbing The process of representing schematically ideas that relate to a central concept and the relationships between those ideas.

Word analysis Analyzing a new word into known elements for the purpose of identification.

Word blindness A label indicating the inability to read words owing to pathological causes, either congenital or acquired.

Word calling Generally refers to the students who pronounce the words correctly but do not demand meaning from the passage. One can "word call" all the words in a sentence correctly but the sentence will make no sense.

Author Index

Subject Index